Sleuthing the Muse:
Essays in Honor of William F. Prizer

William F. Prizer

SLEUTHING THE MUSE:

Essays in Honor of

William F. Prizer

Edited by
Kristine K. Forney and Jeremy L. Smith

Festschrift Series No. 26

Pendragon Press
Hillsdale, New York

Pendragon Press Musicological Series

Aesthetics in Music
Annotated Reference Tools in Music
Bucina: The Historic Brass Society
The Complete Organ
Dimension & Diversity: Studies in 20th-Century Music
Distinguished Reprints
Festschrifts
Franz Liszt Studies
French Opera in the 17th & 18th Centuries
Harmonologia: Studies in Music Theory
The Historical Harpsichord
Interplay: Music in Interdisciplinary Dialogue
The Juilliard Performance Guides
Lives in Music
Monographs in Musicology
Musical Life in 19th-Century France
North American Beethoven Studies

Opera Studies
Organologia: Instruments and Performance Practice
The Complete Works of G.B. Pergolesi
Polish Music History
RILM Retrospectives
The Sociology of Music

Studies in Czech Music
Thematic Catalogues
Vox Musicae: The Voice, Vocal Pedagogy, and Song
Wendy Hilton Dance & Music

Library of Congress Cataloging-in-Publication Data

Sleuthing the muse : essays in honor of William F. Prizer / edited by Kristine K. Forney and Jeremy L. Smith.

    pages cm. -- (Festschrift series ; No. 26)

Includes bibliographical references and index.

ISBN 978-1-57647-148-7 (alk. paper)

1. Music--History and criticism. I. Prizer, William F., honouree. II. Forney, Kristine, editor. III. Smith, Jeremy L., 1962- , editor.

ML55.P755 2012

780.9--dc23

                            2012002056

TABLE OF CONTENTS

PREFACE

The plan for this Festschrift was first hatched in Fall 2007, when Bill Prizer announced his decision to retire from the University of California, Santa Barbara the coming Spring. With the help of his colleagues at UCSB—notably Derek Katz, Stefanie Tcharos, and David Paul—we celebrated his many years of dedicated teaching with a conference entitled *Fêtes de la confrérie amicale de Guillaume Prizer*, featuring papers and performances by students and faculty colleagues. Clearly there was a Toison d'Or theme to the event, honoring the ground-breaking discovery Bill made of the importance of the Order of the Golden Fleece for sacred music and his recognition of the crucial link of the Order to the *L'homme armé* repertory. He was even awarded a life-size replica of the collar worn by the Knights of this esteemed Order, and he was further honored with a performance of music he had edited throughout his career, performed by Les Chapellains du Petit Chapitre. Many of the students and colleagues included in this essay collection were present for this conference, and several presented papers, including Michael Beckerman, Margaret Murata, H. Colin Slim, and Jeremy Smith.

This volume has clearly been a labor of love on the part of the editors—his wife and first PhD student (at UKy) Kristine Forney, and Jeremy Smith, a UCSB graduate, whom Bill also inspired to take up Renaissance studies. The topics included here all relate in some way to Bill's own work and scholarly pursuits, which, in addition to his Golden Fleece work, have contributed significantly to our knowledge of music and performance in Italy during the Renaissance. His interests range from the noble patronage of Isabella d'Este to the raunchy carnival song repertory, some of which were written and performed by courtesans (a continuing interest of Bill's—what he refers to as "his dirty-old-man project"). Nor did we forget his love of mysteries. In all, we strove to pique the readers' interest with diverse and tantalizing categories (Ribaldry in High and Low Places, Enigmatic Women, Gender, Power, Virtù, Mysteries and Secrets Revealed, to name a few) that might succeed in raising this collection above some of the more purely "academic" Festschriften.

As always, there are many people to thank for their assistance and support of this project. First and foremost are the authors of the twenty-seven articles, whose excellent contributions will significantly expand our grasp of scholarship in their respective fields, and thereby ensure the success of the volume, and who have exhibited supreme patience with the long delays in the editing processes. Second, we extend our heartfelt thanks to Claire Brook, our outstanding editor and dear friend at Pendragon Press, and to Robert Kessler, whose encouragement as managing editor of Pendragon has been steadfast, for their unflagging support and dedication to this volume.

Invitation to the conference in honor of William F. Prizer

Finally, and most importantly, we issue our deepest thanks to Bill Prizer from his students, colleagues, and friends, for his dedicated guidance and inspirational scholarly contributions to the field of Renaissance studies. We are all better scholars for his research, publications, and leadership.

Kristine K. Forney and Jeremy L. Smith

Tabula gratulatoria

*Timothy Cooley
Christine Getz
*Derek Katz
Herbert Kellman
Lewis Lockwood
Alyson McLamore
John Nádas
Giulio Ongaro
Susan Parisi

*David Paul
Joshua Rifkin
Craig Russell
Rudi Schnitzler
*Eunice Schroeder
Martin Silver
*Stefanie Tcharos
Henri Vanhulst
Agostino Ziino

Former Students

*Katie Baillargeon
Jonathan Bellman
Grey Brothers
Maureen DeMaio
*Alicia Doyle
*Kristine Forney
*Anita Ip
*Michael Joiner
Deborah Kauffman
David Kidger
*Temmo Korishelli
Marie Labonville

Alison McFarland
James Maiello
Rebecca Giacosi Marchand
Cory Matthews
*Marilee Mouser
Denise Odello
*Randolph Scherp
Jeremy Smith
*Jessica Stankis
*Nathaniel Werner
Sharon and Mark Yeary
*Larry Young

* Member of Les Chapellains du Petit Chapitre, dir. Temmo Korishelli, who performed at the UC Santa Barbara retirement celebration, *Fêtes de la confrérie amicale de Guillaume Prizer,* held on Friday, May 9, 2008.

Liturgical Music and Ceremony

New Sources of the Beneventan Exultet

Thomas Forrest Kelly

More than fifteen years ago I described, in a volume entitled *The Exultet in Southern Italy*, the unusual rites surrounding the blessing of the Paschal candle on the Vigil of Easter as they were practiced in Latin southern Italy in the earlier middle ages.[1]

Briefly, these practices include the use of the well-known Exultet rolls inscribed with the music and the text of the song of blessing, *Exultet iam angelica turba celorum*; these scrolls were usually richly illustrated, the illustrations often placed upside-down with respect to the text and the music. These scrolls have been the source of endless fascination to historians of art and to many other scholars, and were the subject of a major exhibition and catalogue at Montecassino in 1994.[2]

But there is more to the phenomenon. There are, in fact, three further characteristics of the Exultet as practiced in the Beneventan zone—the area of Latin southern Italy that practiced the characteristic Beneventan script.

1. The Beneventan Exultet has a unique text. The ceremony of blessing the Paschal candle is common to the Old Spanish, the Milanese, the Beneventan, and the Franco-Roman liturgies, and in the last three of these the text used for the blessing begins with the words *Exultet iam angelica turba celorum* cited above. But the text has three versions: after the fixed opening portion, the text continues, after a dialogue like that of the preface of the mass (*Dominus vobiscum . . . Sursum corda . . .*), with a text that is unique to the Milanese, the Beneventan, or the Franco-Roman liturgy. The Beneventan text, found only in a handful of documents, including several of the Exultet scrolls[3]--is apparently a feature of the old Beneventan liturgy, widely practiced in southern Italy, and suppressed in the course of the eleventh century.

2. The Beneventan Exultet has a unique melody, different from those usually found with the Milanese or Franco-Roman Exultet, and closely related to a

[1] Thomas Forrest Kelly, *The Exultet in Southern Italy* (New York: Oxford University Press, 1996) (hereafter *TESI*).

[2] Guglielmo Cavallo, with Giulia Orofino and Oronzo Pecere, *Exultet. Rotoli liturgici del medioevo meridionale* (Rome: Istituto Poligrafico e Zecca dello Stato, 1994). Substantial bibliography on the *Exultet* rolls here and in *TESI*.

[3] Beneventan text and translation in *TESI*, 30-35; see also 53-59.

recitation tone used also for other moments in the Beneventan liturgy.[4] This Beneventan Exultet-tone is to some extent independent of the Beneventan text, for it appears in some sources from southern Italy, clearly from within the Beneventan zone, that have adopted the Franco-Roman text of the Exultet, but retained the Beneventan melody.[5]

3. The Beneventan Exultet has a unique ceremony. In the Milanese and Franco-Roman liturgies the Exultet is the first public ceremony of the Paschal vigil; a candle is brought into a darkened church, and it is blessed by a deacon, singing the Exultet. The blessing mentions the mystery of light, the flame of fire that led the people of Israel through the desert, the night of resurrection and of new birth, and the bees who created the candle. The ceremonies continue with a series of readings and canticles, the blessing of the fonts and the baptisms, and the first mass of Easter. In the Beneventan rite, however, the blessing of the candle, with the Exultet, takes place not at the beginning of the rite but between the last two lections.[6]

A source that shows any of these symptoms—the Beneventan text, the Beneventan melody, or the Beneventan placement—is likely to be related to the old Beneventan liturgy, and to have a close connection with southern Italy. Generally we presume that such sources come from a church where the Beneventan liturgy was once practiced, where the Franco-Roman liturgy has since been adopted, and where occasional elements of the vanished liturgy give us a view of its extent before its suppression in the course of the eleventh and twelfth centuries.

* * *

My purpose here is to bring the record up to date, and to note the recent discovery of several further pieces of evidence of the Beneventan Exultet. They increase our understanding of the phenomenon, and give a broader perspective on the dissemination of this Beneventan practice.

There are three new sources to report: two are sources of the Beneventan melody, one from southern Italy and one from a missal of central Italy; the third is a description of the ceremony of the Exultet from the Cathedral of Capua. We shall consider each of these in turn.

---

[4] *TESI,* 82-88; Thomas Forrest Kelly, *The Beneventan Chant* (Cambridge: Cambridge University Press, 1989), 131-32, 156-60.

[5] On the independence of the melody, see Thomas Forrest Kelly, "Structure and Ornament in Chant: The Case of the Beneventan Exultet," in Graeme Boone, ed., *Essays on Music in Honor of David G. Hughes.* Isham Library Papers 4 (Cambridge: Harvard University Department of Music, 1995), 249-76; idem, "L'Exultet: Musica e cerimonia liturgica," in Cavallo et al, *Exultet. Rotoli liturgici del medioevo meridionale,* 19-38.

[6] On the evidence for this placement, see *TESI,* 134-43.

which may be sung to a special melody.

A. Archivio del Pontificio Collegio Irlandese, Rome, MS Music 4 (Plate 1)

This single leaf, evidently used as a book cover, was signaled to me by Virginia Brown in December of 2006, and was subsequently listed in her "A Second New List of Beneventan Manuscripts (V)."[7] It consists of recto and verso from a missal of the thirteenth century, in Beneventan script, and it shows the end of the lections of the Vigil of Easter and the beginning of the Exultet, with its music.

The music of the Exultet has the Beneventan melody, in the version most often associated with documents coming from the area of Montecassino,[8] but its text is the standard Franco-Roman version. The text is unfortunately incomplete, and breaks off (at "sicco vestigio transire fecisti") before the portion where many versions have an elaborate praise of the bees. Likewise we do not have the ending, where Exultets have a number of variants, including sometimes the naming of ecclesiastical and secular authorities that allows a precise localization and dating.[9]

The surviving liturgical elements here are the following:

Lectio *Nabuchodonosor rex*

Tractus *Sicut cervus*

Oratio *Deus qui tribus pueris*

Introductory rubric for the Exultet

Exultet iam angelica turba celorum

This sequence makes clear that the Exultet, in the church for which this missal was designed, was sung after the series of lections of Holy Saturday— or almost at the end, for a further lection probably follows. This is the Beneventan position for the Exultet, as mentioned above, but it represents a combination of Beneventan and Franco-Roman elements. The situation is a complex one, owing to the fact that the number and order of lections varies from manuscript to manuscript, and that the position of the Exultet near or at the end of the sequence makes for a variety of possibilities. Put most simply, the Franco-Roman rite begins with the Exultet and continues with sometimes four, more often twelve lections, usually

Plate 1: Archivio del Pontificio Collegio Irlandese, Rome, MS Music 4.

[7] *Medieval Studies* 70 (2008), 275-355, at 321-22.
[8] See the comparative melodic tables in *TESI*, 99-103.
[9] *TESI*, 65-74.

ending with a reading from Daniel beginning either at *Nabuchodonosor rex* or *Angelus domini descendit cum Azaria*, which depending on its length contains one or two canticles (*Stans Azaria* and *Tunc his tres*), which may be sung to a special melody.

The Beneventan ordo, as nearly as we can reconstruct it, has two principal differences: the Exultet comes before the last lection, and the last lection is *Hec est hereditas* from Isaiah,[10] most often like this:

> Lectio *Nabuchodonosor* or *Angelus*, possibly with canticles
>
> Oratio *Deus qui tribus pueris*
>
> > *Exultet*
>
> Lectio *Hec est hereditas*
>
> Tractus *Sicut cervus*

In this sequence the Exultet comes between the last two lections; it is found in that position in many manuscripts showing the influence of the Beneventan liturgy.[11] The tract *Sicut cervus* provides an appropriate transition to the liturgy of baptism that follows. Occasionally, particularly in later southern sources, the Exultet comes after the last of the lections, rather than before it. We know this only from descriptions of the ceremoniescoming from Benevento, Salerno, and Naples.[12] Now, however, we have a document which gives the Exultet itself, in this liturgical position.

How this manuscript continues would be very interesting to know. Perhaps it continues with the lection *Hec est hereditas*, but without the Tract *Sicut cervus* that normally would follow it to provide a transition to the baptisms. More likely is that the lections are finished here before the Exultet (as with the Naples and Salerno ordinals), and that the liturgy continues with the litany of the saints sung

---

[10] The rubric from Vatican City, BAV lat. 10673, f. 34r-v, seeks to explain the difference: "Lectio Hec est hereditas, que quinta est ordinata secondum romanum legatur hic. Secundum ambrosianum legatur post Benedictionem cerei." Note that "Ambrosian" is the local name for the Benventan rite. Facsimile of the whole manuscript in Joseph Gajard and André Mocquereau, eds. *Le Codex 10673 de la Bibliothèque vaticane, fonds latin (XIe siècle): Graduel bénéventain*, Paléographie musicale 14 (Solesmes, 1931; repr. Berne: Lang, 1971).

[11] They include Vat. lat. 10673 (10th/11th c.), Benevento 33 (10th/11th c.), a fragment now in Farfa (11th c.), Benevento 38 (11th c., with the interesting variant that the prayer *Deus qui tribus pueris*, related to the lection that precedes, is separated from that lection and said only after the Exultet); the lection *Hec est hereditas* is placed last in Benevento 39 (late 11th c.), but there is no indication of the placement of the Exultet. Benevento 40 (11th c.), mixing two versions, seems to skip the lection *Hec est hereditas* at the end of the series (it was not included earlier) and makes no mention of the Exultet). Other sources giving evidence of the Beneventan rites of Holy Saturday are discussed in TESI, 134-143. The very complicated situation of the lections and their associated tracts in south Italian manuscripts is treated by René-Jean Hesbert in "L' 'antiphonale missarum' de l'ancien rit béneventain: Le samedi-saint," *Ephemerides liturgicae* 61 (1947), 153-214 at 153-71; Hesbert treats the same material in his (anonymously written) introduction to Paléographie musicale,14, 337-60.

[12] The monastery of Santa Sophia in Benevento, and one of its daughter houses, in their 12th-century ordinals (Naples, Bibl. Naz. VI E 43; Vat. lat. 4928) place the Exultet after the last lection, *Nabuchodonosor*, the tract *Sicut cervus*, and the prayer *Deus qui tribus pueris*, just as here: see my edition in *The Ordinal of Montecassino and Benevento: Breviarium sive ordo officiorum. 11th century*, Spicilegium friburgense 45 (Fribourg: Academic Press, 2008). A Salerno ordinal reflecting 12th-century practice, and a description of the rites of Holy Saturday at the cathedral of Naples, "which from ancient times have been, and ought to be, observed," each place the Exultet after a standard series of lections; *TESI*, 140-41.

in procession to the font. Perhaps the next folio will turn up in Rome or elsewhere some day. Meanwhile, we can note that at least one further document retains some evidence of the old Beneventan liturgy, in its melody and in its placement of the Exultet. We should note, too, that although the melody has the aspect of Cassinese documents, it was not the practice in the surviving sources of Montecassino to sing the Exultet after the lections, but rather to place it in the Franco-Roman position, at the very beginning of the ceremonies.[13]

B. Milan, Biblioteca capitolare MS E.II.13 (Plate 2)

This manuscript is a fourteenth-century processional-ritual of the Cathedral of Capua, and it contains a description of the ceremonial of the Exultet that places Capua squarely within the Beneventan orbit. This is one of two manuscripts of Capua in the library of the Duomo of Milan, possibly brought there by Charles Borromeo.[14]

After two opening fly-leaves (a notarial document and a table of contents), the manuscript begins with "Incipit liber processionum orationum capitulorum per ordinem totius anni secundum consuetudinem metro-politane ecclesie capue." The following 126 folios are of precious importance for an understanding of the ritual of this cathedral, otherwise little documented. A few additions (ff. 127-32) close the manuscript. I expect to make a further study of the manuscript; for the moment I note that it is in the south Italian tradition in its Holy Saturday ritual. This document describes the rites of Holy Saturday from the point of view

Plate 2: Milan, Biblioteca capitolare
MS EW.II.13, f.43

[13] TESI, 146-50.

[14] The manuscript came to Milan, according to a typescript note pasted to the inside front cover, perhaps as part of the inquiry of Saint Charles Borromeo into the possible relationship of the church of Capua to the Ambrosian liturgy of Milan. The note reads: "Forse è questo uno dei codici della Chiesa di Capua fatto richiedere da San Carlo Borromeo credendo che il rito di quella Chiesa fosse Ambrosiano. (vedi: Sala, Aristide, Documenti circa la vita e le gesta di San Carlo Borromeo. Milano, 1857. Parte II, Documenti: pag. 191, n. 26 e pag. 531, n. 3)." The other Capuan manuscript at Milan, bearing a similar label, is MS E. II. 14, a collectar with votive offices and ritual elements. I am grateful to Angelo Rusconi for calling these manuscripts to my attention. On the possible "Ambrosian" connection between Milan and southern Italy, see Thomas Forrest Kelly, The Beneventan Chant, 181-82; see also Thomas Forrest Kelly, "Beneventan and Milanese Chant," Journal of the Royal Musical Association 112 (1987), 173-95.

of the Archbishop of Capua (it prescribes what the archbishop and his ministers do privately during the reading of the eleventh lection), and it has several unusual features.   The relevant text of the Holy Saturday ritual is transcribed as Appendix 1 below. The uusual features can be summarized as follows:

a. The Exultat is sung twice, once by the archbishop as part of a ceremony during the eleventh lection (thus not apparently a public part of the service) during which new fire is struck and blessed, incense is blessed, a small candle is blessed with the Exultet, and lamps and a triple candelabrum are lit from it; and the Exultet is sung again, by a deacon, shortly afterwards for the large candle.[15] Note that the *Lumen Christi*, here as elsewhere in the south, is not sung in procession, but from a single location.[16]

b. During the procession and the lighting of the large candle the hymn *Veni sancte spiritus* is sung.

c. The lection *Hec est hereditas*, with the tract *Sicut cervus*, follow the public Exultet.

The Exultet is given in full for the archbishop (it is the Franco-Roman text), but given only as an incipit for the deacon; no melody is present, but it is not difficult to suppose the persistence of the Beneventan melody, given its presence in a surviving Exultet roll of the eleventh century still at Capua.[17] The placement of the Exultet between the last two lections is characteristic of the Beneventan ritual; the Franco-Roman text is an import to the south; and the double Exultet, and the use of the hymn *Veni sancte spiritus*, may well be unique to Capua.

The text of the Exultet is not precisely that of any other surviving text. It has multiple variants from that of the Capua Exultet roll; it includes the passage "O certe necessarium Ade peccatum," often omitted from texts of the twelfth century and later; and it omits, like many others, the extended praise of the bees.[18]

There is other evidence of the persistence of the Beneventan practices of the Exultet at Capua. In addition to the eleventh-century Exultet roll already mentioned, a fourteenth-century missal of Capua (Paris, Bibliothèque Nationale de France lat. 829) indicates that the Exultet comes after the lections, although some places do it otherwise ("sed in aliquibus locis primo benedicitur cereus et postea leguntur lectiones"), and that in some churches the lection *Hec est hereditas* comes after the baptisms (another Beneventan symptom: "Completo baptismo, in aliquibus ecclesiis legitur lectio *Hec est hereditas.*")[19]

An even more interesting parallel with this present document is a citation, from abbot Francescantonio Natale's eighteenth-century essay on the re-use of

---

[15] On the use of a triple candlestick, of grains of incense, of lighting candles and lamps during the Exultet , see *TESI*, 165-167; Thomas Forrest Kelly, "Candle, Text, Ceremony: The Exultet at Rome," *Études grégoriennes* 23 (2004), 7-68 at 56-68.

[16] *TESI*, 155.

[17] *TESI*, 218-20; see index at 341-42; description and facsimile in Cavallo, *Exultet*, 291-302.

[18] Versions of all known south Italian texts known at the time are found in *TESI*, 263-89.

[19] *TESI*, 312.

the carved Paschal candle as an outdoor decorative column, of what he calls an "antico breviario Capuano," now apparently lost. In this document precisely the same ceremonies are described as in the Milan ritual, in language very close to that here; but they are not the same document, as a comparison of Natale's quotation, provided in Appendix 2, will demonstrate.[20] There is no indication in Natale's document of the text used to bless the small candle,[21] and thus no indication of the double Exultet; but the other features of the ceremony—including the use of the hymn *Veni creator spiritus,* with its verse *Accende lumen* used for the lighting of the great candle from a triple candlestick, and the reading of the lection *Hec est hereditas* after the Exultet—make it clear that this lost Capuan document reflected the same unusual ceremony as that described in the Capuan ritual in Mil

C. Stroncone (province of Terni), Archivio Storico Comunale, Frammenti, Giudiziario 21-1 (Plate 3)

This is a single leaf from a notated missal of central Italy dating from the first half of the twelfth century. It shows the beginning of the Exultet with the Beneventan melody.

The threefold *Lumen Christi* has the increasingly ornamented melody found also in the central Italian manuscripts Vatican City, BAV Vat. lat. 4770; New York, Pierpont Morgan Library M 379; Rome, Biblioteca Vallicelliana F 29; Rome, Biblioteca Vallicelliana B 32; and Subiaco, Biblioteca del Protocenobio di Santa Scolastica XVIII.[22] These date from the late tenth to the thirteenth century, and share not only the common elaborated opening but also a localized version of the melody of the Exultet itself (save for Vat. lat.

Plate 3: Stroncone (province of Terni) Archivio Storico Communale, Frammenti, Giudiziario, 21-1.

[20] *Lettera dell'abate Francescantonio Natale intorno ad una sacra colonna de' bassi tempi eretta al presente dinanzi all'atrio del duomo de Capua* (Naples: Vincenzio Mazzola-Vocola, 1776). The document has been cited in *TESI*, 311.

[21] "Et dum legitur XI. lectio Nabucodonosor pontifex cum ministris processionaliter euntes ad fores ecclesie benedicant ignem incensum et cereum parvum, deinde accendentes candelas tres imponentesque in arundine revertant ad chorum . . ."

[22] On these see *TESI*, 154-55 and 260-62. A facsimile of the fragment (but not showing *Lumen Christi*) is published in Giacomo Baroffio, Cristina Mastroianni, and Fabrizio Mastroianni, *Frammenti di storia*

4770, where the Exultet is without notation; the Stroncone melody   is closest to that of Subiaco XVIII). They also use the Beneventan melody only for the first portion of the Exultet, up to the *vere dignum*, and the Roman preface-tone thereafter; whether this is true here awaits the discovery of more pages from this missal.

There is evidently a relationship among this group of central-Italian manuscripts, but there is a larger relationship in the fact that they use a version of the melody used at Benevento, and that melody can be shown to be widely used in the Beneventan liturgy, not just for the Exultet.[23] It appears, then, that from the late tenth century (the earliest likely date of Vat. lat. 4770, which in fact has other Beneventan symptoms too[24]), there was the clear influence of the Beneventan liturgy—or at least one of its melodies—to be heard in the monasteries of central Italy.

* * *

These two relatively small fragments, along with the evidence of a ritual transported far from home, serve to underscore the fact that discoveries continue to be made; that the smallest fragment may add something to a larger picture; and that the number of witnesses to the remarkable phenomenon that is the Benventan Exultet are not so few as we once thought.

* * *

Appendix 1: Text from Milan E.II.13

f. 40

Sabbato sancto dicta decima lectione tractu et oratione, dum legitur undecima lectio, *Nabuchodonosor*, Pontifex cum diacono et aliis ministris processionaliter descendens a parte dextra altaris per viam ante sacrarium pergat ad preparatum locum iuxta fores ecclesie, ad benedicendum ignem, incensum, et cereum parvum; et astantibus sibi ministris in circuitu eius cum cruce duobus candelabris et aqua benedicta et decem granis maioribus incensi, quinque pro cereo magno, et quinque pro cereo parvo, carbonibusque accensis igne excusso de lapide in aliquo vase a sacrista preparatis, benedicit novum ignem.

---

medioevale: Mostra di codici e frammenti di codici liturgici dei secoli XI-XIV dall'archivio storico del Comune di Stroncone (Stroncone: Comune di Stroncone, Soprintendenza archivistica per l'Umbria [1998]), 81, description at 18. I cited the fragment previously in my "New Evidence of the Old Beneventan Chant," *Plainsong and Medieval Music* 9 (2000), 81-93 at 90.Another fragment in Stroncone, Notarile 5, is a page from a missal including the beginning of the Exultet without notation; its script, its rubrics (which place the Exultet at the beginning of the ceremony), and its lack of musical notation, give us no reason to associate it with the south-Italian tradition. For a selection of rubrics related to the Exultet at Rome, see Kelly, "Candle, Text, Ceremony: The Exultet at Rome," Appendix 1,44-68.

[23] See above, note 4.

[24] *TESI.*, 262; Kelly, *The Beneventan Chant*, 315-16; see index at 339.

Benedictio novi ignis. Versus. *Adiutorium nostrum.* R. *Qui fecit.* V. *Dominus vobiscum.* R. *Et cum.* Oremus. Or. *Deus qui per filium tuum angluarem scilicet la-* |f. *40v* |*pidem... Or. Domine sancte pater omnipotens lumen indeficiens . . .*

Deinde benedicit incensum cum decem predictis granis maioribus incensi ponendis cereis magno et parvo ab- |f. 41 |solute dicens hanc orationem:

Benedictio incensi. *Veniat quesumus omnipotens deus super hoc incensum . . .*

Et dum benedicitur incensum acholitus assmens de carbonibus predictis ponit in turribulo. Finita vero benedictione incensi, Pontifex ignem benedictum aspergat aqua benedicta et posito incenso in turribulo adolet dictum ignem. Postea pontifex benedicit cereum parvum incipiens absolute.

Incipit benedictio parvi cerei. *Exultet iam angelica turba celorum. . .* |f. 41v-42| *... et curvat imperia.* Hic infinguntur quinque grana incensi predicti cereo a diacono in modum crucis. *In huius igitur noctis . . .* |f. 42v| *. . rutilans ignis accendit.* Hic accenditur cereus parvus. *Qui licet sic divisus . . . apis mater eduxit.* Hic accenduntur lampades et tres candele in harundine pro accendendo cereo magno. *O vere beata nox que expoliavit . . .* |f. 43| *. . .per omnia secula seculorum. Amen.*

Peracta vero benedictione parvi cerei, finitaque predicta prophetia undecima, *Nabuchodonosor* cum oratione, Pontifex accipiens in manu sua supradictam harundinem cum triplici candela accensa ante quam revertatur ad chorum cum ministris flexis genibus congruenti spatio ter incipiat hymnum *Veni creator spiritus* [with musical notation, 1 verse]. Et chorus finiat totum primum versum, quo tertio incepto prosequuntur alternatim predictum hym- |f. 43v| num usque ad versum *Accende lumen sensibus.* Cum autem fuerunt prope pulpitum magnum Pontifex ter incipiens choro presequente Versus *Accende lumen sensibus* [with musical notation, 1 verse]. Predicta triplici candela accendat cereum maiorem, qualibet ipsarum candelarum per se seperata; et finito hymno, Pontificeque ad altare cum ministris reverso, diaconus dalmatica indutus recepta benedictione a Pontifice cum subdiacono portante librum et quinque grana incensi benedicti, ascendens ornatum pulpitum ad benedicendum predictum cereum maiorem ter sic incipiat.

Lumen Christi. R. *Deo gratias.*

Lumen Christi. R. *Deo gratias.*

Lumen Christi. R. *Deo gratias.*

Sequitur immediate *Exultet iam angelica.* cum nota consueta.

Post legitur duodecima lectio *Hec est hereditas,* que legitur per primum diaconem lateris[?] |f. 44|decani.

Qua expleta cantatur tractus *Sicut cervus.* Quo cantato dicitur per Pontificem seu sacerdotem celebrantem v. *Dominus vobiscum.* R. *Et cum spiritu tuo. Oremus.* Or. *Omnipotens sempiterne deus repice propitius ad devotionem populi renascentis . . .* Finita oratione duo ex subcantoribus quorum est chorus incipiant letanis in medio chori modo infra scripto . . .

Appendix 2: from a lost Capuan manuscript

Lettera dell'abate Francescantonio Natale intorne ad una sacra colonna de' bassi tempi eretta al presente dinanzi all'atrio del duomo de Capua (Naples: Vincenzio Mazzola-Vocola, 1776), 33-34, quoting an "antico Breviario Capuano," now apparently lost.

Hora septima, post signum tabule, pontifice seu sacerdote cum ministris vestimentis solemnibus indutis ad altare accedentibus lectiones sine pronunciatione absolute incipiunt legi sic *In principio creavit.* et orationes dicuntur sine salutatione cum *Oremus* absque *Flectamus genua.* Et dum legitur XI. lectio *Nabuchodonosor* pontifex cum ministris processionaliter euntes ad fores ecclesie benedicant [*sic*] ignem incensum et cereum parvum, deinde accendentes candelas tres imponentesque in arundine revertant ad chorum, et pontifex flexis genibus ter incipiat hymnus *Veni creator spiritus.* parum procedendo qualibet vice chorus finiat at sequitur alternatim usque ad V. *Accende lumen.* cum fuerit prope pulpitum magnum pontifex ter incipiens choro prosequente: *Accende lumen sensibus,* predictis tribus candelis accendat cereum majorem quo a diacono benedicto ac finita XII. lectio *Hec est hereditas* cum tractu et Oratio omnes cum processione cantantes Letaniam accedant ad benedicendos fontes, etc.

Four Motets of Guillaume Du Fay in Context

Alejandro Enrique Planchart

My purpose in this essay is to clarify the context of four motets by Guillaume Du Fay: *Apostolo glorioso*, *Rite maiorem*, *Fulgens iubar ecclesiae dei*, and *O sidus Hispaniae*. This will also throw new light into Du Fay's biography, the structure of one liturgical office, and the performance traditions at the Cathedral of Cambrai. I will take the pieces up in chronological order. The first is *Apostolo glorioso*. It is exceptional in two ways: it is the one of two motets by Du Fay with an Italian text, and it is one of two works Du Fay wrote for five voices.

The motet is in honor of St. Andrew, and the texts mention the burial site of the saint in Patras, in the Peloponnesus, which was the see of the last Latin archdiocese in Greece. Pope Martin V appointed Pandolfo Malatesti da Pesaro, the hunchback son of Malatesta dei Malatesti and brother of Cleofe Malatesti, as archbishop of Patras on 10 May 1424.[1] Pandolfo went to Patras to take possession of his see probably in the fall of 1424 and stayed there until 1428, when he traveled to Venice to seek aid against the attacks of Constantine XI, who eventually entered the city on 1 June 1429.[2]

In 1952 Heinrich Besseler showed that Pandolfo restored the cathedral in Patras and rededicated it in 1426,[3] and proposed this event as the occasion for *Apostolo glorioso*. This was a plausible hypothesis and all later scholarship accepted Besseler's interpretation. At the time he was writing Du Fay's whereabouts in 1426 were largely conjectural. The last securely datable work before this time was the ballade *Resvelliés vous* for the wedding of Carlo Malatesti da Pesaro, Pandolfo's brother, to Vittoria di Lorenzo Colonna, in Rimini on 18 July 1424,[4] and the next document was a letter from the papal legate in Bologna, Cardinal Louis Allemand, to the chapter of Saint-Géry in Cambrai, dated 12 April 1427, placing Du Fay in Bologna.[5] Robert Auclou, an important churchman for whom one of Du Fay's early motets was written and whose life was to run parallel to that of Du Fay from

---

[1] Anna Falcioni, "Pandolfo Malatesti arcivescovo di Patrasso (139-1441)," *Bizantinistica. Rivista di studi bizantini e slavi*, ser. 2, 1 (1999), 79.

[2] Kenneth Meyer-Setton, *The Papacy and the Levant, 1204-1571*, 4 vols. (Philadelphia: American Philosophical Society, 1976-84), II: 33-34.

[3] Heinrich Besseler, "Neue Dokumente zum Leben und Schaffen Dufays," *Archiv für Musikwissenschaft* 9 (1952), 159-76.

[4] David Fallows, *Dufay*, rev. ed. (London: Dent, 1987), 216.

[5] Lille, Archives Départementales du Nord, 7G 753, fol. 107v, cited in André Pirro, *Histoire de la musique de la fin du XIV siècle à la fin du XVIe* (Paris: Librairie Renouard, 1940), 63.

the 1420s on, was known to have been in Paris at the University in 1425 and by 1426 in Bologna as secretary of Allemand.[6] Given that that Du Fay's motet for Auclou had an acrostic indicating that Auclou was curate of Saint-Jacques, and that Auclou had at the time the curateship of Saint-Jacques de la Boucherie in Paris, the assumption was that the two had met in Paris in 1425 or thereabouts, that Du Fay had written both *Rite maiorem* and the *Missa Sancti Iacobi* for Auclou, probably in Paris, and that eventually both had found their way to Bologna in 1426. In Bologna Du Fay surely met the Archdeacon of the University, Pandolfo di Galeotto Malatesti (d. 1427), a cousin of both the archbishop of Patras and of Du Fay's first Italian patron, Carlo Malatesti da Rimini, who could have been the conduit of the commission of *Apostolo glorioso* and the transmitter of the work to Greece.

Since 1976, however, a number of details of Du Fay's biography and the transmission of his early works have come to light. The results of these revisions is that we know now that Du Fay was in Cambrai from 1418 to the spring of 1420,[7] in Rimini or Pesaro from before August 1420 to late 1424,[8] in Laon for most of 1425,[9] and in Bologna from early in 1426 to August 1428.[10]

This places a number of works, including a good deal of the *Missa Sancti Iacobi*, the motet *Rite maiorem*, and the *Sanctus papale* in the years 1426-28, which creates a stylistic dissonance with *Apostolo glorioso*, which is written in a style very close to that of the *Missa sine nomine*, which as Fallows has shown must precede the ballade *Resvelliés vous* and was probably composed early in 1422.[11]

A new document changes all of this substantially: it is a papal supplication dated 12 July 1425. Unfortunately the register where it is copied is severely damaged and corroded at the top. What can be seen reads as in Example 1 (p. 15).L Ex.

This petition surely generated a papal bull eventually registered and copied in the Registra Lateranensia, while the original was taken to be presented to the chapter at Saint-Géry. A copy of the papal bull has not turned up, and from it, the only information not available to us from the supplication would be Denis' patronymic, his actual clerical status, and the full name of the saint to whom the altar was dedicated, but nothing more. Two of these we can surmise: Denis had no benefices, only an expectative, which means he was a young *clericus*, and for reasons that will be clear below, the "M" was the initial of "Mariae."

---

[6] Joseph Toussaint, *Les relations diplomatiques de Philippe le Bon avec le Concile de Bâle (1431-1449)* (Louvain: Bibliothèque de l'Université, 1942), 25, and Ursmer Berlière, *Inventaire analitique des diversa cameralia des archives vaticanes (1389-1500) au point de vue anciens dioceses de Cambrai, Liège, Thérouanne et Tournai* (Rome: Institut historique belge de Rome, 1906), 200-1.

[7] Alejandro Enrique Planchart, "The Early Career of Guillaume Du Fay," *Journal of the American Musicological Society* 46, no. 3 (1993), 360-61.

[8] Ibid., 361.

[9] Fallows, *Dufay*, 26-27, Planchart, "The Early Career," 364-65.

[10] Fallows, *Dufay*, 31.

[11] Ibid., 165-67. I prefer not to call it the *Missa Resvelliés vous* precisely because I agree with Fallows that the mass precedes the ballade. The date of the mass can be determined by its presence in the earliest layer of the manuscript Bologna, Civico Museo Bibliografico Musicale, MS Q 15, which was written *ca.* 1422.

Vatican, Archivio Segreto Vaticano, Registra Supplicationum, 188, fol. 292v

(The rigid legal formulas used in these supplications allow the reconstruction of some of the lost text, which is given below with the reconstructed passages in brackets.)

Supp[licat sanctitatis vestrae devotus vester Dionysius ... clericus *vel* presbyter?] Seno[nensis diocesis ... quatenus sibi specialem gratiam facientes de cappellania perpetua] ad altare beatae M[ariae?]... n ... s ... [in] ecclesiae sancti Gaugerici Cameracensis sitis et fundatis cuius fructus etc. duodecim librarum Turonensium parvorum secundum communem extimationem valorem annuum non excedunt vacante per obitum quondam guillermi de fageto in civitate patracensis existenti defuncti ultimi eiusdem cappellaniae possessoris / Seu premisso sive alias quovismodo et ex alterius persona vacet, etiam si generaliter vel specialiter reservati affecti aut devoluti Seu si super eis in Romana curia vel extra inter aliquos lis cuius cause statum hic habere dignemini pro sufficienter expressis pendeat indecisa / Etiam si tanto tempore vacaverit / quod ipsius collatio iuxta lateranensis statuta concilii legitime devoluta existat / eidem dyonisio dignemini misericorditer providere Non obstantibus gratia expectativa si quam habet in cancelleria eiusdem sanctitatis declaranda / Et cum ceteris non obstantibus et clausulis opportunis / Fiat ut petitur O / Datum Romae apud Sanctos Apostolos Idus Iulii Anno octavo.

The papal bull probably reached Cambrai in August 1425, but the chapter acts of Saint-Géry, which survive complete for 1425 and 1426, are absolutely silent on this matter.

The reasons for this are not far to seek: the petition had a number of fatal errors. First and foremost it claimed that Du Fay had died in Patras, and also claimed that Du Fay's benefice was a chaplaincy at the altar of St. Mary in Saint-Géry. There can be no doubt that each of the altars of Saint-Géry was dedicated to one or more saints, and that the chaplaincies in the church had similar dedications and names. But the records of the church throughout the fifteenth century do not ever give the names of the altars or the chaplaincies. The single exception to all of this was Du Fay's benefice, known as "the chaplaincy of the Salve at the altar of Saint-Géry,"[12] the obvious Marian connection with the *salve* would explain the error in the supplication. Further, from what we now know of Du Fay's biography, the canons at Saint-Géry probably knew well that Du Fay was alive and working, as a *petit vicaire* at the Cathedral of Laon, a day's journey away and had probably come to Cambrai a number of times to see his mother and his dying relative, Jehan Hubert Sr., whose nephew, Jehan Hubert Jr., was about to become provost of Saint-Géry.

Under these circumstances, whoever was Denis' representative knew that it would be useless to even present the papal bull to the chapter.

Despite some of the errors in the petition, it is still astonishing that it places Du Fay in Patras, probably late in 1424. Under these circumstances the genesis of *Apostolo glorioso* takes on a different color. Most likely Pandolfo Malatesti traveled to Greece with a retinue of musicians which included Du Fay, and *Apostolo glorioso* would have served as a panegyric to the apostle probably upon the arrival. Two aspects of the piece argue for this interpretation: with a fine diplomatic sense the motet is not about the archbishop, a foreigner, but only about Saint Andrew; and it is in Italian, not in Latin, thus again sidestepping the Greek-Latin antagonism. The text is a sonnet, and it may be more than coincidence that Pandolfo's and Cleofe's father, the Lord of Pesaro, was a very respectable poet, whose name among literary historians is not Malatesta de Malatestis, but Malatesta dei Sonetti. Now the text of *Apostolo glorioso* survives only in the musical setting in Bologna Q 15, which transmits a number of garbled texts. Professor Domizia Trolli, the editor of Malatesta's sonnets, regards *Apostolo glorioso* as too mediocre a poem to be by Pandolfo's father,[13] but I must confess that I do not find Malatesta's securely authentic works so far above *Apostolo glorioso* to preclude his authorship. In terms of the performance of the motet it also makes better sense that Du Fay would have been in Patras to supervise the performance of a particularly ambitious five-voice

---

[12] Lille, Archives Départmentales du Nord, 7G 753, fol. 108r.

[13] Personal communication; see also Malatesta Malatesti, *Rime*, ed. Domizia Trolli (Parma: Studium Parmese, 1981).

work, a texture quite uncommon at the time.[14] This also places the motet in the same period as the *Missa sine nomine*, which resembles the motet considerably in its metric and melodic structure.

The errors in Denis' petition also have explanations in Du Fay's life. The transformation of the chaplaincy of the *salve* into a chaplaincy at the altar *de sancta Maria* is self explanatory. Further, as I noted in an earlier study, what prompted Du Fay to leave the service of the Malatesti was the news of what appeared to be the impending death of Jehan Hubert, and he stayed near Cambrai until shortly after the death. Thus the news of "a death in the family," coupled with Du Fay's disappearance from the region the Adriatic, were transmitted as news of his death.

The second motet is *Rite maiorem* and the early scholarly views of its genesis have been mentioned above. In 1974, while working in Bologna, I realized that there was a church of San Giacomo Maggiore in the city, and that some of its chant books survived and were then in the Archiginnasio. The only catalogue was an old handwritten *schedario* with countless errors and omissions. Manuscripts 598 to 610 were assigned to San Giacomo. I went through them and could find no volume of the Gradual nor the summer volume of the antiphoner. But in several volumes of the antiphoner I found a suffrage for St. James, which normally would be a magnificat antiphon. It is a unique rhymed text.

This called my attention immediately because the quatrain of the antiphon appeared to be metrically compatible with the couplet that serves as the tenor incipit of *Rite maiorem* (cf. Example 2 on p. 18), and the *Missa Sancti Iacobi*, which at the time was assumed to have a connection to *Rite maiorem*, has a rhymed alleluia. I had just spent a number of months looking at the liturgy of St. James in Paris and elsewhere and had tracked down the liturgy for St. James at Saint-Jacques de la Boucherie, which was entirely in prose,[15] and had become aware that the office for Saint James had virtually everywhere an office derived from the *commune sanctorum*. Pieces specific to him were extremely rare and almost always unica in the sources, and rhymed offices were even less common. For these reasons I proposed that both *Rite maiorem* and the mass were written in Bologna, and that Du Fay had used chants from San Giacomo as cantus firmi.

Sometime later Margaret Bent, working on the origins of Bologna, Civico Museo Bibliografico Musicale, MS Q 15, the unique source for both the complete mass and the motet, came up with a series of startling discoveries. A history of her research on this would go beyond the limits of this paper, but the central points she made was that the scribe of Q 15 was a member of the immediate circle around

---

[14] Cf. the commentaries in Fallows, *Dufay*, 23 and Massimo Mila, *Guillaume Dufay*, 2 vols. (Turin: Giappichelli, 1972), I: 132-45.

[15] Alejandro Enrique Planchart, "Guillaume Dufay's Masses: A View of the Manuscript Traditions," *Papers Read at the Dufay Quincentenary Conference, Brooklyn College, December 6-7, 1974*, ed. Allan W. Atlas (Brooklyn: Brooklyn College, 1976), 28-29.

Ex. 2: Antiphon *O doctor et lux Hispaniae*. Bologna, Civico Museo Medievale, MS 598, fol. 166r

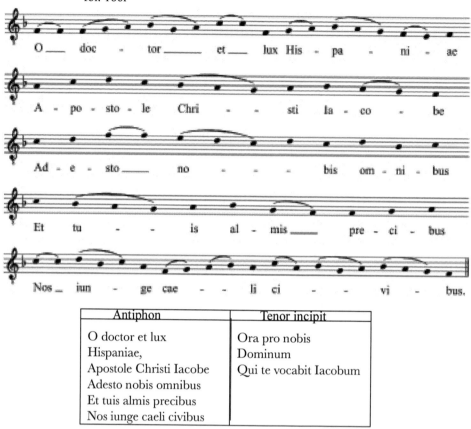

Antiphon	Tenor incipit
O doctor et lux Hispaniae, Apostole Christi Iacobe Adesto nobis omnibus Et tuis almis precibus Nos iunge caeli civibus	Ora pro nobis Dominum Qui te vocabit Iacobum

Bishop Pietro Emilani of Padua. By the middle 1420s the scribe had copied an extensive anthology of sacred music, and *ca.* 1430 he began a second one precisely with Du Fay's *Missa Sancti Iacobi*. At one point he decided to fuse both books into a single one, creating a bibliographic maze worthy of the Minotaur.[16] Bent noted that the compilation of the *Missa Sancti Iacobi* in Q 15 comes shortly after Emiliani, in his will, established a pilgrimage to Santiago de Compostela by four pilgrims, and she found numerous numerical and symbolic congruencies between the mass, Emiliani's will, and his funeral monument.[17] Emiliani's will was drafted in 1429; Bent at first proposed that the final version of the mass and even *Rite maiorem* postdated 1429 and were thus written while Du Fay was in Rome, and that the mass was probably a compilation produced *ad hoc* by the scribe of Q 15, who was known to create such composite cycles.

[16] See Margaret Bent, "A Contemporary Perception of Early Fifteenth-Century Style; Bologna Q 15 as a Document of Scribal Editorial Initiative," *Musica disciplina* 41 (1987), 183-201; idem, "Music and the Early Veneto Humanists," *Proceedings of the British Academy* 101 (1999), 101-30; idem, "Ciconia's Dedicatee, Q 15, Brassart, and the Council of Basel," *Manoscritti di polifonia nel Quattrocento europeo, Atti del convegni internazionale di studi, Trento – Castello del Buonconsiglio*, 18-19 ottobre 2002, ed. Marco Gozzi (Trent: Soprintendenza per i Beni librari e archivistici, 2004), 35-56.

[17] This is extensively detailed in Bent, "Music and the Early Veneto Humanists," 124-29.

By 1988, I had become convinced that, possibly contemporaneous though they might be, the mass and the motet were unrelated,[18] and Professor Bent later reached also the same conclusion.[19] The motet, thus, could have been written in Bologna and the mass, though probably begun in Bologna, did not reach the form it has in Q 15 until after 1429. Throughout all of this, the possible connection with San Giacomo Maggiore remained like some sort of a mirage, a tempting possibility because of the rhymed text of the motet's cantus firmus, but without any confirmation.

Three further chant books of San Giacomo had survived, however. They had been hidden under an altar stone at the time of the confiscation of the books by the Italian government, and were found only two decades later, but they were in a parlous state from mold and humidity and had suffered the loss of many ornamental letters.[20] They were given the numbers 4108-10, but were so damaged they could not be consulted. Ex.3 gives a view of an opening from MS 4109 before restoration.

The hidden chant books in fact complete the entire antiphoner, as can be seen in Table 1.

Giacomo Baroffio and Eun Ju Kim, "La tradizione liturgico-musicale in San Giacomo a Bologna," in I corali di San Giacomo Maggiore: Miniatori e committenti a Bologna nel Trecento, ed. Giancarlo

[18] Alejandro Enrique Planchart, "Guillaume Du Fay's Benefices and His Relationship with the Court of Burgundy," *Early Music History* 8 (1988), 128-29.

[19] Personal communication.

[20] Vania Alessandri, "I corali dalla soppresione del 1866 all'acquisizione communale: Il processo de padre Mazonni," in *I corali di San Giacomo Maggiore: Miniatori e committenti a Bologna nel Trecento*, ed. Giancarlo Benevolo and Massimo Medica (Bologna: Musei Civici d'Arte Antica, 2003), 145-47.

The hidden chant books in fact complete the antiphoner, as can be seen in Table 1.

Table 1
The Books of San Giacomo in Numerical Order

598	Antiphoner, *commune sanctorum*
599	Antiphoner, *de tempore*, Lent 2 to Holy Wednesday
600	Antiphoner, *de tempore*, Saturday after the Octave of Corpus Christi to Pentecost 14, plus Wisdom
601	Antiphoner, *de tempore*, Pentecost 10 to end of the year, with responsories of the months
603	Antiphoner, *de sanctis*, Nativity of BVM to St. Clement
604	Antiphoner, *de sanctis*, Eastertide to St. John Baptist
605	Antiphoner, *de sanctis*, Andrew to Agnes II plus suffrages
606	Antiphoner, *de tempore*, Vigil of Pentecost to Saturday after the octave of Corpus Christi
607	Antiphoner, *de sanctis*, Purification to Annunciation
608	Antiphoner, *de tempore*, Christmas to Octave of Epiphany
609	Antiphoner, *de tempore*, Advent 1 to Vigil of Christmas
610	Invitatories
4108	Antiphoner, *de sanctis*, St. Mary Magdalene to St. Augustine
4109	Antphoner, *de tempore*, Maundy Thursday to Sunday after Ascension
4110	Antiphoner, *de tempore*, Sunday after to Octave of Epiphany to Lent I

The Books of San Giacomo in Liturgical Order

610	Invitatories
609	Antiphoner, *de tempore*, Advent I to Vigil of Christmas
608	Antiphoner, *de tempore*, Christmas to Octave of Epiphany
4110	Antiphoner, *de tempore*, Sunday after Octave to Epiphany to Lent I
599	Antiphoner, *de tempore*, Lent 2 to Holy Wednesday
4109	Antiphoner, *de tempore*, Maundy Thursday to Sunday after Ascension
606	Antiphoner, *de tempore*, Vigil of Pentecost to Saturday after the Octave of Corpus Christi
600	Antiphoner, *de tempore*, Saturday after the Octave of Corpus Christi to Pentecost 14, plus Wisdom
601	Antiphoner, *de tempore*, Pentecost 10 to end of the year, with responsories of the months
605	Antiphoner, *de sanctis*, Andrew to Agnes II plus suffrages
607	Antiphoner, *de sanctis*, Purification to Annunciation
604	Antiphoner, *de sanctis*, Eastertide to St. John Baptist
4108	Antiphoner, *de sanctis*, St. Mary Magdalene to St. Augustine
603	Antiphoner, *de sanctis*, Nativity of BVM to St. Clement
598	Antiphoner, *commune sanctorum*

All of them are from the fourteenth century, but were in use most likely until the end of the Renaissance, if one is to judge from the leaves appended to a number of them. One of the three recovered books, MS 4108, contains the feast of St. James.

Shortly before 2003, in preparation for an exhibit at the museum, the codices were subjected to what amounts to a heroic restoration, which included not only the cleaning and chemical stabilization of the leaves but the restoration of a number of cut out initials that could be found in the museum's collection. With this MS 4108 could be examined and parts of it, including the office for St. James (fols. 19v -51r), were examined by Giacomo Baroffio and Eun Ju Kim.[21] The office is extraordinary in that it goes from first vespers on the vigil through matins, the entire day liturgy, and concludes with second vespers. The *suffragium* I saw in 1974 is the final piece, following the magnificat antiphon for second vespers and carries the rubric "Sequens antiphona dicitur quotidie infra octavas ad magnificat," which also explains why it was used as a *suffragium* for the whole year. Baroffio and Kim note that, even though San Giacomo is an Augustinian church, this office is not that of the Austin canons, which used the *commune apostolorum* for St. James elsewhere, and that virtually the entire office consist of *unica*. Of more than seventy pieces only two have concordances elsewhere: the hymn for first vespers, *Festum colamus die*,[22] and the magnificat antiphon for second vespers, *O lux et decus Hispaniae*,[23] which had an immense diffusion through Dominican sources.

My concern in this case is with the office of matins. The manuscript lost four leaves near the beginning of matins so that the end of the third antiphon, the first three responsories, and the beginning of the fourth antiphon are lost. What remains of the matins office appears in Table 2[24] (see p. 20).

In terms of the text matins is part of a true *historia* that tells us of the *vita et miracula* of St. James and ends with two prayers, the antiphons *O lux et decus* and *O doctor et lux*. From what is left of it it is also clear that matins was a numerical office arranged by mode. Baroffio and Kim came to a similar conclusion, but were mystified by what happens in the eighth and ninth responsories.[25] They were equally puzzled by the presence of the two rhymed responsories in the third nocturn, and wondered if these were perhaps drawn from a different office.[26] You will notice, however, that in the reentrant phrase of the final respond we meet with the words that serve as the incipit of the tenor in Du Fay's motet, "Ora pro nobis dominum / Qui te vocavit Iacobum." They are set, however, to an immense melisma, virtually twice as long as the melody Du Fay used for the tenor of *Rite maiorem*. Ex.4 (see p. 22) gives the ninth responsory and the tenor melody of Du Fay motet.

---

[21] Giacomo Baroffio and Eun Ju Kim, "La tradizione liturgico-musicale in San Giacomo a Bologna," in *I corali di San Giacomo Maggiore: Miniatori e committenti a Bologna nel Trecento*, ed. Giancarlo Benevolo and Massimo Medica (Bologna: Musei Civici d'Arte Antica, 2003), 123-43.

[22] Ibid., 132, n. 29, citing *Analecta Hymnica* 19, 159, and *Repertorium Hymnologicum*, no. 26598, but cf. also *Analecta Hymnica* 11, 144, and *Repertorium Hymnologicum*, no. 26589.

[23] Ibid., 132, note 30.

[24] Vania Alessandri, "Il restauro," *I corali di San Giacomo Maggiore: Miniatori e committenti a Bologna nel Trecento*, ed. Giancarlo Benevolo and Massimo Medica (Bologna: Musei Civici d'Arte Antica, 2003), 166.

[25] Ibid., 133.

[26] Ibid.

Table 2

Matins of St. James the Elder at San Giacomo Maggiore

Inv.   Regem apostolorum dominum Venite adoremus
Hy   Sidus refulsit (incipit)

First Nocturn

A 1	Apostolus Christi Iacobus per synagogas ingrediens eradicando super-stititionem daemonum fallacem Iesu domini praedicabut fidem.	Mode 1
A 2	Docente namque eo contigit auctorem erroris Hermogenem discipu-lum suum mittere ad eum.	Mode 2
A 3	Cum autem venisset Phyletus ad Iacobum asserebat non esse dei filium aeternum euius [lacuna 4 fols.]	Mode 3
R 1	Lost	Mode 1?
R 2	Lost	Mode 2?
R3	Lost	Mode 3?

Second Nocturn

A 4	Lost	Mode 4?
A 5	[Beginning lost] indulgentiam relicto itinere devio et consequeris do-mini gratium.	Mode 5
A 6	Audiens haec ergo Hermogenes carens fide ira commotus nexuit eum dicens videbo si te solvet Iacobus.	Mode 6
Vsc	V. Constitues eos principes super omnes terram. R. Memores erunt no-minis tui domine.	
R 4	R. Facta autem in turba seditione dictum est apostolum debet vocari Et ut reum iniquitatis secundum legem audari. V. in fontem et iustum ac radium veritatis plebs nephanda iudicat adduci. Et.	Mode 4
R 5	R. Gloriosus domini apostoli dixit Hermogeno Accipe tibi baculum itineris mei ac intrepidus cum eo perge securus. V. Lavacro sanctae regenerationis necdum perfusus Hermogenes ait apos-tolo casibus daemonum incidere pavesco dixit ei vir Dei. Accipe.	Mode 5
R 6	R. Istante vero tempore martyrii aspiciens Christi famulus Iacobus vi-dit quaedam languidum Cui misertus mox praebuit sanitatem. V. Dum ergo duceretur ad locum quo erat moriturus respiciens vidit aegrotum iacentem Cui. Gloria patri et filio et spiritui sancto. Cui.	Mode 6

Third Nocturn

A 7	Mox praedicante Iacobo conversus est Hermogenes magus cum suis omnibus factus Christi discipulus.	Mode 7
A 8	Set non ferens incredula gens Iudaeorum improbo rogat Herodem impium ferro perire Iacobum.	Mode 8
A 9	Tunc rex Iudaeis perfidus volens placere invidis electum dei Iacobum mox trucidat apostolum.	Mode 7

R 7	R. Laetetur nam Hispania	Mode 7
	Magno ditata praemio	
	Beati quam fragrantia	
	Claudit honore nimio	
	Membra sacra Iacobi	
	Herodis caesa gladio	
	Ut sic ad regem curreret	
	Ditandus vitae bravio	
	V. Hispanos docens Iacobus	
	Ierusalem revertitur	
	Dum Christum plebi praedicat	
	Herodis telo caeditur.	
	Ut sic.	
R 8	R. Alme perpetui lumini lux apostole Iacobe obscena tuorum intima	Mode 1
	famulorum illumina. Ut valeant tempora sic ducere saeculi quo valeant	
	gaudia captare vitae.	
	V. Sedulus esto Christi benigne apostole intercessor pro hiis quibus da-	
	tus es pater et pastor. Ut valeant.	
	Gloria patri et filio et spiritui sancto.	
	Ut valeant.	
R 9	R. Turbam compescit daemonum	Modes
	Ora.]	

The incipit of Du Fay's tenor sets the text of the phrase that is effectively the climax of the ninth responsory and, by extension, of the entire matins office. This is an immense melody covering the entire extended *ambitus* of the responsory, but its main point of articulation is on d at the end of *dominum* about a fourth into the melody. Du Fay's tenor is also an extended but more modest melody covering the *ambitus* of the first mode, and articulated halfway through the melody. Because it starts at the top of the *ambitus* it is clearly not the beginning of the piece, but since the entire matins is modally ordered, and given where *ora pro nobis dominum* falls in the ninth responsory, it is all but certain that Du Fay took his tenor from the re-entry section of the first responsory. Clearly this was an important textual goal in the office; the repetition of two lines of poetry is an almost unique occurrence in a single office, and the sense of couplet is repeated in the final magnificat antiphon and in the *suffragium* given above. Du Fay clearly understood this, and at the same time he realized that a ninety-seven note melody with a range of a twelfth was not workable as a cantus firmus.

Ex. 4: Responsory: *Turbam compescit daemonum.* Bologna, Civico Museo Medievale, MS 1408, fols. 40v-44r.

The derivation of Du Fay's tenor from the lost first responsory at San Giacomo confirms Du Fay's relationship with that church and the fact that the motet was composed in Bologna. It also allows us to answer some of the questions that Baroffio and Kim posed about the office. First of all it is a modally ordered office, at least for matins. For the antiphons the composer followed one of the normal patterns used to distribute the eight modes among nine antiphons. For the responsories he produced a *sui generis* solution that becomes comprehensible once we understand the function of *ora pro nobis dominum* as the climax of the entire office. The progression from mode 1 to mode 7 involves a gradually ascending *ambitus*. For the eighth responsory the composer goes back to the bottom: *Alme perpetui lumini* is in mode 1, but the respond stays virtually all the time between C and a. This sets off beautifully the immense *ambitus* of the ninth responsory, which stays within mode 8 for most of the respond only to climb into mode 7 territory precisely at the words *ora pro nobis dominum*.

This goes part way to answer Baroffio and Kim's second question: are the two poetic pieces taken from another office? The tonal organization argues against it, and now, knowing from Du Fay's motet that the first responsory included the two lines *ora pro nobis dominum qui te vocavit Iacobum*, we can postulate that this responsory was also in verse, and thus that the lost third responsory was also inverse, creating a completely symmetric distribution of responsories in verse and in prose for the entire office of matins. This entire office is thus most likely the work of one man, an anonymous Bolognese cantor of the fourteenth century with an acute sense of musical and textual drama.

Before moving to the last motets, we need to consider the case of the *Missa Sancti Iacobi*, which Margaret Bent has argued convincingly that, in its final form in Q 15, it is most likely a consequence of Bishop Pietro Emiliani's provision in his will of 1429 for four pilgrims to go to Compostela and thus postdates Du Fay's time in Bologna, although some of the Ordinary movements had been written before 1428.[27] Reopening Du Fay's connection with San Giacomo raises the possibility that he began the *Missa Sancti Iacobi* in Bologna and for San Giacomo. None of the volumes of the Gradual of San Giacomo survive, but the argument that only the alleluia is specific to St. James is a red herring. The masses for the apostles were among the most stable items in the late medieval liturgy. They are given in Table 3 on page 26.

Four of these liturgies are not part of the oldest layer of the Gregorian tradition: that is, they do not appear in the sources for the *Sextuplex*,[28] namely St. Bartholomew, St. James the elder, St. Thomas, and St. Mathias. The liturgy of these was derived, with small variations, from the mass for SS. Philip and Jude, in the course of the tenth and eleventh centuries, but the only one of these derived

---

[27] Bent, "Music and the Early Veneto Humanists," 124-29.

[28] René-Jean Hesbert, *Antiphonale Missarum Sextuplex* (Brussels: Vroomans, 1935. Reprinted Rome: Herder, 1963).

Table 3
Propers of the Apostles

		INTROIT	GRADUAL	ALLELUIA/TRACT	OFFERTORY	COMMUNION
1.	St. Andrew	**Mihi autem**	Constitues eos	Nimis honorati	Mihi autem	Dicit Andreas
2.	St. Bartholomew	**Mihi autem**	Constitues eos	Per manus	Mihi autem	**Vos qui secuti**
3.	St. James the Elder	**Mihi autem**	Constitues eos	Vos estis	**In omnem terram**	**Vos qui secuti**
4.	St. John	In medio	Exiit sermo	Hic est	Iustus ut palma	Exiit sermo
5.	St. Mathew	Os iusti	Beatus vir	Te gloriosus	Posuisti domine	Magna est
6.	St. Peter	Nunc scio	Constitues eos	Tu es Petrus	Constitues eos	Tu es Petrus
7.-8.	SS. Philip & James	Exclamaverunt	A. Confitebuntur	A.Tanto tempore	Confitebuntur	Tanto tempore
9.-10.	SS. Simon & Jude	**Mihi autem**	Nimis honorati	Isti sunt	**In omnem terram**	**Vos qui secuti**
11.	St. Thomas	**Mihi autem**	Nimis honorati	Vos estis	**In omnem terram**	Mitte manum
12.	St. Matthias	**Mihi autem**	Constitues	T. Desiderium	**In omnem terram**	Amen dico

liturgies that coincides with that of SS. Simon and Jude in most of the fourteenth- and fifteenthth-century graduals and missals I have examined is that of St. James the Elder.

Thus, given the liturgical traditions of northern Italy in the early fifteenth century, a mass containing the introit *Mihi autem*, the offertory *In omnem terram*, and the communion *Vos qui secuti*, was not a generic *missa apostolorum* but a mass either for SS. Simon and Jude or for St. James the Elder. With this the possibility should remain open that Du Fay might have begun expanding the three-movement ordinary and even composing a set of propers *for* St. James while he was still in Bologna. These propers might have included a gradual now lost or discarded, and an alleluia that was later discarded. Such removal or exchanges of sections would be compatible with what Margaret Bent has found was the *modus operandi* of the scribe of Q 15.[29]

The mass has two movements written in a style considerably different from the others, the *repetitio* of the introit and the communion, which may indeed be composed after 1429. The alleluia presents a particular case: it is a chant specific only to St. James and it is in verse, which caused me at first to associate it also with San Giacomo. But there is a trait of the alleluia that indicates that Du Fay never saw a plainsong version of it and that most likely no plainsong version of it ever existed. All plainsong alleluias, without exception, are copied as indicated in Ex. 5, and the singers knew that once the cantor intoned the alleluia, the *schola* repeated the opening word and then proceeded to the *iubilus*. With the discovery of Du Fay's proper cycles we have now some fifteen alleluias by Du Fay, and in all of them the melodic substance is present in one of the voices of the polyphony as the word "alleluia" is repeated in polyphony. The only exception to this is the

[29] Margaret Bent, "A Contemporary Perception of Early Fifteenth-Century Style; Bologna Q 15 as a Document of Scribal Editorial Initiative," *Musica disciplina* 41 (1987), 183-201.

alleluia of the *Missa Sancti Iacobi*, where the polyphonic setting of "alleluia" makes no reference anywhere to the intonation. Beyond this there is another trait in this piece that is absent from all plainsong alleluias: the music for the beginning of the verse is identical, note by note, to the music of the intonation of the respond. The plainsong intonations in this alleluia are being used by Du Fay as formal markers for motivic unification. This does not happen in plainsong alleluias, but it happens prominently in the Sanctus and Agnus of the *Missa sine nomine*, and in the Sanctus and Agnus of the *Missa Sancti Antonii de Padua et Sancti Francisci*, the masses written immediately before and after the *Missa Sancti Iacobi*; in both of these cases the plainsong intonations were actually composed by Du Fay. This, I think, is what happened with the alleluia of the *Missa Sancti Iacobi*: Du Fay was provided with a newly fashioned text not associated with any plainsong and he composed the entire piece from scratch. This means he did not see this chant in the books of San Giacomo and that this alleluia can indeed be written after 1429. In all probability the text came to him from Emiliani's circle, as the bishop was sending four pilgrims "to the end of the earth," the *mundi liminis* mentioned in the alleluia itself, thus confirming Margaret Bent's hypothesis about the final shape of the mass.

The context of the last two motets under consideration can be outlined very simply. They are *O proles Hispaniae – O sidus Hispaniae*, for St. Anthony of Padua, and *Fulgens iubar ecclesiae – Puerpera pura parens*, for purification. The first was part of an extended project by Du Fay that included an ordinary of the mass, propers for St. Anthony Padua, propers for St. Francis of Assisi, vespers of St. Anthony of Padua, and vespers for St. Francis of Assisi that Du Fay composed probably in the late 1440s, fragments of which survive in Tr 87, Tr 88, Tr 90, and ModB. At the end of his life Du Fay left a book in large format, in parchment and in black notation, containing presumably all of this music to the Chapel of St. Stephen. More than three quarters of the contents of the book survive. The missing pieces are simple vespers antiphons and the space they took in the book can be easily projected from the size of the ones that survive. In a recent study I have offered a reconstruction of the book, which startlingly appears to have consisted of six sexternios, the exact size of Cambrai 6, one of the two cathedral choirbooks that survive from the 1430s and 1440s.[30] Fallows has argued convincingly that part of this book's contents, the Mass for St. Anthony of Padua, was a work that Du Fay intended to have sung in 1450 at the dedication of Donatello's altar,[31] although all his efforts to find a documentary reference to the performance in Padua itself have proved in vain.[32] I now suspect that no performance took place, that either Du Fay could not reach Padua or his offer was rebuffed. The manuscript in Du Fay's possession at his death was, as I noted, a large manuscript in parchment and in black notation. But from the accounts of the fabric we know that all the manuscripts of polyphony copied at

---

[30] Alejandro Enrique Planchart, "The Books that Du Fay Left to the Chapel of Saint Stephen," *Sine musica nulla disciplina: Studi in onore di Giulio Cattin*, ed. Franco Bernabei and Antonio Lovato (Padua: Il Poligrafo, 2006), 175-212.

[31] Fallows, *Dufay*, 66-67.

[32] David Fallows, "Dufay, la sua messa per Sant'Antonio da Padova e Donatello," *Rassegna Veneta di Studi Musicali* 2-3 (1986-1987), 4.

Cambrai after *ca.* 1445 were on paper. Du Fay's manuscript was therefore a deluxe copy, most likely a presentation copy that was for some reason never presented.

It contained among other things a complete set of vespers for St. Anthony. Now, the text of *O proles Hispaniae – O sidus Hispaniae* consists of two antiphons, the first, *O proles* is by Julian von Speyer, and is the magnificat antiphon for first vespers;[33] *O sidus* is by Simon de Montfort and did not normally form part of the liturgy of the saint.[34] It would be tempting to see it as an antiphon substitute, but it is not. We have a number of vespers antiphons by Du Fay and they are written in a very simple three-voice texture, either in *fauxbourdon* or with a contratenor, and always with the chant paraphrased in the top voice. Moreover, Du Fay refers to this piece in his will, calling it unequivocally "a motet."[35] Its place in the vespers is clarified by a number of entries in the obituaries of the cathedral, Cambrai, Mediathèque Municipale, MS 39, and Lille, Archives Départementales du Nord, 4G 2009.[36] At the end of each there are a number of entries indicating foundations instituted by various canons in the course of the fourteenth and fifteenth centuries, including several for vespers. Virtually without exception the foundations for vespers include the instruction that the choirboys, with their master, and one or two of small vicars, should sing the hymn and "a motet." That then was the function of *O proles Hispaniae,* with its two treble parts in addition to a tenor and contratenor, and indeed, from Du Fay's will we can see that this is the ensemble he assumed would sing it as well.[37] This is also the ensemble he requests for his *Ave regina caelorum,* and we know from Cambrai liturgical traditions, that even though the Marian antiphons belonged at the end of compline, they were also sung at vespers. Thus the vespers he wrote presumably for presentation at the basilica in Padua followed a local Cambrai tradition.

This brings me to the last motet, *Fulgens iubar ecclesiae dei – Puerpera pura parens.* We have no secure date or occasion for it, although it is surely Du Fay's last isorhythmic motet. Du Fay was clearly aware of this, and in a gesture that reveals both remarkable understanding of the high points of both his career and his music, he ends the motet by quoting virtually note for note in all four voices the coda of *Nuper rosarum flores* (see Ex. 5).

Besseler placed this motet in the late 1440s together with *Moribus et genere.*[38] Fallows, however, placed both motets back to 1442, connecting *Moribus et genere* with

---

[33] See See Johannes Evangelista Weiss, *Die Choräle Julians von Speier zu dem Reimsoffizien des Fraziskus- und Antoniusfestes,* Veröffentlichungen aus dem Kirchenhistorischen Seminar München 6 (Munich: J. J. Lentner, 1901).

[34] See Hilaire de Paris, *Saint Antoine de Padoue: sa légende primitive, et autres pièces historiques, avec des sermons inédits et nouveaux et un manuel de dévotion* (Montreuil-sur-Mer, Imprimerie Notre-Dame des Prés, 1890), 326, see also Ulysse Chevalier, *Repertorium Hymnologicum,* no. 31035 (with added note to Hilaire in Vol. V).

[35] Lille, Archives Départementales du Nord, 4G 1313, 73.

[36] A description of these manuscripts, which notes that LAN, 4G 2009 consists of fragments of two obituaries, appears in Barbara Haggh, "Nonconformity in the Use of Cambrai Cathedral: Guillaume Du Fay's Foundations," *The Divine Office in the Late Middle Ages,* ed. Margot Fassler and Rebecca Baltzer (Oxford: Oxford University Press, 2000), 373 and notes 4-6.

[37] LAN, 4G 1313, 73.

[38] Heinrich Besseler, *Guglielmi Dufay Opera Omnia,* 6 vols. Corpus Mensurabilis Musicae 1 (Rome: American Institute of Musicology, 1951-1966), I: v.

Ex. 5: End of *Nuper rosarum flores* and *Fulgens iuber ecclesiae.*

the entrance of Bishop John of Burgundy in Cambrai. He dated *Fulgens iubar* around the same time because an acrostic in the motetus mentions Pierre du Cateau, who was *magister puerorum* at Cambrai from 1437 to 1447, and Fallows found it difficult to believe that a motet using Pierre's name in the text would have been written at a time when he was about to be relieved of his duties as *magister puerorum*.[39] But there are problems with Fallows's assumptions. First, as Laurenz Lütteken has noted, *Moribus et genere* mentions neither John of Burgundy or Cambrai; its text is a panegyric to St. John the Evangelist, one of the patrons of the Sainte-Chapelle in Dijon, and mentions the city of Dijon. Thus Fallows's dating is probably correct, but the motet was most likely written for the Sainte-Chapelle in Dijon, since the Burgundian court was in Dijon during the Christmas seasons of 1441 and 1442.[40] But *Fulgens iubar* is in many ways a different work: its texture, not only in the use of the second tenor, but in the way Du Fay treats the contratenor, bespeaks Du Fay's familiarity with a new kind of four-voice texture exemplified by the English *Missa Caput*.[41] I have argued elsewhere that Du Fay came across at least the last four movements of the *Missa Caput* and several other English masses sometime after *ca.* 1445 as part of his immense project to provide en extensive polyphonic repertory for the cathedral,[42] and *Fulgens iubar* must date from 1445, as Lütteken has proposed,[43] or from 1447 as I suggested in an earlier study.[44] What is interesting is that the acrostic of the contratenor or motetus reads "Petrus de Castello canta," asking Pierre du Cateau to sing the part, and that the cantus uses double notes in several places, so that it was intended for more than one singer to a part. This would fit the description of the ensemble mentioned in the endowments of the obituaries and in Du Fay's will perfectly: reading from top to bottom of the parts, the six choirboys, the *magister puerorum*, and two of the *compagnons*. The function of this piece apparently was not so much an occasional one but that of a vespers motet that could be used every year during Candlemass. In this sense *Fulgens iubar ecclesiae*, with its modern contrapuntal structure and its crystalline sound, is not just the last isorhythmic motet and a relic of the past, but a harbinger of the future of the motet as a genre.

---

[39] Fallows, *Dufay*, 61-62.

[40] Laurenz Lütteken, *Guillaume Dufay und die isorhythmische Motette: Gattungstradition und Werkcharacter an der Schwelle der Neuzeit*, Schriften zur Musikwissenschaft aus Muenster 4 (Hamburg and Eisenach: Karl Dieter Wagner, 1993), 298-99.

[41] See Rob Wegman, "Petrus de Domarto's *Missa Spiritus almus* and the Early History of the Four-Voice Mass in the Fifteenth Century," *Early Music History* 10 (1991), 296-97.

[42] Alejandro Enrique Planchart, "Institutional Politics and Social Climbing through Music in Early Modern France," in *Institutionalisierung als Prozess: Organisationsformen musikalischer Eliten im Europa des 15. und 16. Jahrhunderts—Beiträge des internationalen Arbeitsgespräches im Istituto Svizzero di Roma in Verbindung mit dem Deutschen Historischen Institut in Rom, 9-11 Dezember 2005*, Analecta musicologica 43 (Laaber, Germany: Laaber Verlag, 2009) , 115-52, at 146-47.

[43] Lütteken, *Guillaume Dufay*, 300.

[44] Alejandro Enrique Planchart, "Guillaume Du Fay's Second Style," in *Music in Renaissance Cities and Courts: Studies in Honor of Lewis Lockwood*, ed. Jessie Ann Owens and Anthony M. Cummings (Warren: Harmonie Park Press, 1996), 314.

The Tale of Three Woodcuts: Modeling of Antico in the Mass Prints of Morales

Alison Sanders McFarland

Papal and curial patronage and the possibility of lucrative benefices were among the incentives drawing European musicians to Rome and the papal court in the sixteenth century. The Sevillian Cristobal de Morales was among them, and he spent his most productive decade, 1535-1545, in the papal chapel. As I have described elsewhere,[1] Morales had arrived in Rome earlier than that, most likely during the last years of the reign of Clement VII, in the entourage of the Imperial ambassador to the Holy See. But all known documents relating to his benefices start in 1536, during the reign of Paul III. Evidence from the next decade suggests that Morales was concerned with achieving both recognition of his talents and generous patronage, and his benefice supplications must have been among the enormous number that flooded in during the first year of Paul III's papacy.

In 1544, his last full year in Rome, Morales published two large, ornate, folio choirbooks containing a total of fifteen settings of the Mass Ordinary and one Requiem Mass.[2] Both the choice of genre and the publications themselves were unusual. Mass prints devoted to a single composer were not common at this time, although they had been more so a generation earlier, and the motet had partially eclipsed the Mass as the type of sacred music most anthologized in music prints. A book devoted to the Masses of one composer was therefore designed to be impressive. A copy survives of the printing contract between Morales and his printer, Dorico, which shows that the impetus for publication was the composer's.[3] His were the first Mass prints published in Rome since Andrea Antico's important anthology *Liber Quindecim Missarum* (1516[1]), which contained some of the most prominent composers of the previous generation, including Josquin.[4]

---

[1] Alison Sanders McFarland, "Within the Circle of Charles V: New Light on the Biography of Cristóbal de Morales," *Early Music* 30 (2002): 325-38.

[2] *Missarum Liber Primus* (Rome: Dorico, 1544 = RISM M3580); *Missarum Liber Secundus* (Rome: Dorico, 1544 = RISM M3582).

[3] The contract is reproduced in Suzanne Cusick, *Valerio Dorico: Music Printer in Sixteenth-Century Rome* (Ann Arbor, MI: UMI Research Press, 1981), 297.

[4] On Antico's prints, see Catherine Weeks Chapman, "Andrea Antico" (Ph.D. diss., Harvard University, 1964).

31

It is apparent that Morales intended the publication of his Masses to create a magnificent statement, and hoped they would result in the kind of patronage that had so far eluded him. Efforts to determine the degree of papal favor he enjoyed, as evidenced by the number of benefices awarded, have yielded no certain conclusions, nor are they likely to, given the vagaries of the surviving materials and the hazards of comparison to other musicians. But Morales, certainly, was not satisfied with what he had received, as revealed by the tone of the dedications to his prospective patrons. His first book bears a preface addressed to Duke Cosimo de Medici that promises that all future compositions will be dedicated to him in return for an offer of support. This had been a puzzling dedication until recently, because there were no proven connections between the Duke and Morales, and dedications were often prompted by some familiarity if not an outright invitation. Klaus Pietschmann, however, haas discovered letters from Morales to Cosimo,[5] and I have suggested elsewhere an Imperial connection.[6]

The second volume of Masses is dedicated to the more obvious choice of patrons, Pope Paul III,[7] and asks for the conferring of an ecclesiastical benefice. Since many of those already conferred on him were expectatives, this suggests Morales was not yet in receipt of any benefice income; his dedication to Paul is in effect a benefice supplication that circumvents the curial bureaucratic system. It too, like the plea to Cosimo, apparently fell on deaf ears. A year later Morales left Rome and returned to Spain as choirmaster at Toledo Cathedral.

The two Morales Mass books are similar in format and decoration: they are single-impression prints, in large choirbook format, with woodcut borders and capitals. While the two books are visually similar in many ways, and are designed to be companions, there are, however, important distinctions between them that reveal clues as to their different purposes.

The title pages are, of course, different by virtue of being appropriate to their patrons. Book I features Cosimo's emblem, and Book II presents a finely detailed woodcut of a kneeling Morales presenting his book to the seated pope. The two books share the same ornamental border. The most noticeable distinction between the two Morales books rests in the decorated capital letters that begin each movement or sub-section. The designs are different both for the great initial K and its inset illustration that opens each Mass, as well as the smaller initials throughout. Many of the large Florentine-style initials for Cosimo's book present a standing lion, forming the back of the K, holding the palle of the Medici; two alternate designs omit the lion. The small initials that open every section are in the same Florentine style (Example 1).

The effect of the second Morales print is strikingly different. The style of the great initials has little in common with the ornamented Florentine shapes; they

[5] Klaus Pietschmann, "A Composer Writes to His Patrons," *Early Music* 28 (2000): 383-400.
[6] McFarland, "Within the Circle," 330.
[7] The former Cardinal Alessandro Farnese.

Example 1:
Dorico, Morales Book I,
decorative initials

are still elaborate and detailed, but with clear, sharp lines, and motifs that include columns and capitals. Whereas in Cosino's book there were three basic forms for the incipit **K**, here there is a different design for each Mass. The subsidiary initials, almost without exception, are elaborate script letters (Example 2).

Example 2:
Dorico, Morales Book II,
decorative initials

The significance of these visual designs is striking when the two volumes are compared to Antico's anthology. The resemblance is unmistakable, and it has long been known that a similarity exists between these books.[8] Given that Dorico and his heirs continued to use these decorative materials in subsequent prints, most notably Palestrina's first book of Masses, it has often been assumed that the design elements were Dorico's idea.[9] The purpose of this study is to propose that the similarity was a conscious decision by Morales and that he had very specific reasons for it.

Morales certainly would have known the Antico Mass print well. Besides its unique position in Roman music printing, the book was most likely intended for the papal choir: the contract was witnessed by three papal chapel singers,[10] and the Masses may be from the papal choir repertory.

The woodcut borders used by Antico and Dorico for the first opening of each Mass are virtually identical. The same style of banner, with composer and title, heads every page (Example 3). Antico, too, presents an illustration of the subject of the Mass, in the same location inset into the incipit K, and most of the large K initials are of the same construction as in the Morales Book I, although the lion holds a motto rather than the Medici *palle*. Most of the small initials are also identical to those in Morales's first book (Example 4). And the presentation page from Morales's second book, showing the composer kneeling before his pope, has a

Example 3a: Antico, *Liber Quindecim Missarum*, border

Example 3b: Dorico, Morales Books I and II, border

Example 3c: Antico, *Liber Quindecim Missarum*, banner

---

[8] Cusick, *Valerio Dorico*, 68.

[9] Ibid., 99.

[10] Jane Bernstein, *Music Printing in Renaissance Venice: The Scotto Press, 1539-1572* (New York: Oxford University Press, 1998), 142.

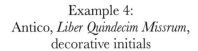

Example 4:
Antico, *Liber Quindecim Missrum*,
decorative initials

precedent in the Antico volume as well: the design is the same, although less well-executed and detailed in the earlier volume (Example 5, see pp. 36 and 37). Antico's anthology too was dedicated to a pontiff, Leo X, and the Medici *palle* are seen at the bottom border, in the same place as Paul III's emblem would be placed twenty-eight years later.

With such similarities established, the question is whether Dorico somehow came into possession of Antico's woodblocks, or if he carefully re-created them for Morales. It is known that Antico left his blocks in Rome when he departed the city for good in 1519, and Cusick suggests that they survived the Sack of 1527 and found their way into Dorico's shop.[11] My superimposition and measurement of images from the books of the two printers reveals few significant differences, more than amply explained by variations in printing materials. And indeed, there is another reason to believe that the blocks used by the two printers were one and the same. Antico's anthology, which was entirely woodcut, took him three years to carve: although much of this time would been required for the music of fifteen Masses, the ornamental borders and capitals are still intricate, painstaking, and time-consuming work. Dorico's shop would likely have been capable of such work:

[11] Cusick, *Valerio Dorico*, 69.

Example 5a:
Antico, *Liber Quindecim Missarum*,
presentation

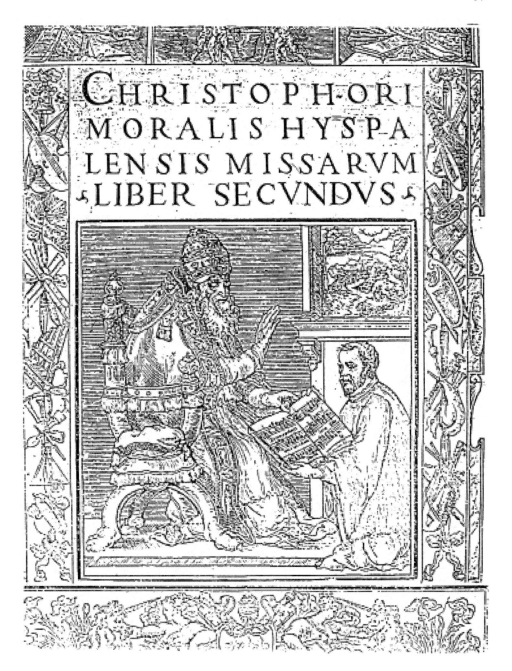

CHRISTOPH·ORI
MORALIS HYSPA
LENSIS MISSARVM
⸡LIBER SECVNDVS⸎

Example 5b:
Dorico, Morales Book II,
presentation

he too was known for his woodcuts, and the quality of his Morales dedication page to Paul III surpasses that of Antico's on the same subject. But to recreate the designs to the exact measurements would undoubtedly be more demanding than the initial carving: and at least the first of the Morales volumes, and probably both, were completed within six months of the contract date, as stipulated in that document. The limited timeframe thus suggests strongly that Dorico would not have had sufficient time to create new woodcuts to such exacting specifications and was, in fact, the inheritor of Antico's blocks.

But if Antico's design elements are found so liberally in the first Morales book, why is an entirely different set of decorative capitals found in the second? They are not re-used in the subsequent Dorico prints, but rather are unique to Morales Book II. The answer lies in the specificity of each print for its prospective patron. Book I, for Cosimo de Medici, makes use of the same materials as did Antico's book dedicated to Giovanni de Medici (Pope Leo X;) this includes not only the Florentine appearance of the designs, but the particular use of the lion initial and the same small initials. Such a reference to his papal relative might well be calculated to be flattering to Cosimo, as well as alluding to this earlier prestigious volume. These materials, however, would have no relevance for Paul III. Entirely new designs were therefore required to distinguish this volume from those intended for Leo X and Cosimo; an illustration mirroring the papal presentation of the Antico would bridge the gap, preserving the effect of the esteemed older print without the Medici connotations, and at the same time flattering the current pope. It can be no accident that the new woodcuts Dorico must have executed for this volume have such a Roman flavor, for they were destined for a Roman pope.

This careful tailoring of book to patron suggests that it was not Dorico but Morales who conceived the idea. In addition, the Morales prints are not only the first but unquestionably the best examples extant of the series of similar Dorico books. The later volumes of other composers do not seem as carefully planned as the Morales editions, and by the time of the five Mass prints produced by Dorico's heirs, the same materials seem to be used haphazardly and lacking an overall design plan, as though whatever was available in the shop had been used indiscriminately.

Although Rome was only a minor center of music publishing in this era, Morales certainly had choices other than Dorico: foremost among them was Antonio Blado, an occasional music printer who held a contract with the Vatican as Apostolic Printer. But no printer then working in Rome had produced a book like this one. With no established tradition of Mass choirbooks since Antico's to guide him, and with no particular reason to favor Dorico that we can discern, Morales's choice of printer might well have been dictated by his knowledge that Dorico had the Antico blocks.

All sixteen Masses, the bulk of his output in that genre, were certainly not written for these two prospective patrons—indeed, three of them seem to be associated with Charles V, as I show elsewhere[12]—but it might be suspected that

[12] McFarland, "Within the Circle," 330-31.

the works could be judiciously divided. And thus, a pattern emerges. Cosimo's book includes several secular-based Masses, more imitation Masses (including the composer's only Mass on a contemporary motet, by Gombert), the only Mass for six voices, and some of Morales's most popular Masses (popular in terms of number of times anthologized previously). Paul, who considered himself musically literate, was favored with archaic tenor-cantus firmus Masses, and the majority of those based on plainchant. The only imitation Masses in his volume are based on composers associated with the French Royal court, Mouton and Richafort, whose works appear frequently in the repertory of the papal chapel. Included also are the two Masses of clear papal significance: *Tu es vas electionis*, the first work in the volume, which, with its cantus firmus incipit including "sanctissime Paule" must have been written specifically for Paul, and the *Quem dicunt homines*, for the feast for the Chair of St. Peter. Table 1 on page 40 shows the contents of each Mass book.

It is puzzling how two such volumes, dividing their repertory evenly, and whenever possible, appropriate to the honoree, could be published in the same year, dedicated to two such diverse patrons. The conventional assumption that Morales executed the extant contract with Dorico for the Cosimo volume, then perhaps after it failed to ensure Morales a patron, hurriedly followed it with another for Paul, is difficult to reconcile logistically and makes little sense in light of the arrangement of repertoire. The volumes must have been planned simultaneously: if that is the case, why does the contract concern only a single book?

A possible solution again lies in the imitation of Antico. The number of Mass Ordinary cycles between the two Morales books is fifteen—the same number, of course, as in Antico. The Morales volumes divide evenly into eight Masses each only with the addition of the *Missa Pro defunctis* in Book II. This number cannot be a mere coincidence, the number of Masses Morales had available to publish in 1544, because at least one other Mass was already written, and the evidence of Morales's biography suggests that at least two other Masses, perhaps several, were written in Spain before the composer came to Rome. It may be speculated that Morales, wishing to publish a successor to Antico's respected volume, selected fifteen of his Mass Ordinaries, with or without the Requiem, and negotiated the contract with Dorico. For some reason, whether for considerations of size (the fifteen Morales Masses would make a far larger and more unwieldy volume than the Antico) or because Morales decided to increase his chances and appeal to two patrons simultaneously, the project became split into two volumes, with all Masses of papal connotations assigned to Paul's. The *Missa Pro defunctis*, if it was not already present, was added for balance, and a different design was chosen for Paul's book.

This suggestion explains several puzzling aspects about these two prints. Unfortunately the contract, however much it can reveal, refuses to answer the questions that would clarify this issue: it specifies no number of pages to the book, nor number of Masses, nor even the expected cost of the paper, from which the rest could be calculated.

This desire to imitate and even to surpass Antico's anthology (for a collection the size of Antico's, all by the same composer, would be a *tour de force*) is quite

Table 1: Contents of the Morales Mass Prints (1544)

Liber I, dedicated to Cosimo de Medici

    M. *De beata Virgine* (a4)
        Plainchant paraphrase
    M. *Aspice Domine* (a4)
        Parody of Gombert motet
    M. *Vulnerasti cor meum* (a4)
        Parody of anonymous (Mouton?) motet
    M. *Ave Maris stella* (a5)
        Canonic treatment of plainchant
    M. *Quaeramus cum pastoribus* (a5)
        Parody of Mouton motet
    M. *L'homme armé* (a5)
        Paraphrase of French secular tune
    M. *Mille regretz* (a6)
        Cantus firmus from chanson by Josquin
    M. *Si bona suscepimus* (a6)
        Parody of Verdelot motet

Liber II, dedicated to Pope Paul III

    M. *Tu es vas electionis* (a4)
        Cantus firmus from plainchant
    M. *Benedicta es celorum regina* (a4)
        Parody of Mouton motet
    M. *Ave Maria* (a4)
        Plainchant paraphrase
    M. *Gaude Barbara* (a4)
        Parody of Mouton motet
    M. *De Beata Virgine* (a5)
        Plainchant paraphrase
    M. *Quem dicunt homines* (a5)
        Parody of Richafort motet
    M. *L'homme armé* (a4)
        Cantus firmus from French secular tune

in keeping with the composer's apparent desire to outdistance his predecessors and contemporaries. His Masses often exhibit a penchant for exceeding the achievements of similar settings, through various techniques like larger numbers of voices, longer maintaining of the cantus firmus, single or double canons, or multiple plainchant melodies.

There is one more visual clue that leads again to issues of repertory. A feature of all three Mass prints is the specific illustrations inset within the incipits that depict the subjects of each Mass. Those for Antico are usually quite general in character, and not particularly detailed—for example, a knight with a bland, rather expressionless face for the *Missa L'homme armée*—but the illustrations for the Dorico editions are often more exacting, and can carry particulars that reveal information about the Mass itself. The two Morales Masses on "L'homme armé" are each illustrated by knights, but the similarity ends there. Each is so detailed as to be more portrait-like, more personal in character; the knight for the five-voiced Mass is young and helmeted, while the drawing for its companion is of a much older man, in armor but without helmet. A banner above him bears the device "plus ultra," the motto of Charles V. Clearly, at least some of these illustrations are more than mere decoration (Example 6).

And indeed, one more small, but important, correlation between the Dorico and Antico prints has until now escaped notice. Of these illustrations, none from Antico are reproduced in the Morales Book I, even while the initials that

Example 6a:
Antico, helmuted knight and Dorico,
Morales Book I, helmeted knight

Example 6b:
Dorico, Morales Book II,
older knight

surround them are the same woodcuts: none, that is, except the illustration of the Madonna and Child used for the *Missa de Beata Virgine* by Josquin, which is identical with that for the Mass of the same name by Morales in Book I. The two other *Missae de Beata Virgine* within these collections are also introduced by Madonna and Child motifs, but these are dissimilar, as are those for all other Masses on Marian subjects in the volumes (Example 7; see page 43).

As visual aspects in the comparison of these Mass collections called for new interpretations of Morales's intent, this potential clue bears further examination. Indeed, analysis of these two Masses reveals a contrapuntal similarity that I argue elsewhere[13] arose from the imitation of Josquin. In the visual modeling of his Mass prints on Antico, we can glimpse not only this hint at a musical relationship, but larger layers of reference. Morales sought to appeal to Cosimo and Paul III by associating their volumes, and by inference the importance of his music, with a collection he hoped would have historical meaning and authority for each.

---

[13] McFarland, "Josquin as Authority in the Masses of Morales," publication pending.

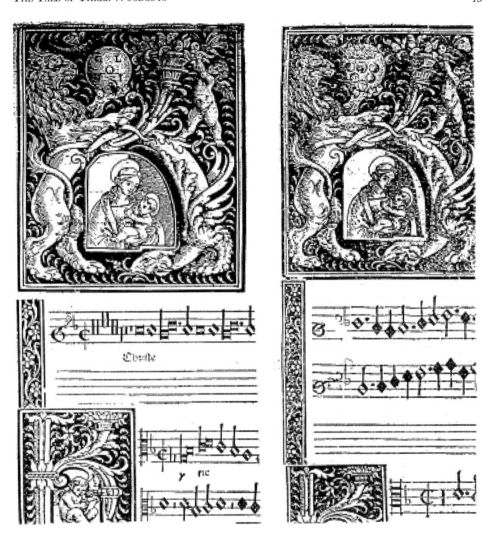

Example 7:
Dorico, Josquin *Missa de Beata Virgine* and
Dorico, Morales Book I, *Missa de Beata Virgine*,
incipits

Words and Music
in the Humanist Era

An Early Example of the Barzelletta-Frottola

James Haar

Among the additions made in 1473-74 by Johannes Bonadies to the early fifteenth-century Faenza Codex[1] is a group of five pieces by the otherwise unknown Johannes de Erfordia, including two Italian-texted songs. In a recently published study John Nádas and I offer an identification, first suggested by Reinhard Strohm, of Erfordia as a German nobleman, Johann von Dalberg, who spent some time in Italy (1472-74, 1476-77) after taking a baccalaureate degree at the University of Erfurt.[2] He seems to have studied music with the English pedagogue John Hothby, in Pavia and/or Lucca, learning enough counterpoint to compose a few sacred and secular pieces. In our study we publish one of the Italian songs, *Non so se l'è la mia culpa*, of which the line just given is all the text that survives. It appears to be an *ottonario*, with room in the music for three more verses, forming the *ripresa* of a barzelletta.

Erfordia's other Italian song, *Doloroso mi tapinello*, is also a barzelletta. It caught the eye of Knud Jeppesen, who included it as an example in the second volume of his magisterial study of the frottola.[3] It was surely the text, a four-line *ripresa* in *ottonari*, corruptly presented but clearly of an earthy popular cast, that interested Jeppesen, who devoted a lot of study to popular song of the frottola period (much of the third volume of *La Frottola* is concerned with this subject).

Doloroso mi tapinello is given here (Example 1, p. 48) after its unique source, the Faenza Codex. It is simple, setting its text syllabically except for line-ending melismas; only line three presents a problem, with its eight syllables set to seven semibreves (an eighth, descending to D, could be discreetly added). The counterpoint is, speaking frankly, amateurish, not a good reflection of Hothby's teaching; the young aristocrat may not have been the most attentive of students. Of more interest is the melodic line of the Cantus, which suggests derivation from a popular tune, perhaps Erfordia's recollection of the melody to which he

---

[1] Faenza, Biblioteca Comunale Manfrediana MS 117. On this source see Oscar Mischiati, "Indice descrittivo del manoscritto 117 della Biblioteca comunale di Faenza," *L'Organo* 20 (1982), 3-35. A full study of the Bonadies section of the Faenza Codex by Pedro Memelsdorff may be found in his doctoral dissertation, "The Filiation and Transmission of Instrumental Polyphony in Late Medieval Italy: The Codex Faenza 117" (University of Utrecht, 2010).

[2] James Haar and John Nádas, "Johannes de Anglia (John Hothby): Notes on his Career in Italy," *Acta musicologica* 79 (2007), 291-358, esp. 318-24. For Strohm's suggestion see his *The Rise of European Music, 1380-1500* (Cambridge: Cambridge University Press, 1993), 292-93.

[3] *La Frottola*, 3 vols. (Aarhus: Universitetsforlaget, 1968-70), 2: 303.

Ex. 1: Johannes de Erfordia, *Doloroso mi tapinello* Faenza, Bibl. Com. Manfrediana, MS 117, fol. 899v

had heard the barzelletta text sung. The opening bars, as well as the frottolistic minims of measure 5, are rhythmically suggestive of the barzelletta. The bare-bones repetition of measures 1-9 in measures 11-14, with the tenor following in rigid and pointless imitation, and the clumsy attempt at contrapuntal texture in the final phrase are, on the other hand, further demonstrations of compositional ineptitude.

Jeppesen's transcription of *Doloroso mi tapinello* is of course correctly done. He did omit one feature of the original: its metrical signature of O2, clearly indicated in all three voices. Hothby may have used the composition of this piece to illustrate for Erfordia the meaning of O2, as defined by him and as used by composers including Dufay: *modus (minor) perfectus* with *tempus imperfectum*, the whole subject in practice to diminution.[4] In Example 1 (on facing page) we can see the imperfect breves of *tempus imperfectum* (the semibreves are also imperfect) as well as their grouping into perfect longs, eight groups in all, indicated by black markers at three-measure intervals and counting from beginning to end of the piece (including a final longa in the original, *ultra mensuram* but here transcribed as three breves). If the signature is also a sign of diminution, the piece could be read at the next lower note level. This is all clear enough; unfortunately it does nothing to support the faint hints of barzelletta style in the song's upper voice. I would guess that Erfordia heard a kind of barzelletta with the 'topinello' text and was attracted to it; resemblance to such a song, probably not familiar to the expatriate Englishman Hothby, was all but lost as he directed a transformation of Erfordia's sketch into a pedagogical exercise.

I have found no other settings of *Doloroso mi tapinello*. Hothby could hardly have given this text to Erfordia, who must have heard it sung by students in Pavia, Lucca, or perhaps Florence, in the early 1470s. But the song, or at any rate its text, was not new; it is found, with a full textual residuum including two eight-line stanzas (each containing *piedi* and *volta*) and with a ripresa beginning "Deh tristo mi topinello," in the Mancini Codex, a musical source copied at the beginning of the fifteenth century.[5] *Deh tristo mi topinello* (Example 2 on p. 50) is in the last section of the manuscript, some of it probably copied in Florence (the body of the manuscript probably comes from the Veneto) beginning c. 1410. *Deh tristo* itself must have been entered into the manuscript no later than the 1420s.

The full text as found in Mancini, fol. XCVIr, is as follows:

> Deh tristo mi topinello
>
> Che sum zunto al dereanpunto
>
> Che non manzarò più d'unto
>
> Se non pane et rafanello.

[4] See the discussion, including references to Hothby, in Anna Maria Busse Berger, *Mensuration and Proportion Signs. Origins and Evolution* (Oxford: Clarendon Press, 1993), 20-23, 148-59 *et passim*.

[5] Lucca, Archivio di Stato, MS 184 / Perugia, Biblioteca Comunale 'Augusta,' MS 3065. See John Nádas and Agostino Ziino, *The Lucca Codex. Codice Mancini*. Introductory Study and Facsimile Edition (Lucca: Libreria Musicale Italiana, 1990), 47-49, 78-79, 198-99.

Ex. 2: *Deh tristo ni topinello* Lucca. Arch. di Stato, MS 184, fols. XCVv-XCVI

El pan serà de mestura,
Sozzo e negro com(o) carbone;
Quella serà (la) mia pastura
De mi, povero compagnone.
Non posso manzar bocone
Tanto è negro e ruzinente;
El me se ficca infra el dente,

[Deh tristo...]
Non manzarò più salcizza,
Nè de grassi caponcelli;
Nanci manzarò panizza
Con de magri buratelli.
Ampo avesse io de tortelli,

Che mi porla ben passare;
Ma el me convirà manzare
(De) la fava a mo' de porcello.
[Deh tristo...][6]

it was more than the opening ripresa. The meaning of the poem, on its surface a mock lament about an enforced vegetarian diet addressed to the author's companion (a mouse, perhaps also his own stomach), is not clear, but it was surely intended to be funny. That it should still have been popular after fifty years or more seems extraordinary, but there are other examples of such survival.[7]

This song has attracted the attention of several modern scholars. Although he is not the first to mention it, I shall give pride of place to William Prizer, to whom this study is dedicated in admiration and friendship. Prizer cites it in his dissertation of 1974 (published in 1980) and again in an article of 1986, the latter of great use to me as I prepared this study.[8] *Deh tristo* is mentioned, slightly misleadingly, in an article by Howard Mayer Brown.[9] Earlier citations mentioning the Mancini Codex as source are those of Mancini, Alfredo Bonaccorsi, and Benvenuto Disertori, the last in the introduction to a volume containing an edition of Petrucci's first three frottola books. Disertori gives a transcription of text and music, together with a commentary oddly wide of the mark, describing the piece both as frottolistic and as reminiscent of troubadour song.

Deh tristo is the only octosyllabic barzelletta in the Mancini Codex; its 'companion piece' cited by Disertori, *De mia farina fo le mie lasagne* (fol. LXVIIr)—though using a food metaphor with clearly obscene meaning—is a ballata with seven- and eleven-syllable lines.[10] Was the barzelletta in *ottonario* an uncommon poetic form in the early decades of the Quattrocento? A brief historical sketch may be helpful at this point.

---

[6] Nádas and Ziino, *The Lucca Codex*, 199. The text as given here is found in Ettore Li Gotti, "Il Codice di Lucca, ii: Testi letterari," *Musica disciplina* 4 (1950), 143. Li Gotti and Pirrotta worked together on the Mancini Codex, Pirrotta writing parts i and iii (*Musica disciplina*, vols. 3 and 5).

[7] A couple of barzellette, of a popular cast, appearing in musical setting in the mid-fifteenth century MS Escorial IV.a.24, are found in a literary codex of the end of the century (Milan, Bibl. Ambrosiana, Cod. C 35 sup.) associated with Filippo Scarlatti. See Nino Pirrotta, "Su alcuni testi italiani di composizioni polifoniche quattrocentesche," *Quadrivium* 14 (Bologna, 1973): 133-57, at 140.

[8] William F. Prizer, *Courtly Pastimes: The Frottole of Marchetto Cara* (Ann Arbor: UMI Press, 1980), 75; idem, "The Frottola and the Unwritten Tradition," *Studi musicali* 15 (1986), 3-37, at 6.

[9] "Fantasia on a Theme by Boccaccio," *Early Music* 5, no. 3 (1977), 324-39, at 337.

[10] *Le Frottole nell'edizione principe di Ottaviano Petrucci*, transcribed by Gaetano Cesari, edited by Raffaello Monterosso, with an introduction by Benvenuto Disertori (Cremona: Athenaeum Cremonense, 1954), xi-xii. The earlier citations are in Augusto Mancini, "Frammenti di un nuovo codice dell' Ars nova," *Rendiconti delle sedute dell'Acccademia Nazionale dei Lincei* 8, no. 2 (1947), 85-94, 92; Alfredo Bonaccorsi, "Un nuovo codice dell'Ars nova': il codice lucchese," *Atti dell' Accademia nazionale dei Lincei. Memorie. Classe di Scienze morale, storiche e filologiche* 8, no. 1 (1948), 539-615, at 593, 602 (Bonaccorsi does not compare the two pieces).

Ottonario verse is said to be found as early as the thirteenth century,[11] having perhaps been composed partly in imitation of contemporary Latin hymns such as the *Stabat mater dolorosa* of Jacopone (?). It became more widespread in the Trecento; a charming use of it may be found in the *Rime* of Franco Sacchetti (mid-late fourteenth century), a nine-stanza *Canzonetta balatella* opening with this ripresa:[12]

> Benedetto sia la state
>
> che ci fa sì solazzare!
>
> Maledetto sia il verno
>
> ch'a città si fa tornare!

The deceptively Petrarchan opening is, like the rest of the poem, half-humorous; as for line two's "solazzare," one wonders whether Simone Prodenzani was thinking of this 'solace' when he set about writing his *Solazzo* in the early fifteenth century (on this see below). The poem continues with Sacchetti's description of a *brigata* of playfully named carefree spirits ("cacciapensieri") who, unlike the learned folk inside the high walls of Florence, devoted themselves to entertaining one another, chiefly through song and dance:

> Sempre danze e rigoletti
>
> con diletti e gioia ciascuno:
>
> vecchi come giovenetti
>
> non è differente alcuno.
>
> Siam cento e siam uno
>
> in un animo e volere,
>
> ciascun grida pur: Godere!
>
> e muoia chi non vuol cantare![13]

The playful reference to Boccaccio is unmistakable. In our context it may be more than casual; at least some of the dances and songs of the *Decameron* preceding or following the *ballate* given in the text may have been barzellette in *ottonari*. A possible example is the opening of Giornata Quinta, in which at mealtime "alcuna stampita et un balatetta o due furon cantate."

Does Sacchetti's *canzonetta balatella* qualify in critical terms as a *ballata*? By the late fourteenth century it would seem that it did. Gidino da Sommacampagna, writing in the early 1380s, has this to say in a summary description of the *ballata grande*:

[11] Pietro Beltrami, *La metrica italiana* (Bologna: Mulino, 2002), 197.

[12] Franco Sacchetti, *Il libro delle rime*, ed. Franca Brambilla Ageni (Florence: Olschki/Perth: Western Australia, 1990), no. [cix], 134-36.

[13] "Always, dances and *rigoletti*, each with joy and delight; old and young, all are alike. We are a hundred and at the same time we are one, united in spirit and will; each of us cries out 'Enjoy!' and let all perish who don't want to sing!'" On the *righoletto* see Robert Nosow, "Dancing the Righoletto," *Journal of Musicology* 24 (2007), 407-46. Nosow cites part of this poem (415-16).

> In conclusion, note that all ballatas of which the *riprese* are composed
> of four lines...are made of eleven-syllable lines, or of eight syllables or
> of seven or of how many one wishes, from six to twelve syllables. As
> long as the ripresa contains four lines they are called *ballate grandi*.[14]

All of Gidino's examples of ballatas feature seven- and eleven-syllable lines, more commonly used in practice and doubtless preferable in theory; but *ottonari* seem to have been allowed as long as the stanzaic structure of the ballata was adhered to.

Simone di Golino de' Prodenzani of Orvieto (c. 1351-1438) is known for his references to Trecento and early Quattrocento music in the sonnets of his *Saporetto* (c. 1410-15).[15] More relevant to our purpose here is another substantial part of his poetic *oeuvre*, a collection of eighteen moralizing tales, written in the form of multistrophic ballatas, of varying length but all *ballate grandi* with four-line ripresas followed by eight-line stanzas (the ripresa is repeated at the end of each ballata). All the poems are cast in *ottonari*, the rhythms and line lengths matching the humorously earthy, colloquial vocabulary and suiting the characters' eating, drinking, fighting, bedding, and their dominating traits *(superbia, invidia, avariçia,* etc.—the seven deadly sins and many more). Here is the ripresa and the first stanza of the third tale (*De avariçia*), about a miser who denied his wife all good things but especially food:

> Se ballate a mia cançone,
>
>   vi dirò di mastro Pece
>
> della moglie e quel che fece
>
>   quando si mangiò el cappone.
>
> Questa giovan Gaudençía
>
>   tutte gente la chiamaro,
>
> senpre visse in penitençia
>
>   del marito, ch'era avaro,
>
> ma facìa vita di cane,
>
>   né da sera, né da mane
>
> carne in casa conparòne.[16]

---

[14] Gidino da Sommacampagna, *Tratttato e arte de li rithmi volgari* [facsimile], ed. Gian Paolo Caprettini *et al.* (Verona: La Grafica, 1993), ch. ii: Trattato della ballata osia cançone, 114-15: "Concludendo, nota che tutte le ballate dele quali li represe sono compillade de quatro versi, siano li ditti versi tutti, osia alguni de quigi, da undexe sillabe, *osia de otto sillabe,* osia de septe sillabe, osia de quante sillabe se voia, da sey sillabe infin a dodexe sillabe per çaschaduno verso, purchè la represa sia compillada de quatro versi, la dicta ballata èe appellada granda." (italics mine) The *Summa artis rythmici* of Antonio da Tempo (1332) from which Gidino's treatise is derived does not contain a version of this passage.

[15] See now Fabio Carboni, ed., *Simone de' Prodenzani. Rime,* 2 vols. (Rome: Vecchiarelli, 2003). Carboni's large bibliography includes, among much else, titles of the pioneering work of Santorre Debenedetti. Of special interest for Prodenzani's musical citations is John Nádas, "A Cautious Reading of Simone Prodenzani's 'Il Saporetto,'" *Recercare* 10 (1998), 23-38.

[16] Prodenzani, *Rime,* i: 67.

The miser, eating, alone, a capon in a food shop, hears from a page that his wife is home doing the same thing; in a rage he returns home and dies on the spot. His young wife immediately summons a *notaio*, and learns that she inherits all her husband's goods; she then consoles herself with a new husband, "giovin, bello e… ben fornito." As in *Deh tristo mi topinello*, food is here made to stand for other good things in life. Whether Prodenzani's barzelletta-fables were widely read we do not know; but it is clear that popular verse in *ottonari*, if not as fashionable as the eleven-syllable *ottava rima* made popular by Boccaccio and used for epic narrative, or the burlesque-sonnet of Burchiello and his contemporaries in Quattrocento Tuscany, had a place all its own in the *poesia per musica* of the time. The "ballare" of Prodenzani, like the "cantare" of the epic poets, may have been metaphorical, but if read aloud the ripresas of his barzellettas could have been sung to a popular or improvised tune.[17]

As the fifteenth century went on the barzelletta appeared in a number of manuscript collections, though until the last decades of the century it seems to have flourished as a musical genre more in the realm of popular, usually unwritten song.[18] Strohm's statement[19] that *Deh tristo mi topinello* as found in the Mancini Codex marks the "first musical appearance" (i.e., notated) of the "octosyllabic line of the barzelletta" is certainly intriguing; I resisted the strong temptation to place it on the opening page of this study out of scholarly caution, but I have not yet discovered an earlier example. From mid-century is *Hora may che fora son,* an evidently popular barzelletta surviving in a four-voice setting close enough to some Petrucci *frottole* to be called a direct ancestor, yet lacking the rhythmic lilt of *Deh tristo*.[20]

Perhaps the most direct poetic ancestor of the North Italian frottola cultivated in Mantua, Ferrara, and the Veneto in the closing decades of the fifteenth century, deftly gathered and published by Ottaviano Petrucci beginning in 1504, was the *canzona a ballo*. This name was used in Florence and, elsewhere in Italy, for strophic ballatas of a popular cast, in various metrical schemes including the barzelletta. Many of these poems include internal repetition of lines from the opening ripresa, and one finds frequent textual references to "ballo" as well as "canto."

We have seen all of this in the work of Prodenzani in the early Quattrocento, and hints of it a generation earlier in the poetry of Sacchetti. It seems no accident that Lorenzo de' Medici (1449-1492) included a good deal of Sacchetti's verse in the *Raccolta Aragonese*, the manuscript anthology of Tuscan verse sent by Lorenzo to Federigo d'Aragona of Naples in 1477.[21] The collection, beginning with Dante

---

[17] For a *canzone a ballo* closely based on a *Decameron* tale, see Hamilton A. Mathes, "*Decameron*, III: 3, and a *Canzone a ballo* of Lorenzo de' Medici," *Modern Philology* 48 (1950), 82-85. The attribution to Lorenzo has been questioned but the poem is of the period.

[18] William F. Prizer, "The Frottola and the Unwritten Tradition," *Studi musicali* 15 (1986), 3-37.

[19] See Reinhard Strohm, *The Rise of European Music, 1300-1500* (Cambridge: Cambridge University Press, 1993), 103.

[20] On *Hora may che fora son* see Pirrotta, "Su alcuni testi," 140, 155; Strohm, *The Rise of European Music*, 571.

[21] On the *Raccolta* see Tiziano Zanato, ed., *Lorenzo de' Medici. Opere* (Turin: Einaudi, 1992), 311-53.

and Cino da Pistoia, extends through the Trecento and includes Quattrocento poets—among them some of the participants in the Certame coronario of 1441 (a Medici-supported event) such as Francesco Altobianco degli Alberti. It ends with contemporary verse, represented by sixteen poems—several of them quite new— by Lorenzo himself.[22] These include eleven sonnets and canzoni from Lorenzo's *Canzoniere*, Petrarchistic in language and 'literary' in tone, followed by five *canzone a ballo*, much more *popolaresco* in theme and vocabulary.

One of these, *Donne belle io ho cercato*, is an ottonario-barzelletta, with a four-line ripresa the last two of which are repeated at the end of every stanza. The poem is a charming acknowledgement of Amor having found the poet's heart (stolen during a dance and locked up in the gaze of "due belli ochi") used his arrows and darts to take the heart and return it to its owner. Here is the ripresa and first stanza:[23]

> Donne belle, io ho cercato
> lungo tempo del mio core.
> Ringrazio sia tu, Amore,
> ch'io l'ho pure alfin trovato.
> Egli è forse in questo ballo
> chi il mio cor furato avia?
> Hallo seco, e sempre arallo,
> quanto fia la vita mia;
> ella è sì benigna e pia,
> ch'ella arà sempre il mio core.
> Ringraziato sia tu, Amore,
> ch'io l'ho pure alfin trovato.

The next poem in the *Raccolta*, also by Lorenzo, is a ballata with seven- and eleven-syllable lines. Its preoccupation with love and dancing nevertheless marks it as another canzone a ballo. Here is its opening ripresa:

> Chi non è innamorato
> esca di questo ballo,
> ché faria fallo
> a stare in sì bel lato.[24]

Donne belle could be sung, needing little if any adjustment, to the soprano line of *Deh tristo mi topinello*, some version of which may have survived into Lorenzo de' Medici's time—and that of Johannes de Erfordia.

Lorenzo's *canti carnascialeschi* include four barzellette, several of them early works; one (late) song is so famous that it has come to represent Lorenzo as poet: the *Canzone di Bacco*, opening with this 'signature' ripresa:[25]

---

[22] Zanato, *Lorenzo de' Medici Opere*, 317-18.

[23] Ibid., 348.

[24] Ibid., 350. It may be translated as "He who is not a lover should leave this dance, since he is mistaken to remain in such a lovely spot."

[25] Ibid., 391 Eleven carnival songs are securely attributed to Lorenzo; many more were at one time thought to be his. See ibid., 357-65.

> Quanto è bella giovinezza,
> che si fugge tuttavia!
> Chi vuol esser lieto, sia,
> di doman non c'è certezza.

The poem is full of lines such as "Donne e giovinetti amanti / viva Bacco e viva Amore! / Ciascun suoni, balli e canti!" It features a characteristic repetition of the last two lines of the ripresa at the end of each of its seven stanzas. Like *Donne belle io ho cercato*, it has the same metric structure as *Deh tristo mi topinello* and could have been sung to its melody or one very like it, late (c.1490) as is its date of composition. Most of Lorenzo's popular verse was sung, as the existence of laude to be sung ("cantasi come") to their melodies testifies.[26]

Angelo Poliziano (1454-1494), the greatest Florentine literary figure of his generation, was for a good deal of their short lives a close friend and mentor to Lorenzo, as well as a teacher of his children. His skills as a classicist were vastly greater than Lorenzo's, and his vernacular poetry, especially the ottava stanzas of *L'Orfeo* and the hundred or so surviving *rispetti*, place him in another class than the Magnifico. But both men seem to have shared an interest in popular poetry; both wrote *canzoni a ballo*, which survive in sources mixing the work of the two.

The poems given under the rubric *Canzoni a ballo* in Daniela Delcorno Branca's critical edition of Poliziano's Italian verse[27] are ballatas of a popular, sometimes didactic, tone. Nine of them are barzellette in form and meter; though not called so in the manuscript and early printed sources, they do appear with the word *ballatetta*, found as early as Boccaccio and Sacchetti (see above).[28] They do not use the mnemonic device of repeating lines of the ripresa in the stanza, nor do they emphasize music-making and dancing. An exception to this last statement is *Ben venga maggio/e'l gonfalon selvaggio* (no. CXXII, 375-77); witness this stanza:

> Ciascuna balla e canti
> di questa schiera nostra;
> ecco che i dolci amanti
> van per voi, belle in giostra.
> Qual dura a lor si mostra,
> farà sfiorire il maggio.

---

[26] Walter H. Rubsamen, "The Music for 'Quant' è bella giovinezza' and Other Carnival Songs," in *Art, Science, and History in the Renaissance*, ed. Charles S. Singleton (Baltimore: Johns Hopkins Press, 1967), 163-84, reconstructs (not altogether convincingly) a musical setting of the poem from materials in the manuscript Florence, B.N.C., Banco raro 230. The text as found in B.N.C. MS Magl. VII, 1225, fol. 45, is prefaced by the remark "Chançona chomposta dal magnificho lorenzo de medici che questo charnasciale fece fare el trionfo di bacho dove chantarano l'infrascritta chançone chomposta da leuto fu choxe bellissime" (cited by Rubsamen, 171).

[27] Daniela Delcorno Branca, ed., *Angelo Poliziano. Rime* (Florence: Accademia della Crusca, 1986), 343-79, nos. CII-CXXIV.

[28] The poems are in early printed sources (see Branca, *Poliziano. Rime*, 90-110) called "ballate, ballatette, canzonette, canzone, canzone a ballo." "Ballatetta" may be a variant form of "Barzelletta."

As the reader will have noticed, this is not a barzelletta but a *ballata minima* with seven-syllable stanzas (and a seven-/eleven-syllable ripresa).

In a sixteenth-century source *Ben venga Maggio* is said to have been sung.[29] As early as 1495 it is described, as are several others of his *canzone a ballo*, as "intonata di Messer Ang. Politiano."[30] Whether this means provided with a tune for singing, or simply brought into poetic sound for reading aloud or for improvisatory singing, I am not sure. As with Lorenzo, Poliziano must have heard or known of his barzellette being sung 'around' Florence.[31]

The frottola repertory printed by Petrucci is largely of North Italian provenance; this includes the barzelletta (examples are pieces in the Table of Contents of Petrucci's Book IV specifically called *frottole*). It can nevertheless be said that the Florentine *ballatetta*, *canzone a ballo*, and *canto carnascialesco*, along with the Spanish / Neapolitan *villancico*, made their contribution to the development of a distinctively Italian popularizing poetic-musical genre akin to the *chanson rustique* and the nascent 'Parisian' chanson of contemporary France. As an early example of the genre *Deh tristo mi topinello* deserves a closer look; we will turn back to it now.

Fig. 1: *Deh tristo mi topinello*, digital image from Lucca, Archivio di Stato, MS 184, fols. XCVv-XCVIr

[29] See Branca, *Poliziano. Rime,* 109: *Canzone a ballo composta da diversi autori...*(Florence: [Sermartelli], 1564): "Canzona dang(elo) Politiano di Maggio: la quale saveva a chantare p(er) donne nellentrare de Giostranti in campo: e coronandogli per loro amore giostravono" (Branca, 375).

[30] Ibid., 92.

[31] For written settings of his verse, see Giulio Cattin, "Le rime del Poliziano nelle fonti musicali," in *Umanesimo e rinascimento a Firenze e Venezia.* 2 vols. *Miscellanea di studi in onore di Vittore Branca* III (Florence: Olschki, 1983), 1: 379-96.

As the facsimile shows, the piece is squeezed into the bottom lines
(three for the Cantus, two for the Tenor) of an opening in the Mancini Codex;
consideration of available space dictated the Tenor to be copied on the verso, the
Cantus with its sizeable text residuum on the facing recto (the opposite of the
usual practice). Both text and music are carefully copied, and both are complete
except for the right margin of the recto page, where trimming and subsequent
damage have sheared off an occasional text letter and one note, a semibreve
A supplied in the transcription (m. 7).[32] The two-voice ballata *O pensieri vani
o sperança fallace,* above *Deh tristo* on fols. XCVv-XCVIr, is an entirely different
kind of piece, a highly melismatic *ballata mezzana* with marked Italian notational
features (frequent dots of division; use of downward and oblique stems; dot of
elision). Both pieces are in the hand of the chief scribe of the manuscript, but
O pensieri would seem to have been copied in northern Italy, *Deh tristo* added at a
later time and probably in Florence.

Another added piece that has been compared in poetic and musical style
to *Deh tristo* is *De mia farina fo le mie lasangne* (see above, at n. 10), a tiny two-voice
song copied on the recto page of an opening (fols. LXVIv-LXVIIr) devoted to
an elaborate madrigal praising a duke (probably Giangaleazzo Visconti, crowned
duke of Milan in 1395).[33] The brief *ballata minima* text of *De mia farina* is earthy in
language, in fact frankly obscene, lacking the charm of *Deh tristo*; its flatfooted music
is notated in a kind of cross between French *tempus perfectum* and Italian *novenari*. I
see little resemblance between the two pieces.[34]

In *Deh tristo* both Cantus and Tenor are completely texted, a feature
characteristic of the Mancini Codex and indeed of Italian music in the early
fifteenth century. The two-voice counterpoint is correctly written—almost too

---

[32] For information about the physical state of the manuscript and about its copying history and scribal
hands, see Nádas and Ziino, *The Lucca Codex.*

[33] Nádas and Ziino, *The Lucca Codex,* 38-39.

[34] For a transcription of *De mia farina* see Disertori, *Le Frottole,* xii; the attribution to Antonello da
Caserta applies *(pace* Disertori and Bonaccorsi) only to the piece at the top of the page. The text is
as follows: De mia farina fo le mie lasangne / Et de queste mi godo / Perche le fo a mio modo. /
Quando io vo molle e quando io vo(glio) stagne / De mia farina…. Mancini, "Frammento," 92,
finds this text "una ballata caratteristica e intelligibile"; Bonaccorsi, "Un nuovo codice," 593, praises
both text and music, admiring its "freschezza," and finding "questo canto…vivo e tutto gentile,"
typical of "un canto materno." Let us hope he did not mean this last phrase to be read literally.

correctly—in the idiom of its time, and is harmonically sound (the one odd spot, the cadence in measure 6, is helped by raising the Cantus a half-step to create a major sixth leading to the octave which opens the next phrase). Whether this song could in another source have had an added third voice, presumably a Contratenor Bassus, it is musically satisfying as it stands. Text underlay is easy in this mostly syllabic piece, with two brief melismas in the upper voice offering the singer some flexibility if all the stanzas are sung.

The rhythmic lilt of the melodic lines, both Cantus and Tenor—almost uncannily evocative of the late Quattrocento frottola—is what gives the piece its charm. There is no metric signature, but the mensuration must be $\mathbb{C}$, *tempus imperfectum* with major prolation: in transcription two perfect (or three colored, hence imperfect) semibreves per measure. The need for alteration in measure 1 of the Tenor, and the dots of perfection (division) occurring several times in the Cantus, confirm this. The Tenor's use of coloration, forming measures of *tempus perfectum* with minor prolation (3/1 against 6/2 or, more familiarly, 3/4 against 6/8), gives the song rhythmic punch; its dance-like character is emphasized by the repeated colored notes marking the cadences.

Whether meant literally for dancing or not, songs like *Deh tristo mi topinello* could have been performed with the sort of easy-going round dance thought to be characteristic of the Trecento ballata. The music must have been equally carefree; when I said above that it seems to have been copied 'almost too carefully,' I meant that the scribe, who was surely an educated musician, must have recognized in his exemplar the style of both poetry and music as local (Florentine) and at the same time the notation as completely French. In copying it he may have tidied things up a bit, especially in the Tenor voice, producing a more civilized version of what might have been a quickly notated popular song.

*   *   *

In order to confirm the resemblance between *Deh tristo mi topinello* and the frottolas of Petrucci's time one should leaf through the surviving published volumes, appearing between 1504 and 1514, perhaps looking at a few manuscript concordances.[35] This is more than can be accomplished here. By way of concluding this essay I will choose a couple of barzellettas from Petrucci's volumes, comparing printed and manuscript sources with modern editions and with my transcription of *Deh tristo*.

L'amor donna ch'io te porto appears in *Frottole libro septimo* (1507), no. 20 in the edition of Lucia Boscolo (Example 3). If one compares this modern edition with Fig. 2, the Cantus of *L'amor donna* as it appears in a manuscript slightly older

---

[35] Modern editions of the Petrucci *Frottole* include books 6-9, and 11, in *Le Frottole Petrucci. Le edizioni dal 1504 al 1514*, vols. 1- 5 (various editors) (Padua: CLEUP Editrice, 1997?). Books 1-3 are edited in *Le frottole nell' edizione principe di Ottavio Petrucci*, ed. Gaetano Cesari and Raffaello Monterosso (Cremona: Athenaeum cremonense, 1954); books 1 and 4 appear, edited by Rudolf Schwartz, in *Frottole Buch I und IV* (Leipzig: Breitkopf und Härtel, 1935).

than Petrucci's print[36] (note the attribution to 'jac. fo.' [Giacomo Fogliano], found only in this source), there are no changes other than the substitution of modern clefs, unavoidable in these notationally effete days (attention should be paid to the original clefs, indicated here); halving of note values, unnecessary for all but the semi-literate reader or performer; and the addition of barlines.

Ex. 3: *L'amor donna, ch'io te porto.* After *Le Frottole Petrucci,* v. 5; *Frottole libro septimo.*
    no.20

These are helpful for music in score, if correctly placed. Are they correct in Example 3? In one sense, yes. The mensural signature ₡ indicates that all note values are duple unless dotted, and that the tactus is on the breve, the down- and upbeats falling on the semibreve (here the whole note and half note respectively). Since mensural signatures indicate note measurement but not necessarily rhythm or (modern) meter, Example 3 is theoretically correct.

---

[36] Paris, B.N.F. Dép. de la musique, fonds du Conservatoire, MS. Rés. Vm7 676, fols. 110v-11r. The example is taken directly from *Manuscrit italien de frottole* (1502). *Facsimilé du Ms de la Bibliothèque nationale, Paris, Rés. Vm7 676* (Geneva: Minkoff, 1979), 20. Notice that the verbal text is slightly different (and wrongly underlaid) in the Paris version of the piece.

Fig. 2: Giacomo Fogliano, *L'amor donna* Paris, B.N.F. Dép. de la musique, fonds du Conservatoire., MS Rés. Vm⁷ 676, fol. 110v

It is, however, unhelpful, even deceptive in reflecting the rhythmic character of the piece. As the reader will recall, what struck me about *Deh tristo* is its close resemblance to the barzellettas of the Petrucci repertory, partly in melodic style but above all in its dance-like rhythmic movement. This rhythm can be seen easily enough in Figure 2, especially in the Cantus voice. It is not as easy to see past the wooden barring of Example 3. I am certainly not the first person to espouse this view of barzelletta rhythm; Alfred Einstein pointed it out and discussed it briefly but lucidly more than sixty years ago, and indeed published a transcription of *L'amor donna* without mensural signature but in lilting 3/4 - 6/8 rhythm and with each phrase beginning with a two-note upbeat.[37]

The next piece in Paris 676 is another barzelletta, *Scopri o lingua el cieco ardore* (Figure 3 on p. 62), printed in Petrucci's *Frottola libro primo of* 1504 (Figure 4 on p. 63), with its music attributed, as in the manuscript, to Bartolomeo Tromboncino. The Petrucci print carries, in all four voices, the mensural signature ₵. The Paris manuscript shows, probably in the Cantus and certainly in the Altus (see Figure 3), the signature O, *tempus perfectum* with implied minor prolation: three imperfect semibreves to the breve (the latter a full measure in transcription). For a number of Petrucci barzellettas the signature I supplied for *Deh tristo* (₵) would be appropriate; for *Scopri o lingua* O does well. Examples 4a-b (see p. 63) show, first, the Cantus of Petrucci's version in modern transcription and, next, the version of Paris 676. It is clear that triple time suits the music better, but since there are no perfect breves the signature ₵ allows a correct if not idiomatic transcription.

---

[37] Alfred Einstein, *The Italian Madrigal*, 3 vols., transl. Alexander H. Krappe, Roger H. Sessions, and Oliver Strunk (Princeton: Princeton University Press, 1949), 1: 80-81 (discussion); 3: no. 5 (transcription).

Fig. 3: Bartolomeo Tromboncino, *Scopri [o] lingua*, Paris, B.N.F., MS Rés. Vm7
676, fols. 111v-112r

Fig. 4: Tromboncino, *Scopri o lingua, Frottole libro primo* (Venice: Petrucci, 1504), fol. 16v.

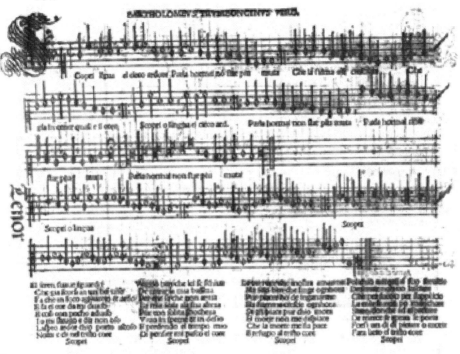

Ex. 4a: Tromboncino, *Scopri [o] lingun*, Cantus, mm.1-13 (*Frottole libro primo*)

Ex. 4b: Tromboncino, *Scopri lingua*, Cantus-Altus (Paris, Vm⁷ 676, fols. 11v-112r)

What we may call *the* barzelletta can thus be seen to last from at least the early fifteenth century (perhaps earlier in the unwritten tradtion) to the early Cinquecento. Indeed it survived for at least another half century,[38] and echoes of it are found in the early seventeenth century. Whether or not *Deh tristo mi topinello* is the oldest written record of this popular dance-song species, it is one that had a very long life, something akin to the pattern-bass lines of Renaissance and Baroque vocal and concerted music.

---

[38] See James Haar, "Arcadelt and the Frottola: The Italianate Chanson c. 1500," in *Res musicae: Essays in Honor of James W. Pruett*, ed. Paul R. Laird and Craig H. Russell (Warren, MI: Harmonie Park Press, 2001), 97-110.

Marriage, Divorce, The Aeneid, *Henry VIII,* *Catherine of Aragon and a Manuscript of Motets*[1]

Richard Sherr

London, British Library MS Royal 8 G. vii (hereafter, London) is a member of a large complex of manuscripts copied and illuminated in the first decades of the sixteenth century in a scriptorium connected to the court chapels of the Hapsburg-Burgundy rulers of Flanders: Philip the Fair, his son Charles (later Emperor Charles V), and Philip's sister, Marguerite of Austria, who acted as regent for Charles after her brother's death in 1506.[2] According to Herbert Kellman, it "… is one of the most important and most interesting of the fifty manuscripts of polyphony produced . . . at the court of the Netherlands . . . for presentation to members of the ruling house of Burgundy-Hapsburg and other sovereigns, nobles, and patricians throughout Europe."[3]

The intended recipients of London are identified by the heraldy that adorns the opening folios as King Henry VIII of England and his first wife, Catherine of Aragon.[4] And if that weren't enough, Henry and Catherine are in fact mentioned by name in the text of the second motet in the manuscript. Further, the text of the

---

[1] This article is based on a paper read at the International Conference: *The Burgundian-Hapsburg Court Complex of Music Manuscripts (1500-1535) and the Workshop of Petrus Alamire,* Leuven, Belgium, 25-28 November 1999, in an expanded version at Smith College (Inaugural Chair Lecture), 25 March 2002, and as the Annual Karl Geiringer Lecturer at the University of California, Santa Barbara, 28 April 2002.

[2] These are generally known as the "Alamire Manuscripts," even though the scribe Petrus Alamire was not responsible for all of them. See Herbert Kellmann, ed., *The Treasury of Petrus Alamire: Music and Art in Flemish Court Manuscripts 1500-1535* (Ludion, Ghent, and Amsterdam: The Alamire Foundation, 1999).

[3] Herbert Kellman, Introduction to *Renaissance Music in Facsimile* [RMF], 9: London, British Library MS Royal 8 G. vii (New York, 1987), v. The manuscript is unique on several counts. Most of the manuscripts that were sent out from the court contained settings of the Mass; London is one of only a few containing motets, and the only one containing motets that is in choirbook format. It is also the only manuscript in the complex in which every work is anonymous.

[4] Henry by the symbols of the Tudor monarchy; Catherine by her emblem, the pomegranate, which is somewhat sexually melded to the Tudor Rose in the lower right miniature. See RMF 9, fol. 2v. A color facsimile of the opening may be found in Kellman, ed. *The Treasury,* 111. There are in fact many sources that referred to Henry and Catherine in this symbolic way. See James P. Carley, *The Books of King Henry VIII and His Wives* (London: The British Library, 2004).

first motet is a prayer to Saint Anne the mother of the Virgin, a barren woman who miraculously gave birth—appropriate to a couple who wanted children and had a daughter named Mary.[5] The reason for these references to the English monarchs in a manuscript prepared at the Hapsburg-Burgundy court is also not hard to find. Catherine of Aragon was Marguerite of Austria's sister-in-law and was also Charles V's aunt; Henry and Catherine were therefore "in the family" (there are other court manuscripts in which their heraldic insignia appear, but London is the only one that reached England).[6]

We also know the period of time during which London had to have been produced. Henry and Catherine were husband and wife from 1509 to 1533. That provides a rather wide chronological window, but I am not concerned with when the manuscript was created. I am more interested in what this object became once Henry and Catherine had it.[7]

Why exactly was London given to Henry and Catherine? After all, by any artistic standards, it is not a particularly fancy book, although it is nice calligraphically. There are no illuminations other than those on the opening folios, and even these aren't particularly interesting from an artistic standpoint. Since it has little artistic value, presumably Henry and Catherine weren't supposed to admire it as an object. The interest, then, must have been in the contents of the manuscript, which are listed in Table I.[8]

Kellman has shown that London consists of eight fascicles, each a quaternion. He has further remarked that the contents seem to exhibit an organizing principle in the third to sixth fascicles, consisting of groups of pieces beginning with some invocation of Mary followed by some invocation of Christ.[9] A principle

---

[5] *Celeste beneficium introivit in Annam per quam nobis nata est Maria virgo. O beata deo grata mater matris nati patris. Anna Anna nos cum filia Cristo reconcilia.*

Adiutorium nostram in nomine domini quis non confitebitur tibi. Orat plorat et exorat Katherina sibi te orantes deprecamur adiuvemur per tuam clemenciam O Georgi tam beate Henricus rex clamat ad te audi queso vocem nostram.

In the *Motetti de la Corona* I, *Adiutorium nostram* is the secunda pars of *Celeste beneficium*, ascribed there to Mouton, but in CambriP 1760 it is a separate motet ascribed to Antoine Févin. In London it is also a separate motet.

[6] See JenaU 9, Kellman, *The Treasury*, 98-100.

[7] The presence of the manuscript in the British Library implies, but of course does not prove, that London actually was in England in the sixteenth century. On the other hand, the call number means that the source came from the Old Royal Library, i.e., the collection given to the British Museum by King George III. That a canon which seems to celebrate the appointment of the Earl of Arundel to the Order of the Garter was stuck into the manuscript at some point may or may not indicate that it was once in Arundel's possession and came to the Royal Library via the Nonsuch music library. John Milsom, for one, is of the opinion that Royal 8 G.vii was not a part of that library. See John Milsom, "The Nonsuch Music Library," in Chris Banks *et. al.*, eds. *Sundry sorts of music books: Essays on the British Library Collections Presented to O.W. Neighbour on his 70th Birthday* (London: The British Library, 1993), 146-82, at 170-71. On the other hand, Arundel did gain possession of other books from Henry's library.

[8] There is no table of contents in the source, and all the motets are anonymous—we know who many of the composers were, but that information is irrelevant to the following discussion, and they have been omitted.

[9] Kellman, RMF 9, Introduction, vii.

Table I
The Contents of Royal 8 G.VII

Superscript numbers indicate fascicles

Fascicle Number. Title	Present Folios	Signature	Final	Text
[1]1. *Celeste beneficium*	2v-4r	b	F	Prayer to Saint Anne, mother of Mary
2. *Adiutorium nostrum*	4v-6r	b	F	Prayer mentioning Saint George, Henry and Catherine
3. *Nesciens mater*	6v-8r	b	F	Virgin
4. *Ave regina coelorum*	8v-10r	b	F	Virgin: Marian antiphon
[2]5. *Descendi in ortum meum*	10v-12r	b	F	Song of Songs (Virgin)
6. *Sancta trinitas*	12v-14r	b	F	Trinity
7. *Vexilla regis*	14v-15r	b	F/D	Christ: Passion/Crucifixion
8. **Fama malum**	15v-17r		A	Aeneid IV: 174-177
9. *Doleo super te*	17v-18r		E	David Lament on death of Jonathan
[3]10. *O domine Ihesu*	18v-20r		A	Christ
11. *Maxsimilla Cristo*	20v-21r		A	Saint Andrew
12 *Sancta Maria/O werder mondt*	21v-22r		D	Virgin
13. *Sancta et immaculata*	22v-23r	b	A	Virgin
14. *Missus est Gabriel*	23v-25r	b	G	Annunciation (Virgin)
15. *Dulcissima virgo*	25v-26r		E	Virgin
[4]16. *Tota pulchra es/Salve*	26v-28r		D	Song of Songs/Beginning of Salve Regina (Virgin)
17. *O Sancta Maria*	28v-30r		A	Virgin: prayer for Charles V
18. *Verbum bonum*	30v-32r		G	Virgin
19. *Recordamini*	32v-34r	b	G	Christ: Crucifixion/Resurrexion

Table 1 (Cont.)

[5]20. *O beatissime domine Ihesu*	34v-38r		E	Christ
21. *Ave sanctissima Maria*	38v-40r		E	Virgin
22. Ecce Maria genuit	40v-42r	b	B♭	Circumcision/Nativity(Christ)/Virgin
[6]23. *Congratulamini michi*	42v-44r		D	Virgin: Nativity
24. *Egregie Cristi martir Christophore*	44v--48r	b	F	Saint Christopher
25. *Alma redemptoris mater*	48v-50r	b	F	Virgin: Marian antiphon
[7]26.**Dulces exuviae**	50v-52r		A	Aeneid IV: 651-654: Dido's last words
27. **Dulces exuviae**	52v-53r		E	Aeneid IV
28. **Dulces exuviae**	53v-54r		E	Aeneid IV
29. **Dulces exuviae**	54v-55r	b	A	Aeneid IV
30. **Dulces exuviae**	55v-56r		E	Aeneid IV
31. *Absalon fili mi*	56v-58r	2b, 3b	B♭	David Lament on death of Absalom
[8]32. *Ihesus autem transiens*	58v-59r	b	D	Christ
33. *Anima mea liquefacta est*	59v-62r		G	Song of Songs (Virgin)
34. *Tribulatio et angustia*	62v-63r	b	G	Psalms
Blank	63v-65v			

of organization might also be determined that covers fascicles 1-6. In any case, whatever organization there may be seems to be jarringly interrupted by two surprising interpolations: the setting of the description of rumor, *Fama malum*, No. 8, lines 174-177 of Book IV of Virgil's *Aeneid*, and most strikingly, fascicle 7 with its five settings in a row of lines 651-54 of Book IV, the beginning of Dido's final lament, commencing with the words "Dulces exuviae," Nos. 26-30, followed by *Absalon fili mi*, No. 31. The "Dulces exuviae" settings, to quote Kellman again, make London "unique not only among the court sources but among all contemporary manuscript and printed sources of Franco-Flemish music."[10]

[10] Ibid., v.

The many Renaissance settings of "Dulces exuviae" have been the subject of several studies.[11] Regarding just the motets in London, it can be remarked that there are musical connections among them: they are all in the same mi tonality, and two of them (Nos. 29-30) even use exactly the same Superius line. One might even argue that the order of the motets is not haphazard, that the text becomes "clearer" as motets progress: the first motets begin in imitation; but by the time we get to the last motet, not only does every line begin with all the voices together, there are even full stops at the end of every line (although the purely chordal declamation of later "Dulces exuviae" motets is not attempted). It is almost as if the motets were meant to be sung one after the other as a kind of five-movement "work."[12]

From a strict point of view, musical settings of lines from the *Aeneid* should not have been included in a manuscript of religious texts. Polyphonic settings of classical Latin poetry in the sixteenth century were more likely to appear in sources of secular music.[13] And there is no source of the sixteenth century that has five settings of "Dulces exuviae" in a row. This raises real questions as to the use London was meant to be put. A motet manuscript in which six out of thirty-four motets (the Virgil settings) could not be sung in any liturgical venue does not look like the kind of thing that was intended to be handed off to Henry's Chapel Royal. Indeed, it might even be argued that the rest of the motets were also so unlike the type of music the Chapel Royal was actually performing, that the chapel would hardly have used this manuscript. This gives London a distinctly private stamp, suggesting that it was actually meant for its recipients, as opposed to being some object that was to be filed away in the library of a household agency. But then, when would these motets be performed? Why give the king and queen of England a choirbook of motets that couldn't be used in the liturgy of the court in England, yet hardly seems suitable for their secular entertainments either?[14] Why would anybody want so many settings of "Dulces exuviae"? Why are they placed in this manuscript where they are? There is something profoundly strange about all of this. It is a situation which, as we say: "cries out for explanation."

When Henry and Catherine received this book, one would assume they opened it and looked at the illuminations in the first motet. But then what? Since there is no table of contents, they would have had to go through the entire manuscript page by page in order to know what was in it; they would have had to read it "like a book," experiencing each motet in the order presented. That the manuscript contains music notation would not have fazed Henry in the least, and perhaps

---

[11] See Helmut Osthoff, "Vergils Aeneis in der Musik von Josquin des Prez bis Orlando di Lasso," *Archiv für Musikwissenschaft* 11 (1954): 85-102.

[12] The motets are transcribed in James Roland Braithwaite, "The Introduction of Franco-Netherlandish Manuscripts to Early Tudor England: The Motet Repertory" (Ph.D. diss., Boston University, 1950), 3: 168-96.

[13] Those are the types of manuscripts in the Hapsburg-Burgundy complex which the other settings of "Fama malum" and "Dulces exuviae" appear, for instance. See BrusBR 228, FlorC 2439.

[14] We know that the pope on regular occasions would have motets sung for him as he was dining, but it is not clear that secular rulers would follow the same custom.

not Catherine either, and in any case it was perfectly possible to read through the texts alone; the advantage of choirbook format is that it makes it possible to see the entire piece at one time and grasp its text if not its music. If we consider the manuscript this way, as an entire document rather than a repository of individually distinct works, certain things stand out.

First, I think it would have been obvious to such readers of London that there was some difference in organization of materials between fascicles 1-6 and fascicles 7-8, and that fascicle 7 stands out in particular as disruptive and peculiar. That might further lead a reader to notice the contrast between the opening "happy" motets of the manuscript with their heraldic references to Henry and Catherine as married, their emphasis on birth, with the concentrated sense of tragedy and loss that begins with the five settings of Dido's lament, continues with *Absalon fili mi*, and ends with the pure anxiety expressed in the text of what became the actual last motet.

> *Tribulatio et angustia invenerunt me. Quia mandata tua meditatio mea est. Tribulationem et dolorem inveni et nomen domini invocavi.*

> Trouble and anguish have taken hold on me.[15] Because your command is in my thoughts.[16] found trouble and sorrow and called I upon the name of the Lord.[17]

From the celebration of birth to death to trouble and anguish caused by someone's commands, this is somewhat disturbing. Is this "progression" of affect merely coincidence or did the people who put this manuscript together have a purpose?

In a recent article Jennifer Thomas has attempted to provide an explanation.[18] She reads the contents of London as a message of sympathy from Marguerite of Austria to Catherine of Aragon. The key to Thomas's interpretation is the five settings of "Dulces exuviae." She sees it as a direct reference to Catherine's "five unfruitful pregnancies," and the whole manuscript as a comment on Catherine's particular situation. She concludes that: "The manuscript, then, may have been Margaret's way of informing Catherine that she was fully aware of every detail of Catherine's circumstances, and thus, that Catherine was not really alone."[19] Attractive as this theory is there are some problems with it. First of all, London by its heraldry seems manifestly directed at Henry more than at Catherine. And Thomas's interpretation of the hidden meaning of the "Dulces exuviae" settings depends on "Dulces exuviae" being somehow divorced from context, somehow viewed as merely a general "woman's lament" instead of the specific lament of woman about to commit suicide having been abandoned by her lover. As it turns out, what little

---

[15] Ps. 118/119KJV: 143.

[16] Source unknown.

[17] Ps. 114/116KJV: end of 3 and beginning of 4.

[18] Jennifer Thomas, "Patronage and Personal Narrative in a Music Manuscript: Marguerite of Austria, Katherine of Aragon, and London Royal 8 G.ii," in Thomasin LaMay ed., *Musical Voices of Early Modern Women: Many-Headed Melodies* (Aldershot: Ashgate, 2005), 337-64.

[19] Ibid., 354.

evidence there is describing people actually singing this text in the sixteenth century implies that the context was not forgotten when people heard those words.

One reference to someone singing "Dulces exuviae" is in a Latin poem by Baldassare Castiglione, which describes a contemporary woman who is clearly compared to Dido herself. The poem is annoyingly entitled "De Elisabella Gonzaga canente;" annoying because there was no such person, which means that "Elisabella" is either a play on Elisabetta (who is "bella"), hence Elisabetta Gonzaga di Montefeltro, duchess of Urbino, or it is a play on Isabella (changing the name by adding Elisa, i.e., Dido's "official" name Elissa, to it) hence Isabella d'Este Gonzaga, marchesa of Mantua.[20] In fact, William Prizer has shown conclusively that the poem was originally written for Isabella, although its printed title may consciously refer to both women.[21] But in any case, it hardly matters who exactly is being depicted. The poem begins with the words "Dulces exuviae" and describes the marvelous effects created by "Elisabella" singing "Dulces exuviae," accompanying herself on a keyboard instrument in what must be a private secular setting. The point of the poem is that, if Aeneas had heard this "new Dido" singing her lament, he would have turned his ships around and returned to Carthage. Obvious flattery, but still it seems very likely that this is inspired by a real occasion in which Castiglione heard Isabella d'Este singing "Dulces exuviae." What she sang was probably quite different from the motets in London, probably very like the simple anonymous setting that appears in a 1519 publication of frottole.[22]

Curiously, the only other reference to the actual singing of "Dulces exuviae" in the sixteenth century known to me concerns Martin Luther, who apparently once sang these words with his friends after dinner, possibly in a polyphonic setting, only slightly more complicated than the frottola and also quite different from the settings in London, transmitted in a German print of 1538.[23] Luther and his friends certainly also were perfectly aware of the context of the lines they were singing. Indeed, Luther used the occasion to remark on the miserable deaths of heathen heroes, like Turnus (Luther at this point quotes the last line of the *Aeneid*) and Dido, who die without the comfort of the Cross of Christ (*crux Christi*) and the Light of the Word (*lux verbi*).[24]

---

[20] The poem is published in *Carmina illustrium poetarum Italorum . . . tomus tertius* (Florentiae: typis Regiae Celsitudinis, apud Joannem Cajetanum Tartinium, & Sanctem Franchium, 1719), 303–5.

[21] An inventory of Isabella's books refers to a manuscript of an "Eligia dil Conte Bathesar da Castione sopra Madama cantante "Dulces exuviae." See William F. Prizer, "Una 'virtù molto convenienta a madonne': Isabella d'Este as a Musician," *Journal of Musicology* 17 (1999): 10-49, at 39.

[22] *Fioretti di Frottole Libro Secondo* (Naples, 1519).

[23] Osthoff, "Vergils Aeneis in der Musik," 91.

[24] The source is Johannes Mathesius, who reports a conversation after the singing of Dido's last words: "Ach Gott, sagt Luther, Arme und ellende leut sind die blinden Heiden mit iren gelerten, wie jemmerlich sterben die leut dahin, *sine crux Christi & lux verbi*, wie der grosse Poet sein Buch auch selbst beschleust, da er des Fürsten Turni tod malet: *Vitaque cum fremitu fugit indignata sub umbras*. Ich sterb mit grimm, und fahr mit ungedult von hinn, drumb rent im mancher selbst sein hertz abe, wie die ellende kurzrethige Dido, Wir dancken Gott für Davidis, Simeonis und Stephani letzte wort, die inn warer erkentnus und anruffung des ewigen Mittlers sein sanfft und frölich einshlaffen, und ire Seelichen

When we consider that anybody hearing a setting of "Dulces exuviae" might automatically consider its context, then the meaning of the contents of London (intended or not) becomes very interesting. And what is interesting concerns what happened to Henry and Catherine beginning in the year 1527. The historical situation may be summarized as follows.

Catherine of Aragon, youngest child of Ferdinand of Aragon and Isabella of Castille, had first been married to, and actually lived for several months with, Henry's elder brother Arthur, who died in 1502. After Arthur's death, Catherine, now a young widow, became a "problem" and Henry VII decided that she should be the wife of the new Prince of Wales, the future Henry VIII. But there was an impediment. The marriage to Arthur had placed Catherine and Henry in the relationship called "the first degree of affinity." It was normally forbidden for people related by the first degree of affinity to marry.[25] Henry VII and Ferdinand of Aragon were well aware of the impediment and also of the remedy: a dispensation from the Pope. That dispensation was duly granted by Pope Julius II in a bull dated 26 December 1503. Catherine then had to wait for six years in trying circumstances for anything to come of this, but on Henry VII's death in 1509, Henry VIII and Catherine were married. For eighteen years they lived together apparently happily as husband and wife and king and queen. Catherine bore Henry a number of children of whom only one, a daughter Mary, survived infancy. By 1518 or so, it became clear that Catherine would have no more children, but there was no reason why things could not go on as they had.

But in 1527, Henry suddenly announced that he had been troubled for a long time about his marriage. He had been considering why God had denied him a legitimate male heir. This was not an idle worry. England had just come out of a period of civil war, the Tudors were not totally secure on the throne, and for Henry to have been succeeded by a "weak" woman (his daughter Mary) left open the distinct possibility of renewed civil strife and the destruction of the dynasty. Why had God done this? The reason, Henry decided, was that his marriage to a person related by the first degree of affinity should not have been allowed. He used as evidence the Biblical origin of the restriction, in two passages from Leviticus that seem to say quite clearly that a brother may not marry his brother's wife.[26] That there was another passage in the Bible, in Deuteronomy, that seemed to say that a brother was required to marry his dead brother's wife if that brother had died without having had children, was conveniently forgotten for the moment.[27] That Henry was also violently infatuated with Anne Boleyn, who was refusing him sex, also did not enter into his stated reasons.

---

dem Herrn Christo auffzuheben und zuuerwaren vertrawen." Quoted in H. J. Moser's chapter on Luther's music in the Weimar edition of Luther's Works, 35: 538-42.

[25] And even if the marriage had not been consummated, there was another impediment known as Public Honesty (i.e., the legal fact that the marriage existed created the impediment) that would have also have made the marriage impossible under normal circumstances.

[26] Leviticus 18: 16 and 20: 21.

[27] Deuteronomy 25: 5.

Since human beings can convince themselves of anything, Henry convinced himself that, regardless of what everybody had thought at the time, his marriage was invalid and that he had literally been living in sin (that is, had not been really married) for eighteen years with the result that he had been cursed by the lack of a male heir. This "false" marriage had to be dissolved, and he be made free to marry again in the sight of God. And so the King's Great Matter (which was actually a request for an annulment, even though we constantly call it a "divorce") began, and was to drag on for six years with momentous consequences that nobody could have forseen at the beginning. For at the beginning, it was merely a legal affair. Henry first tried to overturn Julius II's dispensation on a technicality claiming that it had been granted by *falsa enarratio*, that the pope had not been told the truth when he approved it. This type of objection was a quite standard legal procedure depending on the exact meanings of words and formulas, for if even one word of the dispensation could be shown to be wrong, then the whole thing could be invalidated; and if the dispensation was invalid, so was the marriage that it permitted. It was only when this tactic failed that the process that led to the break with Rome began.

Henry and his advisers added to the opening gambit intense pressure on Catherine to accept the king's will and, without making a fuss, go quietly. This also failed in a big way. Catherine, who was possessed of both a strong character and an honest nature, and who also, even after eighteen years of marriage, clearly did not understand her husband at all, used every means in her power to contest the divorce, resolutely maintaining that her marriage was legal, enlisting her nephew the Emperor Charles V in her behalf, and doing the very opposite of going quietly. In this way she managed to remain the legitimate and recognized Queen of England for six years after the case was instituted. Yet in the end, it was all in vain. The final result, tragic to everybody involved except Henry VIII, is well known: in 1531, Henry finally banished Catherine from court; in 1533, he in effect granted himself a divorce and married Anne Boleyn. By 1536, both Catherine and Anne were dead. By the time of the king's own death by natural causes in 1547, almost everybody who had been involved in his Great Matter as a major player had been executed or was just about to be executed, or (like Thomas Cranmer) would be executed a bit later. But I do not wish to range as widely as that here. Instead, I will concentrate on the beginning of the case and the first tactics, the legal maneuvers and personal pressure that occupied the years 1527-30 or so, because it is this that so strangely resonates in the motets of London. For, viewed in the light of post-1527 England, the aspects of the contents of London that "cry out for explanation" become positively pernicious.

I now ask this question concerning the contents of London: when confronted with five settings of "Dulces exuviae" in a row, might not the consumer of these motets, like Castligione and Luther, have remembered the reason why these lines are said? Would he or she not have remembered what actually goes on in Book IV of the *Aeneid*? And there can be little doubt that they could remember Book IV: the *Aeneid*, after all, was *the* canonical text and Book IV was arguably its most famous episode; furthermore, everybody who learned Latin had probably been forced to memorize these very lines as students (and lines of poetry you memorize in school stay with you forever).

If listeners or readers of five musical settings in a row of "Dulces exuviae" had been spurred by that to remember Book IV of the *Aeneid*, the following would have occurred to them. Book IV is the story of the doomed love of Dido for Aeneas. Dido is the Queen of Carthage, but she is also something else. Dido is in fact a widow who breaks her vow of chastity to her dead husband, Sychaeus, because she is tricked by the gods not merely into falling in love with Aeneas, but into thinking that she has actually taken part in a legal marriage rite. This last, she finds to her tragic dismay, is not the case. Aeneas states in no uncertain terms that even though she may think they are married, he knows they are not, and leaves to pursue his manifest destiny, which is to found a kingdom in Italy that he can pass on to his son and heir. He leaves, she commits suicide and joins her husband in Hades, and Book IV is over. Perhaps this situation sounds familiar. For of course this was precisely the gist of the Henry's case: he claimed that he had been involved in an illegal, in fact non-existent, marriage to a widow that he had every right to break, the reason being that he needed to pass on his kingdom to a son and heir. The only difference in the two cases was that Aeneas actually had a son and heir (Ascanius), while Henry, although he also had a son (the Duke of Richmond), did not have an heir, since that son was illegitimate. The affinity problem is not in the *Aeneid*, but you can't have everything.

And people in the sixteenth century did indeed look upon the story of Dido as a cautionary tale to widows who do not remain "chaste" (faithful to their dead husbands), at least in Italy. "Didone è uno esempio alle vedove di veder quello che fanno" (Dido is a lesson to widows to watch what they do), wrote an Italian owner in his 1514 Aldine edition of the *Aeneid*.[28] Ludovico Dolce's Dido complains that by losing her chastity she has also lost her honor and then has no choice but to kill herself.[29] And the Didonic message to widows also came from another source. It had been known since Virgil's time that there was a "historical Dido" who had had nothing to do with Aeneas. The historical Dido was also a widow, also founded the city of Carthage, and also committed suicide, but for a different reason. This is the Dido in Boccaccio's *De mulieribus claris*, a book aimed at women. As Boccaccio tells it, Dido commits suicide to avoid being forced into a marriage so that she can remain faithful to the memory of her dead husband. The moral he draws is that widows should not remarry but should remain "chaste."[30]

It was of course possible to be sympathetic to Virgil's Dido, as were Ovid, St. Augustine, and Chaucer, as it was possible to admire the "historical" Dido, as

---

[28] See Craig Kallendorf, *Virgil and the Myth of Venice: Books and Readers in the Italian Renaissance* (Oxford: Oxford University Press, 1999), 167.

[29] *Didone* (1547); see Kallendorf, 200-4.

[30] Virginia Brown, ed. and trans., *Giovanni Boccaccio: Famous Women*, The I Tatti Renaissance Library (Cambridge MA: Harvard University Press, 2001), 167-81.

did Boccaccio. In fact, Henry seems to have been sympathetic to Catherine and probably also admired her. But none of that affects the outcome: Dido's death is connected to a loss or future loss of a widow's chastity, and if only Catherine had learned the lesson of Dido, she would not have been placed in the situation she was in 1527. But the correspondences between Book IV of the *Aeneid* and the King's Great Matter go deeper than this, they extend to the details of the case itself.

Let us consider some excerpts from the poem: first, the passages in which Juno tries to convince Venus to allow Dido and Aeneas to marry, Venus agrees, and Juno tells her how she will do it. The translation is by Henry Howard, Earl of Surrey, a man who was intimately connected with everybody involved in the case, and who chose Book IV as one of the two books of the *Aeneid* that he translated (emphasis in the following Latin quotations mine).[31]

Example 1: Juno to Venus (Book IV, lines 99-104 / 124-130)

Quin potius pacem aeternam pactosque hymenaeos	99
exercemus? Habes, tota quod mente petisti:	100
ardet amans Dido, traxitque per ossa furorem.	101
Communem hunc ergo populum paribusque regamus	102
auspiciis; liceat Phrygio servire marito,	103
dotalisque tuae Tyrios permittere dextrae.	104

But rather peace, and bridal bands knit we,	124
Sith thou hath sped of that thy heart desired	125
Dido doth burn with love; rage frets her bones	126
This people now as common to us both,	127
With equal favour let us govern then.	128
Lawful be it to serve a Trojan spouse	129
And Tyrians yield to thy right hand in dow'r.	130

Example 2: Venus to Juno (Book IV, Lines 110-113 / 137-142)

Sed fatis incerta feror, si Iuppiter unam	110
esse velit Tyriis urbem Troiaque profectis,	111
miscerive probet populos, aut foedera iungi.	112
Tu coniunx tibi fas animum temptare precando.	113

But destinies I doubt: lest Jove nill grant	137
That folk of Tyre, and such as came from Troy	138
Should hold one town; or grant these nations	139
Mingled be, or joined aye in league	140
Thou art his wife: lawful it is for thee	141
For to attempt his fancy by request.	142

[31] Geo. Fred. Nott, ed. *The Works of Henry Howard Earl of Surrey and of Sir Thomas Wyatt the Elder,* 2 vols. (New York: AMS Press Inc, 1965), 1: 127-63.

Example 3: Juno to Venus (Book IV, Lines 124-128/157-163)

speluncam Dido dux et Troianus eandem	124
devenient; adero, et, tua si mihi certa voluntas,	125
[conubio iungam stabili propriamque dicabo,]	126
hic hymenaeus erit.'---Non adversata petenti	127
adnuit, atque dolis risit Cytherea repertis.	128

Dido a cave, the Trojan prince the same	157
Shall enter too; and I will be at hand	158
And if thy will stick unto mine, I shall	159
In wedlock sure knit, and make her his own.	160
Thus shall the marriage be: To whose request	161
Without debate Venus did seem to yield;	162
And smiled soft, as she that found the wile.	163

"Let's bury the hatchet, let there be peace and a marriage," Juno basically says, "Let the Trojans and Carthaginians intermingle and everybody will be happy." Of course, she is lying, as Venus well knows. All Juno really wants is to keep Aeneas from Italy. So Venus answers, "Sure, if you can convince Jove, go ahead, let Trojans and Cathaginians form alliances," since she knows it won't work out in the end. Juno responds "Leave it to me and I know just how to do it," and brings up the idea of the cave, to which Venus assents, since she knows this is all false and Juno the Goddess of Marriage is about to create a false marriage to suit her own purposes.

What is worth while noting here is Juno's request to Venus that there be peace (*pax*) between them, and Venus's agreement that there be alliances (*foedera*) between Trojans and Carthaginians, the words I have underlined above. This is what leads to the meeting in the cave and the presumed marriage. Now as it happens, the furthering of "peace and alliances" (*pax, foedera, concordia*) between England and Spain through marriage was the reason, in fact, the only reason, that the dispensation allowing Henry and Catherine to marry was granted. The very words that Virgil uses are to be found in the relevant excerpt from the bull (words underlined).[32]

Example 4: Pope Julius II to Henry and Catherine: Bull dated 26 December 1503

> . . .*Quod cum alias tu Filia Catharina, et tunc in humanis agens quondam Authurus, Carissimi in Christo Filii nostri Henrici Angliae Regis illustrissimi primogenitus, pro conservandis pacis et amicitiae nexibus et foederibus inter carissimum in Christo Filium nostrum Ferdinandum et Carissimam in Christo Filiam nostram Elizabeth. Hispaniarum et Siciliae Catholicos ac praefatum Angliae Regis et Reginam, matrimonium per verba legitime de praesenti contraxissetis. . .Cum autem, sicut eadem petitio subjungebat, ad hoc ut hujusmodi vinculum Pacis et Amicitiae inter praefatos Reges et Reginam diutius permaneat,*

---

[32] This and all other quotations from the documents of the case are taken from Gilbert Burnet, *The History of the Reformation of the Church of England: A New Edition with Numerous Illustrative Notes, and a Copious Index* (London, 1850), vol. II, Collection of Records-Part I. Since the only point of the quotations is to show the use of specific Latin words, translations are not provided.

cupiatis Matrimonium inter vos per verba legitime de praesenti contrahere. . . Nos igitur, qui
inter singulos Christi fideles, praesertim Catholicos Reges et Principes, <u>Pacis et Concordiae</u>
amaenitatem vigere intensis desideriis affectamus. . .(emphasis mine)

The "peace and alliances" rationale was also the first thing that was attacked in the
effort to overturn the dispensation, the argument being that England and Spain
were already at peace at the time of the dispensation so therefore the dispensation
was obtained under false pretences (the *falsa enarratio* argument). It was added that
Henry was too young at the time to be able to consent to this.

Example 5: From the first letter of instruction from Cardinal Wolsey concerning
the divorce

Bulla praeterea Dispensationis fundatur et concessa est sub quibusdam rationibus falso
suggestis et enarratis, in ea namque asseritur, quod haec Regia Majestas Matrimonium
hoc cum Regina percupiebat, pro bono <u>pacis</u> inter Henricum septimum Ferdinandum et
Elizabetham, quam reversa nulla tunc dissensi aut belli suspicio esset inter dictos Principes,
vel Regiam Majestatem praedictam, quae in teneris adhuc annis, nec in discretione aut
judicio constitutis agebat; nunquam deinde assensit, aut quicquam cognovit de hujusmodi
bullae Impetratione, nec unquam hos matrimonium optavit, aut aliquid de eo accepit ante
bullae Impetrationem. (emphasis mine)

These arguments were easily overturned, but the relationship of the stated reason
for Henry VII's and Ferdinand's arranged marriage with Juno's and Venus's reason
for their planned nuptial is uncanny.

Let us continue in the *Aeneid* to the all important scene in the cave, the
"marriage," and its consummation, attended and presumably blessed by
ecclesiastical authority (Juno).

Example 6: The "Marriage" (Book IV, Lines 165-172/211-222)

Speluncam Dido dux et Troianus eandem	165
deveniunt: prima et Tellus et pronuba Iuno	166
dant signum; fulsere ignes et conscius aether	167
<u>*conubiis,*</u> *summoque ululanunt vertice nymphae.*	168
Ille dies primus leti primusque malorum	169
causa fuit; neque enim specie famave movetur,	170
nec iam furtivum Dido meditatur amorem:	171
<u>*coniugium*</u> *vocat; hoc praetexit nomine culpam.*	172

Dido a den, the Trojan prince the same	211
Chanced upon. Our mother then, the Earth,	212
And Juno that hath charge of marriage,	213
First tokens gave with burning gleads of flame;	214
And, privy to the wedlock, lightening skies;	215
And the Nymphs yelled from the mountains top.	216
Aye me! this was the first day of their mirth;	217
And of their harms the first occasion eke.	218

Respect of Fame no longer her withholds,   219
Nor museth now to frame her love by stealth.   220
Wedlock she calls it; under the pretence   221
Of which fair name she cloaketh now her fault.   222

It should be noted that Virgil uses two words to describe what happens here: what Juno blesses is a "*conubium*," but what Dido thinks has happened is a "*coniugium*." Surrey translates both of these with the same word "wedlock," but the meanings of the Latin words are slightly different. *Conubium* was a legal term for the right to marry, or for marriage, or for intermarriage, specifically intermarriage between a Roman and a citizen of a city which had been granted the right of *conubium*. Carthage was not such a city, so in fact this particular *conubium* was illegal, as the Roman readers of the *Aeneid* presumably knew. *Conubium* could also be used to mean simply a physical union that could lead to marriage rites, as Leofranc Holford-Strevens informs me.[33] *Coniugium* was not a term of art, although it could be used to mean marriage, but here it is the term that Virgil uses to describe Dido's self-deception; in fact, he even implies that she had made the word up. He lets us know that while she thinks that she has made a legal marriage which she has then consummated, she is wrong: she uses the wrong word (*coniugium*), a word with which she cloaks her fault (or sin) the fault or sin presumably being the *conubium*, the physical union. The lines that come immediately after this in the *Aeneid* are the description of Rumor, "Fama malum," the first of the Virgil motets to appear in London.

Later, when Dido reproaches Aeneas for wishing to leave his "wife," she again relates *conubium* to marriage (here, *hymenaeos*).

Example 7: Dido to Aeneas (Book IV, Lines 314-324/405-419)

Mene fugis? Per ego has lacrimas dextramque tuam te   314
(quando aliud mihi iam miserae nihil ipsa reliqui)   315
per conubia nostra, per inceptos hymenaeos,   316
si bene quid de te merui, fuit aut tibi quicquam   317
dulce meum, miserere domus labentis, et istam---   318
oro, si quis adhuc precibus locus---exue mentem.   319
Te propter Libycae gentes Nomadumque tyranni   320
odere, infensi Tyrii; te propter eundem   *321*
exstinctus pudor, et, qua sola sidera adibam,   322
fama prior. Cui me moribundam deseris, hospes?   323
Hoc solum nomen quoniam de coniuge restat.   *324*

Shunnest thou me? By these tears and right hand!   405
(For nought else have I, wretched, left myself)   406
By our spousals and marriage begun!   407
If I of thee deserved ever well,   408
Or thing of mine were ever to the lief,   409

---

[33] Personal communication.

Rue on this realm! whose ruin is at hand.	410
If ought be left that prayer may avail,	411
I thee beseech to do away this mind.	412
The Libyans, and tyrants of Namades,	413
For thee me hate: my Tyrians eke for thee	414
Are wroth; by thee my shamefastness eke strained.	415
And good renown whereby up to the stars	416
Peerless I clamb. To whom willt thout me leave,	417
Ready to dye, my sweetest guest! sith this name	418
Is all, as now that of a spouse remains.	419

Conubium leads to *coniugium* in her mind. But Aeneas will have none of this. He throws her own term back at her.

Example 8: Aeneas to Dido (Book IV, Lines 337-339/438-441)

Pro re pauca loquar. Neque ego hanc abscondere furto	337
speravi---ne finge---fugam, nec coniugis umquam	338
praetendi taedas, aut haec in foedera veni.	339

Never meant I to cloak the same by stealth,	438
(Slander me not) ne to escape by flight.	439
Nor I to thee pretended marriage:	440
Ne hither came to join me in such a league.	441

Aeneas basically says to Dido, "Well *you* may think we entered into a binding legal marriage (which you call *coniugium*), but I know we did not, nor did I join you in any alliance," the word *foedera* again.

After this, Dido takes Aeneas's sword, mounts the funeral pyre, and speaks her last words:

Example 9: Book IV, Lines 651-654/871-874

Dulces exuviae, dum fata deusque sinebant,	651
accipite hanc animam, meque his exsolvite curis.	652
Vixi, et, quem dederat cursum fortuna, peregi,	653
et nunc magna mei sub terras ibit imago.	654

Sweet spoils! whilest God, and destinies it would,	871
Receive this sprite! and rid me of these cares.	872
I lived and ran the course fortune did grant;	873
And under the earth my great ghost now shall wend.	874

Now it is not only remarkable how close the specific situation between Aeneas and Dido is to the situation between Henry and Catherine, but it is that *coniugium*, Dido's term of self-deception, had, by the sixteenth century, in fact become precisely what Dido had wanted it to be: the legal term for the sacrament of marriage, the legal marriage, the marriage in Heaven instituted by God, the thing that could not be broken;[34] it is so used in key documents of the case, even though the most commonly used term was the more usual *matrimonium*. Here is Cardinal Wolsey's description of Henry's reasons for beginning the divorce process.

Example 10: From Cardinal Wolsey's first letter of instruction to Sir Gregory Cassali, 5 December 1527

> *Ante hoc tempus vobis apueri, quemadodum Regia Majestas, partim assiduo suo studio et eruditione, partim relatu ac judicio multorum Theologorum, et in omni Doctrinae genere doctorum virorum asservatione, existimans conscientiam suam non esse sufficienter exoneratam, quod in <u>conjugio</u> existeret cum Reginae, Deumque primo et ante omnia ac animae suae quietem et salutem respiciens, mox vero suae Successionis securitatem, perpedendsque accurate quam gravia hinc mala provenirent, aperte sentit quam maxime futurum sit Deo molestum, inhonorificum sibi, et ingratum apud homines, suisque subditis periculosum ex hoc non sufficienti <u>conjugio</u>, si deprehendatur dicta Majestas sciens ac volens in eo perstare, et vivere praeter modum debitum, juxtaque ritum et legitima Ecclesiae Statuta.* (emphasis mine)

What the king now thinks he does not have is a *coniugium*. Catherine, however, like Dido declared that she had entered into *coniugium*.

Example 11: From the Commission of the case to the Curia, presented in Catherine's name by the imperial ambassadors and signed by Clement VII on 16 July 1529

> *Non creditur de mente Sanctitatis Vestrae fuisse aut esse, in causa matrimoniali et ubi agitur de sacramento matrimonii, quod ceteris sacramentis ratione, loci institutionis nobilius existit, quia in paradiso terrestri et in statu innocentiae institutum et ordinatum fuit, et quod <u>coniugium</u> consensu aut confessionibus postquam consumatem est, dissolvi non possit. . .* (emphasis mine)

When the papacy finally pronounced that Henry's marriage to Catherine was in fact legal, Catherine is described as the "legal wife" (*coniuge*), precisely what Dido had called herself.

Example 12: From Clement VII's final sentence in favor of the marriage between Henry and Catherine, 23 March 1534

> *… et praefatum Henricum Angliae Regem teneri et obligatum fuisse, et fore ad cohabitandum cum dicta Catherina Regina ejus legitima <u>coniuge</u>, illamque amaritali affectione et Regio honore tractandum, et eundem Henricum Angliae Regem ad praemissa omnia et singula cum effectu adimplendum condemnandum omibusque juris Remesiis cogendum, et compellendum fore, rpout comdemnamus, cogimus, et compellimus, Molestationesque et denegationes per eundem Henricum Regem eidem Catherinae Reginae super invalidate ac foedere dicti Matrimonii quomodolibet factas, et praestitas fuisse, et esse illicitas, et injustas. . .* (emphasis mine)

---

[34] Mark 10: 9: *quod ergo Deus iunxit homo non separet.*

Mere coincidence of legal language perhaps, but, after 1527, could someone who knew the *Aeneid*, especially if spurred by renditions of *Fama malum* and *Dulces exuviae, Dulces exuviae, Dulces exuviae, Dulces exuviae, Dulces exuviae*, not have failed to notice the connection to present events? Henry certainly knew the *Aeneid*. Catherine is a slightly different matter. She was highly educated and was fluent in Latin.[35] And, even if women's education was not supposed to include the "virile" masculine classics,[36] it is likely that she had read the *Aeneid*. In any case there would have been somebody around to tell her what the *Aeneid* was about, and Catherine could not have failed to know the Dido of *De mulieribus claris*, either in the original Latin or through the Spanish translation that was published in 1494.

Now let us return to the beginning "happy" sections of London and consider what Catherine or Henry might have thought if they visited the opening motets of this manuscript in the years 1527-31. Consider the first motet, *Celeste beneficium*. Even though the opening is emblasoned with their heraldic symbols, the motet none the less celebrates someone named Anne, and does so in a very blatant musical way. At the end of the motet, the name "Anna" is invoked eight times beginning in paired homophonic duets and including a four-voice homophonic invocation.[37] An innocuous prayer to St. Anne in the years before 1527, not innocuous at all in the years following, with its insistence on the first name of a woman the imperial ambassador could only bear to refer to as "la concubine."[38]

And then there is the following motet, *Adiutorium nostrum*, which names Henry and Catherine as well as St. George. I think it possible that Henry or Catherine might have known that their names were not the original ones in this motet, nor St. George the original Saint. If Henry and Catherine had looked at the first volume of the *Motetti de la corona* of 1514 (which they might have seen) or in a manuscript that was already in Henry's possession (now CambriP 1760), or even had been generally aware of the transmission history of this motet, they would have remembered that the original names were Anna and Ludovicus, and the saint, Renatus: that is, King Louis XII of France, his wife, Anne of Brittany, and Saint René. And even if they didn't know that, they might well have seen that the names Anna and Ludovicus had originally been copied in London, only to be erased and overwritten with Katherina and Henricus.

They also certainly knew that Louis XII had married Anne of Brittany in 1498 only after being allowed to divorce his wife of twenty-five years, Jeanne de France, daughter of Louis XI.[39] Jeanne had, in fact, contested the divorce at first,

---

[35] Carley, *The Books*, 109-23.

[36] For instance, Virgil does not appear among the authors recommended for reading by women by Juan Luis Vives in his book *De institutione feminae Christianae* (1523), dedicated to Catherine.

[37] Transcription in Richard Sherr ed., *Selections from the Motetti de la corona [Libro Primo]*, Sixteenth Century Motet 4 (New York: Garland, 1991), 115-17.

[38] J. A. Froude, *The Divorce of Catherine of Aragon: The Story as Told by the Imperial Ambassador Resident at the Court of Henry VIII* (New York, 1891).

[39] Louis XII, of course, had been much luckier in his Great Matter than Henry VIII. He dealt with

but in the end, as Henry and Catherine knew, she did "go quietly," and eventually entered religion as the founder of the Order of the Annonciades. She died in 1505, began to be venerated shortly after her death, and finally was canonized in 1950.[40] This brings up another tactic that was used in the early years of the case in the attempt to convince Catherine to go away quietly. For a while it was thought that the way to do this was for Catherine to enter into religion. St. Bonaventure had declared that entering into religion was a "spiritual death" equivalent to a real one, so just as a widower is released from his marriage vow because of his wife's death, so might a husband be released from his if his wife entered a convent. This was clearly the easiest way out, and pressure was brought to bear on Catherine, not merely from the English side, but from the papal side as well. Cardinal Campeggio, who had been sent to London to "try" the case, attempted to talk Catherine into this. In doing so, he specifically brought up the model of Jeanne de France, the "good" wife of Louis XII: "And I mentioned to her the example 'of the queen of France who was so long with King Louis [XII],' and who later did a similar thing and even now is treated with the greatest honor and respect in the eyes of God and the whole of that country."[41] This attempt failed; Catherine fought to the last, suffered greatly, and has not been canonized.

---

a very different pope (Alexander VI, not Clement VII) and a very different political situation (Alexander VI needed and wanted his support, while Clement VII was under the thumb of the Emperor Charles V, who was Catherine's nephew). Some aspects of the case were similar. For instance, since Louis and Jeanne were related by blood, "by the fourth degree of consanguinity" because of their common direct ancestor King Charles V, a dispensation had been necessary to overcome this impediment. But the legality of dispensations was not the main argument, which was that Louis XII had been forced into the marriage at age twelve by Louis XI against his will on pain of death (which was true), that Jeanne was so deformed that she could not have children (both of these were legitimate reasons for annulment), and that he was so physically repulsed by his wife that he had not consummated the marriage, or if he had or had seemed to (there was some doubt about this), he did not do it "par affection maritalle" but only because he was afraid of Louis XI, who had specifically ordered him to consummate the marriage before witnesses. Everyone agreed that it was not healthy to cross Louis XI; as one of the witnesses remarked, he was, "the fiercest king France has ever had" (que c'estoit le plus terrible Roy qui fust jamais en France), and not only men but even the trees were afraid of him (et quod non solum homines timebant eum, ymo arbores). See Eugène Vouters, Essai juridique et historique sur un procès en annulation de mariage au XVème siècle: Louis XII et Jeanne de France (Lille: Imprimerie Douriez-Bataille, 1931).

[40] Her feast day is 4 February, with most of the texts drawn from the offices and mass of the Common of non-Virgins-not-martyrs.

[41] Cardinal Campeggio's description of a meeting with Catherine on 24 October 1529, specifically mentioning the case of Jeanne de France:

Et per allhora non voleva dare altra risposta, ma che voleva domandare consiglieri al re suo signore et consorte "et che poi ci udiria et responderia, dimonstrando expresse havere inteso, a che andava la persuasion nostra cioè "ad religionem." Il che io non gli negai et mi sforzai persuaderle, che in man sua, facendo questo, era di componere il tutto talmente, che a Dio, alla conscientia sua, alla gloria et fama del suo nome et alli honori et alli temporali beni et ad ogni cosa si satifaria, et in specia "alla sucession di sua figlia, et che non perderia cosa alcuna, se non l'uso del persone del re, qual di già havea perso et per

Given all of this, if London had been picked up and shown to Catherine in the four years after 1527 (and four years is a long time) when Catherine and Henry were living together as king and queen and occasionally meeting to argue about the merits of the case, and if certain of the most striking motets had been sung in her presence, the manuscript could actually have functioned as an instrument of oppression, part of the psychological warfare that was being practiced on the Queen. Imagine what might have been said or implied:

"Let's hear the first motet where the name Anna is repeated over and over. And let's hear the next one: Remember Louis XII and his first wife? She knew the right thing to do. Let's listen to *Dulces exuviae*—five times—Oh, by the way, remember Dido and what happened to her and why? As they say in Italian: 'Didone è uno esempio alle vedove di veder quello che fanno.' " And so on.

Thus confronted with all of this extra baggage that lies beneath or on top of the contents of London, Catherine could easily have exclaimed in concert with the text of the last motet: "Trouble and anguish have taken hold on me. Because your command is in my thoughts. I found trouble and sorrow and called I upon the name of the Lord." It is not God's command, but Henry's that causes the anxiety.

This could be pure coincidence, of course. All the experts on the Alamire manuscripts agree that London was copied before the King's Great Matter began, and it is indeed hard to imagine that Margaret of Austria or Charles V would really have ordered the production of any gift to Henry and Catherine after 1527, especially one that sends the message I am suggesting it sends. Further, "hard evidence" that people of the time made connections between Book IV of the *Aeneid* and the King's Great Matter will probably never turn up. Nor do I think that evidence will be found in which Catherine is linked to Dido. The only literary character with whom she was equated was Griselda, the low born, long suffering wife of Boccaccio's tale, who meekly takes it all and then is rewarded.[42]

On the other hand, the Tudors, and every other ruling house in Europe, had a stake in Aeneas, since they all claimed to be descendents of him or of one of

---

quanto io conoscea, non era per ricuperarlo, et ch'ella dovea più presto pigliare questa via, che mettersi al pericolo della sententia, la quale se venisse contra di lei, considerasse, in quanto dispiacere et disturbo saria, in quanto poco honore et reputatione, et che perderia la dote, perchè nelli trattati del matrimonio fu concluso, che dissoluto matrimonio quomodocunque non repeteret dotem; li scandali et inimicitie che seguirano." Et ex adverso, oltra tutti questi incomodi, che si fugirebbono, conservaria "la dote, il dovario, il governo della figlia et il principato suo" et tutto quello finalmente, che ella sapesse domandare, harebbe dal re, nè offenderebbe Dio nè la conscientia sua. Et gli allegai l'exempio " della regina di Francia, che fu tanto tempo col re Luigi" et poi fece una simil cosa et ancora vive con honore et reputatione grandissima appresso di Dio et tutto quel regno. (emphasis mine). See Stephan Ehses, *Römische Dokumente zur Geschichte der Ehescheidung Heinrichs VIII. von England 1527-1534* (Paderborn: Druck und Verlag von Ferdinand Schöningh, 1893), 55-56.

[42] William Forrest, *The History of Grisild the Second: A Narrative, in Verse, of the Divorce of Queen Katharine of Aragon.* Written by William Forrest, Sometime Chaplain to Queen Mary I, and Now Edited for the First Time from the Author's MS in the Bodleian Library by the Rev. W. D. Macray (London: Whittingham and Wilkins, 1875)

his followers. In other words, the *Aeneid* was basic to the founding myths of their dynasties and of their power and authority. And the preservation of dynasty as well as the enhancement of royal power and authority is what the the King's Great Matter was really all about. I was also struck by Dryden's remark in the introduction to his translation of the *Aeneid* that Aeneas's abandonment of Dido was in fact a "divorce"; he uses the very term and relates it to the divorce of Augustus.[43] So somebody in the seventeenth century saw a connection between this and the idea of a historical divorce. Perhaps somebody in the sixteenth century did as well.

But all that is neither here nor there. Regardless of whether London is actually innocent of the sinister interpretation that I bring to bear on it, that interpretation can still be brought to bear. In other words, even if London was not created to torture Catherine, it could have served that purpose, and if Henry did not use it in that way, he should have.

[43] From Dryden's Introduction:

> Mercury himself, tho' employ'd on a quite contrary errand, yet owns it a marriage by an innuendo: *pulchramque uxorius urben Exstrusis.* He calls Aeneas not only a husband, but upbraids him for being a fond husband, as the word uxorius implies. Now mark a little, if your Lordship pleases, why Virgil is so much concern'd to make this marriage (for he seems to be the father of the bride himself, and to give her to the bridegroom): it was to make away for the divorce which he intended afterwards; for he was a finer flatterer than Ovid, and I more than conjecture that he had in his eye the divorce which not long before had pass'd betwixt the emperor and Scribonia. He drew this dimple in the cheek of Aeneas, to prove Augustus of the same family, by so remarkable a feature in the same place. Thus, as we say in our homespun English proverb, he kill'd two birds with one stone; pleas'd the emperor, by giving him the resemblance of his ancestor, and gave him such a resemblance as was not scandalous in that age. For to leave one wife, and take another, was but a matter of gallantry at that time of day among the Romans. Neque haec in foedera veni is the very excuse which Aeneas makes, when he leaves his lady: "I made no such bargain with you at our marriage, to live always drudging on at Carthage: my business was Italy and I never made a secret of it. If I took my pleasure, had not you your share of it? I leave you free, at my departure, to comfort yourself with the next stranger who happens to be shipwreck'd on your coast. Be as kind a hostess as you have been to me, and you can never fail of another husband. In the mean time, I call the gods to witness that I leave your shore unwillingly; for tho' Juno made the marriage, yet Jupiter commands me to forsake you." This is the effect of what he saith, when it is dishonor'd out of Latin verse into English prose. If the poet argued not aright, we must pardon him for a poor blind heathen, who knew no better morals.

Poliziano and the Language of Lament from Isaac to Layolle

Blake Wilson

In Florence around 1475, the manner preferred by the city's *literati* for performing Tuscan poetry would have been solo, improvisatory song. By 1525, the polyphonic madrigal had become the pre-eminent vehicle. This is a striking development since solo singing was a venerable Florentine practice intimately tied to its literary history, and this same literary history—particularly the late Quattrocento refinement of Tuscan vernacular poetry as cultivated by Angelo Poliziano and other poets in Lorenzo's circles—was celebrated in the early Cinquecento academies that fostered the early madrigal. There is every indication that relations between poetry and music during the intervening half century were as dynamic, complex, and contested as one would expect. Poliziano himself bore witness to this condition in a letter written around 1490, probably from Rome. At a banquet in the Medici circles of the Orsini family, Poliziano recounts having heard the eleven-year-old Fabio Corsini perform first, "together with some experts, certain of those [polyphonic] songs which are put into writing with those little signs of music," followed by a more flexibly-declaimed solo performance of "an heroic song which he [Fabio] had himself recently composed in praise of our own Piero de' Medici."[1] Poliziano waxes rapturous about Fabio's sweet voice and his monodic performance, but expresses indifference, at best, to the polyphonic singing of the "experts." Pirrotta's discussion of this passage is focused upon Poliziano's contrasting attitudes, but of equal interest is the Janus-faced nature of the event, with its calculated juxtaposition of polyphonic and solo song; one might even suppose that this elite audience was being invited to judge the relative merits of the two styles against the common backdrop of Fabio's sweet voice, and at a historical moment when the scales were balanced between them. Poliziano was at the center of a later event involving a confrontation between these two styles, one that reveals how much the Florentine musical scene had changed by the 1520s.

This event involves a text that literate Florentines might have regarded as the *locus classicus* of the solo singer's art: the final lament of Orpheus from Poliziano's

---

[1] Nino Pirrotta, "Orpheus, Singer of Strambotti," in *Music and Theatre from Poliziano to Monteverdi*, trans. Karen Eales (Cambridge: Cambridge University Press, 1982), 36. For a different interpretation of this letter (including an edition and translation), see Elena Abramov-van Rijk, *Parlar cantando: The Practice of Reciting Verses in Italy from 1300 to 1600* (Bern: Peter Lang, 2009), 151-57.

Fabula di Orfeo. At its Mantuan premier in 1480, the title role of *Orfeo* was sung by the famous Florentine solo singer Baccio Ugolini.[2] Sometime during the 1520s, three different madrigal composers set the same, single *ottava* from Poliziano's play, *Qual sarà mai sí miserabil canto*, the first of four stanzas that constitute Orpheus' complete lament (see Example 1a).[3]

Ex. 1:   Poliziano, *Fabula di Orfeo* (lines 261-268)

a. TEXT

Poliziano text (ed. S. Carrai):   Layolle version (ed. F. D'Accone):

1	Qual sarà mai * sí miserabil canto	Qual sarà mai * sì **lacrimabil pianto**
2	che pareggi il dolor * del mio gran danno?	che pareggi 'l dolor * del mio gran danno?
3	O come potrò mai * lacrimar tanto	**Hor** come potrò mai * lacrimar tanto
4	che sempre pianga * il mio mortale affanno?	**che ponga fin * al** mio **crudel** affanno?
5	Starommi mesto * e sconsolato in pianto	Staromi mesto * e sconsolat'im pianto
6	per fin ch'e cieli * in vita mi terranno:	perfin ch' i cieli * in vita mi terranno.
7	e poi che sì crudele è mia fortuna,	**Da** poi che **così vuol la** mia fortuna,
8	già mai non voglio amar * più donna alcuna.	già mai non vogl'amar * più donn'alcuna.

[* marks caesura within poetic line]

How can ever such woeful song
equal the pain of my great suffering?
How can I ever find enough tears
to mourn constantly my mortal affliction?
I shall remain sad and disconsolate in my lament
as long as the heavens keep me in this life.
And since my fate is so cruel,
I do not wish ever again to love any woman.

b. MUSIC

Constanzo Festa (c. 1485/90-1545)	3-part	Brussels, Bibliothèque du Conservatoire Royal de Musique, MS FA VI.5 (1530s), 1542[18]
Francesco Layolle (1492-c. 1540)	4-part	*Cinquanta canzoni a quatro voce* (Lyons, 1540)
Philippe Verdelot (c. 1480/5-after 1530)	5-part	*Libro primo a cinque* (Venice?, c.1536-37) [altus & bassus only]
[Mattio Rampollini (1497-c. 1553)	3-part	*Della scelta di madrigali...Libro primo* (Florence, 1582)]

---

[2] Pirrotta, "Orpheus, Singer of Strambotti," 3-36.

[3] The source of Poliziano's edited text is Stefano Carrai, *Angelo Poliziano: Stanze, Fabula di Orfeo* (Milan: Ugo Mursia, 1988), 155; the variant text used by Layolle is in Frank D'Accone, ed. *Music of the Florentine Renaissance*, Corpus Mensurabilis Musicae 32 ([Rome]: American Institute of Musicology, 1969), 4: xiii. The Verdelot text is very close to Carrai's edition, except for the subsitution of *pianto* for *canto* in the first line.

Each employed a different texture (see Ex. 1b): Verdelot, five voices (of which only the altus and bassus partbooks survive); Francesco Layolle, four; and Costanzo Festa, three. Assuming Verdelot is the composer of the five-part setting, which seems likely, all three composers had strong connections to Florence, though we don't know if they were ever there at the same time.[4] Verdelot was in Florence during the 1520s, and Festa was in Rome by 1517 (if not sooner), where he served two Medici popes and maintained close contacts with prominent Florentines.[5] Before Verdelot's arrival Layolle had left Florence for Lyons, where he was at the center of a Florentine exile community with close ties to the Florentine cultural and intellectual community, through which channels he may have obtained his different version of Poliziano's text (see Example 1).[6] Nevertheless, a Florentine context, perhaps even a commission, is suggested by the subject matter, the composers' Florentine connections, and the apparent nature of the project: three composers, three different textures, one very Florentine text. There is a clear precedent for such a project from the previous decade involving similar circumstances: progressive polyphonic settings by contemporary Florentine composers based on Quattrocento poetic models. In this case, Poliziano's ballata *Questo mostrarsi adirata di fore*, and its original setting by Heinrich Isaac, began a "direct line of descent" leading to a setting of Poliziano's poem by Bartolomeo degli Organi, and to five other musical settings by, among others, the Florentines Bernardo Pisano, Bartolomeo, and Layolle of a ballata text closely modeled on Poliziano's *Questo mostrarsi lieta a tutte l'hore*, by Lorenzo Strozzi.[7]

---

[4] See *The New Grove Dictionary of Music and Musicians*, 2nd ed., s.v. "Verdelot," where it is listed among Verdelot's works. For a more cautious approach, see James Haar and Iain Fenlon, *The Italian Madrigal in the Early Sixteenth Century* (Cambridge: Cambridge University Press, 1988), 304-5. Regarding a later, but possibly related, setting by the Florentine composer Mattio Rampollini, see Ex. 1b, and n. 10 below.

[5] Regarding Festa's biography, see Edward Lowinsky, "On the Presentation and Interpretation of Evidence: Another Review of Costanzo Festa's Biography," *Journal of the American Musicological Society* 30 (1977): 106-28, and *The Medici Codex of 1518: A Choirbook of Motets Dedicated to Lorenzo de' Medici, Duke of Urbino*, Monuments of Renaissance Music 3 (Chicago: University of Chicago Press, 1968), 1: 42-51. For arguments against Lowinsky's thesis that Festa studied in France with Mouton, see Lewis Lockwood, "Jean Mouton and Jean Michel: New Evidence on French Music and Musicians in Italy, 1505-1520," *Journal of the American Musicological Society* 32 (1979): 191-246; and Martin Staehelin, "Review: The Medici Codex of 1518," *Journal of the American Musicological Society* 33 (1980): 575-87. Regarding Festa's connections to Florence, see Richard Agee, "Filippo Strozzi and the Early Madrigal," *Journal of the American Musicological Society* 38 (1985): 227-37.

[6] *New Grove Dictionary*, s.v. "Layolle, Francesco de;" Haar and Fenlon, *The Italian Madrigal*, 63-64, 66-67, 80-81; Anthony M. Cummings, *The Maecenas and the Madrigalist: Patrons, Patronage, and the Origins of the Italian Madrigal* (Philadelphia: American Philosophical Society, 2004), 30-31, 55-56, 174-75.

[7] Frank D'Accone, "Transitional Text Forms and Settings in an Early 16th-Century Florentine Manuscript," in *Words and Music: The Scholar's View*, ed. Laurence Berman and Elliot Forbes (Cambridge, Massachusetts: Dept. of Music, Harvard University, 1972), 29-58, esp. 35-36, and 54-55. All settings of *Questo mostrarsi* but Isaac's are transmitted in Florence, Biblioteca del Conservatorio di Musica, MS Basevi 2440, probably copied in Lorenzo Strozzi's circles around 1515. Lorenzo was brother to the above Filippo, who commissioned Festa for settings in the late 1520s. For modern editions, see D'Accone, ed., *Music of the Florentine Renaissance*, 1: 5-7 (Pisano), 2: 31-35 (Bartolomeo), 2: 47-49 (anon.), and 3: 66-67 (Layolle).

A glance at the music of *Qual sarà mai* strengthens the argument for the workings of a guiding hand, for all three settings share melodic material (see Example 2).[8]

Ex. 2: *Qual sarà mai* motives

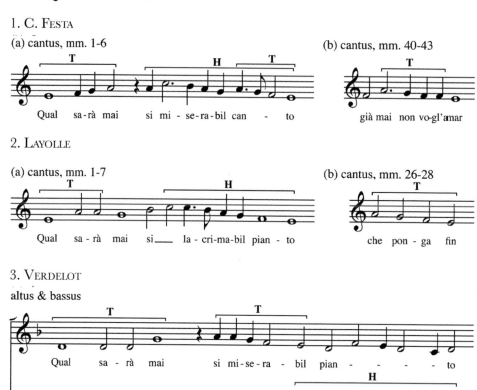

T = Tetrachord; H = Hexachord

It is unfortunate that the unique extant print of the Verdelot madrigal is missing its cantus partbook (along with tenor and quintus parts), but the surviving altus and bassus parts indicate that Verdelot employed melodic figures very similar to those

---

[8] Frederick Sternfeld first drew attention to the thematic links between these three works, particularly to the use of the descending tetrachord, but in the context of a discussions focused upon the rhetorical use of repetition: "Poliziano, Isaac, Festa: Rhetorical Repetition," in *Firenze e la Toscana dei Medici nell'Europa del '500*, ed. Gian Carlo Garfagnini (Florence: Leo S. Olschki, 1983), 2: 562-64; "The Lament in Poliziano's *Orfeo* and Some Musical Settings of the Early 16th Century," in *Arts du spectacle et histoire des idées: Recueil offert en hommage à Jean Jacquot*, ed. Jean-Michel Vaccaro (Tours: Centre d'Études Supérieures de la Renaissance, 1984), 201-4; *The Birth of Opera* (Oxford: Clarendon Press, 1993), 147-51, where Festa's setting is published in its entirety and discussed. Modern editions consulted for this study are Albert Seay, ed., *Costanzo Festa: Opera Omnia*, Corpus Mensurabilis Musicae 25 (Stuttgart: American Institute of Musicology, 1977), 7: 12-13; D'Accone, ed., *Music of the Florentine Renaissance*, 4: 8-11 (Layolle).

of Festa and Layolle at identical places in the text. In the Festa and Layolle settings these figures are shaped by the prevailing Phrygian mode: the basic form of the theme that permeates both works is a tetrachord that descends stepwise from A to E (marked "T" in Ex. 2), which emphasizes the expressive semitone between *e* and *f*. An ascending form of the tetrachord opens all three settings, and forms a gesture suited to the poem's opening question, *qual sarà mai?* The hexachords found in all three settings are extensions of descending tetrachord, and these always involve a dotted rhythm lengthening the note that signals the beginning of the descent (marked "H" in ex. 2).[9] In each case these hexachords are fashioned to suit a longer poetic sub-phrase, the central orphic image of the lament, *sì miserabil canto*, and in the Verdelot and Layolle settings nearly identical hexachordal figures recur with the parallel phrase at the end of line 6, *e sconsolato in pianto*. While our three composers clearly, perhaps deliberately, pursued highly individualized solutions to setting this text—most obviously the differing textures of three (Festa), four (Layolle), and five (Verdelot) voices—what piques interest are the shared features that suggest a common purpose: the poetic text, the tetrachordal figures, and their Florentine context.[10]

1. The Poetic Text

In the context of Poliziano's play, the stanza set by our three composers is technically an *ottava* within a longer series of *ottave* that are the dominant poetic form of *Orfeo*, but in isolation such a single stanza becomes a strambotto, or what Poliziano more precisely called a *rispetto spicciolato* (a detached *rispetto*, or octave).[11] By the time Baccio Ugolini stepped onto a Mantuan stage in 1480, the strambotto was closely associated with the soloistic art of the *improvvisatori*, and would remain the most prestigious form of sung poetry in Italy during the half century we are considering. By the 1520s it was a venerable form in sharp decline, but with a history no poet or musician in Italy could ignore.[12]

---

[9] The term hexachord is used here in the broader sense of any six-note scalar figure, regardless of its solmisation form based on "ut."

[10] A setting of *Qual sarà mai* by another Florentine composer, Mattio Rampollini, is probably related to these other versions (see Ex. 1b). It remains unpublished, but the published incipit in Harry B. Lincoln, *The Italian Madrigal and Related Repertories: Indexes to Printed Collections, 1500-1600* (New Haven: Yale University Press, 1988), 525, indicates a three-part madrigal in the Phrygian mode, opening with an interlocking series of ascending tetrachords, with the opening entries in the outer voices tracing the e to a Phrygian tetrachord. While the date of the work is uncertain (it first appears in a 1582 print), and I was unable to consult a complete version, circumstantial evidence supports the musical evidence to indicate that Rampollini may have composed his setting in direct relation to the others: he worked closely with Verdelot at the Florentine cathedral, and the publication of his Petrarchan canzoni cycles by Moderne in Lyons suggests a previous relationship with Layolle; see Haar and Fenlon, *The Italian Madrigal*, 80-81; D'Accone, "Matteo Rampollini and his Petrarchan Canzoni Cycles," *Musica disciplina* 27 (1973): 77.

[11] Poliziano in fact uses a variety of verse forms in *Orfeo*, but the text is cast primarily in *ottave*, and so invokes a long tradition of *cantari* and their performance by solo singers.

[12] The form is dismissed by Don Harran in his "Verse Types in the Early Madrigal," *Journal of the American Musicological Society* 22 (1969): 51.

That this was true for Verdelot is apparent in one of his few other attributable strambotto settings, *Quando madonna io vengo a contemplarte*. As Colin Slim has shown, Verdelot's setting probably dates from the early 1520s, and exhibits stylistic features that allude clearly to the older strambotto as found in sources dating from the peak years of the genre, *ca.* 1495-1515: a declamatory melody that moves within a relatively narrow range, a homophonic texture built on a cantus-tenor framework and exhibiting frequent parallel imperfect consonances between the cantus and a lower voice, and the musical economy of recycling for subsequent pairs of lines the music of the first two lines.[13] The association of this strambotto with the unwritten practice of its greatest practitioners, like Serafino Aquilano and Benedetto Gareth (*il Cariteo*), is reinforced by the iconography of the painting that is the subject of Slim's article: just behind a woman's outstretched hand resting on a music book open to Verdelot's strambotto, we see the image of a *lira da braccio*, the instrument *par excellence* of the *improvvisatori*. As we shall see, the settings of *Qual sarà mai* by Layolle and Festa exhibit some of these same stylistic markers (the absence of Verdelot's cantus part makes it impossible to judge his version in this regard). Thus the prominence of the strambotto as a vehicle for singing Italian poetry in the decades preceding the rise of the madrigal, its lingering presence in these early madrigals, and its dual nature as both an unwritten, soloistic and written, polyphonic form suggests that it may have functioned in Florence as a medium of transition to the polyphonic madrigal.[14]

As a sung genre, however, the strambotto is generally associated more with areas to the north and south of Florence; what presence did it have in late fifteenth-century Florence? Very little, to judge from the extant musical sources, but these sources are chansonniers which typically did not include native Italian forms. We know the strambotto led a double life at this time as both a written and an unwritten musical form, and while it was rejected from the city's written musical sources, it was absorbed into its oral traditions. Feo Belcari's autograph copy of his own laudario with singing rubrics was completed by about 1478, and shows little interest in the form. But among those works datable to after 1478 and prior to Belcari's death in 1484 is a significant number of laude in this form, and these all drew on secular strambotti as singing models (including many in extant polyphonic settings).[15] The city's vast repertory of devotional songs with singing rubrics, the so-called *cantasi come* sources, record a broad shift at this time, from the use of generic models for poetic modeling and musical borrowing, to the customized modeling

---

[13] H. Colin Slim, "An Iconographical Echo of the Unwritten Tradition in a Verdelot Madrigal," *Studi musicali* 17 (1988): 33-56, esp. 46; the older settings typically provide music only for the first two lines, with the expectation that this will serve the remaining three pairs, whereas Verdelot repeats this music only for poetic lines three and four.

[14] On the strambotto as a musico-poetic form, see G. La Face Bianconi, *Gli strambotti del Codice Estense a.F.9.9* (Florence: Olschki, 1990); Isabel Pope and Masakata Kanazawa, eds., *The Musical Manuscript Montecassino 871: A Neapolitan Repertory of Sacred and Secular Music of the Late Fifteenth Century* (Oxford: Oxford University Press, 1978), 71-82; and Pirrotta, *Music and Theatre*, 3-36.

[15] Blake Wilson, *Singing Poetry in Renaissance Florence: The 'cantasi come' Tradition (1375-1550)* (Florence: Olschki, 2009), 94-95, 136-43.

of lauda verse upon single strophes of Italian poetry in polyphonic settings. The strambotto emerges as a prime mover in this shift of the city's oral singing culture towards the use of customized musical settings for single stanzas of Italian poetry, a condition directly relevant to the early madrigal.[16] These same sources show that sung strambotti entered Florence in two waves that correspond exactly to the geography and chronology of the polyphonic sources: Neapolitan strambotti during the 1480s, and north Italian settings after about 1495.

As a literary form, the strambotto was hardly new to Florence. Luigi Pulci and Angelo Poliziano in particular cultivated the genre during Belcari's lifetime. Poliziano's 100 or so strambotti (*rispetti spicciolati*) are of particular importance, not only because a number of them were set to music, but because they were for Poliziano a site of linguistic experimentation, aligned with the broader Laurentian project to elevate and refine Tuscan vernacular lyric.[17] In large part through delicate inlay of language and vocabulary drawn from Petrarch and other Tuscan poets, Poliziano shifted the strambotto from the regions of popular, oral poetry, towards a more cultivated tradition, thus preparing the way for the *strambottisti*.[18] Serafino's modeling has been shown to be directly dependent upon Poliziano's poetry, as in the case with a Poliziano strambotto, *Contento in foco sto come fenice*, which survives in a polyphonic setting in three north Italian sources.[19] The polyphonic settings applied to both Poliziano's and Belcari's strambotti thus appear to represent the musical side of this very same shift towards a more cultivated and literate tradition. In Dean Mace's well-known article on the origins of the Italian madrigal, his argument that Petrarchan poetry prompted more ambitious music in fact seems much more suited to the late fifteenth-century strambotto.[20]

One sixteenth-century writer noted the kinship of the strambotto and madrigal when he observed that "above all else the madrigal and strambotto must have lovely wit and invention, just like an epigram."[21] Compared to other forms

[16] Pirrotta, "Before the Madrigal," *Journal of Musicology* 12 (1994): 244: "…we have no hint that an 'aria per cantar strambotti' ever existed, as each strambotto appears to have had its own music particularly composed for its text, …a point on which strambotti anticipate madrigals."

[17] Rosella Bessi, "Poliziano e il volgare tra prassi e teoria," in *Poliziano nel suo tempo: atti del VI convegno internazionale (Chianciano-Montepulciano, 18-21 luglio 1994)*, ed. Luisa Secchi Tarugi (Florence: Franco Cesati Editore, 1997), 21-31, esp. 23ff.

[18] Antonino Musumeci, "Poliziano: La poesia dei rispetti," in *Poliziano nel suo tempo*, 81-95; Antonio Lovato, "Appunti sulle preferenze musicali di Angelo Poliziano," in *Poliziano nel suo tempo*, 221-37, esp. 236.

[19] Daniela Delcorno Branca, "Da Poliziano a Serafino," in *Umanesimo e rinascimento a Firenze e Venezia: Miscellanea di studi in onore di Vittore Branca* (Florence: Leo S. Olschki, 1983), 3: 423-50, esp. 423-30.

[20] Dean T. Mace, "Pietro Bembo and the Literary Origins of the Italian Madrigal," *Musical Quarterly* 55 (1969): 65-86. Pre-Bembo Petrarchismo is a complex and understudied topic, but see G. Gerbino, "Florentine Petrarchismo and the Early Madrigal: Reflections on the Theory of Origins," *The Journal of Medieval and Early Modern Studies* 35 (2005): 607-28. For a more nuanced view of Serafino's treatment of both the strambotto and Petrarch, see I. Rowland, "The Antipetrarchismo of Serafino Ciminelli 'L'Aquilano' (d. 1500)," in *Dynamique d'une expansion culturelle: Petrarque en Europe, XIVe-XXe siècle, Actes du XXVIe congrès international du CEFI, Turin et Chambery* (Paris: Champion, 2001), 241-56.

[21] Girolamo Parabosco, quoted in Alfred Einstein, *The Italian Madrigal* (Princeton: Princeton University Press, 1949), 1: 184-85.

of late fifteenth-century Italian lyric poetry, the strambotto was distinguished by
its epigrammatic concision and sentimental tone. The strambotto also shares with
madrigal texts a kind of through-composed rhetorical quality, a tendency to develop a
conceit, often amorous, that crests in a witty point at the end. Of the unwritten music
cultivated by the likes of Serafino we know only what contemporary descriptions tell
us: that the strambotto was distinguished by a particularly refined style of singing
and accompanying, and that, according to Serafino's biographer Vincenzo Calmeta,
the strambotto's "words and music were intertwined with perception."[22] In their
brief discussions of the extant written settings, Nino Pirrotta and James Haar have
drawn attention to the ways in which the strambotto resembles the madrigal. Both
are characterized by customized musical settings, flexible declamation, rhetorical
treatment of individual poetic phrases, and similar functions, that of "condensing in
a concise statement some precious literary thought or compliment to be set to music."[23]

The "dual nature" of the strambotto, and its role as a kind of portal between
the worlds of solo song and polyphonic madrigal, is suggested by its placement
within an important manuscript collection of Florentine secular songs copied
around 1515. D'Accone has described MS Basevi 2440, of the Florentine Biblioteca
del Conservatorio di Musica, as "from the transitional period leading to the rise of
the madrigal."[24] It is dominated by the poetry of Lorenzo Strozzi (1482-1551), in
whose literary circles the collection probably originated, but it opens with a short
run of strambotti that are a clear nod to the solo singer's art.[25] The poet of the first
two, Francesco Cei, was himself a celebrated improvisatory singer and friend of
both Strozzi and the composer Bartolomeo degli Organi. A witness to a Florentine
wedding that took place prior to Cei's death in 1505 recorded hearing Cei sing
one of his own ballate "*in sul la lira*, the way Baccio degli Organi taught him."[26]
This is intriguing, for it means either that Bartolomeo was instructing Francesco
in solo singing to the accompaniment of the *lira da braccio*, or, more likely given
Bartolomeo's credentials, that Cei was singing accompanied song in an unusual
way that required the instruction of a polyphonic composer.[27] Bartolomeo's setting

[22] Vincenzo Calmeta, "La vita di Serafino Aquilano," in *Prose e lettere edite o inedite*, ed. Cecil
Grayson (Bologna: Commissione per i testi di lingua, 1959), 63; trans. and discussed in Ingrid D.
Rowland, *The Culture of the High Renaissance: Ancients and Moderns in Sixteenth-Century Rome* (Cambridge:
Cambridge University Press, 1998), 98-99.

[23] Pirrotta,"Before the Madrigal," 244. Regarding the strambotto/madrigal relationship, see also
Haar, "The Early Madrigal: A Re-Appraisal of its Sources and its Character," in *Music in Medieval
and Early Modern Europe: Patronage, Sources, and Texts*, ed. Iain Fenlon (Cambridge: Cambridge
University Press, 1981), 175, and Paolo Fabbri, "Metrical and Formal Organization," in *Opera
in Theory and Practice, Image and Myth*, ed. Lorenzo Bianconi and Giorgio Pestelli, trans. Kenneth
Chalmers, *The History of Italian Opera, Part II* (Chicago: University of Chicago Press, 2003), 6: 154-
55, concerning the particular declamatory flexibility of the *endecasillabo*.

[24] D'Accone, "Transitional Text Forms," 30.

[25] Ibid., 54, where the index shows that four of the first five settings are strambotti: 1. *Amor, gl'inganni
tua* (Cei), 2. *Pietà, pieta* (Cei), 3. *Ecco la nocte* (Serafino), and 5. *Se ben el fine* (anon.).

[26] D'Accone, "Alessandro Coppini and Bartolomeo degli Organi: Two Florentine Composers of the
Renaissance," *Analecta musicologica* 4 (1967): 52.

[27] On Bartolomeo as a teacher of "singing, playing, and three-part counterpoint" to Niccolò
Machiavelli's son in 1527, see ibid., 53.

of Cei's strambotto *Pietà, pieta* may reveal something of the process of hybridization that was underway in these collaborations: the character of the cantus melody and the provision of music for only the first pair of lines points to Cei's world and reveals Bartolomeo's familiarity with it, whereas the infusion of counterpoint into the traditional domain of the solo singer is probably what Bartolomeo had taught Cei to do.[28]

For Verdelot, Layolle, and Festa, the strambotto was thus a genre that invited both traditional and progressive approaches to musical setting. Discernible in the settings of Layolle and Festa are the traditional elements already exhibited in Verdelot's *Quando madonna io vengo*: declamatory cantus melodies of narrow compass (that tend both to descend, and gravitate to 'A' as a reciting tone), pairs of voices that often proceed in parallel imperfect consonances, and melodic repetition across the whole form (see Appendix, nos. 1 & 2). Repetition of the tetrachordal and hexachordal formations in all three settings has already been noted (and identified in the full transcriptions in the appendix), but Layolle (like Verdelot in *Quando Madonna*) retains a vestige of the strambotto's old habit of repeating music for subsequent lines: lines 1 and 3 resemble each other (though line 3 begins with the semitone oscillations with which line 1 ends, and ends with the ascending tetrachord with which line 1 begins), while lines 2 and 4 are even more clearly aligned. A particular marker of strambotto settings, absent from Verdelot's *Quando Madonna* but present in all three settings of *Qual sarà mai*, is the construction of melodic sub-phrases that observe the poetic *caesura*, the tendency of the strambotto's hendecasyllabic lines to subdivide into a short and long phrase (see Ex. 1).[29] All three composers clearly understood and drew upon the musical conventions of the strambotto, but their training and experience as polyphonists also enabled them to look beyond the strambotto in fashioning more complex musical responses to Poliziano's text.

2. Tetrachords and Laments

The use of the descending tetrachord as an "emblem of lament" is generally assumed to have surfaced in early seventeenth-century vocal music.[30] The immediate antecedents of this *soggetto* appear to be associated with the *passacaglia* in Spanish guitar books of the late sixteenth and early seventeenth century, and perhaps a bit earlier in the Italian dance ritornello (*ripresa*); in this context, the tetrachord seems to coalesce from the world of improvised instrumental music based on formulaic harmonic patterns like the *ruggiero* and *romanesca*.[31] However, our three settings of *Qual sarà mai* present a very different use of tetrachordal figures.

[28] Bartolomeo's music is ed. in D'Accone, *Music of the Florentine Renaissance*, 2: 27-88; Cei's text is ed. on p. xix of this edition, but more recently (and with significant textual variants) in Marta Ceci, ed., *Francesco Cei: Il Canzoniere* (Rome: Zauli Arti Grafiche, 1994), 102.

[29] For analysis of a sampling of strambotto melodies, see Wilson, *Singing Poetry*, 139-42, and La Face Bianconi, *Gli strambotti*, 163-73.

[30] Ellen Rosand, "The Descending Tetrachord: An Emblem of Lament," *Musical Quarterly* 65 (1979): 346-59.

[31] Thomas Walker, "Ciaccona and Passacaglia: Remarks on Their Origin and Early History," *Journal of the American Musicological Society* 21 (1968): 300-20, esp. 311ff. Richard Hudson, "Further

Both the Festa and Layolle settings are cast clearly in the Phrygian mode, which in humanist concepts of modal ethos was generally understood as appropriate to lament.[32] In Festa's three-part version, we hear simple and embellished forms of the tetrachord nineteen times in the space of 47 measures (see Appendix, no. 1). These are mostly descending figures, and are shaped to clear syntactic units (e.g., *Giamai non vogli'amar*) that involve the most expressive words of the lament, such as *danno, lagrimar,* and *sconsolato.* Twelve of these are cast in one of the two specifically Phrygian forms of the descending tetrachord (a-g-f-e, or e-d-c-b), with its poignant semitone between the last two notes of the descent. These figures spread throughout all the voices as the piece unfolds; their density within the overall texture increases as Festa stacks them in pairs near the end, and finally he underpins the harmony with two final statements in the lowest voice, where we hear Orpheus twice utter his fatal rejection of *più donn'alcuna.*

Layolle's beautifully crafted four-part setting is even more saturated with Phrygian tetrachords and their hexachordal extensions (Appendix, no. 2). As mentioned above, strambotto melodies tend to observe the caesura of the individual, eleven-syllable line. The two basic melodic units identified in these madrigals—the tetrachord and hexachord—pervade all four voices of Layolle's setting; the tetrachord is usually assigned to the short, and the hexachord to the

---

Remarks on the Passacaglia and Ciaccona," *Journal of the American Muscological Society* 23 (1970): 282-301; Hudson asserts that the Spanish *paseo* and *passacalle* are both "preceded in Italy by the 16th-century ritornello dance called the *ripresa*, which often displays the same harmonic pattern" (305); idem., *The Passacaglia*, in *The Folia, the Saraband, the Passacaglia, and the Chaconne: The Historical Evolution of Four Forms that Originated in Music for the Five-Course Spanish Guitar,* Musicological Studies and Documents 35 (Neuhausen-Stuttgart: American Institute of Musicology, 1982), 3: xiv-xix. See also John Walter Hill, "*O che nuovo miracolo!*: A New Hypothesis about the *Aria di Fiorenza*," in *In cantu et sermone: for Nino Pirrotta on his 80th Birthday*, ed. Fabrizio della Seta and Franco Piperno (Florence: Olschki, 1988), 283-322, where he makes the intriguing suggestion that a late sixteenth-century bass pattern may have emerged from oral tradition in the early part of the century in the context of a strambotto. Of equal relevance to the present argument is the observation of Palisca and others that the *romanesca* and *Ruggiero* patterns are later manifestations of older oral singing practices, in this case *ottava rima* formula for singing Ariosto's *Orlando furioso*; Palisca, "Vincenzo Galilei and Some Links between 'Pseudo-Monody' and Monody," in *Studies in the History of Italian Music and Music Theory* (Oxford: Clarendon Press, 1994), 346-48.

Another line of transmission of the decending tetrachord was, of course, the later madrigal and related repertories. In his study of the "tear motif" in Dowland's *Lachrimae* (1604), Peter Holman notes that by the late 16th century, the descending tetrachord had become a "standard emblem of grief," to be heard in madrigals by Giovanni Gabrieli, Marenzio, and Wert, among others, as well as in Victoria's 1572 setting of *O vos omnes; Dowland: Lachrimae* (1604) (Cambridge: Cambridge University Press, 1999), 40-42. See also Peter Williams, *The Chromatic Fourth during Four Centuries of Music* (Oxford: Clarendon Press, 1997), which begins with the chromatic madrigals of Vicentino and Rore.

[32] *New Grove Dictionary*, s.v. "Déploration," and s.v. "Mode," III, 4, (iii), where Harold Powers quotes Zarlino on the Phrygian mode having "the character of moving to tears; therefore they set it freely to words that are tearful and full of laments." By Isaac's day, there was a long-standing confusion between ancient Greek and medieval chant modes, especially concerning the nature of Dorian and Phrygian. Even the ancients seem not to have agreed: Gaffurius followed Plato in attributing warlike affects to the Phrygian mode, whereas Aristotle found Phrygian more suited to material of a languid and soft nature; see Claude Palisca, *Humanism in Italian Renaissance Musical Thought* (New Haven: Yale Univ. Press, 1985), 100, 344-48, 407.

long subphrases of Poliziano's lines. The repetition of the tetrachord in the bass line throughout the first half of the poem (mm. 9-27 are formed entirely from it) begins to assume the function of a *basso ostinato* not unlike Monteverdi's *Lamento della Ninfa* and its early operatic relations. The strambotto-like repetition of this melodic material across the first four lines has already been mentioned (line 3 resembles 1, line 4 resembles 2), and this mirrors the typical paired-line rhetoric of strambotto texts, in this case framed as a pair of questions. In the second half of the poem (lines 5-8) questions give way to declarations, as Orpheus commits himself to a life of misery and celibacy. This rhetorical shift is matched by a change in the structure of the cantus melody (see Example 3). These last four melodic lines are all variations of one another: the first half of the caesura in each line consists of a compact up and down traversal of the upper register between a^1 and c^2, while the second half (with the exception of line 7) returns to the lower register by means of the descending hexachord. Line 7 stands apart as a dense field of

Ex. 3: Layolle, *Quai sarà mai*, cantus

polyphonic thematic allusion: between measures 47 and 52, each voice traces a descending tetrachord (cantus c-g; altus a-e, etc.). Here, as *fortuna* spreads her web across Orpheus' fate, the tetrachord is extended across the entire musical texture. In the more extended setting of line 8, the work's predominantly chordal texture comes unraveled; amidst overlapping cascades of descending hexachords, the dismemberment of the texture perhaps evokes Orpheus' ultimate fate at the hands of the Dionysian maenads as punishment for his rejection of women. Layolle's madrigal is an impressive synthesis of two traditions. The strambotto's melodic and formal economy here have been accommodated to the rich thematic, harmonic, and textural possibilities of the new polyphonic style; the music is at once full of repetition and yet through-composed, and it is difficult to say whether the natural and clear declamation heard in every part owes more to the aging strambotto or to the upstart madrigal.

There is a clear sense in these three settings that the tetrachord and its variants have assumed the role of expressive rhetorical *figurae*; they have become emblems of lament, albeit in the purely melodic sense appropriate to a work cast in Renaissance counterpoint, rather than as harmonic patterns of the kind that would emerge across the sixteenth century.[33] To understand how these figures acquired their meaning, however, we must turn to a slightly older secular tradition of polyphonic laments,

Table 1: Tetrachord-Based Laments, ca. 1485-1530

Title (no. of voices)	*Composer*	*Tetrachord disposition*	*Final (flats)*
I. FRENCH ROYAL COURT TRADITION			
A. Chansons & Motets with Latin *cantus prius factus* [cpf]			
Ce povre mendiant/Pauper sum ego (3)	Josquin	cpf?: transposing ostinato (B)	a
Cueurs desolez/Dies illa (5)	de la Rue	cpf. + imitative motive	d (1?)
Cueurs desolez/Plorans ploravit (5)	Josquin	imit. motive	f (1)
Nimphes, nappés/Circumdederunt me (6)	Josquin	cpf + imit. motive	f (1)
Nymphes des bois/Requiem aeternam (6)	Josquin	imit. motive	a (1)
Proch dolor/Pie Jhesu (7)	anon.	cpf in triple canon + imit. motive	d
B. Chansons without cpf.			
Je me complains (5)	Josquin	imit. motive	g (1)
Milles regretz (4)	Josquin?	imit. motive	a
Plaine de duel (5)	Josquin	imit. motive	a
Plus nulz regretz (4)	Josquin	imit. motive (T/B)	d
Plusieurs regretz (5)	Josquin	imit. motive	d
Plusieurs regretz (4)	anon.	imit. motive	g (1)
Secretz regretz (4)	de la Rue	T/B canonic + imit. motive	a

[33] An even clearer example of Verdelot's appropriation of these lament *figurae* is his *Gran dolor di mia vita*, a four-part setting of a true madrigal text (aBAaBCcDD), first published by Antico in 1534[16].

Table 1 (cont.)

Title (no. of voices)	Composer	Tetrachord disposition	Final (flats)
II. Florentine/Early Madrigal Tradition			
A. Secular funeral motet with cpf.			
Quis dabit capiti meo aquam? / *Et requiescamus* (4)	Isaac	imit. motive (STB) + transposing ostinato (B)	a / e
B. Madrigals			
Gran dolor di mia vita (4)	Verdelot	(migrating) ostinato (all parts)	d
Qual sarà mai (3)	C. Festa	imit. motive	a
Qual sarà mai (4)	F. Layolle	imit. motive + ostinato (all parts)	a
Qual sarà mai (5)	Verdelot	imit. motive	d (1)
[*Qual sarà mai* (3)	Rampollini	imit. motive?	a?

the *déplorations* and *chansons des regretz* cultivated by Josquin and his contemporaries. The list of works in Table 1 is not intended to be exhaustive, but rather indicative of the environment in which the descending tetrachord first might have acquired its association with mourning. Not all such works in this tradition feature tetrachordal motives, but all the works examined that exhibit a significant, motivic use of these figures are indeed laments, and these fall into one of two broad categories: *chansons des regretz* without borrowed material, which tend to be amatory complaints (though intensely melancholy ones); and more formal laments based on a Latin *cantus prius factus*, among which are some funeral laments (*déplorations*) for specific individuals. Here we find a very similar complex of attributes: a prevailing Phrygian mode, tetrachordal figures that often dissolve in the later stage of the work into more extended melodic cascades (initiated by a dotted rhythm), semitone oscillations, and the association of these figures with highly expressive and characteristic words such as *plainte, complains, plongez, desolation, regretz,* and *lamentation* (See Example 4 on pp. 98-99).

There is no uniform deployment of these figures within and among these works. Some open with clear tetrachordal figures arrayed as imitative entries; the most conspicuous example is the descending tetrachord that opens Josquin's *Je me*

The work is austerely Phrygian, and so thoroughly permeated by the single e-a form the of the descending tetrachord that it gives the impression of a migrating ostinato; the music is ed. in Jesse Ann Owens, ed., *Philippe Verdelot: Madrigals for Four and Five Voices,* Sixteenth-Century Madrigal 28-30 (New York: Garland, 1989), 1: 96-99. See also Stefano La Via, "Eros and Thanatos: A Ficinian and Laurentian Reading of Verdelot's *Sì lieta e grata morte*," *Early Music History* 21 (2002): 75-116, a discussion of Verdelot's understanding of Florentine poetics of the *Quattrocento*, and his expressive application of Phrygian modal materials to a melancholic text.

Ex. 4: Tetrachordal motives

i. *Plusieurs regretz* (anon.)

plu - sieurs re - gretz de si pi-teu - se sor - te

j. *Plusieurs regretz* (Josquin)

plu - sieurs re-gretz de si pi-teu - se sor - te ne sch-vent plus qu'ils font

k. *Secretz regretz* (de la Rue)

par grief tour - mens en deul et des - plai - san - ce

complains (Example 4c).[34] In Josquin's *Plaine de duel* the motive is not introduced until m. 18, but in various forms it thereafter dominates the texture to the end, interrupted only by several statements of extended scalar descents (Example 4g).[35] Pierre de la Rue's *Secretz regretz* opens with the imitative treatment of an elemental figure that also belongs to the affective world of the lament, an oscillation that emphasizes the semitones between e-f and b-c.[36] Among the ensuing florid contrapuntal lines of de la Rue's chanson, the tetrachord motives in both descending (mm. 9-13) and ascending (mm. 37-45) forms are thrown into relief by being cast in slower, more even rhythms (Example 4k).[37] In Josquin's *Plusieurs regretz* the descending tetrachord is heard fifteen times during the first 24 measures of the piece (Example 4j), and an anonymous setting of the same text opens with a motive identical to that which opens Layolle's *Qual sarà mai* (Example 4i) and Josquin's *Mille regretz* (Example 4d).[38] So

[34] Alan Curtis, "Josquin and *La belle Tricotée*," in *Essays in Musicology in Honor of Dragan Plamenac on his 70th Birthday*, ed. Gustave Reese and Robert J. Snow (1969; repr., New York: Da Capo Press, 1977), 1-8 ; Lawrence Bernstein, "Chansons for Five and Six Voices," in *The Josquin Companion*, ed. Richard Sherr (Oxford: Oxford University Press, 2000), 418-21. Music ed. Albert Smijers, *Wereldlijke Werken*, Werken van Josquin des Prés (Amsterdam: Vereniging voor Nederlandsche Muziekgeschiedenis, 1923), 1: 11 (hereafter Ww).

[35] Bernstein, "Chansons for Five and Six Voices," 400-405, where his analysis of this work identifies the descending 4th as a primary motive. Music ed. in Martin Picker, *The Chanson Albums of Marguerite of Austria: MSS 228 and 11239 of the Bibliothèque Royale de Belgique, Brussels* (Berkeley: University of California Press, 1965), 362-67; Ww 4.

[36] Also a feature of the *Qual sarà mai* settings; see Festa (Appendix, no. 1), mm. 18 (altus), 19-21 and 27-28 (cantus, where an A♭ could be justified), 43-47 (altus) and Layolle (Appendix, no. 2), mm. 8-11 and 18-22 (cantus), and 32-35 (altus).

[37] Music ed. in Picker, *The Chanson Albums*, 192-94.

[38] Editions of *Plusieurs regretz* may be found in Ww 1: 7, and Picker, *The Chanson Albums*, 339-42 (anon.). Apart from the shared melodic shape of these figures, the opening dactylic rhythmic figure (long-short-short) is even more pervasive (for ex., 4b, 4f, Verdelot's *Qual sarà mai*, and the openings of both *Cueurs desolez* settings), and evokes the elegiac couplet that was the primary meter of lament in antiquity.

much attention has been paid to issues of authorship regarding the most famous of *chansons des regretz* that discussions of *Mille regretz* overlook the fact that this compact work is built almost entirely of tetrachordal motives. The superius and altus parts are saturated with the motive, and nearly half the work is constructed from stacked pairs of descending tetrachords harmonized by a bass that itself leaps down twice by a fourth (Ex. 4d$^{2\text{-}3}$), configured to cadence on the primary Phrygian tonal centers of e (mm. 7-12) or a (mm. 12-15, 34-38). Pairs of hexachordal cascades initiated by dotted rhythms make a conspicuous appearance exactly halfway through the work (mm. 19-24; Ex. 4d^4).[39]

Table 2 Possible Liturgical Sources of the Descending Tetrachord

Cantus prius factus	*Composer/primary title*	*Music source/text source (LU = Liber usualis)*
Anxiatus est me	Moulu, *Fiere atropos*	Good Friday Lauds, antiphon/Ps. 142:4 (LU 691)
Circumdederunt me	Josquin, *Nimphes, nappés*	?/Ps. 18:5-6
Dies illa, dies irae	de la Rue, *Cueurs desolez*	Burial Service, responsory *Libera me*, 3rd verse (LU 1767)
?Pauper sum ego	Josquin, *Ce povre mendiant*	?8th psalm tone (cadence)/Ps. 87:16
Pie Jesu	Festa, *Super flumina Babylonis* anon., *Proch dolor*	Mass for the Dead, sequence *Dies irae*, final verse (LU 1813)
Plorans ploravit	Josquin, *Cueurs desolez*	?/Lamentations 1:2
Requiem aeternam	Josquin, *Nymphes des bois*	Mass for the Dead, introit (LU 1807)
Et requiescamus in pace	Isaac, *Quis dabit capiti meo aquam*	Compline, antiphon *Salva nos, Domine*, final phrase (LU 272)

[39] David Fallows, ed., *The New Josquin Edition: Secular Works for Four Voices* (Utrecht: Koninklijke Vereniging voor Nederlandse Muziekgeschiedenis, 2005), 28: 25 (hereafter, NJE). Osthoff, Noble, and Picker favor attribution to Josquin; Litterick does not ("Chansons for Three and Four Voices," in the *Josquin Companion*, 374-76). Fallows recently has come out in favor of Josquin in "Who Composed *Mille Regretz*?," in *Essays on Music and Culture in Honor of Herbert Kellman*, ed. Barbara Haggh (Paris: Minerve, 2001), 241-52, where he also states his belief that the chanson was among Josquin's last works and probably written for Charles V (252). Owen Rees, in "*Mille regretz* as Model: Possible Allusions to 'The Emperor's Song' in the Chanson Repertory," *Journal of the Royal Musical Association* 120 (1995): 44-76, characterizes the motives of *Mille regretz* as "built from…commonplace elements" too simple to form the basis of determining correspondences with other works (45). Rees's goal of determining specific instances of modeling and borrowing is indeed made difficult by the "common-place" nature of the material (the Phrygian tetrachordal motives discussed in this article, for example, emerge quite naturally from the mode). More attainable is the goal of showing

The more formal group of cantus firmus-based laments is similar to the *chansons des regretz* with respect to the varied deployment of tetrachordal motives among the non-cantus firmus voices. This is most evident in the two settings of *Cueurs desolez* by Josquin (Ex. 4a) and de la Rue (Ex. 4b), and in Josquin's *Nymphes des bois* (Ex. 4e) and *Nimphes, nappés* (Ex. 4f).[40] However, they differ in that they use texts and melodies borrowed primarily from the Latin liturgy (see Table 2). That all but one of these Latin texts concern death and suffering suggests that they might be a source of our lament emblems, but in fact only one of them—*Pie Jesu*—is promising. This cantus firmus for *Proch dolor/Pie Jesu*, an anonymous seven-voice setting of a Latin elegy mourning the death of Maximilian I (d. 1519), is the final verse of the sequence *Dies irae* from the Mass for the Dead.[41] Its first four notes form an a^1 to e^1 descending tetrachord in the Phrygian mode, and this figure is arrayed in triple canon and repeated across the first 56 measures of this massive motet. This cantus firmus appears in two other funeral laments: Ockeghem's *Mort tu as navré/Miserere* (for the death of Binchois), and C. Festa's *Super flumina Babylonis/Pie Jesu*, but the absence of tetrachordal motives in the non-cantus firmus voices in all three *Pie Jesu* works (and their absence in the cantus firmus melodies of the other works in Table 2) suggests that these particular liturgical melodies were chosen for the affective resonance of their texts, not their music.

The pieces in Table 1, part I, appear to be the work of composers associated with the French royal court, and are mostly datable to the period *ca.* 1505-20. A number of these can be found in the chanson album, MS 228 of the Royal Library, Brussels, copied around 1520 for Marguerite of Austria, where they share the pages with the most doleful collection of music and poetry ever assembled.[42] The collection as a whole almost certainly is a reflection of Marguerite's "melancholy disposition" and unhappy life, and given her discerning taste in music and the rhetorical sensitivity of the more progressive composers represented in the collection, particularly Josquin, it is entirely possible that Marguerite was in some way the muse of this musical emblem.[43]

---

these works as "drawing upon the same elements of a general musical language" (46), though I would argue "shared" rather than "general," since this material develops quite specific rhetorical significance in the context of these texts. Rees also identifies three primary motives in *Mille regretz* (48-50), though none of them is a descending tetrachord.

[40] See Patrick Macey, "An Expressive Detail in Josquin's *Nimphes, nappés*," *Early Music* 31 (2003): 400-11, esp. 409, where his analysis reveals the pervasiveness of the Phrygian tetrachordal motives he identifies as "y" and "z."

[41] Picker, *The Chanson Albums*, 56, 135; music ed. 304-15.

[42] Ibid., 4, argues the MS was copied between 1516 and 1523, and certain portions were added in or after 1519; the earliest datable works in the collection he assigns to 1508. Howard M. Brown and Jaap van Benthem, *NJE 27: Secular Works for Three Voices, Critical Commentary* (Utrecht: Koninklijke Vereniging voor Nederlandse Muziekgeschiedenis, 1991), 31: "copied in Mechlin by members of the scriptorium of Alamire before 1516; small portions of the manuscript were added no earlier than 1519." See *The Chansons Albums*, 9-20 for a summary of the tragedies in Marguerite's life.

[43] Brown, "Josquin and the Fifteenth-Century Chanson," *Proceedings of the British Academy* 71 (1985): 119-58, esp. 136-37, argues that the earliest examples of *regret* chansons and motet chansons pre-date Marguerite, and may have originated south of the Alps, perhaps in Milan.

There is, however, one anomalous piece from this tradition that complicates the above picture, Josquin's motet-chanson, *Ce povre mendiant/Pauper sum ego*. Presumably it was included in Marguerite's collection because it is a lament of sorts, but it stands apart for several reasons: there is no known source for the melody, and the casting of a beggar's complaint about economic status in the more formal guise of a motet-chanson suggests a mock-serious tone.[44] *Ce povre* is also the only three-part piece in Table 1, part I; it probably predates all of them, datable most likely to Josquin's Milan period (*ca.* 1484-9), if not earlier, and so was composed not for the French royal court, but in Italy.[45] The structure is distinctive: a transposing ostinato squarely based on a descending Phrygian tetrachord (see Example 5a) is stated six times in a stepwise descent from a to d, with a final return to a. This supports two florid upper voices in non-imitative counterpoint that are thematically unrelated to the cantus firmus in the bassus.

Ex. 5: Josquin and Isaac, transposing ostinati

a. Josquin, *Ce Povre mendiant/Pauper sum ego*

Pau - per sum _____ e - go

b. Isaac, *Quis dabit capiti meo aquam/Et requiescamus*

Et re - qui - e - sca - mus in pa - ce.

There does happen to be another piece that employs an identical structure, also composed in Italy, and it is the most famous polyphonic lament of the late fifteenth century. Upon the death of Lorenzo de' Medici in 1492, Poliziano wrote a Latin funeral elegy, *Quis dabit capiti meo aquam*, which was set to music by Heinrich Isaac. As Martin Staehelin has shown (and Taruskin confirmed), Isaac borrowed music from his own *Missa Salva nos* in creating the two outer sections of his three-part motet, including the plainchant phrase *Et requiescamus in pace* (the final section

---

[44] For autobiographical interpretations of the texts of *Ce povre mendiant/Pauper sum ego*, see Brown, "Josquin and the Fifteenth-Century Chanson," 131-38 (as a plea for a position in the Hapsburg court), and of *Fortune destrange plummaige/Pauper sum ego*, see Litterick, "Chansons for Three and Four Voices," 339, and *NJE 27, Critical Commentary*, 34.

[45] Litterick, "Chansons for Three and Four Voices," 338-39. Brown dated the work to the 1470s or earlier, based in part on style, but also the belief, now no longer valid, that Josquin was in Milan around that time; "Josquin and the Fifteenth-Century Chanson," 135. Fallows has recently argued for a later date for the work, in *Josquin*, Epitome musical (Turnhout: Brepols, 2009), 305, 330. For a modern edition, see *NJE* 27: 5, and Picker, *The Chansons Albums*, 389-90. Most commentators, including *NJE 27, Critical Commentary*, 33, follow Picker (143) in seeing the ostinato melody as related to the cadence formula of psalm tone VIII (Liber usualis, 133). While the Mode VIII cadence formula (c-c-c-b-c-a-g-g) resembles the melodic shape of Josquin's ostinato, it is unlikely to have been a model, since the interval content and modal character are quite different from the Phrygian version found in *Ce povre*.

of the Compline antiphon *Salva nos* upon which the mass is based), which migrates continuously among the cantus, tenor, and bassus voices of these sections.[46] In the middle section of *Quis dabit*, however, the tenor part, marked "tenor laurus tacet," falls silent as Poliziano's text invites the reader to ponder Lorenzo's death ("Lightning has struck our laurel tree, our laurel so dear to all the muses and dances of the nymphs"). While the upper two voices weave gracefully in florid, non-imitative counterpoint, the *et requiescamus* melody (bearing the antiphon's original text)—a slightly decorated version of a Phrygian descending tetrachord—symbolically sinks downwards in precisely the same manner as Josquin's *Pauper sum ego*, in stepwise descent from a to d, with a return to a (see Example 5b). That this middle section is an entirely original work is suggested by the particular circumstances of its composition: the plainchant melody was borrowed from Isaac's own prior mass, the tenor part was eliminated in response to the text, and the downward-spiraling ostinato was inspired by the death of Isaac's great patron to give structure to the only part of the motet composed entirely from scratch.

What, then, are we to make of the relationship between Josquin's *Ce povre mendiant* and the middle section of Isaac's *Quis dabit*, which are so alike in mode, texture, and the shape and deployment of the transposing ostinato? Josquin's is almost certainly the earlier work, but its source tradition (it appears in no extant sources before the first decade of the sixteenth century) suggests that it achieved limited circulation in the late fifteenth century.[47] While the possibility of direct modeling cannot be ruled out, Isaac may have gotten his ideas from elsewhere. The texture of the motet-chanson is found in a group of works by Compère and

---

[46] Allan Atlas, "A Note on Isaac's *Quis dabit capiti meo aquam*," *Journal of the American Musicological Society* 27 (1974): 102-10; Martin Staehelin, "Communications," *Journal of the American Musicological Society* 28 (1975): 160; Richard Taruskin, "Settling an Old Score: A Note on Contrafactum in Isaac's Lorenzo Lament," *Current Musicology* 21 (1976): 83-93. Both Taruskin, 84, and Wolfgang Osthoff, *Theatergesang und darstellende Musik in der italienischen Renaissance*, 2 vols. (Tutzing: Hans Schneider, 1969), 2: 177-79, provide detailed analyses of the cantus firmus migration in Isaac's motet, though Osthoff overlooks its presence in the tenor at measures 33-37 (part I), and neither author notes its appearance in the final four measures of the bass. For a detailed analysis of the cantus firmus treatment in Isaac's motet, see Warren Drake, "The Ostinato Synthesis: Isaac's Lament for Il magnifico," in *Liber amicorum John Steele: A Musicological Tribute*, ed. Warren Drake, Festschrift Series 16 (Stuyvesant, NY: Pendragon Press, 1997), 57-85, esp. 66-70. For counter-arguments favoring the precedence of the motet, see Atlas, "Communications," *Journal of the American Musicological Society* 28 (1975): 565-56, and Drake, "The Ostinato Synthesis," 74-76.

The unusually prominent role of the "et requiescamus in pace" phrase in the original *Missa salva nos* remains unexplored. Taruskin's table 2 (p. 86) shows the disposition of the "Salva nos" antiphon phrases in the tenor voice of Isaac's mass, but not its migrations to the other voices. From this latter perspective, it becomes clear that this final phrase (Taruskin's phrase "E") is given special prominence: it appears more frequently (often out of the sequence the first four phrases [A-D] tend to observe), migrates more aggressively among all the voices, and more thoroughly saturates the textures of certain sections (e.g., the Credo beginning with the Crucifixus).

[47] Moreover, the work appears in Florence, Biblioteca del Conservatorio di Musica "Luigi Cherubini," MS Basevi 2439 (copied in Brussels/Mechelen, *ca.* 1508; hereafter Florence 2439) with a different French incipit, *Fortune destrange plummaige*, and there seems to be no consensus among scholars about which French text Josquin set originally, or whether the work is even by Josquin; see Brown, "Josquin and the Fifteenth-Century Chanson," 124-25; Litterick, "Chansons for Three and Four Voices," 339; and *NJE 27, Critical Commentary*, 34.

Agricola probably originating in Milan during the 1470s or early 1480s,[48] and though still rare in the 1480s, transposing ostinati had been used in mass settings by several composers, including Isaac.[49] Clearly Isaac drew his cantus firmus, its text, and even chunks of its original polyphonic setting from his own Mass, and the similarity to the *Pauper sum ego* cantus firmus may be coincidental, due to the relative ubiquity of its Phrygian melodic formula (a tetrachordal descent cadencing on e), found alike in the final phrases of the *Salva nos* antiphon, *Dies irae* sequence (*Pie Jesu*), and psalm tone IV.[50] Despite (or perhaps because of) its occasional nature, the Poliziano/Isaac *Quis dabit capiti meo aquam* seems to have attracted widespread attention. Petrucci included it in his *Motetti B* print (1503¹), and subsequent settings of *Quis dabit* texts by Pierre de la Rue (*Quis dabit pacem*), Jean Mouton and C. Festa (*Quis dabit oculis meis*), and Nicholas Payen (a setting of Polizano's text), as well as adaptations by German composers, all pay homage both to Isaac's Poliziano setting, as well as his setting of a second lament for Lorenzo, *Quis dabit pacem*.[51] The

---

[48] Brown, "Josquin and the Fifteenth Century Chanson," 136-41. Since Brown's article, recent evidence has removed Josquin from Milan until the 1480s, but his main arguments about the style and its origins remain valid.

[49] Timothy J. Dickey, "Rethinking the Siena Choirbook: A New Date and Implications for Its Musical Contents," *Early Music History* 24 (2005): 1-52, esp. 36, where he cites the first Naples *L'homme armé* mass, and masses by Isaac, Compère, de Orto, Obrecht, and Josquin. A more detailed study is Stephanie Schlagel, "The Sequential Ostinato in the Music of Josquin and his Circle" (MA thesis, University of North Carolina at Chapel Hill, 1991).

[50] Until Staehelin's correct identification of the source of Isaac's ostinato, a number of differing plainchant sources had been proposed: the versicle of the respond *Libera me* from Matins in the Office for the Dead, in Osthoff, *Theatergesang und darstellende Musik*, 1: 177 (*Liber usualis*, 1799); a respond from the office of St. Cecilia, in Atlas, "A Note on Isaac's *Quis dabit*," 106; and the fourth psalm tone, in Martin Just, *Studien zu Heinrich Isaac's Motetten* (Ph.D. diss., Tübingen, 1961), 162 (*Liber usualis*, 130). The relatively generic nature of this cadential figure may explain the mystery of how a scribe ignorant of the *Salva nos* antiphon came to enter and erase the St. Cecilia text in the Cappella Giulia chansonnier; of the several possible sources, this happened to be one known or provided to him. Its character as a cadential figure, and thus a symbol of finality, or death, may have contributed to its rhetorical force.

[51] The text of Isaac's second Lorenzo lament, *Quis dabit pacem populo timenti* (the same text set by La Rue) is a funeral chorus from a Latin tragedy attributed to Seneca, *Hercules Oetaeus*, but with lines added and arranged so as to refer to Lorenzo. Both motets are edited in Johannes Wolf, *Heinrich Isaac: Weltliche Werke*, Denkmäler der Tonkunst in Österreich, JG. 14/1, vol. 28 (Vienna: Artaria, 1907), 1: 45-52. Atlas's otherwise welcome edition of *Quis dabit capiti* in his *Anthology of Renaissance Music* (New York: Norton, 1998), 166-170, is marred by a printing error resulting in the exclusion of mm. 106-113; there are two other modern editions: Drake, "The Ostinato Synthesis," 77-85; and Noah Greenberg and Paul Maynard, *Anthology of Early Renaissance Music* (N.Y.: W. W. Norton, 1975), 266-76. Jean Mouton and C. Festa set adaptations of Poliziano's text as laments to mourn the death of Anne of Brittany in 1514. Payen was a South Netherlandish composer serving in the Spanish court of Charles V; he set Poliziano's text with music that pays homage to Isaac's setting, perhaps the result of a trip Payen made with the court to Italy during 1535-8; Laura Pollie McDowell, ed., *Nicolas Payen: Motets and Chansons*, Recent Researches in the Music of the Renaissance 144 (Middleton, WI: A-R Editions, 2006), xi (discussion), 47-60 (edition). For more on Isaac's motets and their sources, including later *Quis dabit* settings by Jean de Chainée and Michael Deiss for the death of Emperor Ferdinand in 1564, see Just, "Heinrich Isaac's Motetten in italienischen Quellen," *Analecta musicologica* 1 (1963): 1-19; Alexander Main, "Maximilian's Second-Hand Funeral Motet," *Musical Quarterly* 48 (1962): 173-89; Sternfeld, "Poliziano, Isaac, Festa," 551-59, and *The Birth of Opera*, 205-11, and Albert Dunning, *Die Staatsmotette*, 1480-1555 (Utrecht: Oosthoek, 1970), 93-98.

first of many printings of Poliziano's poem was issued by Aldus Manutius at Venice in 1498, and these typically bore a rubric alluding to Isaac's setting: "Monodia in Laurentium Medicem, intonata per Arrighum Isac."[52]

It may well be that Isaac's inspired setting of Poliziano's seminal elegy forged the first significant association between lament and its musical emblems, including ostinato, for this is the earliest and most famous work in which we find the essential ingredients assembled together: tetrachordal motives cast in the Phrygian mode, and deployed both throughout the musical texture (parts I and III), and as a transposing ostinato in the bass (part II), all in response to a classicizing lament text. The latent association of the *Et requiescamus* text and melody with Compline themes of sleep and departure, and the potential of the descending Phrygian tetrachord, with its poignant half-tone cadence to represent a descent into silence, mourning, and eternal rest, are explicitly realized in *Quis dabit capiti me aquam*. About a decade later, while in the service of the Ferrara court (1503-4), Josquin composed an extraoardinary work that suggests he, too, now understood these lament emblems as appropriate to the elevated rhetoric of a motet associated with death. In both mood and mode, *Miserere mei, Deus* is an elegiac work that ostensibly reacts to the dark tone of a penitential psalm, but it also may have functioned both as a work for its dying patron, Ercole d'Este (d. 1505), and a lament for the death of Girolamo Savonarola. Macey has demonstrated its structural links to Savonarola's own meditation on Psalm 50, and the likelihood that the pious Duke would commission such a work is strengthened by his known admiration for the friar: he corresponded with Savonarola beginning in 1485, and intervened in vain with the Florentine Signoria to prevent his execution in 1498.[53] Musically the motet is cast in the Phrygian mode, uses a transposing ostinato throughout (based on a semitone oscillation), and is built from motives identified by Patrick Macey that include a tetrachord as well as a cascading descent commencing with a dotted rhythmic figure.[54]

3. The Florentine Context

At this point it is tempting to posit an evolutionary development of our musical emblems that begins with their forging in the humanist circles of Poliziano, Isaac, and Lorenzo, passes to Burgundian-Hapsburg court circles through the agency of Josquin and his fellow Hapsburg court composers, and having there undergone a

---

[52] On the particular fame of the poem, see John Sparrow, "Latin Verse of the High Renaissance," in *Italian Renaissance Studies*, ed. E. F. Jacob (London: Faber, 1960), 405-8, and Sternfeld, *The Birth of Opera*, 205-9. The *Quis dabit* incipits ultimately recall two ancient sources, one biblical ("Quis dabit capiti meo aquam, et oculis meis fontem lacrimarum?"), from Jeremiah 9: 1, the other the above-mentioned ancient Roman source. On the textual and musical sources of *Quis dabit capiti meo aquam*, see Drake, "The Ostinato Synthesis," 60, notes 7-8.

[53] Macey, *Bonfire Songs: Savonarola's Musical Legacy* (Oxford: Clarendon, 1998), 184-86.

[54] See ibid., 186-92; and more recently, idem., "Josquin and Musical Rhetoric: *Miserere mei, Deus* and Other Motets," in *The Josquin Companion*, 492-523, where he offers a detailed analysis of the motet's four principal motives. It was with reference to the motets of both Josquin and Isaac that Reinhard Strohm observed a link between ostinato and "serious matters, such as life and death;" *The Rise of European Music* (Cambridge: Cambridge Univ. Press, 1993), 635-38.

more varied and refined motivic treatment in the *chansons des regretz* and *déplorations*, then returns to Italy through chanson *collezionismo* to form a strand that crosses over into the strambotto-laments of our three composers. Doubtless the reality is much messier and more complicated; music and musicians traveled constantly in both directions throughout this period, many works are lost to us, and other composers and patrons probably had a hand in gradually shaping a musical *lingua franca* of lament. However they were forged and synthesized, the primary strands seem clear, and are directly relevant to the musical language of our three settings of *Qual sarà mai*.

The significance of the Isaac/Poliziano *Quis dabit* can by measured by the enduring fame it achieved both abroad and within Florence. Alexander Agricola and Johannes Ghiselin were in Florence in Medici employment immediately after Lorenzo's death, and upon their subsequent return north to pursue their careers at the French and Burgundian courts, they surely would have brought with them knowledge of Isaac's *Quis dabit capiti meo aquam*, if not an actual copy of the music.[55] Both of Isaac's Lorenzo laments circulated actively in Florentine sources right up to the 1520s, and their juxtaposition with the *Quis dabit* laments of Mouton and de la Rue is entirely consonant with a Florentine political and cultural temperament of the period that exalted the pre-eminence of their Laurentian past, and that measured Medici aspirations and accomplishments on a European scale following the ascendancy of Leo X.[56] Florentine sources also record the influx into Italy of French royal court music and musicians arising from the repeated incursions of French armies, and in particular the historic event of December 1515 in Bologna, when Leo X and Francis I met to discuss peace.[57] Among the musically literate in Florence, polyphonic chanson literature had been avidly collected and well-known since the late fifteenth century, and increasingly it came from French royal court circles. The earliest of the surviving manuscripts from Burgundian-Hapsburg court, the "Basevi Codex," was actually prepared in the Alamire workshop for a Tuscan patron, and transmits a number of *déplorations* and *chansons des regretz*, as well as Josquin's *Ce povre mendiant* (though with a different French text, *Fortune d'estrange plummaige*).[58] Florentine chanson manuscripts of the period *ca.* 1505-25 generally

[55] On the frequent movement of Isaac's music to northern Europe, and northern music to Florence, both through commercial courier networks, see my "Heinrich Isaac among the Florentines," *Journal of Musicology* 23 (2006): 97-152.

[56] Both Isaac motets as well as Mouton's are preserved in Florence, Biblioteca Nationale Centrale, MSS Magliabechi XIX. 164-167 (*ca.* 1515-20); Cortona, Biblioteca Comunale, MSS 95-96/Paris, Bibliothèque National de France, Nouvelles Acquisitions Français, MS 1817 (ca. 1519-23); and Florence, Biblioteca Nationale Centrale, MS II. I. 232 (*ca.* 1516-21), which also includes La Rue's *Quis dabit pacem*. On the dating, provenance, and contents of each see, respectively, the studies of Anthony Cummings: *Ms. Florence, Biblioteca nazionale centrale*, Magl. XIX. 164-167 (Aldershot, England: Ashgate, 2006); "Giulio de' Medici's Music Books," *Early Music History* 10 (1991): 65-122; "A Florentine Sacred Repertory from the Medici Restoration," *Acta musicologica* 55 (1983): 267-332, esp. 280, 291 -92 concerning Isaac's *Quis dabit* motets.

[57] Lockwood, "Jean Mouton," *passim.*

[58] Florence 2439; Herbert Kellman, ed., *The Treasury of Petrus Alamire: Music and Art in Flemish Court Manuscripts, 1500-1535* (Ludion: University of Chicago Press, 1999), 78-79.

include, among other repertoire stemming from the French courts, a cluster of *chansons des regretz*, and a favorite seems to have been Josquin's *Plus nulz regretz* (Ex. 4h), an occasional piece commemorating the Treaty of Calais (21 December 1507), and based on a text by Margaret's court poet and Josquin intimate, Jean Lemaire.[59] Exposure to French court repertory can have been no less vital by the time our three composers were contemplating Poliziano's Orpheus lament: Layolle was living in Lyons, where he was involved in music publishing with Jacques Moderne; Verdelot *was* French; and as the composer of a *Quis dabit oculis* motet commemorating the death of Anne of Brittany, Queen of France (1514), as well as *Super flumina Babylonis/Pie Jesu*, Festa clearly had experience with northern motet procedures, probably acquired in the Roman circles of Leo X.[60] The opportunities for all three to encounter French court music were manifold,[61] and was abetted not only by Medici papal tastes, but also by their direct contact with other influential Florentines like Filippo Strozzi who were keenly interested in French music.[62]

To return to the music of our three *Qual sarà mai* settings, I believe we can now see these in greater detail as products of the eclectic, experimental environment in which the early madrigal arose. As a Poliziano lament for Lorenzo, and cast in

---

[59] Fallows, *NJE 28: Secular Works for Four Voices, Critical Commentary*, 342-68; Picker, "Josquin and Jean Lemaire: Four Chansons Re-Examined," in *Essays Presented to Myron P. Gilmore.*, ed. Sergio Bertelli and Gloria Ramakus, Villa I Tatti 2 (Florence: La Nuova Italia Editrice, 1978), 448; Litterick, "Chansons for Three and Four Voices," 374-76. The music is ed. in Picker, *The Chanson Albums*, 280-4, and Fallows, ed., *NJE* 28: 28. Josquin may have set the poem at Lemaire's request, and text and music were probably performed at the celebration marking the return of Maximilian's ambassadors to Mechelin (Malines) on 1 January 1508. *Plus nulz regretz* is transmitted in three Florentine sources of the time, two in the Biblioteca Nazionale Centrale of Florence, MSS Magliabechi XIX. 164-167, and MS Magliabechi XIX. 117 (1513-18), and in Florence, Biblioteca del Conservatorio Luigi Cherubini, MS Basevi 2442 ("Strozzi Chansonnier," *ca.* 1518-28; hereafter Florence 2442). Clusters of *chansons des regretz* can be found in these latter two sources, as well as in Florence, Biblioteca Nazionale Centrale, MS Magliabechi XIX. 107 (*ca.* 1505-13). On an earlier cluster of *regretz* chansons in a Florentine source of the early 1490s, Bologna, Civico Museo Bibliografico Musicale, MS Q 17, see Irena Cholij, "Borrowed Music: *Allez regrets* and the Use of Pre-existent Material," in *Companion to Medieval and Renaissance Music*, ed. Tess Knighton and David Fallows (New York: Schirmer, 1992), 165-76.

[60] Given evidence that the primary sources of Festa's *Super flumina Babylonis* (the Medici Codex) and *Quis dabit oculis* (Bologna, Civico Museo Bibliografico Musicale, MS Q 19) are, respectively, of Roman and north Italian (possibly Paduan) origin, the more likely context in which Festa wrote the latter and gained exposure to a wide range French Court music is Leonine Rome. Leo X knew French court music at first hand, and favored Mouton's music in particular, and surely he would have fostered the setting of a funeral text with strong Medicean associations; see *The New Grove Dictionary*, s.v. "Mouton [de Holluigue], Jean." Festa joined the papal chapel in Rome on 1517, but it is likely that his association with Roman circles dates back at least to *ca.* 1514, as suggested some time ago by Lockwood, "Jean Mouton and Jean Michel," 218. The relationship between the Festa and Mouton motets is carefully worked out in Dunning, *Die Staatsmotette*, 93-98.

[61] See the studies on Florentine sources and patronage by Cummings: "Giulio de' Medici's Music Books," 95-97; "A Florentine Sacred Repertory," 274, and 278ff.; and "Medici Musical Patronage in the Early Sixteenth Century: New Perspectives," *Studi musicali* 10 (1981): 197-216, esp. 209-14.

[62] For arguments that Florence 2442 was compiled for Filippo ca. 1518-28, see H. M. Brown, "The Music of the Strozzi Chansonnier (Florence, Biblioteca del Conservatorio di Musica, MS Basevi 2442)," *Acta musicologica* 40 (1968): 115-29, and Agee, "Filippo Strozzi," 229, n. 12. Staehelin mentions that the Medici Codex can be traced to the library of the Strozzi after the death of its first owner in 1519, Lorenzo de' Medici, Duke of Urbino; "Review: The Medici Codex," 576.

a famous musical setting still very much in circulation, Isaac's *Quis dabit* cannot
have been far from the minds of all three composers as they approached the text
of Poliziano's *Qual sarà mai*. However, it is the setting by the native Florentine
among them that bears the most recognizable traces. Only in Layolle's setting do
we hear the tetrachordal themes continuously, and in all four voices. As in Isaac's
setting, the descending tetrachord is arrayed as an ostinato in the bass (albeit less
systematically), and all of this material in both settings is cast almost exclusively
in the Phrygian mode, to the extent that the e-a tetrachord is unusually pervasive
in both. The distinctive *fauxbourdon* passage in the Layolle version heard for line 7
(mm. 47-52), in which all four parts trace a protracted descent through a tetrachord,
has its counterpart in measures 9-13 of Isaac's motet, where all four voices make a
similar descent in conjunction with the text *quis oculis meis* (see Example 6).[63] Here
Isaac presents a different solution to the voice-leading problem posed by two voices
beginning on the same pitch and following the same melodic descent: the cantus and
bass parts make staggered, rather than simultaneous, entries on a[1] and a, allowing
Isaac to shape them as identical, imitative statements of the cantus firmus in the
Phrygian mode. The *fauxbourdon* texture heard at this point in Isaac's setting, a style
that around this time also begins its association with a mournful affect, also resounds
in several parts of Layolle's madrigal, each time in conjunction with statements of
the descending Phrygian tetrachord (mm. 18-21, 23-25, 25-28, 58-60).[64]

Ex. 6: Isaac, *Quis dabit capiti*, mm. 9-14

On the other hand, the deployment in all three madrigals of the tetrachordal
themes as short motives, their manipulation in various descending and ascending

---

[63] As Staehelin has shown, Isaac's passage began life as the opening measures of the second Osanna,
in the Sanctus of his *Missa salva nos* (mm. 168-73); "Communications," 160.

[64] Strohm, *The Rise of European Music*, 637, cites Isaac's motet as an early example of such usage, with
Ockeghem's *Mort, tu as navré* as a possible precedent.

formations, and their extensions into longer, cascading figures appears to be derived directly from the French tradition of *chansons des regretz* and *déplorations* considered above. What is novel, of course, is the casting of these lament emblems within the form of the strambotto, but as we have seen this was a conjunction occasioned by a text clearly associated with the topic of lament, the poetry of Poliziano's *Orfeo*, and a Florentine cultural environment that combined an interest in contemporary French music with poetic and musical traditions of the Laurentian era.

But what might have been the specific conditions that brought about these interrelated settings? Although there is no record of efforts to mount a production of Poliziano's *Orfeo* in early sixteenth-century Florence, a new edition of *Orfeo* in 1524 was perhaps the occasion for one; there was a tradition of "theatrical madrigals" composed specifically for dramatic productions, such as Verdelot's settings of choruses for Florentine productions of Machiavelli's *La Mandragola* (1524) and *La Clizia* (1525).[65] In the early 1490s, there were plans afoot at the Mantuan court to mount new performances of *Orfeo*, and once again a famous Florentine solo singer, this time Atalante Migliorotti, was sought for the lead role.[66] A Florentine production in the 1520s might have been undertaken as an effort to repatriate a Florentine cultural treasure to which the Gonzagan court laid a defensible (and ongoing) claim. Less clear is why a production of *Orfeo* would call for three different settings of only the first of the lament's four stanzas, and the mildly contrapuntal styles of all three versions render them less suitable to theatrical recitation.[67] A plausible explanation that arises from circumstantial evidence is that Verdelot's setting may have been composed first; modally it stands apart from the other two settings, and may be contemporary with his other datable strambotto setting, *Quando madonna*, which Slim placed in the early 1520s. The Layolle and Festa versions thus would come later, but in response to Verdelot's. The prime candidate as agent in bringing these latter two together is Filippo Strozzi (1488-1538), a keen patron of the early madrigal, and the only one we know to have been in direct contact

[65] H. Colin Slim, *A Gift of Madrigals and Motets* (Chicago: University of Chicago Press, 1972), 1: 100-104; Pirrotta, *Music and Theatre*, 120-54, 283-98.

[66] Alessandro D'Ancona, *L'origini del teatro italiano*, 2nd ed. (Turin: Ermanno Loescher, 1891), 2: 358-64; Povoledo, "From Poliziano's *Orfeo* to the *Orphei tragoedia*," in *Music and Theatre*, 289-90. Productions were planned for 1490 and 1491; Migliorotti, traveling from Florence where he was in the service of the Medici, failed to reach Mantua in time in 1490. Migliorotti continued his association with the Medici, both with Pope Leo X in Rome, and through his membership in the Sacred Academy of the Medici in Florence. When he was elected *perpetuo cytharedo* of the Academy in 1515, he was "compared extravagantly to Orpheus" (Cummings, *The Maecenas and the Madrigalist*, 86). This raises the interesting prospect that Migliorotti formed a direct link between the musical traditions of the original Orfeo production and the environment of the early madrigal.

[67] See Slim, "Un coro della Tullia di Lodovico Martelli messo in musica e attribuito a Philippe Verdelot," in *Firenze e la Toscana dei Medici nell'Europa del '500*, ed. Gian Carlo Garfagnini (Florence: Leo S. Olschki, 1983), 2: 487-511, where he reaches a similar conclusion regarding Verdelot's *Fuggite l'amorose cure acerbe*, a madrigal (from the same print as his *Qual sarà mai*) that Einstein and Osthoff had suggested might be intended for a performance of a *Medea* play. He also cites evidence (511) that choral singing in tragedies, as opposed to comedies, was a new phenomenon around 1524.

with both composers, *ca.* 1528-36.[68] As husband to Lorenzo the Magnificent's granddaughter and Medici supporter through the papacy of Leo X, Strozzi had reason to engage in a project that glorified the Laurentian era. On the other hand, Strozzi also became disillusioned with Medici rule and in 1528 moved to Lyons, home to another republican sympathizer, Francesco Layolle.[69] Given Verdelot's anti-Medicean position during the last republic (1527-30), and Festa's close dealings with Strozzi after this time, there remains the intriguing possibility that the *Qual sarà mai* complex was intended to carry a double political meaning as both a tribute to the Florentine republic of the past, and a lament for its temporary recovery and second loss, a fate not unlike that suffered by Orpheus.

While we cannot be certain of precisely what forces of politics and patronage gave rise to these three settings of Poliziano's famous lament, we can be more confident about their musical and poetic patrimony. They conjoin elements of the Josquin-era chanson, ongoing efforts (rooted in the works of Isaac) to apply the polyphonic *maniera* to Florentine poetic texts, a humanist interest in the affective force of rhetorical *figurae*, a classicizing cultivation of the ancient and recent traditions of lament, and the suggestive history of the strambotto as both a vehicle of a specifically Florentine tradition of orphic solo singing as well as a genre susceptible to musical experiments in text setting. As such, they record something of the highly eclectic and Janus-faced environment in which the musical language of the early madrigal was forged. They are also perhaps a swan-song to the older strambotto tradition; for a literate Florentine audience, the madrigals of all three composers—three of the era's best interpreters of Italian texts—summoned the image of the archetypal solo singer at the same moment they exhibited the polyphonic transformation of that practice. Orpheus "singer of strambotti" had become Orpheus singer of madrigals.

[68] Festa actively sought texts from Filippo, who in turn received settings from both composers; Agee, "Filippo Strozzi," 230-37. Filippo certainly would have recalled brother Lorenzo's earlier involvement with the multiple settings of the latter's poem *Questo mostrarsi* (see above), another Poliziano project with which Layolle, too, was involved. Yet another Strozzi-inspired collaboration took place when Layolle, Willaert, Gerolamo Scotto, and Simon Boyleau all wrote musical settings of one of Filippo's poems, "Rompi l'empio cor;" see Agee, "Roberto Strozzi and the Early Madrigal," *Journal of the American Musicological Society* 36 (1983): 11, n.35.

[69] Brown, "Chansons for the Pleasure of a Florentine Patrician: Florence, Biblioteca del Conservatorio di Musica, MS Basevi 2442," in *Aspects of Medieval and Renaissance Music: A Birthday Offering to Gustave Reese*, ed. Jan LaRue (New York: Norton, 1966), 56-66, esp. 63-64; *The New Grove Dictionary*, s.v. "Layolle, Francesco de."

Appendix 1:
Costanzo Festa, *Qual sarà mai* (RISM 1542[18], fols. 51v 52)

Appendix 2:
Francesco Layolle, *Qual sarà mai* (Cinquanta canzoni, no. 5)

Ribaldry in High and Low Places

Lorenzo de' Medici and the Carnal in the Carnival*

Leofranc Holford-Strevens

I. Carnival Carnality

Imagine a world in which a man as a matter of course has not only what is called natural sex, but also anal sex with both men and women, but never masturbates; in which women do occasionally masturbate, though only with fruit or dildos, but never have sex with each other. Welcome to the world of the Florentine carnival songs, the *canti carnascialeschi*.

How far was this the real Florentine world? As Michael Rocke has shown, court-records pay no attention to what women did with other women, but prove that sodomy between males, often cross-class, was as rife in Florence as foreigners said it was.[1] Anal intercourse with women, disliked, tolerated, enjoyed, or even demanded by them, was employed, not only for reasons of pleasure, but for avoiding pregnancy or syphilis, and also so that sex might continue during menstruation. The *canti*, it appears, amuse the public by distorting reality in a circus mirror, not by creating an imaginary world for private fantasy.

They do so, not by explicit description, but by pervasive sexual images,[2] some virtually transparent, such as tilling the soil, some less obvious, but nevertheless

---

*A version of this chapter was delivered on 19 May 2007 at the Conference on "Sexualities, Textualities, Art and Music in Early Modern Italy" organized by Dr. Melanie L Marshall in the Department of Music, University College Cork. I am grateful to all those who participated in the discussion, in particular to Dr. Laurie Stras for the suggestion cited below, and also to Professor William F. Prizer for sending me the text of his paper cited in n. 9; I am happy to offer this study in tribute to the scholar who has made the topic of carnival his own.

[1] Michael Rocke, *Forbidden Friendships: Homosexuality and Male Culture in Renaissance Florence* (New York: Oxford University Press, 1996). Flaws in Rocke's statistics have been detected by Samuel K. Cohn, Jr., review, *Speculum* 74 (1999), 481–83; but see Trevor Dean, *Crime and Justice in Late Medieval Italy* (Cambridge: Cambridge University Press, 2007), 145–46 (references I owe to Sean Gallagher). In any case, sodomy manifestly flourished, even if deemed a sin and a crime; the resulting frisson is essential to the relish with which the facts are stated in our texts.

[2] Charles S. Singleton, *Nuovi canti carnascialeschi del Rinascimento* (Modena: Società tipografica modenese, 1940), 40; William F. Prizer, "The Music Savonarola Burned: The Florentine Carnival Song in the Late 15th Century," *Musica e storia*, 9 (2001): 5–33; idem, "Reading Carnival: The Creation of a Florentine Carnival Song," *Early Music History*, 23 (2004): 185–252 at 189 n. 5. The nature of the metaphors is explored by Giulio Ferroni, "Il doppio senso erotico nei canti carnascialeschi fiorentini," *Sigma: Rivista quadrimestrale*, N.S. 11, nos.2-3 (1978): 233-50, who also observes their uniformity of sexual reference and their utter incompatability with Bakhtinian models of carnival (I thank Judith Testa for the reference and for a copy of the article).

familiar to all and sundry, such as the fig for the female organ, a metaphor also known to the ancient Greeks though strangely not to the Romans, who applied it to the piles. Birds may be the penis, fish either the penis or the vagina depending on which they more resemble. In addition, ever since Burchiello Florentines had been confronted with ever more imaginative and recondite euphemism, which has been elucidated in exhaustive detail by Jean Toscan.[3]

The typical *canto carnascialesco* purports to be sung by artisans or shopkeepers offering their wares and services to the ladies of the city, but in fact boasting of their sexual prowess with the invitation to sample it. Artisans or shopkeepers they are not; suffice it to cite the supposed locksmiths who do not know how to make locks, only how to open them with their "keys" (Example 1);[4] rather, the gentlemen have the keys to the ladies' locks.

Ex. 1: Anon., *Canzona de' chiavaioli* (1482), ll. 13–16

Toppe far no' non sappiàno,	We don't know how to make locks
e non abbiam mai imparato,	And we have never learned;
ma di chiavi lavoriàno	We work only with keys
e faciànne buon merchato.	And we do it very cheaply.

l.1. For the vagina as lock (T 1: 341, cit. 410; *Diz.* 588) cf. the ancient Greek vulgar name κύσθος related to Latin *custos* and English *hoard*. (In the plural *toppe* may refer to both nether orifices, T 3: 1381–2, cit. 2548.)
l.3. *chiave* "penis"; T 4: 1678; *Diz.* 104; *chiavare* is still current Italian slang.
l.4. " 'Buon mercato' [. . .] also branded with a hot iron." An obvious play on words (Prizer, citing Florio). It also indicates vaginal intercourse (T 1: 436, cit. 637).

II. Lorenzo de' Medici

However contested the assertion that the *canto carnascialesco* was invented by Lorenzo de' Medici,[5] his own *canti* are excellent illustrations of the world I have described. For manageability's sake I shall confine myself to those now accepted

---

[3] Jean Toscan, *Le carnaval du langage: le lexique érotique des poètes de Burchiello à Marino*, 4 vols. (diss. Paris, 1978; Lille: Atelier National de Reproduction des Thèses, 1981), hereafter cited as "T" with volume, page, and either section or citation as is more useful in each case. For tilling the soil, see T 2: 1065, cit. 1897–98; for the fig, 4: 1695 s.vv. fica, fico 4: 1695; for birds, 3: 1540–83, §§1111–44; for fish 3: 1595–1608, §§1152–63. Also useful, but not confined to the Renaissance, is Valter Boggione and Giovanni Casalegno, *Dizionario letterario del lessico amoroso: metafore eufemismi trivialismi* (Turin: Unione Tipografico-Editoriale Torinese, 2000), hereafter "*Diz.*"

[4] Quoted and translated by William F. Prizer, "Petrucci and the Carnival Song: On the Origins and Dissemination of a Genre," in Giulio Cattin and Patrizia Dalla Vecchia (eds.), *Venezia 1501: Petrucci e la stampa musicale/Venice 1501: Petrucci, Music, Print and Publishing* (Venice: Fondazione Levi, 2005), 215–51 at 225.

[5] Anton Francesco Grazzini, detto il Lasca, *Tutti i trionfi, carri, mascheaate [sic], ò canti Carnascialeschi andati per Firenze. Dal tempo del Magnifico Lorenzo vecchio de' Medici; quando egli hebbero prima cominciamento, per infino à questo anno presente 1559* (Florence: [Lorenzo Torrentino]), sigs. aiiv–aiiir. See T 1: 99–131; Giovanni Ciappelli, *Carnevale e Quaresima: comportamenti sociali e cultura a Firenze nel Rinascimento* (Rome: Edizioni di storia e letteratura, 1997), 195–211; Prizer, "Reading Carnival," 237 n. 110; idem., "Petrucci," 216–28.

as his,[6] though he has been credited with more, for instance one set by Agricola (Example 2),[7] about makers of oil who never spill a drop "outside," each of whom has his own "equipment" in good condition; they do their job with great *letizia* and know how to extract oil in plenty from the ladies' olives. *Ulive* are the two female lower orifices (T 3: 1494–95, §1081), *letizia* may denote the joy of sex in general (T 2: 1170–2, §814), but is also code for sodomy (T 3: 1172–78, §§816–17). The boast is thus: "every one of us is fully erect; we do the deed in front and behind, and can extract great enjoyment from both places."[8]

Ex. 2: *Canzona dei facitori d'olio*

Donne, noi siam dell'olio facitori,	Ladies, we are makers of oil,
né mai versiànne una gocciola fuori.	and never spill the teeniest drop outside.
Ciascun di noi ha la sua masseritia	Every one of us has his equipment
in punto bene, et con assai letitia	in tip-top condition, and are very happy
compiam nostr'opra, et dell'olio a dovitia	to accomplish our work, and we know how
sappiamo di vostre ulive cavar fori.	to extract oil in plenty from your olives.

l.3. *masseritia* = penis (T 3: 1371–72, §974).
l.4. *in punto* = "erect" (T 2: 1157–58, §798). *bene* indicates vaginal intercourse (T 1: 449–50, §276) especially when set against a term that can refer to sodomy.
l.5. *compiam* = "we ejaculate" (T 2: 1061–63, §734). For *dovizia* of sex see T 1: 350–52, §167.

In some songs straightforward metaphors prevail: in the *Canzona dello zibetto* (Example 3), evoked by the civet given Lorenzo de' Medici in November 1487,[9] statements that the animal lives in marshy places and enjoys boneless meat—plenty of it in large pieces—but needs three or four days' rest each month indicate that it represents the vagina, all the more so when we learn that the civet's musk is extracted with a prod *un terzo lunga*; a third of a braccio—about 19.455 cm or just

[6] Ed. Riccardo Bruscagli, *Trionfi e canti carnascialeschi del Rinascimento*, 2 vols. (Rome: Salerno, 1986), and Paolo Orvieto, *Lorenzo de' Medici: Canti carnascialeschi* (Rome: Salerno, 1991).

[7] Ed. Edward R. Lerner, *Alexandri Agricola* [sic] *(1446–1506) Opera omnia*, 5 vols. ([Rome]: American Institute of Musicology, 1961–70), 5: 67–68, #46.

[8] See T 2: 1170–2, §814. *Olio* may be either sperm (T 3: 1492, §1078; Diz. 357, Singleton, *Nuovi Canti*, 148) or vaginal secretion (T 3: 1491–2, §1077); *far l'olio* = to have intercourse (T 3: 1492–93, §1079; *Diz.* 357). Lines 4–5 mean "we know how to make your vaginas exude abundant secretions and our penises to emit abundant sperm in both vagina and anus." Similarly the "oil" whose production is described in the *Canzona de' profumi* will be applied behind as well as before: ll. 25–26 "L'olio è una cosa santa, | s'è stillata in buona boccia" ("Oil is a holy thing, if it is drizzled into a good round jug"), where sodomy is implied by *santa, buona*, and (roundness being associated with the anus) *boccia*; see T 1: 692–96, §477, esp. cit. 1216; 3: 1362–63, cit. 2489; ll. 41–42 ("Evv'egli accaduto mai, | donne, aver l'anella strette"? ("Has it ever befallen you, ladies, to have tight rings?"), where *anella* (an -*a* plural, see below) = "anuses"; see T 2: 900, §625, cf. *Diz.* 16.

[9] Bernard Toscani, "I canti carnascialeschi e le laude di Lorenzo: elementi di cronologia," in Piero Gargiulo (ed.), *La musica a Firenze al tempo di Lorenzo il Magnifico: congresso internazionale di studi, Firenze, 15-17 giugno 1992* (Florence: Olschki, 1993), 131–42 at 134–35; William F. Prizer, "Behind the Mask: Patrons and Performers of Florentine Carnival and the Carnival Song," unpublished paper given at Johns Hopkins University (2006).

Ex. 3: *Canzona dello zibetto*, ll. 1–14, 19–30, 39

Donne, quest'è un animal perfetto
a molte cose, e chiamasi zibetto.

Ladies, this is a beast perfect
for many things, and is called civet.

E' vien da lungi, d'un paese strano,
sta dov'è gemizion over pantano,
in luoghi bassi, e chi 'l tocca con mano,
rade volte ne suole uscir poi netto.

It comes from afar, from a strange land,
it dwells where there is spring or marsh,
in lowlying places; whoever puts a hand to it 5
rarely comes out clean.

Carne sanz'osso sol gli paion buone,
ma vuolne spesso, e se può gran boccone;
poi duo dita di sotto al codrione,
come udirete, si cava il zibetto.

Meat without bone is all that it likes,
but it wants it often, and in large bites if it can;
two fingerbreadths below the base of the spine,
as you shall hear, the civet-musk is extracted.

Hassi una tenta, ch'è un terzo lunga,
spuntata acciò che drento non lo punga
Caccisi drento, e convien tutta s'unga,
o donne: e' vi parrà dolce diletto. . . .

It has a prod, which is a *terzo* long,   11
blunted so as not to prick it inside
Drive it in, and it must get smeared all over
ladies; it will seem to you a sweet delight.

Bisogna al metter drento ben guardare;
il luogo ov'è 'l zibetto non scambiare,
ché si potria d'altra cosa imbrattare
la tenta, e fassi male al poveretto.

In putting it in one must take great care   19
do not mix up the place where the civet is
for the prod might get stuck in something else,
and the poor little creature gets hurt.

Chi non ha tenta pigli<a> altro partito;
truova stran modi, o almeno fa col dito,

She who has no prod takes other measures;
she finds strange ways, or at least uses her
                finger,
                                                     24

e poi lo dànno a fiutare al marito,
se non ha tenta o vien da lui il difetto.

and then they give it to their husband to sniff,
if he has no prod or the want comes from him.

È certe volte a trar pericoloso,
perché gli ha il tempo suo, e vuol riposo
tre giorni o quattro; pure un voglioloso
non guarda a quello e trae un stran. . . .
    brodetto

On occasion it [the musk] is dangerous to draw
for it has its "time," and wants to rest
three or four days; only a hothead
pays no heed to that and draws a strange
    broth. . . .
                                                     30

Di far ingravidar ha gran virtue . . .

It has great virtue for making pregnant .
                                                     39

Bruscagli 1: 13–14; Orvieto 71–2, 99–100. Wet and marshy places represent the vagina:
    T1: 598–602, §415 (for *pantano* see cits. 1025, 1027). *Trarre* for sexual intercourse: T
    2: 1060–61, cits. 1880–2.

under 7.66 inches—is the standard length in Florentine folklore for the penis.[10] Not only that, it is also important to put the prod in the right place. Furthermore, we have a glimpse into the Florentine bedroom: in the absence of a prod, a woman finds alternatives, such as the finger, which she then gives her husband to sniff if he still needs inspiration.

And yet part of the humour resides in the use of language that might suggest sodomy even though that is manifestly warned against. The civet dwells "two fingerbreadths below the base of the spine"; the obvious meaning apart, *duo* and plurals in *-a* such as *dita* often point in that direction (T 2: 954–61, §§668–72; 2: 964–66, §675), as *perfetto*, *poi*, *strano*, and *almeno* normally would.[11] But the anus does not need a monthly rest, nor does it confer pregnancy; our sexual taste is being teased.

Contrast the *Canzona de' confortini* (Ex. 4), which in fact says very little about sweets; indeed, the singers will not waste time explaining how they are made, because loss of time reduces one to simple pot-meals—except that *tempo* is the menstrual period and *pentolini* are the buttocks: at that time of the month sex had better be anal. The ladies are bidden still to do the business, but let neighbour help out neighbour, that is to say the anus should take over the work of the vagina. We then pass to a complex analogy with the card-game basset (*carte* are the buttocks, T 1: 687–88, cit. 1195; *Diz.* 88), in which one player lifts and the other puts; that is one player turns a card and the other bets on it, or one partner erects his organ (T 2: 1148, §787; *Diz.* 11–12) and the other inserts and envelops it (*Diz.* 327). The original audience knew what it was to play "without a man" (without court cards?) or "underneath" or "on top" (bets on low or high?); the latter two decode as anal and vaginal respectively (T 1: 424–25, §251; cf. *Diz.* 55), and sex *sanz'uomo* will have to be masturbation if it is true that Florentine men (unlike Aretino) never envisaged lesbianism.

Attention then passes to another game, *primiera*, otherwise known as *flusso* after the flush: a four-card hand all of one suit,[12] but also an attack of diarrhea. The gambler who has staked everything on his high-value primiera (all four cards of different suits), only to be called (Italians say "seen") by a player with a flush, is equated with the over-enthusiastic sodomite who has provoked such a flux in the receiving party. This section culminates in a curse on Sforza Bettini, an agent

[10] See T 1: 304, cit. 336 with 4: 1858 n. 124. In the 1560s Garzia de' Medici had a codpiece 20.6 cm (8.11 in.) long and 19 mm (0.75 in.) wide at the base: Janet Arnold, *Patterns of Fashion: The Cut and Construction of Clothes for Men and Women, c1560–1820* (London: Macmillan, 1985), 52 with pl. 76 (16).

[11] See respectively T 1: 512–13, §349; 1: 417–18, §246; 1: 223–24, §65; 1: 353–5, §171. Even *pantano* may be the anus when the vagina is spoken for (T 1: 600–1, cit. 1029).

[12] The game is played with a pack of forty cards, having no eights, nines, or tens. There is considerable variation in the rules, but any flush beats any primiera. For an extended erotic allegory of the game see Francesco Berni, "Commento al capitolo della primiera," *Poesie e prose*, ed. Ezio Chiorboli (Geneva and Florence: Olschki, 1934), 203–64 (available online at http://www.nuovorinascimento.org/n-rinasc/testi/pdf/berni/primiera.pdf, consulted 17 Sept. 2007).

Ex. 4: *Canzona de' confortini*, ll. 3–10, 15–22, 35–42

Non bisogna insegnar come si fanno,	There is no need to explain how they are made,
ch'è tempo perso, e'l tempo è pur gran danno;	for it is lost time, and time is a great waste;
e chi lo perde, come molte fanno,	and she who loses it, as many women do, 5
convien che facci poi de' pentolini.	will afterwards have to do things with pots.

Quando gli è 'l tempo vostro, fate fatti,	When it is your time, do your stuff,
e non pensate a impedimenti o imbratti:	and don't think of hindrances or blockages;
chi non ha il modo, dal vicin l'accatti;	whoever hasn't the means should get it next door;
e' preston l'un all'altro i buon vicini. . . .	good neighbours lend to one another. 10

No' abbiam carte, e fassi alla bassetta,	We have cards, and it's sit down to basset 15
e convien che l'un alzi e l'altro metta;	and one has to lift and the other put;
poi di qua e di là spesso si getta	and then the cards are often tossed this way
la carte; e tira a te, se tu indovini.	and that; and take (the money) if you guess right.

O a sanz'uomo, o sotto o sopra chiedi	You ask for "without a man," "below," or "on top" 19
e ti struggi dal capo infin a' piedi	and twist and turn from your head to your feet
infin che viene; e quando vien poi vedi	until it comes, and when it comes then you see
stran visi, e mugolar come mucini. . . .	strange faces, and people mewing like kittens.

Il flusso c'è, ch'è giuoco maladetto.	There is "flush," which is a cursed game; 35
ma chi volessi pure uscirne netto,	but let anyone wishing to come out unscathed
metta pian piano, e inviti poco e strietto;	"put" very gently, and id small and tight
ma lo fanno oggi infino a' contadini	but nowadays even peasants do it.

Chi mette tutto il suo in invito,	He who stakes his all in one bid,
se vien flusso, se truova a mal partito;	if flush comes, finds his game wrecked; 40
se lo vedessi, e'par un uom ferito;	if you should "see" him, he seems a stricken man;
che maladetto sie Sforzo Bettini!	cursed by Sforzo Bettini!

Bruscagli 1: 3–4; Orvieto 59–60, 87–92; *bassetta* is also a sexual position in which the man stands
    behind the woman, who bends forwards (*Diz.* 42); cf. T1: 294, cit. 318 and for
    games in general 2: 1056–8, §731.

    l.17. *Gettare* = to ejaculate (T 2: 1083–4, cits. 1891–4; *Diz.* 225).

    l.18. *tirare* = to have intercourse (T 2: 1060, cits. 1878–9), ejaculate (*Diz.* 585).

    l.21. *viene*: also in the sexual sense as in English (T 4: 1765; cf. *Diz.* 613–14).

    l.37. *Poco* and *stretto* are sodomitic (T 1: 350–3, 373–4, §§168–9, 196).

of Lorenzo's during the 1470s; puns on his name there may be,[13] but the literal
reference is primary, arising from some immediate occasion unknown to us. That

[13] "Rapist of boys" (T 1: 316, cit. 361); "effort (*sforzo*) of defecation" (Orvieto 91).

poses a problem of chronology. Lasca asserts that Lorenzo's first song in his new style was the *Canzona de' confortini*, "set to music for three voices by one Arrigo the German, chapelmaster at San Giovanni, in those times a most renowned musician."[14] But if the setting (now lost) was indeed made by Heinrich Isaac—who in any case was never chapelmaster at S. Giovanni, only a singer—the song must date from the mid-1480s, several years after Sforza Bettini's departure; it seems better, having found Lasca in error on the composer's employment, to suppose him wrong too on his authorship.[15]

In Florentine burlesque, the vogue for anal sex is further expressed by such words as *oggi* (T 1: 227–9, §68), as in the *Canzona de' visi addrieto* (Ex. 5), which states that nowadays you have to watch your back, because we are all traitors (another code-word, T 1: 493, §328). Those who trust a man's front by allowing him to stand behind them are likely to be sodomized.

Ex. 5. *Canzona de' visi addrieto*, ll. 5-10

E' bisogna oggi portare	It is necessary nowadays to have
gli occhi drieto e non davanti;	your eyes behind you not in front;
né così possi un guardare:	not even so can one look after oneself:
traditor siam, tutti quanti;	we are traitors every one;
tristo a chi crede a' sembianti,	woe to him that trusts appearances,
ché riceve spesso inganno.	for he is often deceived.

Buscagli 1: 23-24; Orvieto 85-86. 112-15 (who wrongly denies the sexual interpretation).

The singing persona is not always male. In the *Canzona delle forese* (Example 6), six country girls in town for carnival have lost their husbands, and offer the ladies a reward for finding them. These rewards are fruits and vegetables, which are sweet and do no harm; they are described in loving and manifestly phallic detail. Country girls might perfectly well have brought such things with them in the literal sense, but are obviously not so equipped in the metaphorical; and although there is at least one hint at a dildo,[16] gourds kept for seed (l. 23) cannot be that. These are male organs, belonging not to the *forese* but to the singers; yet the identification goes so far that the country girls end by saying: "we are still of tender age; if they [the husbands] turn

[14] Lasca, *Tutti i trionfi*, sig. aiiir: "e il primo canto, ò Mascharata che si cantasse in questa guisa fu d'huomini, che vendeuono Berriquocoli, e confortini; composta à tre voci da vn certo Arrigo Tedesco; Maestro all'hora della Capella di San Giouanni; e musico in quei tempi, riputatissimo."

[15] On the chronological problem see Ciappelli, *Carnevale*, 202 n. 24; but Prizer, "Petrucci," 228 and "Behind the Mask" is inclined to accept a date in the 1470s, which would exclude him.

[16] At ll. 29–36 their *bacelli* (beans, i.e., penises, T 3: 1452, cit. 2682, *Diz*. 33) are good both cooked (*cotti* = used for sex, T 1: 541–43, §374) and with the top cut back to form a movable hood; Toscan sees in them a kind of dildo (4: 1810 n. 94; cf. 1: 113 on female masturbation). One may suspect the same at ll. 25–28, where the *melloni*, traditionally carved into fancy shapes for carnival, take on the form of a dragon reinterpretable as a penis (no doubt with testicles for wings), "a vederlo e fiero e vago" (27), both proud (or erect, T 3: 1364–65, cit. 2492) and attractive to look at.

Ex. 6. *Canzona delle forese*

Lasse, in questo carnasciale	Alas, in this carnival,
noi abbiam, donne, smarriti	ladies, we have lost
tutt'a sei nostri mariti;	our husbands, all six of us;
e sanz'essi stiam pur male.	and without them we're in a bad way.
Di Narcetri noi siam tutte,	We are all from Arcetri, 5
nostr'arte è l'esser forese;	our skill is being country girls;
noi cogliemo certe frutte	we gather certain fruit
belle come dà il paese;	as fine as our country yields;
se c'è alcuna sì cortese,	if there is any lady so courteous,
c'insegni i mariti nostri:	let her point out our husbands to us: 10
questi frutti saran vostri,	these fruits shall be yours;
che son dolci e non fan male.	they are sweet and do no harm.
Cetriuoli abbiamo e grossi,	We have cucumbers, and big ones,
di fuor pur ronchiosi e strani;	gnarled on the outside and odd;
paion quasi pien di cossi,	they look all but full of bumps, 15
poi son apritivi e sani;	but then they keep you open and healthy;
e' si piglion con duo mani:	and they are taken in two hands;
di fuor lieva un po' di buccia,	peel off a little skin outside,
apri ben la bocca e succia;	open your mouth wide, and suck; 19
chi s'avezza, e' non fan male.	once you get used to them, they do no harm.
Mellon c'è cogli altri insieme	We have serpent-melons in with the rest
quanto è una zucca grossa	the size of a thick gourd;
noi serbiam questi per seme,	we keep them for seed,
perché assai nascer ne possa. . . .	so that plenty can grow from them. . . .
Queste frutte oggi è usanza	Nowadays it is the custom
che si mangia drieto a cena:	to eat these fruit after dinner;
a noi pare un'ignoranza.	we think that's ignorance,
a smaltirle è poi la pena:	they're a trouble to digest afterwards. 40
quanto la natura è piena,	so abundant is nature,
de' bastar: pur fate voi	it should suffice; all the same,
dell'usarle innanzi o poi;	make use of them before or after;
ma dinanzi non fan male.	but before, they do no harm.
Queste frutte, come sono,	These fruits, just as they are, 45
se i mariti c'insegnate,	if you point out our husbands to us,
noi ve ne faremo un dono.	we shall give you for a present.
Noi siam pur di verde etate;	We're just in the bloom of youth;
se lor fien persone ingrate	if they turn unpleasant,
troverem qualche altro modo,	we shall find some other ways 50
che 'l poder non resti sodo;	of seeing the farm does not remain
	unploughed;
noi vogliam far carnasciale.	we want to make Carnival.

Bruscagli 1: 15–17; Orvieto 73–5, 100–2.16–20. T 3: 1218, cit. 228: "Les phallus que voici employés par derrière (*poi*) savent pénétrer les lieux les plus secrets (*apritivi*), où ils font merveille (*sani*). On les reçoit (*piglion*) entre les fesses (*con duo mani*); rabattez d'abord le prépuce (*lieva un po' di buccia*), présentez un orifice bien disposé (*apri ben la bocca*) et absorbez-les (*succia*). Avec un peu d'habitude on ne trouve pas qu'ils font mal malgré ce qu'on dit."

> 21–4. The *mellone* at Florence is not (as at Rome) the ordinary melon, there called *popone*, but the cucumber-shaped serpent-melon, *Cucumis flexuosus*, and hence stands for the penis; see T 3: 1448–51, §1048.

nasty, we shall find some other way of seeing the field does not go unploughed; we want to make Carnival." That is, understanding the field to be ours, the girls', we shall find lovers (and leave you with our husbands?); or is it your, the ladies', fields that will be ploughed by us, the singers? The song has reached that stage in the proceedings when everyone is too much aroused to worry about "who whom?"

But if *whom* does not matter, *what* does. The *forese* protest against the custom of eating these fruits after dinner, in other words anal sex; that is in their rustic character, for even after the elegant joys of sodomy had trickled down from the nobility to the urban élites, the burgesses, and even the artisans (so that the city ladies may suit themselves), they were still notionally too good for peasants. The fruits, accordingly, *son dolci e non fan male*, taken afore not abaft.[17] But peasants too were aping this urban custom, even if only as a second course.[18] *Cortese* in l. 9 (T 1: 390, §212), *buon* in l. 32 (T 1: 509–11, §347), and *dono* in l. 47 (T 2: 1013–16, §710) stand for sodomy; in l. 16 *apritivi* is manifestly anal; in 17 *duo mani* are the buttocks, [19] to sex in which quarter Toscan refers *bocca* and *succiare*.[20] Not indeed that one will exclude fellatio, which, though to a classical scholar shockingly rare, occasionally relieves the Renaissance diet of "Wham bam, thank you sir or ma'am."

III. "Free of All Indecency"?

Three of Lorenzo's texts are described by Toscan (1: 112) as "nettes de toute grivoiserie." Two are *trionfi* from the Carnival of 1490: of these, the *Canzona de' sette pianeti* (Example 7) appears to consist of two extracts from a greater whole, the introduction and the stanzas relating to Venus. It is undeniably in a more elevated and learned style, appropriate not only to astrology as a supposedly scientific discipline (elementary as the content is) but also to Ficino, to whom Orvieto 43–4 sees the poem as a compliment. And yet, when the planets declare that they use force when defied but gently lead those who comply ("sforziam chi tenta contro noi far pruova,|conduciam dolcemente che ci crede"), echoing Seneca's line

---

[17] *Dolce*, especially in contrastive contexts, = vaginal sex (T 1: 823–27, §§570–71); far male = sodomize (T 4: 1714).

[18] On peasants and sodomy in Florentine writing see T 1: 201–10, §53–6; cf. Ex. 4, l. 38.

[19] For sodomitic duo see above; for *mani* "buttocks" see T 1: 387, cit. 518.

[20] *Bocca* "anus" T 3: 1208–10, §847; *succiare* "envelop" 3: 1215–19, §854.

Ex. 7: *Canzona de' sette pianeti*, ll. 1–2, 7–20

Sette pianeti siam, che l'alte sede	Seven planets are we, who are leaving
lasciam per far del cielo in terra fede.	our lofty seats to make earth believe in heaven.
Sforziam chi tenta contro a noi far pruova;	We force whoever tries to defy us;
conduciam dolcemente che ci crede.	we lead gently whoever trusts us.
Maninconici, miseri e sottili	Melancholics, misers, and subtle persons,
ricchi, onorati, buon prelati e gravi,	rich, honoured men, prelates good
	and grave, 10
sùbiti, impazienti, fèr, virili,	impetuous, impatient, proud, and manly men;
pomposi re, musici illustri, e savi;	gorgeous kings, renowned musicians,
	and sages;
astuti parlator, bugiardi e pravi;	clever talkers, liars, and scoundrels;
ogni vil opra alfin da noi procede.	in a word, every base deed comes from us.
Venere graziosa, chiara e bella	Venus the gracious, bright, and beautiful 15
muove nel core amor e gentilezza	stirs in the heart love and courtesy:
chi tocca il foco della dolce stella,	whomso the fire of the sweet star touches,
convien sempre arda dell'altrui bellezza:	must ever burn with another's beauty;
fère, uccelli e pesci hanno dolcezza:	beasts, birds, and fishes enjoy sweetness;
per questo il mondo rinnovar si vede.	thereby the world sees itself renewed. 20

Bruscagli 1: 20–21; Orvieto 83–84, 110–12.

1. *sette* suggests sodomy T 2: 936–40, §655–7; planets are *stelle*, i.e., buttocks, T 1: 768–70, §535; for astrology as sodomy T 1: 771–72, §537; *Diz.* 569–70.

2. *cielo* vs. *terra* = vagina vs. anus T 1: 689–21, §475; *fede* = penis (T 4: 1694; *Diz.* 186). Given that *di* was not radically distinguished from *da* (see the *Grande dizionare della lingua italiana*, 4: 304, sense 6), we may understand a descent from one mode of intercourse to the other.

8. For *dolcemente* used in a sexual sense T 1: 299, cit. 323; 1: 339, cit. 405.

9–13. The characters are those produced respectively by Saturn, Sun, Mars, Jupiter, and Mercury. Sodomy is suggested by *sottili* (T 1: 364–6, §184; cf. *Diz.* 553), *prelati* (T 1: 196, cit. 117), *re* (T 1: 197–8, §50), *bugiardi* (T 1: 463, §291); also by *savi*, which like other terms denoting wisdom implies the savoir-faire of the elegant sodomite (T 3: 1276–87, §§894–900); one will suspect the same of *astuti* and also of *subiti*, *impazienti* given the coded use of terms for haste (T 1: 289–96, §§111–15); although *vile*, when opposed to *gentile*, denotes vaginal sex (T 1: 385–6, cit. 514, 2: 984. cit. 1738), here, like *pravi*, it occupies the semantic field of *malo* (T 1: 455–6, §285), for otherwise why should the planets boast of causing baseness? *Onorati* = "well-hung" (T 2: 999, cit. 1765); *fèr* "erect" (T 3: 1364–65, cit. 2492).

17. Or "he who sodomizes the anus" (*toccare* 1: 303–4, §125; *fuoco* 1: 611–15, §424).

19. *fiera* may denote the penis (T 1: 643, cit. 1107) or in the plural the nether orifices (T 3: 1582, §1143), *pesce* and *ucello* the penis (T 3: 1595–97, §1153; 3: 1541–42, §1111; *Diz.* 401, 599–600; Singleton 148, 150).

the unwilling drags," we also recall that *far pruova* means "sodomize" (T 2: 1012, §710) and *credere* "consent to sodomy" (T 2: 1027–30, §716), yielding: "Don't you dare try it on with us, but let us do it to you." Seven was a sodomitical number, the great Galileo himself used *strologare* for that practice, and although *pianeta* is not in T's index, planets counted as a class of star (Venus in the poem is *la dolce stella*), and *le stelle* are the buttocks; even the collocation *in terra fede* is capable of such a meaning. When the planets state what kind of people they produce, we recognize several classes of presumptive sodomites (*sottili* under Saturn, *buon prelati* under the Sun, *re* and *savi* under Jupiter), for the standing joke is that all elites, whether "ducunt uolentem fata, nolentem trahunt" (*Epistulae morales* 107. 11), "Fate leads political, clerical, or intellectual, are so inclined,[21] and *sottili* and *buon* mean the same. Nor would elegant homoeroticism be inappropriate to the Platonist Ficino; but the remaining stanzas are given over to Venus, who bids "donne vaghe" and "giovinetti adorni" to make the most of their "dolce tempo," an uncoded incitement to heterosexuality, which of course does not exclude the anal intercourse perhaps hinted at in l. 17. There is *grivoiserie*, in short (for Lorenzo can hardly have failed to notice what he was writing), but it is served as a side-dish to keep the merrier souls happy.

The other *trionfo* pronounced clean by T is the famous *Canzona di Bacco*, "Quant'è bella giovinezza" (Ex. 8). This would be surprising, since the part played by wine in the promotion of sexual activity stands in no need of learned footnoting, and satyrs in love with nymphs in caves and woods are unabashedly physical: but there are abundant linguistic clues in such apparently innocent features as the diminutive endings and the number one hundred that the satyrs do not shrink from serving the nymphs as they sometimes serve each other in their celebration of unbridled sexuality.

For Orvieto 109–10 this poem is a Christian Platonic allegory: the Silenus who comes along behind on his donkey is really Jesus Christ, since it is to Silenus that Socrates is likened in Plato's *Symposium*, Socrates was taken for a precursor of Christ, and Christ rode into Jerusalem on a donkey, a gesture Lorenzo was to emulate in 1492. Rather than explain why the Messiah should be so drunk he cannot stand on his own two feet, Orvieto brings in the carnivalesque *fête de l'Âne* celebrated in France, a country (he might have added) with which the Medici traditionally had good relations. All this—based on the bare words *asino* and *Sileno*—is to be a tribute to Ficino.

Doubt is in order. In a Bacchic parade Silenus could not well be absent, and the donkey is his traditional mount (e.g., Ovid, *Fasti* 1. 399, 6. 339); on the surface the description is as appropriate for him as it is inappropriate for either Socrates (whose capacity to hold his liquor is emphasized at the end of the *Symposium*) or Jesus Christ. Nevertheless, it is hard, on hearing "vien drieto," not to think of sodomy. Although the phrase is normally said of the penetrator (T 1: 416–17, §245), the continuation "sopra l'asino," given what donkeys are famous for, suggests "has an orgasm from receiving a penis *a tergo*," a pleasure to be enjoyed even by one who cannot *star ritto*, manage an erection (T 2: 1149, §789, *Diz.* 481–2). Silenus' donkey would remain a symbol of virility for Alessandro Striggio in *Il cicalamento delle donne al bucato*, published in 1567.[22]

---

[21] T 1: 195–201, §§49–-52; they take their cue from the gods,1" 194–95, §48.

[22] Transl. Christina Fuhrmann (unaware that Silenus' steed is his donkey), "Gossip, *Erotica*, and the Male Spy in Alessandro Striggio's *Il Cicalamento delle donne al bucato* (1567)," in Todd M. Borgerding (ed.), *Gender, Sexuality, and Early Music* (London: Routledge, 2002), 167–97 at 182.

Ex. 8: *Canzona di Bacco*

Quant'è bella giovinezza,	What a lovely thing is youth,	
che si fugge tuttavia!	which nevertheless is fleeting!	
Chi vuol esser lieto, sia:	Let who would be merry be so;	
di doman non c'è certezza.	there's no assurance of tomorrow.	
Quest'è Bacco e<d> Arianna,	This is Bacchus and Ariadne,	5
belli, e l'un dell'altro ardenti:	handsome, and burning for each other:	
perché 'l tempo fugge e inganna	because time flees and deceives,	
sempre insieme stan contenti.	they stay ever content together.	
Queste ninfe ed altre genti	These nymphs and other folk	
sono allegre tuttavia.	are cheerful all the time.	10
Chi vuol esser lieto, sia:	Let who would be merry be so;	
di doman non c'è certezza.	there's no assurance of tomorrow.	
Questi lieti satiretti,	These merry little satyrs,	
delle ninfe innamorati,	in love with the nymphs,	
per caverne e per boschetti,	through caverns and woodlets,	15
han lor posto cento agguati,	have laid a hundred ambushes for them;	
or da Bacco riscaldati,	now heated by Bacchus,	
ballon, salton tuttavia.	they dance and leap all the time.	
Chi vuol esser lieto, sia:	Let who would be merry be so;	
di doman non c'è certezza.	there's no assurance of tomorrow.	20
Queste ninfe anche hanno caro	These nymphs, too, love it	
da lor essere ingannate:	when the satyrs deceive them:	
non può fare a Amor riparo,	no one can resist Love	
se non gente rozze e ingrate:	except rough and unpleasant persons;	
ora insieme mescolate;	now mixing together (with them)	25
suonon, canton tuttavia.	they play and sing all the time.	
Chi vuol esser lieto, sia:	Let who would be merry be so;	
di doman non c'è certezza.	there's no assurance of tomorrow.	
Questa soma, che vien drieto	This burden that comes behind	
sopra l'asino, è Sileno:	on the donkey, is Silenus:	30
così vecchio è ebbro e lieto,	at his great age he is drunk and merry,	
già di carne e d'anni pieno;	now full of meat and years;	
se non può star ritto, almeno	if he cannot stand up, at least	
ride e gode tuttavia,	he laughs and rejoices all the same.	
Chi vuol esser lieto, sia:	Let who would be merry be so;	35
di doman non c'è certezza.	there's no assurance of tomorrow.	
Mida vien drieto a costoro:	Midas comes behind them:	
ciò che tocca, oro diventa.	what he touches becomes gold.	
E che giova aver tesoro,	And what's the use of having a treasure,	
s'altri poi non si contenta?	if another is not contented then?	40
Che dolcezza vuoi che senta	What sweetness do you expect one to feel	
chi ha sete tuttavia?	who is thirsty all the time?	
Chi vuol esser lieto, sia:	Let who would be merry be so;	
di doman non c'è certezza.	there's no assurance of tomorrow.	
Ciascun apra ben gli orecchi,	Let everyone open his ears wide,	45
di doman nessun si paschi;	let no-one feed on tomorrow;	
oggi sian, giovani e vecchi,	now let young and old	
lieti ognun, femmine e maschi;	be merry everyone, women and men;	
ogni tristo pensier caschi:	let every serious thought fall away;	

facciam festa tuttavia.	let us have a festival all the same. 50
Chi vuol esser lieto, sia:	Let who would be merry be so;
di doman non c'è certezza.	there's no assurance of tomorrow.
Donne e giovinetti amanti,	Ladies and young lovers,
viva Bacco e viva Amore!	Long live Bacchus, long live Love!
Ciascun suoni, balli e canti!	Let everyone play, dance, and sing! 55
Arda di dolcezza il core!	Let the heart burn with sweetness!
Non fatica, non dolore!	No weariness, no pain!
Ciò c'ha a esser, convien sia.	Whatever's to be must be.
Chi vuol esser lieto, sia:	Let who would be merry be so;
di doman non c'è certezza.	there's no assurance of tomorrow. 60

Bruscagli 1: 17–19; Orvieto 80–82, 106–10.

1–12. Although *lieto* and *allegre* may suggest sodomy (T 2: 1172–78, §§816–17; cf. *fuggire* "be sodomized" 2: 1143–44, §762; *ingannare* "sodomize" 1: 493, cit. 773), since *contento* points to vaginal intercourse (T 2: 929, cit. 1629), the reference is rather to sexual enjoyment in general (T 2: 1169–72, §§813–15).

13–20. Diminutives may suggest sodomy (T 1: 378–81, §§203–5), as may *caverna* (anus 1: 596–97, cit. 1015; but vagina *Diz*. 96), *boschetto* anus (T 3: 1583, §1145; but vagina 3: 1534, §1107), *cento* (T 2: 927–31, §§649–51), *agguati* (T 4: 1659; but a woman's nether orifices 1: 425, cit. 609); however, *ballon* (T 2: 1055–56, §729; *Diz*. 37), *saltare* (T 3: 1510–11, cit. 2792; *Diz*. 499) suggest vaginal sex; as if a new draught of wine gave them new energy for that. It is manifest that they have it both ways.

21–28. For *ingannare* "sodomize" see on 1–12; *suonare* may denote either form of sex 2: 1054–55, §728 (cf. *Diz*. 551), as may *cantare* (vaginal *Diz*. 81, anal T 1: 361–2, §180).

29–36. Both *asino* (T 3: 1512, cit. 2797; *Diz*. 25) and *carne* (T 4: 1676, *Diz*. 85–86) are the penis; *almeno* "in the anus" (T 1: 353–55, §171; cf. above, n. 11), *ridere* = "have an orgasm" (T 2: 1179–81, §819).

37–44. *toccare* sodomize (see above), but *oro* = vagina 1: 590, cit. 1001 (penis 1: 723–24, §499); *tesoro* penis *Diz*. 583. *Contentarsi* is normally vaginal (T 1: 325, cit. 376) but is here redefined by *poi*, a procedure attested by T *passim* (e.g., 1: 164–68, §27. 2). *Dolcezza* sexual pleasure (T 2: 805–6, §556); *sete* lust (T 1: 584–85, §407).

45–52. *tristo* sodomitic (T 1: 455, cit. 678); *pensier* penis (T 3: 1263, §882; *caschi*: cf. *cadere* of sodomy or switching thereto (T 1: 428–29, §254).

57. *fatica* (T 1: 334–6, §152) and *dolore* (T 1: 320–23, §139) may represent sodomy; but here the carnivalesque wish is that it not be painful.

e che 'l destrier del vecchiarel Sileno,	and that the nimble steed of silly old Silenus,
d'amor tutto ripieno,	all full of love,
si duol, né vede l'hora	is in pain, and cannot wait
di trovar l'orme de la sua signora.	to find his lady's path.

*3. Or "is dying for sex (*dolere* T 2: 1116, cit. 1998), and cannot have congress (*vedere* T 2: 1079–81, §743) with his lady's orifice (*ora* T 1: 766–68, §534)."

After the nymphs and Silenus, Midas too *vien drieto*; readers of Ovid would recall that once, when Silenus had strayed from Bacchus' company, he was found by Phrygian peasants and brought to their king, Midas, who having feasted him for ten days brought him back to the god and was rewarded with a choice of reward, only to wish in his folly that everything he touched should turn into gold.[23] Since

---

[23] Ovid, *Metamorphoses* 11. 85–145. In another tale, Midas, having asked Silenus what was the

Midas is "coming behind" Silenus, sodomy, also suggested by *tocca*, seems more plausible than vaginal intercourse *a tergo* even though "gold" in code means vaginal sex (T 1: 720–24, §§498–99); rather, the implication is that his partners effeminize themselves. In the next two lines, we all know what a man's treasure is, and *poi*, which commonly indicates the physical as well as the temporal posterior, imposes the sense that this treasure is a waste if it gives no-one pleasure in the rear. Then, "what sweetness do you expect him who is always thirsty to feel?"; Midas was always thirsty because his drink turned to gold before he could swallow it, but is he not also the sexually insatiable person who is always wanting more?

The next stanza begins "Ciascun apra ben gli orecchi"; "listen to me," but the line has more point when we recall that the "ears" may be the female orifices (T 2: 1221–24, §857). After that, the summons to young and old, female and male, to be merry, and the cry "viva Bacco e viva Amore," take us beyond drinking, though just to be sure Lorenzo writes "Ciascun suoni, balli e canti," where all three verbs refer to sexual activity, and *suonare* and *cantare* may be sodomitical.

The third supposedly uncoded poem is the *Canzona delle cicale* (Example 9), in which the girls, *le fanciulle*, complain that the cicadas (or gossips) are always speaking ill of them; too bad, we're like that, say the cicadas, but often enough it's your fault for tattling and for tormenting your lovers with waiting instead of doing it right away; well, say the girls, we shall just ignore your chattering. Although Toscan finds no extra meaning for *cicala*, if the grasshopper, *el grillo* in the famous frottola, can be the penis (T 4: 1704, *Diz.* 241), it is hard to see why the cicada cannot be too; and Burchiello couples *cicale* with *granchi*, literally "crabs," which certainly has that meaning.[24] Men do not brag the less about their sexual conquests if they achieve them quickly; but there are codewords enough to suggest a lament that the "cicadas" prefer anal sex to vaginal, countered by "you enjoy it but won't admit it; and it protects you against the danger of *parlare*," that is vaginal sex.[25] When the girls surrender and cry "Viva amore e gentilezza," "gentilezza" is code for sodomy, the supposed speciality of noble birth (T 1: 383–85, §208).

More startlingly, the cicadas' retort in l. 18, if addressed to men, would undoubtedly mean "you sodomize us back";[26] the *fanciulle* either wear strap-ons, or more economically are addressed as the male singers they are. We encountered a similar oscillation between singer and character in the *Canzona delle forese*; an attractive explanation of the oscillation between singer and character is due to Laurie

---

best thing for a human being, received the answer: "not to be born, and next best to die as soon as possible" (e.g., Cicero, *Tusculan Disputations* 1. 114), a thought that might have struck home to Lorenzo in his decline even as it did to Sophocles, who at some ninety years old gave it to a chorus sung by old men on the miseries of age (*Oedipus at Colonus* 1224–27).

[24] Burchiello, *Rime* 2.6 "vidi cicale e granchi in val de Pisa"; for *granchi* see T 3: 1604–6, §1161. *Val di Pisa* is the vagina: T 1: 684, §469.

[25] T 2: 1105–6, §758; so *parole* l. 28 (2: 1116–18, §766). The danger is still pregnancy, not pox.

[26] For *ridire* in a sexual sense see T 3: 1257, cit. 2292.

Ex. 9. *Canzona delle cicale*

Le fanciulle incominciano:
Donne, siam, come vedete
giovanette vaghe e liete.
Noi ci andiam dando diletto,
come s'usa il carnasciale:
l'altrui bene hanno in dispetto
gl'invidiosi e le cicale;
poi si sfogon col dir male
le cicale che vedete.

Noi siam pure sventurate!
Le cicale in preda ci hanno,
che non canton sol la state,
anzi duron tutto l'anno;
a color {o} che peggio fanno,
sempre dir peggio udirete.

Le cicale rispondono:
Quel ch'è la natura nostra,
donne belle, facciam noi;
ma spesso è la colpa vostra,
quando lo ridite voi;
vuolsi far le cose, e poi
saperle tener secrete.

Chi fa presto, può fuggire
il pericol del parlare.
Che vi giova un far morire,
sol per farlo assai stentare?
Se v'offende il cicalare,
fate, mentre che potete.

Le fanciulle rispondono:
Or che val nostra bellezza,
se si perde per parole?
Viva amore e gentilezza,
muoia invidia e a chi ben duole!
Dica pur che mal dir vuole,
noi faremo e voi direte.

The girls begin:
We are ladies, as you see,
young, charming, and cheerful.
We go giving pleasure.
as is done at Carnival:
others' welfare counts for nothing   5
with the envious and the cicadas,
then the cicadas whom you see
exert themselves in speaking ill.

We really are unfortunate!
The cicadas have made us their prey,   10
they do not sing only in summer,
but last all year round,
those who do the worst
you will always hear say the worst.

The cicadas reply:
That which is our nature,   15
fair ladies, is what we do;
but often it is your fault,
when you repeat it;
you want to do things, and then
to find a way to keep them secret.   20

One who acts quickly can escape
the danger of speaking.
What good does it do you to cause death,
simply to make the man suffer great pain?
If gossip offends you,   25
act while you can.

The girls answer:
What is our beauty worth now,
if it is lost through words?
Long live love and nobility,
death to envy and him who is aggrieved!   30
Let who will speak ill,
we shall do and you will tell.

Bruscagli 1: 21–22; Orvieto 78–79, 105–6.

2. *liete*: "fond of sex" or "fond of sodomy"; see on Ex. 8, ll. 1–12.

5. *bene* is code for the vagina (T 1: 448, §273); but since it may also be the anus (T 1: 449, §275) and *dispetto* is the act of sodomy (T 2: 1074–76, §740), we have a double meaning: "they despise other people's vaginas" and "they sodomize other people's anuses."

7. *dir male* = sodomize (T 1: 453, cit. 674).

11. *La state* is vaginal sex (T 1: 263–64, §90); *tutto l'anno* that and anal sex together (T 2: 941, cit. 1650; 2: 1016, cit. 1795).

13–14. "You will always submit to being sodomized by sodomites" (*udire* T 3: 1224–25, §858).

20. *secrete* of sodomy (T 2: 1099–1102, §755).

21–2. *Far presto* is sodomy (T 1: 287–90, §§108–11). On the surface ll. 23–24 refer to the tortures of the lover by his unrequiting mistress; but *morire* is also "to be sodomized" (T 1: 501, cit. 794) and *stentare* is the resultant pain (T 1: 323, §140).

Stras,[27] namely that the performers, whom we know to have been young noblemen performing a *rite de passage*, were marking the transition from the adolescent state in which they served older men as "passive" and "feminine" sexual partners to the adult state in which they were to be homo- and heterosexually "active."[28]

Thus the real difference is not that some of the poems are saucy and some are not, but that in one of them the double meaning is not pervasive; as a *trionfo* written in the traditional *endecasillabi* it thus shows fewer marks of genre-crossing than the *Canzona di Bacco*, in the *ottonari* characteristic of *canti carnascialeschi*, into which conversely Lorenzo introduced the longer metre as in the *Canzona de' confortini* and the *Canzona dello zibetto*. Even so, he had learnt a lesson in public taste when the the long narration set by Isaac on a Medici victory, *Alla battaglia*, performed at young Piero's expense, proved a flop.[29] He was free to admit learned subject-matter (already present in a *trionfo* possibly of 1464),[30] and not restrict himself to playing shopkeeper; what the audience wanted was sex, and he made sure they got it.

---

[27] On the sexual ambivalence of young mn in Renaissance Italy, and its especial tolerance in Florence, see Guido Ruggiero, *Machiavelli in Love: Sex, Self and Society in the Italian Renaissance* (Baltimore, MD: Johns Hopkins University Press, 2007) 25–28.

[28] Noble *giovani*: Prizer, Reading Carnival," 242–44; idem, "Behind the Mask." *Rite de passage*: Ciappelli, *Carnevale*, 242–44.

[29] See Blake Wilson, "Heinrich Isaac among the Florentines," *Journal of Musicology*, 23, no.1 (2006):97-152, esp. 109–110.

[30] See Prizer, "Petrucci," 225–27.

[31] Or, since *sano* is used of vaginal sex (T 1230–32, § 71), "they operate both ways."

Games of Fame:
Street Cries, Birdsong, Gossip, and Other Remnants in Renaissance Secular Music[1]

Susan Forscher Weiss

Ti, ti piti, ti chouthi, thoui, chouthi. You say to yourself, little darling, it is Corpus Christi, it is time for drinking. To the Sermon, mistress, mine! To Saint Trotin to see Saint Robin…Quick to the Sermon…Up, madame, to the Mass of Saint Chatter who chatters.[2]

The title of this essay is a play on William F. Prizer's "Games of Venus: Secular Vocal Music in the Late *Quattrocento* and Early *Cinquecento*," published in 1995.[3] In so doing, I am emulating my mentor and referencing another type of imitation. The literary device of *onomatopoeia*, or imitating the sound of nature, was defined by Henry Peacham (1546-1634), writing in *The Garden of Eloquence* (1593, for perhaps

---

[1] A version of this paper, "Musical Pastiches: Imitating the Sounds of Everyday Life in Renaissance Secular Songs," was delivered at the Annual Meeting of The Renaissance Society of America, Chicago, April 5, 2008. I am particularly indebted to William F. Prizer, to whom I owe my earliest professional mentoring, as well as an understanding of Italian secular music of the Renaissance. In addition, I draw on previous work done on the folk song tradition, quodlibet, and centone by Knud Jeppesen, "Venetian Folksongs of the Renaissance," in *Papers Read at the International Congress of Musicology, Held in New York, September 11th – 16th, 1939*, ed. Arthur Mendel, Gustave Reese, and Gilbert Chase (New York: Music Educators' National Conference for the American Musicological Society, 1944): 62-75; and Fausto Torrefranca, *Il segreto del Quattrocento: Musiche ariose e poesia popolaresca* (Milan: Hoepli, 1939). Other pertinent studies include Kate van Orden, "Sexual Discourse in the Parisian Chanson: A Libidinous Aviary," *Journal of the American Musicological Society* 48, no. 1 (Spring 1995): 1-41; Donna Cardamone Jackson's work on *canzone villanesche, Adrian Willaert and his Circle: Canzone Villanesche alla Napolitana and Villotte*, Recent Researches in Music of the Renaissance 30 (Madison, Wisconsin, 1978), and her article, "Erotic Jest and Gesture in Roman Anthologies of Neapolitan Dialect Songs," *Music and Letters* 86, no. 3 (2005): 357-79; Howard Mayer Brown, *Music in the French Secular Theatre, 1400-1550* (Cambridge, MA: Harvard University Press, 1963). Musical borrowing and pastiche has been a focus of my research and teaching in the past couple of decades. The exchange and sharing of popular repertories in Italy and Germany with an emphasis on the quodlibet and centone resulted in an unpublished paper delivered at a conference in 1996. I am also grateful to Virginia Newes and to the late Martin Picker for sharing unpublished papers on descriptive vocal music.

[2] Clément Janequin, "Chant des Oyseaux: Réveillez vous, cœurs endormis," in *Chansons polyphoniques, édition complète*, eds., A. Tillman Merritt and François Lesure (Paris: Éditions de L'Oiseau-Lyre, 1971), vol. 1.

[3] William F. Prizer, "Games of Venus: Secular Vocal Music in the Late Quattrocento and Early Cinquecento," *The Journal of Musicology* 9, no. 1 (Winter 1991): 3-65. Of the Roman gods and goddesses mentioned, the least known, Fame, is one who plays an important, if somewhat underestimated role in the music of the Renaissance. Fame (Pheme, according to Greek mythology)

the first time in an English treatise), in two categories: imitations of sounds, such as rattling and creaking, or imitation of voices such as "croking of frogs, the chattering of Pies [magpies], the chirping of sparrows, the howling of dogs."[4]

By acknowledging sources of sound outside of the mainstream, artists and composers were able to create their own identities, establishing a new language that merged popular and courtly styles. The sounds of nature, birds and animals, the hunt, the battlefield, and the market place are depicted in programmatic musical compositions, beginning as early as the thirteenth century. By studying the surviving polyphonic assemblages, it becomes possible to tease out the voices of those whose social status didn't account for preservation of their culture.

In his now infamous essay, Milton Babbitt stated "a popular song would appear to retain its germane characteristics under considerable alterations of register, rhythmic texture, dynamics, harmonic structure, timbre and other qualities."[5] Add to this commonplace sounds—birds warbling and singing, dogs barking, horses galloping, market vendors chanting street cries advertising their wares, gossip mongers, and musical instruments, such as trumpets sounding a call to arms—and you find playful, witty assemblages of courtly, popular, and rustic traditions blended together. What follows is a study of the sounds of nature and the voices of common folk prevalent in some programmatic chansons and other secular works of the late Middle Ages and Renaissance.

Animals and humans engaging in sexual activities, dancing, singing, and playing instruments are common themes not only in sixteenth-century music, but also in literature, in such works as François Rabelais (1494-1553) tales of *Gargantua and Pantagruel*, as well as in the visual arts, in particular the paintings of Hieronymous Bosch (1450-1516) and Peter Brueghel, the Elder (*ca.* 1525-1569). The sounds and images are often filled with double meanings. Birds, hens, eggs, flutes, bagpipes, sticks, and other symbols reference a world closer to the barnyard than to the court.[6]

The world of popular festivals and games can be mined from a study of a wide variety of sources including settings of *chansons rustique, canzone villanesche*, street

---

was a shadowy winged woman, often depicted holding a trumpet, and known for eavesdropping and then spreading gossip. She worked hand in hand with Ossa, the messenger of Zeus.

[4] Henry Peacham, on Onomatopoeia in *The Garden of Eloquence* (London, 1593): "Onomatopeia, this figure of the Latines is diversly named, as Nominatio, Nominis fictia, Procreatio. It is a forme of speech whereby the Orator or speaker maketh and faineth a name to some thing, imitating the sound or voyce of that it signifieth, or else whereby he affecteth a word derived from the name of a person, or from the originall of ye thing which it doth expresse. And this form of fayning, & framing names is used diverse wayes. First, by imitation of sounds, as to

1. By imitation of sound. say, a hurliburly, signifying a tumult or uprore: likewise, rushing, lumbring, ratling, blustring, creking, and may such like.

2. Secondly, by imitation of voyces, as the roaring of Lyons, the bellowing of buls, the blating of sheepe, the grunting of swine, the croking of frogs, the chattering of Pies, the chirping of sparrows, the howling of dogs, the neighing of horses, ye hissing of serpents. . . . Yet the English tongue endevoreth what it can so speake by this part, as where it saith, I can not court it, I can not Italian it, that is, I can not performe the dutie or manners of a courtier, I can not imitate the fashion of an Italian." http://www.perseus.tufts.edu/hopper/text?doc=Perseus:text1999.03.0082

[5] Milton Babbitt, "Who Cares If You Listen?" *High Fidelity* 8, no. 2 (1958), 39.

[6] Beckett refers to the scraps or trifles in his last poem "Mirlitonnades" (from mirliton, a reed pipe

cries, and dances, as well as from literature and the visual arts.[7] The smells and noises of nature emanate from and intertwine with courtly conceits. A Bolognese eclogue by the aristocrat Cesare Nappi (fl.1490-1510), written in 1508, catalogues popular songs as it describes a day in the life of some peasants who are picnicking, singing, dancing, and complaining about government and taxes.[8] One of the dances mentioned, "tentalora," is quoted in the Renaissance programmatic chanson *La bataille* by Clément Janequin (1485-1558). Modeled on Vergil's eclogues, Nappi's rustic poem represents the literary counterpart of musical pastiches composed from the late fourteenth through to the end of the sixteenth centuries. In music, the logical places to look for the remnants of popular tunes, as well as a myriad of other sounds associated with early modern European music, is in the surviving repertoire of musical "stews," such as quodlibets, centone, ensaladas, and fricassées.[9]

---

or primitive whistle similar to a kazoo, but also the name of a type of eggplant indigenous in French cuisine) as "gloomy doggerel." A pipe in the sixteenth century symbolized a phallus. For more on instruments and the body see Keith McGowan, "The Prince and the Piper: Haut, Bas and the Whole Body in Early Modern Europe," *Early Music* 27, no. 2, *Instruments and Instrumental Music* (May 1999): 211-32. "Lirum bililirum," also known as "un sonar de piva in fachinesco" (A Sound of Bagpipes from a Lout) by the early sixteenth-century Mantuan composer Rossino Mantovano (published by Ottaviano Petrucci in 1505), is a parody of the *amour courtois*, depicting a bagpiper (in lieu of the courtly string player) serenading his lover under her window. The sound of the bagpipe ("lire lire") serves as a refrain that follows a rather vulgar text written in Bergamesque dialect. William Prizer states that the piece is not removed from the courtly world, but is rather an example—as in other satires—of the *amour courtois* "turned upside down." See Prizer, "Games of Venus," 50-52. The rites of communion and harmony celebrated by the civic wind player's growing musical and social integration associated with Corpus Christi ceremonies, the laity's access to the Eucharist and Marian devotion, flourished on territory that would be fought over in conflicts arising from pressure for social and religious reform during the sixteenth century; see McGowan, "The Prince and the Piper," 211-32.

[7] The phenomenon of street cry pieces was especially popular in England *ca.* 1600 in the genre of consort song—Weelkes, Gibbons, Dering, etc. See Kristine Forney (Gibbs), "A Study of the Cries of London as Found in the Works of English Renaissance Composers" (MA Thesis, University of Kentucky, 1974); unfortunately I was not able to consult this work prior to this publication as it is not available electronically.

[8] Susan F. Weiss, "Bolognese Theater ca. 1500: Where's the Music?," Paper read at the Fifty-Eighth Annual Meeting of the American Musicological Society, Pittsburgh, PA, November, 1992.

[9] Quodlibet: also in other languages: *fricassées, ensaladas, misticanzas, centone, incatenature,* a play upon words, a low joke. Academic festivals as far back as the late thirteenth century consisted of the arts faculty getting together in lecture halls to hold their annual disputatio de quolibet, a series of orations on various subjects, humorous as well as serious, led by a quodlibetarius. These sessions often ended with magnificent and elaborate banquets and musical entertainments. One debate centered on whether herbs or harmonies could drive away evil spirits. Although the first definition of quodlibet as a musical form doesn't appear until Praetorius' *Syntagma Musicum* in the early seventeenth century, examples exist from much earlier periods. Theorists such as Tinctoris, Glareanus, Zarlino, and others used quodlibets to demonstrate pedagogical concepts in their treatises. Tinctoris, for example, illustrated his point with "Vrai dieu d'amer" a contrafactum of "La bella Franceschina," one of the more popular centone, in his *De arte contrapuncti*; see Torrefranca, *Il segreto del Quattrocento*, 97, 120. Students in German-speaking lands would collect songs in liederbuchen. One of these, the Glogauer Liederbuch, compiled in around 1460, contains a quodlibet titleed "O rosa bella" that includes twenty-two snatches of German folk song, many of which appear in complete polyphonic versions elsewhere in the manuscript. There are types of quodlibet in which musical and textual materials are patched together. They fall into three

A number of regions in Europe, particularly in France, provided artists, writers, and musicians with environments conducive to producing these humorous and often satirical works. An important *locus amoenus* for artists and writers in the sixteenth century was Lyons, one of the largest and wealthiest cities in France, if not all of Europe. The popular book fairs provided authors such as François Rabelais and Clément Marot (1496-1544), among others, with inspirations for their stories and characters, and with audiences savvy enough to be able to laugh at the witticisms in their satires, poems, and plays. The Valois court of François I (1494-1547) frequented Lyons, where they came to know many writers and musicians, a number of whom were friendly with the King, his sister Marguerite of Navarre (1492-1549), and their court printer Pierre Attaingnant (1494-*ca.* 1552). Another patron and protector of writers, musicians, and artists—in particular Erasmus, Marot and Rabelais—was the dissolute brother of Duke Antoine of Lorraine (1489-1544), Jean (1498-1550), archbishop of Lyons, bishop of Metz and other cities. There is evidence for an Italian-French interchange, as Ippolito d'Este of Ferrara (1509-1572) became archbishop of Lyons and was also a patron of a number of artists and writers.[10] The poet Eustorg de Beaulieu (*ca.* 1495-1552), a friend of both Marot and Marguerite, lived in Lyons for a period of time. In 1536 Marot encouraged Eustorg to contribute to a collection of blasons for Ferrara that was subsequently published in Paris in 1543.[11] Eustorg also visited Bordeaux, where he dined and sang three-

---

categories: catalogue, simultaneous, or successive. The Italians, the French, and, to an even greater extent, the Germans in the sixteenth century turned what had been a serious "debate" in Paris in the Middle Ages, into a humorous recitation of lists of loosely-related items organized by a comical theme, a catalogue of poems, sometimes called "Priamel" or "Durcheinandermischmäsch." One theme concerned the objects left behind by women as they fled from a harem. Of the twenty-five pieces included in Schmeltzl's anthology, fifteen are of the catalogue type. One is Matthaeus Greiter's "Von Eyren," another is "Von Secken" and another is Puxstaller's "Von Nasen," a catalogue of noses that was also set by Lassus in the sixteenth century and again in a late seventeenth-century German collection. The simplicity of musical style suggests that the pieces may have been written-down exemplars of improvised musical entertainment. There are six pieces in Wolfgang Schmeltzl's collection, *Guter, seltzamer, und künstreicher teutscher Gesang* (Nuremberg: J. Petreius,1544) [modern edition, ed. R. Flotziner, *Denkmäler der Tonkunst in Österreich*, Bd. 147-148 (Graz, Austria: Akademische Druck- u. Verlagsanstalt, 1990)] that fall into the category of successive quodlibet, where one voice, usually the tenor, consists of a patchwork of short musical or textual quotations while the other voices provide a homophonic accompaniment. The most complex of the quodlibet types is the simultaneous or polyphonic cento where several different patchworks of successive quotations are combined polyphonically. Schmeltzl includes only three of them, including an anonymous "Ade mit leyd" and Greiter's "Elselein leibstes Elselein," the latter composed entirely of quoted melodies."

[10] Ippolito was also a patron of Marot. Another commemorative musical composition, a four-voice "Bataglia taliana," celebrated the other side, the defeat of France at the Battle of Pavia (1525), which ensured Milan's independence. It was first published in Nuremberg in 1544 in the Schmeltzl quodlibet anthology with the German title "Die Schlacht vor Pavia" and an attribution to the Flemish-born Matthias Herman Verecorensis [Werrecore, who succeeded Gaffurius at Milan Cathedral], who was himself in the line of battle and witnessed the worst miseries, composed this on the way. Connections between Italy and Germany in the late fifteenth and early sixteenth century as in part a result of German humanists sending their sons to study in Italian universities are discussed in my unpublished paper, "Quodlibets and Centone: A Sharing of Folk Repertories," *Austria 996-1996 Music in a Changing Society*, International Conference, Ottawa, Canada, 6 January 1996.

[11] Frank Dobbins, *Music in Renaissance Lyons* (Oxford: Clarendon Press, 1992), 48. Marot was

part chansons with Clément Janequin, who worked not only in Bordeaux, but also in Paris and Angers (the capital of Anjou and home of an important antecedent, the thirteenth-century trouvère Adam de la Halle). Eustorg may well be the link in a chain that included Rabelais and a number of musicians he represented in Book IV of *Gargantua*, among them, Janequin and Henry Fresneau (fl. 1538-54). The latter's music appears in among other manuscripts, Paris, Bibliothèque Nationale, f.fr. 1597, the so-called Lorraine chansonnier, a miscellany containing a number of novelty chansons. Included in the manuscript is the anonymous "Il estoyt ung bon homme qui venoit de lion [Lyons]," with a text made up of solmization syllables that do not always correspond to the pitches of the gamut, as well as the unique "L'autre jour my chevauchoye tout du long d'une montaine," with its onomatopoetic refrain, "La hipela houpela houpedondaine," an imitation of the song of a feathered creature.[12] Fresneau composed a number of the novelty pieces including a fricassée that quoted over one hundred contemporary chansons.[13] Add to this network the Florentine composer Francesco de Layolle (1492- *ca.* 1540), who worked in Lyons for Jacques Moderne (*ca.* 1495- *ca.* 1560), the transplanted Italian publisher of music by Janequin, Fresneau, and others.[14] Eustorg published a rondeau in praise of "a beautiful garden on the Saône in Lyons belonging to maistre François Layola, a most expert musician and organist."[15] Eustorg's network spread to Switzerland where, while studying at the University of Basel in the late 1540s, he had occasion to teach French to the son of the Rector of the University, Bonifacius Amerbach (1495-1562). While teaching young Basilius Amerbach, who undoubtedly had read his Rabelais, Eustorg copied a number of French chansons into Basel University library manuscripts, including pieces by Janequin.[16]

As is well understood, Rabelais had numerous models and inspirations for the characters and materials in his novels *Gargantua and Pantagruel*. Aside from the books he bought at fairs in Lyons, he owned volumes of the plays of Aristophanes. Those fifth-century allegorical comedies (448-380 BCE) used sounds as much

considered to be the inventor of blasons, a type of satiric or metaphoric catalogue verse in which parts of women's bodies are praised or in which one culture raises its own self-esteem by belittling another.

[12] Jonathan Paul Couchman, "The Lorraine Chansonnier: Antoine de Lorraine and the Court of Louis XII," *Musica disciplina* 34 (1980): 85-157. See also Richard Freedman, "Music, Musicians, and the House of Lorraine during the First Half of the Sixteenth-Century (France)" (PhD diss., University of Pennsylvania, 1987).

[13] Jacques Moderne published Fresneau's fricassée in *La Parangon des chansons*, RISM 1538.[17] Attaingnant ascribed some pieces by Fresneau to Janequin, possibly because they wrote in a similar style of novelty pieces featuring rapid notes to effect patter.

[14] This provides one explanation for the Italian influence on Janequin and the French influence on Layolle.

[15] In the poem Eustorg describes Layolle and other musicians gathering to join the birds in song: "You will hear the birds sing here and there,/And divide their Ut- re- mi- fa- sol- la/ In all the places that could be composed by musicians." Dobbins, *Music in Renaissance Lyons*, 48.

[16] Dobbins, *Music in Renaissance Lyons*, 48 and note 80. Basle, Universitätsbibliothek, MSS F. IX. 32-35, 59-62; F.X. 5-9, 17-20, 22-24. See also John Kmetz, "The Piperinus-Amerbach Partbooks: Six Months of Music Lessons in Renaissance Basle," in *Music in the German Renaissance* (Cambridge: Cambridge University Press, 1994): 106-7.

"to evoke an interspecies contrast as to parody Socratic discourse."[17] In *The Birds* (414 BCE), perhaps the most intensely political, if not also sexual of his comedies, the characters Aeschylus, Euripides, and Dionysus toss about wordy phrases, such as "unfettered, uncontrolled of speech, unperiphrastic, bombastiloquent" and "thou chattery-babble-collector," or "this cripple-maker who crows so loudly."[18] Epops, King of the Birds, a hoopoe or lapwing, chants a variety of warbles interspersed with words. Tereus sings to Procne to sexually arouse her. A contrast is set up between their utopic garden of delight on the one hand and the evils of the city of Athens on the other. The cuckoo had been King of Egypt and Phoenicia, and now he and other birds are looked upon as "fattened up" slaves and fools. "Again, if they would but serve you up simply roasted; but they rasp cheese into a mixture of oil, vinegar, and laserwort, to which another sweet and greasy sauce is added, and the whole is poured scalding hot over your back, for all the world as if you were diseased meat." Anyone reading this would become a hardened vegetarian.[19]

In her article "Sexual Discourse in the Parisian Chanson: A Libidinous Aviary," Kate van Orden demonstrates the links between birds and sex, particularly in sixteenth-century French literature, science, and music.[20] The importance of Aristophanes' model cannot be overestimated. Aristophanes' difficult and controversial text, based on the terrifying myth of *Tereus and Procne*, embodies many of the same tropes—bucolic fertile landscapes, gluttony, sex, topsy-turvy worlds—and techniques—allegory and onomatopoeia, particularly birdsong and chatter—as the satires and parodies of Rabelais, the music of Janequin and Fresneau, and the paintings of sixteenth-century artists such as Bosch (d. 1516), and Brueghel (d.

---

[17] *Imagining Language: An Anthology*, edited by Jed Rasula and Steve McCaffery. (Cambridge, MA: MIT Press, 1998): 100ff. Rassula and McCaffery assemble examples of 20th-century avant-garde writing as a starting point to demonstrate a continuum of creative conjecture on language from antiquity to the present. Some examples of imaginary languages, such as found in works by James Joyce, were considered scandalous and unreadable. I would add to their lists works by Samuel Beckett and Stephane Mallarmé, each of whom treat warbles, babble, chatter, and other verbal expression as if they were music. Beckett's playscripts recall musical scores. Lucky's speech at the end of Act One of Godot is a word salad, a parody of scholastic pedantry harkening back to Ovid's frog peasants who have been deprived of human speech, or Dante's sinners and gluttons, such as the farting Malacoda, howling like dogs "Urlar li fa fa pioggia come cani." See also note 6 above.

[18] Aristophanes. *Birds*, in *The Complete Greek Drama*, vol. 2, edited by Eugene O'Neill, Jr. (New York: Random House, 1938) (accessed 16 June 2011), http://www.perseus.tufts.edu/hopper/text?doc= Perseus:text:1999.01.0026. The first sounds a baby makes when learning to speak, a babble that fills both the speaker and listener with delight, elicits an imitative babble in the older child or adult playing with the infant. But babble also connotes the failure of powers—in mental illness and senility. Stephane Mallarmé's lists, acoustic chains with variations, include words about speaking that capture his attention: babble and blab lead off the b's; gabble jibberish, jabber the g's; tittle tattle and chit chat; jangle jangle jaw; and so on. Roger Pearson has called it Mallarmé's "music of the Spheres," but it is also word and game playing. Mallarmé reveals his excitement in the potential of alliteration, assonance, onomatopoeia, and a version of linguistic mimicry, a kind of semantic synaestheisa." See Marina Warner, Commentary: "Who can shave an egg?" in *Times Literary Supplement*, 29 February 2008, 14-17.

[19] Aristophanes, *Birds*.

[20] van Orden, "Sexual Discourse," 2. The author includes a table of birds and their human counterparts.

1569).[21] Bosch was known for his imagination, his depiction of devils, and scenes of seeming nonsense filled with satirical meanings. Brueghel, whose style was reminiscent of Bosch and was referred to in an epigram following his death as "this new Hieronymous Bosch," depicted peasants, birdnesters, and carnivalesque creatures. The vices and devils appearing in his allegories were usually more comical than terrifying; sin was caused not by the machinations of these devilish creatures but by the misuse of human reason. This concept appealed widely to the secular society of the early sixteenth century. Mikhail Bahktin asserted "in this new canon, such parts of the body as the genital organs, the buttocks, belly, nose, and mouth cease to play the leading role."[22]

Rabelais, perhaps in defiance of the new canon and safe in the environs of Lyons where he enjoyed the protection of sympathetic patrons, represented the giants of antiquity in the material acts and eliminatons of the body—eating, drinking, belching, farting, defecating, fornicating, and of course singing. Rabelais' entertaining writing, lewd though it might be, carries with it serious religious, political, and social undertones. Trained as a physician, Rabelais was also well versed in, and perhaps even obsessed by, music, musical instruments (such bagpipes, hautboys, hurdy gurdies, drums, organs, and virginals), and musicians (he names numerous contemporary composers in two groups: those of the Josquin era; and those of his own, among them Claudin (de Sermisy), Janequin, Arcadelt, Willaert, Verdelot, Gombert, Morales, and Passereau (whose very name translates as sparrow, a symbol of a lewd and carnal man).[23] In Book IV, Rabelais describes the musicians singing an erotic catch filled with puns that begins "Big Ted went to bed that night, With his new wedded wife, He hid a mallet out of sight."[24] Further along Rabelais describes those composers named above and "other jovial musicians, in a private garden, under a pleasant arbor, and surrounded by a rampart of flagons, hams, pasties, and various sorts of tufted quail, as they, in the most charming fashion, rendered the following:

> Since a hatchet or a tool is of no use
> Unless it has a handle that will match it
> Let's put a handle in, and not too loose
> You play that I'm the handle, you're the hatchet." [25]

[21] Dora C. Pozzi "The Pastoral Ideal in 'The Birds' of Aristophanes," *The Classical Journal* 81, no. 2 (December1985 - January1 986): 119-29.

[22] Mikhail Bahktin, *Rabelais and His World*, trans., H. Iswolsky (Bloomington: Indiana University Press, 1984), 321. Rabelais's other influences may have known Teofilo Folengo's Italian macaronic poetry with its lists that rattle off delicious dishes and songs or Luigi Pulci's giant in *Morgante* or possibly even Antonio Vignoli's scatological *La Cazzaria* ("The Book of the Prick"), trans., Ian Frederick Moulton (New York: Routledge, 2003).

[23] van Orden, "Sexual Discourse," 2.

[24] *François Rabelais, The Portable Rabelais*, trans. Samuel Putnam (New York: The Viking Press 1977), 541.

[25] Rabelais, 542. Numerous satires on government and the laxity of monastic orders appear in litera-ture and art of the Middle Ages and Renaissance. In the fourteenth century, the *Roman de Fauvel*, a political satire on corruption in government and the church examines the topsy-turvy world in which a donkey named Fauvel, an acrostic for six of the seven deadly sins, rules. A certain artistic freedom of the late fourteenth and fifteenth centuries (evidenced in the novels of Giovanni Boccaccio and a bit later in the poetry of Jean Molinet) came to an abrupt end in the mid-sixteenth century in Europe.

Aspects of carnival, burlesque, popular, and festive forms work together as a means to conquer terror with laughter in Rabelais.[26] The hedonism depicted in Rabelais's writings has its roots in Angevin poetry, particularly in the works of the trouvère Adam de la Halle. Aristophanes' song of the missel-thrush—trai-trai, trai-trai—finds itself only slightly altered in a dialogue between the knight and Marion in Adam's thirteenth-century play. Both text and music are restricted to a narrow compass of five notes and five syllables (Ex. 1).

Ex. 1: Adam de la Halle, "Trairi" from *Le jeu de Robin e Marion*, vv. 96-97, 99-100

Ardis Butterfield suggests that the many displacements in Adam's play—social, sexual, linguistic, musical, generic—lead to questions of how cross-cultural tensions might relate to the crisis then present in Angevin Naples, where the play was first performed.[27]

> If Angevin Naples is indeed the setting, then the "jeu" is playing on a courtly stage, which was itself under threat, attempting to adjust rapidly from a position of power to one of vulnerability in the face of hostility… its linguistic misunderstandings speak to a situation where the cultural power of one language (French) is being questioned aggressively by a less culturally significant vernacular.[28]

One of the earliest attempts to imitate a cuckoo's call in notated music is found in the ostinato, "Sing cuckoo" of the well known thirteenth-century English *rota*, "Sumer is icumen in." Johannes Vaillant's virelai, "Par maintes foys," a May

---

[26] Bahktin, *Rabelais*, 326.

[27] Ardis Butterfield, "Historicizing Performance: The Case of *Jeu de Robin e Marion*," in *Cultural Performances in Medieval France, Essays in Honor of Nancy Freeman Regalado*, ed., Eglal Doss-Quinby, Roberta L. Krueger, and E. J. Burns (Cambridge: D.S. Brewer, 2007): 104-6. Marion's very next refrain summoning her lover Robin also contains an untranslatable or perhaps unprintable text. Adam's use of sung babble is very effective as a means of connecting all three characters. They also emphasize the playful quality of the drama. Game playing, double entendre, and sexual innuendo echo Aristophanes' bird dialogue. Adam's advantage is having composed music and dance to accompany the babble. The opening snatches of song are actually quotations that add another dimension of hidden meaning to the play.

[28] The Bible states that humanity originally shared a common language, but when the Babylonians tried to build a tower to reach the heavens God disrupted the project by making the workers speak in many tongues so they wouldn't understand each other. Genesis 11: 1-9 is depicted in Pieter Brueghel's "Tower of Babel," painted in 1563.

song with its characteristic call to awake, to love and to enjoy the sounds of the birds, is also among the earliest in this genre. It was widely copied in the fourteenth century.[29] "Der Mai" is a slightly later contrafact by the German composer Oswald von Wolkenstein who adds the sounds of other species, perhaps native to German-speaking lands. Once again the musical composition is repetitive and confined to a narrow range. Each species of bird (nightingale, cuckoo, raven, lark, etc.) has its own distinctive musical pattern, notated most frequently as quadruplet sixteenth notes or triplet eighths, and as we shall see, its unique association.(See Ex. 2 on page 142.)

Virginia Newes has described the fourteenth-century programmatic virelais that employ birdcalls and other sounds in a kind of rhetorical play, suggesting that these so-called "realistic" pieces "evoke a complex web of associations that extends far beyond the literal interpretation of onomatopoeic motives."[30] In Francesco Landini's "Ecco la primavera," for example, Landini's birds may be imitating his organ playing, but perhaps too, they are engaged in conversations about the advantages of divine love over the carnal and earthly variety. Another instance of this duality is the birds' performance of mass presided over by the Goddess of Love. Newes also suggests that a hierarchy among the birds places the nightingale, with its ability to sing more complex polyphonic music, above a bird like the cuckoo, which is limited to one rhythm and one pitch.[31] According to Richard Jensen, one of the most realistic treatments is that of the cuckoo, one of the few birds whose name derives from his song.[32] Symbolically the cuckoo means at least two things: on the one hand, it is a harbinger of spring; and on the other, it symbolizes an unfaithful bird who lays eggs in other birds' nests, an allegorical representation of a man who seduces the wife of his neighbor.[33]

Jensen asserts that musical notation offers "a more accurate representation of birdsong" than the verbal descriptions and onomatopoeia. One of the earliest examples of notated bird sounds in a nonmusical context is found in a seventeenth-century source: Athanasius Kircher's *Musurgia Universalis,* published in 1650. Kircher not only notates the song of the nightingale, but also provides cartoons of this and various other avian species. (Se Fig. 1 on p. 143.)

---

[29] Jae Num Lee, "Scatology in Continental Satirical Writings from Aristophanes to Rabelais" and "English Scatological Writings from Skelton to Pope," *Swift and Scatological Satire* (Albuquerque: University of New Mexico Press, 1971): 7-22; 23-53.

[30] Virginia Newes, "The Cuckoo and the Nightingale: Patterns of Mimesis and Imitation in French Songs of the Late Middle Ages," unpublished paper, 162.

[31] Ibid., "The Cuckoo," 169.

[32] Richard Jensen, "Birdsong and the Imitation of Birdsong in the Music of the Middle Ages and Renaissance," *Current Musicology* 40 (1985): 50-65. Think of cuckoo clocks with their familiar falling minor third.

[33] Jensen, "Birdsong," 55, and van Orden, "Sexual Discourse," 2.

Ex. 2: Oswald von Wolkentein, "Der Mai," mm. 37-81

Fig. 1: Athanasius Kircher, *Musurgia Universalis*, Rome, 1650[34]

Our timeless fascination with birds may have to do with a human desire to fly and sing like these creatures. Recalling Milton Babbitt's comment on the immutability of popular song, some birdsong is treated with an amazing degree of consistency. The songs of owls, hens, and roosters have also been imitated in the compositions of French, Italian, and German composers from the fourteenth through sixteenth centuries (to say nothing of examples in the works of the Elizabethan composer Giles Farnaby (1563-1640) as well as Rameau, Vivaldi, Mozart, Haydn, Beethoven, Dvorák, Respighi, Messaien, and John Adams to

[34] Athanasius Kircher, *Musurgia Universalis* (Rome: Corbelletti, 1650), Book I, opposite p. 30. Permission Sheridan Libraries Special Collections, The Johns Hopkins University. His parrot imitates a human saying "hello" in Greek (⬚⬚⬚⬚⬚).

name only a few later composers with a fascination for birds). Many compositions show striking similarities in both their verbal and musical representations. Pierre Passereau's (fl. 1509-47) chanson, "Il est bel e bon," for example, portrays the clucking of chickens, using the realistic "cococococodac" to imitate the hen's song.[35] Some birds, such as nightingales and larks, have more complex songs and therefore reveal less consistency in their imitative patterns.[36] This duality is also manifest in general references to birds as both spiritual (i.e., the myth of the dove and Pope Gregory) and sensual creatures.

Birds were special signifiers linking song and sex in unique sets of references that played both sides of the courtly-carnivalesque bifurcation. These complex associations polarized the body itself along a vertical axis: speech, the spiritual aspects of love, and lyric creation were situated in the upper bodily stratum while sexuality, the physicality of love, and procreation were confined to the lower bodily stratum. In this paradigm, the proscriptions against sex so fundamental to northern French formulations of *l'amour courtois* resulted in a language of unrequited love that handles erotic discourse in one of two ways. First, courtly love lyrics employ a series of conceits that accommodate the treatment of sexuality through double-entendre. The poet's love-death is understood simultaneously as the result of moral languishing and sexual climax. The second mode of erotic discourse allows for explicit depiction of sexual acts in carnivalesque language, engaging popular characters, such as libidinous shepherds and shepherdesses or amorous birds, in its satires of bucolic sexual encounters.[37]

Rabelais' closest musical counterpart may well be his contemporary, the composer Clément Janequin, who also turned towards parody, fantasy, and wordplay to provide an outlet for creative expression outside the mainstream of chanson composition. The text to Janequin's *Le chant des oyseaux* (Example 3) sets up a dualism between the celestial and the earthly. This is seen primarily in the combination of holy imagery—ministers, sermons, and the feast of Corpus Christi—with earthly, sexual imagery. There is, of course, also drinking and merry making, not your typical Sunday worship service.

The text of this work is set around Easter, the time of the Resurrection when paschal laughter would have been allowed, if not even encouraged. This is indicated by the repeated mention of Corpus Christi, the feast that would have occurred on Holy Thursday, three days before Easter Sunday. Not unlike its earlier counterpart in the fourteenth-century virelai, the birds seem to be preaching this paschal humor to the world: "to the Sermon, mistress, mine! To Saint Trotin to see Saint Robin…Quick to the Sermon…Up, madame, to the Mass of Saint

[35] The phenomenon is called "nest parasitism" in the scientific literature. Kirchner, *Musurgia*, 59.
[36] Newes, "The Cuckoo," 170-72; see pp. 14-15 and note 30.
[37] van Orden, "Sexual Discourse," 4-6.

Ex. 3: Janequin, *Le chant des oyseaux*

Reveillez vous, cueurs endormis,	Wake up sleep hearts[38]
Le dieu d'amours vous sonne.	The god of love is calling you!
A ce premier jour de may	On this first day of May
Oyseaulx feront merveilles	Birds will perform wonders
Pour vous mettre hors d'esmay.	Put off your misery
Destoupez vos oreilles	And plug your ears
Et farirariron, ferely ioly.	And faririron….etc
Vous serez tous en ioye mis	You will all be made happy
Car la saison est bonne.	For it is a good season.
Vous orrez, à mon advis,	You will hear, in my opinion
une doulce musique	A sweet music
Que fera le roy mauvis	Which the redwing will make
Le merle aussi	The blackbird too
Lestoruel sera parmy	The starling will be there
D'une voix autentique:	With an authentic voice
Ti ti ti ti ti ti pyti, etc.	Ti ti ti ti etc.
Le petit sonsonnet de Paris	The little starling of Paris
Le petit mignon.	The little darling
4 voices split	
{*Soprano*} Sancte teste Dieu!	By God's holy head
Il est temps d'aller boire.	It's drinking time
Au sermon ma maistresse	To the sermon, my mistress
A saint Trotin	To St. Trotin
Voir saint Robin	To see St. Robin
Monstrer le tetin	To show the tits
Le doulx musiquin	The sweet musician
{*Alto*}Qui, Tost tost, au sermon, din, dan	Up up to the sermon
Sus, ma dame â la messe	Up my lady to Mass
Sancte Caquette	St. Gossip
{*Tenor*} Guilemette, Colinette	Guilemette, Colinette.
Il est temps d'aller boire	It's drinking time
{*Bass*} Qu'est là bas passé, villain	Someone's walking past
Saige courtoys et bien apris	Wise, courteous and well-brought-up
Il est temps que di tu.	It's time, don't you say?
Rire et gaudir c'est mon devis,	Laugh and rejoice, that's my motto
Chacun s'i habandonne.	Let everyone give into it.
Rossignol du boys joly,	Nightingale of the pretty wood
A qui la voix resonne,	In which your voice resounds
Pour vous mettre hors d'ennuy	To arouse yourself from boredom
Vostre gorge iargonne:	You warble in your throat
Frian, frian, frian, etc.	Frian etc.
Fuyez, regretz, pleurs et souci	Be gone regrets, complaints and cares.

---

[38] Translation by the author.

Car la saison l'ordonne.	For the season commands it
Arriere, maistre coucou,	Back off, mister cuckoo
Sortez de no chapitre,	Leave our chapter
Chacun vous est mal tenu	Everyone holds you in contempt
Car vous n'estes qu'un traistre.	For you are nothing but a traitor
Coucou, coucou, coucou, etc.	Cuckoo etc.
Par traison, en chacun nid	By treason in every nest
Pondez sans qu'on vous sonne.	You lay your egg without invitation.
Resveillez vous, cueurs endormis	Wake up, you sleepy hearts
Le dieu d'amours vous sonne.	The god of love is calling you.

Chatter who chatters" (see Ex. 3 above). The holy words of the sermon are here fused with the earthly gossip of Parisian chatter. Now, evangelism of the Word is replaced with evangelism of words—glossalalia to be precise.

There is an interesting parallel here, then, that the all-encompassing Word is replaced with the all-questionable "non-lexical vocables" that are so useful in children's rhymes. These have an all-inclusive nature of their own, though: they can mean almost anything, just as the birds can represent both themselves and the different lover tropes of Parisian culture. Here there is also a link between birds and the celestial. One should not overlook the fact that, despite being earthly creatures, the birds are able to fly into the heavens. They bridge the gap between the humans they represent and the "heavenly bowl" to which the mere creatures of Prometheus are unable to gain access. Thus the chant of the birds is both the holy chant that would have been intoned in the worship service—the "authentic mode" sung by the royal thrush—but also the chant of chatter in the city streets.[39] As one enters the High Mass of Chatter, there is the question of how much the chatter matters, a question that would certainly have been ripe in many a bored parishioner's mind as they eagerly awaited the relief of paschal laughter and the end of Lent, when drinking can begin again in earnest. We will return to the topic of chatter shortly.

Janequin's *Le chant des oyseaux*, or "Resveillez vous," was one of a number of his attempts at writing songs that feature bird sounds. His earlier "Alouette" is from an Italian collection to which he added a fourth voice, while a later revision of his "Resveillez vous" appeared following a publication by Tylman Susato (ca. 1515-ca. 1570) to which Philippe Verdelot (*ca.* 1480-85 – before 1552) added a fifth voice.[40] Nicolas Gombert (c. 1495-c. 1560) composed a three-voice version, very much modeled on the same source as the one used by Janequin. The same bird sounds—"tue tue, oci oci, lire lire, etc."—surface in all of these pieces, many

[39] To cement the aspect of the celestial that overlays/undergirds the earthly, there is a little hint to the passion play at the end: Mister Cuckoo, who is called the owl. Amidst an atmosphere that evokes the divine, is the earthly chatter of the gossiping birds. The owl was the symbol of Lillith, Adam's first wife in Kabbalistic texts. She is most infamous for being cast out of Eden and spawning a multitude of demons, Lilim, a multitude that probably would have chattered not unlike the chatter we hear in the piece. I am indebted to Douglas Buchanan for drawing my attention to this symbolism.

[40] *Le dixiesme livre des chansons* (Antwerp: Susato, 1545); see facsimile ed. (Brussels: Éditions Culture et Civilisation, 1970) and modern ed. in *Chansons polyphoniques, édition complète*, eds., A Tillman Merritt and François Lesure (Paris: Éditions de L'Oiseau-Lyre, 1971).

of them identical to those used in the virelais of the fourteenth century. As noted earlier, "lire lire" may be a reference to sounds made by a bagpipe,[41] and "tirelire" and "turelure" refrains are prevalent in French chansons of the sixteenth century as well.[42] Eventually composers were able to depict the sounds of birds absent of a text. In the variations written by the blind Dutch composer Jacob van Eyck (*ca.* 1589- 90- 1657), there is a sense that two birds are engaged in conversation, each trying to outdo the other, each representing one side of a debate (as in a quodlibet).[43]

Other topics were also explored through musical onomatopoeia, including the hunt, warfare, games such as chess, and gossip. The appeal of these to the same underlying passions is made clear from the graphic account of "a ball in the manner of a tournament" that Rabelais gives in the fourth book of *Gargantua.*[44] Here, the hunt and tournaments surrounding it produced an entire repertoire of sounds, such as the barking of dogs and neighing of horses in Lorenzo da Firenze's "A poste messe," a fourteenth-century caccia.[45] (See Ex. 4 on p. 148.)

Janequin's *La chasse* is, of course, a sixteenth-century French elaboration on this theme; it is in itself a mini-drama, alternating lyrical passages with chaotic and primal sounds that employ rhythmic displacements not unlike hocket to depict dogs barking and horses galloping as they converge on and eventually slaughter the stag.[46] (See Ex. 5 on p. 149.)

[41] See Peter Woetmann Christoffersen, "*Or sus vous dormez trop.* The Singing of the Lark in French Chansons of the Early Sixteenth Century," in *Festskrift Henrik Glahn*, ed. Mette Müller (Copenhagen: Dan Fog Musikforlag 1979): 35-67 and endnote no. 38.

[42] Howard Mayer Brown, *Music in the French Secular Theatre*, 91, 162ff. Words like "tirelire," or "turelure," are refrains of jingles that have, like many other examples in the chanson rustique, double meanings. The expression "C'est toujours la meme turelure" means "it is always the same thing, over and over." "Turelure" can also be "tol-de-rol, fol-de-rol," the *burden* of a song, or a *morisque* ("Moor's dance"). Another commonly used sound is "trique," which can mean a bat or stick used to beat or cudgel. The double meaning of a stick is implied in "mazacrocca," a word used in a number of Italian *villotte*, such as Niccolò Piffaro's "Per memoria di quell giorno," or Henrich Isaac's *incatenatura* or quodlibet, "Donna di dentro/Dammene un pocho de quella mazacrocca," based on the popular tune "Famene un poco de quella mazacrocca," an obvious reference to a lower body part. See Prizer, "Games," 38.

[43] Jacob van Eyck, *Der fluyten lust-hof*, complete edition with full commentary by Marijke Oostenkamp and Bernard Thomas (England: Dolce, 2002), 4 vols.

[44] Alexander Ringer, "Proxy Wars and Horns of Plenty: Music and the Hunt at the Time of Francis I," in *Music and Civilization: Essays in Honor of Paul Henry Lang* (New York: W. W. Norton and Co., 1984), 298. Accompanied by two sizable bands of musicians, thirty-two young persons performed intricate moves and countermoves on a "large piece of velveted white and yellow checkered tapestry."

[45] See *Canons and Canonic Techniques, 14th-16th Centuries: Theory, Practice, and Reception History. Proceedings of the International Conference Leuven, 4–5 October 2005.* Katelijne Schiltz and Bonnie J. Blackburn (eds.) Analysis in Context: Leuven Studies in Musicology 1 (Leuven and Dudley, Massachusetts: Peeters, 2007). I am also grateful to the late Martin Picker for sharing with me typescript of an unpublished paper, "Some Cacce of the Late 15th-century Reconsidered," (1995). He, along with certain other musicologists, disagreed with Alfred Einstein who argued that descriptive music of the fourteenth, fifteenth, and sixteenth centuries respectively were discrete genres and did not represent a continuum. Professor Picker believe that the caccia should be viewed "as a conceptual unity passing through the various stylistic phases of these centuries." In this respect Renaissance musical parody and quotation of works from the distant past parallel literature and the visual arts in their homages to their classical and medieval antecedents.

[46] Ringer, "Proxy Wars," 30.

Ex. 4: Lorenzo da Firenze (d. ca. 1373) "A poste messe," mm. 67-97

Calls to battle spawned a number of well-known compositions, including the late-fourteenth-century virelai "A l'arme" by Magister Grimace (fl. late 14th century). Its battle cries present a *double entendre* on "all' arme" or "à l'arme," meaning both "to arms" and "alarm," and "wacarme," to battle. (Example 6 on p.150.) Grimace also evokes fanfares that symbolize the warfare of love and conjure up the image of mortal wounds inflicted by Cupid's arrows ("To arms, quickly, sweet love, I have been struck by such an arrow.").[47]

Janequin's famous battle pieces are, like his *La chasse,* mini-dramas. In *La bataille,* first published in 1528, he recreates not only the call to arms ("all' arme"), but also military trumpets and drums and battle cries such as "Fan frere le le fan fan fan feyne, farirarira, tarirarirarira reyne, ponpon,ponpon, la la la… poin poin, larileron" from the wounded while human shouts of "courage" function as a cantus firmus.[48] (See Ex. 7 on p. 150.)

Written to commemorate the battle of Marignano on 13-14 September 1515 (and sometimes referred to as *La bataille de Maarignan*), the piece is fillled with onomatopoeic sounds such as those in the example, as well as words and phrases like "frisques mignons," "haquebutiers," "à l'estandart," "bombardes et canons,"

---

[47] Jeremy Yudkin, *Music in Medieval Europe* (Englewood Cliffs: Prentice Hall, 1989), 563-67.

[48] *La bataille,* also called *La Guerre* or "Escoutez tous gentilz," Merritt/Lesure (1967 and 1971) vol.1, no.3 (version à 4) and vol.6, no. 234 (version à 5), written to celebrate the French victory over the Habsburgs at the Battle of Marignano in 1515, imitates battle noises, including trumpet calls, cannon fire, and the cries of the wounded. Other of his battle pieces earned him benefices and titles. On returning home in 1530 via Bordeaux, after Frances I's defeat at the Battle of Pavia some years before, his sons were greeted by Janequin's "Chantons, sonnons, trompettes." Other battle pieces include *La bataille de Mets* ("Or sus branslés"), Merritt/Lesure, vol. 6, no. 235.

Ex. 5: Janequin, *La chasse*, mm. 113-116

Ex. 6: Grimace "A l'arme," opening

Ex. 7: Janequin, *La guerre* ("Escoutez tous gentilz"), mm. 103-108[49]

[49] The combination of verbal and musical onomatopoeia, as well as the play on the words "all'arme"

Ex. 8: Janequin, "Chantons, sonnons trompetes," opening

"faulcons." "toute relore la tintelore," that permeate not only Rabelais' writings, but those of other early sixteenth-century authors. Janequin followed this with his "Chantons, sonnons, trompettes" in 1530, a piece that attempts to imitate the actual sound of trumpets with a triadic motive in all four voies. (See Ex. 8).

Janequin not only revised *La guerre* in 1555 adding a fifth voice, but he continued with his excursions into battle music with his *La bataille de Mets* ("Or sus branslés"), published in the same volume as the revised *La guerre*. The editors added words in italics in an effort to make possible a purely vocal interpretation of passages where the composer specified an instrument, i.e., "tabourin de Suisse" (*"Pon pon pon pon pon"*), "le phifre" (*"farirariralelalela"*), "trompette" (*"trique traque trique traque, crique crac bre de dac"*), and charge (*"bre de dac flic flac crique crac"*). In another place, four trumpets sound polyphonically to accompany a single fife.[50]

Street cries made up of simple melodic formulas served as advertisements for the wares peddled by merchants and small tradesmen as they worked in the marketplace or peddled from door to door. An anonymous motet from a codex in Montpellier (the seat of the medical school attended by Rabelais) is among the earliest surviving polyphony with a secular cantus firmus based on a street cry of a fruit vendor: "frèse nouvele, muere franca" (fresh strawberries, fresh blackberries). Above this, the top two voices describe scenes in thirteenth-century Paris:

(recall the Grimace) made it a favorite on both sides of the Alps. In the third part of the piece, the text includes imitations of instrument sounds, non-lexical vocables, and a mixture of German and Italian characteristic of the Italian carnival songs that desctibed the German mercenary solider. Because of its folk-like simplicity and tonal structure, this piece was also popular in the lute literature. Mathias' composition with its Italian text (perhaps a tribute to his native Milan) is preceded in the anthology by a German-texted version of the Italian madrigal "Dormend un giorno a Baia" by Philippe Verdelot. Schmeltzl chose the five-voice version, published in 1535, rather than the four-voice one published two years later. Verdelot's madrigal was also paarodied by a contemporary Spanish composer F. Guerrero.

[50] Francisco Guerrero composed a parody of Janequin's *Missa La bataille* (published in 1532 and based on his *La guerre*). Guerrero's *Missa de la batalla escoutez* was published in Book I of his Masses in 1582, See Harry Gudmundson, "Paroldy and Symbolism in three Battle Masses of the Sixteenth Century" (Ph.D diss,, University of Michigan, 1976). 132ff. Vincent d'Indy made a modern transcription in 1916.

Ex. 9: Montpellier Codex, "On parole/A Paris/Frèse nouvele," mm. 1-9

By the fourteenth century, works could be found in French, Italian, English, and German sources, a number sharing texts and music containing market cries advertising many victuals.[51] Trades depicted in contemporaneous illustrations included shoe repairs, chimney cleanings, or knives sharpened by itinerant hawkers. Wine or water, new or used clothing, inexpensive popular books, the texts and sometimes the music for the latest hit tunes, and all manner of fruits and vegetables, as well as prepared foods like hot pasties, were among the multitude of things offered for sale in the streets.[52]

The chansons of Janequin and his contemporary Jean de Servin (ca. 1530 – ca. 1595 or later) were made up entirely of street cries; these imitate the voices of market vendors selling many things, such as fresh butter, hot cakes, peas, vinegar, herrings, and tarts, and even describe where to buy them. Servin's *Fricassée des cris de Paris* contains the popular tune, with its obvious double meaning: "Rammoneur de cheminées" ("Sweep your chimneys, young ladies").[53] Janequin's "Voulez ouir les

---

[51] In the caccia "Cacciando per gustar," in the Squarcialupi Codex, there are cries that advertise mustard, oil, and vinegar.

[52] Brown, *Music in the French Secular Theatre*, 84-87.

[53] Ibid., 85.

[54] Bahktin, *Rabelais*, 104-5; 114-15. Bahktin describes the relationship between this speech and Rabelaisian

cris de Paris" (first published in Paris by Pierre Attaingnant in 1530, the same year as "Chantons, sonnons, trompetes"), advertised many products in the text of the chanson. In Janequin's *Les cris, moustarde* (mustard) may serve a similar function as the cry of fresh strawberries in the Montpellier motet, described earlier. Or possibly, the ostinato on *moutarde* is Janequin's wry parody of that earlier work. (See Ex. 10.)

Ex. 10: Janequin, *Les cris de Paris*, mm. 53-60

My final example of a composer mimicing the sounds of nature, in this case, human speech, are musical depictions of chatter or gossip. Caquets (literally "cackles," as in the clacking of hens, but more precisely chitchat and gossip) became quite fashionable in the liteature and iconography at the beginning of theseventhcentury;[54] this British broadside (Fig. 2 on p.154) depicts the several branches of gossiping.

Janequin's chanson "Le caquet" begins like many works in the *amour courtois* tradition, with rhythmic note values (long-short-short), but then gradually shifts away from the homorhythmic style of the Parisian chanson, almost parodistically, to eighths and sixteenths in an effort to depict uncontrolled speech that borders on babble. At times only some of the five voices are heard singing the same text,

[54] Bahktin, *Rabelais*, 104-05, 114-15. Bahktin describes the relationship between this speech and Rabelaisian "swabs," symbols of the material bodily lower stratum, "one of the widespread images of scatological literature, of anecdotes, familiar colloquial genres, curses, billingsgate metaphors and analogies." In some seventeenth-century caquets, "the popular frankness of the marketplace with its grotesque ambivalent lower stratum is replaced by chamber intimacies of private life, heard from behind a curtain."

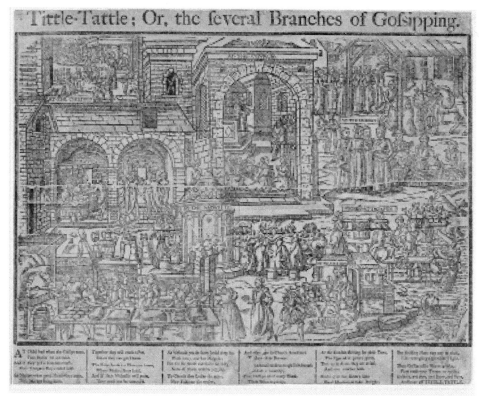

Fig. 2: *Tittle-Tattle: Or, the Several Branches of Gossiping*[55]

but more often there is great overlap, and, on occasion some voices sing entirely different texts (as if several women are speaking simultaneously). (Ex. 11a)

Ex. 11a: *Le caquet des femmes*[56]

Estant oysif quelque journée,	One day I had nothing to do
Que dames feirent assemblée	And ladies were gathering.
Je m'approchay et me mussay	I approached and was hanging around
Pres d'elles vis a vis,	Near them
Pour ouyr leur devis.	To hear what they were talking about.

[55] "Tittle-Tattle: on the several branches of gossiping," British Museum 1973, U.216, in *British Printed Images to 1700*. a late impression (probably eighteenth century) of a late fifteenth or early sixteenth-century English version of a French broadside, now in Magdalene College, Cambridge. http://www.bpi1700.org.uk/research/printOfTheMonth/december2006.html, accessed 26 June 2011.

[56] Translation by the author. Each voice has its own text, resulting in a rather long string of phrases. Merritt/Lesure (1967), vol. 3, no. 108. First published in *Inventions musicales de Jannequin: premier, second, troisième et quatrième livres ou sont contenus le Caquet des femmes a cinq parties, la Guerre, Bataille, Jalouise, Chant des oiseaux. . .* (Lyon, J. Moderne, 1545.)

De fort bien caqueter ouy merveilles

Je vous en diray

Ouvrés vos oreilles.

Perrette viendras-tu vieille vesse

Ma maistresse

Viens ça ma robe est elle nette,

Et de mon chapperon la cornette!

J'ay la chemise perfumée,

Et votre cotte descrottée.

Mais qu'as tu plus faict, courte fesse?

Le chapperon est mis en presse.

La la apres m'amye.

J'ay si tres grand'envie de dire un mot,

Plus je ne le sçaurois celer.

Ma commere, m'amye, gardés vous
       bien de reveler ce que sçavés

Pourquoy non, si fera vrayement qui
       m'en gardera,

On le sçait bien, elle le peult bien dire.

Ha je le diray car ce n'est que pour rire.

Or dites la gente bourgeoise

Ces jours passés une galloise

Prioit son grand jenin dando

Je croy qu'il en valoit bien vingt.

Il ne demandoit que dodo.

Or dittes nous qu'il en advint.

La jeune dame son conte faisant

De trois mots l'un, c'estoit en soupirant,

Son cueur estoit il si doulent

Or fut enquise qu'il avoit au corps

Elle estoit bien faschée

La jeune mariée

Et que respond elle

O povre fumelle

En plaurant respond qu'elle n'estoit records,

D'en avoir eu quelque liqueur,

Ho le meschant! quel crevecueur

(Ho le meschant, meschant, hou hou hou

I heard some amazing talk.

Open your ears:

I'll tell you about it

Perette, are you coming, you old fart?

My Mistress [quote from Ockeghem?]

Come here. Is my dress clean?

And my coif and hood [the sort of things
       nuns wore until Vatican II]

My shirt is perfumed

And your skirt is clean.

But what else did you do, you bum?

My hood is folded in the clothes press

I am very eager to a talk with my friend,

I can't keep it to myself.

That I am incapable of sealing my lips.

My chrony, my friend, watch out

That you don't reveal what you know

Why no, I'll really be careful not to.

We know very well that she is capable of
       talking about it.

Ha, I'll say it, because it's just a joke.

Now say, gentle lady,

Recently a gallic woman

Asked [was begging] her [big errant ninny]

I think he was worth twenty.
All he asked was dodo [to go to bed]

Now tell us what happened.

The young lady told her story
[sighing every third word]
Her heart was so sad [anguished]
Now she was asked what he had on his body

She was quite angry
The young bride,
And what does she reply
Poor woman
Weeping she replies

[it seems to be saying that she "hadn't had
any moisture". . . .inepret that as you wish!]

What a jerk! [Oh, the wretch!]what a cruelty

Ho le mescahnt meschant!)	
A ceste bonne dame!	To that nice lady
D'avoir un corps sans ame.	To have a body without a soul
Baillés, luy du clou de girofle.	He was taken by cloves [Give him some cloves]
Avancés vous le cueur lui faut,	Advance, he needs heart
Je vous jure par Saint Christofle,	I swear to you by St Christopher
Quand du mari vient le deffaut,	When the flaw comes from the husband
C'est un grand mal qui est bien laid.	It's an ugly business
Sus sus, dames, sus a ce plaid	On [onward, onward ladies, to the pleading [altercation, contention, debate]
Une sage femme y estoit,	A midwife was there
Qui tous ces propos escoutoit,	And heard it all
Chascune son mari louoit,	Each one praised her husband
Et sur ce point l'une disoit:	And one of them said
Ma foy, j'ai un mari galland,	My faith, I have a gallant husband
A deux bras il me prend, et me couche,	He takes me in his two arms and beds me
Et me jette, et me met sur un lict branslant	And throws me down, and puts me on a shaking bed
Puis me dict de la la la m'amye,	Then, my friend, he tells me
Je fais les dents à mon vilain claquer	I make his teeth rattle, the villain,
S'il devoit tout vif enrager,	If he were to get mad
Le vilain n'oseroit bouger	He wouldn't dare move
Quand je le tiens, il n'oseroit grongner	When I hold him, he wouldn't dare to growl
Voire, deust-il perdre la vie.	Even if it cost him his life
Avec le mien je ne m'ennuye,	I'm not bored with mine.
A le baiser prens mon deduit toute la nuit.	I enjoy kissing him all night long
Le mien me serre, baise	Mine hugs and kisses me,
Et moy je suis tant aise,	And I feel great,
Quand bien fort il m'accole,	When he embraces me strongly
Voila tres bonne escolle	That's a very good school
Dit la saige sus ce passage,	Says the wise man on this subject
Elle en parle comme tres saige,	She talks about it in a wise way
De bien aymer l'affection,	That she likes the affection
A eu en recordation,	She has in her recollection
Tout le temps de sa vie.	All the time of her life
Je meurs ma sceur m'amye,	I'm dying, my love,
Ha quel mal j'endure,	What pain am I enduring
C'est quelque froidure	What coldness is it
Qu'elle a pris a son gésir.	That makes her lie down
Helas, je m'en vois mourir,	Alas, I will die
Las vueillés moy secourir,	Alas, please come to my rescue
Il luy faudroit pour sa douleur oster	To get rid of his [her?]pain
Estre aupres d'elle et la réconforter,	It is necessary to be near her and comfort her,
Quand aura eu plaisir de son mary,	When she has had pleasure from her husband

Son povre cueur plus n'en sera marry,
Et n'en fera que mine,
Il luy faut pour allegement
Avoir d'amour contentement
C'est douce médecine.
La ferme amour de la femme et de
    l'homme
Assoupit toute douleur et consomme,

O très doux bien tant douce chose

Quand ferme amour au cueur enclose,
Est entre amans, ô quelle joye!
Parlés plus bas qu'on ne vous oye.
J'en parleray c'est mon office,
Car c'est la chose plus propice
Que je désire tant.

Si j'ay parlé, ou caqueté

Du caquet que je veux caqueter,
Faut-il qu'on en tienne caquet
Trop caquetés et si criés haut comme une
    trompette
Et en eust parlé Trupette?
La, la, langue friette.
Badin, badault, badine,
Finette, fine mine,
Baveuse qui bavarde,
Langue qui chascun larde,
Lourde faulse vilaine,
Tant que j'auray haleine
Je chanteray, je parleray,
Et le tout par despit de vous
Ce n'est pas parlé à propos.
Appoinctement fy de couroux
C'est trop presché sur la besongne,
Allés tancer en autre lieu.

Qui voudra grongner si en grongne,

Je jourray, jourray a beau jeu

Vous jourres jourrés le naturel jeu.

Femmes sont faites pour tancer et braire.

Il vous fait taiser,

Et tost rapaiser,

Non pas ainsi crier et braire.

Par le benoist Dieu je suis d'aussi grand
    bien que vous,

Her poor heart no longer will be sad
And will only make a pretense of it
In order to find relief
She must have contentment of love
It's a sweet medicine

The strong love between a man and a
    woman
Makes every pain drowsy and consumes
It is very sweet to be lovers

When strong love is enclosed in the heart
O what joy
Talk quietly so that people don't hear you
I'll talk about it, that's my job
Because it's the most propitious thing
That I desire so much
If I have talked or gossiped
About the gossip that I want to gossip
about, Is it necessary that we gossip

And cry out loud like a trumpet
Would Trupette have talked about it?
La la fried tongue [play of sounds: based
on the word "clown around"]
cunning lady, fine countenance
baveux = bavard [a spineless fish who chats]
tongue that is greased by everyone
dull, false villain
as long as I have breath
I'll sing, I'll talk
And all just to spite you
It is not appropriately spoken
Peace, fy on anger
Too much preaching about work!
Go and tease elsewhere.

Someone who wants to grumble will
    grumble,

I will play, I will play a fine game,

and you will play the natural game

Women are made to tease and bray,

You must be quiet.

And quickly calm down,

Not cry out and bray like that,

By the blessed God, I am as fine as you,

Vous ne me ferés taire	You won't make me be quiet,
Laissés moy, meslés vous de votre affaire.	Leave me alone, mind your own business,
Mais je les feray bien taire	But I'll make them be quiet,
La la la c'est tousjours à refaire.	La, la, la, you have to keep doing it over again,
Or je les vois bien tost faire taire.	Now, I am going to make them be quiet soon
Je vous conjure par Vénus,	I implore you by Venus,
Dont souhaits d'amour sont venus,	From whose wishes came Love [Cupid?],
Que vous taisés si vous povés	To please be quiet if you can,
Mettés nous donc en un lieu reclus,	Put us, therefore, in some hidden place,
Et de langues soyons perdus,	And let our tongues be lost,
Lors conjurés si vous povés,	Then conjure, if you can,
Vous avez beau crier, et braire,	You cry in vain and you bray,
Quelque part que je soye,	Wherever I am,
Joyeuse seray et caquetteray	I'll be joyous and will gossip
Affin que plus on ne vous oye	So that no one will be able to hear you
Chascune de vous devienne oye,	Each of you becomes a goose,
Vole vole Dieu vous convoye	Fly, Fly, God who accompanies you,
Oye, oye, oye,	Hear, Hear, Hear, [Goose, Goose, Goose],
Jart, jart, jart,	Gander, Gander, Gander
Apart, apart, apart,	Apart, Apart, Apart,
Va, va, va,	Go, Go, Go,
Vole, vole, vole,	Fly, Fly, Fly
Perrette, Perrette, Perrette,	Perrette, Perrette, Perrette,
En voyage à Saincte caquette,	On a journey, blessed gossip,
Voyés vous point ceste tempeste,	Don't you see this storm
Dela la mer va son sablat tenir,	that from the sea is going to keep its sand
Mais quelque fois la verrés revenir	But sometimes you see it return.

Here the music matches the language, the chattering babble and gossipy patter with its static melodic material and rapidity of movement (more like cuckoos than nightingales or larks). Janequin seems to be mimicking the chit-chat and gossip of members of the working class, a type of *coq-à-l'âne* (literally "from rooster to *ass*") *an absurdity and inconsequence of speech, a game of words.*[57] Le caquet, like the street-cry compositions, contains elements of a quodlibet or fricassée. Among the quotations in this work are Johannes Ockeghem's "Ma maitresse," and a snippet from Janequin's own *Le chant des oyseaux* ("Sus ma dame a la messe Sainct Caquette qui caquette"

[57] Rabelais, 422-23.

referencing the blessed gossip).   The only sounds approaching onomatopoeia come towards the end of the piece, with musical and textual iterations on a series of rhyming words *vole, oye, jart, apart, va, vole, perrette* (Ex. 11b). Apart from the title's pun (hens), there are other double entendres such as *oye/oie* (goose and to hear), and some plays on words such as *trumpet/trupette* (trumpeting, both musical and verbal), and *badin, badault badine*, (clowning around). In other places, Janequin privileges our understanding of the types of conversations that took place in mid-sixteenth-century France, such as discussion of having a body without a soul. Janequin's text stresses the importance of the body: notably tongues and vaginal secretions. He also incorporates crude slang expressions including old fart (*vielle vesse*), you bum, (*courte fesse*), and ninny (*dando*). Occasional references to religion poke through, such as the description of a nun's coif or praying to St. Christopher.

Ex. 11b: Janequin, *Le caquet*, mm. 218-22

Women's gossip, their cackling, and boisterous laughter posed a tangible threat to a patriarchal society. Christina Fuhrmann begins her essay on Alessandro Striggio's *Il cicalamento delle donne al burato*, noting "During the Renaissance, an ideal woman was a silent woman."[58] In Anton Woensam's broadsheet, "The Allegory

[58] Christina Fuhrmann, "Gossip, Erotica, and the Male Spy in Alessandro Striggio's *Il Cicalamento delle donne al bucato* (1567). Chapter 6 in *Gender, Sexuality, and Early Music*, ed. Todd Borgerding (New York: Routledge, 2002), 167.

of a Wise Woman" (Vienna, 1525), the figure is depicted with signs and images on parts of her body. On her mouth is a padlock (with a large key next to her face) and the following warning: "Every hour, day and night, I wear a golden lock upon my lips so that they say no harmful words or wound another's honor."[59] Janequin's *Le caquet* is arguably the first French musical representation of the gossips, but the *canti carnascialeschi* associated with Florence include at least one earlier composition on the subject. Lorenzo de' Medici's "Canzone delle donne e delle cicale" depicts women gossips trying to win younger women over to their evil ways, but to date no one has located a musical setting.[60]

It was not until an Italian madrigal comedy of 1567 that the sounds of cackling made their way into the music itself. Christina Fuhrman credits Janequin as the model for Striggio's earlier madrigal "La caccia," based on Janequin's *La chasse*. In another of his works, the madrigal comedy *Il Cicalamento delle donne al bucato*, Striggio employs a Petrarchan conceit at the beginning with a fourteen-line introduction before breaking into the uncontrolled speech of the women at the well. The structure resembles Janequin's opening allusions to the courtly Parisian chanson. Like Janequin, a male narrator plays both the role of storyteller and voyeur. Also like Janequin, the women are working-class, lacking in manners and morals and in the ability to curb their tongues. They speak using explicit language sprinkled with puns and babble.[61] The comedies were probably meant as entertainment for aristocratic male audiences "offering them erotic titillation beneath a thin veil of double meaning…as well as an opportunity 'to imitate and mock the stereotypically garrulous women of the lower classes.[62] Yet, in some ways, each celebrated the very loquacious liberty they sought to condemn.[63] Clearly, the town gossip, like the cuckoo (or cuckolded husband), was one of the most fascinating, if somewhat reviled characters of the Renaissance (and continues to be today). Imitations of uncontrolled babble, as well as the various sounds of the birds and animals, the hawkers in the market, the hunters in the woods, the wounded on the battlefield, coupled with the word games and tune salads of the fricassées, paint musical pictures of the world that artists, writers, and musicians imitated again and again. Our knowledge of the popular traditions of the early modern are aided by a study of its surviving art, literature, and music that contain street cries, dance melodies, lullabies, and other remnants of the natural sounds heard by courtly folks walking in the streets and listening to the songs of their caretakers.

[59]Anton Woensam's "Allegory of a Wise Woman" (Vienna, 1525), online. sfsu.edu/~tgetz/Hist%20 115%20Readings%201.doc (accessed 3 July 2011).
[60]Charles S. Singleton, ed., *Canti carnascialeschi del Rinascimento* (Bari: Laterza, 1936), 117.
[61] *Il Cicalamento delle donne al bucato: Commedia armonica in cinque parti a 4 e 7 voci*, first published by Girolamo Scotto in 1567 and reprinted by the same firm in 1569 and 1584. A modern edition was published by Bonaventura Somma, *Capolavori polifonici del secolo XVI*, vol. 4 (Rome: Edizioni de Santis, 1947).
[62]Fuhrmann, "Gossip," 182.
[63]Ibid.

On State in Church and Theater

An Honest and Virtuous Recreation: Two Theatrical Academies in Seventeenth-Century Venice

Beth Glixon and Jonathan Glixon

Academies, both formal and informal, played a vital role in the creation and spread of opera in seventeenth-century Italy. The role of the gathering of intellectuals and artists around the Florentine nobleman Jacopo Corsi in the production of the first two operas, Peri's *La Dafne* and *L'Euridice*, is well known, as is that of the Mantuan Accademia degli Invaghiti as the sponsor of Monteverdi's *Orfeo*. After the development of commercial opera in the 1630s, academies were responsible for productions in many Italian cities, most famously in Florence, where the Accademia degli Immobili, under Grand Ducal protection, and the Accademia degli Infuocati both operated theaters and were the major producers of opera in the city in the 1640s and 1650s.[1] Also notable were the activities of the Accademia dei Riaccesi in Bologna, which created an opera theater in the Palazzo Formagliari in 1640. Academies were the principal sponsors of opera in many less central cities as well, such as Lucca, Brescia, Faenza, and Siena.[2] It has often been argued that even in Venice, where entrepreneurial commercial opera dominated, one academy played a central role in defining the genre, the Accademia degli Incogniti.[3] While

---

[1] For a detailed description of the activities of the Immobili, see John W. Hill, "Le relazioni di Antonio Cesti con la corte e i teatri di Firenze," *Rivista italiana di musicologia* 11 (1976): 27-47.

[2] Colleen Reardon has recently discussed the production of the Accademia degli Intronati's first opera in Siena. See her "The 1669 Sienese Production of Cesti's *L'Argia*," in *Music Observed: Studies in Memory of William C. Holmes*, eds. Colleen Reardon and Susan Parisi (Warren, MI: Harmonie Park Press, 2004), 417-28.

[3] See Ellen Rosand, *Opera in Seventeenth-Century Venice: The Creation of a Genre* (Berkeley: University of California Press, 1991), Chapter 2. The Incogniti was the most influential academy of its time in Venice; its members were among the most important authors of mid-seventeenth-century Italy (most of them not Venetian), and several of them wrote opera librettos, most famously Giovanni Francesco Busenello, who penned *L'incoronazione di Poppea* for the 1642/43 season at Venice's Teatro SS. Giovanni e Paolo. They were most active in the 1630s and 1640s, and the Venetian presses published numerous books by a variety of members, encompassing both fiction and polemical prose, and addressing some of the hottest topics of the day (feminism, women's rights, etc.). The bibliography concerning the Incogniti is vast. For a comprehensive overview and discussion, see Wendy Heller, *Emblems of Eloquence: Opera and Women's Voices in Seventeenth-Century Venice* (Berkeley: University of California Press, 2003). On the academies of Venice, see Michele Battagia, *Delle accademie veneziane: dissertazione storica* (Venice: Orlandelli, 1826).

there is no doubt that members of that academy, notably Giovanni Francesco Busenello, Giulio Strozzi, and Maiolino Bisaccioni, were major figures during the first decade of Venetian opera, more recent research lends little support to the idea that the academy itself was involved, leaving La Serenissima as one of the few operatic centers in the peninsula in which academies were not a driving force in the presentation of the genre.[4]

Although Venetian opera remained a resolutely commercial enterprise, with theaters run by impresarios with the backing of investors, for a brief period in the 1650s and 1660s two academies made an effort to enter the scene and provide an alternative source of entertainment to that available in the large public theaters.[5] These two, the Accademia degli Imperturbabili and the Accademia degli Angustiati, were closely linked both in their purpose and, in one instance, their personnel, and they shared similar fates. Although the extant documentation for these two groups is quite different, their similarities allow them to be discussed together. For the earlier of the two, the Imperturbabili, active in Venice from 1656 to 1659, we have, in addition to librettos for two of their three productions (the anonymous *Tolomeo* and Domenico Gisberti's *La pazzia in trono*[6]), a series of legal documents, including contracts and lawsuits. The Angustiati, founded in Murano in 1660 and operating until 1664, left behind no such extended legal trail. On the other hand we are fortunate to have a manuscript in the hand of one of the academy's founders and its prime mover, the same Domenico Gisberti, which includes a copy of the group's bylaws.[7] Extant also is one libretto for the Angustiati, Gisberti's *La barbarie del caso*.[8]

---

[4] See Beth L. Glixon and Jonathan E. Glixon, *Inventing the Business of Opera: The Impressario and His World in Seventeenth-Century Venice* (New York: Oxford University Press, 2006).

[5] According to Cristoforo Ivanovich, who published a chronicle of Venetian theatrical life in the 1680s, the seventh theater to appear in Venice was the Saloni, which was opened "through the efforts of some academicians [to present] dramas in recitative" (...per opera d'alcuni Accademici per Drami recitative). Cristoforo Ivanovich, *Memorie teatrali di Venezia*, ed. Norbert Dubowy (Venice, 1688; reprint. Lucca: Libreria musicale italiana, 1993), 400. The dramas produced there during the 1650s were by Giacomo Castoreo, who also wrote dramas for S. Aponal. Eleanor Selfridge-Field writes that "the Accademia ai Saloni built its own theater," and she states that the plays were performed by the academicians, in *A New Chronology of Venetian Opera and Related Genres, 1660-1760* (Stanford, CA: Stanford University Press, 2007), 632. Unlike the texts of the plays performed by the Imperturbabili and the Angustiati, those done at the Saloni do not feature the name of any academy on the title page itself, nor does Castoreo refer to one in the opening pages of his librettos. Selfridge-Field's *A New Chronology* includes a separate supplement for theatrical works produced for academies and societies, beginning in 1658, but does not list the first libretto discussed in our article, *Tolomeo*. Ibid., 632.

[6] *Il Tolomeo, Drama de gl'Academici Imperturbabili, Rappresentato nel Theatro di S. Apollinare Di Venetia, L'Anno 1658* (Venice: Valvasense, 1658); and *La Pazzia in Trono, overo Caligola Delirante, Opera di Stile Recitativo Comparsa Nel famoso Teatro Di S. Apollinare in Venetia. L'Anno 1660. Per virtuosa ricreatione Delli Signori Academici Imperturbabili*, in Domenico Gisberti, *Talia* (Munich: Jecklino, 1675).

[7] *Costituzioni delle Accademie degli Angustiati e degli occulti di Murano* (Venice, Biblioteca nazionale marciana, Ital. X, 121 (7197)).

[8] *La Barbarie del Caso, Tragedia di Domenico Gisberti... Dall'Academia Delli Sigg. Angustiati Rappresentata in Murano nel MDCLXIV* (Venice: Valvasense, 1664).

The founders of both the Imperturbabili and the Angustiati were inspired by the same idea, that Carnival, the famous annual period of merrymaking and rule breaking, posed real perils for young men. The unsigned foreword of the Imperturbabili's 1658 *Tolomeo* states the academy's *raison d'être*: "to pass, in honest and virtuous recreation, the most dangerous days of the year."[9] Gisberti explains the origins of the Angustiati similarly:

> Every city or country, no matter how small, if inhabited by citizens of some genius and civilization, has always chosen and maintained the honorable custom of employing its more spirited youth, during the Carnival period, in the profitable and wise recreation of Academies, particularly theatrical ones. Therefore ... [the founders] thought it a good idea ... to erect in our city of Murano an honorable academy, and thus provide the opportunity for youths to occupy themselves in virtuous and modest recreation, and at the same time avoid many pernicious distractions to which most young people are easily drawn.[10]

Academies such as these signaled their philosophies in several ways beyond their activities, most visibly in their names: the Imperturbabili (the imperturbables) clearly intended to persevere in their goals no matter the difficulties (which, as we will see, were many), and the Angustiati (the restricted or constrained ones) probably indicated both their status as inhabitants of the small island of Murano and their desire to keep to the narrow path of good behavior. It was also the convention for an academy to choose a motto and an emblem. Battagia (repeated by Maylender) reports, without providing a source, that the emblem of the Imperturbabili was a flaming mountain with hunting dogs, with the motto, apparently misread, as *Aelent ne doleant*.[11] This should be, possibly, *Valent ne dolent*, or "they are strong so that they do not suffer," which fits well with their name. Gisberti's manuscript records the emblem of the Angustiati: a thermometer (presumably to measure increasing difficulties) with the motto *Rigore crescit*, or, roughly, "things get harder."[12]

The membership of both academies, as far as can be ascertained, consisted primarily of young men, thus calling to mind the famous *compagnie delle calze* of the fifteenth and sixteenth centuries, who sponsored and staged carnival

---

[9] "...di passare in honesta, e virtuosa ricreatione i giorni più perigliosi dell'anno..." *Tolomeo*, 5.

[10] "Qual si sia Cittade ò Terra, anche minima, da Cittadini di qualche ingegno, e civiltade habitata, sempre mai s'ha trascelto, e mantenuto l'honorevole costume di trattenere ne' tempi di Carnovale la Gioventude più spiritosa nella profittevole, e savia ricreatione dell'Academie, e particolarmente recitative: quindi è, che ... hanno stimato bene ... di erigere nella Patria nostra di MURANO un'honorata Academia, e così porgere occasione a Gioveni d'impiegarsi in virtuose, e modeste ricreationi, et evitare parimenti molti perniciosi trattenimenti ne quali per lo più la Gioventude facilmente inclina." *Costituzioni*, f. 2.

[11] Battagia, *Delle accademie veneziane*, 49-50; Maylender, *Storia delle accademie d'Italia* (Bologna: Cappelli, 1926-1930), 2: 177-78 . No motto or emblem appears in either of the two publications of the Imperturbabili.

[12] *Costituzioni, op. cit.*; see also Maylender, *Storia delle accademie d'Italia*, 1: 185.

entertainments.[13] Unlike the members of the *compagnie delle calze*, however, who were all wealthy noblemen, those of the Imperturbabili and Angustiati were of mixed background, with both artisans and businessmen, Venetians and non-Venetians, and in one case, just a hint of nobility.

Among the first acts of any academy would have been the drafting of bylaws, and those recorded by Gisberti for the Angustiati are particularly detailed. The members, both founders and other academicians, were to elect, "following the practice of other academies," officers, including *principe*, *vice principe*, councillors (*consiglieri*), censors (*censori*), a treasurer (*cancelliere*), and a custodian (*bidello*). Similarly, the officers of the Imperturbabili included the *capo* (also referred to as *principe*), *vice capo*, treasurer, and vice treasurer. One hint that Gisberti might have founded the Angustiati specifically on the model of the Imperturbabili is his statement that the founders drafted the bylaws "following the model of our own predecessors."[14]

Although the main function of this organization would be to produce theatrical works, the constitution also affirmed the underlying goal of regulating behavior:

> If one of our academicians or performers should dare to speak curses or obscene words, insult a companion, or do any other indecent act whatsoever, he should be immediately removed from our Academy and be marked as infamous...[15]

The membership, by a two-thirds majority, would select a work to be performed, and the founders (who remained distinct from the others) elected members to serve as protector, collector (who received the mandated contributions of the members), cashier, paymaster, supervisors, and other necessary offices.[16] The roles in the drama were assigned to the members by a committee composed of the *principe*, the poet, and one censor, and could be taken away for unexcused absences.

It seems that the actors were responsible for their own costumes, but the rest of the production was paid for by the required contributions of the members. Performers who failed to show up for a performance would be fined ten ducats, but if the absence were intentional, they could be brought to court to enforce a fine of one hundred ducats. Since the performers were amateurs, the constitution recognized that it would probably be necessary to make adjustments after each performance, perhaps even necessitating a delay before the changes could be implemented:

---

[13] Two of the most spectacular entertainments, sponsored by the Sempiterni in 1542 and the Accesi in 1567, are discussed in Franco Mancini, Maria Teresa Muraro, and Elena Povoledo, *I teatri di Venezia e il suo territorio* (Venice: Corbo e Fiore, 1996), 1: 41-66 and 67-85.

[14] "...seguendo lo stile degli stessi nostri antepassati." *Costituzioni*, f. 2.

[15] "Che si si sia de' nostri Accademici, o Recitanti, il quale havrà ardimento di proferire bestemmie, parole oscene, ingiuriare il Compagno o fare qualsivoglia altro atto indecente sii immediatamente cancellato dalla nostra Accademia con titolo d'infame..." *Costituzioni*, ff. 3v-4.

[16] "Prottettore, scuotitore, cassiere, spenditore, soprastanti, od altro bisognoso uffitio." *Costituzioni*, ff. 4v-5.

that after the performance, that same evening, or no later than the next day, the Academy should meet to discuss there, and fix, any problems that might have occurred, and then establish, based on the proposal of the *principe*, counsellors, and censors, when the next performance should take place...[17]

The members were not to discuss their parts, the scenery, or the costumes with anyone outside of the academy, nor let anyone see the costumes in the theater before the performance, with a penalty of two ducats for violations.

Also regulated was the number of tickets available to the members of the academy. According to the size of the performance hall, the leading officers, the poet, and protector would receive twelve tickets each, other officers and functionaries would receive eight, the performers six, and others involved in the production two each, with the remainder distributed based on the contributions each made to the production. With the members deeply involved in the production, as managers, backstage, and as performers, they would have had little time for less virtuous recreation. Their required monetary contributions undoubtedly also made it less likely that they would stray from the straight and narrow.

Membership

As mentioned above, these two academies shared several characteristics, but they also differed in some ways, perhaps most significantly in their membership. Many members of both were quite young, and probably comfortably situated, if not wealthy. Those of the Angustiati, however, were all *muranesi*, while the Imperturbabili included both Venetians and foreigners. During the time between 1657 and 1658, when the Imperturbabili were involved in several legal disputes that generated a considerable amount of paperwork, the leadership of the group changed regularly. Gasparo "alli tre savi," a goldsmith, was the *principe* in early 1657, or so the complainant asserted on 14 March 1657. Two months later, Felippo Cesari, characterized as "newly elected," was in charge, and only one month later the Bolognese Lauro Tamburini had evidently replaced Cesari.[18] Unfortunately we have no sense of the size of the group. Other known members over the three-year activity of the academy included Lorenzo Mazzocco, the goldsmith Giacomo de Franceschi, Giacomo Renier (most likely the son of the noted artist, Nicolò Renier), Giacomo Rizzardi, Michel dall'Acqua, and Dolfin Quartano, a student at the

---

[17] "Che doppo recitato la sera stessa, ò almeno il giorno dietro sij ridotto Academia, per discorrere in essa, e rimediare a qualche inconveniente, che potesse essere accaduto, poscia stabilire quando si doverà di nuovo recitare il che sarà proposto dal Principe, Consiglieri, Censori..." *Costituzioni*, f. 6.

[18] Archivio di Stato di Venezia (henceforth ASV), Giudici di petizion, Dimande. b. 39, 14 March 1657; ASV, Archivio notarile, b.8021, f. 39v, 15 May 1657; ASV, Archivio notarile, b. 12047, f. 64v, 16 May 1657. Tamburini may have been the member with the most exposure to the Venetian theatrical system, as he was the confidant of Caterina Zane, one of the renters of the comedy theater S. Luca during the 1650s; Tamburini frequently represented Zane when problems occurred regarding the theater; perhaps that experience led to his increased participation in the Imperturbabili.

University of Padua. Paolo Vedoa, who was active during the group's last theatrical production, would act for many decades as the consul of France in Venice. As we shall see, one of the most generous of the group was Emanuel Calafati, whose family had attained the status of nobility in Crete.

We learn of the membership of the Angustiati only from Gisberti's manuscript. He lists the founders, besides himself, as Pietro Beltrame, Paulo Baris, Ettore Bigagia, Alvise Calice, Tomaso Untepergher, Nicolò Pallada, Andrea Darduin, Giacomo Bagatin, and Bernardo dalla Balia, all from Murano.[19] The first officers elected, on 17 October 1660, were Giovanni Antonio Rota, *principe*, Giacomo Trivisan, *vice principe*, Paulo Baris, Vincenzo Gatteschi, and Ettore Bigagia, *consiglieri*, and Reverendo Vincenzo Giuliani, *censori*, and Francesco Schiaonetto, *bidello*. Gisberti provides, as well, the names of sixteen honorary members, among them the well-known Muranese lawyer and librettist Aurelio Aureli.[20]

Cost of Membership

Surviving documentation suggests that the members of the Imperturbabili would have contributed thirty ducats towards the season's entertainment. The clearest reference is the statement of debt signed by Paulo Vedoa after the production of *La pazzia in trono*.[21] In March 1657, following the group's first presentation, *Argenide*, however, Felippo claimed to be the creditor of the group for his share of forty ducats, plus thirty more laid out for the purchase of wood.[22] Perhaps as an officer he owed a higher fee; it is likely that he, like Calafati in 1659, had laid out more than his assessment, and was therefore due some reimbursement. The only other documentation regarding membership fees concerns the fifty-five-and-a-half lire (about fifteen ducats) that the student at Padua, Dolfin Quartano, still owed; this lower amount might represent the unpaid half of a regular fee, or perhaps a reduced assessment because Quartano was living outside of the city.[23] Thirty ducats was a rather sizable sum for those times: one Lorenzo Mazzocco, quite possibly the member mentioned earlier, paid thirty-one ducats for his yearly house

[19] *Costituzioni*. Beltrame succeeded Gisberti as the chaplain of the nunnery of Santa Chiara (see below), and was responsible for the memorial stone for Gisberti placed in the church of Santo Stefano in Murano. See Giannantonio Moschini, *La chiesa e il seminario di Santa Maria della Salute in Venezia* (Venice: Tipi di Giuseppe Antonelli, 1842), 90.

[20] Among the honorary members were also the composer Pietro Molinari and Gisberti's relative, Don Domenico Gisberti, son of Giovanni (see below) (*Costituzioni*, f. 7v). The manuscript also gives the names of four other regular members, accepted in later meetings: Giovanni Mazzolà, Domenico Darduino, Andrea Marinoni, and Giovanni Battista Bembo (*Costituzioni*, ff. 8v-9). The size of the membership is unknown, but at one meeting of the Angustiati in November 1660, sixteen members were present (*Costituzioni*, f. 9).

[21] ASV, Giudici del Mobile, Sentenze a legge, b. 432, 27 January 1661; registration of declaration of debt dated 28 January 1658, *more veneto* [with the new year beginning on March 1 rather than on January 1].

[22] ASV, Giudici di Petizion, Dimande, b. 39, f. 15v, 17 March 1657. It is unclear why Cesari should have been reimbursed for his portion, or dues.

[23] ASV, Archivio notarile, b. 12047, f. 247v, 14 December 1657.

rent near Sant'Aponal.[24] Indeed, the stiff fees necessary to support the activities of the academy may well have kept the young members away from the gaming tables, a popular carnival pastime.

The Imperturbabili, 1656-1659

The existence of the Imperturbabili has been recognized since the seventeenth century because its name appeared on the two librettos mentioned above; until the discovery of additional papers regarding the theatrical activities of the impresario Marco Faustini, however, nothing more was known about the academy, and other recent research has unearthed the performance of an earlier work.[25]

The first documented activity of the Imperturbabili came during the 1656/57 season, with the mounting of *Argenide*. At that time five theaters were active in Venice: S. Moisè (comedy) and S. Samuele (comedy) in the district of S. Marco; S. Cassiano (comedy) and S. Aponal (opera) in the district of S. Polo; SS. Giovanni e Paolo (opera) in the district of Castello; and the Saloni in Dorsoduro.[26] *Argenide*, however, was presented in an area far removed from these others, in the meeting hall of the confraternity of the Misericordia (the Scuola and Abbazia della Misericordia lie in the outer region of Cannaregio, not far from the church of Madonna dell'Orto).[27] Although we know nothing of the author of this work, nor of its dramatic sensibilities, it was a staged drama with "real" scenery, and is thus remarkable for a noncommercial work at that time and in such a location.[28] It is the scenographer himself who left traces of the Imperturbabili's earliest activities, for the Bolognese Lorenzo Gennari (1595-1665/72) undertook a series of legal actions against various members of the academy. Gennari, born in Cento (between Ferrara and Bologna, but under the jurisdiction of Ferrara), came from an extended family of artists, and was the disciple and a relative of Guercino (Giovanni Francesco Barbieri), under whom he trained and worked during the early stages of his professional life. It should be noted that the latter part of Gennari's artistic career is almost entirely unknown; moreover, his presence in Venice during the 1650s has

---

[24] ASV, Dieci savi sopra le decime, Catastico di Venezia. S. Polo, b. 423. S. Aponal, no. 70, Calle da Ca Cucina.

[25] Some of the Faustini materials relating to the Imperturbabili were discussed in Glixon and Glixon, "Oil and Opera Don't Mix: The Biography of S. Aponal, a Seventeenth-Century Venetian Opera Theater," in *Music in the Theater, Church, and Villa: Essays in Honor of Robert Lamar Weaver and Norma Wright Weaver*, ed. Susan Parisi (Warren, MI: Harmonie Park Press, 2000), 131-44. See also Mancini, Muraro, and Povoledo, *I teatri di Venezia e il suo territorio*, 1: 363, 372-73.

[26] No libretto survives for a work performed at the Saloni during the 1656/57 season, but a document concerning the scene painter Simon Guglielmi shows that he had been hired to produce the scenery for the upcoming season there. ASV, Archivio notarile, b. 8020, f. 387, 26 September 1656.

[27] ASV, Archivio notarile, b. 8021, f. 39v, 15 May 1657.

[28] Evidence of "private" dramatic entertainments of this time is usually limited to published librettos. As most of those entertainments for which librettos were published had been presented in the homes of the nobility, we have little indication of carnival activities in the homes of the cittadino and merchant classes.

thus far escaped notice.[29] Gennari signed a contract with the Imperturbabili on 17 November 1656, before the carnival season, and the following March claimed to be owed fifty-two ducats for the scenery. Although Gennari turned to one of the Venetian courts, the Petizion, in order to obtain his fees, the case was eventually settled outside of the court system, with the assistance of independent arbitrators. As always, each party chose an arbitrator. The Imperturbabili picked the artist Pietro Vecchia (the brother-in-law of member Giacomo Renier), while Gennari chose the painter Francesco Ruschi; both of these artists were among the most important then active in Venice. The arbitration was not completed until June 1658, by which time Gennari had approached the courts once again in search of funds he had expended for the scenery.[30]

While the dispute between the academy and Gennari continued, the members made plans for the next season. The Imperturbabili were evidently quite dedicated to their goal of occupying themselves with a theatrical production during carnival, and when the Teatro S. Aponal became available shortly after the performance of *Argenide*, they successfully obtained the theater for their own use.[31] Details of the rental agreement between the Imperturbabili, and the lawyer, impresario Marco Faustini (who had continued the lease initiated by his brother, the librettist Giovanni Faustini, in 1650) point up both the advantages and disadvantages of mounting a production in a "real" theater. In the Teatro S. Aponal, the academicians found a much more central location, and one that by

---

[29] The most thorough account of Gennari's life and career appears in Prisco Bagni, *Guercino a Cento: Le decorazione di Casa Pannini* (Bologna: Nuova Alfa Editoriale, 1984), 223-38. Gennari was in Venice at least by 1653 (ASV, Archivio notarile, b. 12665, f. 105v, 15 November 1653). In 1651, in Rimini, where he lived before coming to Venice, he and the artist Guido Cagnacci collaborated on a work dedicated to S. Antonio in the eponymous church; Cagnacci executed the painting itself, while Gennari did the "decorazione prospettica a chiaro-scuro" into which the painting was inserted (thus, he was known as a practitioner of "prospective art," on which seventeenth-century scenery was based). Gennari knew Cagnacci as far back as 1622, when the two of them shared a residence in Rome with Guercino (Bagni, *Guercino a Cento*, 231). (Gennari had been working with Guercino for some time, while Cagnacci probably joined them as an assistant). Cagnacci had moved to Venice by 1648, so that Gennari may have come to that city based on Cagnacci's recommendation. The last documents that mention Gennari concern business transactions about a house in Rimini between him and his wife, on the one hand, and two sisters of Cagnacci, on the other. On Cagnacci and his participation in Venice, see Beth Glixon, "'Fortuna instabile': Francesco Lucio and Opera Production in Seventeenth-Century Venice," forthcoming. Genari was still (or again) living in Venice in 1663. The Venetian careers of Cagnacci and Gennari will be discussed in a future article.

[30] Gennari specified additional expenses he had borne at the instruction of the academy members, for which he demanded twenty-five ducats, plus ten more for expenses such as the transport of canvas to the theater, wood, and charcoal for the fire necessary for the manufacture of the scenes. ASV, Giudici di petizion, Dimande, b. 40, no. 72, 16 November 1657. In a separate dispute, one of the officers, Felippo Cesari, acting as guarantor, claimed to have laid out thirty ducats for wood. ASV, Giudici di petizion, Dimande, b. 39, f. 15v, 17 March 1657.

[31] Marco Faustini had been running the Teatro S. Aponal with the Venetian noblemen Alvise Duodo and Marc'Antonio Correr. Following the carnival season of 1656/57, they moved their company to the Teatro S. Cassiano. See Glixon and Glixon, *Inventing the Business of Opera*, 48-58.

now had acquired the sheen of presenting "respectable" entertainment for carnival. Undoubtedly, however, this new venue far exceeded the cost of the previous one, for Faustini took great advantage of the situation, charging the academicians 120 ducats, twice the reasonable fee that he and his brother had paid to the owners. The contract, dated 20 June 1657, had numerous specifications, and many of them were to the advantage of Faustini rather than to the Imperturbabili. The theater rental comprised the stage itself, two rooms beneath it, the "orchestra" (*parterre*) with its seats, and the use of all the opera boxes except Faustini's own. The rent was to be paid in two installments, the first due at the time of the agreement, and the second on 1 December 1657, i.e., before the beginning of the carnival season. Among Faustini's other stipulations were the following:

> Faustini himself would select the person who would sell snacks (*scalleter*), but he forbade the sale of wine. (Perhaps he feared the damage that might result from the drunkenness of the young men.)

> Performances were forbidden at S. Aponal on those nights that performances were taking place at Faustini's new opera theater, S. Cassiano. (Faustini specified that without this condition the agreement would not have been drawn up.)

> Faustini would notify the members the evening before a night when a performance would not take place at S. Cassiano, so that they would have time to dispense the tickets; once dispensed, the permission could not be withdrawn. (This stipulation and the one preceding it could have significantly interfered with the academy's ability to mount their drama; in the event, however, performances at S. Cassiano usually occurred only every other night that season.)

> The members must reconsign the theater in its original state at the end of the rental period, without damage and with new lamps.

Perhaps most importantly, the academy could not charge for their entertainment.[32]

Giovanni Faustini had characterized S. Aponal as a small and humble theater, but the academicians proudly displayed the name of their new home on the title page of their libretto. The anonymous *Tolomeo* (the text for which had been sent to Venice from an undisclosed location about one hundred miles away) comprises a prologue and three acts, in the manner of an opera.[33] The libretto

[32] ASV, Scuola Grande di San Marco, b. 113. For dates of the performances, see Glixon and Glixon, *Inventing the Business of Opera*, 356. The contract's validity was to expire at the end of May 1658, rather than after the conclusion of the carnival season.

[33] Giacomo Castoreo, in his plays for S. Aponal and other theaters, often resorted to the more "classical" five acts.

specifies that Pier Simone Agostini–then about twenty-three years old, and thus quite close to the age of the members–composed music for the prologue and ballets, as well as some canzonette; these represent his earliest datable pieces (see below).[34]

Unable to charge admission for their offering, the academicians apparently ran short of money. Moreover, they failed to turn back their keys to the theater after their year's rental; eventually, in September, Faustini had the locks on the theater changed, and he threatened to dismantle the boxes and the stage. The academy was determined (imperturbably, one might say) to continue its mission in the same manner, however, and one of the members came forward to make special arrangements with the impresario. On 11 January 1659, Emanuel Calafati, then twenty years old, agreed to turn over to Faustini the interest from some of his investments in order to cover some of the previous debts, and on 26 January, well into the traditional carnival season, Faustini rented the theater to Calafati (not to the academicians as a group), but only through the period of Lent.[35] In extending the rental agreement for another season, however, Faustini slightly relaxed some of his previous prohibitions: he granted the academy the right to present entertainment on the same nights as the Teatro S. Cassiano two times during the last week of carnival. Had he not done so, S. Aponal would have remained dark for much of February, for the show at S. Cassiano (Cavalli's *Antioco*) ran for seventeen consecutive nights, from 8 February through 24 February (carnival ended that year on 25 February).[36] The Faustini/Calafati rental contract was drawn up just one day after Cavalli's opera had commenced performances at the Teatro S. Cassiano. Thus, Faustini managed to take in 120 ducats (still with a sixty-ducat profit), and the Imperturbabili found a venue for their third carnival presentation.

---

[34] See *New Grove Dictionary of Music and Musicians* (New York: Macmillan, 2001), s.v. "Agostini, Pier Simone." Following his musical training, Agostini undertook a military career, and served in Crete, fighting against the Turks. It is likely that he traveled to Venice on his return from his military duties, and found this small job composing for the Imperturbabili.

[35] This contract renewal is partially transcribed in Mancini, Muraro, and Povoledo, *I teatri di Venezia e il suo territorio*, 1: 372. We have interpreted the date of the renewal as *more veneto* (i.e., January 1659), while Mancini, Muraro, and Povoledo place it in the previous year. Regarding Calafati's age, in testimony given at the time of his marriage in 1656, his father said that the two of them had come to Venice in 1647. The younger Calafati's age is given as seventeen years old. Archivio Storico del Patriarcato di Venezia, Curia patriarcale, Sezione antica, Examinum matrimoniorum, b. 59, f. 33, 8 February 1656. A copy of the notarial document between Faustini and Calafati drawn up by Ascanio Scarella (11 January 1658, *more veneto*) can be found in ASV, Scuola Grande di San Marco, b. 117, mazzo A. Extending the rental period through Lent would have given the academicians ample time to return the theater to its proper and original condition.

[36] The performance dates for Cavalli's *Antioco* at S. Cassiano are taken from Faustini's account book, found in ASV, Scuola Grande di San Marco, b. 194. See Lorenzo Bianconi and Thomas Walker, "Production, Consumption and Political Function of Seventeenth-Century Opera," *Early Music History* 4 (1984): 209-96, at 223-24.

The academy presented *La pazzia in trono overo Caligula delirante*, an "opera di stile recitativo" by the Muranese Domenico Gisberti (at that time around twenty-four years old); this is his first known dramatic work.[37] Either time, money, or both were short, and the academy published no libretto for their short run (had he so wished, Gisberti could have paid for the printing of his own libretto; it is possible that some sort of scenario was printed for the audience to consult).[38]

That the Imperturbabili rented the Teatro S. Aponal for two years at such an elevated price speaks of their commitment to pass the dangers of the carnival season in a well-established theater. One hundred-twenty ducats, in itself, was not such a high rate compared to the rental of most theaters (although Faustini himself had paid only half that amount), but the provision in the contract that admission not be charged, and an additional lack of income from the sale of wine, meant that the members were forced to make many expenditures with no hope of reimbursement. It is not surprising, then, that the group apparently ceased to function after three years, and it is telling that no other group followed them at the Teatro S. Aponal. The academy's last librettist, however, did not remain silent. Rather, as we saw earlier, perhaps influenced by his experience with the Imperturbabili, he went on to form his own academy the next year. The Angustiati's constitution, discussed above, was drawn up in Gisberti's home in October 1660.

Domenico Gisberti and the Angustiati, 1660-1664

Domenico Gisberti has not yet inspired an extensive study; he is most well-known for the works he wrote and published while he lived in Munich, serving as the secretary to Ferdinand Maria, Elector of Bavaria (indeed, *La pazzia in trono* was published amidst his later works, many of them issued in Munich in a series of nine volumes dedicated to the Muses). It is Gisberti's formative years, however, that are particularly intriguing, given the journey he travelled, both literally and figuratively, from Murano to Munich.

Gisberti was a native of Murano, a priest and eventually the chaplain of the nunnery of Santa Chiara di Murano.[39] The earliest reference to him that we have

---

[37] The much later publication of the work–in Gisberti's *Talia* of 1675–gives 1660 as the year of the performance. Nonetheless, a document concerning money loaned by Calafati to Paulo Vedoa regarding expenses for *Caligula delirante* leaves no doubt regarding the date of the performances: Vedoa's statement regarding his debt is dated 28 January 1658, *more veneto* (1659 modern style). ASV, Giudici del Mobile, Sentenze a legge, b. 432, f. 25. Gisberti's dates are traditionally given as 1635-1677.

[38] On the economics behind the publishing of opera librettos, see Glixon and Glixon, *Inventing the Business of Opera*, 120-25. Gisberti's name has been linked for centuries with a different libretto of 1672 entitled simply *Caligula delirante* (set by Giovanni Maria Pagliardi), but the two works are unrelated. See Thomas Walker, "'Ubi Lucius': Thoughts on Reading Medoro," in Francesco Lucio, *Il Medoro, Drammaturgia musicale veneta* 4 (Milan: Ricordi, 1984), clvii.

[39] He was appointed to the post some time before late 1662. ASV, Archivio notarile, b. 11070, f. 517, 28 February 1662, *more veneto*.

found dates back to 1656: on 13 October testimony was heard at the Sant'Uffizio (the Holy Office, the Venetian branch of the Inquisition) regarding pre Domenico Gisberti, "who runs a school for grammar and reading." The witness, Antonio Marinetti, claimed that Gisberti had read to him from a prohibited book that dealt with love.[40] Another witness testified that Gisberti had written the work presented at the Teatro S. Aponal in Venice the previous carnival.[41] The latter testimony, while perhaps less troubling to the Holy Office than the reading of prohibited books, creates problems for the music historian, as the only opera known to have been presented at S. Aponal for the 1655/56 season was Aurelio Aureli's *Erismena*. Whether or not Gisberti was involved in *Erismena*, the testimony may speak towards Gisberti's interest in, and probable attendance at, opera in Venice. One wonders if the witness had confused Gisberti with the Muranese poet Aureli, who did write that libretto.[42] After the demise of the Angustiati, Gisberti was with the Venetian ambassador, Giorgio Cornaro, in Austria. Upon the ambassador's death in 1667, the dowager empress Eleonora found some employment for Gisberti until he joined the service of elector Ferdinand Maria in Munich.[43]

The constitution that Gisberti drew up for the Angustiati in 1660 specified the initial performance of the work *Maria Stuarda*, but it seems likely that it was not performed until 1664, the date of the publication of the libretto, now entitled *La barbarie del caso*. Gisberti must have been pleased to see his drama reach the stage, but he was generally disappointed in the activities of his academy, as he expressed in a letter to the reader appended to the *Costituzioni*:[44]

> It began in confusion, and ended with disorder. For three years it was silent. Finally, in 1664, regaining spirit, it made itself heard, and it reappeared with *La barbarie del caso*. It ended its life with this performance, even more tragic for that than for the death of Mary Stuart. This virtuous congress lasted four years, and justly ended its splendor with a tragedy, as it was born in comedy, and by chance.[45]

---

[40] ASV, Savi all'Eresia (Santo Ufficio), b.108, 13 October 1656. Our Domenico Gisberti, who was the son of Pietro Gisberti, had a relative also named Domenico, whose father was named Giovanni. The document under discussion here fails to name the accusant's father, but the context makes the identification clear.

[41] "Ha fatto il Carneval passato l'opera recitata nel Teatro di S. Aponal di Venezia." ASV, Savi all'Eresia (Santo Ufficio) , b.108, 13 October 1656.

[42] Although Aureli lived in Venice, his family still owned property in Murano, and from 1665 to 1667 he was chancellor of Murano. ASV, Podestà di Murano, b. 201.

[43] At this point the most reliable source of biographical information on Gisberti must be *La virtù fra i cipressi nell'essequie funebri Del signor Domenico Gisberti*, an oration by Antonio Lupis published after Gisberti's death in 1677 (Venice: Antonio Tivanni, 1677). Gisberti's funerary stone provided by Pietro Beltrame, mentioned earlier, also refers to Gisberti's service to the Empress Eleonora and to the Elector of Bavaria.

[44] Published with some small omissions and slight inaccuracies in Maylender, *Storia delle accademie d'Italia*, 1: 185-86.

[45] "Cominciò nelle confusioni, e finì con disordine. Tacque tre anni. Finalmente nel 1664 ripigliato

The Theatrical Productions

The works produced by these two academies, if not true operas, were certainly far more than amateur theatricals. As mentioned above regarding the first of the Imperturbabili productions, *Argenide*, they employed real operatic scenery. They also were fully costumed, included ballets, and even utilized machinery and special effects. The three extant librettos, two for the Imperturbabili and one for the Angustiati, provide good evidence of how these works resembled the operas performed at other Venetian theatres, and how they differed.

In terms of plot and characters, *Tolomeo* and *La pazzia in trono* are quite close to those of ordinary operas: based loosely on historical events and personages, they include the usual love triangles, often with disguised or misidentified characters, with all resolving happily in the end. *La barbarie del caso*, however, is quite unusual. Its setting is not ancient or exotic, but relatively recent, sixteenth-century England, and the ending, befitting the description on the libretto, is tragic: Mary Stuart, true to history, is decapitated (although in this version as a result of a long series of deceits and misunderstandings) and all hopes are dashed. All three works contain the standard sorts of comic characters, including lecherous old women, hunchbacks, doddering servants, and lovesick young men, and the latter two (*La pazzia in trono* and *La barbarie del caso*) also have madmen (Caligula driven mad by love and James of Scotland feigning madness to be near to his imprisoned mother).[46] The comic characters in *Tomoleo* and *La pazzia in trono*, both with happy endings, serve to prevent the audience from getting too emotionally involved in the apparent tragedies of the serious characters, while those in *La barbarie* only make the ultimate tragedy more shocking. In addition to the speaking characters, each libretto requires the participation of considerable numbers of extras, including soldiers, courtiers, judges, and the English parliament, perfect for those academicians without the time or ability to learn roles. One question that remains unanswered is whether the female roles were played by male academicians or by women.

The appearance of these works on stage must have been virtually indistinguishable from ordinary operas, although the costumes, provided by the members themselves, may not have been as uniformly designed or as elaborate (although the documentation is entirely lacking for this aspect, so it is impossible to be sure). Like standard operas of the time, the works featured seven to eleven different sets, some quite elaborate, such as *Tolomeo*'s scene of the Egyptian pyramids with the walls and gate of Memphis, or the island prison with bridges and a river in *La barbarie del caso*.[47] The painters for the two Imperturbabili works are not known,

---

lo spirito, si fece sentire e la sua Comparsa fu la <u>Barbarie del Caso</u>. Terminò la sua vita con questa recita, più Tragica per la medesima, che per la morte di Maria Stuarda. Durò questo virtuoso congresso quattr'anni, et a ragione morì con una Tragedia il suo fasto, che nacque in una Comedia et a caso." *Costituzioni*, f, 10.

[46] On operatic conventions in Venice, see Rosand, *Opera in Seventeenth-Century Venice*, Chapter 11.

[47] For scenery in Venetian operas, see Glixon and Glixon, *Inventing the Business of Opera*, 227-39.

but for *La barbarie*, the libretto credits Simon Guglielmi, well known for his work for Marco Faustini,[48] along with "Michiel."

Not surprisingly, these works also call for some special effects.[49] Those for *Il Tolomeo* are the simplest, limited to flights (by Conone, the court wise man–and apparently also a wizard–and Venus and Cupid) in the ballets at the ends of the first two acts. *La pazzia in trono* employs no flying machines, but calls for some unusual special effects involving fire and light. Many of the scenes are done in the dark (either during the night time or with shuttered windows to simulate night, at the request of Caligula), with lamps and torches being carried on and off stage, windows opening and closing, sometimes revealing the set and sometimes obscuring it. There is also a prominent sacrificial bonfire in Act II. *La barbarie del caso* is the only one for which we know the creator of the machines, Anastasio Marchiori, like Guglielmi one of Marco Faustini's former collaborators. These are also the most elaborate of the three. The prologue of the opera opens with a curtain reproducing the engraved title page of the libretto, which, after a brief discussion by Terror and Compassion, is torn in half by the two characters who fly off in opposite directions, revealing the Palace of Poetry. The end of Act I is equally dramatic: at the conclusion of the trial of Mary Stuart, as she is on the brink of being declared guilty of murdering her husband, a pageboy flies on stage and writes glowing characters in the air declaring the Scottish queen's innocence (we later discover that this was one of the enchantments of Queneda). Act II ends with a marine ballet of dancing Nereids, and in Act III the old woman Queneda calls up spirits who carry her away after agreeing to obey Queen Elizabeth's commands. Elsewhere in the opera characters enter and exit in boats, and the ghost of the Duke of Norfolk makes an appearance. The final scene includes an image worthy of the Grand Guignol: the backdrop opens to show a funereal chamber with the decapitated body of Mary Stuart.

As in operas performed in the commercial theaters, the first and second acts of each of these works conclude with a ballet, those for *La barbarie* choreographed by Olivier Vigasio (another of Faustini's collaborators).[50] Each of these has a solo or choral song, and *Tolomeo* and *La barbarie* also begin with a sung prologue.

It is in the musical aspect that these works differ the most from true operas. It seems likely that the dialogue was all spoken (although the description of *La pazzia in trono* as "opera di stile recitativo" is somewhat confusing).[51] The basic texts of all three are in *versi sciolti*, and are considerably longer than the average opera

---

[48] Ibid., 260-61 and 263-66.

[49] For stage machinery and special effects in Venetian opera, see ibid., 239-48.

[50] On dance in Venetian opera, see Irene Alm, "Theatrical Dance in Seventeenth-Century Venetian Opera," (Ph.D. diss., University of California, Los Angeles, 1993); idem (ed. Wendy Heller and Rebecca Harris-Warrick), "Winged Feet and Mute Eloquence: Dance in Seventeenth-Century Venetian Opera," *Cambridge Opera Journal* 15 (2003), 216-80; and Glixon and Glixon, *Inventing the Business of Opera*, 215-20.

[51] This view is suggested in Thomas Walker, "'Ubi Lucius,'" clvii.

libretto: while standard librettos of this period have sixty or seventy pages of text, *Tolomeo* and *La pazzia* have about 115 each, and *La barbarie* more than 150. This extended dialogue is relieved by songs in rhymed, strophic poetry with shorter lines (usually five or eight syllables).

In *Tolomeo*, the six songs (besides those in the prologue and two ballets) are not printed with the main text, but are appended at the end of the libretto, after the end of Act III, with a separate title: "Canzonette per musica composte insieme col prologo, e introduttioni de' balli dal Signor Pier Simon Augustini." No character is named for these songs, but one is indicated to be sung in each of the six physical locations of the main drama (for example, the pyramids), and their exact placement in the play is not certain. They are all light in character, and typical of songs that might be sung by servants or other comic roles. Unfortunately, the music of Agostini, as he is usually known, is lost (see also above).

La pazzia in trono seems to have featured the least music of the three, and the libretto gives no indication of the composer of this small amount of music. There is no prologue, and the two ballets, although they certainly had music (the second specifies trumpets and drums), are not provided with songs. Within the drama itself there are only three songs (in I/15 Cherea is given a series of rhymed seven-syllable lines that may also be a song) and one chorus, performed by the imperial musicians to the sound of trumpets and drums while a peace treaty is being signed. This decrease in the amount of music could have been the result of the hasty preparations for the production, as the theater was only rented in late January. *La barbarie del caso* is at the other end of the spectrum: besides the prologue, two ballets, and two special scenes (a dialogue between Queneda and the spirits, and the suffering of Pauleto after he puts on an enchanted cloak), there are twenty-one songs and two choruses, all composed, according to the libretto, by Pietro Molinari.[52]

The songs themselves reveal another key difference from standard opera: all of the singing is done by comic or secondary characters. The one assigned song in *Il Tolomeo* is sung by the sage/magician Conone. In *La pazzia in trono*, Palante the eunuch and Macrone the hunchback sing (and perhaps Cherea, the tribune). The vast majority of the songs in *La barbarie del caso* are performed by the old servant woman/sorceress Queneda, the hunchback jailer Pauleto, the singer and page Melvino, and the inept conspirator Gissar. With notable exceptions in *La pazzia* and *La barbarie*, none of the principal characters sing—unlike, of course, in the more usual operas of the day, which were dominated by the star *prime donne* and *primi uomini*, who played the major roles and sang the bulk of the arias. The exceptions are Caligula and James of Scotland: the former sings while driven mad by love, and

---

[52] Molinari had previously composed music for *Hipsicratea*, also performed at Murano (1660), and he was active as a music teacher in Venice. In 1669 he attested to having taught one Felice Margarita Raimondo at the house of her companion Andrea Vendramin (not the theater owner) for about ten years. ASV, Archivio Storico del Patriarcato di Venezia, Curia patriarcale, Sezione antica, Examinum matrimoniorum, b. 84, f. 2548, 25 August 1669.

the latter while in disguise as the mad Amiltone—what better way to demonstrate insanity than to sing?[53]

Despite the elaborate production, the theater and the actors were not up to the level of those in a professional production, as Gisberti warned his audience in a poem at the end of the libretto:

SCUSA.

Se di questo Mar nero,

Che una selva di carta quasi inonda

Si perde in picciol onda

Qualch'INTERLOCUTOR fatto nocchiero:

Se frà tanti Palaggi,

Ch'al par d'altre Città, vanta Murano,

Dentro breve HABITURO

S'han ricovrato i nostri PERSONAGGI,

E voglion con due GIORNI

Misurar le fatiche di due MESI.

Se del TORCHIO medemo, che gemendo,

Per si lamenti tano

De vitij naturali

Ne men ponno volar co le bell'ALI

Ad asciugare il pianto;

Deh spettator cortese;

Non rimaner confuso,

Poiche nel'ACADEMIA MURANESE,

Se non fosse quest'uso

Non sariano Chiamati

Veramente ANGUSTIATI.

(If in this dark sea, almost drowned in a forest of paper, some actor made into a sailor gets lost in a small wave; if among all the grand palaces of which, like other cities, Murano is proud, our characters have taken refuge in a small cottage, and try in two days to measure the work of two months; if the same printing press, which

---

[53] These restrictions echo some of the principles of verisimilitude that governed the use of aria in earlier opera. See Rosand, *Opera in Seventeenth-Century Venice*, 45, 248, 272, 275, 279. See also John Walter Hill, "'Ov'e il decoro?' Etichetta di corte, espressione degli affetti e trattamento dell'aria nell'Orontea di Antonio Cesti," in *La figura e l'opera di Antonio Cesti nel Seicento europea*, ed. Mariateresa Dellaborra (Florence: Olschki, 2002), 3-14.

groaning, because of both the laments and the expected errors, cannot even fly with beautiful wings to dry its tears; then, courteous spectator, don't be confused, because the Muranese Academy, if it weren't that way, would not truly be worthy of the name Angustiati.)[54]

* * * * *

Nothing is known of the end of the Accademia degli Imperturbabili, which seems simply to have ceased functioning after the performances of *La pazzia in trono*, although the legal problems generated by their productions dragged on for some time. The Angustiati's end, however, as shown above, is mournfully and angrily described by Gisberti. He attributes the short life of the Angustiati to the nature of Murano itself:

> Everything in Murano bears the fragility of being made of glass. According to some Greek peoples, even the wheel or globe of Fortune herself was made of thinnest glass. All of [Murano's] good things, all of its blessings have short lives. Riches have never reached the fourth generation, and virtues never last to old age [*terza età*] in one who studies. If some apply themselves as youngsters, they cease to care when they are old. The majority start school, but finish in the glass factories. All begin, but very few continue to learn. They are all inclined by nature to the arts, but they do not cultivate the intellect. Murano is the noblest and most spirited district of Venice, but also the laziest, most inconstant, and most depraved. As a result of everything I have said, and I swear to it, our times are totally deprived of every Academic entertainment and any sort of virtuous exercise.[55]

Gisberti's cynicism aside, these two academies show the ends to which the young men of Venice were prepared to go to provide themselves and their friends with

---

[54] Gisberti, *La barbarie del caso,* 167.

[55] "Tutte le cose in Murano traggono la fragilità dell'esser loro dal Vetro. Anche la fortuna medesima par che vanti come un tempo tra certi Popol della Grecia, la sua Ruota, od il suo Globo di sottilissimo Vetro. Ogni suo Bene, ogni sua benedittione è poco durevole. Le Ricchezze non hanno mai veduta la quarta Generatione, e la Virtù non mai la terza età della Persona studiosa. Se taluno s'applica Giovanetto, non sen' curan da vecchi. La maggior parte comincia dalle Scuole e finisce nelle Fornaci. Tutti principiano, ma pochissimi continuano l'imparare. A tutte le bell'Arti sono inclinati dalla Natura, ma non coltivano il Genio. Murano è la Contrada più nobile, e più spiritosa di Vinetia, ma la più otiosa, incostante e vitiosa. Di tutto ciò l'esito il dica, ne ne faccia fede, la miseria del nostro Secolo priva totalmente d'ogni Accademico Trattenimento, e di qualsiasi virtuoso esercito." *Costituzioni,* ff. 10-10v. The Angustiati name appears in two other publications signaled by Maylender in his *Storia delle accademie d'Italia*. One was a work in memory of the Venetian nobleman Giovanni Battista Ballarino: *Epicedio in morte di Giamb. Ballarino gran Canc. della Rep. di Venezia* (Venice: Valvasense, 1666); in a   second appendix to the *Costituzioni,* f. 10v, Gisberti provides a brief description of this event, praising the decorations, the music, and the poetry, but referring to his own oration as "orrida e oscura." The other is *Il focile. Discorso di Domenico Gisberti recitato alli Signori Angustiati di Murano* (Venice: Valvasense, 1666). We have not yet located copies of either of these works. Gisberti also refers to himself as "fra gl'Angustiati l'Accademico liberato" in the 1667 Munich publication of *I trionfi di virtuosa bellezza.*

special entertainment during a perilous time of the year. Moreover, in a certain sense, the members of both lived up to their names. The Imperturbabili forged ahead through three seasons, imperturbable through lawsuits, changes of venue, and who knows what other impediments. The Angustiati, viewed through the eyes of its founder, were certainly constrained, and failed to achieve their potential. Both provide a fascinating look at popular entertainment in the city famous for its carnival celebrations.

Theatri intra theatrum
or,
The Church and the Stage in Seventeenth-Century Rome

Margaret Murata

In the year 1697 at the end of the month of July, on the advice of the Sacred Congregation of the Reform, Pope Innocent XII ordered the demolition of the famous Teatro Tor di Nona, built several years back by Count d'Alibert. The supporters of drama cited a passage by St. Thomas that says dramas are neutral things and actors are not prohibited by divine law…. Other learned people said that generally all types of spectacle are prohibited as being temptations to sin, and they brought forward a passage by Tacitus which said that although plays and spectacles were approved in [ancient] Rome, Pompey was nonetheless condemned by the censors, because he built a permanent theater, which appeared to outsiders a monument to scandal…. The Roman people, great lovers of spectacles, were extremely displeased by said demolition…. After the theater was destroyed and dramas prohibited, they feared disturbances much worse than those that could occur on account of the theaters: no one doubts that the courtesans, hitherto so famous in this city, have been laughing over being re-established like this. It's certain that the very thing has disappeared that used to lure people away from their moments destined for pleasures.[1]

When Innocent XII had Rome's first public opera house destroyed—the building licensed in 1669 by Pope Clement IX—was he ignoring both St. Thomas and

---

[1] Vatican City, Biblioteca Apostolica Vaticana (hereafter BAV), Fondo Vaticani latini MS 8518, f. 99r-v: "Notizie della demolizione del Teatro di Tor di Nona," cited (but transcribed only in part) in the still-fundamental documentary study of the theater by Alberto Cametti, *Il Teatro di Tordinona poi di Apollo*, 2 vols. (Tivoli: A. Chicca, 1938), 1: 97. For the Italian text, see Appendix 1. A version of this essay was presented at the Fiftieth Annual Meeting of the American Musicological Society in Philadelphia, Pennsylvania in 1984. I thank Stefanie Tcharos for a reference to Andrea Penna, "Il primo teatro pubblico di Roma. Le vicende del Teatro Tordinona nel XVII secolo," in *Studi Romani* 46 (1998): 337-68, which relates contractual and financial aspects of the theater's history, beginning with the original proposal made to Alexander VII in 1666. For a brief discussion of the demolition, see Maria Grazia Pastura, "Legislazione pontificia sui teatri e spettacoli musicali a Roma," in *La musica a Roma attraverso le fonti d'archivio. Atti del convegno internazionale, Roma 4-7 giugno 1992*, B. M. Antolini, A. Morelli, and V. Vita Spagnuolo, eds. (Lucca: LIM, 1994), 167-75, at 168-69. For the physical fortunes of the theater, see Sergio Rotondi, *Il Teatro Tordinona. Storia, progetti, architettura* (Rome: Kappa, 1987); for the history of the edifice and its urban environment to the present day, see V. Quilici, A. Cappabianca, and C. Coraggio, eds., *Tor di Nona, storia di un recupero* (Rome and Bari: Editori Laterza, 1991).

the renewal of business for Rome's courtesans in the hopes of eradicating a greater evil? Immoral stories? Immoral performers? Perhaps monetary gain from the sale of entertainment? Or wasting money on unnecessary luxuries? Or, was the Tor di Nona a shameful blotch on the image of the very center of Catholic Christendom?

Like-minded arguments against the stage on the grounds of morality were at the time, and continue to be, well known and have been widely discussed in the annals of the European theater.[2] Numerous seventeenth-century tracts and treatises, filled with citations from the Church Fathers, urged Protestants and Catholics alike to avoid corruption and infection by Lust, Ambition, and Vengeance, who reigned in comedies, tragicomedies, and tragedies alike, not to mention the harm, as one Roman put it in 1676, "of seeing women perform and witnessing their extravagance, shamelessness and unruliness, which have excited so much ferment in our Roman youth."[3] Of course, the theater was not alone in offering such incitements to sin. An anonymous Roman advocate of "heroic dramas, honest fables and deeds of great men" wrote, "I am not talking about either [the activities on] the Corso, or the parties, or other carnival licenses, since I could well demonstrate that the theater is the lesser of every other evil."[4]

This is not the place to present or even try to summarize the intellectual positions on the morality of the theater that were and are available in seventeenth-century tracts and discourses. In Catholic countries, their positions range from complete non-acceptance of representations in any form to hair-splitting discussions that try to set the limits of Christian and social acceptability.[5] All of the ink expended,

[2] Studies of polemics for and against the theater in the various European countries in the seventeenth century are too numerous to indicate here. Most examine textual materials, which in turn typically focus on the content (scripts) of what was produced on public, academic, collegiate, convent, and private stages, which is not the path of the present essay. For excerpts from Italian tracts for and against the theater *ca.* 1600 (at its various levels of influence), see Ferdinando Taviani, *La fascinazione del teatro. La commedia dell'arte e la società barocca*, vol. 1 (Rome: Bulzoni, 1970); Taviani follows these by an examination of the multi-volume *Della Christiana moderatione del theatro* (Florence 1646-52; repr. 1655) by the Jesuit Giovanni Domenico Ottonelli, with extensive transcriptions. For a concise survey of the theatrical terrain in Italy, see Silvia Carandini, *Teatro e spettacolo nel Seicento*, Biblioteca Universale Laterza 306 (Rome and Bari: Editori Laterza, Gius. Laterza & Figli, 1990, with seven reprints to 2007).

[3] From *Avvisi di Roma* for 22 February 1676, from the passage quoted in note 37 below.

[4] BAV Vat. lat. MS 8623, "Discorso sopra i teatri aperti in Roma e della convenienze di essi," (undated), ff. 446, 449: "Io non parlo o del Corso, o delle veglie, o d'altre licenze carnevalesche, che potrei ben mostrare d'ogn'altro male esser minore il teatro.... Dico ben sempre, che degl'abusi romani questo è sì picciolo, ch'appena ne merita il nome, et a' zelanti avviso, che questa loro autorità non è in tutto lodevole ..." (This essay in general supports the entertainment value of the theater, reasoning that the modern stage is not like the theater condemned by the ancients and that the moral person who knows that he is susceptible to the wiles of the contemporary theater ought to refrain from attending.)

[5] When it was decided not to reopen the Tor di Nona after Holy Year of 1675, one set of Avvisi noted that decision along with the publication of a book by Father Girolamo Fiorentini that "detested similar comedies, *Theatrum contra theatrum*" (19 August 1675, quoted in Arnaldo Morelli, "La musica a Roma nella seconda metà del Seicento attraverso l'archivio Cartari-Febei," in *La musica a Roma attraverso le fonti d'archivio*, Doc. 36, 126. See also Morelli's subsequent documents, nos. 37-39, and 41, which describe one of the pope's objections to the public opera house as the appearance of women

however, needs to be considered in the light of unceasing theatrical activity in most cities—including Rome—for the duration of the seventeenth century. The changing tensions between the theatrical policies of each papacy, such as they were, and what might be considered the "inevitable" development of Italian drama and theater constitute a necessary aspect of the slowly changing social and political climate of the city.[6] The influence of the Sacred Palace amounted to more than the presence or refusal of patronage, in the form of licenses, benefices to writers and musicians, or outright subsidies to private "sponsors." Many important changes in the history of drama in Rome can be attributed, of course, to circumstances not directly related to the papal administration itself, such as the rectorship of Father Filippo Merelli at the Collegio Clementino, which brought the Corneilles and Racine to the Roman stage,[7] or the forming of an academy of Arcadians. We also need to consider that the severe anti-theatrical positions of Innocent XI and Innocent XII failed to effect their ends, except for a few outstanding actions, like the destruction of the Tor di Nona. The Vatican was never so puritan as to ban completely the publishing or staging of plays. The demolition of the Tor di Nona has been seen in moral terms as a sign of the influence of religious reformists, in political terms as an overreaction to Gallic criticism of the leadership of the papacy, as well also as mere anecdote—as an act of personal authority by a cranky, embattled pope. More recently, the austerity measures of Innocents XI and XII have been discussed as measures to reform the social structure of the court by attacking privileges and abuses exercised by the resident nobility.[8] The comments in the Roman *Avvisi*, commonly shared news circulated weekly in manuscript throughout Italy,[9] also point to a social context, a question of temporal governance over the unusual mix of nobles in Rome, who owed fealty to no single sovereign.

* * *

In its lists of activities banned during carnival seasons, the Sacred Palace certainly considered the theater one of the potential occasions to sin. In Holy Years, for example, comedies were normally banned, along with other traditionally Roman

---

singers in its productions, as was the norm in Venice). Fiorentini's Latin treatise is *Comoedio-Crisis sive Theatri contra theatrum censura* (Lyon, 1675); cf. Taviani, *La fascinazione del teatro*, 263-84, which translates the first section into Italian.

[6] For the altered relation between Church and stage in the next century, see Bruno Cagli, "Produzione musicale e governo pontificio," in *Le muse galanti. La musica a Roma nel Settecento*, Bruno Cagli, ed. (Rome: Istituto della Enciclopedia Italiana, 1985), 11-21.

[7] Free prose versions of *Stilicone* by Thomas Corneille performed at the Clementino in 1698 (Franchi 1698/11); and in 1699, *Eraclio* by Pierre Corneille (*Héraclius*; Franchi 1699/6) and the *Bérénice* by Racine (Franchi 1699/5). For references to Franchi, see note 12 below.

[8] Renata Ago, "Hegemony over the Social Scene and Zealous Popes," in *Court and Politics in Papal Rome*, Gianvittorio Signorotto and Maria Antonietta Visceglia, eds. (Cambridge: Cambridge University Press, 2002), 229-46.

[9] On the *Avvisi di Roma*, see Mario Infelise, "Roman *Avvisi*: Information and Politics in the Seventeenth Century," in *Court and Politics in Papal Rome*, 212-28.

carnival entertainments.[10] In Holy Year of 1600 only two plays were allowed, one at the church of Sant'Eustachio and another at the Collegio Clementino. The prohibitions for 1650 extended the theatrical ban to all private performances, but exempted the staging of spiritual plays and tragedies. These two genres, of course, comprised the bulk of the repertory of the convents, monasteries, colleges, and seminaries, which could be relied upon for propriety in content and presentation. Not only were the actors in the colleges all boys and men, but the productions were also as a rule open only to men. In 1676, Clement X however allowed some women *(dame ordinarie)* to attend plays at the Seminario Romano, although this upset the rector and caused a lot of argument.[11] In the changing edicts for various years, however, we see that the actions of the Vatican did not make consistent policy. In 1682 under Innocent XI, the Seminario Romano and the Collegio Clementino were permitted to stage plays during carnival only on the condition that no outsider attend. In carnival of 1695—two years before he ordered the demolition of the Teatro Tor di Nona—Innocent XII himself attended a "commedietta" played by the boys of the newly founded hospice of S. Michele a Ripa. These few instances (from among many) show that the staging of plays was not condemned outright, nor did the Vatican seem ever to doubt the efficacy of drama as a vehicle for persuasion. At the least, each of the seventeenth-century popes recognized that under certain circumstances, plays could edify. For most of the century, lack of evidence to the contrary suggests that most of the popes considered academic plays in themselves harmless, both as scripts and productions.

This is substantiated by the sheer quantity of plays and opera libretti published in Rome and the Papal States with the necessary imprimatur. Furthermore, any general survey of theatrical prints shows that, in terms of content, official policy accommodated much and easily.[12] If we turn to improvised or unpublished dramas, where there could be no pre-performance censorship, cases of official intervention that captured public notice also appear surprisingly rare in the course of the century. In 1611, members of a professional Spanish troupe were temporarily

---

[10] Elisabetta Natuzzi cites a collection of *bandi* in Rome, Archivio Storico Capitolino, Deputazione dei Pubblici Spettacoli, busta 8, in her *Il Teatro Capranica dall'inaugurazione al 1881. Cronologia degli spettacoli con indici analitici,* Quaderni de "La musica e la danza," 12 (Naples: Edizioni Scientifiche Italiane, 1999), 15, note 5. Edicts were promulgated to cover a variety of city activities, including the closing of shops when the *Porte Sante* at St. Peter's were opened; see for example, Francesca Barberini, and Micaela Dickmann, *I pontefici e gli Anni Santi nella Roma del XVII secolo. Vita, arte e costume* (Rome: Ugo Bozzi Editore, 2000), 219-20.

[11] BAV Barb. lat. 6381, *Avvisi di Roma,* 22 February 1676, f. 126: "I padri gesuiti del Seminario Romano sono più di tutti stati angustiati dalle sudette licenze, già che andato l'Eminentissimo Vicario a sentir i trattenimenti s[c]enici carnevaleschi de' loro convitori adinò nel partire a quel Padre Rettore, che per gli altri giorni rimanenti [of Carnival] si contentasse lasciar entrare anche le dame ordinarie, il che mal soffrendo detto Rettore cominciò a portare delle controversie; ma il Cardinale gli verificò, che essendo il Papa dispotico assoluto di tutto, egli come suo Vicario poteva arbitrare per tutto."

[12] For a catalogue of print material for theatrical performances in Rome in the seventeenth century (and printed literary editions), see Saverio Franchi, *Drammaturgia romana,* 2 vols. Sussidi Eruditi 42 (Rome: Edizioni di Storia e Letteratura, 1988, 1997), vol. 1: *Repertorio bibliografico cronologico dei testi drammatici pubblicati a Roma e nel Lazio: secolo XVII.*

jailed in Rome for having played clerics in costume. Implying that good luck, not virtue, got promotions for priests, they lost their license to perform in public.[13] In another later instance (1666), the pope punished some comedians whose depiction of the death of a queen had offended a French cardinal, despite the fact that the players brought forward their original scripts to demonstrate that their material was "old stuff" *(tutte cose vecchie)* and not performed to be topical.[14] They could not have known that the queen mother of France would die two weeks later. These are examples of specific, circumstantial censorship, not the implementation of an anti-theater policy. Plays not given publicly did not require scrutiny or intervention, nor did they generally motivate official comment. The Sacred Palace ignored the reportedly obscene and nauseating plays staged by Christine, the former queen of Sweden, in 1666 and 1678. One public notice of direct intervention on a "morals" question comes from 1699, under Innocent XII's reign. This was the censorship of an intermedio performance in a private palace.

> The ... governor [of Rome] has prohibited any more performances in Ruspoli's theater of a certain intermedio he wrote himself, in which two spinsters learn the true craft of the bordello. When a German comes to their salon, they take everything off him little by little with great nonchalance.[15]

The scarcity of actions against the theater should not surprise: throughout the century, the general attitude of the cardinals and prelates who ran Rome is for the most part indistinguishable from that of the learned aristocratic class from which a good many came. Outweighing the dangers of intellectual and spiritual infection were the habits of education and the importance of social ceremonies that affirmed prestige and status.[16] Cardinals and prelates wrote, gave, and attended private operas and plays. As princes of the Church, their presence at theatrical performances was noted as an indication of the social importance of the event. In Rome, it was the unremarkable familiarity with drama on the part of educated ecclesiastics that provided the starting position for the two notable, opposing and diverse responses to the problem of the Church and the stage. Cardinal Francesco Barberini (elev. 1623) combined every theatrical resource with Christian themes. Innocent XI, and

---

[13] See BAV Fondo Urbinati latini, MS 1079, *Avvisi di Roma*, 22 January 1611, ff. 71, 77, 97.

[14] BAV Fondo Chigiani MS C.III.73, untitled journal, entry for 15 [January] 1666, ff. 5-6v. This journal notes the January death of Anne of Austria, mother of Louis XIV, on 5 February; the *Avvisi di Roma* reported it much later (e.g., 13 February in Vatican City, Archivio Segreto Vaticano [hereafter ASV], Segretariato di Stato, vol. 113, f. 238).

[15] *I-Rli* MS 1693, *Avvisi di Roma*, 28 February 1699, f. 20: "Sabbato della passata Sua Santità mandò a chiamare Monsignor [Pallavicini] Governatore e li diede alcuni ordinij positivj per la quiete publica in occasione de' baccanali; et in tanto il suddetto Governatore ha prohibito, che nel teatro di Ruspolij non si rappresent[a] più certo intermedio d'una sua mano, la quale insegna a due citelle [zitelle] il vero mestiere del bordello; e venendo uno Tedesco in conversatione, lo spogliano a poco a poco di quanto tiene con gran disinvoltura."

[16] Although in terms of the social order in France, pertinent to this social context is Henry Phillips's discussion "The Theatre, the Church and the State," in his *The Theatre and its Critics in Seventeenth-Century France* (Oxford: Oxford University Press, 1980), chap. 10, esp. 204-8.

later Innocent XII, maneuvered to withdraw the social, and therefore political, presence of the Church's princes and intellectuals from theatrical performances, considerably weakening their importance as social events, especially from 1680 to 1686.

Barberini's means for co-opting the stage and making it worthy of Christian admiration involved his direct influence on the content and form of dramatic works. Under the combined influences of the Spanish *comedias de santos,* Florentine sacred operas, and Roman Jesuit tragedy, he initiated a series of spiritual operas produced on the model of private entertainments. His innovation was not his espousal of moral themes or hagiographical stories, which had appeared frequently on private and academic stages before 1628; it was his promotion of these subjects in the exorbitant form of the drama in music that placed the potential function of the stage in a new relationship with the ruling princes of the Church. His productions, in turn, affected the staging of dramatic works in the colleges and seminaries. With his protectorship of the Seminario Romano, the English College, and the Seminario Vaticano, the clerical public was exposed consistently to a single basic type of play, which acquired theatrical ornaments and flourished, thanks to the resources of the near-monopoly of their Barberini patron. Barberini perhaps can be blamed for introducing the prestige and luxury of private opera to a city of nobles quite capable then of imitating the form if not his content—to the benefit of their own prestige and magnificence. After the reign of the Barberini in spiritual, temporal, and operatic matters, opera in Rome ceased to be a monopoly of the Sacred Palace. But its importance as status entertainment persisted, especially after members of the Roman secular nobility became acquainted with opera in other cities, especially in Venice.[17]

The aura of private entertainment penetrated the commercial theater. Before the Tor di Nona opened for its first season, the 1670 subcontract to impresario Filippo Acciaiuoli stipulated that not only was Queen Christina of Sweden entitled to five *palchetti* on the second tier, but that also the architect had to build a separate entrance way to those boxes.[18] Thus, the Queen and her guests would not have to mix with other auditors or unnecessarily encounter them. When the re-modeling

[17] Valeria De Lucca traced the venues of operas given in Rome in the 1670s in "On the Emergence of Semi-Private Theater in Rome after 1675: Lorenzo Onofrio Colonna's Theater," unpublished paper given at the 16th Annual Conference of the Society for Seventeenth-Century Music, San Marino, CA 2008, reflecting research in her dissertation, "'Dalle sponde del Tebro alle rive dell'Adria': Maria Mancini and Lorenzo Onofrio Colonna's Patronage of Music and Theater between Rome and Venice (1659-1675)" (Ph.D. diss., Princeton University, 2009).
[18] See Penna, "Il primo teatro pubblico," from Rome, Archivio di Stato. Archivio di S. Girolamo della Carità, vol. 191, f. 27, after Cametti, *Il Teatro Tor di Nona.* Ludovico Zorzi is one of few who discuss the mixture of social classes in the public opera house, albeit in those of Venice. The *borghese e l'artigiano,* he observes, "acquired the illusion of being admitted to a collective rite on a footing that was finally not subaltern but relatively equal" (247); but this is a view from below looking up, in "Venezia, la Repubblica a teatro" in his *Il teatro e la città. Saggi sulla scena italiana* (Turin: Giulio Einaudi, 1977), 235-83, esp. 246-48.

and restoration of the same theater was being contracted in 1695, the Marchesa Ruspoli paid 3,500 *scudi* for five boxes—along with rights to "parking" space for two carriages, a stall for two horses, and two ground floor rooms in which a private staircase to the boxes would be built.[19]

The importance of the social setting is demonstrated by the later actions of Innocents XI and XII, who had no interests in weakening the theater by tinkering with scripts. Innocent X had already discovered in Holy Year of 1650 that if comedies were banned in the city, the nobles and prelates just went out to the suburban principalities to stage and enjoy them. Innocents XI and XII therefore attempted to reduce the audiences. In 1678, Innocent XI forbade women from singing on stage, taking away a major attraction.[20] In 1680, he forbade cardinals from attending operas, taking away some social cachet. The effect was noted in the *Avvisi:*

> The Queen of Sweden has honored both operas with her presence, but up to now there has been only a single cardinal. Many are planning to stay a-way completely, with the certainty of pleasing the pope.[21]

In 1681, he forbade women from attending performances and sent spies to control the situation.[22] In 1682, he allowed comedies in the two of the colleges but banned all outside guests.[23] In 1686, his Camera Segreta pleaded to be allowed to hear

---

[19] At the price of 3,500 scudi (*moneta*); see Penna, "Il primo teatro pubblico," 360, note 45, from a copy of the sale contract in *I-Ras*, Camerale III, busta 2126, fasc. 3, f. 45. On the Colonnas' private quarters at the Teatro Tor di Nona, see De Lucca, "Dalle sponde del Tebro," chap. 4.

[20] Bans against women performers in private productions and later in public ones resurface throughout the century. Women are notably absent under the reign of Urban VIII (1623-44), except at the foreign embassies, which being extraterritorial were not subject to municipal ordinances.

[21] BAV Barb. lat. 6422, *Avvisi di Roma,* 10 February 1680, f. 69: "Si è dato principio alle due opere in musica che riescono di gran sodisfattione, e specialmente quella che si recita nel Teatro del Palazzo Capranica [*L'Idalma* by Bernardo Pasquini]. La Regina di Svetia le ha onorate ambedue della sua presenza, ma fin'hora non vi è stato che un' sol cardinale; molti pensano d'astenersene affatto con certezza d'incontrare il gusto del Papa."

[22] *I-Rli* MS 1756, *Avvisi di Roma,* 1 February 1681, f. 57v: "Anco la medesima sera si cominciorno le comedie in musica a Capranica con mediocre applauso, ed adesso s'aspetta di sentir come riuscirà l'altra nel Teatro della Pace, di cui si ha miglior relatione. Successe qualche rissa fra Antonio Gabrielli, e lo stesso Capranico doppo fatto il prologo, che servì d'intermedio, di modo che li due notarij, e giudici, che si fanno assistere perché non accadino inconvenienti, poco serviranno all'intentione di chi l'ha comandato, e Pompeo Azzolino per spartir restò leggermente ferito in una gamba, e mano. Nostro Signore ha mandato ordine che non s'ammettono dame in recitamenti di comedie, in cui anche si sa haver mandato persone incognite a' teatri per sapere se i suoi ordini sono esseguiti."

[23] Vatican City, ASV, Segretariato di Stato, vol. 46, *Avvisi di Roma,* 3 January 1682, f. 41v: "A Superiori del Seminario Romano, e del Collegio Clementino è stato ordinato per parte del Papa, che ne l'uno ne l'altro di detti luoghi si faccino comedie nel prossimo carnevale, eccettuato se volessero farle tra di loro, senza dar addito ad alcun forastiere di qualsisia conditione." The opera season that year was promised to consist of only two productions, both staged at the Palazzo Colonna (where *commedie all'improvviso* were also offered): one was sponsored by Duke [Alessandro] Caffarelli (*Il falso nel vero,* Franchi 1682/2) and the other given by Filippo Acciaiuoli (*Chi è cagion del suo mal pianga se stesso,* Franchi 1682/1). One set of Avvisi declared the Casa Colonna "divenuta l'arsenale delle feste baccanali" (*I-Rli* MS 1729, 31 January 1682, f. 60). Another set deemed the Caffarelli opera "tediosa" (*I-Rli* MS 1757, 14 January 1682, f. 31).

an opera, but the pope refused.[24] In 1699, Innocent XII struck an aesthetic blow, forbidding singers of his Cappella Sistina to sing in any production, even in the seminaries and colleges.[25] These tactics are not the same as censuring any theatrical works themselves. However clearly they were intended to chip away at the theater, they still do not reveal the specific reasons for them or the reason why later one public venue (the Tor di Nona) was singled out for destruction.

In January of 1697, Cardinal Carpegna policed the theaters to prevent dining and gambling, but this is a rare notice of such Venetian-style activity in seventeenth-century Rome.[26] One finds objections to extravagance more frequently. In 1676, Innocent XI considered turning the Tor di Nona into a conservatory on the Venetian model for poor, unmarried girls.[27] In 1678 and 1680, he demanded that admission to certain theaters be free.

> Our Lord, who understands the misery in the city, has banned those plays where you rent boxes and where you pay for places, wanting that whoever does them, does them *gratis,* so as not to tax the poor, who, in order to enjoy such amusements have gone to bed many times without supper—a poor excuse, for being all the more possible nowadays, since the tithe-bread that the bakers used to give [at] eight loaves a julie, after the rise in the price of grain, they began to give seven, and in this week, six and a half.[28]

---

[24] ASV Segr. di Stato, vol. 49, *Avvisi di Roma,* 23 February 1686, f. 42v: "La Camera Segreta alla quale … fu prohibito di non uscire dal Palazzo Apostolico, fece supplicare il papa per la licenza di poter' andar a sentire la commedia in musica, ma gli fu negata." At least four operas were staged in Rome that carnival season; a candidate for this request could be *Il silenzio d'Arpocrate,* a Minato libretto (Vienna 1677) set to music by Bernardo Pasquini (cf. Franchi 1686/1).

[25] *I-Rli* MS 1693, *Avvisi di Roma,* 10 January 1699, f. 7: "Ha Sua Santità prohibito a' musici di Cappella [Sistina] di non potere in questo carnevale cantare ad alcuna comedia, come nemeno, né seminarij, né colleggi."

[26] I-Rli MS 1691, vol. 1: *Avvisi di Roma,* 19 January 1697, f. 9r-v: "Il cardinale Carpegna è stato alla visita de' teatri per impedire che non si diano stanze ad alcuno come prima per farvi cena e giochi volendo la Congregatione della Riforma levare tutti li scandali vi potessero nascere, e soltanto ha ordinato, che li soldati di guardia ne' detti teatri non lascino fermarsi più due assieme ne' luoghi di passo, per levare l'abbuso de' cicisbei che vi si fermano con soggettione delle dame, tanto, che possino entrare in carozza nel partirsi." Earlier in 1693, though not in conjunction with theaters, the pope objected to card gambling in one women's gathering, threatening to close it down: "Seguono li festini in diverse camerate di dame, et avendo Nostro Signore saputo, che in una si giocava alla bassetta all'ingrosso gl'ha fatto intimare lo sfratto, quando non se ne astenghino" (*Avvisi di Roma* for 3 January 1693, BAV Ottob. lat. 3358, f. 2).

[27] BAV Chigi MS O.III.37, [*Avvisi diversi*], 26 December 1676, f. 456: Innocent XI, recently elected, "inoltre ha fatto visitare il teatro dell'opere in musica di Monsù d'Arimbert [Giacomo Alibert, impresario], con disegno di farvi un conservatorio delle povere zitelle disperse." Shortly thereafter, the pope annulled Alibert's previous license for the Tor di Nona (see Barb. lat. 6417, entry for 9 January 1677, f. 12).

[28] BAV Barb. lat. 6385, *Avvisi di Roma,* 5 February 1678, f. 35v: "Nostro Signore, che compatisce le miserie di questa città, ha proibito le comedie, dove s'affittano li palchi e si fanno pagamenti luoghi volendo, che chi le fa, le facci gratis per non interessare (?) li poveri huomeni, che per godere di tali spassi sono andati molte volte a letto senza cena, cattivo incontro, che tanto più hora li potria succedere, poiche il pane a decina, che prima i fornari davano 8 pagnotte per giulio, doppo cresciuto il prezzo del grano cominciorno a darne 7, et in questa settimana, 6 e mezzo."

> And since the pope does not want any admission charged [for the operas], there doesn't lack a crowd at the gates, where the cutpurses are having a good harvest, slitting purses; not that, however, the purses yield many coins.[29]

In 1699, buyers as well as sellers of *bollettini* to comedies were jailed.[30] The pope of course could never demand open admission to privately given productions— and, in a seeming contradiction, why block cardinals from private productions and open the public house to all? While no disdain for the commerciality of the public theaters is evident on the part of the *Avvisi* writers, the notion of the "Church's" intent to save people from the costs of their pleasures is more paternalistic than economically aware. Its humanitarian impulse is pre-capitalistic: grandeur and pleasure are nobler when distributed and enjoyed as gifts, as largesse. The equation of nobility with magnanimity colors a comment prompted by a similar conjunction of moral didacticism and incidental asceticism experienced in conflict with the social values of the aristocracy:

> There were only a few cardinals Thursday evening for the meal at the Sacred Palace, probably because food was scarce. But His Holiness did this to set an example, not to save.[31]

The distinction here between "example" and "economizing" is not a subtle one. In reality, spending for private productions or public ones, for a price or for free, seems not to have come under control under Innocent XI; the pace of private productions seems indistinguishable from the previous decade. As Renata Ago has succinctly put it, "Having absented himself from the festive scene without succeeding in ending its pomp, the pope [Innocent XI] had in effect yielded its resources to his nobles."[32] The Vatican's assertion of a moral position most often concerned the areas of theater surrounding the stage: the audience, the "box office," and non-theatrical activities taking place on the premises. Most of the public notices of papal interventions concern the public theater of the comedians and opera impresarios. Were the barons in Rome so powerful that their palaces did not need to obey the Sacred Palace? Was there an official double standard, one for public productions and another for those *inter domesticos parietes?* Or were the private resources for private productions so vast in Rome that the public theaters were superfluous, rendering them dispensable targets for the Vatican's public image

---

[29] BAV Barb. lat. 6422, *Avvisi di Roma*, 24 February 1680, f. 104: "Intervenne in queste opere musicali la Regina [Christine of Sweden] quasi ogni sera, e perche non vuole il Papa che si paghi niente, non manca di folla alle porte, ove fanno buona raccolta i borsaroli, tagliando le borse, non però quelle doneriano a molti zerbini."

[30] "Si recitino quantità di comedie con innumerabili festini, ma essendosi penetrato d'esser stati venduti alcuni bolettini si sono carcerati li curiosi compratori, e gli avidi venditeri de mede[si] mi," from the *Avvisi Marescotti*, 28 February 1699, in Gloria Staffieri, *Colligite fragmenta. La vita musicale romana negli 'Avvisi Marescotti' (1683-1707)* (Lucca: LIM, 1990), 137-38.

[31] ASV Segr. di Stato, vol. 46, *Avvisi di Roma*, 26 December 1682, ff. 429v-430: "Pochi furno giovedì sera i cardinali, che si trovono alla colatione in Palazzo; e fosse perche era molto scarsa la tavola, ma Sua Santità ha voluto, che questo serva ad'essempio, e non per sparmio."

[32] Renata Ago, "Hegemony over the Social Scene and Zealous Popes," 240.

program? Considered as a campaign against the public more than the private stage, the problem of the Church and Stage enters another area, the temporal-civil control of theater zones.

Sifting through and attempting to categorize such scattered notices about the Roman stage lead to a conclusion that the problem of the theater in Rome lay not so much in the Vatican's spiritual duty to uphold morals but rather in its temporal responsibility to govern the city, which lay in the hands of the *Governatore*, appointed by the pope. He and the city police, the *sbirri*, were responsible for public order, a concern of particular importance during the theatrical and carnival season. New edicts and prohibitions were issued every year during carnival, and although modern historians prefer juicy events to recount, all of the writers of Avvisi and presumably every Roman welcomed a "quiet carnival," one without serious accidents, altercations, or upheavals. The Governor's prohibitions in 1602 were so numerous—including an injunction against throwing eggs—that one had to be very careful not to commit an infraction unwittingly. In 1619 the prohibitions, in effect for all of carnival and eighteen days thereafter, banned "carrying any sort of arms after the Ave Maria."[33] Such ordinances were designed to avoid the potential violence caused by tempers crossed due to the special license of carnival (so romanticized by some later historians). Seventeenth-century pride and the sword ready to defend it are well and widely recognized. In 1625, to give only one characteristic example here, during a rite for a woman becoming a nun, Duke Caetani invited the young Prince of Venosa and the Duke of Selci to a comedy at the palace of the Marquis Olgiati, as they were standing apart in the church. Prior Aldobrandino mocked Caetani for consorting with such youngsters. Insulted, Caetani provoked the prior into accepting the challenge of a duel. A bloody end was avoided by physical restraint on the part of some gentlemen in the household of Cardinal Maurizio of Savoy, as well as verbal pacification by Barbarini, the pope's nepew, who had to leave the rite to quell the incident.[34] The attempts of governments to control similarly hotheaded nobles only serve to show how

---

[33] BAV Urb. lat. 1087, *Avvisi di Roma* (di Bartolomeo Dardano), 6 February 1619, f. 56v: "Lunedì mattina furno publicati li soliti bandi delle maschere, corso de' palij, et simili trattenimenti del carnevale che cominciorno il medesimo giorno doppo pranzo con grandissima quiete, sendo in particolare per tutto questo carnevale et 18 [15?] giorni dopo prohibito il portare qualsivoglia sorte d'armi sonata l'Avemaria, sendo sospese et rivocate per detto tempo qualsivoglia sorte di licenze." For a brief list of edicts culled from Avvisi from 1683 to 1707, see Staffieri, *Colligite fragmenta*, Scheda 8 "Editti o disposizioni contro la musica," 207-8.

[34] BAV Urb. lat. 1095, *Avvisi dell'anno 1625*, 8 February 1625, ff. 79v-80: "Mentre giovedì sera si vestiva monaca nella chiesa di Santa Lucia in Selice [sic] la figliuola del signor Ottavio Costa, stavano in disparte discorrendo in un circolo alquanti signori titolati et havendo il duca Caetano invitato per la sera a sentir una comedia in casa del marchese Olgiati, il principe di Venosa et il duca di Selci, figliuolo del duca di Ceri, il priore Aldobrandino, motteggiando, punse il duca Caetano, ch'andasse con quei giovanotti, et il Duca rispondendogli se diceva da vero, o pur burlasse; et egli affermando dirlo da vero, detto Duca lo disfidò a questione, et il Priore accettando la disfida uscì di chiesa. Ma il Duca fu ritenuto da alcuni gentilhuomini del cardinal di Savoia. Il che arrivato all'orecchie del signor cardinal [Francesco] Barberino, che si trovava in chiesa a quella cerimonia, subito corse al rumore, e con la sua autorità li fece repacificar' insieme."

serious the problem seemed. Two incidents outside of Rome illustrate municipal responses. Insulted by a man who only bowed his head without removing his cap, the Marchese Serra once lashed out and struck the hat off his head, striking the man. The Genoese authorities imprisoned the marchese.[35] In the years before the public theaters, this kind of incident could arise in the collegiate theaters. In 1608 at the Jesuit college in Milan, feeling impeded and half crushed by the crowd of people, the Marchese Sfrondato drew his dagger to clear space for himself. We might consider this typically arrogant behavior from a seventeenth-century cavalier. The nub of the incident, however, reveals the expectations of the Spanish governor. The "secret police" immediately jumped on the haughty marchese, with pistols drawn. Thus was it discovered that twenty detectives were among the crowd, and "fu sturbata la festa, et dimessa tutto."[36] In addition, swords were not the only arms carried in public. The *Avvisi* in 1676 noted that firearms were to be seen in public, carried by not only the nobility but also by "mascalzoni" (scoundrels).[37] At the public Teatro Capranica in Rome in 1681,[38] two notaries and judges were posted in order to turn any incipient fight into a paper dispute. Nevertheless, an argument arose between a Capranica and a Gabrielli in which a third nobleman, who tried to separate them, was wounded in the leg and hand.

Year after year, the edicts remind us that social behavior in the public theaters had the potential tensions of the dance at the high-school gym in *West Side Story*, except that the noted trouble-makers were the upper, not the lower, classes.

---

[35] BAV Urb. lat. 1098, *Avvisi dell'anno* 1628, 12 January 1628, f. 22: "... che in Genova era stato carcerato il marchese Serra per havere la mano percosso uno in testa, et fattoli cadere il cappello con alcune parole ingiuriose, perche l'haveva solamente salutato con abbassarsi il capo senz'essersi scoperto."

[36] Reported as news from Milan in BAV Urb. lat. 1076, *Avvisi di Roma*, 23 February 1608, f. 126v.

[37] BAV Barb. lat. 6381, *Avvisi di Roma*, 22 February 1676, f. 125v-26: "La metropoli di Roma è convertita nella città di Bologna, mentre si vedono publicamente portare l'armi da fuoco non meno dalla nobiltà ordinaria, che dalli mascalzoni, indizio manifesto della poca stima della giustizia. Similmente nel Corso per la poca autorità de' sbirri, si sono mascherate tutte sorte di donne, e sono mede[si]mamente comparse le notti intiere ne' festini fatti in gran numero con rancore di quelli, che avevano lodato il divieto fatto delle publiche opere del teatro per veder recitare le donne, e scorgere il lusso, e la sfacciataggine, et il disordine di esse, che hanno eccitato tanto bollore nella romana gioventù. Si crede, che l'opere sudette del publico teatro non conceduto quest'anno, debbano in quest'altro rifarsi al certo, mentre gl'inconvenienti succeduti nell'opere private sono stati insoffribili alle persone, che hanno operato, et imparticolare [sic] alli Bernini, li quali dovendo ogni volta volevano far recitare la loro opera musicale, dare i palchetti al terzo, e quarto principe, sì come alle principesse, e dare i bolettini dimandatili, risolsero finalmente sotto il pretesto di malatie ne i recitanti di terminare la funzione con molte inimicizie."

[38] A summary of research resources for this family-run theater (for which, nevertheless, boxes had to be paid for) is John Rosselli, "I teatri di dipendenza della famiglia Capranica," in *La musica a Roma attraverso le fonti d'archivio*, 177-82. More recent than Luigia Cannizzo, "Vent'anni di storia di un teatro romano: Il Capranica (1678-1698)," in *Il libro di teatro*. Annali del Dipartimento Musica e Spettacolo dell'Università di Roma, 1990, Roberto Ciancarelli, ed. (Rome: Bulzoni Editore, 1991), 31-46, is Natuzzi, *Il teatro Capranica* cited in note 10 above. Natuzzi includes a chronological catalogue of works performed at the Capranica from 1679 to 1881, with transcriptions of printed dedications and other front matter in the libretti (for seventeenth-century productions, see 104-30).

1653: Since a company of outside comedians have begun to stage their plays in a room in Strada Giulia, Monsignor Illustrissimo the Governor has given out a public edict to avoid the disorders that could occur and has declared that no person of any rank may carry in or bear on his person arms of any kind whatsoever, except a plain sword, and that "bad women" cannot enter.[39]

1660: The Governor has published an edict which gives out the order of Our Lord to both players and spectators, as well as to coachmen of all conditions, that under pain of punishment, no other arms may be brought into locations where comedies are performed, except the sword, and no disturbances or obstructions are to occur around or inside these areas.[40]

1667: On the order of ... Governor Borromeo, an edict has been published with heavy penalties to players and spectators who cause disturbances and problems in the theater for public comedies.[41]

Aside from the dangers of personal disputes, political factions contributed to the governor's task. Every change in the balance of the influence of France and the rule of Spain in the Italian peninsula was reflected in the contest between their respective allies and supporters in Rome. In 1673 the trumpeters of the French ambassador skirmished with the servants of the Cardinal "Lantgravio," leaving two dead.[42] This hostility often reached the theaters. Already mentioned was a complaint made to the pope by the Cardinal de Retz in 1666, asking for punishment for "some actors for having done a piece that mocked France."[43] In 1672, the visiting Bishop of Laon asked the Sacred Palace to have a French air removed from an intermedio to the opera *La prosperità di Seiano*, staged at the Tor

[39] *I-Rli* MS 1752, *Avvisi di Roma*, 18 January 1653, f. 14r-v: "Havendo una compania de' comici forastieri cominciato a rappresentare le loro opere in una stanza in Strada Giulio [sic], questo Monsignor Illustrissimo Governatore per ovviare alli disordini che vi potess[er]o nascere, ha con publico bando ordinato, e prohibito che non si possi da qualsisia persona portare né tenere in essa armi di sorte alcuna eccettuato la semplice spada, [e] che non vi possino andar donne di malavita."

[40] ASV Segr. di Stato, vol. 109, *Avvisi di Roma*, 17 January 1660, f. 14: "Da questo Monsignor Illustrissimo Governatore è stato publicato bando col quale anco d'ordine di Nostro Signore commanda tanto alli comedianti, quanto agl'ascoltanti, come anco a cocchieri di qualsivoglia conditione, che sotto gravi pene non portino ne' luoghi, ove si fanno comedie altr'armi, che la spada, e non diano all'intorno, o dentro d'essi alcun disturbo, o impedimento."

[41] BAV Barb. lat. 6368, *Avvisi di Roma*, 15 January 1667, f. 544: "D'ordine di questo Monsignore Illustrissimo Governatore Borromeo è stato publicato bando con gravi pene ai comici et uditori che cagioneranno disturbi et inconvenienti nel teatro della comedia publica che si cominciò a rappresentare da lunedì sera per divertimento e passatempo della città."

[42] Reported in BAV, Barb. lat. 6376, *Avvisi di diversi luoghi*, Roma, 14 January 1673, f. 336: "Tra li trombetti di quest'Ambasciatore francese, et alcuni servitori dell'Eminentissimo Lantgravio vennero in un incontro a contesa, di modo che quelli ne uccisero uno di questi." Em.mo Lantgravio or the "cardinal d'Assia" was Friedrich, Landgrav von Hessen-Darmstadt (elev. 1652; in 1637 he had been the dedicatee of the Barberini opera *Chi soffre speri*).

[43] BAV Barb. lat. 3524, *Nouvelles de Paris*, 16 March 1666, f. 40: "On ecrit de Rome que le Pape qui est tousjours un peu indisposé a faict punir quelques comediens pour avoir joué une piece à la risée de la France, sur les plaintes que le Cardinal de Retz en fit à S. S[antité]."

di Nona. The *Avvisi* noted, "There are trouble-makers who are urging a boycott of the comedies to hang this disturbance onto the French."[44] In other words, protest could easily backfire. A protest could cause a crackdown, which could, in turn, direct sentiment against the protestor. In 1697—our focal year—the nephew of the Commissioner of Arms was wounded at the Teatro Capranica in an incident involving a slave of the Polish legate. The *primo cavaliere* of the Imperial ambassador was later killed in the same theater by three local shopkeepers. In response, the city immediately closed down *both* public opera houses, the Capranica (where the incidents had occurred), as well as the Tor di Nona. The Imperial ambassador, however, had the Capranica reopened so that the closing of the theaters would not excite more hostile feelings against the Empire. The subsequent destruction of the Tor di Nona, as related by Cametti, was urged by the Congregation for Ecclesiastical Reform. The *Avvisi* mention that both opera houses were accused of bad moral example and suggestive acting, but they stress the death of the Austrian knight (at the hand of commoners) as the real trouble. The Capranica could not be destroyed, because it was located in a private building.

Why were the theaters so often the site of such disturbances, or disorder, when blows and challenges were a commonplace of seventeenth-century life? The answers lie in the nobility's elaborate code of social behavior, which they jealously observed, and in their arrogance of privilege, which often disregarded the municipal government. This contradiction surfaced in the theater, because the nobles' code did not adequately cover personal action in a non-select assembly. That is, not tradition, written constitution, or rules of hospitality could completely control behavior in a venue like the public theater. Most other types of public appearance were predicated on guidelines for behavior. Ceremonies in Church were strictly ordered and controlled by diplomatic protocol. Placement in both ecclesiastical and civil processions were worked out, discussed, and announced in advance. Public games, such as jousts, were presented following artificial formalities of chivalry. Nobles who stood together on palace balconies to watch carnival parades were bound by the rules of hospitality, and were, to begin with, judiciously invited by their host. An anecdote from a 1686 *avviso* illustrates both the problems caused by admission by "ticket" alone and the code of hospitality in action. A monk gave his *bollettino* for a comedy to a gardener *(ortolano)* in exchange for a few vegetables.[45] The gardener was admitted to the Palazzo Colonna, rough as his appearance was. When the Contestabile Colonna was about to throw him out but discovered how the poor man had obtained his *bollettino,* he laughingly reseated him in a place apart from, but in full view of, the noble guests, so that they would not scorn him.

Codes for behavior even covered chance encounters on the streets, either on horseback or in carriages. In 1675, the Imperial, Spanish, French, and Venetian ambassadors systematically mortified Cardinal nephew Altieri—for example, by

---

[44] *I-MOe* Archivio di Stato, *Carteggio Caprara,* 27 January 1672, quoted in Cametti, *Il Teatro Tor di Nona,* 334.

[45] From the *Avvisi Marescotti* for 23 February 1686, Doc. 37 in Staffieri, *Colligite fragmenta,* 67.

drawing their carriage curtains when encountering his carriage. The scandal caused even ordinary people to gather in the streets just to observe the snubs.[46] The values of the social code are apparent in the deliberations of constitutionally organized entities, for example, the sessions of the Cappella Sistina, whose members all had regular contact with the nobility. One is struck by the punctiliousness and the great satisfaction with which decisions were reached and disputes were settled, within the framework of and with constant recourse to constitutional principles. There is consciousness of civility and pride in it, even though to us the proceedings may seem tortuous or bureaucratic to the point of absurdity. The century's frequent recourse to lawsuits is another sign of the triumph of code over force.

Norms for courteous or "civilized" behavior at a public event seem not so rigid. From early in the century comes an anecdote from the performance of a play at the French embassy in Rome.

> A play was given at the French embassy, but it would be better to say that one was supposed to be performed, because those French nobles made so much noise that it was not possible to understand anything, even though the ambassador himself rose several times and begged everyone to be silent, in the end *ordering* them in the name of His Majesty (but completely in vain), and thus the *festa* went cold.[47]

In 1671, Queen Christina and the Contestabilessa Maria Mancini Colonna held up the curtain at the Tor di Nona by arriving late and were whistled at when they entered. (Four wretches suffered later.)[48] In 1694, the sons of Duke Sforza tried to force the doors of the Teatro della Pace, in order to see the rehearsals of the opera *Roderico.*[49] Here is a description of another incident from 1680:

> While the show was going on at the Teatro al Fico, there arose a great disagreement between Cavalier Vaini and the Governor's police. As young men will, Vaini and some other lords were making a commotion. They were yelled at twice by the corporal, who was down below, but he finally went up to the box with the whole cohort. And because Vaini threw a lantern in his face, the policeman took his sword from him and bound him; and they would have taken him to prison, if the Governor hadn't ordered him free on bail.[50]

---

[46] The public behavior reflected diplomatic differences with the cardinal nephew; see Barb. lat. 6380 *Avvisi di Roma,* for the months of March and April, 1675, ff. 40-113 passim, esp. for 16 March.

[47] BAV Urb. lat. 1074, *Avvisi di Roma,* 8 February 1606, f. 50: "Dall'Ambasciata di Francia dove la domenica si recitò una comedia, ma era meglio dir si doveva recitare, perché quelli nobili francesi fecero tanto rumore, che non se ne potè intender mai niente, nonostante che l'Ambasciatore stesso si levasse più volte et pregasse tutt'a star quiete, et in fine ordinandolo anco loro (ma il tutto in vano) per parte di Sua Maestà, e così la festa andò molto fredda."

[48] Recounted in Cametti, *Il Teatro Tor di Nona,* 2: 329.

[49] ASV Segr. di Stato, vol. 57, *Avvisi di Roma,* 23 January 1694, f. 34v: "Sono stati sequestrati in casa li figli del duca Sforza per haver voluto sforzar il Teatro della Pace per veder la prova dell'opera."

[50] BAV Barb. lat. 6422, *Avvisi di Roma,* 10 February 1680, ff. 69v, 74: "Mentre se ne recitava una nel Teatro al Fico, vi nacque un gran bisbiglio tra il cavalier Vaini e li sbirri di monsignor Governatore.

In addition to such rudeness and violence, there was constant rancor among the nobles for the allocation and borrowing of theater boxes and for rights and precedence at the entrance, amidst the chaos of carriages and entourages.

> This evening the Teatro Tor di Nona opens with the first performance, and tomorrow night, the Capranica will open, whenever the problem of the boxes *(palchetti)* is settled…, because of which, the Governor rightly refuses to give the license for the theater, until the princes' ministers can be satisfied…. There was a controversy over the second [theater], as the Imperial Ambassador wanted another box, and Cardinal Fourbin also wanted one facing the stage; so just like that, it was necessary to take down the balustrade and to make the theater square, where before it was round.[51]

In 1676, the Bernini brothers cancelled a private opera production, with the excuse that the performers were ill, rather than deal with requests for presumably free admission from this and that prince and princess (see note 37). Incidents in public theaters could quickly develop into serious problems, whereas in a private context they would have been more readily settled by instant recourse to the authority of the host (remember the Contestabile Colonna and the unexpected gardener). Two more examples should suffice. In 1698, after the opera *Camilla* at the Capranica, the carriage of Count Capizucchi caught against that of the Marquis Serlupi, and

---

Il suddetto Vaini con altri signori facevono all'usanza de' giovani un poco di chiazzo, furono sgridati due volte ad alta voce da un cap[ora]le de' sbirri, che stava da basso, ma finalmente salì al palchetto con tutta la sbiraglia; e perché il Vaini gli diede la lanterna nel viso, lo sbirro li fece levar la spada, e solennemente ligarlo, e l'haverebbe condotto [in] prigione se non veniva ordine dal Governatore di lasciarlo con sicurtà…. (f. 74): Detto Vaini è stato sequestrato in casa, con sicurtà di 2 mila scudi, per doversi rappresentare." Another report of the Vaini incident is in Alessandro Ademollo, *I teatri di Roma nel secolo decimosettimo* (Rome, 1888; repr. Bologna: Forni Editori, 1969), p. 161, from an unidentified document, likely *Avvisi* in *I-Fas*. (This is the same Vaini who created a well-known scandal nine years later entering the rooms of La Giorgina, one of Christine of Sweden's singers.) Another incident in 1680 began with a scuffle at the opera between the pages of two noblewomen; it continued in the courtyard another day, when the opera was performed privately at the residence of Queen Christine of Sweden. She had them beaten and thrown out; as a result, both sets of pages were released from their respective households (10 February, Barb. lat. 6422, f. 72).

[51] BAV Fondo Ottoboniani latini MS 3358, *Avvisi di Roma*, 3 and 10 January 1693, ff. 2v, 4v: "Questa sera s'apre il Teatro in Torre di Nona con la prima recita, e dimani sera s'aprirà quello di Capranica quando per altro s'accordino le differenze de' palchetti [between the Imperial Ambassador and Cardinal Fourbin], …onde con ragione monsignor Governatore non vuole dar licenza per tal teatro, se prima non siano stati contenti li ministri de' principi…. (4v) Si sono già sentite le prime due opere in musica ne' teatri di Tor di Nona, e di Capranica: nel primo recitano tutti maestri, e nella seconda tutti scolari, fra questi però vi sono 4 voci superiori a quell'altre. In quella poi macchine, balletti, scene, e comparse assai cattive, et in questa assai buone, ma l'orchestra assai ordinaria, dove quella è perfetta. Vi fu contradittione per il secondo, stante che l'Ambasciatore Cesareo voleva altro palchetto, et il cardinal Fourbino lo voleva anch'egli in faccia, onde all'improvviso bisognò gettar a terra il parapetto, e ridur in quadro il teatro, dove prima era circolare." The operas were *Il Seleuco* (Venice 1691) by Carlo Fr. Pollarolo, rev. by Bernardo Pasquini, and a version of *Il Vespasiano* (Venice 1678) that probably reflected revisions made to Pallavicino's original score by Bernardo Sabadini, Pietro Porfirii and an unknown Roman composer (cf. Staffieri, *Colligite fragmenta*, 109, notes 76-77, and Franchi 1693/2 and 1693/5; the various composers' interventions worked out by Lowell Lindgren, private communication).

Serlupi beat Capizucchi's coachman. Capizucchi waited a day for an apology, which did not come. So he sent his men to Serlupi's, to beat up *his* coachman. Capizucchi then waited for the challenge. This argument escalated up to the College of Cardinals, and the pope exacted a huge fine for every day that passed without a settlement; but in the end, Serlupi escaped to Modena.[52] More amusing is an incident from 1680 in which Filippo Acciaiuoli, former impresario of the Tor di Nona, disagreed over a box at a theater with Monsignor Del Giudice. In retaliation, he stole all the costumes that he had loaned the company, which wasn't discovered until the curtain was about to go up before a full house. Everyone was sent home.[53]

These disturbances within and without the public theater—noble versus noble, noble versus commoner, noble versus municipal law—had nothing to do with anything that was happening on stage. And the Vatican's inability to control them had nothing to do with the growth of opera. The fact that the Tor di Nona remained closed from 1675 through 1689 did not succeed in suppressing opera. Under Innocent XI, when all Rome recognized his hostility to amusements, including the theater, the number of *private* productions increased tremendously. Noble families like the Colonna, Orsini, Barberini, Caffarelli, and Rospigliosi sustained the original Roman habit of private representations through the 1680s—and even after three public houses and other prose theaters were in full swing again after 1692. Indeed, less than six months after the pope had torn down the Tor di Nona, the Capranica was back in business with the customary two operas for the carnival season. In the end, the pope's violent action in 1697 worked against him. Cametti has summarized the report of how the pope:

> refuses to talk to the subscribers of the already demolished Teatro Tor di Nona, although he has elected a deputy congregation to hear them and give them satisfaction.... On Monday at the first meeting, it was resolved that the artisans, building supplies, iron-work, carpentry and painting not already paid for should be paid, and Thursday ... at the second meeting, it was resolved that His Holiness should pay over 40,000 *scudi* for the boxes already paid for (less the two years already run) and the unpaid artisans, as 20,000 were spent on the boxes, beyond the 14,000 invested by Count d'Alibert in the building and beyond the 16,000 [*sic*] for the price of a fief sold in Corsica, which was

---

[52] One account of this "rissa" is in *I-Rli* MS 1692, *Avvisi di Roma*, 25 January 1698, f. 9.

[53] Recounted in *I-Rvat Barb*. lat. 6422, *Avvisi di Roma* for February and March, 1680, esp. ff. 81-83, and elsewhere: "Domenica sera dovendosi fare l'operetta in musica al Teatro della Pace, essendo pieno di gente, e di molta nobiltà, con l'intervento della regina di Svetia, quando si volsero vestire i musici, trovorno mancargli gli habiti quali si erano stati imprestati dal cavalier [Filippo] Acciaioli e dal medesimo quella sera di nascosto portati via acciò non si recitasse l'opera per un disgusto havuto da Mons. [Del] Giudici a causa di un palchetto. Il disturbo fu grande, e mandato a cercare, e non trovato, convenne a tutti ritornarsene a casa; la regina si mostrò offesa, e dava segni di risentimento onde convenne al card.l [Niccolò] Acciaioli, con l'assistenza del sig.r card.l [Decio] Azzolino far il possibile per placarla, che vi condussero l'istessa sera il cavalier Acciaioli ad umiliarsi, e si recitò poi nella seguente sera" (Barb. lat. 6422, 17 February 1680, f. 83).

part of his wife's dowry. And the Holy Father, now having to pay out such a large sum, is now also complaining about the Reformers, who have invisibly ensnared him in such a great chain of expenses.[54]

This report confirms the suspicion that none of the popes after 1671 had considered the subscription theater as a fiscal entity, nor understood—or perhaps did not approve of—the extent that the nobles had invested money in the enterprise, in hopes of return revenue.[55] Litigation to settle damages real and future continued for years after the 1697 demolition of the fabric. Likewise, Innocent XI's earlier austerity measures had economic repercussions that could not be silenced by free tickets. In carnival of 1677, the *Avvisi* narrated

> Now that every artisan is out of work (due to the closing of the theaters), they spend their time singing songs. The other day, some clever ones made two ballads: "No skill is worth a nickle, and we are all in a pickle," and the other against the Governor: "Wages, wages! To start the day there's debts to pay." They sent two boys to sing these ditties at the doorway of the Palazzo Odescalchi, and then all through Rome, perhaps to show that the spirit of the desperate is in their shoes.[56]

---

[54] *I-Rli* MS 1691, *Avvisi di Roma*, 7 September 1697, f. 74: "Nostro Signore ricusato di voler parlare agl'interessati del già demolito Teatro di Torre di Nonna [sic], ma ha bensì eletto una Congregatione Deputata per sentirli, e sodisfarli, cioè monsignor Spinola viceregente, monsignor Giacometti auditore, monsignor Meola commissario, e monsignore Filipetti sottodataro, e lunedì tenutasi per la prima volta detta Congregatione, fu risoluto doversi pagare le maestranze, e materiali di fabrica, ferri, legname, pitture non peranco pagate; e giovedì tenutasi di nuovo essa Congregatione per la seconda volta fu risoluto dovere Nostro Signore pagare sopra 40 mila scudi di spese de' palchetti compratj, da quali se ne deve detrahere due annate di recita, e maestranze non pagate, dalle quali somme devono detrahersi le partite incerte, che si suppongono sodisfatte, havendosi speso più di 20 mila scudi nei comprati palchetti, oltre li 14 mila, e più, che ha presi ad interesse il conte d'Aribert per detta fabrica, oltre li 16 mila d'uno prezzo d'un feudo venduto in Corsica, che era della dote di sua moglie; e Nostro Signore dovendo hora fare sborsare così grosse somme, strepita anco contro li zelanti, che l'hanno invisibilmente illaqueato in una così gran catena di spese, essendosi contro il gusto universale." Further sessions of the deputized congregation were reported on ff. 76 and 78v (Avvisi for 14 and 21 September). Cametti summarizes the parallel text from I-MOe Archivio di Stato, busta 72, in *Il Teatro Tor di Nona*, 1: 99; see also the *Avvisi Marescotti*, in Staffieri, *Colligite fragmenta*, 130-32.

[55] Ludovico Zorzi's characterization of Venetian society's economic grasp of the business of opera theaters contrasts with its marginal recognition in Rome (in "Venezia: la Repubblica a teatro," 242-46). Furthermore, rather than escalating differences over theater boxes to international diplomatic crises, Venetians seem to have resorted excessively to the non-violent arena of the lawcourts; Zorzi notes that at least a third of surviving documents relating to Venetian theaters deal with suits over the ownership and leasing of boxes (244). He then, however, goes on to correlate the alteration (or decadence) of the genre in Venice to the heterogeneity of its audiences. Also invisible to the papacy was the economic opportunity the commercial theater presented to nobles with small or no estates, "senza feudo ma con il titolo in tasca," as described and discussed in "La mercatura teatrale e le corti," chap. 3, §3 in Siro Ferrone, *Attori, mercanti, corsari. La commedia dell'arte in Europa tra Cinque e Seicento* (Turin: Giulio Einaudi, 1993), 108-15, esp. 111. In the Roman scene, the Florentine Filippo Acciaiuoli could fit this profile.

[56] BAV Barb. lat. 6417, *Avvisi di Roma*, 13 February 1677, f. 92: "Già che si sta in otio ogni artista s'ingegna cantar la sua canzona; e l'altr'hieri certi ingegnosi, che fecero due historie, una intitolata

But these artisans were little people, not a Polish cardinal accusing a libretto of obscenity and the Imperial ambassador denying it—questioning the Pole's Italian, when in fact the issue was two murders. Not Cardinal Ottoboni and the Cardinal de Bouillon pleading for Marchese Serlupi against Cardinal Marescotti, when the issue was—a jolted carriage. Not the Governor himself contravening the pope's orders that women were not to perform, because the Baronessa del Nero (Anna Carusi) is a "lady of quality,"[57] or Cavalier Vaini flauntingly breaking his house arrest. The history of the theater in Rome is not simply a story of expansion under art-loving regimes and constriction under less liberal ones. The theaters were not microcosms of real life: Rome, theater of the world, was much less manageable than the theaters in it.

'Ogni arte più non vale, e per tutti la va male,' e l'altra contro Monsignor [Governatore], 'Paga, paga, ch'incominciar bisogna pagar le debiti,' mandorono due ragazzi a cantar queste rime sul portone del Palazzo Odescalchi; e poi per tutta Roma forse per dimostrare con queste, che l'animo de' disperati sta nelle scarpe."

[57] Recounted in Ademollo, *I teatri di Roma,* 156.

APPENDIX 1
Notizie della demolizione del Teatro di Tor di Nona
Vat. lat. 8518, ff. 99r-v

Nell'anno 1697 sul fine del mese di luglio N. Papa Innoc.o XII col consiglio della S. Congregaz.e della Riforma ordinò s'abbattesse il famoso Teatro di Tor di Nona, fabricato qualch'anni prima dal sig.r conte d'Alibert.

Li partegiani delle comedie citavano un passo di S. Tommaso, il quale dice, le comedie esser cose indifferenti, e l'istrioni non esser proibiti dalla legge divina, adducevano ancora l'esempio di S. Carlo, il quale si contentava di rivedere le comedie, che si dovevano rappresentare, scena per scena.

Altri eruditi dicevano esser proibiti generalmente tutti li spettacoli, come occasione prossima di peccare, e portavano un passo di Tacito, il quale dice, che benché fossero approvati a Roma le comedie, e li spettacoli, però fu biasimato dalli censori Pompeo per aver fatto fabricare un teatro stabile, il quale si mostrava a' forestieri, come una pietra di scandalo.

Ebbe il popolo di Roma amatore grandissimo de' spettacoli un grande disgusto di detta demolizione, e si fecero pasquinate contra quelli che furono stimati autori di simil risoluzione: La malignità s'attaccò principalmente a Monsig.r Fabroni, segretario della Congregaz.e de Propaganda [Fide], prelato stimato di costumi santissimi, e d'un zelo ardentissimo. Si fece alla sua occasione una medaglia, dove si rappresentava, da una parte la superba fabrica di Montecitorio, con quelle parole, *Pius Faber*, le quali si riferivano al pontefice Innocenzo XII, che l'aveva fatta fare; dall'altra parte della medaglia si vedeva quel magnifico teatro rovinato, et abbattuto col motto *Impius Fabronus*, volendo significare, che come il Papa (99v) aveva fabricato Montecitorio, questo qui avesse procurato la demolizione di quel teatro.

E benché la parola *Impius* non potesse cadere sulla demolizione del detto teatro, la quale più presto potrebbe dirsi *Pia che Empia*, nulladimeno si sosteneva esser bene posta la detta parola, dovendosi riferire all'empio intento di Monsig.r Fabroni, il quale si pretendeva volesse per quel mezzo buscare un cappello rosso.

Simili pasquinate sono usitatissime in Roma, ove le azioni più sante, sono alcune volte interpretate in sinistra parte da maligni, e critici, e dove non si perdona, nemeno a Sommi Pontefici, e perché si credeva da molti esser stato fatto detto teatro col chirografo e consenso sottoscritto dal Papa istesso furono adoperate le parole dal cap. X di Giobbe vers. viii per farne una 2.da pasquinata, e queste sono le parole *Manus tuae fecerunt me, et plasmaverunt me totum in circuitu; et sic repente praecipitas me.* Essendo distrutto quel teatro, e proibite le comedie, si tem evano disordini più grandi che quelli, che potevano accadere all'occasione de' detti teatri: et è cosa indubitata che le corteggiane altre volte così famose in questa città avevano da ridere per esser così ristabilite; essendo certo, che era tolto quello che ne' tempi destinati a' piaceri conduceva la gente altrove, e per questo si fece la seguente inscrizione.

Teatro ad ripam fluminis everso
spadonum turba profligata
meretricio contubernio, ac turpi questu restitutis
pellices romanae
inhonesti beneficij memores
clarissimis benefactoribus
posuere
Anno MDCXCVII.

Siena Cathedral and Its Castrati

Colleen Reardon

Although many accounts of the great singer Francesco Bernardi generally include a sentence explaining that the castrato's stage name "Senesino" derived from the city in which he was born, most tend to concentrate on his singing career after 1707.[1] The glossing over of the period between the singer's birth and his maturity is understandable for until now little information has come to light about his formative years. Although we will probably never have a truly detailed account of Bernardi's childhood, we can at very least affirm that his hometown gave him more than a nickname. As it turns out, Siena Cathedral played an important role in creating and training Bernardi and a number of other castrati, many of whom went on to have careers in opera. What follows is a brief overview of what is known about that tradition and the singers who emerged from it in the period between 1670 and 1775.[2]

The first castrato recorded in the Duomo's payment records was Girolamo Gulini, who joined the choir in 1595 and whose wonderful voice and long career were the stuff of legend in his native city.[3] By the 1630s, the choir had at least four adult castrati on the payroll and the presence of a number of castrato singers in

---

[1] This is not only true for older publications such as Patrick Barbier, *The World of the Castrati*, trans. Margaret Crosland (London: Souvenir Press, 1996), 85, 118, 120, 151, 175, 176, 182, 210; Angus Heriot, *The Castrati in Opera* (1956; repr. New York: Da Capo Press, 1974), 91-95; William C. Holmes, *Opera Observed: Views of a Florentine Impresario in the Early Eighteenth Century* (Chicago: University of Chicago Press, 1993), 131-50; and John Rosselli, *Singers of Italian Opera: The History of a Profession* (Cambridge: Cambridge University Press, 1992), 51, 84, 122, 123, 130; but also for newer studies, including Elisabetta Avanzati, "The Unpublished Senesino," *Handel and the Castrati*, catalogue of the exhibition, 29 March-1 October 2006 (London: Handel House Museum), 5-9, reprinted in *Handel*, ed. David Vickers (Surrey: Ashgate, 2011), 305-09; and David Vickers and Carlo Vitali, "Senesino," in *The Cambridge Handel Encyclopedia*, ed. Annette Landgraf and David Vickers (Cambridge: Cambridge University Press, 2009), 581-84.

[2] My heartfelt thanks to Frank D'Accone and to Stefano Moscadelli, who started me on this subject by bequeathing to me the documents they had found on their initial forays into the Archivio dell'Opera della Metropolitana di Siena (hereafter AOMS). I am also grateful to Susan Scott, who keeps the Siena Cathedral archive open so that scholars can consult its rich sources, to my husband, Nello Barbieri, without whose help as researcher, transcriber, and translator this article would not have been possible and to Beth Glixon, who made a number of helpful suggestions that improved the essay.

[3] Frank A. D'Accone, *The Civic Muse: Music and Musicians in Siena during the Middle Ages and the Renaissance* (Chicago: University of Chicago Press, 1997), 370; Colleen Reardon, *Agostino Agazzari and Music at Siena Cathedral, 1597-1641* (Oxford: Clarendon Press, 1993), 51-52; idem, *Holy Concord within Sacred Walls: Nuns and Music in Siena, 1575-1700* (Oxford: Oxford University Press, 2002), 36.

the soprano and alto sections was a regular feature of the ensemble right through much of the eighteenth century. Precisely when the cathedral administration began to subsidize the operation that turned boys into castrati is unknown. The earliest Sienese record I have been able to find comes not from the Duomo but from the Hospital of Santa Maria della Scala; it is dated 1623 and concerns an orphan there. The wording of the document indicates a certain squeamishness about the entire process; it suggests that the administration of the charitable organization was willing to pay for the operation only because the youngster was Jewish, for it specifies that the boy was to be baptized immediately after being castrated.[4]

By the last quarter of the seventeenth century, however, no such reticence was in evidence. Cathedral rectors openly entered into legal agreements with the fathers of talented boys.[5] (We can only speculate as to what the boys felt about the arrangement.) The contract prepared for Francesco Bernardi on 17 November 1699 is typical:

> Let it be stated for the present document that the magnificent Giuseppe Bernardi, a barber, has resolved to castrate his son Francesco, who is approximately twelve years old, because the boy has both the talent and the desire to advance in the profession of music and to serve our church. For that reason, the illustrious sir Alessandro Nini, our most worthy rector, out of pure generosity obligates himself to pay the usual expenses for the *norcino* from the funds of our Opera. He is doing so because he wishes to enhance and promote music for the greater honor of our church. And in exchange, said Giuseppe Bernardi promises that said Francesco, his son, will serve the same church as a musician and singer for the term of the next six years with the salary that he deserves and that our most illustrious rector thinks that he deserves. The rector will make sure that he receives instruction from the chapel master who is appointed during that time to serve our Opera. And if in the space of those six years, it happens that said Francesco decides to leave the church's employ of his own will or is fired for his own faults and failures, in that case said Giuseppe Bernardi is obligated to repay to the Opera half the salary that Francesco received from the aforementioned Opera and half of the fifty lire paid by the Opera to the *norcino* for the castration of said Francesco…. (Doc. 1)

The very same terms and conditions are present in a legal agreement drawn up for Andrea Martini three-quarters of a century later, on 11 October 1775; the cost of the operation was still fifty *lire*, the boy had to promise to sing in the cathedral choir for six years, and the penalty for leaving the service of the church earlier than this

---

[4] Reardon, "*Insegniar la zolfa ai gittatelli*: Music and Teaching at Santa Maria della Scala, Siena, during the Late Sixteenth and Early Seventeenth Centuries," in *Musica Franca: Essays in Honor of Frank A. D'Accone*, ed. Irene Alm, Alyson McLamore, and Colleen Reardon (Stuyvesant, New York: Pendragon, 1996), 133-34.

[5] Such contracts were not unusual; see Thomas Culley, "The Influence of the German College in Rome on Music in German-speaking Countries during the Sixteenth and Seventeenth Centuries (II)," *Analecta musicologica* 9 (1970): 43 (Doc. 15); Cristina Pampaloni, "Giovani castrati nell'Assisi del Settecento," *Musica/Realtà* 8 (1987): 133-54; and Rosselli, *Singers of Italian Opera*, 37-39.

was a repayment of half the cost of the operation as well as half the salary that the boy had earned during his tenure.[6] The prevailing cultural climate in the late eighteenth century appears, however, to have changed since Bernardi's time. The historical record shows that the cathedral's rectors had been disengaging themselves from direct involvement with the procedure itself for a number of years but that Martini presented too good an opportunity to pass up. Fortunately for them, two surgeons were able to confirm that the boy had an inflammation in his left testis and a hernia—perhaps epididymo-orchitis and an inguinal hernia—and thus they had a medical justification for proceeding with the radical "cure" of castration.[7]

Table 1 shows the boys named either in contracts such as the one given above or boys whose names appear in payments for the cost of the operation.[8] At first, the cathedral's financial officers disbursed money directly to the *norcino*, a general term for a man who specialized in this particular kind of surgery. In Siena, all the men who were engaged in this business actually did come from Norcia; Giovanni Domenico Tolesani of Poggio alla Croce, Norcia, was the surgeon of choice for the nineteen-year period from 1683 to 1702. But starting in 1708, officers made restitution to a male relative (generally the father, or in Francesco Gai's case, an uncle or grandfather) for already having had the boy castrated; this payment was generally disbursed the same day that the contract for the boy's services was drawn up. In this way, the rectors tried to put themselves at arm's length from the disfiguring, life-changing operation (although the change in *modus operandi* would later be recognized as a mere ploy).

None of the boys were members of the aristocracy. Giovanni Battista Tamburini, Giovanni Britii, and the Bernardi brothers were all born to barbers, but most of the boys came from modest families of tradesmen.[9] Giuseppe Lafini's father was a tailor, Matteo Gaetano Tozzi's was a shoemaker, and Giuseppe Rossi's was a baker. Agostino Perotti's father made his living as a stone grinder (*arrotatore di pietre*) and both Francesco Cioncolini and Girolamo Ghinelli were sons of

[6] AOMS 41, Contratti 1743-sec. XIX, Part III, document 94. The catalogue numbers used in this article are those from Stefano Moscadelli, *L'Archivio dell'Opera della Metropolitana di Siena: Inventario* (Munich: Bruckmann, 1995).

[7] AOMS 86, Carteggio (sec. XVIII), fascicle 10, unn. fol.: "Adì 27 settembre 1775. In Siena. Noi infrascritti chirurghi in questa città abbiamo visitato Andrea Martini in età d'anni quattordici e abbiamo trovato che il medesimo, oltre ad essere allentato [*sic*] ha un ernia acquosa dalla parte sinistra, ed in fede della verità, Io Muzio Rigacci mano propria; Io Antonio Bruni mano propria." The fact that the surgeon's exam was the excuse for going ahead with the operation is confirmed by the fact that Paolo Salulini, the chapel master, appended a note to the certificate confirming Martini's musical talent and the possibility of the boy becoming a good singer (see n. 18 below). For more on castration as a "cure" for injuries, see Rosselli, *Singers of Italian Opera*, 39; and Heriot, *The Castrati in Opera*, 38 n. 1.

[8] Other castrati who were members of the Siena Cathedral choir, among them singers who had careers on the operatic stage—Salvatore Mellini, Torquato Ricci, and Dionisio Buonfigli, for example—are not considered here because I was unable to find contracts or payments for their castration among extant cathedral records.

[9] Pampaloni, "Giovani castrati nell'Assisi," 135-36; Rosselli, *Singers of Italian Opera*, 39; Heriot, The *Castrati in Opera*, 38.

Table 1: Singers Named in Cathedral Contracts and/or Payments for Castration, 1673-1775

Name	Contract/ Payment	Age	Cathedral service	Operatic career
Graziani, Gio. Domenico	4/12/1673[1]		1671-90	1684-98
Graziani, Damiano	*6/15/1679*[2]			
Bigelli, Girolamo	*7/21/1679*[3]		1680-82	1690-96
Macchioni, Jacomo	*8/8/1679*[4]		1680-1750	
Britii, Giovanni Simone	*10/1/1683*[5]		1683-1717	1690
Tamburini, Gio. Battista	*12/6/1683*[6]	14	1683-95	1690-1719
Bartali, Matteo	*6/20/1687*[7]	12	1686-93; 1710-16	1690
Minelli, Giovanni Carlo	*11/9/1689*[8]		1689-c.1741	
Cioncolini, Francesco	7/15/1693[9]	15	1694-1761	
	8/6/1693[10]			
Bernardi, Giovanni Carlo	11/9/1696[11]	14	1695-1705; 1718-40	1700-34
	11/23/1696[12]			
Bernardi, Francesco	11/17/1699[13]	13	1695-1708; 1709	1700-40
	12/2/1699[14]			
Fontani, Domenico	6/16/1702	14	1704-07	1695-1715
	6/20/1702[15]			
Lafini, Giuseppe	6/11/1708[16]	12	1708-17	
Rossi, Giuseppe	10/9/1709[17]	13	1709-18	1718-50
Perotti, Agostino Gio. Ant.	9/27/1710[18]	11-12	1710-34	
Rapinzi, Antonio	5/30/1714[19]	13	1717-22	1723-29
Tozzi, Matteo Gaetano	6/1/1714[20]	11	1717-22	
Angeli, Giovanni Battista	*7/3/1725*[21]	13[22]	1726-33; c.1749-78	1732-46
Ghinelli, Girolamo	*6/27/1726*[23]		c.1728-34	
Angeli, Giuseppe	*5/23/1732*[24]		1733-40	1740-42
Ciaccheri, Francesco	*9/23/1740*[25]		c.1749-54	
Coli, Giovanni Lorenzo	4/30/1750[26]	9		1762-86
Savoi, Gaspare Gio. Batt.	4/5/1752[27]	14	c.1754-57	1758-92
Gai, Francesco	9/16/1760[28]	15	c.1763-87[29]	
Martini, Andrea	10/11/1775[30]	14	c.1775-79[31]	1781-1800

[1] AOMS 34, fol. 43r. This contract specifies an eight-year obligation, unlike later ones, which ask for six years' service.
[2] AOMS 633. fol. 83r.   [3] AOMS 633, fol. 84v.   [4] AOMS 633, fol. 85r.   [5] AOMS 633, fol. 119v.
[6] AOMS 633, fol. 119v.   [7] AOMS 633, fol. 144r.   [8] AOMS 713, doc. 23.   [9] AOMS 634, fol. 15r.
[10] AOMS 713, doc. 110.   [11] AOMS 634, fol. 41r.   [12] AOMS 714, doc. 161.   [13] AOMS 634, fol. 68r.
[14] AOMS 714, doc. 173.   [15] AOMS 714, doc. 81 preserves both the contract and the payment to the *norcino*.
[16] AOMS 634, fol. 146r; reimbursement to the father for the expense of the operation is in AOMS 715, doc. 96.
[17] AOMS 634, fol. 161r; reimbursement in AOMS 715, doc. 294.
[18] AOMS 634, fol. 170r; reimbursement in AOMS 715, doc. 78.
[19] AOMS 634, fols. 188r-v; reimbursement in AOMS 716, doc. 61.
[20] AOMS 634, fol. 188v-89r; reimbursement in AOMS 716, doc. 62.

woodworkers.[10] We do not know what trade Antonio Martini plied but we do know that he was not an educated man. In 1775, he had to bring a witness to sign the legal agreement for his son Andrea's castration as he himself could not write.[11] Three fathers—Lorenzo Graziani, Francesco Angeli, and Giuseppe Bernardi—sacrificed more than one child to the *norcino*'s blade. The gamble paid off differently for each family. Graziani probably lost a son in the process because the only cathedral record we have for his younger boy, Damiano, is the payment for his castration. The Angeli and Bernardi boys all survived, but as we shall see, their subsequent careers took greatly divergent paths.

Although the youngest child to undergo castration under cathedral sponsorship was nine years old, it seems to have been common in Siena to wait until the singers were at least twelve, if not in their teens. Giovanni Battista Tamburini, Giovanni Carlo Bernardi, Domenico Fontani, Gaspare Savoi, and Andrea Martini were apparently all fourteen years old when they were castrated and at least two boys were even older at the time they were consigned to the *norcino*.[12] In the absence of birth records, it is prudent to assume that the ages given in the contracts are rough estimates. For example, Francesco Gai was supposedly fifteen when he was castrated in 1760, but a list of chapel members from eight years later gives his age at that time as twenty.[13] Even if the latter document is correct, however, Gai was already twelve when he submitted to the operation that preserved his high

---

[10] Both contracts and payments for castration often record the trade of the boy's father.

[11] See Pampaloni, "Giovani castrati nell'Assisi," 136.

[12] This would seem to contradict Barbier, *World of the Castrati*, 12: "The operation was never performed before the age of seven and rarely after twelve."

[13] AOMS 87, Carteggio (1768-83), unn. fol.

Continuation of notes from Table 1:

[21] Reimbursement to father in AOMS 717, doc. 86.

[22] Angeli's approximate age at the time of castration can be calculated from a document of October 1768 listing members of the chapel and their ages; at this time, Angeli was 56 years old, making him about 13 in 1725. See AOMS 87, Carteggio (1768-83), unn. fol.

[23] AOMS 717, doc. 78. [24] AOMS 718, doc. 49. [25] AOMS 719, doc.4

[26] AOMS 41, Part III, doc. 28; reimbursement in AOMS 720, doc. 132.

[27] AOMS 41, Part III, doc. 37; reimbursement in AOMS 721, doc. 120.

[28] AOMS 41, Part III, doc. 60; reimbursement in AOMS 722, doc. 53.

[29] I did not find Francesco Gai in the salary registers I consulted, but a list of chapel members from October 1768 includes his name and credits him with five years service to the organization; see AOMS 87, Carteggio (1768-83), unn. fol. Gai's service as a soprano in the choir is mentioned in a document from 1774; see AOMS 135, fasc.10. He was still on the cathedral payroll in 1787, the probable year of his death (see no. 36 in the text).

[30] AOMS 41, Part III, doc. 94; reimbursement in AOMS 725, doc. 74.

[31] Martini never appears in the extant salary registers, but his two requests for pay rises allow us to trace his career at least partially. In the first petition, written sometime before 14 January 1778, Martini notes that he has been serving the Duomo for two and a half years; see AOMS 135, fasc. 46. The later petition is transcribed as Doc. 2 in this essay.

voice. On the other hand, some boys were not as young as the age stated in the agreement. Francesco Bernardi was described as "about twelve years old" when he went under the knife; he had actually just turned thirteen.[14]

The majority of the contracts or payments for castration predate any paid musical position for the boys at the cathedral. Extant salary registers show that only Domenico Graziani, Matteo Bartali, and the two Bernardi brothers were part of the choir before they were castrated.[15] The rectors did not, however, enter into any such agreements blindly, doubtless because they wanted to avoid the heart-breaking situation of discovering a boy to be without musical gifts only after he had been castrated.[16] As a result, they relied heavily on the advice of the chapel master who, in addition to his other duties, ran a music school in which Sienese boys with good voices received their first singing lessons.[17] In 1775, for example, the director Paolo Salulini wrote to the rector about Andrea Martini, who had been "attending the music school for about six months" and who showed all signs of "developing over time into a fine singer as he has a small but good voice."[18] The castration contracts for Giovanni Lorenzo Coli, Gaspare Savoi, Francesco Gai, and Andrea Martini specifically mention that the boys were already studying with the director of the cathedral's musical organization. In all the extant agreements, the *maestro di cappella* promised to devote time to instruct the boy or, in these four cases, to continue teaching the boy.

The rectors and chapel masters who made an investment in these boys did so with an eye to maintaining a high level of music making in the church,[19] all

[14] Avanzati cites the document that establishes Bernardi's date of birth as 31 October 1686; see "The unpublished Senesino," in *Handel*, ed. Vickers, 305.

[15] Girolamo Ghinelli, too, was on the cathedral payroll before his operation but in the capacity of a clerk. Salary registers from Siena Cathedral series ("Distribuzioni e salari") are fairly complete from 1578-1774. In the period between 1743-49, however, no musicians' salaries are listed, and after 1741, singers' names appear only if they received rations of wine and wheat. Information on the boys' tenures and salaries, cited in the text and in Table 1, come from the AOMS 1089 (1670-79), 1090 (1679-89), 1091 (1689-98), 1092 (1698-1708), 1093 (1708-17), 1094 (1717-23), 1095 (1723-29), 1096 (1729-35), 1097 (1735-41), 1098 (1741-55), and 1099 (1755-74).

[16] Charles Burney was not the only one to lament this unhappy state of affairs; see Heriot, *The Castrati in Opera*, 45-47. Pampaloni cites a specific case in which a young castrato was dismissed from a training program for "lack of talent"; see "Giovani castrati nell'Assisi," 143.

[17] The music school was of long standing (see D'Accone, *The Civic Muse*, 44-45 and Reardon, *Agostino Agazzari*, 42-45) and it continued to function during the period under consideration here. In 1680-81, for instance, church registers preserve payments for tuning and adjusting the harpsichord in the music school and for buying music books for the students there. See AOMS 633, fols. 92r, 96v, 101r.

[18] The contract for Martini, cited in Table 1, refers to the boy's studies with Salulini. AOMS 86, Carteggio (sec. XVIII), fascicle 10, unn. fol., contains Salulini's postscript to the surgeons' report on Martini's hernia (see n. 7 above): "Illustrissimo Signor Rettore. Adì primo ottobre, io Paolo Salulini, maestro di cappella dell'Opera, ho l'onore di rappresentare a Vostra Signora Illustrissima come il sopradetto Andrea Martini da circa a sei mesi in qua ha frequentato la scuola della musica e l'ho ritrovato tale che mostra e dà speranza di poter diventare a suo tempo un buon musico, avendo poca voce ma buona…"

[19] Rosselli, *Singers of Italian Opera*, 41: "Whether in an institution or not, these boys were being trained for careers as, in the first place, church singers."

the while recognizing that the most talented would eventually go on to careers on the stage. This explains the terms of the castration contract, which sought to impose financial penalties on boys who left the service of the cathedral before six years were up. Although the threat of having to repay a large sum of money may have certainly motivated families to insist that their sons fulfill the stipulations of the pact, access to private lessons may have encouraged many of the ambitious young singers to stay on and grow into well-rounded musicians at the cathedral's expense before cutting all ties and venturing out as free-lancers in the risky world of opera.

Certainly, the men who taught these youngsters were both talented and dedicated to their mission of producing singers with solid vocal technique and first-rate musicianship skills. Francesco Piochi, who was *maestro di cappella* at Siena Cathedral from 1646 until his death in March 1677, set the bar very high for all who followed him. His last three publications, books of *Ricercari* (issued 1671, 1673, 1675), contain untexted, two- and three-part contrapuntal singing exercises. The first two volumes were dedicated to his "dear disciples" in the cathedral music school and all three were meant to refine their ability to read at sight.[20] One of Piochi's pupils, Giuseppe Cini, who sang soprano and played violin in the ensemble during the 1670s and early 1680s and eventually assumed its directorship for a brief period in 1706 and 1707, composed a book of *Solfeggiamenti* for the youngsters in the church's training program. The twenty-four textless pieces, scored for nearly every combination of two voices, strive to expand singers' ranges, to put them at ease with passagework, and to familiarize them with different key signatures and various metric permutations.[21] Giuseppe Fabbrini, who directed the choir for all but three years between 1685 until his death in 1708, also wrote *Ricercari* that were probably in a similarly didactic vein. He simply may not have found the time to submit these (and indeed, most of his works) to the press because he was in such demand for his pedagogical skills. In addition to his duties at the cathedral, he taught nuns at three different convents and composed dramatic music for the theatrical productions performed by the young gentlemen enrolled in the local Jesuit institution of learning, the Collegio Tolomei.[22] In the later eighteenth century, the chapel masters Fausto

---

[20] The titles and dedications of all three of Piochi's volumes of *Ricercari* are reproduced in Gaetano Gaspari, *Catalogo della Biblioteca musicale G.B. Martini di Bologna* (1905; repr. Bologna: Forni, 1961), 4: 220-21. An excerpt from one of Piochi's exercises is published as Example 11.6 in Reardon, "*Cantando tutte insieme:* Training Girl Singers in Early Modern Sienese Convents," in *Young Choristers, 650-1700*, ed. Susan Boynton and Eric Rice (Woodbridge, UK: The Boydell Press, 2008), 213.

[21] For the complete title and dedication to the volume, see Gaspari, *Catalogo della Biblioteca musicale G.B. Martini di Bologna*, 1: 316-17. Excerpts from two of Cini's exercises are published as Examples 11.7 and 11.8 in Reardon, "*Cantando tutte insieme*: Training Girl Singers in Early Modern Sienese Convents," 214-15.

[22] See Fabio Bisogni, "Fabbrini, Giuseppe," *Grove Music Online, Oxford Music Online*, http://www. oxfordmusiconline.com/subscriber/article/grove/music/09162 (accessed 7 September 2010); Reardon, *Holy Concord within Sacred Walls*, 40-42; idem, "I monasteri femminili e la vita musicale a Siena, 1550-1700 circa," in *Produzione, circolazione e consumo: consuetudine e quotidianità della polifonia sacra nelle chiese monastiche e parrocchiali dal tardo medioevo alla fine degli antichi regimi*, ed. David Bryant and Elena Quaranta ([Bologna]: Il Mulino, 2006), 176, 179.

Frittelli and Paolo Salulini seem to have been able and inspiring teachers, although they, like Fabbrini, published no pedagogical works. Frittelli's pupils included Giovanni Battista Angeli, Giovanni Lorenzo Coli, and Gaspare Savoi[23] and it was Paolo Salulini who discovered and championed Andrea Martini.

Most of the boys who can be traced in the Duomo's payment records completed at least the stipulated six years of service, whether out of fear or lack of opportunity (see Table 1). One exception is Domenico Fontani, who already had a surprisingly mature operatic résumé for such a young boy when, in 1702, his stepfather signed the contract with Siena Cathedral.[24] By 1707, either Domenico or his stepfather might have thought it was worth repaying the £. 197 he would have owed to the church administration at that point for the chance to earn an operatic salary.[25] Adequate compensation may have encouraged the majority of the boys without such professional backgrounds to complete the terms of their contracts. In the late seventeenth century, the youngsters' talents and value to the organization were recognized with frequent salary raises. For example, it took only four years (1670-74) for Giovanni Domenico Graziani to go from earning two *lire* monthly to taking home fourteen *lire* every month. By 1678, Graziani's monthly payment had reached £. 20 month, making him one of the highest paid members of the choir.

The financial situation of the Cathedral was apparently less rosy in the late eighteenth century. Those who failed to fulfill the stipulations in the contract found themselves dealing with a long administrative memory. Gaspare Savoi, returning to his hometown sometime in 1778, was presented with a request to pay back the Duomo for half the cost of the operation and half of his salary because he had not fulfilled the last six months of the required six-year tenure. Savoi hastily wrote the appropriate petition to the Grand Duke of Tuscany asking for his debt to be forgiven and his request was just as quickly granted, some twenty-one years after he had left the choir to make his fortune as an operatic singer.[26] Around that

---

[23] The contracts cited in Table 1 specify that Coli and Savoi had been studying with Frittelli. Antonio Mazzeo cites Frittelli as Angeli's voice teacher; see *I tre "Senesini" musici ed altri cantanti evirati senesi* (Siena: Centro Studi per la Storia della Musica Senese, 1988), 47.

[24] For information on the operatic careers of Fontani and the other castrati listed in Table 1, I have relied primarily on the information transmitted in Claudio Sartori, *I libretti italiani a stampa dalle origini al 1800*, Vol. 6: Indici, II (Cuneo: Bertola e Locatelli, 1994), which lists singers alphabetically and cites all librettos known to Sartori in which those singers' names can be found. Some libretto collections were not adequately catalogued when Sartori was putting together this monumental project, so the citations are not always complete. It is quite possible that singers also performed in other venues where they were not identified in the librettos.

[25] Domenico Fontani was the stepson of Girolamo Lippi and although the castration contract identifies him by his birth name, the salary registers from the Duomo refer to him as "Domenico Lippi." He used his biological father's name, Fontani (or Fontana), in his operatic career, which began as early as 1695. Fontani was a "virtuoso" under the protection of Prince Ferdinando de' Medici; see Robert Lamar Weaver and Norma Wright Weaver, *A Chronology of Music in the Florentine Theater, 1590-1750*, Detroit Studies in Music Bibliography 38 (Detroit: Information Coordinators, 1978), 68.

[26] AOMS 124, Ordini e rescritti 2 (1777-88), fascicle 22, fols. 176r-v: "Altezza Reale, Gaspero Savoi professore di musica senese...espone come in età non anco giunta alla pubertà fu obbligato per

same time, the younger singer Andrea Martini, still in the Duomo's employ, needed to lobby the institution's administrators in order to receive better compensation. Early in 1778, for example, Martini informed the rector that notwithstanding the fact that Giovanni Angeli's recent death left Martini the first soprano in the choir, his salary was only ten *lire* a month. As he was rather poor, he needed a larger remuneration to continue to advance in his studies.[27] The rector raised his salary to fourteen *lire* a month and there it remained until early 1779, when Martini felt once again compelled to petition the rector. Here, he presented his case more forcefully, citing not only his poverty, but also his specific nutritional and educational needs as a singer, as well as the touchy subject of pay equity:

> Andrea Martini of Siena…puts before you the fact that for some years he has had the honor of serving the cathedral chapel as first soprano with the monthly salary of only fourteen *lire*. With this sum, he cannot pay all his necessary expenses, not only for food and special nourishment that his profession and his frail constitution demand but also for his harpsichord lessons, which are necessary for him to improve at his profession. And since the petitioner has no other income, and his parents, who are very poor, cannot take care of those expenses, he calls on the great generosity of Your Most Illustrious Lordship to deign to concede to the supplicant a larger monthly salary amounting to at least five *scudi*, which would be equal to the salary enjoyed by some other musicians who do not render greater service to the chapel than that provided by the supplicant… (Doc. 2)

On 6 January 1779, the rector responded to Martini's request by authorizing a salary of twenty-four *lire* a month for the singer.[28]

---

contratto a servire nella cantoria della Metropolitana con la condizione fattagli stipulare dal rettore dell'Opera di quel tempo di dover servire per corso d'anni sei, con l'onorario di lire due il mese e mancando a terminare il sestennio fosse obbligato rifondere all'Opera la metà dei salari percetti, al quale contratto accedé fideiussore Giuseppe Savoi padre del supplicante. Espone che doppo aver servito per anni cinque e mezzo circa gli convenne passare in Pisa, né gli fu permesso terminare residuali mesi sei, onde presentemente essendo tornato in Siena è stato richiesto dal rettore attuale a pagare la metà dei salari percetti nella somma di lire ottantasei: Perciò supplica la real clemenza voler restar servita di concedere all'oratore la condonazione…Io Gaspero Savoi supplico, mano propria." Following the petition is a note on fol. 177r that the request has been approved, with the date 30 November 1778.

[27] AOMS 135, Affari diversi 1 (1770-88), fascicle 49, Aumenti di salari a' diversi musici: "Illustrissimo signor rettore, Andrea Martini di questa città di Siena, servitore umilissimo di Vostra Signoria Illustrissima reverentemente le rappresenta come per la morte accaduta ultimamente del signor Giovanni Angioli è restato egli primo soprano della cappella di questa Metropolitana e che nonostante che sia in oggi il primo soprano di essa non retrae di provisione più della somma di lire dieci il mese, compresovi anche l'aumento ottenuto nel caduto mese di gennaio. L'espone inoltre umilmente ritrovarsi esso in istato assai povero e che perciò li sarebbe necessario per potersi tirare avanti con profitto e decoro, come ardentemente desidera, un maggiore sussidio o provisione….Io Andrea Martini supplico mano propria." A note follows in the rector's hand, dated 15 February 1778, authorizing a salary rise to £. 14 a month.

[28] AOMS 135, Affari diversi 1 (1770-88), fascicle 59. If 18th-century monetary practices followed those of the 17th century (1 *scudo* = 7 *lire*), then Martini received less than he requested.

Earlier in the eighteenth century, however, Siena Cathedral was still able to reward the young men handsomely without the stimulus of written petitions and this may have generated loyalty and perhaps even affection in return. The most famous case is offered by Francesco Bernardi, who began singing with the choir in December of 1695 at a salary of three *lire* a month. After his castration, which took place sometime in late November or early December of 1699, his salary immediately soared to ten *lire* a month. Bernardi continued to garner pay regular pay raises nearly every year until late 1703, when his salary settled in at £. 20 monthly. In mid-1707, his compensation increased to £. 28 a month. Francesco continued to sing as a member of the organization right through August 1708, even as he began to perform on stage. He appears for the last time on the payroll for one month's service in March 1709. The Duomo administrators not only rewarded Francesco with an excellent stipend (by their own lights), they also gave him room to pursue a career in opera by permitting him to leave town during Carnival season.[29] Salary records show absences in January 1706, from November 1706 through February 1707, and from November 1707 through June 1708.[30] From 1708 on, the singer known as "Senesino" did not need to hang on to his day job at Siena Cathedral. He eventually took London by storm and, as is well known, inspired Georg Frideric Handel to write some of his finest music. We can now give credit to Giuseppe Fabbrini, the *maestro di cappella* at Siena Cathedral, for the years of vocal training that gave Bernardi such secure technique, thus assuring his success and longevity on the international operatic circuit.

Francesco Bernardi was not the only boy among those castrated at the cathedral's expense who managed to achieve fame. Giovanni Battista Tamburini sustained a long career as a *secondo uomo* in operas performed in Milan, Turin, Venice, Bologna, and Naples, not to mention his many appearances in the Marches and in his native province of Tuscany.[31] Gaspare Savoi—the singer who almost found himself in hot water for not fulfilling the terms of his cathedral contract— sang in most of the important centers in Italy during the years from 1758 to 1765 and, like Francesco Bernardi, worked extensively for more than a decade in London (1765-77). He had returned to Italy by 1779 where he continued to

[29] In this matter, Siena Cathedral seems to have been much less severe that, for example, San Francesco in Assisi, which forbade the castrati admitted to its school to perform in opera until they had reached the tenth year of their contract. See Pampaloni, "Giovani castrati nell'Assisi," 138. Newly discovered documents show, in fact, that both Bernardi brothers made their first appearance on the operatic stage in a Sienese production of 1700; see Reardon, "*Camilla* in Siena and Senesino's Début," *Studi musicali* (forthcoming).

[30] Payments to Francesco Bernardi, as well as his absences during specific months, are recorded in AOMS 1091, fols. 217 right, 247 right, 277 right; AOMS 1092, fols. 24 right, 57 right, 87 right, 119 right, 149 right, 179 right, 208 right, 268 right, 300 right; AOMS 1093, fol. 28 right.

[31] Tamburini's correspondence with his patron, Cardinal Francesco Maria de' Medici, is the subject of my article, "Launching the Career of a *secondo uomo* in Late Seventeenth-Century Italy" *Journal of Seventeenth-Century Music* (forthcoming).

perform in opera through 1792.[32] Andrea Martini, also nicknamed "Senesino," had a stellar career performing opera up and down the Italian peninsula from 1781 until at least 1800.[33]

Most of the boys listed in Table 1 did not, however, rise to such great heights. Ten of the young men castrated at the cathedral's expense seem to have dedicated their lives and careers to the institution. They either never sang in opera or they took one or two minor roles in dramatic works performed in their hometown.[34] Of these, Jacomo Macchioni and Francesco Cioncolini offer the most dramatic examples. After his castration in 1679, Macchioni began at the bottom rung of the choir hierarchy with a monthly salary of £. 2. It took him seventeen years to work his way up to earning £. 20 a month. He had been a member of the chapel for seventy years when he died in 1750. His colleague Cioncolini rose through the ranks faster but did not go as far. By September of 1702, only eight years after beginning his career with the choir, he was taking home £. 16, the highest salary he would ever earn. He faithfully discharged his duties as a soprano in the musical organization until his death in February 1761 at the age of eighty-three. Cioncolini owed money to the Duomo when he died, but the debt was forgiven because his heirs were so poor.[35] Francesco Gai likewise spent all his life singing at Siena Cathedral and apparently died on the job.[36]

Of the remaining castrati in Table 1, several were talented enough to have minor careers in opera or to make operatic performance at least one facet of their professional lives.[37] Domenico Fontani is a case in point, as is Giovanni Domenico Graziani who, like Fontani, went on to become one of the "virtuosi" of Prince Ferdinando of Florence. Graziani mounted the stage in operas at Pratolino as well as in Rome and in Naples during the 1680s and 1690s.[38] Girolamo Bigelli, after a very brief stint at the cathedral, entered the service of the Rospigliosi

---

[32] See Dennis Libby, "Savoi, Gaspero," in *The New Grove Dictionary of Opera*, edited by Stanley Sadie, *Grove Music Online, Oxford Music Online*, http://www.oxfordmusiconline.com/subscriber/article/grove/music/O006102 (accessed 7 September 2010); and Antonio Mazzeo, *I tre "Senesini" musici*, 51.

[33] See Heriot, *The Castrati in Opera*, 160-61; Mazzeo, *I tre "Senesini" musici*, 39-46. Martini appeared frequently in Florence during his career and entered the service of the Grand Duke by 1792; diarists' notes praising his Florentine performances in both opera and in private academies can be found in Weaver and Weaver, *A Chronology of Music in the Florentine Theater, 1751-1800* (Warren, Michigan: Harmonie Park Press, 1993), 445, 478, 506, 514, 530, 531, 574, 592, 594, 602, 616, 646, 672, 674, 808, 812.

[34] The production and patronage of dramatic musical works in Siena is the subject of my forthcoming book, *A "Sociable Moment": Sienese Opera Patronage and Performance, 1669-1733*.

[35] AOMS 1099, fol. 109 right.

[36] I do not know for certain when Gai died, but I do know that on 30 March 1787, he was described as "sick and incapable of writing" and that he authorized that his salary be assigned to Antonio Petroni. See AOMS 135, Affari diversi 1 (1770-88), fascicle 202.

[37] Most of the information in this and in following paragraphs comes from Sartori, *I libretti italiani*, with other sources cited when appropriate.

[38] See Weaver and Weaver, *A Chronology of Music in the Florentine Theater, 1590-1750*, 68; see also the Weavers' notes on the following productions: 1685[3], 1686[4], and 1698[5].

family.[39] Giuseppe Rossi can be traced throughout Italy from 1718 to 1750 and traveled as far as Brussels for at least one operatic performance. Giovanni Lorenzo Coli was popular on the Berlin stage from 1774 to 1786.

Less is known about Antonio Rapinzi, Giovanni Angeli, and Giuseppe Angeli, although documents suggest that fortune was only intermittently kind to the Angeli brothers. In a letter of 15 August 1772, Giuseppe, then in Florence, complained to his brother Giovanni in Siena about the fact that he had just received a letter from Giovanni with a note informing him that he was a creditor to his home town cathedral for three months provision of wine given to him back in 1740 (the long institutional memory again). Giuseppe protested that this could not be true, as he had left Siena on 12 July 1740 and if his memory served him after thirty-two years, he had never accepted wine from the cathedral. He furthermore alluded to problems within the family and expressed a desperate hope that divine providence would come to his aid (perhaps a veiled plea for his brother to lend a hand).[40] Giovanni responded to this note from his brother with one of his own to an administrative officer at Siena Cathedral, lamenting the fact that he had been charged with informing Giuseppe of the debt. "It would have been better if you had written my brother and left me in peace because I have enough sadness and melancholy in my life without adding new troubles." He ended the letter by informing the official, "Whether he pays up or does not, it does not concern me, because I know of no law that says a man is responsible for his brother."[41]

---

[39] Lowell E. Lindgren and Carl B. Schmidt, "A Collection of 137 Broadsides Concerning Theater in Late Seventeenth-Century Italy: An Annotated Catalogue," *Harvard Library Bulletin* 28 (1980): 188, 212, 213, 214.

[40] AOMS 135, Affari diversi 1 (1770-88), fascicle 35, (letter addressed to "Giovanni Battista Angeli, virtuoso di musica, Siena"): "Carissimo fratello. Firenze, questo dì 15 agosto 1772. Passando ieri dalla posta mi fu data una vostra scritta del dì 23 passato, nella quale trovo un curiosissimo biglietto mentre in esso vi sono cose che non possono essere. E in primo io non so di aver preso mai vino dall'operaio, né io né mio padre, che mi ricordi doppo 32 anni. In secondo luogo (e questo è più bella) io sono partito di Siena il dì 12 luglio 1740 e il biglietto mi fa debitore del dì 6 settembre 1740. Quasi due mesi doppo la mia partenza dunque si rileva che almeno per tutto settembre mi correva la provvisione e in questo caso vo creditore io di tre mesi di provvisione non avendo tirato la provvisione che di giugno 1740. Onde vedo che questo è uno sbaglio per le ragioni antedette, e basta. Io già so tutte le disgrazie di nostra casa, ma ancora le nostre non sono piccole e se Iddio per sua misericordia non provede, le cose vanno assai male. Salutate tutti ed a mia madre la santa benedizione. E resto di Vostra Signoria affezionatissimo fratello, Giuseppe Angeli."

[41] AOMS 135, Affari diversi 1 (1770-88), fascicle 35, "Molto illustre signore, signore padrone colendissimo. L'aver trasmesso nelle mani di Vostra Signoria la lettera di risposta di mio fratello Giuseppe, mi pare che da ciò doveva conoscere e la mia pronta obbedienza alle premure dell'illustrissimo signore rettore e altresì ch'io non volevo entrare mallevadore di questo debito. Onde ne sarebbe parso meglio che lei ne avesse scritto a mio fratello e lasciare in pace a me che non mi mancano altre tristezze e malinconie senza aggiungermene delle nuove. Circa poi a quello che mi dice che questo vino sia venuto in sua casa, li dirò che questa casa non ci è più e questo co[n]sta per rinunzia fattami fare da mio padre vivente, ed io non ho fatto acquisto di beni paterni. Oltre di ciò essendo un debito di così lungo tempo e di così tenue somma mi maraviglio come Vostra Signoria non ne abbi fatto mai parola con il medesimo mio fratello che si trattenne qui in Siena per alcuni giorni. Non mancherò di far sapere al medesimo i suoi sentimenti e dell'illustrissimo signor rettore. Ma poi se paga o se non paga io non vi voglio entrare, perché credo che non vi sia legge che il fratello sia obligato per il fratello. E pieno di stima mi dico di Vostra Signoria molto illustre devotissimo et obbligatissimo servitore Giovanni Angeli. Siena, di casa 28 agosto 1772."

Both Giuseppe and Giovanni had tried their hand at operatic careers. Giuseppe is named in two extant librettos from 1741 and 1742. Giovanni either was more talented or more adventurous than his brother, because after having mounted the stage in Pistoia (1732) and in Siena (1733), he departed for Lisbon on 22 May 1733, perhaps to take a role in one of the Italian operas mounted in the Portuguese capital.[42] Giovanni probably decided to return home shortly after 1742 when King João V's illness prompted a moratorium on all theatrical performances in Lisbon, for his name appears in cast lists for two Florentine productions during Carnival 1745-46.[43] These performances were probably Giovanni Angeli's last on the operatic stage. A few years later, he rejoined the Siena Cathedral choir and died on the job sometime in late 1777 or early 1778.[44] We can only imagine the tribulations, perhaps both professional and personal, that the brothers suffered and the incident or incidents that seem to have so soured Giovanni Angeli's relationship with his younger brother Giuseppe.

Senesino's brother, Giovanni Carlo Bernardi, experienced a longer period of success as an operatic singer than did his much younger colleagues the Angeli brothers. The older Bernardi's career took him to Palermo, Messina, Rome, and Venice. At some point, he was taken under the patronage of the Marchese de los Balbases, the Duke of Sesto, who seems to have inherited his father's role as an ardent patron of opera.[45] Even though the elder Bernardi was also known as "Senesino," he could not dream of competing with his younger brother Francesco. Unlike Giovanni Angeli, Giovanni Carlo Bernardi either had a more realistic idea about his talent or a greater affection for his native city because he decided to return to Siena Cathedral while he was still in some demand as a dramatic singer. From 1718 until at least 1733, he fulfilled his duties as a member of the choir and obtained leaves of absence to perform in opera. Giovanni Bernardi's swan song probably occurred in the 1734 Sienese production of *Semiramide riconosciuta*. After this performance, he settled into his job at the cathedral, where he died on 2 March 1740.[46] Documents that might shed some insight into the relationship between the Bernardi castrati have not yet surfaced.[47]

[42] The date of Angeli's departure is noted in AOMS 1096, fol. 192 left. For more about opera in Lisbon, see Manuel Carlos de Brito, *Opera in Portugal in the Eighteenth Century* (Cambridge: Cambridge University Press, 1989), 1-23.

[43] An account of Giovanni Angeli's life and career (largely undocumented) is in Mazzeo, *I tre "Senesini" musici*, 47-48.

[44] Andrea Martini mentioned the recent death of Giovanni Angeli in his first petition asking for a higher salary (see n. 27 above). Since the rector approved that petition in February 1778, it seems logical to assume that Angioli died within the dates given in the text.

[45] This was probably Ambrogio Gaetano Spinola, the fifth in his family to hold the title. The Marchese de los Balbases is named as Giovanni Carlo Bernardi's patron in the libretto for the opera *Semiramide riconosciuta* (Siena, 1734).

[46] For Giovanni Carlo's career at Siena Cathedral, see AOMS 1091-92; 1094-97. His death is recorded in AOMS 1097, fol. 231 left.

[47] Avanzati describes Francesco Bernardi's less-than-ideal relationships with his married brother Gaetano and with his nephew Giuseppe; see "The unpublished Senesino," in *Handel*, ed. Vickers, 306-08.

The long-established way of doing business so as to ensure soprano voices for the musical organization at Siena Cathedral came under high-level scrutiny in the late eighteenth century. A case involving a soprano singer in the choir prompted Grand Duke Pietro Leopoldo I to examine the church's policies and to lay down the law regarding its involvement in the process of castration:

> On this occasion His Most Serene Royal Highness understood that in the past the chapel masters had a policy of inducing boys to be castrated for the purpose of teaching them music and making them capable to serve the church; that the Opera paid them fifty *lire* for the operation; that the rectors hired them as members of the chapel with a monthly salary that increased in proportion to their skills and behavior; that in return the castrated boy (or one of his relatives on his behalf) formally obligated himself to serve the church for six years; and that if he were fired for his own failings or went to serve elsewhere before the end of the six-year period, he was to repay the Opera half of the fifty *lire* and half of all the salary received.
>
> Therefore the Royal Sovereign, with a decree of 26 [March 1778] recently ordered that such an abusive custom, censored by all laws, contrary to a good political system and shameful for a holy institution (which should have never authorized it) be abolished completely, and that the Opera not be involved at all in such abominable contracts for mutilation, much less employ its finances to such ends.
>
> His Royal Highness is also aware that the above-mentioned practice was abandoned many years ago and there is now a policy of not inducing children to be castrated; however, if the boys present themselves already mutilated, they are reimbursed fifty *lire* from the funds of the Opera and the Opera and the boys enter into agreements with the same conditions. That notwithstanding, [the sovereign] realizes that any time mutilated children are paid the same sum of money and are admitted to the service of the chapel with the same conditions, this boils down to manifest collusion; in substance the only difference is the one that the rectors managed to introduce in order to save face and distance the holy institution from such a monstrous practice. Therefore, in order to provide a better service to the church His Royal Highness has also ordered that in the future, at least when the position of first soprano becomes vacant, the practice of hiring children be abandoned, not only in the abusive form already abolished, but also in the other form which is still legal. The rectors of the Opera should instead think about hiring singers for the chapel who are already established in the profession and who cannot perform in theaters anymore, but are able to give the church a useful service. They should give them, if necessary, a higher salary than usual, as long as this does not negatively affect the finances of the holy institution.... (Doc. 3)

The strong language in the decree leaves no doubt that Pietro Leopoldo found castration repugnant. He framed the rectors' complicity in the practice as corrosive to good government in general and forbade the hiring of any castrated children (all the while paradoxically recognizing that it was still legal for a father to castrate his son). As for the problem of finding soprano voices for the choir, the grand duke could offer no better solution than to advise the administrators to do what they were already doing: to seek out former opera singers who could no longer sustain a career on the stage and to pay them off-scale compensation if necessary.[48] Apparently, it was fine for the organization to benefit from the musical services of a castrato only if it had not been involved in financing the operation, before or after the fact.

Andrea Martini was, then, the last boy castrated with the official blessing of Siena Cathedral's rector—not that many boys would have followed in Martini's footsteps even if Pietro Leopoldo had remained silent on the issue. The grand duke's official decree simply administered the *coup de grâce* to a practice that had already begun to decline, most likely because of changing social and cultural philosophies and rising economic tides, not to mention new musical tastes.[49] It is, however, a testament to the strength and depth of the musical tradition at Siena Cathedral that during the heyday of *opera seria* its training program turned out so many fine castrati, including one of the greatest singers ever to grace the operatic stage.

[48] See Rosselli, *Singers of Italian Opera*, 47.
[49] Ibid., 54-55, 130.

Appendix

Doc. 1: AOMS 634: Giornale H (1692-1714), fol. 68r [contract for castration of Francesco Bernardi].

Condizioni per l'assunzione di Francesco Bernardi.

Adì 17 novembre 1699.

Dichiarasi per la presente come il magnifico Giuseppe Bernardi barbiere, havendo resoluto di far castrare Francesco suo figlio d'anni 12 in circa per la disposi[zi]one e desiderio che il medesimo ha di tirarsi avanti nella professione della musica e servire alla nostra chiesa, di qui è che l'illustre signor Alessandro Nini nostro dignissimo rettore per sua mera liberalità s'obbliga di fare le spese solite del norcino delli denari della nostra Opera e tutto con il motivo che ha di accrescere e promuovere la musica per onorevolezza maggiore della nostra chiesa. Et all'incontro detto Giuseppe Bernardi promette che detto Francesco suo figlio servirà la medesima di musico e cantore per lo spatio d'anni sei prossimi futuri con quello stipendio che meritarà e parerà che meriti al detto nostro illustre signor rettore, cura del quale sarà sempre che sia instruito dal maestro di cappella che per li tempi servirà la nostra Opera. Et in caso che detto Francesco dentro lo spatio di detti sei anni spontaneamente lassasse il servitio o per suoi mancamenti e colpa fusse licentiato, in tal caso detto Giuseppe Bernardi si obbliga di restituire alla nostra Opera la metà di quello che detto Francesco suo figlio havesse percetto dalla medesima per suo salario e la metà delle lire cinquanta che si doveranno pagare dalla nostra Opera al norcino per la castratura di detto Francesco. Per le quali cose tutte e ciascheduna di esse osservare detto Giuseppe Bernardi obbliga se stesso, suoi eredi e beni presenti e futuri e beni dell'eredi, in forma etc., renuntiando etc., et in fede soscriverà la presente fatta da me Persio Landi scrittore dell'Opera d'ordine dell'illustre nostro signor rettore Nini.

Io Giuseppe Be[r]nardi affermo e m'obligho a q[u]anto sopra.

Doc. 2: AOMS 135: Affari diversi 1 (1770-1788), fascicle 59 [petition and salary rise for Andrea Martini].

Illustrissimo signore rettore,

Andrea Martini di Siena umilissimo servo di Vostra Signoria Illustrissima con il più umile ossequio le rappresenta come ha l'onore da qualche anno di servire nella cappella della Metropolitana in qualità di primo soprano col mensual salario di sole lire quattordici, con la quale somma non può supplire alle spese che necessariamente gli occorrono non solo per il vitto e sostentamento particolare ch'esige e la sua professione e la sua gracil complessione, ma ancora per la squola del cimbalo, necessaria per meglio riescire nella sua professione. E siccome l'oratore è mancante di qualunque altro assegnamento né possono i di lui genitori, che sono miserabili, supplire alle dette spese, supplica la bontà somma di Vostra Signoria Illustrissima volersi degnare di concedere al supplicante un maggiore mensuale stipendio almeno di cinque scudi, uguale a quello che gode qualche altro della cappella medesima che non presta ad essa un servizio maggiore di quello che vi presta il supplicante…

[Following is a note in rector Giovanni Borghesi's hand, dated 6 January 1779, authorizing a payment of twenty-four *lire* a month to Martini.]

Doc. 3: AOMS 124, Ordini e rescritti 2 (1777-1788), fasc. 20, document 2, fols. 162r-163v [orders issued by Grand Duke Pietro Leopoldo I to the Opera of Siena Cathedral regarding the hiring of sopranos for the choir].

...

In quest'occasione la Reale Altezza Serenissima ha potuto restare intesa che in passato dai maestri di cappella si stilava di disporre i fanciulli alla castrazione per istruirli nella musica e renderli idonei per il servizio della chiesa; che l'Opera pagava loro per le spese dell'operazione lire cinquanta ed i rettori gli ammettevano al servizio della cappella con una provvisione mensuale che si aumentava a proporzione dell'abilità e condotta; e che in corrispettività il fanciullo castrato o qualche suo parente si obbligava nelle forme di servire la chiesa per anni sei con dovere restituire all'Opera la metà delle lire cinquanta e di tutti i salari percetti nel caso che fosse stato licenziato per demeriti, o fosse passato ad altro servizio prima del compimento del sessennio.

Ha ordinato pertanto il Real Sovrano con rescritto de' 26 del caduto [marzo 1778] che un costume così abusivo, riprovato da tutte le leggi, contrario al buon sistema politico e vergognoso per un luogo pio che non avrebbe dovuto autorizzarlo, resti intieramente abolito, e che l'Opera non si mescoli in alcun conto in simili abominevoli trattati di mutilazione, e molto meno v'impieghi le sue rendite.

E sebbene sia Sua Altezza Reale egualmente informata che, da molti anni abbandonata l'accennata pratica, si stila non di disporre i fanciulli alla castrazione, ma se si presentano già mutilati si fanno rimborsare dalla cassa dell'Opera delle lire cinquanta e si stabiliscono con i medesimi le condizioni sopraccennate, ciò nonostante tutte le volte che ai mutilati si passa l'istessa somma e si ammettano al servizio della cappella con le stesse condizioni, apprende che l'affare si riduce ad una manifesta collusione e che in sostanza non vi è altra differenza che quella che si è procurato di mettervi, acciò resti apparentemente salva per la parte del luogo pio una pratica così mostruosa.

All'effetto perciò di provvedere al miglior servizio della chiesa ha parimente comandato la Reale Altezza Serenissima che in avvenire in occasione di vacanze almeno de' posti di primi soprani, tralasciata la pratica di eleggere dei ragazzi, non meno nella forma abusiva che resta abolita ma in altra ancora legittima, si facciano i rettori dell'Opera un pensiero di destinare per la cappella soggetti che già si siano acquistati un credito nella professione e che, non essendo più al caso di recitare ne' teatri, si trovino in quello di poter prestare un servizio utile alla chiesa, con fissarli, occorrendo, quella provvisione maggiore del solito che non possa fare un disappunto all'economia del luogo pio....

Plate 1: Engraving of Nancy Storace (London, 1791) by Jean Condé
after a painting by Samuel De Wilde (1751-1832)

Nancy Storace, Mozart's Susanna

Daniel Heartz

Anna Selina Storace, familiarly called Nancy, was born on 27 October 1765 in London, where, by coincidence, the Mozart family was then in residence. Her Italian father, Stefano Storace, was trained as a violinist at Naples in the 1730s and settled in Britain (first Dublin) before 1750. Finding many good violinists there he switched to double bass and quickly became one of its outstanding players, employed as such, among other places, at the King's Theatre in the Haymarket and London's pleasure gardens. He became director of music at Marylebone Gardens and in 1761 married Elisabeth Trussler, the owner's daughter. Their first child was the future composer Stephen (born 4 April 1762), followed by Nancy. A vocal prodigy as a child and very vivacious, Nancy sang in public by age eight and was placed eventually under the guidance of the eminent castrato and composer Venanzio Rauzzini and the even more eminent Antonio Sacchini, principal composer at the King's Theatre from 1772. Rauzzini was engaged there in 1774, one year after creating the *primo uomo* role in Mozart's *Lucio Silla* at Milan. He could have told young Nancy much about the amazing sixteen-year-old composer from Salzburg.

In or about 1776, Stephen Storace was sent to finish his musical education at Naples. There he enrolled in the San Onofrio Conservatory where his father had been a pupil. Next it was Nancy's turn. The program of her London benefit concert on 27 April 1778 announced that she was "going to Italy the ensuing summer for improvement."[1] The parallel is not only with her brother Stephen but also with the tenor Michael Kelly, another pupil of Rauzzini, who sailed from Dublin to Naples in 1779 and was taken under the wing of the famous soprano Giuseppe Aprile.[2]

---

[1] Geoffrey Brace, *Anna . . . Susanna. Anna Storace, Mozart's First Susanna: Her Life, Times and Family* (London: Thames Publishing, 1991), 24.

[2] Michael Kelly, *Reminiscences*, 2 vols. (London, 1826), ed. by Alec Hyatt King (New York: Da Capo, 1968). Kelly's memoirs were ghost-written by Theodore Hook. For a recent assessment of their reliability (poor), see Daniel Heartz, *Mozart, Haydn and Early Beethoven 1781-1802* (New York: W. W. Norton, 2009), Appendix I, "An Irish Tenor in the Burgtheater."

Accompanied by both parents Nancy embarked for Naples in mid-1778. During the 1778-79 season at the city's huge Teatro San Carlo, the *primo uomo* was one of the most famous of all castrato sopranos, Luigi Marchesi (1755-1829). Although still quite young he was the logical choice of aspiring parents as a mentor for such a high-spirited daughter as Nancy. In later years Nancy, always a great mimic of other singers' vocal and thespian mannerisms, did not spare even Marchesi. Yet they remained on friendly terms, singing together, for instance, in the same charity concert when Marchesi came to London in 1788.[3] Nancy's first professional engagement, in fall 1779, suggests another connection with Marchesi. It was not at one of the smaller Italian centers, as would normally have been the case, but at the Pergola Theater in Florence, as *seconda donna* in a serious opera by Francesco Bianchi, *Castore e Polluce*. The *primo uomo* role of Castore was sung by none other than Marchesi. He likely had taken her with him and had her promoted to greater status than could have been expected for a beginner just turned fourteen. The least that can be said is that Nancy would not have been engaged without Marchesi's approval, for that is how the system worked.

Besides the circumstantial evidence implying that Nancy was a pupil of Marchesi, there is one documentary clue. Count Karl Zinzendorf, finance officer at the Habsburg court in Vienna during the 1780s, kept a diary over several decades in which he detailed among many other things his theater-going, which was often nightly. In August 1785, when Marchesi was in Vienna, Zinzendorf referred to Nancy as his student (*son ecolière*).[4]

At Florence Nancy was still accompanied by family, her parents as well as brother Stephen, who was engaged by the Pergola Theater as second cembalist. He remained with her for another year or more. After Florence, Nancy followed a more normal course for so young a singer, playing comic roles at several theaters in smaller centers such as Lucca and Livorno, where, in 1781 Nancy and Stephen first encountered Michael Kelly, at dockside, as amusingly told by Kelly in his memoirs. The three of them became friends at once and remained so for life. Kelly was on his way to sing at the Pergola in Florence, his appointment having been secured by his teacher Aprile.

In 1782 Nancy graduated to her first major comic role, and at one of Italy's grandest theaters, La Scala in Milan. She created the *prima buffa* part of Dorina at the premiere of Giuseppe Sarti's *Fra i due litiganti il terzo gode*, one of the roles with which she next conquered Venice, then Vienna. Stephen was not with her for this triumphant progress. Father Stefano died in Italy, probably in 1781, and his decease may be bound up with his son's return to London about this time. Mother Elisabeth remained with Nancy and would do so throughout the nearly four years in Vienna, from March 1783 to February 1787. Nancy's partner on the stage of La Scala was the most sought-after *primo buffo* of that time, Francesco Benucci (c. 1745-1824), a handsome and dashing figure as well as a great actor and singer. He must count as one of Nancy's mentors too, and it was perhaps asking too much of a

---

[3] Brace, *Anna . . . Susanna*, 74.

[4] Dorothea Link, *The National Court Theatre in Mozart's Vienna. Sources and Documents 1783-1792* (Oxford: Clarendon Press, 1998), "*Le soir au théâtre* from the Diary of Count Karl Zinzendorf, 1783-92)," 250.

headstrong young woman like Nancy not to fall for him. The Italian public did not expect its favorite female singers to be towers of virtue and perhaps even relished seeing the adored sirens indulge in dalliances.[5]

Benucci and Nancy were both engaged at Venice for the Carnival season of 1783. At the San Samuele and San Moise theaters they sang various comic operas, including Antonio Salieri's *La scuola de' gelosi* on a fine libretto by Caterino Mazzolà, a work that had been making the rounds of Italian opera houses since 1778. In early 1783 Emperor Joseph II sent word via his theater director Count Rosenberg to Giacomo Durazzo, his ambassador to Venice, of his desire to reinstate Italian opera in the Burgtheater. No expense was to be spared, and only first-class singers hired, specifically to put on opera buffa, not opera seria. Durazzo engaged Benucci, Nancy, Michael Kelly, and the versatile baritone-tenor Stefano Mandini, along with his wife. Salieri, as court Kapellmeister for theater music, was the Burgtheater's music director, so it comes as no surprise that he chose for the new troupe's Viennese debut his own *Scuola de' gelosi*.

Thus Nancy's first role in Vienna was that of the Countess in *La scuola*, the *prima buffa* part she had just been singing in Venice. It was a serious role, at least in the first half of the opera. Although Nancy had some seria credentials from roles played in Italy, she did not resemble the noble ladies portrayed in opera seria. She was small, plump, and looked more like a maidservant. As the Countess in this opera, she makes a late appearance, after the proceedings are well underway, singing a slow Cavatina, a complaint about her husband's coolness. If this situation rings a bell it may be because Mozart and his librettist Lorenzo Da Ponte held back their Countess from the first act of *Le nozze di Figaro* (contrary to their model in the play by Beaumarchais) and had her open Act II with a slow Cavatina complaining of her husband's neglect. Later in *La scuola* the Countess disguises herself as a gypsy and tells her husband's fortune, giving Nancy a chance to act and sing in more lively fashion.

The operas presented by the new troupe during the spring and summer of 1783, all new to Vienna but not to Italy, were in order: Salieri's *La scuola* (22 April); Cimarosa's *L'Italiana in Londra* (5 May); Sarti's *Fra i due litiganti* (28 May); Anfossi's *Il curioso indiscreto* (30 June); Cimarosa's *Il falegname* (25 July); Paisiello's *Il barbiere di Siviglia* (13 August); and Sarti's *Le gelosie villane* (17 September). Nancy sang in most of them. She performed as often as four times a week and kept several roles in her memory. Once produced, the operas stayed in repertory for a few months generally. The Burgtheater did well to bring out a new Italian opera production about once a month, along side of all the plays in German constantly being added and kept in repertory. Operas took more planning, as scores had to be procured, parts copied, librettos printed, often with translations. Joseph II was a hard taskmaster with his theatrical forces and expected as much discipline from them as he demanded of himself.

---

[5] In Italy famous women singers were equated with high-class whores since at least Renaissance times, a subject deftly explored by Professor Prizer, most recently in "Cardinals and Courtesans: Secular Music in Rome, 1500-1520," in *Italy and the European Powers. The Impact of War, 1500-1530*, ed. Christine Shaw (Leiden and Boston: Brill, 2006), 253-77.

Count Zinzendorf, a bachelor who was particularly attentive to the ladies in his social circle, was captivated by Nancy, and not only by her acting and singing. On her first night in *La scuola* he was there and noted in his diary, "L'Inglesina, jolie figure voluptueuse, belle gorge, bien en Bohemienne" (the little Englishwoman, pretty and voluptuous figure, beautiful neck [or bosom], good as a Gypsy).[6] At the Viennese premiere of *Fra i due litiganti* on 28 May he wrote more along the same lines: "La Storace y joua comme un ange. Ses beaux yeux, son cou blanc, sa belle gorge, sa bouche fraiche faisoient un charmant effet" (La Storace acted to perfection. Her beautiful eyes, her white neck, her lovely bosom made a charming effect). Whatever Nancy's physical limitations she did not lack sex appeal.

No portrait of Nancy from the time of her residence in Vienna during the mid-1780s is now known, although they must have existed then, given the amount of enthusiastic response she generated. From the time after her return to London in 1787 there are several depictions of her. None captures the charms and freshness of which Zinzendorf speaks better than that of De Wilde, who painted her from life in Milton's *Mask of Comus*, a stage scene in which she holds a glass of wine and sings "But the Nymph disdains to pine, Who bathes the wound in rosy wine," as set to music by Thomas Arne. The engraving by Condé in my possession has the added charm of color, perhaps provided by some admirer, giving Nancy a rose-colored gown under her white shift, rosy cheeks, and a deep-red glass of wine (Plate 1).

Besides Nancy, it was Benucci who provided the spark that fired the Italian troupe in the Burgtheater to its best efforts. Zinzendorf often sang his praises too, both for acting and singing. At the performance of *Litiganti* on 2 June 1783 Zinzendorf noticed that Nancy and Benucci were indulging in pranks and gestures of affection that were not called for by the parts they were playing. She had a song to sing while skipping about (*saltellar*) in which she was supposed to make fun of him, instead of which she applauded him. Two days later she fell ill during another *Litiganti* performance, and the opera had to be ended before the third act.[7] The strain of giving so many performances resulted in quite a few cancellations by her during the months that followed. Besides the frequent stage appearances the pair of Nancy and Benucci were in demand for private concerts. At one of these, given by the British Ambassador Sir Robert Keith, Zinzendorf was present and inscribed this account in his diary.

> 1 July [1783]. With Countess Palfy to the Chevalier Keith. There La Storace sang an aria from *Giulio Sabino*, opera seria by Sarti, for which Benucci played the keyboard, then she played the keyboard and he sang an aria from *Il pittor Parigino* by Sarti [recte: by Cimarosa] "Ma il pittor non c'ha da Star." He was charming. Then they sang the duet from *L'amor costante* by Cimarosa: "Bella, bella gioja, gioja" which enchanted us. La Storace has a striking countenance, a stocky figure, beautiful eyes and skin, the naiveté and petulance of a child. Benucci is good looking.[8]

[6] Link, *The National Court Theatre in Mozart's Vienna*, 204.
[7] *Fra i due litiganti* is everywhere described as being in two acts, yet at the Burgtheater on this occasion is was presumably divided into four acts. The case is instructive with regard to *Le nozze di Figaro*, originally in four acts, but performed subsequently in some early productions in two acts.
[8] Link, 207. "La Storace a beaucoup de physionomie, une figure trapûe, beaux yeux, belle peau, la naïveté et la petulance de l'enfance. Benucci a bonne façon."

Both artists were finished musicians clearly, and no strangers to the keyboard (at a time when many opera singers were nearly illiterate in musical matters). The instrument they played when accompanying is called "clavecin" by Zinzendorf, and it may be that the residence of Ambassador Keith was so old-fashioned as to still maintain a harpsichord. Most up-to-date music lovers had replaced the older instrument with a fortepiano by this time. "Clavecin" (like "cembalo") can be a general term that does not exclude the newer instruments.

The practice at the Burgtheater operas was to allow as many encores as the audience demanded, unless expressly forbidden by Joseph II, who, when he was in Vienna, often attended in his box on the right side, above the orchestra. The leading singers bore the brunt of audience-demand for encores. At the *Litiganti* on 9 July 1783 Zinzendorf noted "they made poor Storace repeat the scene with hand-kissing and skipping three times." It became clear during the following year that "poor Storace" was losing her health from the strains she was under.

Mozart was another spectator-auditor of the new Italian troupe in the Burgtheater. He had no suitable opera of his own to offer the company, nor was he asked by Joseph or Rosenberg to provide one. He did get his foot in the door, as it were, by providing two insert arias (K. 418-419) for Aloysia Weber Lange (his sister-in-law) to sing at her debut with the company in Anfossi's *Il curioso indiscreto*. The production was not very successful. Mozart began searching for a libretto to set, although he had no commission. One that he lighted upon was *Le donne rivale*, an intermezzo for five characters that had been set by Cimarosa for Rome in 1780. To it Mozart had two characters added, bringing the revised libretto, renamed *Lo sposo deluso*, to the seven exemplified by Salieri's *La scuola* and most other comic librettos then in favor. Tying it securely to the Burgtheater troupe, Mozart wrote singers' names in a copy of the text. The first three were Signor Benucci as *primo buffo*, Signor Mandini as *primo mezzo carattere*, and Signora Fischer as *prima buffa*. The last was Nancy herself, after she married John Abraham Fisher in March 1784, which helped give a precise date for this unfinished torso of an opera (K. 430).

What possessed Nancy to marry a man twice her age? She was eighteen, he forty. The wishes of widow Elisabeth Storace were paramount according to Michael Kelly in his memoirs. Possibly she was worried about where Nancy's affair with Benucci was leading, and surely she wanted to gain more financial security than reliance on her son or on Nancy guaranteed. Fisher looked like a good catch. With a Doctor of Music degree from Oxford as a *bona fide*, he was a former business partner of her late husband, a successful composer, and a virtuoso violinist who was on a concert tour of the Continent.

The marriage license was signed on 21 March 1784 in the Parish Registry of the Schottenkirche, not far from where the Storaces resided in the Herrenstrasse. As for the wedding ceremony, it took place a few days later in the Chapel of the Dutch Ambassador, officiated by a Protestant German clergyman.[9] Nancy was led to the altar by Prince Adam Auersperg and Lord Mount Edgcumbe as proxy for British Ambassador Keith. The rather exalted circumstances confirm what an important figure Nancy had become in Vienna's cultural life. They would seem to bode well for the marriage. Alas, it quickly turned sour. Within a month troubles

---

[9] Brace, *Anna. . . Susanna*. Appendix 2,142-44.

became apparent. The earliest witness to them we have is Zinzendorf, who noted in his diary entry for 15 April 1784 "Fisher beats his wife" (*Fischer rosse sa femme*). One possible explanation could be that Dr. Fisher was irate about Nancy's behavior with Benucci.

Nancy's appearances on stage dwindled in number and at some of them she had to conserve her forces. In order to spare herself she cut some numbers short. On 14 July 1784 Zinzendorf noted that, in Anfossi's *I viaggiatori felici* she ended the rondò with the initial slow part, the Cavatina, omitting the fast part, often more demanding technically (*La Storace jolie resta court au rondeau, a la Cavatina*). The great operatic event of the year happened this same summer, a new opera for Vienna written on command from Joseph by the poet Giambattista Casti, *Il re Teodoro*, and set to music by Paisiello, Joseph's favorite composer. Both poet and composer were in attendance for the event, as were a number of foreign dignitaries especially invited to the premiere on 23 August. The rehearsals had been lengthy for this complex work, and Nancy worked hard to prepare the *prima buffa* part of Lisetta. At the premiere she was too ill to go on and had to be replaced by another soprano, who proved unsatisfactory. Shortly thereafter, word got out that Nancy was pregnant.

In consequence, the call went out for another *prima buffa* as a possible replacement. It brought Luisa Laschi, a Florentine soprano perhaps a year or two younger than Nancy and the daughter of a famous family of opera singers. She proved to be a first-class musician and made her Viennese debut to acclaim in October 1784. The *Wienerkronik* reported her success in glowing terms.

> She [Laschi] is still very young, has a lovely clear voice which will grow rounder and stronger with time; it is very musical with an attractive timbre; she acts with more expression than the usual opera singer and has a pretty figure. Madame Fischer [Storace] is only superior in experience to Mlle. Laschi, who is in every respect a great acquisition for Vienna.[10]

Zinzendorf did not rate her acting quite so highly as Nancy's but praised her singing without reservation. Looking ahead to *Le nozze di Figaro* we can begin to comprehend why Vienna needed both Luisa and Nancy, the first to play the Countess, the second Susanna, a role that demanded skilled acting in nearly every scene.

At some time in late 1784 or early 1785 Joseph II declared Dr. Fisher *persona non grata* in the Habsburg realms, upon which he betook himself elsewhere and was not heard from again until years later in London. Nancy reverted to being Signorina Storace. Her pregnancy was not subject to reversal. She continued on bravely earning praises for acting and singing although subject to frequent illness. Zinzendorf noted that on 21 January 1785 Benucci had her sit while delivering her big aria in *Il re Teodoro*. In the Lenten season that followed there were many benefit concerts as usual but no operas. At Nancy's benefit on 20 March she sang a German text praising Joseph II to the music of "Saper bramate," the Count's serenade in *Il barbiere di Siviglia*. The Italian troupe was due to take the stage again two days after Easter (27 March). It could not do so because Nancy was ill and Luisa Laschi

[10] Ibid., 43.

had returned to Italy in order to fulfill prior engagements. Zinzendorf, in a letter to his sister dated 29 March, did not conceal his boredom with the Lenten fare of concerts. "Here you are delivered from monotony and once again in the season of spectacles. The most perfect of ours, that is to say the Italian comic operas, are not beginning because of the illness of our best actress, whom everyone loves, because she is good and sings well."[11] The German singers were summoned to fill in with Singspiel performances, which Zinzendorf disdained. On 6 April Laschi's replacement, called from Italy, was another Tuscan soprano, the veteran Celeste Coltellini, who made a successful debut in Paisiello's *La contadina di spirito*. All in all, she was not liked as much as Laschi, who returned for the 1786-87 season. Nancy sang again on 20 April her role of Lisettta in *Il re Teodoro*, eliciting from Zinzendorf the remark that "she gave the impression of having suffered. They had her exit after the stage was darkened."

Stephen Storace returned to Vienna in the spring of 1785 with the commission to compose an opera, his first, surely due to the good offices of his sister and the high esteem in which Joseph II held her. The opera, *Gli sposi malcontenti*, was in rehearsal throughout May. Nancy played a fairly serious part in it, that of an unhappy wife. At the premiere on 1 June the worst fears of any singer came true. She managed to struggle through her part in the initial trio, then during her first aria she lost her voice and could not sing at all. She did not return to the stage until nearly four months later. On 3 June Zinzendorf heard Stephen explain his sister's illness "avec sensibilité" and reveal that for her lying in she was supposed to go either to Spa or to England, but that she was "stubborn," for which he used the Italian expression *testarda*.

The baby, a girl, was born sometime later in June and died within a month. On 20 July Zinzendorf repeated a rumor he heard, gossip to the effect that the baby died of starvation because Elisabeth Storace fired the wet-nurse as an economy measure. If true, it could mean that Nancy gave care of the baby over to her mother, who was avaricious (perhaps increasingly so after the departure of Dr. Fisher). Who fathered the baby? Nancy's modern biographer writes "Presumably, though by no means certainly, it was Fisher's . . . ."[12]

On 12 October 1785 Nancy created the role of Ofelia, the serious and studious daughter in *La grotta di Trofonio* by Casti and Salieri. Coltellini played the light-hearted daughter Dori, while Benucci sang the title role. Nancy's illness led to a cancellation of *Il re Teodoro* scheduled on 28 October. Then at the performance of *Teodoro* on 28 November Zinzendorf observed that "La Storace acted with a great deal of care and taste but her singing was very different from what it once was. She no longer reached those high and veiled tones" (*elle n'atteint plus ses sons hauts et couvres*). Count Zinzendorf obviously was capable of saying more about what he heard than he usually did, and the same can be deduced from his remark on the two-tempo rondò, cited above.

[11] Link, 509, note 77. "Vous voila hors de la monotonie et de nouveau dans les spectacles. Les plus parfaits des nôtres, c. a. d. les operas comiques italiens ne commencent pas encore a cause de la maladie de notre meilleure actrice, que tout le monde aime, parce qu'elle est bonne et chante bien."

[12] Brace, *Anna . . . Susanna*, 47.

The year 1786 began with rehearsals for Salieri's short opera *Prima la musica e dopo le parole* in which Nancy sang the part of a *prima donna seria*, and Coltellini sang the soubrette role. The work was being readied for first performance at the Orangerie of Schönbrunn Palace on 7 February. On 26 January when visiting Count Rosenberg, Zinzendorf encountered Nancy and Coltellini rehearsing what must have been the scene where they sing together in the finale. One of the highlights of *Primo la musica* is a scene in which Nancy did an imitation of Luigi Marchesi, who had sung at Vienna the previous summer in six performances of Sarti's *Giulio Sabino* at Joseph's command, staged to take advantage of Marchesi's passing through Vienna on his way to Russia. Nancy had mimicked Marchesi's acting and singing as far back as her stint with him at Florence in 1779, according to the memoirs of Michael Kelly.[13] It is to be doubted whether Nancy's voice was still capable of Marchesi's feats of bravura singing, or of his great vocal range, especially as to his extremely high tones. Salieri's score calls for her to make a few sallies up to high A, and one high B-flat, with one low G at the bottom, but overall the tessitura is a moderate, middle-range one.

Easter 1786 fell on 16 April. After it the Italian troupe gave few performances, and only of works already in repertory. The reason for this slow start is clear. They were faced with learning the longest and most complicated opera buffa yet attempted, *Le nozze di Figaro*. The original intention was probably to stage it in Carnival season. Perhaps the music was not finished in time for that. In any case the ideal singer for the part of the Countess was not on hand until Luisa Laschi returned to the troupe in April. There were many rehearsals. The final one, on 29 April, was attended by Joseph. Two days later, on the first of May, came the premiere, at which some pieces did not go smoothly. Zinzendorf was present and said almost nothing about the experience except that it bored him, perhaps in reaction to the opera's inordinate length. He can be forgiven for his inattention because on that day his mind was occupied by his lady-love, Louise van Diede, who was about to leave Vienna.

How the work fared at its first performances, at the hands of the cast and of the public, is a tale told elsewhere.[14] Suffice it to say here that, at the third public performance on 8 May, Joseph forbad encores of any pieces with more than one voice. Seven more performances were given in 1786, one on 3 June at Laxenburg Palace where the court had gone to spend its usual summer holiday. The total of ten performances was about average for an operatic success.

Mozart asked of Nancy as Susanna a vocal range that was quite moderate and in line with what Salieri required of her in *Prima la musica* a few months earlier. The tessitura is mid-range, concentrated in the octave and a half between D (one tone above middle C) and G, an eleventh above. The two opening duets with Figaro require even less. In her third duet, with Marcellina, the top note is pushed up to A. Her first aria, sung while dressing Cherubino as a girl in Act II, covers precisely the tones from D up to G. The next number, a trio sung with the Count and Countess

---

[13] Kelly, *Reminiscences*, 49. The passage is quoted and put in context by John A. Rice, *Antonio Salieri and Viennese Opera* (Chicago: University of Chicago 1998), 378-81.

[14] Among other places in Daniel Heartz, *Mozart's Operas* (Berkeley and Los Angeles: University of California, 1990), 190.

(No. 13 in the *NMA* edition), is in C, and Mozart wished to have a vocal climax that would carry the vocal line up to a high C (at mm. 116-118 and mm. 131-32). In the autograph this is assigned to the Countess, but in the *Directionsexemplar*, the authoritative score from which the parts were made, Mozart switched the passage to Susanna. In both versions he notated an alternate solution avoiding high C by turning back at A and resolving via F to E.[15] Either Nancy or Luisa Laschi should have been able to sing this rare foray up to high C, which is made easier by being smooth and stepwise. Possibly one may not have been in as good voice as the other when Mozart made the switch. Many discussions of the case in the literature seem to ignore that he left open the possibility of not ascending to high C at all. Whatever the singer did, Mozart resolved B natural, the leading tone, up to C in the first violins.

The lowest tone in Susanna's part is an A below middle C in the Sextet (No. 19). It recurs in her final solo, the Garden Aria (No. 28) where there is one low A and an ascent briefly touching her high A. In the Letter Duet (No. 21) it is Susanna who eventually reaches high B-flat, while the Countess trails along in thirds below her. In sum, Mozart treated Nancy's voice carefully by keeping it within a limited, middle range, with only occasional sorties above or below the staff. Of bravura passage-work there is scarcely a hint. Perhaps Mozart thought it inappropriate to the character of so candid and clever a maidservant as Susanna. While her social rank is far below that of the noble Rosina, Countess Almaviva, Susanna outranks everyone else in the cast as to brain power, including her spouse Figaro (Benucci).

Mozart earlier wrote for Nancy's voice when he drafted an aria for her part as Eugenia and inscribed it "Signora Fischer" in his unfinished *Lo sposo deluso* (1784). This *prima buffa* role portrayed a young lady of spirited character, who describes herself as a noble Roman, "Born in the Campidoglios's triumphant clime." Mozart sets these pompous words to an unspecified but evidently moderate tempo in cut time, and in the key of E-flat (Example 1). The vocal line is most memorable for the triumphant striding passage in descent through tones 8-5-1, and the rather ungainly leaps between high and low. There is also a low A-natural further on but mostly the tessitura is moderate, concentrated in the middle. At measure 51 the

Example 1. Aria (draft) from Mozart, *Lo sposo deluso*, mm. 13-21

[15] Ulrich Leisinger, *Kritischer Bericht* to *Le nozze di Figaro*, ed. Ludwig Finscher (Kassel: Bärenreiter, 2007), 349-50 (Mozart, *Neue Ausgabe sämtliche Werke*, II/5/16).

tempo changes to Allegro at the words "Ah! son furia delirante," set to flurries of eighth notes, and imitated in the bass. The aria has some trappings of the two-tempo rondò although it is shorter than that typical showpiece of opera seria and lacking the repetition of both slower and faster parts. In the final section the voice breaks into triplet eighth notes in figures outlining the tonic triad, with long and scalar melismatic extensions, a coloratura passage that confirms the role's seria pretensions. Approaching the final cadence Mozart gives the voice a high B-flat, yet hedges by providing an alternative B-flat an octave lower, just in case.

At some late stage in the composition of *Figaro* Mozart sketched Susanna's Garden Aria as a "Rondo" in E-flat to the text "Non tardar amato bene." Eugenia's aria apparently lingered in his mind as he imagined Susanna impersonating the proud and lofty Countess. He resorted again to the key of E-flat and cut time, with another descent through the tonic triad, 8-5-3-1, for "Non tardar" (Do not delay!) with a more yielding figure in dotted rhythm for the endearment "amato bene" (Example 2). At this moment Susanna is attempting a double deceit. Figaro, listening, knows that it is Susanna, dressed as the Countess and imitating her voice and manner; he does not know that Susanna taunts him by pretending to welcome the Count's embraces. This draft was completed as to voice and bass only through the initial slower part of the rondò, which ends with the customary return of initial text and music, at which point it breaks off. Once it became clear that Figaro's previous (at one stage subsequent) aria, the diatribe against women (No. 27), would be in E-flat, a recurrence of the same key for Susanna's aria was impossible. Not only did Mozart substitute F for E-flat in his final decision about Susanna's Garden Aria, he gave up the idea of a grand rondò such as the Countess might sing, and substituted the simpler but sublimely subtle piece that we know as the opera's final aria, "Deh vieni, non tardar." Yet he did not abandon all semblance of the descending triad melodic idea; he only made it more delicate and appealing.

The last piece Mozart wrote for Nancy is the Scena and Rondò "Non temer, amato bene" (K. 505), performed at her farewell concert on 23 February 1787, which took place in Vienna's Kärntnertor Theater. K. 505 is in fact a superb duo-drama between Nancy's voice and a solo concertante part for fortepiano, played by Mozart. A precedent for this unusual kind of duet in Mozart's earlier works occurs in *Il re pastore* (K. 208) for Salzburg in 1775. In its second and final act, the action stops while Aminta, the shepherd king of the title, proclaims his undying love for Elisa, "L'amero sarò costante" (I shall love her and be faithful). This is the opera's big moment and Mozart makes it special in a number of ways. He chooses the key of E-flat and projects it softly with a magical blend of flutes, English horns, bassoons, horns in E-flat, upper strings with mutes, and an unmuted solo violin (*violino principale*). There is not the slightest doubt in my mind that Mozart himself played the violin solo. He was at the height of his violin playing and composing

Example 2. Rondò (draft) from *Le nozze di Figaro*, mm. 1-3

Example 3. Rondeaux, from Mozart, *Il re pastore*, mm. 9-12

for the instrument at that time, from which his violin concertos date, and he was then concertmaster of the Salzburg court orchestra. He chose for the piece a moderate speed, Andantino in ¾ time, which in combination with E-flat and the orchestral sonorities, produced an aura of devotion and rapture.

The melody Mozart chose (Example 3 above) forecasts what he wrote later for Nancy as Eugenia (Example 1), an initial descent outlining 8-5-1 and a flurry of sixteenth notes falling to the repeated E-flat of the cadence. The solo voice for which Mozart wrote "L'amerò" was that of soprano Tommaso Consoli, a young castrato and very fine singer who was borrowed for the occasion from the Munich court. I call "L'amero" a love duet between the voice and solo violin not to imply any amorous link between Mozart and Consoli, although they did become good friends later, but to suggest that the solo violin personifies the beloved Elisa, who is engaged in a dialogue with Aminta conducted by exchanges of melodic material, until the two are ultimately united in the chains of thirds that lead rapturously to the cadence.

On 13 March 1786, Emperor Joseph's forty-fifth birthday, Mozart presided over a performance of his *Idomemeo* in the theater of Prince Adam Auersperg sung by non-professional but expert performers. For the part of Idamante, a castrato in the original performances at Munich, Mozart had young Baron Pulini, one of his pupils and a tenor. To enhance Idamante's part, and the opera as a whole, he substituted for the *aria di sorbetto* of Arbace opening Act II a new *Scena con Rondò*, a scene between Ilia and Idamante in which he protests his love for her and then sings an elaborate aria with concertante violin (K. 490), played by Mozart's dear friend Count Hatzfeld. The text of this rondò begins "Non temer, amato bene," a close verbal parallel to "Non tarder, amato bene," sung by Susanna in the discarded earlier version of the Garden Aria, and perhaps from the same time, that is to say about a month before *Figaro* went into rehearsal in April. The poet of the discarded Garden Aria was surely Da Ponte, who was also in all probability the poet of the new *Scena con Rondò* for *Idomeneo*. It is the violin solo that first states the themes, both the slow initial one and the faster one, thematically related to the first. As in "L'amerò" of eleven years earlier, the violin plays the role of a partner with the voice, proposing, answering, sometimes cajoling, and ultimately joining the voice in consonant intervals for rapid passage work. In other words, voice and violin act very much like lovers in a duet, and the piece can be compared profitably with Mozart's actual love duets. "Non temer, amato bene" is in the key of B-flat, a choice probably having something to do with Baron Pulini's voice. It could not have been in E-flat for sure, as that was the key of the very next aria, Ilia's "Se il padre perdei."

Nancy and Benucci were no strangers to the Lenten concerts and operas given in the theater of Prince Auersperg. Indeed, they may very well have heard the *Idomeneo* on 13 March 1786. Ten days later, on the same stage, they sang Paisiello's new setting of the old two-voiced intermezzo *La serva padrona*, to the delight of Zinzendorf.

Mozart composed K. 505, the aria for Nancy's farewell to Vienna, in late December 1786, well in advance of the February concert. Having received and accepted an invitation to visit Prague, Mozart and his wife Costanza left Vienna on or about 8 January and did not return until 12 February. In choosing for K. 505 the text of the new *Scena con Rondò* for Idamante, he had a ready-made artifact with which to begin. All he did by way of alteration was to shorten the initial scena by removing Ilia's lines. K. 505 is longer and more complex than K. 490 in regard to their arias. At the same time, as might be expected of pieces departing from identical texts, the two settings have several musical ideas in common, besides the formal layout and special textures that emanated from having disparate soloists— one vocal, the other instrumental. Apparently pleased with the result, Mozart inscribed the autograph score of K. 505 "Composto per la Sig^ra Storace dal suo servo ed amico W. A. Mozart, Vienna li 26 di dec^bre 786." A day later he entered the incipits "Recitativ" and "Rondò" in his thematic catalogue with the accompanying label "Scena con Rondò mit klavier solo. für Mad^selle storace und mich." Thus from one day to the next he transformed Nancy from Mrs. to Miss—from Signora to Mademoiselle, i.e., Signorina.

The recitatives of both K. 490 and K. 505 end with a cadence in g minor, arrived at by poignant chromatic descent, appropriate to the final words of a lover at the thought of losing his beloved: "Ah I should die of grief" (*Ah di dolor morei*). In K. 490 Mozart extends the chromatic descent of the bass by one measure so that it arrives via D, C-sharp, C-natural at B-flat for the beginning of the aria. In K. 505, the recitative cadence in g minor is transformed subtly into a two-measure preparation for the arrival of E-flat and the beginning of the aria. These finely wrought and brief transitions exemplify the care Mozart took with every detail in both pieces.

The violin first proposes the slower theme of K. 490, an Andante in common time. Then the tenor sings the nearly identical notes, a regular eight-measure phrase divided into antecedent and consequent phrases (Example 4). Attractive features of this melody are the return of the peak tone G before the descent of the cadence, and the way "sem-pre" receives an agogic accent on the second syllable. In K. 505, the instrument also proposes the initial theme, again an Andante in duple meter but in cut time. It is in the high range of the piano

Example 4. Rondò (K. 490), from *Idomeneo* (March 1786), mm. 9-16

Example 5. Rondò (K. 505), (December 1786), mm. 12-21

Idamante: Non te - mer,⎯ a - ma - to be - ne, per⎯ te⎯

sem - pre, sem - pre il cor - sa - rà.

and elaborated so as to help sustain the instrument's sound. Then the soprano (Nancy) sings a plainer version an octave lower without the decorations (Example 5). The theme is another antecedent and consequent, the latter being lengthened to emphasize the word "sempre," which is sustained by the voice for two extra measures with a held B-flat, against which the piano fills in changing chords.

After the first phrase is extended and brought to a cadence, the concertante instruments are called upon to illustrate two ideas in the text, "L'alma mia mancando vo" (My soul is drooping) and "Tu sospiri?" (You are sighing?). The solo violin utters little melodic sighs at the latter, as does the piano. Mozart makes more of a case for the former, which the tenor interprets by a small chromatic rise and fall. The soprano, on the other hand, sings "mancando" to a veritable wail, descending an entire octave by chromatic steps, each harmonized by the full chords of Mozart's piano. K. 505 goes far beyond K. 490 in expressive power here, so that it becomes a more intense experience. Not that Mozart's piano can compete in sonority with the soulful intensity of an expertly played violin. It cannot, yet Mozart makes up for the disparity by stretching out the moment with greatly enriched harmonies. He also does more to dramatize the text. At the words "che istante è questo!" (what a moment this is!), the piano rushes headlong by a rapid scalar ascent and dotted rhythms to a cadence in c minor (m. 42.)

What happens following this in K. 505 is a proposal by Mozart's piano that is at once wordless, and secretly texted (Example 6). In the earlier version of the Garden Aria, Nancy received a nearly identical melody at the words "amato

Example 6. Rondò (K. 505), mm. 42-44

bene" (see Example 2). Even the rhythm is nearly the same. Only the upbeat has been moved ahead a measure. Those searching to find evidences of an intimate relationship between composer and soprano have overlooked this tiny clue.

The two concertante arias, K. 490 and K. 505, correspond to many of the norms of the two-tempo rondò. In each, the slower initial theme is repeated after tonal contrast and is brought to a conclusion on the tonic, followed by the faster themes, Allegro moderato in K. 490, Allegretto in K. 505. Both of these faster themes are in gavotte rhythm, as is typical of the form and style. K. 490 has two episodes, providing the needed tonal contrast with the refrain, and the second one adds a nice touch by bringing back words and thematic remnants of the initial slower section. K. 505 does this even more beautifully in the second episode, which bring back, in A-flat, the initial words "Non temer, amato bene," and alludes melodically to their setting in K. 490. After further ruminations and the final return of the Allegretto theme, K. 505 concludes with a generously proportioned coda, with many more sallies of voice and piano. Perhaps on the mind of at least some of the auditors who were assembled in the Kärntnertor Theater on the evening of 23 February 1787 were questions about its star. Could Nancy still sing coloratura? Could she still reach high B-flat for the big climax at the end? Whether she could or not, or how well, these are present in Mozart's score. At many points in the piece Mozart's right hand had scampered up and down the keyboard in rapid scalar passages. As the end neared it joined with Nancy's voice for sixteenth-note passages in parallel thirds. At the very end Nancy's penultimate tone is a high B-flat. Notated also in her part is the B-flat an octave lower, just in case.

Zinzendorf was of course in the theater on that gala night, devoted as he was to Nancy ever since her arrival, and overcoming his dislike for concerts. His comments are disappointingly brief and off the mark: "To Storace's concert at seven . . . the duet from *Una cosa rara* was repeated three times, a bravura aria she sang was a little boring. Her compliment sung in German from *Gli equivoci* made a good effect" (*Le soir a 7ʰ au Concert de la Storace . . . "Le Duo de la Cosa rara fut repeté trOois fois, un air de bravoure qu'elle chanta un peu ennuyeux. Son compliment allemande tiré des Equivoci fesoit un joli air*). *Una cosa rara, o sia Bellezza ed onestà* by Da Ponte and Martín y Soler, first performed on 17 November 1786, quickly eclipsed *Figaro* and every other opera in repertory. The Spanish composer Martín was the man of the hour in Vienna and, according to Da Ponte's memoirs, Nancy cast tender glances in his direction, much to the displeasure of Benucci. Nancy sang the opera's main role, embodying the rare combination cited in the title. The duet in question was a simple little piece more notable for its sexually suggestive text than anything else—audiences went wild for it, reacting mainly perhaps to how Nancy performed it with Mandini, who sang the tenor part. It was likely Mandini who also sang the fervid duet with Nancy at her concert, meaning that he may have had solo music for himself to sing as well, for such was the custom. Benucci apparently did not take part in the benefit concert for Nancy. He may have been ill. On Friday, 16 February, one week before Nancy's concert, Zinzendorf reported that Benucci had a cold and was in bad voice, also that "Storace was unfaithful to him and went off with Lord Barnard" (*La Storace lui est infidele et s'en va avec Lord Barnard*). At last Nancy had a beau of her own age in the person of this young Lord, future Duke of Cleveland, then visiting Vienna.

Stephen Storace had returned to Vienna in the fall of 1786 to compose a second opera for the Burgtheater, *Gli equivoci*, on a text by Da Ponte derived from Shakespeare's *The Comedy of Errors*. The first performance was on 27 December 1786 and it was a success. Nancy drew from its music, according to Zinzendorf, the compliment she sang in German to the audience at her concert, no doubt thanking the Viennese for their support. It was a large audience that evening, very large for it earned her, according to one witness, more than 4,000 gulden.[16] Neither this source nor Zinzendorf say anything that would confirm Mozart's participation in the concert or that K. 505 was indeed performed. With only these documents to go on Otto Eric Deutsch was cautious in his documentary biography of 1961, saying only that Storace "probably" sang K. 505 on this occasion, "perhaps" accompanied by Mozart at the piano.[17] Not until thirty years later, in 1991, did another witness come forward, so to speak, almost like a miracle.

Thomas Attwood, Mozart's pupil in composition from August 1785 to February 1787, was very close to the Storaces and lived with them in the Count Clary house on the Herrenstrasse. He was the same age as Nancy and traveled back to England after the benefit concert with the three Storaces, Michael Kelly, and Lord Barnard. Around 1830 an unknown correspondent asked Attwood to recall what he could about Mozart. In reply Attwood wrote: "The last time I heard him, he play'd his Concerto in d minor & 'Non temer' at Storace's Benefit for whom he composed that Cantata with Pianoforte solo."[18]

Earlier in the same letter Attwood had mentioned Mozart's "Pianoforte with Pedals," which had particular relevance to Piano Concerto No. 20 in d minor (K. 466) because its autograph includes some deep bass tones that could have been played only by foot pedal. Thus Attwood not only confirms what had previously been no more than presumed about K. 505, he also reveals that Mozart chose to perform one of his greatest and most passionate concertos as a further tribute to Nancy, his beloved Susanna.

---

[16] Otto Eric Deutsch, *Mozart. Die Dokumente seines Lebens* (Kassel: Bärenreiter, 1961), 271-72; idem, *Mozart. A Documentary Biography*, translated by Eric Blom, Peter Branscombe, and Jeremy Noble (Stanford, CA: Stanford University Press, 1965), 309.

[17] Deutsch, *Mozart. Die Dokumente seines Lebens*, 251; idem, *Mozart, A Documentary Biography*, 285.

[18] Cliff Eisen, *New Mozart Documents. A Supplement to O. E. Deutsch's Documentary Biography* (Stanford, CA: Stanford University Press, 1991), 39, and *Mozart, Die Dokumente seines Lebens*. Addenda. Neue Folge zusammengestellt von Cliff Eisen (Kassel: Bärenreiter, 1997), 90-91.

Gender, Power, Virtù

Anna Inglese and Other Women Singers
in the Fifteenth Century:
Gleanings from the Sforza Archives*

Bonnie J. Blackburn

On 4 June 1468 Galeazzo Maria Sforza, Duke of Milan since 1466, ordered his treasurer to pay one hundred gold ducats to "la Inglese cantarina" as a gift so she could travel to her home.[1] No women singers ever appear on the few lists of singers that survive from the Milanese court in the late fifteenth century, and of Galeazzo's and Ludovico's consorts, Bona of Savoy and Beatrice d'Este, only the latter is recorded as singing, though she greatly appreciated music, especially the singing of Jean Cordier.[2] Thus a woman's musical voice was rare in formal events at court. This

* This article is a present from one "archive rat" to another; over the decades, Bill and I have both been assiduous in our search for documents that would cast light on musical practice in the years around 1500. It has been a long time since I worked in the Milanese archives, and with the appearance of the very comprehensive book by Paul and Lora Merkley, *Music and Patronage in the Sforza Court*, I thought I would never return to the study of the Milanese court musicians that I had started in Milan while Edward Lowinsky was researching the life of Ascanio Sforza (and both of us desperately searching for sightings of Josquin). And yet, there were interesting unpublished documents that fell outside the Merkleys' remit, some of which I present here in honor of Bill, though unfortunately none concerns Mantua. Exceptionally, Bill kindly read the article once the secret Festschrift had been revealed and offered me useful advice. My warm thanks also go to Keith Polk for information on women musicians, and to Lewis Lockwood for his kind help and suggestions on the Ferrarese aspects. A condensed version was read at the seventy-fifth annual meeting of the American Musicological Society, Philadelphia, 14 November 2009, and at the Graduate Colloquium at Oxford University, 17 November 2009.

[1] "Antonio de Placentia, camerario theuxario nostro. Siamo contenti et così volemo che tu day a la Inglese cantarina cento ducati de horo dagandogli come nuy ge li donamo voluntera perché la posa andar a casa sua. Papie die 4 Iunii 1468." Milan, Archivio di Stato (hereafter ASM), Reg. Missive 83, fol. 205v. Transcribed in Paul A. Merkley and Lora L. M. Merkley, *Music and Patronage in the Sforza Court*, Studi sulla storia della musica in Lombardia, vol. 3 (Turnhout: Brepols, 1999), xxvi n. 47.

[2] Beatrice is reported to have sung more than 25 songs with her two companions on a trip in 1491. See William F. Prizer, "Music at the Court of the Sforza: The Birth and Death of a Musical Center," *Musica disciplina* 43 (1989): 141–93 at 173. On Beatrice's visit to Venice in 1493,

is the more surprising, given all that we know of the musical prowess of Beatrice's sister Isabella at the Mantuan court, as William Prizer has amply documented.[3]

Who was this Englishwoman, and what was she doing in Milan? A hundred ducats is a huge payment: when the Marquis of Mantua's three trumpeters and four *pifferi* came to Milan in the following month to honor Galeazzo's marriage to Bona of Savoy, they were given a gift of thirty-two ducats and the harpist Jacomo d'Asti four ducats.[4] The singer must have been at the court for some time, or else she was being paid for future services, because her presence at the wedding festivities in July would seem to have been highly desirable. Indeed, this is precisely the idea that Marquis Guglielmo Paleologo VIII of Monferrato had in mind when he recommended the same singer to Galeazzo in a letter of 24 June, from which it appears that the Englishwoman had gone to Guglielmo's court at Casale after leaving Milan (App., Doc. 1):

> Most illustrious prince and excellent lord, our father most to be honored. Anna the singer, bearer of the present letter, has decided to come to your illustrious lordship to honor you at your marriage in the near future, and to perform various pleasant games and entertainments, which we think will please your aforesaid illustrious lordship. For which reason, because we understand the said Anna is an honorable person and very apt and sufficient for such games and festivities, we beg your illustrious lordship to accept her as recommended among her equals, as we believe your aforesaid lordship does. To whom, with sincere affection, we commend ourselves. Given at Casale on the twenty-fourth of June 1468.
>
> Guglielmo, Marquis of Monferrato, etc.

Guglielmo's letter of recommendation is curiously distant: he seems to know Anna only by reputation, and not that she had just been in Milan. Had Anna set out for England but changed her mind when she reached Casale?[5] When the payment was ordered, Galeazzo was in Pavia, some thirty-five miles distant from Milan, and perhaps the route through Savoy and France was the normal way to travel to England. Had Guglielmo wished to curry favor with Galeazzo, implying that Anna's change of mind was prompted by him? The letter, however, indicates that it was Anna herself who decided to go to Milan. She comes across as very

---

accompanied by members of the ducal choir including Cordier, see Emilio Motta, *Musici alla corte degli Sforza: Ricerche e documenti milanesi* (Geneva: Minkoff, 1977; repr. from *Archivio storico Lombardo* 14 (1998), 29–64, 278–340, 514–61), 537–38. Ludovico was enchanted with Beatrice's playing the clavichord, as we learn from a touching letter written by the Ferrarese ambassador in August 1491; see Merkley and Merkley, *Music and Patronage*, 422. I am not aware of any mention of Bona performing music, though she thought it important to retain the best singers in the chapel after Galeazzo was assassinated.

[3] See in particular "Una 'virtù molto conveniente a madonne': Isabella d'Este as a Musician," *Journal of Musicology* 17 (1999): 10–49.

[4] 19 July 1468. ASM, Potenze Sovrane 124, published in Guglielmo Barblan, "Vita musicale alla corte sforzesca," in *Storia di Milano* (Milan: Fondazione Treccani, 1961), 9: 789–852 at 793–94.

[5] The date of the payment is accurate, because it was copied into a register among other documents of the same date.

much of an entrepreneur, seeking out opportunities to ingratiate herself at princely courts. No mention is made of a husband or companion. That a woman—and a foreigner at that—should be able to travel and work on her own in Quattrocento Italy is astonishing. This letter is one of the rare fifteenth-century documents concerning independent professional women musicians;[6] with the flourishing of courtesan culture in the sixteenth century, women who made their living at least partly through music come into their own.

In fact, as we learn from other documents, Anna was not alone. She had her own ensemble, which included a tenorista, and she had been in Milan for some time before the farewell payment of June: on 24 May 1468 the Milanese singer Donato Cagnola complained to Galeazzo that he had lodged Anna and her "brigata" for about four months at the duke's request, for which he had been reimbursed only "con gran preghere," but had received nothing at all for the past forty days.[7] Judging from Cagnola's difficulty in extracting money from the duke, Anna may have left Milan for Casale because she too had not been paid sufficiently to cover her expenses, or perhaps she herself had not been hired: a payment to her accompanist (the tenorista), who apparently stayed, is recorded on 10 June for a suit and a jacket. Contemporary documents reveal that there was intense competition among musicians eager to be retained for the wedding festivities, and perhaps to obtain a post at court. "Johanne Todesco, tenorista" and his companions auditioned, and were apparently engaged in April.[8] Vincenzo de' Medici and his companion, the gentleman Lanceloto dala Croce, made a bid for patronage on 15 June, boasting that they could sing French songs as well as or even better than any French singers who might come.[9]

---

[6] Howard Mayer Brown cites it in "Women Singers and Women's Songs in Fifteenth-Century Italy," in *Women Making Music: The Western Art Tradition, 1150–1950*, ed. Jane Bowers and Judith Tick (Urbana and Chicago: University of Illinois Press, 1986), 62–89 at 68. There are references to women musicians throughout the fifteenth century, but these are often daughters and wives who perform incidentally; Keith Polk has collected a number of references, especially to German musicians, in "Voices and Instruments: Soloists and Ensembles in the 15th Century," *Early Music* 18 (1990): 179–98. For women musicians see in particular 194–95.

[7] "son circa quatro mesi che lo nostro Signore me dette alogiare in casa d. Anna Anglese con sua brigata . . . e da la prima volta o fora may non ho havuto dinari salvo con gran preghere, per fare le spese a predicti, pur adesso son piu de quaranta zorni ch'io non hebbi un dinaro"; Milan, ASM, Archivio Sforzesco, cart. 884. In a letter to Ludovico Suardo of 10 June 1468 Galeazzo ordered him to "dar al tenorista de la Inglese panno fino per uno vestito et veluto verde o alexandrino per uno zuparolo" (ASM, Registri delle Missive, no. 83, fol. 236v). Gregory Lubkin drew attention to these documents in his review of the Merkleys' book in *JAMS* 55 (2002): 346–53 at 350 nn. 12 and 13.

[8] Ibid., 352, citing AMS, Archivio Sforzesco, cart. 883, 27 and 28 April 1468. The number of singers needed to be augmented by "uno bono soprano, che senza quella non fanno niente," which Giorgio tenorista would be able to fetch (from Germany?) in fifteen to eighteen days (ibid., n. 11, citing cart. 884, 25 May 1468). The soprano may be a woman, since the reference is to "quella."

[9] "Anchora venendo de li francesi come credo vegnara havereano ad intendere et cognoscere in Lombardia essere chi saperano così ben cantare cantione de li loro linguagi como loro e meglio." The letter is published in Evelyn S. Welch, "Sight, Sound and Ceremony in the Chapel of Galeazzo Maria Sforza," *Early Music History* 12 (1993): 151–90 at 161 n. 34, citing ASM, Archivio Sforzesco, cart. 884; I have checked the original and added a missing phrase.

We gain some knowledge of Anna's skills as well as her first name from Guglielmo's letter, but we know nothing more about her personally. The trajectory of her career, however, confirms that she was an independent woman with considerable initiative, and that she was completely at home in Italy: she turns up in Ferrara and Naples as well, and perhaps even in Venice. At Ferrara in 1465 the name "Anna cantarina Anglica" appears once in court records.[10] As was the case in Milan, she is the only woman singer known to have been paid at the Este court in the fifteenth century. The connection with Ferrara may be significant in explaining Anna's status and her presence in Italy, for this is the only fifteenth-century Italian court I know of that employed English musicians.[11] There are three references to Johns: "Johannes cantor," a priest, the son of another John, of London, at both the court and the cathedral in 1448; "Giovanni d'Inghilterra cantore" at the court in 1449 (very likely the same); and "Giovanni dall'arpa Inglese," a harpist attached to Leonello d'Este in 1448–50.[12] The most important musician, however, is a Robert: Roberto Inglese, the son of Petrus Suchar de Anglia, was in the service of Rinaldo d'Este, commendatory abbot of Pomposa, when he witnessed a document on 19 August 1454;[13] in September 1460 he was hired for one year as a singer in Ferrara Cathedral and to teach the clerics singing, and was re-elected for another year in October 1463.[14] From April 1467 to September 1474 he was *magister cantus* in San Petronio at Bologna.[15] He was very likely the compiler of the chansonnier Porto

---

[10] See Lewis Lockwood, *Music in Renaissance Ferrara 1400–1505: The Creation of a Musical Center in the Fifteenth Century* (Cambridge, MA.: Harvard University Press, 1984), 317. The reference was given to Lockwood by Adriano Franceschini, and remains unpublished (nor is the source known, as Lockwood has kindly informed me; Franceschini's papers are scattered in various locations). This is one of only two payments listed to musicians in 1465 in Lockwood's book. Possibly Anna performed in connection with the festivities arranged by Borso d'Este during the visit of Ippolita Maria Sforza in May 1465, as she traveled to Naples to marry Alfonso, Duke of Calabria (ibid., 93).

[11] St. Peter's in Rome had a "Roberto Anglico" in service from December 1484 to April 1485, and an Andreas Tardiff (Tardis) de Britania from April 1486 to June 1488 and March 1489 to February 1493; see Christopher A. Reynolds, *Papal Patronage and the Music of St. Peter's, 1380–1513* (Berkeley, Los Angeles, and London: University of California Press, 1995), 335 and 330. In 1499–1503 a "Roberto Inglese," whose surname was Frost, appears in Ferrarese court records: see Lockwood, *Music in Renaissance Ferrara*, 153, 326–28.

[12] Johannes cantor: see Lockwood, *Music in Renaissance Ferrara*, 61 and 316, and Enrico Peverada, *Vita musicale nella chiesa ferrarese del Quattrocento* (Ferrara: Capitolare Cattedrale, 1991), 118. Giovanni d'Inghilterra: Lockwood, 317. Giovanni dall'arpa: Lockwood, 60 and 317; in 1450 Niccolò Tedesco, the main singer at court, was pursuing the harpist for money owed him (Lockwood, *Music in Renaissance Ferrara*, 60–61). Curiously, in 1462 the same Niccolò wrote to Francesco Sforza, Duke of Milan, complaining about the duke's harpist Jacomo da Bologna, who had borrowed money from him as surety to bring some books from Bologna and failed to repay him; see Motta, *Musici alla corte degli Sforza*, 54–55. This Jacomo is probably the same Jacomo da Bologna *sonadore* who turns up in Ferrara in 1470; see Lockwood, *Music in Renaissance Ferrara*, 97 and 318.

[13] Lockwood, *Music in Renaissance Ferrara*, 112; Peverada, *Vita musicale*, 131. Rinaldo lived in Ferrara, "in Castello Novo," which is where the document was signed.

[14] The document is transcribed in Peverada, *Vita musicale*, 15–16 n. 51, who notes that "presbiter secularis" has been struck out. See also 131 and (for his re-engagement) 134.

[15] Osvaldo Gambassi, *La cappella musicale di S. Petronio: Maestri, organisti, cantori e strumentisti dal 1436 al 1920* (Florence: Olschki, 1987), 52–74. Some of these notices were originally published by Gaetano

714, which includes his music, as well as songs by Galfridus de Anglia and John Bedyngham.[16] This manuscript is prefaced by two treatises based on the *Declaratio musicae disciplinae* of Ugolino of Orvieto, whom Robertus de Anglia succeeded at Ferrara Cathedral, and was most likely written in Ferrara.[17] Could Anna have been the wife or daughter, or possibly the sister, of one of these Englishmen? The most likely candidate, given the date of the Milanese document, 1468, would be Robertus; as we know from a scribal alteration in the document drawn up when he was hired, he was not a priest, though it appears that he was a cleric, since he is referred to as "dominus" and had a "mansionaria."[18] As *magister cantus* at San Petronio, he did not need to be a priest: Giovanni Spataro, who became *maestro di canto* there in 1512, was not even a cleric. If Anna was the wife (or "femina," as in the case of the singer and cleric Jean Cordier in Milan) of Roberto Inglese, home might have been Bologna rather than England.

Gaspari in "La musica in S. Petronio. A continuazione delle memorie risguardanti la storia dell'arte musicale in Bologna," *Atti e memorie della R. Deputazione di Storia Patria per le Provincie della Romagna,* ser. 1, vol. 5 (1867), 21–60, repr. in *Musica e musicisti a Bologna,* Bibliotheca Musica Bononiensis, sez. 3, no. 1 (Bologna: Forni, 1969), 119–20. On p. 120 Gaspari refers to "manoscritti del p. Martini" for the information that Roberto received a "mansioneria" in S. Petronio a month after he was hired, and that he resigned to return to his country.

[16] See David Fallows, "Robertus de Anglia and the Oporto Song Collection," in *Source Materials and the Interpretation of Music: A Memorial Volume to Thurston Dart,* ed. Ian Bent (London: Stainer & Bell, 1981), 99–128; repr. in idem, *Songs and Musicians in the Fifteenth Century* [Aldershot and Brookfield, VT: Variorum, 1996], essay II), who suggests that the MS "must be closely connected with Robertus or his circle" (104), and the facsimile with introduction by Manuel Pedro Ferreira, *Porto 714: Um manoscrito precioso* (Porto: Campo das Letras, 2001), 60–63, where the literature on the provenance and dating is reviewed. See also James Haar and John Nádas, "The Medici, the Signoria, the Pope: Sacred Polyphony in Florence, 1432-1448," *Recercare* 20 (2008): 25–93 at 77–81. Reinhard Strohm has proposed that the three English Johns in Ferrara are the same person and may possibly be John Bedyngham; see *The Rise of European Music, 1380–1500* (Cambridge: Cambridge University Press, 1993), 546. David Fallows saw evidence of Roberto's involvement with Porto 714 in the absence of a mensuration sign for pieces in perfect tempus; according to Bartolomé Ramos, "Robert the Englishman" argued that when no mensuration sign is found, the time is perfect (see the discussion in "Robertus de Anglia," 103–4). But there is also evidence that the scribe was English, for he drew flats on b' and e' in an idiosyncratic English fashion, as a capital B with a stem (see, e.g., fols. 54v, 56v, 66v). It is true that the handwriting does not look English; however, an Englishman in Italy might (with good reason) have conformed his script to Italian style. For an example of this, see the tragedies of Seneca copied by John Gunthorpe (later dean of Wells) while he was a student of Guarino da Verona in Ferrara in 1460, pl. 107 in S. Harrison Thomson, *Latin Bookhands of the Later Middle Ages, 1100–1500* (Cambridge: Cambridge University Press, 1969).

[17] The second treatise is a condensation of Book III of Ugolino's *Declaratio,* a glossed version of the *Libellus cantus mensurabilis* attributed to Johannes de Muris. The first treatise (the first leaf of which is missing), on the fundamentals of music, seems to have been filtered through an English consciousness, since it uses a peculiarly English term, "proprius cantus," in conjunction with the natural hexachord: "Et potest dici natura sine [*sic;* should be *sive*] proprius cantus quia naturaliter et proprie cantatur sine ulla variacione tonorum et semitonorum" (fol. 01r). On this usage see Bonnie J. Blackburn, "Properchant: English Theory at Home and Abroad, with an Excursus on Amerus/Aluredus and his Tradition," in *Quomodo Cantabimus Canticum?: Studies in Honor of Edward H. Roesner,* ed. David Butler Cannata, with Gabriela Ilnitchi Currie, Rena Charnin Mueller, and John Nádas (Madison, WI: American Institute of Musicology, 2008), 79–96.

[18] See above, n. 14.

Another possibility is that Anna was connected with one of the English students at the Studio in Ferrara. Since many of the students had studied elsewhere before attending the university, it was not uncommon, especially for foreigners, to receive a degree quickly.[19] Thus the students could well have been older than one might expect.[20] As to one of them being a musician we should recall that the famous Dutch humanist Rudolf Agricola was an organist in Ercole's chapel in 1476–77, while he was studying at the university.[21]

Anna next turns up in Naples in 1471. In the "musica del S[enyor] R[ey]" a payment to "madama Agna Anglesa" is registered in the treasury on two occasions.[22] In the account books of the Strozzi bank in Naples, "madama Anna" was paid thirty ducats on 9 March 1476.[23] Edmond vander Straeten saw a register of 1480, apparently no longer in existence, with a payment to "Madama Anna Inglese, musica del S. R."[24] She was still on the payroll in 1499, with the very high sum of 150 (ducats? the currency is not specified). Following next on the list is "Galderi de Madamma Anna," who is paid thirty-four. If he is her son (Walter?), as Allan Atlas speculates, he is not mentioned in any other documents surviving from Naples.[25] It is difficult to tell how old Anna was; if she was about twenty years old in 1465, she would have been fifty-four in 1499 and could have had a teenage son. Alternatively, Galderi could have been her tenorista.

---

[19] See Paul F. Grendler, *The Universities of the Italian Renaissance* (Baltimore and London: The Johns Hopkins University Press, 2002), 104–5, who calls the university "something of a diploma mill" (p. 105). In the 1460s Ferrara awarded 129 degrees in law, 114 in arts and medicine, and 30 in theology (p. 104 n. 128). Lewis Lockwood discusses some prominent English students, suggesting that they or others may have been the conduit for the English music in ModB (*Music in Renaissance Ferrara*, 58–61).

[20] For example, the English student William Nykke, who witnessed the conferral of a doctorate on William Fitzherbert in 1475, was then age 27. John Young, born in 1467, received his doctorate in 1500. See R. J. Mitchell, "English Students at Ferrara in the XV. Century," *Italian Studies* 1 (1937–38): 75–82, at 77–78. Five English students are recorded in the 1450s, though others may have studied there without receiving a degree.

[21] See Lockwood, *Music in Renaissance Ferrara*, 151–52. By 1478 he had become a "familiaris" of the duke; see Giuseppe Pardi, *Titoli dottorali conferiti dallo Studio di Ferrara nei sec. XV e XVI* (Paris, 1890–94; repr. Bologna: Forni, 1970), 68–69.

[22] *Frammenti di cedole della Tesoreria (1438–1474)*, ed. Anna Maria Compagna Perrone Capano, Fonti aragonesi 10 (Naples: Bardi Editore, 1979), 63 ("Frammenti di cedole," 5, fol. 10).

[23] Carlo Galiano, "Nuove fonti per la storia musicale napoletana in età aragonese: I musicisti nei libri contabili del banco Strozzi," in *Musica e cultura a Napoli dal XV al XIX secolo*, ed. Lorenzo Bianconi and Renato Bossa (Florence: Olschki, 1983), 47–59 at 56. All three of these Neapolitan documents were known to Allan W. Atlas, *Music at the Aragonese Court of Naples* (Cambridge: Cambridge University Press, 1985), 105–6, who speculates that Anna came to Naples from Monferrato and Milan between 1468 and 1471.

[24] Edmond vander Straeten, *La musique aux Pays-Bas avant le XIXe siècle* (Brussels: G.-A. van Trigt, 1878), 4: 31.

[25] For the source (a late copy), see Atlas, *Music in Aragonese Naples*, 105 n. 46. I saw another 18th- century copy of this "Diarii di Silvestro Guarino d'Aversa," covering February 1477 to June 1507, in the Biblioteca Apostolica Vaticana, MS Cappon. 73, fols. 39–74, some years ago. Here the name is spelled "Galteri." The list of Musici in this version also includes an "Antonio musico," paid 49. Moreover, the names of the twelve Ministeri et Trombetti and three more Trombetti, missing in the manuscript cited by Atlas, are included. It should be borne in mind that documents surviving from this period are very few.

But there is also a possibility that she is even older, if she is the same as the young English singer Galeazzo Maria Sforza heard when he was in Venice in November 1455. In a letter to Galeazzo's father, Duke Francesco Sforza, describing a banquet arranged for the eleven-year-old count, the six Milanese gentlemen who accompanied him report: "And there was all the more pleasure because they had arranged for some very notable singers to come, among whom was an English damsel, who sang so sweetly and suavely, that the voice appeared to be not human but divine."[26] The appellation 'damisela' implies that she was very young, and certainly unmarried, so if she is the same as Anna Inglese, she might be a daughter rather than the wife or sister of Roberto Inglese, or an English student in Ferrara.

In all of these documents Anna herself remains a rather shadowy figure, except for the letter of recommendation by Guglielmo of Monferrato, where we learn of her ability to entertain as well as to sing. To be an entertainer requires a certain type of personality, and this fits in well with Anna's ability to pursue an independent professional career. She might therefore have devised games, or told stories, or danced.[27] A hitherto unpublished letter throws new light on her. It is one of the regular reports from the Milanese ambassador to Naples, Francesco Maletta, writing to Galeazzo Maria under the date 20 March 1472. After mentioning the arrival of Ugolotto de Facino, the Ferrarese envoy sent by Ercole d'Este to Naples, Maletta reports that Facino has been to visit Ippolita Maria, Galeazzo's sister and the wife of Alfonso, Duke of Calabria (App., Doc. 2):

> Then, teasing him, the aforesaid Madona asked why his lord Duke Ercole was not taking a wife. He told her that Duke Ercole was totally determined to get married, and as soon as his Majesty the King returned to Naples he [Facino] wished to speak with him about the matter. And he tells [will tell] him that he [Ercole] has given himself body and soul and placed his state under his protection. He also said that he had brought here a portrait of the said Duke Ercole, and that the king was of the opinion that he was about 45 years old, but he guesses he is not yet 40. Later. The English woman singer who used to be at your court, and is very affectionately disposed to you, is here in the service of Madona Leonora. She told Ippolita that finding herself recently in the garden with Madona Leonora, and jumping about and dancing with her, she said to her: "Well, Madona, when will the day come when I accompany you to Milan to your husband?" To which Madona Leonora responded in a low voice: "My husband is not at Milan, but elsewhere. And he is 40 years old."

[26] "Et che è havuto molto mazore piacere, hanno facto venire lì alcuni notabilissimi cantatori, fra li quali gliera una damisela anglese, che cantava tanto dolcemente, et suavemente, che pareva una voce, non humana, ma divina." The document was cited by Howard Brown, "Women Singers," 68, and has now been published in Welch, "Sight, Sound and Ceremony," 155–56. The source is Paris, Bibliothèque nationale de France, f. ital. 1585, fol. 90.

[27] An excellent article on patrician women dancing and performing music in public is Judith Bryce, "Performing for Strangers: Women, Dance, and Music in Quattrocento Florence," *Renaissance Quarterly* 54 (2001): 1074–1107.

Poor Eleonora! She was then twenty-two years old, though this was not an uncommon age gap. But this was not her only hesitation, for at that time she was in fact already married, to Galeazzo's younger brother, Sforza Maria Sforza, Duke of Bari, a marriage arranged many years earlier by Francesco Sforza and stipulated by proxy in 1465. When Francesco died in 1466, Galeazzo's undiplomatic dealings with the King of Naples created mutual ill will, and Ferrante became reluctant to send Eleonora to Milan for the formal marriage. Early in 1472 it was decided by mutual agreement that the marriage should be dissolved, and soon rumors were circulating that Eleonora would instead be married to Ercole. Sforza Maria, under pressure from Galeazzo, renounced the marriage in October, and a papal bull dissolving it (since the marriage had not been consummated) was issued on 15 October.[28] By November Eleonora was married by proxy in Naples to Ercole, then age forty-one.

It was not really very kind of Anna to mention accompanying Eleonora to *Milan* in March, alluding to the long-expected formal wedding to Sforza Maria, who was Eleonora's age. Clearly Eleonora did know that she was being wooed by Ercole, with her father's approval. Once the marriage with Ercole took place by proxy, she had to wait another seven months before she was conducted to Ferrara, which took her by way of Rome, Siena, and Florence, with elaborate receptions in all the cities, and on 4 July 1473 the formal wedding took place in the Duomo in Ferrara. Although we are informed of the Ferrarese delegation that was sent to accompany her, including Pietrobono and other instrumentalists,[29] we do not know if Anna was part of the Naples contingent conducting Eleonora to Ferrara. She might well have been: her status at this point, as this letter shows, is that of a companion, not merely a hired singer, and one on such familiar terms with the princess that she could tease her, using the familiar "voi" rather than "Your Ladyship."[30]

Naples seems to have been the only court where Anna was on the payroll. She may very well have traveled to other courts as she did to Milan, to enliven social festivities. Such notices will be hard to find, however, because they will be occasional payments, which may not have been preserved. Of the reports of her activities that we do know, it is characteristic that the most informative documents do not emanate from Milan. Conversely, Milanese documents concerning women singers, with the exception of two documents mentioning Anna in 1468 and one other, report on performances in Naples, Venice, Florence, Fiorenzuola d'Arda, Bologna, and Savoy.

Some of these notices are known to scholars, so I will present them briefly, in chronological order. In April 1459 the fifteen-year-old Galeazzo Maria Sforza was sent with a Milanese delegation to Florence to honor Pius II, who was on his way to the Congress of Mantua. He greatly impressed the pope:

[28] See Nicola Ferorelli, "Il ducato di Bari sotto Sforza Maria Sforza e Ludovico il Moro," *Archivio storico lombardo*, ser. 5, 41 (1914), 389–468, at 389–433.

[29] Costantino Corvisieri, "Il trionfo romano di Eleonora d'Aragona nel giugno del 1473," *Archivio della Società Romana di Storia Patria* 1 (1878): 475–91 at 480 n. 1, quoting the diary of Ugo Caleffini.

[30] We do not know if Eleonora had music lessons with Johannes Tinctoris, as did her younger sister Beatrice, but she was acquainted with the instruments in the music room of the palazzo in Ferrara, which she showed to a guest; see Lockwood, *Music in Renaissance Ferrara*, 145.

This handsome youth was not yet sixteen, but his character, eloquence, intellect and diligence were such that he seemed wiser than many a grown man. In his expression and bearing he had the dignity of a prince; he gave extemporaneous speeches which most men could scarcely have declaimed after long preparation; there was nothing frivolous or immature about him. It was astounding to hear sentiments of great age issue from the mouth of a child and to listen to a beardless boy express the ideas of a grizzled old man. His father has sent him together with a splendid and magnificently accoutred escort of five hundred horsemen from Milan to Florence to meet the pope.[31]

Such praise would undoubtedly have gratified his parents, but as he grew older Galeazzo was severely criticized for his headstrong indulgence in pleasure.[32] In 1459, however, he was still the perfect prince. On the way to Florence he stopped in Fiorenzuola d'Arda, where he reported to his mother on one of the many entertainments put on in his honor: "Again we danced, but it was a round dance in which the girls sang in a delightful and pleasing way."[33] Four days later he was in Florence, where he was entertained by Cosimo de' Medici (App., Doc. 3):

> After dinner I went to visit the Magnificent Cosimo, who had a daughter of Piero, his son, play a pipe organ that was a delightful thing to hear, which in fact she has done every day since I have been here, and he also arranged for some of his singers to sing, all these things with singular pleasure. But more important, he treats me like one of the family, and lets his womenfolk be where I am, which means that he loves me with all his heart. Then, having heard these sounds and songs, at which Signore Hector, who sang, and whose son played, was always present . . . .

The young woman must be Bianca de' Medici, who played the same pipe organ and sang for Pius II in February 1460 when he returned to Florence after the congress of Mantua.[34]

Galeazzo then went on to Bologna as the commander-in-chief of a large body of cavalry and armed men whose duty was to keep peace in the city as the Pope passed through on his way to Mantua. There, he reported to his mother, at the home of Virgilio Malvezzi (the Malvezzi were the major opposition party to the Bentivoglios and friendly with the Sforzas) (App., Doc. 4):

> There was given the very great pleasure of various sounds, and among other things he had a young woman sing many times, and especially between one *imbadisone* and another,[35] which truly was a sweet thing to hear. Then, having

---

[31] Pius II, *Commentaries: Volume I, Books i–ii*, ed. and trans. Margaret Meserve and Marcello Simonetta, The I Tatti Renaissance Library (Cambridge, MA and London: Harvard University Press, 2003), 311.

[32] See Welch, "Sight, Sound and Ceremony," 158–60.

[33] 15 Apr. 1459. ASM, Pot. Sov. 1461: "una altra volta si ballò. Ma al ballo ritondo nel quale cantandose per le puce in uno modo tropo zentile et piacevele . . ."

[34] See the document cited in William F. Prizer, "Games of Venus: Secular Vocal Music in the Late Quattrocento and Early Cinquecento," *Journal of Musicology* 9 (1991): 3–56 at 3–4 (document on 53–54).

[35] I have not been able to discover what an *imbadisone* is; perhaps a course in the banquet.

dined here with very great pleasure, I watched the women dance, of whom there were fourteen, who had also dined there, and after the young woman sang again, this time in the company of a young man, I had supper and came home.

All these women heard by Galeazzo were probably court ladies or at least, in the city of Bologna, daughters and wives of the upper classes. It is interesting that Galeazzo remarks on women singers, which he clearly appreciated; whether he afforded the same pleasure to his visitors to Milan is unknown, except in 1468 when Anna Inglese entertained the court. But Anna may have given him a taste for English singers, because England was the destination of one of his early attempts at securing singers. On October 1471 he wrote to Edward IV requesting his assistance to Raynerio, "musico nostro," and Aluysio, "nostro familiari," who were traveling to England to seek singers and musicians, and passports were issued on the same day.[36] We do not know if they went, and no English musicians came to the court as far as is known.

Before Galeazzo decided at the end of 1472 to form a court chapel to rival those of Ercole d'Este and King Ferrante, he had borrowed the chapel of his close neighbor, Yolanda of Savoy, several times, sometimes demanding the singers in rather imperious terms, expecting them to be with him on the following day.[37] Eventually he lured Antonio Guinati, who had served in the Savoy chapel since 1457, and who was to become the head of Galeazzo's chapel for many years. Savoy had a flourishing musical chapel even before 1450,[38] undoubtedly on the French model, and it is not surprising that Galeazzo looked to that court first, especially since his wife came from the house of Savoy. The close connections between Milan and Savoy may explain the Milanese ambassador's very detailed description of the week-long festivities devised to entertain Federico, the natural son of the King of Naples, in Turin in February of 1475. Federico had just been in Milan, and was on his way to Burgundy to ask for the hand of Charles the Bold's daughter, Mary, in marriage.[39] On the 7th Yolanda hosted a splendid banquet (see App., Doc. 5):

> Most illustrious and excellent Lord, commending myself always to your lordship's good graces. I will write this letter saying briefly something about the festivities arranged for this illustrious lord Don Federico. I report that Tuesday evening, which was carnival, this illustrious lady [the Duchess, Yolanda] held a banquet at which 93 people, men and women, were seated at a table. And this same lady and Don Federico sat at the head of the table as equals, and at another table there were 26 people. And while they were at table there was brought in a castle with four towers, all painted, and elegant, with all the singers of her chapel, dressed in black velvet tunics and gold chains, singing, and every tower had four shields with arms on them, that is, the arms of

---

[36] Motta, *Musici alla corte degli Sforza*, 301. The passports are in Reg. Duc. 107, fol. 109r.

[37] See Motta, *Musici alla corte degli Sforza*, 302–3.

[38] See Marie-Thérèse Bouquet, "La cappella musicale dei duchi di Savoia dal 1450 al 1500," *Rivista italiana di musicologia* 3 (1968): 233–85. Du Fay was one of its luminaries.

[39] His lengthy (and in the end unsuccessful) trip is summarized in Ronald Woodley, "Tinctoris's Italian Translation of the Golden Fleece Statutes: A Text and a (Possible) Context," *Early Music History* 8 (1988): 173–244 at 182–85 and 191. Woodley suggests that Tinctoris may have accompanied him.

France for Madame, those of the lord King Ferrante, those of your excellency, and those of Savoy, and they carried them singing around the table. Then was brought in a live sheep, with four horns, in a garden, all gilded with carved gold leaves, all trembling, hanging down to his feet, and it was presented along with a strambotto in song.[40] Thirdly there came six men and six women, elegantly dressed, hand in hand in a row, and each was holding a torch, singing, and performing a basse danse in a dignified manner around the table. Lastly were brought in eight little boys, each in his little garden, on a table, dressed in the form of angels; it appeared that they were holding little plates in their hands, and they were placed on strong posts in the little garden, and they sang two by two very fittingly. After the table was removed, armed men appeared on foot, though it appeared they were on horseback, that is, they had bards [horse armor] and tunics down to the ground, and painted lances in their hands, and suddenly there was set up a standard, and they broke their lances, so that it appeared they were jousting. Then there was dancing past midnight, and while dancing there came to the festivities many farces of various kinds,[41] and many men and women dressed very appropriately; in conclusion, it was a beautiful festivity. And Madame said to me: "Tell the lord our brother about this festivity," and I promised I would, and she repeated: "Go, do it."

The first day of Lent, after dining, the lord Federico came to the castle, and there was dancing again, saying that as long as carnival lasted in Milan,[42] one could dance. Thursday, after dinner there was again dancing, sometimes in the hall, sometimes in the chamber of Duke Filiberto himself, where Don Federico retired with the young people, and they were joined by many court and city ladies, and now they danced and now they sang, and they enjoyed other pleasures and entertainments. Yesterday too he was at court, but didn't dance, owing to the Friday devotion, and he was engaged familiarly with laughing and joking with these ladies, and enjoying various pleasantries. Now that his personal customs and manners have been praised to the skies, tomorrow, which is old carnival, there will be more festivities, and Monday (God willing) he will be on his way. I recommend myself to your lordship with devotion. Turin, 11 February 1475.

Of the same excellency your most devoted little servant, Antonio Appiano

Galeazzo must have read this report with interest, comparing the entertainment he himself had offered Federico during his stay in Milan. His own chapel, of course, could have performed in similar manner, and surely the dance was organized along the same lines. Court ladies and gentlemen might well have rehearsed some ceremonial dances, though such dancers do not normally

[40] I take the gilded sheep to be an allusion to Ferrante's having been elected to the Order of the Golden Fleece, in May 1473; perhaps the gold chains worn by the singers were another allusion. Unfortunately, no music manuscripts have survived from the court of Savoy; however, the text and music of the strambotto were probably devised for the occasion.

[41] These were a regular feature of the Savoyan court; see Bouquet, "La cappella musicale dei duchi di Savoia," 280–81.

[42] In the Ambrosian rite, carnival extends to the Saturday before the first Sunday in Lent, referred to later in the letter as "old carnival."

sing at the same time.[43] Thus there is a possibility that the court at Savoy had professional women singers. But in one aspect Galeazzo could not compete: the Milanese chapel had no choirboys, whereas the Savoy court had eight.[44] In the entertainment for Federico they were dressed as angels, and appear to have sung alternating duets. Galeazzo in fact does not seem to have appreciated the singing of children. When he asked to borrow the Savoy chapel on 18 January 1472 he requested "the singers alone; it is not necessary to send anyone else with them" ("li cantarini soli, et non bisogni mandi altra compagnia con loro"), adding in a letter the next day that he wanted "the big singers and not the little ones" ("li cantori grandi et non li picolini").[45] The duchess was somewhat taken aback: the ambassador reported that she wanted the little ones to have their share, and the whole chapel would be sent unless he heard to the contrary.[46] Evidently Galeazzo was adamant, since in October of that year, when he wanted to borrow the chapel again, he specified that the little singers should be left behind, as was done before.[47]

Yolanda's insistence that the ambassador report to Galeazzo Maria in detail about the entertainment offered to Federico in 1475 may reflect a certain undercurrent of rivalry: if Galeazzo had lured the director of her choir and some of her singers for his own chapel a few years earlier, she was still able to put on splendid festivities, with elaborate dancing and singing of men, women, and children, perhaps on a scale that Galeazzo rarely attempted.

These Milanese documents mentioning women singers offer tantalizing glimpses into performance practice, but one that is hard to pinpoint. What exactly did Anna and the other women musicians sing? None of the documents tells us that, but we know that they sang alone, in Anna's case with a tenorista playing the lute or viol, and probably with other instrumental accompaniment, and they also sang with

[43] For example, in Urbino in 1474 singing and dancing took place in alternation. See Alfredo Saviotti, "Una rappresentazione allegorica in Urbino nel 1474," in *Atti e memorie della R. Accademia Petrarca di Scienze, Lettere ed Arti in Arezzo*, n.s. 1 (Arezzo, 1920), 180–236, cited in Wolfgang Osthoff, *Theatergesang und darstellende Musik in der italienischen Renaissance (15. und 16. Jahrhundert)*, 2 vols. (Tutzing: Hans Schneider, 1969), 1: 33–36. Barbara Sparti kindly drew my attention to this reference.
[44] See Bouquet, "La cappella musicale dei duchi di Savoia," 261–75. They were a long-standing choral foundation called the "Innocents." Although they were not formally members of the ducal chapel (see her n. 43), they often sang with them.
[45] ASM, Sforzesco 487 (new 393), partly transcribed in Motta, *Musici alla corte degli Sforza*, 302.
[46] 19 January 1472, ASM, Sforzesco 487 (new 393). "Et madama volse che li petiti, ne havesserono la particella loro; Hor concludendo, li farò parechiare tutti per domane, così li petiti col loro Magistro, como li grandi." Earlier in the letter, the ambassador reports that the duchess had sent one of her singers to clarify what Galeazzo had in mind by the "cantarini." This singer explained that "the little singers with the white robes are not to be understood as being chapel singers" ("li petiti cantarini cum le cappe bianche, non se intendano essere cantarini dela capella"). Perhaps the confusion came about because of the Milanese habit of calling all singers "cantarini," which was the standard terminology until Galeazzo formed his own chapel in 1473, when the term "cantori" become more normal.
[47] "et lassino li picolini come fecero lanno passato"; Motta, *Musici alla corte degli Sforza*, 303.

men, in which case they were surely singing polyphonic songs.[48] In 1472 one of Galeazzo's singers, Pietro da Oli (or Holi), was paid 40 ducats to copy what was probably a choirbook of sacred music (given the price) that belonged to the duchess of Savoy. In the same year four books of French and Spanish songs were purchased, also for forty ducats.[49] The 'libri iiii' were probably not partbooks, a format that would have been unusual though not impossible at this early date;[50] besides, three-voice music would have been more normal, and the cost suggests that these were substantial manuscripts. Spanish songs would have been heard frequently at court, since the chamber singers in the 1460s and early 1470s came from Naples. One of them, Raynerio, copied three Spanish songs and sent them to Galeazzo in 1473, saying that he was sure they would please, and he could send more; if there were any mistakes in them it was not his fault. Possibly the songs were acquired through the intermediation of Anna in Naples. He suggests that they be sung sweetly, softly, and slowly ("dolcemente et sotto voce, et ben pianamente"; *pianamente* could also mean "simply").[51] This was the ideal performance of chamber music, one for which women's voices were well suited. "Dolcemente, et suavemente" were the words used to describe the angelic singing of the "damisella anglese" in Venice in 1455; this may well have been Anna Inglese at the beginning of her illustrious career.

[48] Keith Polk has gathered together a number of references to musical ensembles, especially in Germany, in "Voices and Instruments: Soloists and Ensembles in the 15th Century," *Early Music* 18 (1990): 179–98. For women singers, see 193–95. Most intriguing is the payment in August 1480 of 1 gulden to "4 englisch cantoribus zu Bonomese zu singen" (194). Polk kindly informs me that "Bonomese" is "der Kirche im Dorf Bonames bei Frankfurt," according to Gerhard Pietzsch, whose Nachlaß this notice comes from. His reference in turn is "sA [Stadtarchiv] Frankfurt, Baumeisterrechnung Mgb B 32 No. 9," published in Rudolf Jung, "Stiftungen Jakobs zu Schwanau und seiner Treuhänder zum Bau und zur künstlerischen Ausschmückung von Frankfurter Kirchen 1473–1480," *Einzelforschungen über Kunst- und Altertumsgegenstände zu Frankfurt am Main*, ed.. von Staedt. histor. Museum, Band 1 (Frankfurt a.M., 1908), 1:87–107 at 103. I give the full reference since the Frankfurt archives were destroyed and Pietzsch's Nachlaß (in the music library at the University of Cologne) seems to have been mislaid (Keith Polk, pers. comm.). The occasion was the dedication of the church by the bishop (evidently of Frankfurt), who may have brought the singers with him.

[49] "Per libri iiii da canzone Franzese et Spagnole . . . d. 40. Item per lo libro mandato a tore d. Petro da Oli da la Ill.ma Madama de Savoya secundo il mercato ha dicto domino Petro . . . d. 40." Another undated note mentions "libro uno de canzone spagnole et franzose per tenire in camera." Quoted in Welch, "Sight, Sound and Ceremony," 173 n. 73, from C. d'Adda, *Libreria viscontea et sforzesca del Castello di Pavia* (Milan, 1875), 134.

[50] The Glogauer Liederbuch of *ca.* 1480 is the most significant source, but see also "Stimmbuch" by Ludwig Finscher and Jessie Ann Owens in *Die Musik in Geschichte und Gegenwart*, 2nd ed., Sachteil, 8: 1765–75.

[51] "I vi mando tre canti spagnoli in nela presente interclusi, li quali certamente credo serano boni et dolci. Se ve piacerano ve ne mandarò deli altri, et si alcuno mancamento et discorectione se trovasse in dicti canti, Vostra Excellentia non lo voglia imputare a me che li ho scripti et notati; faciateli cantare dolcemente et sotto voce, et ben pianamente, che son certo ve piacerano." Quoted in Motta, *Musici alla corte degli Sforza*, 530. William Prizer (pers. comm.) cautions against reading "sotto voce" in the modern sense, suggesting that it might mean falsetto: in 1491, when Isabella d'Este was seeking a good soprano, Giovanni Martini replied that he could not find one, but he recommended a contratenor singer: "Il xarà bone cantare sovverano; sotto vose il cante bene" (the letter, of 24 October 1491, is published in Stefano Davari, "La musica a Mantova," *Rivista storica mantovana* 1 [1885], 53–71, 63 n., under the wrong date, 4 October; the source is Archivio di Stato di Mantova, Archivio Gonzaga, Busta 1232, fol. 183). Martini immediately goes on to mention another contralto who sings well but doesn't have a good voice for the chamber; in that case, "sotto voce" may indicate the type of voice and performance best suited to chamber singing.

APPENDIX
Documents

All of the documents except no. 3 are in the Archivio di Stato in Milan. I have added accents and lightly regularized the punctuation.

Doc. 1. Casale, 24 June 1468. Guglielmo Paleologo, Marquis of Monferrato, to Galeazzo Maria Sforza. Sforzesco, Potenze sovrane 124. Transcribed in Motta, *Musici alla corte degli Sforza*, 299–300 and in Merkley and Merkley, *Music and Patronage*, xxvi n. 47. The letter appears in facsimile in *Storia di Milano*, 9:821.

Illustrissime princeps et excellentissime domine pater noster honorandissime. Ha deliberato Anna cantatrice portatrice de la presente venire da vostra illustrissima Signoria per honorarla in queste vostre noze proxime davenire, et fare qualchi belli giochi et solacij, quali credemo piacerano a vostra antelata illustrissima signoria. Per la quale cosa per che como intendemo, dicta Anna è persona honorevole et molto apta et sufficiente a simili giochi et feste, pregamo essa vostra Illustrissima signoria se degni de haverla interceteras soe paregie per ricomendata, come credemo havere la prefata vostra signoria. Alaquale sincero cordis affectu se arricomendiamo. Datum Casali die xxiiij Junij Mcccclxviij.

Guilielmus Marchio Montisferrati etc.

Doc. 2. Naples, 20 March 1472. Francesco Maletta to Galeazzo Maria Sforza. Sforzesco 221 (Naples).

Deinde tentandolo la p.ta M.a perché il S.re suo Duca Hercule non pigliasse dona: Gli disse, ch'esso Duca Hercole havea totalmente deliberato de maritarse: & che gionta la M.ta del Re ad Napoli ne voleva parlare & fare instantia cum quella: Ad la quale dice: che quello signore s'è dato in anima et in corpo: et misso el stato in sua protectione. Disse anchora che 'l havea portato qui retracta la ymagine del p.to Duca Hercule: et chel Re havea opinione, ch'ello havesse circha xlv anni et luy fa cunto: che non è gionto anchora ad xl. Appresso. La Anglese cantarina quale è stata altre volte da v. subl.ta et se mostra molto afectionata ad quella: è qui a li servitij de Madona Leonora. Ha dicto a [cipher sign for Ippolita] che trovandosse questi dì nel giardino cum essa M.a Leonora: et saltando et tripudiando fra loro, essa cantarina gli disse, Dho Madona, quando venirà quello dì ch'io ve accompagni ad Milano da vostro marito. Alche respose M.a Leonora cum sumissa voce: mio marito non è ad Milano: Ma altrove. et ha xl anni. . . .

Doc. 3. Florence, 19 April 1459. Galeazzo Maria Sforza to Francesco Sforza. Paris, Bibliothèque nationale de France, f. it. 1588, fol. 225. The document has also been published by Evelyn Welch, "Sight, Sound and Ceremony," 156.

. . . Nanday ad visitare el M.^{co} Cosmo quale fece sonare una figliola di Piero suo figliolo uno organo de cane che era una zentil cosa da oldire, la quale cosa pero l'ha facto ogni dì dopo ch'io sono qui, et fece anchora cantare per alcuni soy cantatori non senza singulare piacere tute queste cose. Ma molto magiore l'usare la domesticheza con mi, che egli fa in fare stare le donne sue dove jo sto, però che per tal acto me significa che 'l mi voglia bene da bon seno, or olditi quisti sono et canti ali quali el S.^{re} m. Hestor [*sic*] anchora luy era sempre presente et cantò et fece sonare uno suo figliolo . . .

Doc. 4. Bologna, 8 May 1459. Galeazzo Maria Sforza to Bianca Maria Sforza. Sforzesco, Pot. Sov. 1461.

fu dato grandissimo piacere de varij suoni et tra l'altre cose di fare cantare de molte volte una damisella, et maxime fra l'una imbadisone et l'altra, che in vero fu una dolce cosa da oldire. Or quivi cenato con grandissimo piacere, vidi ballare le done, che a numero erano xiiij, quale haveveno cenato anchora lì et cantato una altra volta per la dicta damisella, quale cantava in compagnia con uno Giovane[;] facto colazione ne sono venuto a casa. . . .

Doc. 5. Turin, 11 February 1475. Antonio Appiano to Galeazzo Maria Sforza. Sforzesco 492 (new 398) (Savoy).

Illustrissimo et Excellentissimo Signore mio. Ricommandandome sempre ala bona gratia de vostra sublimità. Scriverò per questa discurrendo breve qualche cosa de le feste facte a questo Illustrissimo Signore don Federico: Et dico che martesdì sera che fu carnevale, questa Illustrissima Madama [Yolanda of Savoy] gli fece un bancheto, dove erano 93 persone assetate tra homini et donne, ad una tavola. Et ipsa prefata Madama, et Signore don Federico, in capo de tavola de pari, et ad un'altra tavola, erano persone 26: et stando a tavola fu portato un castello de quatro torre, tutto depincto, et polito, cum tutti li ciantri de la sua capella, travestiti cum turche de veluto negro et colane d'oro, cantando, et ogni torre haveva quatro scuti, cum l'arme suso, videlicet l'arma di Franza per Madama, quella del Signore Re Ferrando, quella di vostra excellentia et quella di Savoya, et lo portarono cantanto [*sic*] intorno la tavola: poy fu portato un moltono [*sic*] vivo, cum quatro corne, in un zardino, tutto dorato cum folie d'oro, intagliate, tutte tremante, et pendente fin ali pedi, et fu presentato cum una canzone de stramotti. Tercio venerono sei homini, et sey donne, travestiti dignamente, tenendosi tutti ala filla per mane, et ciaschuno havea la sua torza in mane, cantando, et facendo bassadanza dignamente intorno la tavola. Ultimate [*sic*] forono portati octo petiti garzoneti caduno nel suo zardineto, su la tavola, ornati in forma d'angeli, che pariva tenessero li piatelli in mane, et erano posti su forti bastoni nel zardineto, et cantavano a duy, a duy molto dignamente. Doppo levata la tavola, comparseno homini armati a pede che pariva fosserono a cavallo, cioè le barde et sopraveste fin a terra, et le lanze depincte in mane, et subito fu piantata una tella, et rompevano quelle lanze, parendo che giostrasserono: deinde se ballò, fin passata meza nocte, et ballando, venerono su la festa de molte farse, in diversi modi, et molti homini, et done travestiti dignamente, concludendo fu una bella festa. Et Madama me disse, Avisareti vuy el Signore nostro Frare, di questa festa; dixigli, de sì: Me repplicò, hor fatelo.

El primo giorno de quaresima presso disnare, venne in castello el prefato Signore don Federico, et se ballò anchora, dicendosi che fin al carnevale de Milano, se può ballare. Zobia doppo disnare, pur si ballò, quando in sala, et quando in la camera del Signore duca Philiberto, ove ipso Signore don Federico se reduceva cum la brigata zovene, et la andavano de molte Madame de la corte, et de la cità, et quando si ballava, et quando si cantava, et se facevano altri piaceri et solazi. Heri etiam stete in corte, ma non si ballò, per la divotione del venere, et stete molto domesticamente ridendo et solazando cum queste Madame, et facendosi qualchi solazi. Adeo, che tanti suoi humani costumi et maynere, sonno laudati fin al celo, domane che sarà carnevale vechio, se farano altre feste, et poy lune (deo dante) se partirà. Ala Signoria vostra divotamente sempre mi ricommando. Ex Thaurino xj. Februarij 1475.

Eiusdem Excellentiae vestrae divotissimus servulus Antonius de [Aplano]

Music for Margherita Farnese

Anne MacNeil

This essay comprises three stages in the life of a Renaissance princess. It offers a cultural analysis of the musical and theatrical entertainments written and performed by and for Margherita Farnese, princess of Parma. The three stages of her biography reflect Margherita's changing relationship to the Gonzaga court in Mantua, the home of her husband Vincenzo Gonzaga. The first phase relates to her preparations for entering Mantuan life as Vincenzo's bride. The second phase focuses on the Gonzaga court's reception of Margherita as its future duchess. And the third phase concerns the divergence of Margherita's and Vincenzo's lives after the wedding is annulled, when she enters the convent of St. Paul in Parma and he weds Eleonora de' Medici, the eldest princess of the Grand Duchy of Tuscany. When Margherita's biography and the entertainments which narrate it are considered together, a remarkable conception of these works and their significance unfolds. These musical and theatrical compositions portray the anxieties of the Farnese and Gonzaga families with regard to the marriage of Margherita and Vincenzo and its importance for the political landscape of northern Italy. Moreover, they portray Margherita's personal anxieties about coming of age and assimilating herself into a new family and a new culture, and about her own obligations as a representative of the Mantuan state and an author of its image.

The story of Margherita Farnese's wedding to Vincenzo Gonzaga in 1581 and its subsequent annulment is a prophetic tale with respect to the political fortunes of the northern Italian courts of Mantua and Parma. Marred by a series of gruesome medical examinations, Margherita's marriage was initially heralded as a monument to the unification of two of northern Italy's most strategic courts. But after two torturous years, Margherita relented to pressures from the Gonzaga family and signed over her dowry as she entered the Convent of Saint Paul in Parma.

Documentation of the bride's journey to Mantua and her brief time at the Gonzaga court is filled with reports of her music-making, dancing lessons, performances attended, and compositions made in her honor. The cast of characters is impressive: court composer Giaches de Wert dedicated his seventh book of madrigals to Margherita and dancing master Isachino da Mantova taught her to dance in the latest Mantuan style. She heard concerts sung by members of Alfonso II d'Este's renowned *concerto delle donne*, and she was offered performances of comedies by the famous *commedia dell'arte* troupe, i Gelosi. These were among the very best composers and performers in all of western Europe, who, in the 1580s, were at the height of their careers.

The Mantuan agent Cesare Cavriani was charged by Guglielmo Gonzaga (Vincenzo's father and the reigning Duke of Mantua) with making daily reports of Margherita's activities. These include her responses to purges and medical examinations, in addition to descriptions of what she did to pass the time. Together with reports made by Aurelio Zibramonte (another Mantuan secretary) concerning his negotiations on Guglielmo's behalf for musicians from the Farnese court and with the letters written by Margherita herself to various members of the Mantuan establishment, Cavriani's letters provide us with the bulk of our information regarding Margherita Farnese during the first and second phases of her biography.[1]

I. The Marriage, the Newlywed's Medical Problems, and Their Political Impact

Margherita Farnese (1567-1643) was the first daughter of Alessandro Farnese, third Duke of Parma, and Maria of Portugal. Maria died in 1577, and from this date Margherita was raised by her paternal grandmother, Margherita of Austria. In 1580, when the child was only thirteen years old, her grandmother took her on a trip to the Low Countries. During that year, negotiations took place for Margherita's betrothal to Vincenzo Gonzaga (1562-1612), crown prince of Mantua, and the contracts were finalized on 23 November 1580.

Margherita and Vincenzo did not meet until 25 February 1581—one week following her return from Namur and one week prior to their wedding at the Duomo in Piacenza. On 30 April, the newlyweds entered Mantua together. Margherita was fourteen years of age and Vincenzo, nineteen. Within a matter of days, it was discovered that Margherita and Vincenzo were unable to consummate their marriage. The doctors consulted (they came from Mantua, Parma, and Rome) maintained that Margherita suffered from a congenital impediment which might be cured (depending on which doctor was being consulted), either with the application of various purges and unguents, or with a delicate, but simple surgical procedure which, by November 1582 (a year and a half after the wedding and after the discovery of these problems), had yet to be performed. At the same time, the Farnese family insisted that it was Vincenzo who suffered some defect which prevented consummation of the union. And, in fact, medical reports show that he did have a fistula in an inconvenient location.

The stakes in this confrontation were high. Vincenzo's father, Guglielmo Gonzaga, had fathered only one son among three children, and if Vincenzo's marriage failed to provide an heir, the Duchy of Mantua would pass to a distant, French branch of the family, which would introduce Protestantism into the region.

---

[1] Chiefly, these documents are preserved in the Archivio di Stato di Mantova (ASMN), Archivio Gonaga, buste 201, 202, , 410B, 1255, 2212, 2615, 2624, 2625, 2626, 2952, 2954, 2955. See also Maria Bellonci, *Segreti dei Gonzaga* (Milan: Arnoldo Mondadori, 1947).

On the part of the Farnese, the Duchy of Parma was in competition with Mantua for the protection of Emperor Charles V at a time when control over various regions in northern Italy was under contention. Moreover, as relative upstarts among north-Italian nobility (the Duchy of Parma being established only in 1545), the Farnese needed to marry their daughters into prestigious families in order to build the strength and allegiances of the nascent duchy.

Thus, in the matter concerning the medical response to Margherita's condition, Duke Alessandro Farnese and his mother, Margherita of Austria, were fervently opposed to the surgery because they feared it might result in Margherita's death. At the same time, they insisted the marriage continue. The Gonzaga, surprisingly enough, were similarly against the surgery, but for a very different reason: because it would not guarantee them a fertile union for Vincenzo and the continuation of their own dynastic line. The debate raged on through 1582 and into 1583, with Margherita taking purges and undergoing medical examinations throughout. She submitted to all this willingly: her letters and the daily reports written by Cavriani all tell of her unending love for Vincenzo and her fervent desire to fulfill the roles of wife and mother.[2]

Finally, with the third anniversary of the marriage looming, time was running out for the possibility of declaring it annulled. Guglielmo Gonzaga enlisted the aid of the Pope, advising Gregory XIII of the dangers of allowing Mantua to fall into the hands of Protestants. Gregory, in turn, authorized Cardinal Carlo Borromeo in January of 1583 to investigate the situation, with a strong cautionary note that the current Gonzaga hereditary line must remain intact. On 9 October (1583), after Margherita had already entered a convent in Parma, Borromeo officially declared the marriage annulled.

Vincenzo Gonzaga was now in the position of having to undergo his own set of embarrassing examinations, in anticipation of a second wedding to Eleonora de' Medici. These were dictated by Grand Duke Francesco de' Medici in order to ensure that it was not Vincenzo's deficiencies that prevented consummation of his marriage to Margherita Farnese. Vincenzo was required to prove his virility before witnesses. He did so in Venice on 7 March 1584 and he married Eleonora six weeks later.

II. Women as Conservators of Manners—Women as Authors of Monarchic Power

Music, dance, and theater serve in the late sixteenth century as some of the primary modes by which a noble woman might express herself. Women often organized important musical and theatrical spectacles at court and, in so doing, upheld the manners, style, and self-fashioning of the monarchy and its rulers. Such spectacles circumscribed the kinship of the court, distinguishing between its insiders and

---

[2] Margherita could have been excommunicated if she were found to be trying to end her marriage, in which case she would not have been able to enter a convent—the only viable alternative for a single noblewoman.

outsiders, delineating lines of heredity, paternity, and orders of succession. They also instructed audiences in modes of civic responsibility, adult behavior, and the ways to live well. As Stephen Orgel writes, in reference to the English court masque, "every masque is a ritual in which society affirms its wisdom and asserts its control of its world and its destiny."[3] The presentation of grand, staged spectacles is thus virtually synonymous with the perceived power of the court that sponsors them. A female monarch, in assuming an organizational or advisory role in court-sponsored musical-theatrical events, put herself in the position of conserving the court's image and, in effect, writing the history and culture of the ruling family and its dominions for a contemporary audience.

Margherita of Austria, wife of Philip III and Queen of Spain until her death in 1611, is an excellent case in point—more so for the purposes of this study because she was a member of the Gonzaga family and her wedding in 1598 was celebrated at the Mantuan court. Margherita's personal desires regarding music and spectacle profoundly affected the perception of her husband's regency and the potency of Spanish rule. Queen Margherita's disapproval of theatrical court entertainments, and especially of theatrical music, helped to undermine the perceived strength of her husband's regime. As Louise Stein has noted, "Philip III is known to have been a weak and impressionable young king, and it is thought that the real power of state (and the authority in matters of court life) lay not with him but with his first minister and *valido* the Duke of Lerma."[4] Coincidentally, the Duke of Lerma organized sumptuous theatrical entertainments, while Philip III and Margherita did not, although they did produce stately social dances, or *saraos*, which helped to define and maintain courtly manners.

Queen Margherita demonstrated her distaste of theatrical productions also during her wedding festivities in Italy. Her biographer, Diego de Guzmán, wrote in 1617 that the new queen attended the entertainments performed for her in Ferrara, Mantua, and Milan out of a sense of obligation rather than pleasure. When she and Philip settled into their regency, she discouraged such spectacles and the Spanish court remained relatively arid of these monumentalizing musical-theatrical productions. After her death in 1611, however, grand, staged entertainments again became part of life at the Spanish court.

A noblewoman's desires regarding grand court spectacles may be seen not only in her sponsorship of them (or lack thereof), but also in the editorial censorship of entertainments. The position of advisor (or, as we might call it today, artistic director) often fell to the female monarch: examples include the festivities organized by Catherine de' Medici at Fontainebleau in 1564 and at Bayonne in 1565, as well as Eleonora de' Medici's involvement in the festivities produced in

---

[3] Stephen Orgel and Roy Strong, eds., *Inigo Jones: The Theatre of the Stuart Court*, 2 vols. (Berkeley and London: University of California Press, 1973), 1: 13.

[4] Louise K. Stein, *Songs of Mortals, Dialogues of the Gods: Music and Theatre in Seventeenth-Century Spain* (Oxford: Clarendon Press, 1993), 68.

Mantua in honor of the wedding of her son Francesco and Margherita of Savoy in 1608.[5]   In Mantua, Eleonora served as the advisor for the performance of Claudio Monteverdi's *Arianna*. "It's very dry," she is reported to have said after witnessing a run-through of the play in March of 1608. And as Tim Carter relates, the comedy's creators (the poet Ottavio Rinuccini and the composer Claudio Monteverdi—and potentially "entertainment director" Federico Follino and the *commedia dell'arte* actress who sang the role, Virginia Andreini, significantly modified its structure to conform to Eleonora's desires.[6]

Margherita Farnese, like Queen Margherita of Spain, understood very well the position she would assume as Princess of Mantua in conserving Mantuan manners through music and dance. In the month leading up to her entrance into the city in March 1581, she took lessons from the dancing master Isachino da Mantova, and she declared her desire to comport herself in a well-mannered fashion for the dances that would be performed as part of her wedding celebrations. She was *assuming* Mantuan manners and culture in learning how to dance in Mantuan style. This kind of cultural induction into the bride's new court often extended to clothing as well. For the Medici wedding of 1589, for example, Christine of Lorraine was greeted at the Medici villa at Poggio a Caiano during the week before her formal entry into Florence by, among things, a full wardrobe of dresses made in Florentine style—a wardrobe that she then adopted as the Grand Duchess of Tuscany.

The fourteen-year-old Margherita Farnese, however, seems not to have understood, as her successor Eleonora de' Medici did so very well, the relationship of music, dance, and spectacle to the greater vision of the Mantuan court. Nor does she seem to have comprehended the symbiotic relationship of the performative arts and politics, which was increasingly crucial to the strength and perception of the Mantuan state.

III. The Princess of Mantua's Personal Desires Regarding Music and Spectacle

When we see in the young Margherita Farnese a preference for quiet, intimate music-making—she sang songs to the simple accompaniment of a recorder and she sang *ottave* from Ariosto's *Orlando furioso*, probably to a simple bass accompaniment like the Ruggiero, named for one of the protagonists in Ariosto's epic—and when we see in her a distaste for the performance of comedies and the raucous masquerades and other theatrical festivities given in Ferrara during carnival in 1582, we recognize a rasping friction between her personal tastes and those of her new husband, Vincenzo Gonzaga.

Vincenzo's penchant for grand, often bawdy, musical-theatrical entertainments is well documented. Having been kept on a short financial leash by his father during most of his adolescence, Vincenzo spent much time at the more lively court

---

[5] See my "Weeping at the Water's Edge," *Early Music* 27, no. 3 (Aug. 1999): 406-17.

[6] Tim Carter, "Lamenting Ariadne?" *Early Music* 27, no. 3 (Aug. 1999): 395-405.

of Ferrara, especially after the marriage of his sister Margherita to Alfonso II d'Este in 1579. Once Vincenzo inherited the Duchy of Mantua in 1587, however, he paid lavish sums to sponsor theatrical spectacles at court and to ensure that Mantua was home to the best theatrical musicians and actors in western Europe. Indeed, Vincenzo's desire for such spectacles may have been fueled in part by the fallout of his marriage to Margherita Farnese and the subsequent shadow that was cast over his potency as both man and ruler. In addition to the theatrical entertainments Vincenzo sponsored throughout his regency—including the monumental performances of Battista Guarini's *Il pastor fido* (1598), of Monteverdi's *Arianna* in 1608, and the numerous performances by various *commedia dell'arte* troupes that eventually resulted in his naming the Compagnia de' Gelosi "The Duke's Comedians" and making citizens of the Andreini family—the strength of Vincenzo's image-making may also be seen in his commissioned portraits, which present him as a robust man with a bold stance, in full armor and with a prominent codpiece. Indeed, it is remarkable in Renaissance portraiture that Vincenzo Gonzaga is so rarely represented out of armor.

Inherent in Margherita Farnese's choices of entertainment during the period of her betrothal to Vincenzo is her serious misunderstanding of precisely this importance of bold musical and theatrical display to the image of the Mantuan state. Perhaps this was a result of her age and inexperience. And perhaps it was a result of the fact that the Duchy of Parma, in 1581, was quite new: established only in 1545 by Margherita's great-grandfather, it had yet to become identified with specific styles of theatrical activity, although construction of the famous Teatro Farnese would soon be initiated by Margherita's brother, Ranuccio.

Music-making at the court of Parma during the reigns of Margherita's grandfather, Ottavio, and her father, Alessandro, had become quite well-established. As may be seen in the chronology for March 1581 (see Appendix 2), the Farnese court sponsored a number of carnival activities, in which Margherita participated or not, depending on her physical reactions to purgation. One such *ballo*, given on 27 March, is described in a sonnet written by the *commedia dell'arte* actress Isabella Andreini, "È danza, or pugna questa?" Here, Andreini portrays the dance as a glorious, marshall victory for Love.

> *Sonetto LXIX*
> *Sopra La Corrente, Ballo nel quale i Cavalieri rubano le Dame*

> > *È Danza, ò pugna questa? ecco s'io miro*
> *Mover Dive, & Heroi con arte il vago*
> *Leggiadro piè, di lieti balli appago*
> *Il cor, ne chiede altr' esca il mio desiro.*   4
>
> > *Se predar veggio in questo breve giro*
> *La bella amica al valoroso vago.*
> *Scorgo del Frigio involator l'imago.*

> *O di quei ch'à Sabini il bel rapiro.*   8
>   *Amore, e Marte han quì lor misto impero*
> *L'un'arde, e l'altro invola, ed ambi il crine*
> *Cingon fastose, ed honorate palme.*   11
>   *O fortunate, ò nobili rapine,*
> *Com'hoggi fate il gran trionfo altero*
> *Vincendo Marte i corpi, ed Amor l'alme.*   14

Sonnet 69
About "La Corrente," a dance in which the knights steal the women

>   Is this a battle or a dance? Lo, if I watch
> The goddesses and heroes move with skill
> Their graceful, nimble feet, I please my heart
> With joyous dance, and no bait else asks my desire.   4
>   If in this brief whirl I observe
> The valorous lover carry off his sweetheart,
> Scenes of the Phrygian rapists I behold,
> Or those who stole the Sabine men's delight.   8
>   Love and Mars have joined their empires here,
> One burns, the other steals, and both bind round
> Their locks the splendid and the venerated palms.   11
>   O you abductions noble, fortunate,
> How great a triumph proud you've made today,
> Mars vanquishes your bodies, Love your souls.[7]   14

As Richard Sherr notes, negotiations between Alessandro Farnese and Guglielmo Gonzaga in the early days of Margherita's and Vincenzo's marriage concerned the acquisition by the Mantuan court of various singers from the Farnese musical establishment. Two were male: a castrato and a bass, neither of whom were released from service in Parma. Others, however, were female and specifically designated as musicians and companions for Margherita: Laura Bovia and Ippolita Mezzovillani. Negotiations concerning the illegitimate Bovia's suitability to serve as a companion to the young princess came to nothing, but Mezzovillani entered Mantuan service on 25 June 1581. A year later, Margherita declared herself to be less interested in music than she had thought (11 July 1582, "la Serenissima Signora Principessa per servitio della quale fu presa non s'è dilettata della musica come si credeva"), and Mezzovillani was dismissed.[8]

The documents concerning the singer Mezzovillani, together with others from 1581 and 1582, show Margherita to be gradually losing interest in entertainments during the years when medical scrutiny into her congenital impediment was most

---

[7] *Selected Poems of Isabella Andreini,* introduction and edition by Anne MacNeil, translations and notes by James Wyatt Cook (Lanham MD: Scarecrow Press, 2005), 184-85.

[8] Richard Sherr, "The Publications of Guglielmo Gonzaga," *Journal of the American Musicological Society* 31 (1978): 118-25.

intense. In July of 1581, when Margherita had been taking purges for over four
months, she indicated to Guglielmo Gonzaga that she had no interest in seeing
comedies performed by the Compagnia de' Gelosi, in spite of the fact that he had
already commanded them to come to her. Six months later, in January of 1582,
after ten days of carnival activities in Ferrara with her husband, his sister, and
his sister's husband Alfonso II d'Este, Margherita grew weary of the continuous
celebrating and yearned to return to Mantua. On the 21st of that month, the
Duchess of Ferrara and her ladies organized a special entertainment in which they
would dance, but Margherita did not participate. After another six months, she
would lose interest even in the small-scale, intimate music-making she had once
loved and would send Mezzovillani away.

IV. Giaches de Wert's Musical Homage to the Young Bride

One of the foremost compositions reflecting the Mantuan court's embrace of
Margherita as its future duchess is Giaches de Wert's *Settimo libro de madrigali*.
Comprising a collection of thirteen madrigals, Wert's book serves as a primer to
instruct the young princess about the combat between Love and Scorn, and Love's
eventual triumph. While many scholars have discussed individual madrigals from
this collection—most notably the stunningly beautiful setting of Torquato Tasso's
"Giunto alla tomba" and the rather crude musical representations of love-making
in Battista Guarini's "Tirsi morir volea"—none have looked on the book as a
comprehensive statement about love and marriage. Indeed, several scholars have
noted that the contents of Wert's *Settimo libro* seem particularly *in*appropriate to the
celebration of a wedding.

When placed in the context of other wedding entertainments, however,
the narrative thread of Wert's madrigal book becomes clear. The enactment of
conflict and, in particular, the representation of conflicting desires, such as Love
and Scorn, is an omnipresent construct in sixteenth-century music and literature.
Dialogical structures (and by this I mean forms which are based on the presentation
of conflicting ideas and their eventual reconciliation) are not foregrounded in our
historical narratives, and so we do not often recognize the number and importance
of sources that are cast in this form. And yet, a moment's thought allows our
recollection of such sources to multiply. Baldassare Castiglione's *Il cortegiano* is set
in the form of a dialogue, as are Ercole Bottrigari's *Il desiderio*, Giordano Bruno's
La cena dei ceneri, Boccaccio's *Decameron*, Machiavelli's *Dell'arte della guerra*, Lodovico
Dolce's *Dialogo della institutione delle donne* among his five others, Leone de' Sommi's
Quattro dialogi in materia di rappresentazioni sceniche, Galileo Galilei's seminal scientific
essay *Dialogo sui massimi sistemi del mondo* and his father Vincenzo's *Dialogo della
musica antica et della moderna* of 1581 (which is the foundational document of the
Florentine Camerata), Giraldi Cinzio's *Dialoghi della vita civile*, Stefano Guazzo's
La civil conversazione, Antonio Minturno's *L'arte poetica*, Francesco Patrizi's twenty-
three dialogues on history, philosophy and honor, Alessandro Piccolomini's *Dialogo
della bella creanza delle donne*, among others, Annibale Romei's *Discorsi*, Giovan
Maria Artusi's diatribe against Claudio Monteverdi's compositional practices, and

Torquato Tasso's dialogues, written in the last fifteen years of his life. These are just a few of the dialogues that inform courtly discourse in the sixteenth century.

Dialogues such as these allude to the didactic purpose of the genre, which allows, at the same time, for an emphasis on the art of persuasion, in contrast to more pedantic demonstrations of authority, as may be seen in monological treatises. An overview of the genre also shows a remarkable wealth of dialogues written about manners, life at court, and women. Both observations go a long way toward answering a central question about sixteenth-century dialogues that is posed by Virginia Cox in her excellent, but limited, treatment of the subject in *The Renaissance Dialogue*:

> It seems reasonable to assume that, when any age adopts on a wide scale a form which so explicitly "stages" the act of communication, it is because that act has, for some reason, come to be perceived as problematic. The causes of this crisis in communication may be epistemological or sociolinguistic, or a combination of the two: the breakdown of traditional certainties, a failure of confidence in the concept of certainty itself, a major shift in the medium or audience of literary discourse.[9]

All of the options Cox offers ring true in various contexts. Discovery and translation into Latin of Aristotle's *Poetics* in the last years of the fifteenth century caused a comprehensive renovation of Renaissance thinkers' conceptions of literature and its significance, thereby undermining communal ideas of certainty; Galileo Galilei's dialogue on the earth's systems even more so. The advent of printing and, later, of music printing, expanded a writer's audience of readers beyond the confines of his known circle of friends and colleagues, thus presenting a major shift in the audience of literary and musical discourse. The establishment of permanent ambassadorial practice among the courts of Europe gave rise to a constant influx of strangers to local custom, which would contribute to a breakdown of traditional certainties; and the inexplicable attention to women in courtly settings in the sixteenth century provided an audience with little or no commitment to traditional avenues of education, thus drawing Cox's epistemological and sociolinguistic reasonings together. With regard to a wedding ceremony, which serves as a coming-of-age ritual for its participants, dialogues are a way of educating the bride and groom into their new responsibilities as adult members of court and society.

Poetic dialogues that have been set to music are more prevalent than our mainstream historical narratives will allow. The frottola repertory, for example, contains numerous dialogues, set to music by Bartolomeo Tromboncino, Ruffino d'Assisi, Pietro da Hostia, and Bernardo Pisano, among others, and Serafino dall'Aquila's strambotto-dialogue "Crudo Caronte" achieved lasting popularity throughout the continent, inspiring variant settings by numerous composers. Somewhat loftier dialogues may also be found among the works of Phillipe Verdelot.

---

[9] Virginia Cox, *The Renaissance Dialogue: Literary Dialogue in its Social and Political Contexts, Castiglione to Galileo*, Cambridge Studies in Renaissance Literature and Culture 2 (Cambridge: Cambridge University Press, 1992), 7.

The great composer and teacher of the Renaissance, Adrian Willaert, set a far-reaching precedent for the representational use of musical textures in his settings of sonnet-dialogues from Petrarch's *Canzoniere*, and he instilled these compositional techniques in his pupils Perissone Cambio, Baldassare Donato, Cipriano da Rore, and Nicolà Vicentino, all of whom also wrote dialogues in a northern style favored by Venetian academies. Other, still later, composers in this style include Andrea and Giovanni Gabrieli, Claudio Monteverdi, and Heinrich Schütz. The primary offshoot of this central tradition of the genre reaches out to the nearby cities of Ferrara, Mantua, and Modena in the works of Orazio Vecchi and Giaches de Wert.

In outline, the narrative structure of Wert's *Settimo libro* follows this plan:

1. "Sorgi e rischiara"—an introductory paean to Margherita's and Vincenzo's marriage and its luminous prophecy for the Mantuan court.

2, 3, 4, 5. "Misera, che farò," "Donna, se ben le chiome," "Vive doglioso il core," and "Vani e sciocchi"—four variations on the theme of love scorned. Note that the second of these, "Donna, se ben le chiome," presents the expression of a man too old to decorously pursue his desires.

6. "Vaghi boschetti"—a luscious invocation to love consumated. The heady sensuousness of this madrigal, with its recollection of sweet laurels, myrtles, cedar, and citrus exuding perfume in the sultry heat of the noonday summer sun, and in the last two lines, the refreshing, playful flight of the two nightingales among the shady branches of the trees, offers us a clearly erotic scene in which two lovers enjoy each other in the shade of an intimate bower. This scene mimics the setting of Phaedrus's love-making with Socrates in Plato's erotic dialogue on the madness and transcendence of Love in the *Phaedrus* dialogue.

7, 8, and 9. "Io mi vivea del mio languir," "Solo e pensoso," "Giunto alla tomba"—three madrigals on the theme of love known, then lost. This theme encompasses, especially in "Giunto alla tomba," a simultaneous reading of the idea of lost love as a confrontation with the concept that the human body in the end presents an obstacle to the fulfillment of true, or pure, love, in that it imprisons Love within the heart of the beloved.[10] As you may see from the text of "Giunto alla tomba" within the context of Tasso's *Gerusalemme liberata* (Appendix 1), Wert's decision to set only two *ottave* from Tasso's epic stops short of including the passage that refers explicitly to mortal death and the departure of the soul from the body. Thus, with regard to the enactment of a Neoplatonic ascent or transcendance to the divine, these three madrigals represent that stage when the lover realizes that achievement of divine love entails the separation of the soul from the corporeal realm.

10 and 11. "Voi volete ch'io muoia" and "Grazie ch'a pochi il ciel"—two madrigals on the reawakening of love and its relationship to feminine grace.

---

[10] The translation and interpretation offered here are somewhat different than those of Jessie Anne Owens in "Marenzio and Wert Read Tasso: A Study in Contrasting Aesthetics," *Early Music* 27, no. 4 (Nov. 1999): 555-74.

12. "Tirsi morir volea"—a celebration of the joys of shared love and the benefits of mutual orgasm.

13. "In qual parte sì ratto"—a concluding hymn in praise of the expected procreative results of love-making and their significance for the dynastic fortunes of the Gonzaga line.

I have alluded, now, to the dialogues of Plato, with regard to "Giunto alla tomba" and its companions under the rubric of love known, then lost. Plato's dialogues, and especially *Phaedrus* and the *Symposium*, stand at the heart of my argument concerning the overall narrative structure of Wert's seventh book. They do so because, in these works, Plato expresses a conception of the cosmos that places Eros, or Love, among the three originary gods. This is Hesiod's vision of the universe, which also gives us the imagined realm of Arcadia. In addition to underlying Plato's conception of Eros, and Renaissance writers's conceptions of the pastoral landscape, this Hesiodic cosmology lies also at the foundation of the Orphic literature, wherein Orpheus is the singer of theogony (the genealogy of the gods) and eschatology (death and judgement, heaven and hell). Here, Orpheus's compelling song encompasses epic poetry, healing, oracles, and rites of initiation with regard to puberty and sexuality—all intimately linked with the power of his songs to persuade.[11]

Plato utilizes this conception of Eros several times in his writings, but nowhere more evocatively than in the *Phaedrus* dialogue, where Socrates explains to the boy Phaedrus the nature of divine madness.

> And we made four divisions of the divine madness, ascribing them to four gods, saying that prophecy was inspired by Apollo, the mystic madness by Dionysus, the poetic by the Muses and the madness of love, inspired by Aphrodite and Eros, we said was the best.[12]

Plato further elucidates the process by which this love-madness is achieved, which inspires the soul's transcendance. The soul, he describes as a tripartite conception, embodied in the figure of a charioteer and his team of horses.

> Now when the charioteer beholds the love-inspiring vision, and his whole soul is warmed by the sight, and is full of the tickling and prickings of yearning, the horse that is obedient to the charioteer, constrained then as always by modesty, controls himself and does not leap upon the beloved; but the other no longer heeds the pricks or the whip of the charioteer, but springs wildly forward, causing all possible trouble to his mate and to the charioteer, and forcing them to approach the beloved and propose the joys of love.[13]

---

[11] *The Oxford Classical Dictionary: The Ultimate Reference Work on the Classical World,* 3rd ed., edited by Simon Hornblower and Antony Spawforth, s.v. "Heriod," "dialogue," "Orphism," "Orphic literature" (Oxford: Oxford University Press, 1996).

[12] Plato, *Euthyphro, Apology, Crito, Phaedo, Phaedrus,* translated by H. N. Fowler (Cambridge MA: The Loeb Classical Library, 1982), 533.

[13] Ibid., 495. Note that in the Homeric and Anacreontic interpretations of Eros, he is depicted as cruel and unruly, flaying the lovestruck with a whip.

Representation of this process as an enactment of the simultaneous expression of conflicting desires allows for an analogy to be made with regard to Plato's choice of genre for his dialogue, for Socrates and Phaedrus, engaged in dialogue regarding the nature of Eros and the soul, represent the very love-madness of which they speak. This allows us to tease out further an analogy with dialogues written by Renaissance writers who show a particular interest in and affinity for the dialogues of Plato. This is especially true of the Ferrarese and Mantuan writers mentioned earlier. Tasso, for example, acknowledges a profound debt to Plato in his *Discourse on the Art of the Dialogue* and even includes close readings of portions of Plato's dialogues in that text. Among these is an explicit reference to the scene in *Phaedo* where Socrates rubs his leg and later entwines his hands in Phaedo's beautiful locks while offering a discourse on the interrelatedness of pleasure and pain. This clearly is a variation on the theme of the Phaedran charioteer and his unruly, erotic team.[14]

Reference to the Orphic literature draws blood from two particular veins that associate the Orpheus legend with Renaissance dialogues and impute cultural meaning to them. Recall that in Ovid's *Metamorphoses*, Virgil's *Georgics*, and Monteverdi's *Orfeo*, Orpheus's songs are, above all, forms of persuasion which can, famously, entice all of nature to bend to his will. Born of the god Apollo and one of the Muses, Orpheus selects the beautiful but mortal Eurydice to be his bride, thereby foresaking his right to immortality in favor of their love. When Eurydice dies of a snake-bite before she and Orpheus have had the opportunity to consumate their love, he travels to the gates of Tartarus and entices the boatman Charon to ferry him across the river Styx so that he may sing his desire to Pluto and Persephone. Imitation of these moments in the Orpheus legend, when Eros draws Earth and Tartarus together, forms the foundation of much of music history, let alone an entire genre of madrigal-dialogues.

Thus, much of the madrigal-dialogue literature accesses in a substantive way the musical arts of persuasion attributed to Orpheus by direct reference to the moment when he stands at the gates of Tartarus, binding the Earth to the Underworld by virtue of his song. Finally, it is worth noting that the subject of Orpheus's songs of persuasion before the gods of Tartarus is the rite of sexual initiation for himself and Eurydice, which had been prevented by her death. As he sings to Pluto and Persephone in Book 10 of Ovid's *Metamorphoses*, "I ask as a gift from you only the enjoyment of her."[15] This binds the art of persuasion and Orpheus's love-madness to rites of sexual initiation.

This connection of the art of persuasion with the dialogue brings us full circle to one of the central characteristics of the form: that unlike a monological treatise or musical composition, the dialogue seeks to persuade to its purpose by adopting a

---

[14] Ibid., 209, and Torquato Tasso, *Tasso's Dialogues: A Selection, with the Discourse on the Art of the Dialogue*, translated with introduction and notes by Carnes Lord and Dain A. Trafton (Berkeley, Los Angeles, and London: University of California Press, 1982), 39.

[15] Ovid, *Metamorphoses*, translated and with an introduction by Mary M. Innes (London and New York: Penguin Books, 1955), 226.

conversational approach. The dialogue's composer forecasts his audience's idealized resistence to his theme, thereby showing us the process by which Renaissance readers might have interpreted the ideas placed before them. The friction between the author's ideas and his readers' imagined responses creates the heat typically associated with both dialogues and love's madness. The adoption of a dialogical structure also allows the author to distance himself from the overweening, pedantic, and even intrusive relationship with his readers implied in monological discourse. In a dialogue, the author may offer opinions for consideration rather than dictating rules, and he may allow his characters to talk intimately, in ways that allow ideas to steal into the minds of his listeners.[16]

This is the case with Wert's "Tirsi morir volea" and "In qual parte sì ratto," where the poetic texts and musical settings offer an undecorous mode of communication between Wert and Margherita Farnese, the volume's dedicatee. We may giggle at the clear musical representations of trembling and love-making in "Tirsi morir volea," but what an irreverent way for an artisan to address his prince's bride! And yet, in adopting a dialogical structure for "Tirsi morir volea," and the book of madrigals in its entirety, Wert is able to accomplish the delicate task of persuading the fourteen-year old Margherita Farnese to perform her sexual initiation with her new husband, without committing any breach of decorum. His book fulfills its didactic purpose by creating a conversational friction and heat designed to inspire the young princess to love's madness.

I wrote at the beginning of this essay that the story of Margherita Farnese's marriage to Vincenzo Gonzaga is profoundly sad. It is also unique, in that the confluence of events surrounding the marriage and Guglielmo Gonzaga's need to document them provide us with the materials necessary to write a biography of Margherita Farnese that demonstrates the incorporation of personal desire with the representation of state and the interaction of musical and theatrical performance with both.

Had the Gonzaga family not been in such a precarious position regarding its heirs and the continuation of its dynasty, Guglielmo Gonzaga might not have felt compelled to arrange for Cavriani's constant supervision of Margherita or to command that he make written reports on her activities—sometimes as many as four a day. And had he had even one female musician in his employ, Guglielmo Gonzaga might not have entered into such protracted negotiations for female singers from Parma to entertain his new daughter-in-law and to keep her company. Guglielmo's intrusions into Margherita's personal life—in one instance, a caring gesture of music to guard against her potential feelings of isolation and ennui, but in another, a brutal physical attack against her person in order to save his hereditary line— highlight the bifurcated role of the female monarch as both individual and representative of the state. In the end, Margherita failed the Gonzaga *twice* along these lines.

---

[16] Tasso, *Tasso's Dialogues*, 41.

What was seen to be (and unfortunately later proven to be) Margherita's incapacity to engender an heir contrasted arrantly with her position as Vincenzo's wife and the future Duchess of Mantua. Similarly, her individual desires regarding music and theater seriously contrasted with her responsibility to convey the image of monarchy through massive musical and theatrical display. In the grossest terms, Margherita's inability to produce, in spite of the lessons offered in Wert's *Seventh book of madrigals*—both physically, in the birth of heirs, and aesthetically, in the presentation of Mantuan honor—signaled her more profound incapacity to rule.

Appendix 1

Excerpt from Torquato Tasso, *Jerusalem Delivered: An English Prose Version*, translated and edited by Ralph Nash (Detroit: Wayne State University Press, 1987).

> *XII.96 Giunto alla tomba, ove al suo spirto vivo*
>
> *Dolorosa prigion' il ciel prescrisse;*
>
> *Di color, di calor, di moto privo*
>
> *Già marmo in vista al marmo il viso affisse,*
>
> *Al fin sgorgando un lagrimoso rivo,*
>
> *In un languido oimè proruppe, e disse:*
>
> *"O sasso amato tanto, amaro tanto,*
>
> *Che dentro ha le mie fiamme, e fuor' il pianto!*
>
>
> *XII.97 "Non di morte sei tu, ma di vivaci*
>
> *Ceneri albergo, ov'è nascosto Amore.*
>
> *Sento dal freddo tuo l'usate faci*
>
> *Men dolci sì, ma non men cald'al core.*
>
> *Deh prendi questi piant' e questi baci,*
>
> *Ch'io bagno di doglioso umore,*
>
> *E dalli tu poich'io non posso, almeno,*
>
> *All'amate reliquie ch'ai nel seno.*

XII.98 "Dalli lor tu, ché se mai gli occhi gira

L'anima bella a le sue belle spoglie,

Tua pietate e mio ardir non avrà in ira,

Ch'odio o sdegno là su non si raccoglie.

Perdona ella il mio fallo, e sol respira

In questa speme il cor fra tante doglie.

Sa ch' empia è sol la mano; e non l' è noia

Che, s'amando lei vissi, amando moia.

XII.96 Arrived at the tomb, where Heaven ordained a sorrowful prison for his living soul, pale cold and mute, and almost deprived of motion, he fixed his eyes upon the marble. At last, releasing a stream of tears, he broke out in a languishing *Ay me!*, and said "O stone so honored and so much loved, that holds my flames within, my tears without;

XII.97 "you are the shelter not of the dead, but of live ashes wherein Love lies concealed; and truly I feel from you in my heart the accustomed flames—less sweet, it is true, but no less warm. Ah! take my sighs and take these kisses that I bathe in sorrowful tears; and do you at least (since I cannot) bestow them on the beloved relics that you hold in your bosom.

XII.98 "Bestow them there, for if ever that lovely soul should bend her eyes upon her lovely remains she will bear no resentment against your pity and my daring, for scorn or anger finds no place up there. She pardons my mistake; and only in the hope of this does my heart continue to breathe amid so many sorrows. She knows that only my hand was irreligious, and is untroubled if (as loving her I lived) loving I die.

Appendix 2

Chronology of events

1562	Birth of Vincenzo Gonzaga (d. 1612) to Guglielmo Gonzaga and Eleonora of Austria.
1567	Birth of Margherita Farnese (d. 1643) to Alessandro Farnese and Maria of Portugal.
1577	Death of Maria of Portugal; Margherita Farnese enters the care of her paternal grandmother, Margherita of Austria.
1580	Margherita accompanies her grandmother on a trip to the Low Countries.
	Nov. 23, the marriage contract for Margherita and Vincenzo is finalized.
1581	Feb. 17, Margherita returns to Piacenza.
	Feb. 25, Piacenza. Margherita and Vincenzo meet for the first time. Vincenzo declares that Margherita is more beautiful than her portrait.
	Mar. 2, Piacenza. Margherita (14) and Vincenzo (19) are married at the Duomo by Vescovo Ferrante Farnese.
	Mar. 3, Torquato Tasso's epic *Gerusalemme liberata* is printed by Erasmo Viotti in Parma (ed. Angelo Ingegneri) and given to Vincenzo. Tasso is confined at S. Anna.
	Mar. 18, Margherita and Vincenzo return to Parma.
	Mar. 26, Parma. Margherita begins to undergo a series of purgations to cure her of the congenital impediment that keeps her from being able to consummate the marriage. After the day's hunt, there is music (*"cantorno una bella compita con la musica del s.or Duca"*).
	Mar. 27, Parma. Margherita willingly takes a purge, which makes her quite ill; there is a big banquet and a dance in the evening (*"il ballo del robbarsi le donne"*).
	Mar. 30, Parma. Margherita dances in the garden with the other women and enjoys the exercise; she takes dancing lessons from Isachino da Mantova and shows every diligence in wanting to appear well-mannered in the dances for the wedding.
	Mar. 31, Parma. Margherita continues with the purgation, gladly following doctor's orders as well as she can.
	Apr. 4, Parma. Cavriani is charged with making an inventory of Margherita's clothes and finds most of them old and worn.
	Apr. 5, Parma. Margherita is lively, dining and dancing at the fountain.
	Apr. 10, Mantua. Wert dedicates his *Seventh Book of Madrigals à 5* to Margherita Farnese.

Apr. 18, Parma. After dining until the third hour of night, Margherita stays up a long time, happy because the moment of her entry into Mantua is drawing near.

Apr. 20, Parma. Margherita remains lively in anticipation of her arrival in Mantua. After the doctors leave, she does nothing but sing, and Cavriani accompanies her on the recorder [*flauto*].

Apr. 23, Cavriani writes that, if Margherita wanted to give money to musicians or to the poor, she doesn't have a dime.

Apr. 30, Margherita and Vincenzo enter Mantua.

Jun. 25, Mantua. Ippolita Mezzovillani enters Mantuan service as a singer for Margherita.

July 5, Saileto. Guglielmo Gonzaga calls the Compagnia de' Gelosi to come perform comedies to pass the time.

July 6, Genza. Margherita changes her mind about the Gelosi.

July 6, Porto. Regarding the Gelosi, Margherita thanks Guglielmo Gonzaga for sending them, but she does not care to hear comedies now. Vincenzo leaves for Gonzaga, while Margherita remains in Porto.

July 8, Genza. The Gelosi are unable to come.

July 9, Genza. Rain has washed out the roads and Margherita will not travel in such weather.

1582   Jan. 11, Ferrara. Everyone goes *in maschera*. There is a big banquet with dancing afterward that lasts until the 5th hour of night.

Jan. 12, Ferrara. The Duke and Duchess of Ferrara go in the Bucintoro with Margherita and Vincenzo. There is loud music of trumpets, pipes, cornets and trombones. All go *in maschera*, and attend comedy by zanni, after which the four retire to Margherita Gonzaga d'Este's rooms for an intimate dinner.

Jan. 14, Ferrara. There is a joust followed by a beautiful banquet.

Jan. 15, Ferrara. Everyone goes *in maschera*, except to eat and sleep.

Jan. 20, Ferrara. Everyone goes *in maschera*; there is a banquet and a dance. Margherita is tired of the festivities and wants to be in Mantua.

Jan. 21, Ferrara. All go *in maschera*; there is a dance with special music composed and directed by Maestro Ballarino, with Luzzasco, Milleville, Peverara and Guarina. The duchess and seven other ladies of the court dance, but not Margherita.

Jan. 30, Margherita and Vincenzo leave Ferrara.

Jul. 11, Mantua. Margherita declares a lack of interest in music and Ippolita Mezzovillani is dismissed from service.

Nov. 21, Parma. Margherita thinks only of Vincenzo. She commands Cavriani to write a canto part to an ottava by Ariosto ("*Mi parea sù una lieta et verde riva*").

1583   Jan. 13, Carlo Borromeo leaves Rome for Loreto, then Fer-
        rara, Mantua and Parma, to make an end of the marriage, as
        commanded by Pope Gregory XIII.
        Feb. 7, Mantua. Marcello Donati affirms that Margherita cannot
        be cured of her impediment.
        Apr. 19, Parma. Margherita often sings ottavas adapted from
        Ariosto's *Orlando furioso*. Burattino [the comedian Carlo de
        Vecchi] indicates that he and his company are ready to come to
        serve Margherita, if she desires it.
        May 11, Parma. Cavriani reports on the merits of the singer
        Giulio Cima.
        May 18, Parma. Margherita and her brother Ranuccio attend a
        banquet.
        Aug. 14, Guglielmo Gonzaga commands Cavriani and Salomone
        di Vita to ensure the return of Mantuan jewels that were given to
        Margherita.
        Sept. 23, Parma. Margherita enters the Convent of St. Paul
        under the name suor Maura Lucenia.
        Sept. 28, Camillo Gatico, Parma, to Theodoro San Giorgio,
        writes that, this morning, at the 17th hour, Margherita took the
        veil.
        Oct. 9, Borromeo pronounces the formal annulment of the
        marriage.
1584   Mar. 7, Venice. Vincenzo proves his virility with a Florentine
        orphan, Guilia Albizzi, witnessed by the Mantuan agent Belisario
        Vinta.
        Apr. 28, Mantua. Wedding of Vincenzo Gonzaga and Eleonora
        de' Medici (1567-1611).
1586   May 25, Parma. Margherita indicates to Salamone di Vita that
        she cannot return certain jewels (worth 100 scudi) which she gave
        to Leonora Musona in Mantua as a symbol of her gratitude for
        service rendered.

Class, Gender, Accomplishment:
Laura Netzel in Nineteenth-Century Sweden
Katherine Powers

Our understanding of women's lives as musical performers and composers in nineteenth-century European society continues to develop, including the significance of class and its relationship to gender as contexts within a woman's biography. Though class is rarely mentioned in most modern biographical dictionary entries on women performers and composers, social constructs would have played an important role, basic to a woman's experiences. Class as well as gender influenced the working life of pianist and composer Laura Netzel (Plate 1), a noble woman in nineteenth-century Stockholm, whose status affected the choices she made, the treatment granted her by others, and the reputation awarded her later. This study will investigate Laura Netzel's working life as a composer in late nineteenth-century Sweden, assessing her particular position as a noble woman promoting women's accomplishment through her own work, while attempting to maintain a boundary of class decorum.[1]

Laura Netzel (1839-1927) was born Laura Constance Pistolekors, the last of five children, into a Swedish-speaking untitled noble family in Finland.[2] Following her mother's death, a few months after Laura's birth, the father moved his five young children to Stockholm and married a noble Jägerhorn af Spurila woman,[3] who had never been married before and was six years his elder. Laura's new stepmother supervised the children's education, and Laura enjoyed privileges of her class, including home schooling. She undertook serious piano study under

---

[1] I am currently preparing a monograph on women composers in nineteenth-century Sweden.

[2] This study clarifies details of Netzel's life as given in Eva Öhrström, *Elfrida Andrée, ett levnadsöde* (Stockholm: Prisma, 1999), 319-22. Laura's father, Georg Fredrik, is among the Pistolekors family included in Gustaf Elgenstierna, *Den introducerade svenska adelns ättartavlor* (Stockholm: Norstedt, 1928), 5:736. Reliable synopses of Laura's life are found in Tobias Norlind, *Allmänt musiklexikon* (Stockholm: Wahlström & Widstrand, 1927), 2: 205; Walborg Hedberg and Louise Arosenius, *Svenska kvinnor från skilda versamhetsområden. Biografisk uppslagsbok* (Stockholm: Bonnier, 1914), 73; Lars Öberg, "Netzel, Nils Wilhelm," *Svenskt biografiskt lexikon*, ed. Göran Nilzén (Stockholm: Norstedt, 1989), 26: 555-56; "Laura Netzel," *Idun*, 23 January 1891, 25; and "Lago (Laura Netzel)," *Svensk musiktidning*, 1 June 1897, 91. Laura's father held the rank of *kollegieassessor*, a public or government position. Svenska Akademien, *Ordbok över svenska språket* (Lund: Gleerup, 1937), 2, col. 2513, and 4, col. 1875.

[3] Elgenstierna, *Svenska adelns ättartavlor*, 4: 57. Her stepmother's full name was Antoinette Fredrika Jägerhorn af Spurila.

the tutelage of master teacher Mauritz Gisiko (1794-1863) and gave her public debut as soloist with orchestra at age seventeen. In 1859 she traveled to Vienna to study with Anton Door, Professor at the Music Conservatory.[4] Netzel's abilities as a pianist were strong; her debut work was Moscheles' Piano Concerto in G Minor and throughout her life her abilities are reviewed positively.[5] Within her repertoire Netzel cites as favorite works Schumann's Piano Quartet in E-flat Major, Mendelssohn's Piano Trio in D Minor, and Chopin's C-sharp Minor Polonaise.[6] But rather than attempt a professional career as a pianist, Netzel, like many high-born women, limited her public appearances, performing primarily chamber music within a variety of private or semi-public venues, including concerts in upper class salons[7] and performances sponsored by private organizations for its members. In 1860 Netzel was the pianist for the premiere performance of Elfrida Andrée's first piano trio, a semi-public concert held at Brunkebergs Hotel; her chamber music partners were violinist Joseph Dente (1838-1905) and cellist Fritz Söderman (1838-85), both from the Royal Opera Orchestra (Hovkapellet).[8] She also performed in concerts at meetings of the New Artist's Society (Nya Konstnärsgillet), an organization for discussion of the arts whose members came from both genders of upper class Stockholm society.[9] She did occasionally perform on a Stockholm public concert stage but only in charity events.

In 1866 Laura married Nils Wilhelm Netzel (1834–1914), the son of a merchant and bank director from a "bourgeois aristocratic" family.[10] Wilhelm had

---

[4] Many sources mistakenly state that she studied with Door only during his visits to Stockholm in 1857 and 1865. Sources written or edited by Netzel herself, however, mention her traveling to Vienna for lessons with Door.

[5] Reviews include "Svenska musikkonstnärinnor i Paris," *Svensk musiktidning*, 27 June 1886, 95, which describes her playing as "skillful" (*skicklig*), and *Stockholms dagblad*, 19 May 1890, which commends her performance with difficult collaborative pieces: "the more difficult violin numbers were accompanied well by the composer Lago" (*De svårare violinnumren ackompagnerades förtjenstfullt af tonsättarinnan Lago*).

[6] "Laura Netzel," *Idun*, 26.

[7] Netzel is listed as one of three music directors in Calla Curman's salon, for example, the others being conductor Andreas Hallén (1846-1925) and piano pedagogue Richard Andersson (1851-1918). Gurli Linder, *Sällskapsliv i Stockholm under 1880- och 1890-talen. Några minnesbilder* (Stockholm: Norstedt, 1918), 23, and Lotten Dahlgren, *Interiör från 1870- och 80-talets konstnärliga och litterära Stockholm* (Stockholm: Wahlström & Widstrand, 1913). Martin Tegen, *Musiklivet i Stockholm, 1890-1910* (Stockholm: Haeggströms Boktryckeri, 1955), 87-96, presents an overview of Swedish salons in the nineteenth century as does also Eva Öhrström, "Borgerliga kvinnors musicerande i 1800-talets Sverige" (Ph.D. diss., Gothenburg University, 1987), 131-34.

[8] Öhrström, *Andrée*, 85. Andrée was a noted Swedish composer, organist, and conductor.

[9] The New Artist's Society is described in Claes Lundin, *Nya Stockholm . . . dess . . . konstnärer . . . sällskapslif . . . under 1880-talet* (Stockholm: Gebers, 1890), 654, and Linder, *Sällskapsliv*, 94.

[10] "Bourgeois aristocratic" is drawn from the description in William Weber, *Music and the Middle Class. The Social Structure of Concert Life in London, Paris, and Vienna* (New York: Holmes & Meier, 1975), 8. Nancy B. Reich borrows the term "bourgeois aristocratic" in her discussion of nineteenth-century women musicians and class in her "Women as Musicians: A Question of Class," in *Musicology and Difference: Gender and Sexuality in Music Scholarship*, ed. Ruth A. Solie (Berkeley: University of California Press, 1993), 126. Wilhelm Netzel's family history is presented in [Birgit Ekman], *Anteckningar om släckterna Richert och Netzel* (Stockholm: Haeggströms Boktryckeri, 1923), part 2.

Plate 1: The young Laura Netzel (courtesy of Musikmuseet, Stockholm)

an extraordinary career as a practicing doctor as well as researcher and professor in the fledgling discipline of gynecology. His doctoral dissertation led to research visits in Vienna, Prague, Berlin, France, England, and Scotland, and to the development of new treatments on which he published more than forty publications. In 1864 he joined the medical staff at the Carolinian Institute (Karolinska Institutet), eventually becoming Professor of Obstetrics there in 1887 as well as Director of the Public Obstetrics Hospital (Allmänna Barnbördshuset) in Stockholm (to 1899) and Chief of Gynecology at Sabbatsberg Hospital (Sabbatsbergs Sjukhus) from 1879 to 1895, then Chief of Gynecology from 1895 to 1899 at Seraphim Hospital (Serafimerlasarettet). He was attending physician to Crown Princess Viktoria during the birth of her three children in the 1880s. His honors and awards are many: in 1882 he was made Knight of the Royal Order of the North Star (Kongliga Nordstjerneorden) and in 1889 commander first class of both the Royal Order of Vasa (Kongliga Vasaorden) and the Badenische Zähringen-Löwen Order; he was president of the Swedish Doctor Society (Svenska Läkaresällskapet), editor of its journal *Hygiea*, and honorary member of the Augusta Medical Society.[11]

Laura Netzel continued to perform as a pianist following her marriage and the birth of her three children, but gradually turned her attention to composing. By the time she retired after the turn of the century, she had composed, by her own count, ninety-two pieces.[12] Netzel's varied *oeuvre* comprises many genres: songs for voice and piano (several with obbligato violin), vocal duos and trios, and works for women's choir. Her chamber music repertoire encompasses more than a dozen violin and piano duos, two pieces for cello and piano and two for flute and piano, and three piano trios; her solo piano *oeuvre* includes a number of character pieces, such as the *Salon Pieces* op. 24, *Concert Etudes* op. 52, *Six Morceaux* op. 57, and a Sonata in E-flat Major op. 27. She also composed two orchestral works and a piano concerto as well as several large mixed works: in particular, the Ballad "Die Bergstimme" on a text by Heinrich Heine for baritone, eight-part choir, organ, and piano; a Cantata for solo voice, double choir, and harp (with an arrangement for two pianos); and a Stabat Mater for choir, soloists and orchestra or organ.[13] Her early biographers note in particular her Ballad, Stabat Mater, and Cantata, for which she won a prize in Copenhagen. Her chamber settings of character pieces display imaginative melody and ingenuity of harmony. About half of her works feature voice, hence her music fits well into Sweden's (and especially Stockholm's) music tradition, wherein vocal music dominated the concert stage.[14]

---

[11] "Netzel, Nils Wilhelm," *Sveriges Läkare-historia*, 3d ed. (Stockholm: Norstedt, 1895), 2: 596; 4th ed. (Stockholm: Norstedt, 1933), 3: 525. Netzel's publications include *Om uppkomsten och utbildningen af placenta praevia totali* (Stockholm: Norstedt, 1867), the subject of his dissertation. At least one of his books was translated and published abroad: *Operation cesarienne rendua neessarire par un myome incarceer dans lel petit basin* (Paris: n.p., 1876).

[12] Netzel's known *oeuvre* contains about eighty works; her statement that she composed ninety-two as well as an opus 87 suggests that some pieces are now lost.

[13] A (nearly complete) list of Netzel's works is given in Öhrström, "Borgerliga kvinnors musicerande," 218-20.

[14] An overview of late nineteenth-century Swedish music is found in Tegen, *Musiklivet i Stockholm*;

From the beginning of her career as a composer, Netzel's works were performed under the pseudonym "Lago," a practice widely employed by women of the nobility.[15] Her composing debut had taken place in 1874 with the premiere of two *a cappella* choral works for women's voices at one of the concerts of the New Harmonic Society (Nya Harmoniska Sällskapet), an amateur choral group of which she was a member; the New Harmonic Society had been founded in 1860 by composer, teacher, and conductor Ludvig Norman (1831-85), who himself was a major force in music in Stockholm. Netzel continued to compose songs and choral pieces for friends to perform in Stockholm's private salons and semi-public concerts; in 1875 her song "Fjäriln" (The Butterfly) was premiered.[16] Though Netzel received much encouragement from composers Ludvig Norman, August Söderman (1832-76), and Louise Héritte-Viardot (1841-1918), daughter of Pauline Viardot, as she herself explains, the lack of formal training in composition made her hesitant to allow her music to be published.[17] But her unwillingness to release her music stemmed also from her wish to avoid the appearance of being a professional through earning money. She describes changing her mind when Stockholm music publisher Abraham Lundqvist, in 1884, suggested that she allow some works to be issued to benefit charity. Any proceeds from the publication would be donated to Pastor Henri Bach, of the French church in Stockholm, and Lina Nordwall, who was planning to open a dwelling for homeless women with the Pastor.[18] At least one of the chosen songs had been performed already at a charity concert at the French church organized by Netzel and Pastor Bach. Netzel's sense of decorum allowed her efforts to be philanthropic: money earned from her publications would go directly to charity.

Not yet allowing her real name to appear in print, however, she continued to use the pseudonym "N. Lago," in all publications of her music. Newspaper notices and reviews (of which there were a good half dozen a year in the 1880s and 1890s) followed suit, referring to her as "Lago" and "the well known pseudonym Lago"[19] or another description, including "a woman from society,"[20] and "a positively known

---

Tobias Norlind, *Svensk musikhistoria* (Stockholm: Wahlström & Widstrand, 1918); and Bo Wallner, *Wilhelm Stenhammar och hans tid* (Stockholm: Norstedt, 1991).

[15] The practice of using a pseudonym was wide and its reasons many; among nineteenth-century upper class Stockholm women pseudonyms were used by Fredrika Peyron (1845-1922) ["Ika,"] Calla Curman (1850-1935) ["Eli Rem,"] and Aurore M. G. Ch. von Haxthausen (1836-88) ["G********."] *Sällskapet Nya Idun 1885-1913. Historik och medlemsförteckning* (Stockholm: Central-tryckeriet, 1914), 9. A. J. Nosnikrap, "Pseudonimity," *The Musical Times* 126, no. 1706 (April 1985): 202-203, offers a historical survey.

[16] "Laura Netzel," *Idun*, 25; "Lago (Laura Netzel)," *Svensk musiktidning*, 1 June 1897, 91.

[17] Undated letter from Laura Netzel to Elfrida Andrée held in the Stenhammar-Andrée Archive, Statens Musikbibliotek, Stockholm.

[18] Described in letters from Laura Netzel to Elfrida Andrée, from the second half of 1884, held in the Stenhammar-Andrée Archive, Statens Musikbibliotek, Stockholm. See also Öhrström, *Andrée*, 320.

[19] "af den välkända pseudonumen Lago." "Teater och musik," *Dagens nyheter* (Stockholm), 18 March 1889, 2.

[20] "en dam ur societeten." Adolf Lindgren, "Teater och musik," *Aftonbladet* (Stockholm), 8 February 1886, 4.

woman composer from the capital city's circles."[21] Netzel's wish to withhold her real name from publication stemmed primarily from her view of behavior proper to a noble woman, and not from her gender. Full names of women performers and composers were printed with regularity in the Stockholm press throughout the late nineteenth century: these include names of singers Dina Edling (1854-1935), Dagmar Sterky Möller (1866-1956), and Annie Pettersson Norrie (1860-1957); pianist Sigrid Carlheim-Gyllensköld (1863-1938), and others. Music by composers Elfrida Andrée (1841-1929), Valborg Aulin (1860-1928), and Helena Munktell (1852-1919) was also published under the composers' full names.

The Stockholm press kept Netzel's real name out of print until the late 1880s, when *Svensk musiktidning* gave "Laura Netzel" as the accompanying pianist for a concert held in Paris in June 1886 at which some songs of "Lago" were sung.[22] *Svensk musiktidning* also printed her real name in a review of a concert of the New Artist's Society in 1888, in which she is cited also as the organizer for the event.[23] Netzel and the editor of *Svensk musiktidning*, Frans J. Huss, were acquaintances; she corresponded with him regularly, and therefore she must have allowed the magazine to release her real name. In 1891 the magazine *Idun* published a biographical interview of Netzel, describing her youth, her music activities and charitable work in Stockholm, and even a list of her compositions; thus the general public came to know who she was.[24] About that time, other newspapers made public the connection between Lago and Laura Netzel as well. Wilhelm Peterson-Berger, music journalist for the *Dagens nyheter*, reviewed a concert on which violinist Sven Kjellström performed: "He [Kjellström] performed . . . and also Lago, under which pseudonym, as is known, hides *professorskan* Netzel. This composer accompanied the works."[25] In 1897 Adolf Lindgren and Nils Personne included her portrait and brief biography under her own name among the hundreds in their collection of composers and musical artists.[26] Clearly Netzel's balance between decorum and public notice had changed and she now sought acknowledgement of her work. Years later she explained in a letter that she allowed her name to be given not to gather accolades for herself but to demonstrate women's ability: "Yes, women's

---

[21] "i hufvudstadskretsar fördelaktigt känd tonsättarinna." Tor Andrée, "Musikpressen," *Svenska dagbladet* (Stockholm), 23 December 1884, 3. "Lago, the known Swedish woman composer" (Lago, den bekanta svenska tonsättarinan), "Teater och musik," *Aftonbladet* (Stockholm), 22 April 1891.

[22] "Svenska musikkonstnärinnor i Paris," *Svensk musiktidning* 27 June 1886, 95: "The composer (professor's wife Laura Netzel from Stockholm, who is now well known) is also a skillful pianist" (*Tonsättarinnan professorskan Laura Netzel från Stockholm hvilket nu är allmänt kändt) är äfven en skicklig pianist*).

[23] *Svensk musiktidning*, 15 February 1889, 31.

[24] "Laura Netzel," *Idun*, 25-26.

[25] "Han [Kjellström] utförde . . . samt Lago, under hvilken pseudonym, som bekant, döljer sig professorskan Netzel." Wilhelm Peterson-Berger, "Musik hos kronprinsen," *Dagens nyheter* (Stockholm), 16 January 1897, 2. The exact same review appeared also in *Vårt land* (Stockholm), 16 January 1897, 3. "Professorskan" was the title given to the wife of a professor.

[26] Adolf Lindgren and Nils Personne, *Tonkonstnärer och sceniska artister* (Stockholm: Tullbergs Boktryckeri, 1897), 81.

[27] "Ja, kvinnans erkännande som kompositör var ju drifkraften till mitt stora steg att obekant resa ut

recognition as composers was indeed the driving force for my great step to venture out into the unknown with my best works. It was not to gather praise for myself," as she says, but rather that she tired of bias against women.[27]

Although girls had been accepted as students at the Music Conservatory (Kungliga Musikaliska Akademien) in Stockholm by 1854, mostly studying voice and piano, [28] Netzel's social status prescribed that her schooling be largely private, including her education in music. Her music training did not include composition lessons and she had no tangible experience as a composer prior to the performance of her works in the 1870s. Once her music was committed for publication, however, Netzel wrote for help to her childhood friend, Elfrida Andrée, then principal organist for the Gothenburg cathedral and a respected composer. Netzel and Andrée knew each other through their participation in the Harmonic Society (Harmoniska Sällskapet, an organization supporting premieres of new music) in the mid-1850s, when Andrée studied at the Music Conservatory (including composition lessons with Norman and Niels Gade).[29] Though Netzel and Andrée had lost contact over the years, now Netzel sought Andrée's help in editing her songs. Throughout the summer and fall of 1884, the two women corresponded, with Netzel sending works for Andrée's review and Andrée returning the edited works.[30]

After Netzel's first works appeared in print in late 1884, she began studying composition privately with Wilhelm Heintze (1849-95), organist, composer, and teacher. Netzel and Heintze had a supportive relationship: he premiered her works for organ and she collaborated with him on a new Swedish hymnbook, the *Koralbok för kyrkan, skolan och hemmet* (1889).[31] Eventually she took lessons with Charles-Marie Widor (1844-1937) in Paris during her many trips there beginning in 1885.[32]

The chronology of Netzel's creative work shows evidence of careful planning for her own development as a composer on the public stage. Her first attempts at composition, in the 1870s and 1880s, were songs for herself and friends to sing as well as short choral works for amateur choral societies to which she belonged.

---

med mina största verk—det var ej håg att skörda eget beröm." Letter from Laura Netzel to Elfrida Andrée, 18 September 1921, held in the Stenhammar-Andrée Archive, Statens Musikbibliotek, Stockholm.

[28] Öhrström, *Andrée*, 69, and Gustaf Hilleström, *Svenska musik perspektiv: Minneskrift vid Kungl. Musikaliska Akademiens 200-årsjubileum* (Stockholm: Nordiska Musikförlaget, 1971). The Music Conservatory comprised part of the Kungliga Musikaliska Akademien, or Royal Music Academy, until the late twentieth century; I use "Music Conservatory" rather than "Royal Music Academy" to distinguish the organization's education branch from its other activities.

[29] Öhrström, *Andrée*, 234.

[30] Letters from Laura Netzel to Elfrida Andrée held in the Stenhammar-Andrée Archive, Statens Musikbibliotek, Stockholm.

[31] Wilhelm Heintze, *Koralbok för kyrkan, skolan och hemmet med svenska messan jemte et urval af rytmiska melodier för sång, orgel, harmonium eller piano* (Stockholm: Lundholm, 1889), preface, and "Musikpressen," *Svensk musiktidning*, 15 December 1889, 157.

[32] "Svensk musik i Paris," *Svensk musiktidning*, 12 June 1891, 96. Öhrström, *Andrée*, 439 n. 59. In April 1891, Swedish newspapers reported successful performances of Netzel's songs in Paris, the

---

278 — KATHERINE POWERS

In the late 1880s she completed the Stabat Mater and Ballad—both larger works involving solo voices, choir, and keyboard or orchestra. She had moved into string writing by first adding obbligato violin to songs for voice and piano, and in about 1890 she began to compose short duos and trios for string instruments, flute, and piano. Eventually, she wrote piano trios, violin sonatas, and solo piano music including a piano sonata. Late in the 1890s she composed a piano concerto, a movement of which was premiered in Paris in 1897, and an orchestral work.[33]

Netzel's earliest publications were allotted a fuller portrayal of their style in the "Musikpressen" (Music Press), newspaper columns describing newly issued compositions, in part due to her lack of reputation. The reviewers' overall general reception offered praise and encouragement; the *Stockholms dagblad* reviewer wrote in 1884 that Netzel's songs "have earned a deserved reputation, and we have noted the quality of these works." The writer "takes, for example, [the song] *Lofsång* and finds it to be exquisite . . . [with a] fitting melody and brilliant accompaniment."[34] The writings of Adolf Lindgren (1846-1905), a well-respected music journalist, are particularly reliable, given his overall lack of gender bias.[35] He wrote an exceptionally positive review of Netzel's first publications, which he claimed "reveal . . . an exceptional talent. . . . [One] wishes her all success in a composition career with a promising start."[36] To be sure, Netzel's social status affected the treatment she received. In this case, Lindgren's criticism is gently put, mentioning only "a warning . . . for the danger of careless text setting."[37]

composer herself at the piano, mentioning that she is in Paris for studies with Widor. *Aftonbladet* (Stockholm), 22 April 1891 and *Stockholms dagblad*, 22 April 1891 (the latter further listing the *Journal des debats* (Paris) and *Echo le Paris* as sources on 10 May 1891).

[33] Hedberg and Arosenius, *Svenska kvinnor*, 73 and Norlind, *Musiklexikon*, 2: 205. She composed her orchestral work at about the point in her life at which she might have further explored music for orchestra, but instead, she turned her attention away from composing altogether, it seems, to devote her attention to social work, organizing inexpensive concerts for the working class.

[34] "der väckt ett berättigadt uppseende, och vi hafva vid dessa tillfällen framhållit dessa sångsverks förtjenster. . . . taga t. ex. Lofsången och finna der en förträffligt . . . stämmande melodiföring och ett praktfullt ackompagnement." "Musikpressen," *Stockholms dagblad*, 22 December 1884, 8.

[35] Lindgren was the *Aftonbladet*'s music reviewer from 1874 to his death and was known for being discerning, knowledgable, and fair; his writings are important contributions to the founding of Swedish musicology. Lindgren studied music theory and philosophy at the university in Uppsala and founded the *Svensk musiktidning* in 1881, serving as its editor until 1884. He wrote articles for numerous Scandinavian journals and newspapers, was music correspondent for several music journals in Germany, and authored several books on Swedish music and musical style. Kathleen Dale and Axel Helmer, "Lindgren, Adolf," *Grove Music Online*, ed. L. Macy, http://www.grovemusic.com (accessed 15 January 2008). To be sure, there is ample evidence within the Swedish press of a different standard for women's accomplishments from men's. The subject is described in some detail in Margaret Myers, *Blowing Her Own Trumpet: European Ladies' Orchestras and Other Women Musicians, 1870-1950, in Sweden* (Gothenburg: Novum Grafiska, 1993), especially 95-112.

[36] "Dessa alster . . . röja . . . en ovanlig talang. . . . önskas henne i öfrigt all framgång i den så löftesrikt påbörjade kompositionsverksamheten." Adolf Lindgren, "Från musikpressen," *Aftonbladet* (Stockholm), 30 December 1884, 3.

[37] "en varning . . . för oaktsam textbehandling." Adolf Lindgren, "Musikpressen," *Aftonbladet* (Stockholm), 30 December 1884, 3.

But newspaper reviews also note that Netzel's music was often well received by the audience with strong applause; for example, on a concert in December 1892 the *Aftonbladet* and the *Stockholms dagblad* recorded that Netzel's new piano concert etude, *Feu follet,* "awakened lively response"[38] and was "applauded most."[39] In 1893 "the lively response after" [*Chanson slave*] "led to a repeat of the work."[40] Indeed, Sweden's most respected musicians performed Netzel's music in a variety of public and private venues; these performers included opera singers Mathilda Grabow Taube, Dina Edling, Augusta Öhrström, Anna Klemming (1864-89), and Dagmar Sterky Möller; violinists Hugo Alfvén (1872-1960) and Sven Kjellström; and pianist Sigrid Carlheim-Gyllensköld. Andreas Hallén (1846-1925), founder of the Philharmonic Society (Filharmoniska Sällskapet) in 1885 and its conductor to 1895, led the choirs in performances of Netzel's music in the 1880s, including multiple performances of her two most appreciated works: the Stabat Mater and the Ballad. Conrad Nordqvist (1840-1920), conductor and director of the Royal Opera, also performed her music. Sven Scholander (1860-1936), famed "troubadour" lutenist, made appearances on many of Netzel's concerts whether she served as composer, performer, or organizer.

Though it can be argued that Netzel's social status encouraged the support of these musicians, her music must have played a significant role as well: Taube, Sterky, Kjellström, and Carlheim-Gyllensköld all kept Netzel works in their repertoire, performing them on numerous occasions. Nonetheless, her social status eased access to the royal family and noble circles. King Oscar II (r. 1872-1907), himself a writer and amateur musician, enjoyed the arts and attended many concerts with his family. In January 1897 Netzel organized a violin recital with Kjellström at the Crown Prince's studio, marking the young violinist's departure for studies in Paris, and she served as collaborating pianist for the recital as well. Her status also ensured her position on committees in which members were chosen from high society, for example, the Swedish committee for the Woman's Building for the World's Columbian Exhibition in Chicago in 1893. Among her committee responsibilities was the organization of a display containing music and biographical material of Swedish women composers within Sweden's exhibit.[41] And class helped Netzel promote herself within artistic circles, dedicating works to music friends and supporters abroad, including violinists Emile Sauret (1852-1920) and violinist Leopold Auer (1845-1930), mailing her newly published pieces directly to performers abroad, and sending foreign press clippings to the editor of *Svensk musiktidning* and many of Stockholm's major papers for re-publication.[42] Her

---

[38] "den väckte ock lifligt bifall." "Teater och musik," *Stockholms dagblad,* 7 December 1892, 6.

[39] "till de mest applåderade." "Teater och musik," *Aftonbladet* (Stockholm), 7 December 1892, 3.

[40] "Det lifliga bifallet efter [*Chanson slave*] . . . föranledde en bissering." *Stockholms dagblad,* 18 January 1893, 5.

[41] Ellen Fries, *Reports from the Swedish Ladies' Committee to the World's Columbian Exposition at Chicago 1893* (Stockholm: Central-tryckeriet, 1893), 18..

[42] For example, letters to Frans J. Huss, editor for *Svensk musiktidning,* held in the F. J. Huss Auto-grafer-Brev collection, Statens Musikbibliotek, Stockholm.

connections within high social circles and with the city's most respected musicians helped her to organize and conduct concerts within the music associations to which she belonged, and arrange and participate in public concerts for charity.[43] One of her greatest accomplishments was the creation of the Saturday Worker's Concerts (Musikaftnar för Arbetare or Lördagskonserter), a series of weekly classical music concerts with inexpensive ticket prices open only to the proletariat; from 1892 to about 1907, she directed the programming and chose the musicians for this series. In these situations Netzel participated in the philanthropic activities expected of her social position.

Despite her social and musical connections, Netzel lacked the traditional network of support among the conservative and influential music leadership in Stockholm, a situation due not only to her education but also her musical style, which was decidedly French in model. The *Stockholms dagblad* described her songs as representing an "elegant new French style."[44] The *Aftonbladet*'s Lindgren, despite his general encouragement for Netzel's music, still found it important to point out that her "creativity and style [are] primarily French."[45] He continues, noting that "one would almost swear" Netzel herself "to be French."[46] Her "French style" was point of criticism as well for Wilhelm Peterson-Berger (1867-1942), a composer and music writer whose championing of Wagner and outspoken opposition to French style was pervasive and influential. Indeed, from the 1860s Swedish music life was heavily influenced by continental styles as a result of touring foreign virtuosos in Stockholm and Swedish musicians studying abroad. Many leaders in Stockholm's music—composers, teachers, writers, and administrators—promoted a German style, whether Wagnerian or more conservative. Peterson-Berger's opinionated essays made a significant contribution to Sweden's growth towards higher international music standards, helping develop a Romantic nationalist style.[47]

But not only did Peterson-Berger criticize Netzel's French-style but also her "dilettantism." In a pointed review for the *Dagens nyheter*, he declared his "suspicions" "that one of Stockholm's music dilettantes' more hysterical and

---

[43] Within her role in the New Artists' Society, for example, Netzel helped organize a charity concert for composer Per August Ölander's (1824-86) surviving family. *Svensk musiktidning*, 1 December 1887, 153.

[44] "en elegant, något nyfransk." "Musikpressen," *Stockholms dagblad*, 22 December 1884, 8.

[45] "skaplynnet och stilen öfvervägande franska." *Aftonbladet* (Stockholm), 30 December 1884, 3.

[46] "man nästan ville svära på vore till börden franskt." "Från musikpressen," *Aftonbladet* (Stockholm), 30 December 1884, 3. On at least one occasion, Lindgren complained that Netzel's harmony "is too French," saying that the harmonies were "too full" for the "simple Nordic content" (hennes skaplynne är så att säga för mycket galliskt . . . för att fullt harmoniera . . . den nordiska enkla innerligheten). "I musikhandeln," *Aftonbladet* (Stockholm), 23 December 1887, 3. Netzel's harmonic language and musical texture, however, are not Wagnerian, *Grove Music Online*'s characterization notwithstanding. Eva Öhrström, "Netzel, Laura," *Grove Music Online*, ed. L. Macy, http://www.grovemusic.com (accessed January 10, 2008).

[47] Peterson-Berger was critic for the *Dagens nyheter* (Stockholm) for much of the period 1896 to 1930, and also produced other writings on music. Rolf Haglund, "Peterson-Berger, Wilhelm," *Grove Music Online*, ed. L. Macy, http://www.grovemusic.com (accessed January 10, 2008).

French-crazy patronesses was behind the [concert's] undertaking," naming Lago and her "tedious pieces" in the subsequent sentence.[48] Properly speaking, however, Netzel was not a *dilettant*, as that Swedish word described a person with extreme passion for a subject, but uneducated or self taught; *dilettant* is distinct from *amatör*, someone who is not paid for work.[49] The descriptor *dilettant* is better applied to Helena Gustava Tham (1843-1925), for example, an aristocratic woman lacking systematic training in music composition whose musical *oeuvre* comprises only songs and short piano pieces.[50] Though Netzel is, properly speaking, an amateur, she was extraordinary in the amount and quality of music she composed. Peterson-Berger's negative view of Netzel's music, however, likely represents an opinion held by other leaders, thus limiting recognition for her work. Though many women performers and composers were honored for their work, Netzel's accolades from official Swedish musical agencies were few. She had no compositions published by the Musical Art Association (Musikaliska Konstföreningen) for their series of recent music,[51] for example, nor was she elected to the honor rolls of the Royal Music Academy.[52] In 1921, long after she had retired, Netzel wrote to Andrée admitting her frustration with the music establishment, that she had become "tired of seeing all those [men] who thought they were creative artists—young gentlemen with the academy's counterpoint studies in their pocket but little talent within."[53] She lamented that her work, in her view, seemed to be recognized more in other countries than at home: her 1921 letter to Andrée expresses the desire early in her life to prove that an unknown "woman, that is, unknown in other countries, inspired by a great purpose, but without reputation and without press could be given a place even in Berlin as a 'student' of counterpoint."[54] Her Cantata had won first prize at the Women's Exhibition in Copenhagen (Kvindernes Udstilling)

---

[48] "osökt den misstanken att någon af den stockholmska musikdilettantismens mest hersklystna och fransosgalna skyddspatronessor stod bakom företaget. Det ledsamma sakerna af Lago." *Dagens nyheter* (Stockholm), 23 April 1897, 3. Peterson-Berger wrote for the *Dagens nyheter* from 1896 and signed his early writings simply –t-.

[49] At the end of the eighteenth century, the terms "dilettant" and "amatör" entered the language, initially having the same usage even though from different sources. Later their meanings grew distinctly different: while the opposite of "amatören" (amateur) was "professionisten" (professional), the opposite of "dilettantten" was "sakkunnige, kännaren" (specialist, expert). "Dilettant," Svenska Akademien, *Ordbok över svenska språket* (Lund: Gleerup, 1914), 6, col.1376-77.

[50] Elgenstierna, *Svenska adelns ättartavlor*, 8: 33.

[51] Founded in 1859, the association issued recently composed Swedish music, paying costs of printing; women composers whose works were published include Andrée, Aulin, and Amanda Maier.

[52] Between 1771 and 1893 forty-three women were elected as first class honorary members and thirteen as second class or associate members to the Royal Music Academy, about ten percent of its membership. Fries, *Reports*, 18.

[53] "led vid att se all dem som trodde sig skapade till konstnärer, dessa unga herrar med Akademiens kontrapunkt i fickan och föga egen inneboende skapande kraft." Letter from Laura Netzel to Elfrida Andrée, 18 September 1921, in the Stenhammar-Andrée Archive, Statens Musikbibliotek, Stockholm.

[54] "ville jag visa hur kvinnan, om ock obekant i andra länder, besjälad af ett stort mål, utan reklam, utan press, blott med stöd af framvisandet af sina verk, blef gifven en plats redan i Berlin som en 'studerad' i kontrapunkt." Letter from Laura Netzel to Elfrida Andrée, 18 September 1921, held in the Stenhammar-Andrée Archive, Statens Musikbibliotek, Stockholm. Öhrström, *Andrée*, 321-22.

in 1895.[55] Her Stabat Mater, Ballad, and piano concerto, in addition to her songs, were performed in Paris, where she was awarded the *Cour artistique* for several of her works in 1891,[56] and in 1906, *Les Palmes académiques*.[57] Her compositions were mostly issued by foreign publishers, in particular Simrock in Berlin, as well as in Paris, Lyon, and Copenhagen.

In short, Netzel had a full life in music: composing, conducting, performing as a pianist, singing in choirs, and arranging concerts. Her working life was on a high artistic level, both as a pianist and a composer, and she collaborated with many of the finest musicians in Stockholm. Yet, by definition, she was an amateur, strictly speaking, as she allowed her social class to discourage her from attempting a professional career in music with employment as a teacher, performer, writer, or composer. She did not accept payment as a pianist, performing instead only within amateur associations and for charity concerts, nor did she accept the proceeds from publication of her work. Hence, Netzel was never a professional "artist-musician," to borrow the term created by Nancy B. Reich for women musicians who worked for a living as either performers or composers.[58] Professional "artist-musician" is better applied to women composers such as Andrée, Munktell, and Aulin, all from middle class families, working in late nineteenth-century Sweden. As noted earlier, Andrée was employed as principal organist for the Gothenburg cathedral from 1867 until her death, and was also a composer and a conductor, producing works for orchestra, choir, chamber ensembles, solo piano and organ, and arranging concerts where she frequently conducted; furthermore, she was elected to the Royal Music Academy in 1879. Andrée was the most accomplished composer of these four women and had the strongest feminist views, seeking and obtaining professional opportunities otherwise granted to men. Munktell studied at the Music Conservatory in Stockholm, including composition with Norman and Johan Lindegren, and later in Paris with Benjamin Godard and Vincent d'Indy. She composed works for voice, choir, and orchestra, and her comic opera, *I Firenze*, was well received by audiences in Stockholm and performed many times in the years around 1890; she too was elected to the Royal Music Academy, in 1915. Aulin also attended the Music Conservatory in Stockholm where she studied composition with Norman, later studying in Copenhagen with Gade and in Paris with Massenet and Godard on a Jenny Lind scholarship. Returning to Stockholm, she taught piano and composed works for voice, solo piano, and chamber ensemble as well as a suite for orchestra; in 1903 she relocated to Örebro and apparently ceased composing.

[55] *Svenskt dam-tidning*, 13 September 1895, 300; "Från in- och utlandet," *Svensk musiktidning*, 1 June 1895, 88.

[56] "Lago (Laura Netzel)," Svensk musiktidning, 1 June 1897, 91.

[57] Hedberg and Arosenius, "Netzel, Laura," 73.

[58] Artist-musician class" is a category that "includes actors, artists, artisans, dancers, writers, and practitioners of allied professions. They all had in common an artistic output and a low economic level. Above all, they depended on their work for a livelihood." Reich, "Women as Musicians," 125. The influence of class is also described in idem, "The Power of Class: Fanny Hensel," in *Mendelssohn and His World*, ed. R. Larry Todd (Princeton: Princeton University Press, 1991), 86-99.

The professional work of Andrée, Munktell, and Aulin forms part of the public record; their working lives and their accomplishments are documented through school records, newspaper reviews and magazine articles, histories and descriptions of music life in Sweden, professional association minutes, and other sources. Netzel's lack of professional employment limited record of her work or recognition of her accomplishment, both during her life and later. If allotted space within standard reference works could be viewed as a sign of reputation, then lexicographic treatment of Netzel, Andrée, Aulin, and Munktell is telling. Writing in the early twentieth century, musicologist Tobias Norlind allotted more than one-half of a column to Netzel and her work in his *Allmänt musiklexikon*, where he favorably acknowledged her contribution to music life in Sweden as composer, performer, and concert organizer.[59] In fact, Norlind's lexicon grants Netzel and Andrée the same amount of space, and slightly smaller articles to Munktell and Aulin. (Other amateur upper class women composers—Tham, Curman, and Peyron—receive only brief mention.) Decades later, after her death, Netzel is treated much differently in other biographical dictionaries. *Sohlmans musiklexikon* (with a socialist point of view) does not include Netzel at all in either of its editions, but allots a paragraph with worklists to each Aulin and Munktell, and nearly a full column to Andrée.[60] *Svenskt biografiskt lexikon* (1918-) finally arrived in the 1980s at that point in the alphabet to publish entries on Munktell and Netzel. The biographical dictionary allots over two pages for Munktell and includes a worklist. Netzel, however, receives only a couple of paragraphs, and those are within her husband's entry, wherein she is described as an "amateur."[61] The *New Grove Dictionary of Women Composers*, compiled in the 1990s, ranks Andrée highest among these four women composers, and appropriately so, presenting her in one full page including a worklist.[62] Both Aulin and Munktell each receive about one-half a page, also with worklists. Netzel, however, is allotted only a quarter of a page and no worklist.[63] The situation is similar in *Grove Music Online*. With time, therefore, Netzel's work lost value in comparison to other women composers whose accomplishments are arguably similar.

---

[59] Norlind, *Musiklexikon*, 2:205. Norlind (1879-1947) was one of the first musicologists in Sweden. Following studies at the universities in Munich and Berlin with Adolf Sandberger, Johannes Wolf, and Max Friedlaender among others, he earned his doctorate in 1909 at the University in Lund. In 1919 Norlind became director of the Museum of Music (Musikmuseet) in Stockholm and eventually taught music history at the Music Conservatory. He was secretary of the Swedish section of the International Musicological Society from 1901 to 1914. His *Allmänt musiklexikon* was a "standard reference work." M. Elizabeth C. Bartlet, "Norlind, Tobias," *Grove Music Online*, ed. L. Macy, http://www.grovemusic.com (accessed January 15, 2008).

[60] Gösta Morin, Carl-Allen Moberg, and Einar Sundström, eds., *Sohlmans musiklexikon* (Stockholm: Sohlmans Förlag,1948-52; 2d. ed., 1975-76).

[61] Eva Öhrström, "Munktell, Helena," *Svenskt biografiskt lexikon*, ed. Göran Nilzén (Stockholm: Norstedt, 1989), 26:25-28; Öberg, "Netzel, Nils Wilhelm," in ibid., 26:555-56. To be sure, the evolving meaning of "amateur" is problematic and one that historians have not always dealt with satisfactorily.

[62] Eva Öhrström, "Andrée, Elfrida," *The New Grove Dictionary of Women Composers*, 16.

[63] Rolf Haglund, "Aulin, Valborg," *The New Grove Dictionary of Women Composers*, 27; Eva Öhrström, "Munktell, Helena," in Ibid., 340; and idem, "Netzel, Laura," 346.

Upper class women's opportunities and choices seem to have been limited to "amateur" activities by a sense of decorum appropriate to their class, thus affecting notice of their accomplishment and, eventually, historical reputation. Netzel had a full life in music at the highest artistic standards, yet maintained her own view of upper class propriety governing public acknowledgement: as a pianist she performed under an amateur's guise; as a philanthropist, she organized charity events and concerts for the proletariat; as a composer, she guardedly published under a pseudonym. Yet, she gradually sought a public arena for her compositions, carefully planning the development of her artistic achievements and eventually allowing her real name to be known publically. In this manner, Netzel expanded the typical upper class woman's sphere of activity, and her life illuminates the complexity involved in evaluating issues of gender, social class, and accomplishment among high-born women musicians.[64]

[64] Furthermore, Netzel serves as an example of a continuing need to evaluate approach in writing biography. For the musicologist, a good starting point is Marian Wilson Kimber's discussion on biography in her "The 'Suppression' of Fanny Mendelssohn: Rethinking Feminist Biography," *19th-Century Music* 26, no. 2 (2002): 125-28.

Enigmatic Women

Imitation as Cross-Confessional Appropriation: Revisiting Kenneth Jay Levy's "History of a 16th-Century Chanson"

Jeremy L. Smith*

Fifty-five years ago Kenneth Jay Levy published an essay on a set of related musical works that were based on a setting of "Susanne un jour" from the mid-sixteenth century.[1] Thus far the "Susanne complex" (as Levy dubbed it) has not been discovered to relate to enigmatic dragonheads or meetings of the Order of the Golden Fleece. Nor did it inspire the cutting edge compositional qualities so prominent in the early history of the famous complex of *L'homme armé* masses.[2] Yet it was still an unusually rich musical tradition. In addition to a plethora of instrumental arrangements, the late sixteenth century alone witnessed over thirty original settings of related works on Susanna poems. Many of the composers were relatively obscure, like the founder of the series, Didier Lupi Second. Yet the complex also featured such recognized greats as Cipriano de Rore, Claude Le Jeune, Pierluigi Palestrina, Philippe de Monte, William Byrd and, perhaps most importantly, the prolific and influential Orlando di Lasso.

Levy's was a valiant attempt to introduce an unwieldy corpus of material with some thoroughness. Perhaps for this reason his essay has been treated as if it were the last rather than the first word on the topic. But Levy had warned his readers that he had listed works he had not seen or studied; indeed over the years some of his omissions and misidentifications have been sporadically noted in print, while others have not. In sum they alter the picture considerably, at least from the present point of view, as discussed below. But the main issue introduced by Levy that was subsequently left undeveloped had to do with his theory of appropriation.

* Jeremy L. Smith is Associate Professor of Music at University of Colorado, Boulder and co-editor of this volume.

[1] Kenneth Jay Levy, *"Susanne un jour:* The History of a 16th-Century Chanson," *Annales Musicologiques* 1 (1953): 375-408 (hereafter, Levy).

[2] See Anne Walters Robertson, "The Savior, the Woman, and the Head of the Dragon in the *Caput* Masses and Motet," *Journal of the American Musicological Society* 59 (2006): 537-630; William F. Prizer, "Music and Ceremonial in the Low Countries: Philip the Fair and the Order of the Golden Fleece," *Early Music History* 5 (1985): 113-53; idem, "Brussels and the Ceremonies of the Order of the Golden Fleece," *Revue belge de musicologie/Belgisch Tijdschrift voor Muziekwetenschap* 55 (2001): 69-90; and Alejandro Enrique Planchart, "The Origins and Early History of 'L'homme armé,'" *Journal of Musicology* 20 (2003): 305-57.

Levy was among the first to stress the preponderance of modeling practices in sixteenth- century music. He was also acutely aware of political issues surrounding music in the Reformation era. He had rightly emphasized that Lupi, the founder of the series, was a Protestant and that he had worked with a Protestant poet. But Levy found it impossible to ignore the great number of Catholic musicians who followed in Lupi's path.[3] Later, Howard Brown would dispel concerns that something political might underlie this intriguing phenomenon. In his view the noticeable participation of Catholics in a series founded by Protestants simply showed how musicians of the era might cast aside confessional divisions as they developed collectively a "central musical tradition."[4] But Levy was less congenial. Accusing Catholic composers of "burglary"— "of pillaging ... [the enemies'] ... musical arsenal" and offering them "musical slap[s]" that could only have been intended as "mock[ing]... insult[s]"— he cast a rather dark cloud over the imitative process.[5] Since then scholars have tended to follow Brown rather than Levy in spirit. Competition, emulation, and homage are now assumed to be the motivating forces that propelled the practice of musical imitation in the sixteenth century.[6] But, as I will attempt to show, it was appropriation as much as anything else that spurred the key patterns of parody in the Susanne complex.

Levy had no difficulty in establishing a context for his theory. Before he turned to the Catholics, he argued with support of concrete evidence that Protestants had been up to their own acts of "parody" and "perversion." He noted that they had promulgated "malignant political caricatures," "derisive chansons" and "virulent exchanges of poetic broadsides." Most significantly, Levy found that Guillaume Guéroult, the poet who had authored the verse Lupi set to start the series, was prominently featured in a deviously titled collection *Les dixains catholiques*, one that purposely "misrepresented the content of what was, in reality, a very Protestant publication."[7]

This would seem an auspicious start to an exploration of appropriation in the complex. Why is it that apparently no one, not even Levy, took this matter much further? One reason may have been the nationalistic point of view that Levy adopted when he turned to the extraordinary number of Catholics that had participated in the Protestant-based musical tradition. Levy pointed to the fact that "Susanne was the Hebrew word for *lily*" and that it "emblemized the religious orthodoxy of the house of Valois." Catholic composers, Levy hypothesized, were incited by a wish to "pillag[e] the Huguenots' musical arsenal by appropriating

---

[3] Levy, 376-81.

[4] Howard Brown, "The *Chanson spirituelle*, Jacques Buus, and Parody Technique," *Journal of the American Musicological Society* 15 (1962): 145-73, at 151-52.

[5] Levy, 380-81.

[6] Howard Mayer Brown, "Emulation, Competition, and Homage: Imitation and Theories of Imitation in the Renaissance," *Journal of the American Musicological Society* 35 (1982): 1-48; and Honey Meconi, "Does Imitatio Exist?" *Journal of Musicology* 12 (1994): 152-78.

[7] Guillaume Guéroult, *Les dixains catholiques* (Basle: Wilmach, 1561); Levy, 380-81.

Susanne as a symbol of their own, royalist, party."[8] French royalists, however, were not alone in adopting the fleur-de-lis as a national symbol. Lyons, for example, also used the flower as an emblem of allegiance; and Lyons was hardly uniformly Catholic at this time.[9] But Levy stuck with the idea that it was a "Catholic fleur de lis," even though he had only established that it was a *French* royalist symbol.

Almost immediately after advancing his provocative theory, Levy revealed that in any case Susannes were not easily confined to Parisian presses and musicians, but rather that they fell distinctly into three groups, which he designated as "French, 'Northern,' and English."[10] A cursory glance at Levy's list of publications reveals that the "Northern" presses of Antwerp and Louvain were far busier with Susannes than any others, especially with those by Catholic composers, and that the presses of Paris and Lyons tended to serve the rather few Protestant musicians that were actually involved in the series.[11] Certainly Catholics in the Spanish provinces of the Netherlands were battling Protestants along with their coreligionists in French territories, but to see them all flying the royalist flag of the Valois was to blur the very real tensions that persisted throughout this era between the "Most Christian" king (of France) and the "Most Catholic" (of Spain).

Still, Guéroult had indeed been involved in anti-Catholic activities and since Lupi was closely associated with him, it seems fair to ask: Did the Protestant composer participate in this kind of parodic mischief too? This path seemed unpromisingly blocked, for scholars have been rather certain that he did not. Brown, for example, emphasized that Lupi's music for "Susanne" was "newly invented." He proclaimed that, unlike monophonic works that used secular tunes, and with the key exception of Jacques Buus, the polyphonic *chansons spirituelles*, like "Susanne," were all characterized by "newly invented texts and freshly composed music."[12] But perhaps Brown was searching in the wrong place. Rather than to check for Catholic models, it seems that he was only looking to see if Lupi had used a *timbre* from the secular sphere for his spiritual chanson.

In searching through the chant repertory I discovered that a case could be made for casting Lupi as a musical appropriator.[13] A standard office responsory for the third nocturne of Matins in the first Sunday of November (Prophets) opens musically in a manner that suggests it could well have been Lupi's model.[14] It begins

[8] Ibid.

[9] Jean Tricou, *Armorial de la Généralité de Lyon*, 2 vols. (Lyons: Société des Bibliophiles Lyonnais, 1958-60), II: 262.

[10] Ibid., 381.

[11] Ibid., 398 and 402. Levy mistakenly includes Byrd among the Protestants.

[12] Brown, *"Chanson spirituelle,"* 149.

[13] Medieval Music Database: An Integration of Electronic Sources, dir. John Stinson, La Trobe University, 2004, http://www.lib.latrobe.edu.au/MMDB/Feasts/l11111000.htm (accessed 9 December 2007).

[14] Ibid. Further study may reveal that Lupi's direct source was a motet based on the *Angustiae mihi undique* text, as there were at least two of these that contain the same *Angustiae* chant melody as a

with the following two motives: a) a triadic gesture with a passing tone between the third and the fifth scale degree that is followed by, b) a series of repeated notes, the penultimate one inflected by an upper neighbor (see Ex. 1). Although the mode is distinct and the intervals are not fully replicated in Lupi's tenor, his first nine notes correspond rather closely to this chant motivically; Lupi even inserted a rest to distinguish the two gestures (see Ex. 2).

Example 1: "Angustiae mihi"

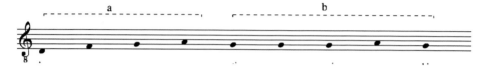

Example 2: Didier Lupi Second, "Susanne un jour," Tenor, mm. 1-4

More importantly, the text of this chant was clearly derived from the Susanna story (Daniel 13: 22-23) and it captures the same dramatic moment that Guéroult highlighted in his poem:

First Sunday of November (Prophets), Third Nocturne, Responsory
Angustiae mihi sunt undique et quid eligam ignoro: Melius est mihi incidere in manus hominum quam derelinquere legem Dei mei.
(I am straitened on every side, I know not which to choose: It is better for me to fall into the hands of man than to disobey the law of my God.)[15]

Daniel 13: 22-23
Ingemuit Susanna et ait: Angustiae mihi undique si enim hoc egero mors mihi est si autem non egero non effugiam manus vestras. Sed melius mihi est absque opere incidere in manus vestras quam peccare in conspectu Domini.
(Susanna sighed, and said: I am straitened on every side: for if I do this thing, it is death to me: and if I do it not, I shall not escape your hands. But it is better for me to fall into your hands without doing it, than to sin in the sight of the Lord.)[16]

cantus firmus. These include an anonymous setting in *Musica quinque vocum: motteta materna lingua vocata* (Venice: Scotto, 1543) (RISM 15432 and 15496) and one by Dominique Phinot, which appeared in *Musica quatuor vocum, que materna lingua moteta* (Venice: Gardano, 1549) (RISM 1549/09). On Phinot's connections with Lyons and Lupi himself see Frank Dobbins, *Music in Renaissance Lyons* (Oxford: Oxford University. Press, 1992), 284-50 and V. L. Saulnier, "Dominique Phinot et Didier Lupi musiciens de Clement Marot et des marotiques," *Revue de musicologie* 43 (1959): 61-80.

[15] Ibid. I wish to thank Dr. Rebecca Maloy for her generous advice and assistance with the translation and the matter of this poem's relationship to the biblical text.

[16] Latin Vulgate. Com, Mental Systems Inc., http://www.latinvulgate.com/verse.aspx?t=0&b=32&c=13 (accessed 9 December 2007). The English translation is from the Douay-Rheims bible of the 16th century.

"Susanne un jour" by Guillaume Guéroult

Susanne un jour d'amour solicitée
Par deux viellardz, convoitans sa beauté,
Fust en son coeur triste et desconfortée,
Voyant l'effort fait à sa chasteté.
Elle leur dict, Si par desloyauté
De ce corps mien vous avez jouissance,
C'est fait de moy. Si ie fay resistance,
Vous me ferez mourir en deshonneur.
Mais j'aime mieux périr en innocence,
Que d'offenser par peché le Seigneur.[17]

(Susanna faire, sometimes of love requested
By two old men, whom her sweet looks allur'd,
Was in her heart full sad and sore molested,
Seeing the force her chastity endur'd,
To them she said: If I by craft procur'd,
Do yield to you my body to abuse it,
I kill my soule; and if I do refuse it,
You will me judge to death reproachfully.
But better it is in innocence to choose it,
Than by my fault t'offend my God on high.)[18]

Missing in the responsory is Susanna's name and the explanation that this was a direct quotation ("Ingemuit Susanna et ait: ... ," see p. 288). Such a cut, though, was surely performed at least in part for the practical purpose of allowing those singing the chant to adopt Susanna's plea as their own in prayer. Homilies and other commentary of the early church strongly suggest too that the subject was more likely to be seen as the Christian church itself (as Ecclesia) instead of the biblical Jewess *per se*.[19] Nonetheless, the responsory preserves the sense as well as some of the specific words Susanna spoke at the dramatic moment when the two men started to attack her. The words "angustiae undique" with which it began were so closely linked to Susanna that the phrase had in fact become by the sixteenth century something of the biblical heroine's "motto," so to speak. This emblematic treatment is reflected obliquely in the prophesies of the Florentine Girolamo Savonarola, who used the phrase as a means to conjure images of threatening

---

[17] Levy, 375.

[18] *English Madrigal Verse, 1588-1632*, 3rd ed., ed. E. H. Fellowes, rev. and enl. Frederick W. Sternfeld and David Greer (Oxford: Clarendon Press, 1968), 323. Fellowes's translation is based on the *Musica Transalpina, Madrigals Translated of Foure, Five and Sixe Parts ...*, pub. Nicholas Yonge (London: Thomas East, 1588), Cantus, C2r.

[19] Valerie I. J. Flint, "Susanna and the Lother Crystal: A Liturgical Perspective," *Early Medieval Europe* 4 (1995): 61-86; and Kathryn A. Smith, "Inventing Marital Chastity: The Iconography of Susanna and the Elders in Early Christian Art," *Oxford Art Journal* 16 (1993): 3-24.

circumstances as a social corrective.[20] It appears quite explicitly in an image of Susanna depicted in the rosary worn by Mary Queen of Scots in the so-called Sheffield portraits, where the words "angustiae undique" surround an image of Susanna threatened by the elders (see Figures 1 and 2).[21]

It would probably have required some special effort on Lupi's part to find the relevant text in the chant repertory and determine the means by which to use the chant's two opening musical motives in a multi-voiced composition. Whether

Lupi was so inspired, this kind of action fits in well with other acts of appropriation that Protestants were involved with at the time. And even if Lupi were unaware of the striking musical similarities, they could of course have occurred to a Catholic composer who had encountered Lupi's music, especially one who had decided to study the piece in some depth for the purposes of emulation.

It is intriguing that the first Catholic composer we know to have so studied Lupi's music was Lasso, for the latter was surely just as adept in the game of religious appropriation as Guéroult and Lupi. Lasso, for example, took upon himself and his son a formidable musical project of setting three-part music for Kaspar Ulenbach's German psalter, a book designed to compete with the ubiquitous Protestant staple musical

Figure 1: Mary, Queen of Scots. 1578. Panel. 193.5 by 112 cm. Hatfield House (copyright, The Marquess of Salisbury, Hatfield House).

[20] Villani Pasquale, *Life and Times of Girolamo Savonarola*, translated by Linda Villari (London: T. Fisher Unwin; New York: Scribner, 1889), 308.

[21] See Lionel Cust, *Notes on the Authentic Portraits of Mary Queen of Scots, Based on the Researches of the Late Sir George Scharf* (London: John Murray, 1903), 69-91; *Roy Strong, Tudor and Jacobean Portraits: National Portrait Gallery*, 2 vols. (London: HMSO, 1969), I:216; and Jeremy L. Smith, "Revisiting the Origins of the Sheffield Series of Portraits of Mary Queen of Scots,"*Burlington Magazine* 152 (2010): 212-18.

text.[22] But does it follow from this that Lasso picked Lupi's work to emulate because of the lily, as Levy suggested? Given the extraordinary international scope of his career, it would be reasonable to assume Lasso might wish to show allegiance to the French king and to have noted that the name Susanna and the French royal emblem were linked by the Hebrew word for lily.[23] But a closer look at the situation suggests instead that Lasso was probably responding not to French issues but to those of the Wittelsbach Dukes of Bavaria. Within their palace in Munich Susanna was regarded as a symbol of dynastic power, one well expressed through the arts of painting and architecture.

Figure 2: Detail of Figure 1, showing "Susanna and the Elders" within a rosary

There are two striking depictions of Susanna now in the Alte Pinakothek in Munich that were originally in the Wittelsbach palace, specifically in a Kunstkammer famously full of extraordinary curiosities and major works of music and art.[24] One of these is a panel by Albrecht Altdorfer titled *Susanna and the Elders* that was completed in 1526 (see Figure 3).[25] It seems to have been the inspiration for an extensive series of history paintings—eight male heroes and eight heroines

[22] Orlando di Lasso, *Komposition mit Deutschem Text: Drei- bis achtstimmige deutsche Lieder aus verschiedenen Drucken sowie aus hanschriftlicher Überlieferung*, rev. ed. Hortst Leuchtmann, vol. 20 of *Sämtliche Werke* (Wiesbaden: Breitkopf and Härtel, 1971), xviii.

[23] Potential ties of Lasso's to France at this time are suggested in Donna G. Cardamone, "Orlando di Lasso and pro-French Factions in Rome," in *Orlandus Lassus and His Time, Colloquium Proceedings Antwerpen 24-26.08.1994*, ed. Ignace Bossuyt, *et al.*, Yearbook of the Alamire Foundation 1 (Peer: Alamire, 1995), 23-47.

[24] See Jessie Ann Owens, "An Illuminated Manuscript of Motets by Cipriano de Rore (München, Bayerische Staatsbibliothek, Mus. Ms. B)," 2 vols. (Ph.D. diss., Princeton University, 1978).

[25] Cordula Bischoff, "Albrecht Altdorfer's *Susanna and the Elders:* Female Virtues, Male Politics," *RACAR, Revue d'art canadienne / Canadian Art Review* 23 (1996): 22-35.

Figure 3: Albrecht Altdorfer. *Susanna an ihrem Bad und Der Steinigung von den Alten Männern.*1526. Panel. 74.8 x 61.2 cm. Die Pinakotheken im Kunstareal München (copyright, Bayerische Staatsgemäldesammlungen).

of ancient and biblical fame—that were commissioned by Wilhelm IV and his wife Maria Jacobäa of Baden and completed over the period from 1528-44.[26] This set included another Susanna portrait, a panel by Hans Schöpfer that was completed

[26] Gisela Goldberg, *Die Alexanderschlacht und die Historienbilder des bayerischen Herzogs Wilhelm IV. und seiner Gemahlin Jacobaea für die Münchner Residenz,* Künstler und Werke / Bayersiche Staatsgemäldesammlungen 5 (Munich: Hirmer, 1983), 55-59.

Figure 4: Hans Schöpfer, *Die Geschichte der Susanne*. 1537. Panel. 100.8 x 149.9 cm
Die Pinakotheken im Kunstareal München (copyright, Bayerische Staatsgemäldesammlungen).

in 1537 (see Figure 4). As art historians have noted, both well exemplify a "crucial
function of art to fashion political identity."[27]

Significantly, when Johann Finkler described Altdorfer's *Susanna* in a 1598
inventory, the first thing he mentioned was the "huge splendid palace with a tower."
After this Finkler noted that the painting depicted some simultaneous scenes including
"chaste Susanna" at the bath and the "two old wantons who afterwards were stoned
because of Daniel's judgment."[28] In viewing Altdorfer's work today, the first thing
one indeed notices is that fabulous building, an architectural conglomerate of palace,
church, and town hall, all depicted by an artist who was also an architect.

It was the prominence of this fantasy building that spurred Cordula Bischoff
to conclude, "the architecture in the painting can be equated with Wilhelm's claim

---

[27] Pia F. Cuneo, *Art and Politics in Early Modern Germany: Jörg Breu the Elder and the Fashioning of Political Identity, ca. 1475-1536* (Boston, Leiden and Köln: Brill, 1998), 4.

[28] Quoted in Bischoff, "Albrecht Altdorfer's *Susanna*," 25.

to control jurisdiction in his country," for "obviously the patron ... attached great importance to establishing 'the court' as a jurisdictional institution and, in doing so, showed himself to be a just sovereign."[29] Perhaps just as importantly for our purposes Bischoff explained too that these Wittelsbach paintings were imbued with hidden meanings and only an elite few had access to them. Musicologists would quickly appreciate that this relates to some of the exclusionist practices surrounding Lasso's compositional and publishing activities in Bavaria. Lasso himself was certainly among the privileged few to see these paintings of Susanna and appreciate their political messages. Important visitors as well as court figures such as Hans Jacob Fugger, the superintendent of music and court librarian, and his brother and fellow Catholic music collector Georg II probably had privileged access to them as well.

The Fuggers's connection to the Susanne complex rests on the evidence of a rather enigmatic manuscript of chansons now found in the Austrian State Library in Vienna. Despite the lack of many of the traditional forms of identification, Jerry Max Call has established that this manuscript was copied in Lyons. He based this view on sources that included two printed collections of 1559, which set the *terminus post quem*.[30] But Call also argued that Georg II obtained it rather soon thereafter (*ca.* 1560). Unmentioned in Call's otherwise thorough study was that some time earlier Levy had made note of this manuscript too. Levy believed it to be the source of an independent setting of Guéroult's poem.[31] It turned out instead merely to have been an un-attributed version of Lupi's chanson. The manuscript's provenance and timing suggest, however, that it may have served an important purpose, as the source Lasso used to study Lupi's work.

The late 1550s was an eventful time at the Wittelsbach palace in Munich. In 1558 Albrecht V had taken decisive steps to strengthen the Catholic cause and his own authority by taking strong actions against reformers.[32] Sometime in the 1558-60 era, too, Hans Meilich had illuminated a manuscript with twenty-six motets by Cipriano de Rore while Lasso had completed his famous settings of penitential psalms for the duke that were copied also into two splendid manuscripts and illuminated by Meilich. (Incidentally, Meilich was the teacher of the artist Schöpfer who had painted a Susanne mentioned above.)[33] Hans Jacob Fugger was to marry (again) in Munich in 1559 and Lasso probably wrote some specific pieces for the

[29] Ibid., 29.

[30] Jerry Max Call, "A Chansonnier from Lyons: The Manuscript Vienna, Österreichische Nationalbibliothek, Mus. Hs. 18811," 2 vols. (Ph.D. diss., University of Illinois at Urbana-Champaign, 1992), 1: 185-91.

[31] Levy, 399 and 402.

[32] Philip M. Soergel, *Wondrous in His Saints: Counter-Reformation Propaganda in Bavaria* (Berkeley: University of California Press, 1993), 75ff.

[33] See Owens, "An Illuminated Manuscript of Motets" and Orlando di Lasso, *The Seven Penitential Psalms and Laudate Dominum de caelis*, ed. Peter Bergquist, Recent Researches in Music of the Renaissance 86-87 (Madison, WI: A-R editions, 1990). Intriguingly, Mielich himself used the "Susanna and the Elders" image to illuminate Rore's setting of *Pater noster*, specifically at the phrase, "...and lead us not into temptation, but deliver us from evil," see Owens, "An Illuminated Manuscript," 100-2.

occasion.[34] Based on this evidence, one might hazard a guess that if Georg II did find and collect the Vienna chansonnier in something of a hurry, as Call suggested, his brother's marriage might have been the reason why.

All of these threads of circumstantial evidence tend to suggest that the Fugger manuscript might have been what Lasso saw when he studied Lupi. If so, one may posit that Lasso treated Lupi with less reverence than was typical for a parodic gesture of this nature. Since the work in the Vienna manuscript was unattributed, Lasso may not even have known who the composer was that he had copied. Such a Stravinskian disregard for the work's (Protestant) origins would have well pleased a patron whose political career would "culminate in a total Catholic state, that aimed at complete confessional homogeneity."[35]

But without direct evidence it is impossible to be certain of the circumstances surrounding how and when Lasso took to the task of emulating Lupi's chanson. We do know, however, that Lasso's work had to have been composed before 1560 when it was published. Given the Kunstkammer setting and prominence of the paintings on the theme it seems perverse to suggest that the composer's efforts would have had nothing to do with the Wittelsbach's special view of the Susanne story. Less certain, but still plausible, is the suggestion that further impetus may have come from the "discovery" of the chanson in a Fugger manuscript, and that it all might have had to do with the duke's interest at this time in commissioning music and illuminated manuscripts for his chapel and Kunstkammer.

Meanwhile, a letter of Rore's, discovered by Jessie Ann Owens, revealed that this composer too had been in contact with Hans Fugger and Albrecht V not long before Lasso's "Susanne un jour" was published.[36] The letter Rore wrote to Albrecht V in early 1559 was in response to one the composer had received from Hans Fugger. In his reply Rore mentioned an unidentified Mass that he had composed for Albrecht, and he enclosed with his note another unnamed composition he had written for the duke as well, one which Owens has recently proposed to have been Rore's motet *Mirabar solito*.[37] Following in the tradition of the architect and painter Altdorfer, Rore took the opportunity of a Wittelsbach commission to champion his particular field of endeavor. Rore claimed his works were "worthy of being offered to [Albrecht's] ears" not only because they were the finest things he had ever written but also because Apollo had aided him in his task.[38]

---

[34] James Haar, "A Wedding Mass by Lasso," *Journal of Musicology* 17 (1999): 112-35, at 120.

[35] Alexander J. Fisher, *Music and Religious Identity in Counter-Reformation Augsburg, 1580-1630* (Aldershot, Hants and Burlington, VT: Ashgate, 2004), 18.

[36] Owens, "An Illuminated Manuscript of Motets," 74-76 and 83-85.

[37] Jessie Ann Owens, "Cipriano de Rore's New Year's Gift for Albrecht V of Bavaria: A New Interpretation," *Die Münchner Hofkapelle des 16. Jahrhunderts im europäischen Kontext*. Bericht über das internationale Symposium der Musikhistorischen Kommission der Bayerischen Akademie der Wissenschaften in Verbindung mit der Gesellschaft für Bayerische Musikgeschichte, München, 2.–4. August 2004, Bayerische Akademie der Wissenschaften, Philosophisch–historische Klasse, Abhandlungen, Neue Folge, Heft 128 (Munich, 2006): 244-73.

[38] Ibid., 247.

What is fair tentatively to surmise from all this, I believe, is that Lasso and Rore were not working independently so much as engaging in a friendly form of competition for a single purpose: to please a musical patron who had a particular view of the Susanna theme. Albrecht V was ultimately one of the most successful post-Tridentine Catholic leaders. If he was aware of Lupi's appropriation of chant, one suspects he would have been very pleased to see Susanna "counter-reformed" so adeptly by two esteemed composers whose work he had the wherewithal to direct. In light of their close association with both musicians and perhaps the Vienna manuscript too, one might imagine that the idea was suggested by one of the Fuggers? In any case, it would have been a conceit worthy of the two composers and fitting as a tribute to a duke well aware of the political uses of art and music and keen on establishing his power over reformers at this time.

Soon after his dealings in Munich, Rore took a position at the court of Margaret of Parma, who had herself just been appointed Governor of the Netherlands.[39] It seems that Rore was disappointed there. After serving at the resplendent court in Ferrara and meeting with the duke in the glamorous Wittelsbach castle, Rore might well have regarded his new post as a bit of a backwater. As far as Protestants were concerned, however, Rore had gone to the very heart of enemy territory. Although Philip II had left Margaret with limited authority, she was nonetheless in charge of a region that soon became embroiled in the most violence yet to be witnessed under the banner of religious reform. Already in 1566 the Protestant-led "iconoclastic fury" had driven Margaret to report to Philip II that the entire Netherlands were in revolt. Philip responded, most ominously, by replacing her in 1567 with Fernando Álvarez de Toledo, the Spanish Duke of Alva. Soon Alva more than earned his epithet "Black Legend" for his brutal methods of Protestant repression.[40] But to Catholics he looked rather like a hero. Despite his own reticence to engage England in a full-scale war, for example, the staunchest supporters of the English prisoner Mary Queen of Scots saw in Alva's might the greatest hope for her cause. But Rore died in 1565 before these matters had come to much of a head. Thus it was not Rore himself but his reputation, if anything, that may have helped spur the phenomenal surge of interest among composers— first in the Netherlands and then elsewhere— in setting pieces on Guéroult's "Susanne" that parodied the music of Lasso and Lupi.

The simple question, "Who was first to follow Lasso and Rore"? cannot easily be answered. Turning to Levy, one discovers that he had set certain limits for his study. Levy wisely did not even attempt to account for all of the re-printings and instrumental adaptations, but focused instead on the compositional activity

---

[39] Jessie Ann Owens, "Cipriano de Rore a Parma (1560-1565): nuovi documenti," *Rivista italiana di musicologia* 11 (1976): 5-26. On Margaret of Parma see Seishiro Niwa, "'Madama' Margaret of Parma's Patronage of Music," *Early Music* 33 (2005): 25-37.

[40] William S. Maltby, *Alba: A Biography of Fernando Alvarez de Toledo, Third Duke of Alba, 1507-1582* (Berkeley and Los Angeles: University of California Press, 1983). Maltby devotes a chapter to Alva's image as "England's Protector" (182-204). Alva, as Maltby establishes, was not at all eager to satisfy the much-expressed wishes of the English Catholics who rested so much hope on him.

surrounding direct interactions with the Guéroult/Lupi source. Thus Levy discussed, but did not list, a few Latin-texted works that nearly fit his criteria as well as a few reprinted editions that surely sparked some new compositions, such as Thomas Vautrollier's London edition of Lasso's *Mellange* in 1570.[41] Otherwise, however, he kept his purview limited to what he described and tabulated as "vocal settings of *Susanne un jour.*" It was an approach that served well to show when a *new* work appeared with the Guéroult text (or one based on it) and whether the composer in question made "use of Lupi."[42] With some important exceptions, however, Levy could only establish when works were published, not composed; and even under those limited conditions, he was inevitably plagued by a lack of bibliographical control.

As noted above, Levy mistook a manuscript copy of Lupi's work for an independent version. Levy similarly erred with two others: one he dated 1562 and another "after 1642." These were both un-attributed copies of Lupi that derived from a single source first published not in 1562 but 1560.[43] On another front, Levy was unaware that Gérard de Turnhout's three-voiced Susanne was first published in 1569 because he mistook a reprint of 1577 for a first edition.[44] Finally, Levy, as must be expected, missed altogether some Susannes composed in this era that he would surely have added to his list had he known about them.

In his study of the "Linköping-Faignient" manuscript Frits Noske discussed a number of works by Noë Faignient and one by Nicolas Lefebure that fit the basic criteria. Noske was struck by the linguistic variety in the material at hand. Lefebure's was a setting of the same German poem Lasso had published in 1575.[45] Faignient's Susannes included a Latin "Eximie castitatis exemplar Susanna," a Dutch "Susanna schoon" and an Italian madrigal, whose title included the name Susanna. Except for the Italian piece "Alma Susanna," these were all based on Guéroult or the same two biblical verses on which Guéroult's were based (Daniel 13: 22-23).[46]

---

[41] Levy, 383, note 1. Along with Palestrina's motet, Levy made note of "Susanne"-based musical material in a Mass by Lasso, a Mass by Palestrina's Roman colleague Marc'Antonio Ingegneri, a Magnificat by Lasso, and quite a number of instrumental adaptations (p. 379, note 3). In his *Orlando di Lasso: A Guide to Research*, Garland Composer Resource Manuals 25 (New York and London: Garland, 1990), James Erb added motets by Thomas Crequillion and Christian Hollander to Levy's list (p. 279). Only the latter of the two works in question, however, was clearly based on music by Lupi or Lasso. In addition to these, a setting by Jacobus Handl was noted by Marko Motkin in his very useful "*Susanne un jour*: Geschichte einer Chanson spirituelle" (Diplomarbeit für IG II, University of Vienna, 2004). Neither Erb nor Motkin seem, however, to have been aware of Noske's findings (see n. 93). As far as I know, Alfonso Ferrabosco The Elder's "Ingemuit Susanna" has not been mentioned in the literature relating to the "Susanne complex." No doubt there will be many more works to add.

[42] Ibid., 408.

[43] See Frits Noske, "The Linköping Faignient-Manuscript," *Acta musicologica* 36 (1964): 152-65, at 165.

[44] I have not seen this mistaken view of Levy's noted in print as such, but see Gérard de Turnhout, *Sacred and Secular Songs for Three Voices*, ed. Lavern J. Wagner, 2 vols., Recent Researches in the Music of the Renaissance 9 and 10 (Madison WI: A-R Editions, 1970).

[45] Noske, "Linköping," 157, note 23.

[46] Ibid., 155-59.

All of Faignient's works appeared in a manuscript dated 1568 that Noske argued was a copy of a lost printed edition (or "ghost").[47] In the same manuscript Noske discovered a work by Faignient that Levy had listed but Noske noted that because he had found it in a source of 1568, "in the column of publication dates, Faignient's Susanne has to change place with [the Fleming, Jean de] Castro's from 1569."[48] But even Noske was unaware that Turnhout's chanson might have fit in between Faignient and Castro's, as it too was published in 1569 (as noted above).

Once these additions, subtractions, and re-orderings are performed on Levy's list three particular aspects of Lasso's influence tend to emerge: 1) judging by the conspicuous gap in publications from 1560 to 1568 (or 1569), it seems that Lasso did not generate much immediate interest in the theme;[49] 2) when things finally picked up again, there were three composers involved in a noticeably reinvigorated series, namely Castro, Faignient, and Turnhout, all of whom were centered in the Low Countries; and 3) most of those who followed from this point forward made conspicuous use of Lupi's music. Was this all because of Lasso or his followers; or did it have more to do with Lupi?

Lupi should not too readily be written out of the series he had begun. After exposing a few more re-printings of Lupi's original version, Noske, for example, went so far as to claim that this one chanson spirituelle "became a symbol ... of early Protestantism ... [one strong enough to] hold its own against numerous brilliant settings by the most eminent of sixteenth century composers."[50] Significantly, however, in musical terms at least, it was the eminent Protestant Frenchman Claude Le Jeune who produced the most ambitious of all settings of the Géroult poem. In 1585 he set the verse once again. His seven-voiced version of 1572 featured a rigorous canonic approach that no other composer followed. And Levy emphasized that Lupi's "tenor appeared more exactly as a cantus firmus than in any Susanne before Le Jeune's own five voice setting of 1585."[51] Especially when compared, for example, to the free treatment of the material in the adamantly Catholic Philippe de Monte's Susanne of 1570, both of Le Jeune's Susannes are indeed striking in their faithfulness to Lupi. Even if Le Jeune was not attempting here to reclaim Susanna through musical rather than bibliographical force, his effort seems obviously designed to resurrect a link to Lupi's original music through its careful reproduction.[52] Nevertheless, compositional ties like these to Lupi tend to fade away fast as we move back to the first works to revive the tradition in 1568-69.

---

[47] Ibid., 154.

[48] Ibid., 157.

[49] This would seem to hold even in the realm of instrumental music, as there were apparently only two published lute intabulations based on Lasso's chanson in the 1560-68 era, see Motkin, "*Susanne un jour,*" 144.

[50] Noske, "Linköping," 165.

[51] Levy, "*Susanne un jour,*" 389.

[52] Along with a six-voiced version, another Protestant, Jean Servin, wrote the only eight-voiced work in the complex (see Levy, 402). I would argue that Servin was following Le Jeune's lead in reclaiming the Lupi tradition for the Protestant cause.

Although Castro had connections to Lyons, where Lupi's fame was concentrated, his professional relationship to Lasso was much closer. Castro, for example, was in contact with Jean Pollett, a copyist who had worked with Lasso (and Meilich) in the 1550-60s in Bavaria.[53] More to the point, Castro topped the list of composers Frank Dobbins described as engaged in "the quite exceptional emulation of [Lasso's] settings."[54] In his 1569, 1574, and 1575 publications Castro had set a record thirty of the same poems as had Lasso; and, of these, twenty-seven were modeled on the latter's music. From this it seems fair to conclude that Castro's interest in Guéroult's "Susanne" might have had little to do with anything other than his method of looking for "texts that had already proved their musical efficacy" and, on that score, to trust Lasso.[55] Since Castro's popularity would eventually rate second only to the master himself, it would seem fair to conclude that if anyone else beside Lasso might have reenergized a tradition based purely on the strength of its popularity, Castro was the best choice for the task.[56]

But Castro was just beginning his career in 1569 and the new prominence subsequent scholarship had placed on Faignient and Turnhout opens some new perspectives on Lasso's effect on the Susanne complex. Faignient can hardly be shown to have lacked an awareness and respect for Lasso— in Dobbins's list, for example, Faignient's name does appear, if only once.[57] But the composer's demonstrated interest in the Susanna theme itself was the more striking phenomenon. Noske rightly emphasized that Faignient had featured a work with the name in each of the four linguistic sections of the manuscript (French, Flemish, Italian, and Latin) and he surely meant to suggest that Faignient's choice to saturate a source with Susannes like this should be seen as the composer's rightful claim to fame.[58]

In regard to Lasso and "Susanne," Turnhout stood somewhere between his two "Northern" colleagues. On the one hand, Turnhout set seven of the same poems as Lasso, which exceeds Faignient's by five.[59] But this falls rather short of Castro's extraordinary total of thirty. On the other hand, Turnhout demonstrated a special interest in the Susannes that went well beyond Castro's, who set only one. Turnhout set Guéroult's poem twice—in versions for two and three voices— and a Dutch translation of the verse for five.[60] Indeed, with three different Susannes to his

---

[53] See Jeanice Brooks, "Jean de Castro, the Pense Partbooks and Musical Culture in Sixteenth-Century Lyons," *Early Music History* 11 (1992): 91-149.

[54] Frank Dobbins, "Lassus — Borrower or Lender: The Chansons," *Revue belge de musicologie/Belgisch Tijdschrift voor Muziekwetenschap* 39-40 (1985-86): 101-57, at 101.

[55] Ibid.

[56] On Castro's popularity see Katrien Derde and Saskia Willaert, "Jean De Castro in Antwerpen," *Musica antiqua* 10 (1993): 63-66.

[57] Dobbins, "Lassus — Borrower," 102.

[58] Noske, "Linköping," 155-59. Noske rightly emphasizes that the lady referred to in "Alma Susanna" had nothing to do with the biblical character (p. 158). It is nonetheless intriguing to find the name again in a manuscript where it appears in all other sections, and to note that Rore (who had also set "Susanne"), had set the same Italian poem.

[59] Dobbins, "Lassus — Borrower," 102-05.

[60] Levy, 402.

credit, Turnhout exceeded every other composer but Lasso on Levy's list, although thanks to Noske we now know that Faignient demonstrated as much interest. Thus in the matter of choosing between Lasso-tested poems and poems that evoke the name Susanna, these three composers demonstrated both tendencies, if to a rather different degree. The distance between them diminishes, however, as we turn to their politics.

Turnhout's career was the one most obviously linked to the Spanish party in 1569. Paul Doe emphasized that Turnhout was actually serving as the "*maitre de chant* of the Antwerp Cathedral ... when the organs and music library were destroyed by religious fanatics ... and [Turnhout] thereupon began the formidable task of making good the loss by copying new material and supervising the rebuilding of the [instruments]."[61] In his 1569 publication Turnhout set a prayer for Philip II and joined the Spanish court in Madrid in 1572. In light of these facts it would be difficult to dispute a contention that Turnhout used his music to express his support for Catholic Spain. Noske had found room, however, to suggest that Faignient, at least, might have been expressing the views of a crypto-Protestant.

Noske discussed two Flemish works in the Linköping manuscript that, like Faignient's Susannes, featured some of the same music and text. Both of these were psalm-based and included an ominous reference to "dese benaude tijden ('these fearful days')" that Noske interpreted as "an allusion to the arrival in the Netherlands of the Duke of Alva." Noske finds corroboration for this view in a letter by a Calvinist who requested one of Faignient's non-political works ("Joli mois de may") along with an indisputably Protestant one ("Wilhemus van Nassouwe").[62] But the only biographical fact Noske could furnish concerning Faignient directly had to do with the position the composer held in 1580 as "Sanghmeester" for Eric II of Brunswick-Lüneburg and Noske then admitted, "it seems unlikely that [the Duke] should have engaged a Protestant *Kapellmeister*."[63]

Noske had not come across Guillaume de Poetou's sonnet, "A Maistre Nouel Faignient, no moins gentil Musicien qu'excellent compositeur de Musique." In the poem Faignient was treated as a fellow member of "L'église Catholique" in a publication closely linked to an ultra-Catholic association of traders and bankers known as the Genoese Nation.[64] Poetou published his tribute to Faignient in a volume he had dedicated to Jan vander Noot. Van der Noot would later establish himself as the "most favored" poet of the Antwerp-based Genoese Nation and dedicated his works to a record twenty-two members. Even earlier, in 1565,

---

[61] Paul Doe, "Flemish Songs," Review of Turnhout, *Sacred and Secular Songs, Musical Times* 113, no. 1548 (1972): 183-184, at 183. See also Kristine K. Forney, "The Netherlands, 1520-1640," in *European Music, 1520-1640*, ed. James Haar (Woodbridge: Boydell Press, 2006), 246-79.

[62] Noske, "Linköping," 153.

[63] Ibid.

[64] Guillaume de Poetou, *Suite du Labeur en Liesse...* (Antwerp: Aeg. Diest, 1566), f. 33v. See Karel Bostoen, *Dichterschap en Koopmanschap, in de zestiende eeuw: Omtrent de dichters Guillaume de Poetou en Jan Van der Noot*, Deventer Studiën 1 (Deventer: Sub Rosa Deventer, 1987), 160.

Poetou had addressed his first volume of poems, *La Grande Liesse*, to two prominent members of the same corporation, Stefano Gentile and Giovanni Grimaldi, and another volume to Giovanni Giacomo Fiesco, whose uncle Tommaso was elected to the Consul of the Nation in 1567.[65]

Lasso had preceded the poets in securing the patronage of these Genoese-born Netherlanders. After pointing out that Castro's 1569 publication shared many traits with so-called 'Opus 1," *Primo Libro dovesi* ... of 1555, Igance Bussuyt noted that both included a "dedication in Italian addressed to a leading member of the Genoese Nation."[66] In a bibliographical study of Lasso's edition Kristine K. Forney had already emphasized the importance of the Nation as likely madrigal consumers in the Low Countries. She also noted that Lasso's debut work was reprinted in 1560 with the same dedication and much of the same content, but with the addition of Lasso's "Susanne un jour" and that it thus "should be added to the bibliographic study of the piece by Levy ... [because it] released the famous chanson at the same time it was published in Paris."[67] It is indeed suggestive of their intimate knowledge of this reprinted set that all three of the first composers to follow Lasso—Castro, Faignient and Turnhout — were closely associated with Antwerp and had set the poem that appeared in the first position of the chanson section of "Opus 1," "Las voulez vous," as well as "Susanne," which Lasso's printer Susato, had placed last in the third edition of 1560.[68]

Bossuyt and Forney have made a strong case for the important role played by the Genoese Nation in the "spread of Renaissance culture in the Low Countries."[69] But these gentlemen merchants had more than cultural interests at the center of their attention. Along with the Fuggers, they were deeply enmeshed in the Catholic suppression of rebellions in the late-1560s. As one scholar recently noted, they were "hailed as saviors of the Spanish government. Their money was needed in the first place for the maintenance of Spanish troops in the Netherlands."[70] The Nation's interests, both financial and political/religious, were keenly involved in August 1567 when Alva arrived in the Lowlands and again in late-November 1568 when the English seized a flotilla of Spanish treasure ships, placing in jeopardy the money intended for Alva and his military efforts. This latter act was viewed throughout the trading world as an astonishingly bold move, a maneuver that would

[65] See Katrien Derde, *Recevez ce mien petit labeur:* Jean de Castro: Music and Patronage in the 16th Century, University of Louvain, http://fuzzy.arts.kuleuven.be/decastro/en/n_06.htm (accessed 11 December 2007).

[66] Ignace Bossuyt, "Orlando di Lasso as a Model for Composition as seen in the Three-Voice Motets of Jean de Castro," in *Orlando di Lasso Studies*, ed. Peter Bergquist (Cambridge: Cambridge University Press, 1999), 158-182, at 162.

[67] Kristine K. Forney, "Orlando di Lasso's 'Opus 1': The Making and Marketing of a Renaissance Music Book," *Revue belge de musicologie/Belgisch Tijdschrift voor Muziekwetenschap* 39-40 (1985-86): 33-60, at 60, note 4.

[68] Ibid., 49 and 25; Dobbins, "Lassus — Borrower," 102.

[69] Bossuyt, "Orlando di Lasso as a Model," 162.

[70] Derde, *Recevez ce mien petit labeur.*

lead not only to an embargo on English trade with Flanders (and vice versa) but also become the *casus belli* for an Anglo-Spanish "cold war."[71] Thus with seriously vested financial interests at stake, members of the Genoese Nation turned their eyes to the British Isles in 1568, adding yet another element to those already drawn into the maelstrom of Elizabethan religious and political affairs at the onset of an international crisis that would ultimately lead to the execution of Mary, Queen of Scots and the ill-fated journey of the Spanish Armada.

That Mary herself was identified with the biblical character Susanna in English Catholic propaganda at the time suggests there may have been a musical link between the Genoese nation and the English political situation.[72] Space does not permit a full treatment of this subject. But I might note that Vautrollier's aforementioned edition of Lasso's *Mellange* that included his setting of "Susanne un jour" was produced in London at the height of the Marian crisis in 1570; and that the later published works on this theme by Catholic composers in England, like Alfonso Ferrabosco and William Byrd, corresponded in tone and timing with a great surge in Marian propaganda at the time of her execution.[73]

Since their fates were so different—one executed and the other exonerated— it may seem odd to us today that Mary was linked to Susanna of biblical Babylon. As far as her contemporary supporters were concerned, however, Mary's situation was aptly and (especially after her execution) poignantly reflected in the story of a beautiful, innocent victim of an attempted rape and blackmail by two old men who, after failing to accomplish their crime, falsely accused her of adultery in an effort to avoid recrimination. It was a compelling connection, but interest in the Susanna theme in the musical world must surely have extended beyond its potential application to a persecuted co-religionist. As the chant "Angustiae mihi" reminds us, in the early Christian church the story was used to remind a beleaguered sect of the value of justice, the triumph of virtue, and the efficacy of prayer, and when new forms of slander and heightened desires for vindication arose in the turmoil of the Reformation era, the Susanna story took on a new life in tracts and homilies as well as in the pictorial and dramatic arts.[74] It was in this latter context, I believe, that we find a vibrant form of cross-confessional appropriation spurring the growth and development of the great complex of musical works based on "Susanne un jour."

---

[71] Conyers Read, "Queen Elizabeth's Seizure of the Duke of Alva's Pay-Ships," *Journal of Modern History* 5 (1933): 443-64.

[72] See Jeremy L. Smith, "Mary Queen of Scots as Susanna in Catholic Propaganda," *Journal of the Warburg and Courtauld Society* 73 (2011): 209-20 and idem, "Revisiting the Origins."

[73] Jeremy L. Smith, "A 'Parable in Many Men's Opinion': Mary Queen of Scots as Susanna in Music and Propaganda," paper read at the Medieval & Renaissance Music Conference 2007, Vienna, 11 August 2007.

[74] Dan Clanton, *The Good, the Bold and the Beautiful: The Story of Susanna and its Renaissance Interpretations*, Library of Hebrew Bible/Old Testament Studies 430 (New York and London: T & T Clark, 2006).

Memorial for a Mysterious Matron:
The Funeral Cycle of Gaspar de Albertis

Gary Towne

In the city of Bergamo, almost 500 years ago, there lived and died a great and good woman. Her identity may always remain conjectural, but her death was commemorated with three exquisite works of polyphony by Gaspar de Albertis, the first *maestro di cappella* of the Basilica of Santa Maria Maggiore.

These signed works occupy most of a single fascicle of Bergamo, Biblioteca Civica MS 1209 (BGbc 1209), one of three surviving books of polyphony largely copied by Albertis for the basilica between 1524 and 1541.[1] David Crawford and Scott Messing, in their analysis of the Bergamo manuscripts, noted that the three funerary works occupied the first six leaves of a *quarternion* near the end of the book, the remaining two leaves containing the beginning of a set of eleven Vespers psalms by Albertis and Ruffino Bartolucci, for which they postulate a date in the mid to late 1520s.[2] The funeral cycle includes two motets, *Oremus fratres carissimi* and *Ne reminiscaris*, and a concluding Litany of the Saints. None of the pieces exactly fits a liturgical situation in the Mass or Office as we know it, but collectively they comprise an elegant set of polyphonic works suitable for commemorating the death of a highly esteemed woman in a deeply reverent paraliturgical devotion. The texts of the motets are as follows:

---

[1] Bergamo, Biblioteca Civica MS 1209, with its companions, MSS 1207 and 1208, comprise what remains of the sixteenth-century manuscript repertory of polyphony at the Basilica of Santa Maria Maggiore, which originally included nine or ten choirbooks, as discussed in Gary Towne, "Gaspar de Albertis and Music at Santa Maria Maggiore in Bergamo in the Sixteenth Century," (Ph.D. diss., University of California, Santa Barbara, 1985), 1: 154-71; and David Crawford and J. Scott Messing, *Gaspar de Albertis' Sixteenth-Century Choirbooks at Bergamo*, Renaissance Manuscript Series 6 (Neuhausen-Stuttgart: American Institute of Musicology/Hänssler Verlag, 1994), 61-81.

[2] Crawford and Messing, *Albertis' Choirbooks*, 56, locates the works in the foliation analysis; 168-70 discusses the works in their manuscript context. Their dating, (69-72), arises from analysis of the manuscript structure and copying practices as related to the few associated dates.

Oremus fratres carissimi   BGbe MS 1209, 105v-106r

Oremus, fratres carissimi, sororesque dilecte,   Let us pray, dearest brothers and beloved
pro anima matris nostre, quem Dominus de   sisters, for the soul of our mother, whom the
laqueo huius seculi liberare dignata est, cuius   Lord has esteemed to release from the snare
depositionis diem commemoramus: ut eam   of this world [and] whose day of burial we
pietas Domini in sinu Habrae, Isaac et Jacob   commemorate, that the compassion of our
collocare dignetur: ut cum juditii dies advenerit   Lord may deem her worthy to place in the
inter sanctos et electos suos eam in parte dextera   bosom of Abraham, Isaac, and Jacob, that
collocandam resuscitari atque sedere fatiat. Per   when the day of judgment has come, he may
Christum Dominum nostrum.[3]   make her, being worthy, to be raised again
                                                        and to sit at [his] right hand among his saints
                                                        and elect. Through Christ our Lord.[4]

Ne reminiscaris   BGbc MS 1209, 106v-107r

Ne reminiscaris, Domine. Dicite cantores,   Remember thou, O Lord. Declare singers,
plorate matres, et orate simul pro anima   lament mothers, and pray likewise for the soul
matris nostre. Opus est enim misericordie   of our mother. For it is a duty to implore for
pro defunctis exorare, ergo nobiscum orate   mercy for the dead; therefore, pray with us
devotis cum orationibus, optime sorores.   with devout entreaties, best of sisters. Weep
Flete nobiscum matrem nostram quem   with us for our mother whom we have lost.
perdidimus. Erat enim gemma ecclesie,   She was indeed the jewel of the church, the
castitatis exemplum, norma doctrine,   model of chastity, the standard of doctrine, the
caritatis speculum, vas omnium virtutum.   mirror of charity, the vessel of all virtues. And
Et ideo virtutes celorum nobis rapuerunt   therefore the Virtues of heaven have stolen her
eam. O mater nostra, nostrum solamen, o   away from us. O our mother, our consolation,
quam desolatos nos derelinquisti. Eyulate!   oh how desolate you have left us. Lament! Let
Cantores dicite, orantes dicite, matres orate: singers declare, supplicants affirm, mothers
Requiem eternam dona ei Domine, et lux   pray: Rest eternal grant her, Lord, and let
perpetua luceat ei.[5]   light perpetual shine upon her.

[3] Crawford and Messing, *Albertis' Choirbooks,* 168-69, note that this text is "nearly identical to a prayer
after lowering a body into a grave, given in Jean Deshusses, *Le sacrémentaire grégorien: ses principles formes
d'après les plus anciens manuscrits, Spicilegium Friburgense* 16 (1971), 1: 461, and also *Breviarium predicatorum
. . .* (Venice: Giunta, 1515), f. 411v."

[4] I am very grateful to Daniel Erickson of the University of North Dakota Foreign and Classical
Languages Department for his assistance with these Latin translations.

[5] Crawford and Messing, *Albertis' Choirbooks,* 169, note that portions of this text relate to others, the
first three words to "the antiphon for the seven penitential psalms [*Liber usualis,*] 1840, CAO [*Corpus
antiphonalium officii*], ed. Renato-Joanne Hesbert (Rome: Herder, 1963-79), no. 3861, and three later
words, 'nos desolatos derelinquis' derive from an antiphon for St. Martin of Tours, [*Liber usualis,*]
1748 and CAO, no. 2262." They note that the attributions of virtues may be commemorative of
the deceased and, because they are the only lines that rhyme, that they may derive in part from
an unidentified litany like one for Albertus Magnus, found in Benjamin Musser, *Kyrie eleison: Two
Hundred Litanies* (Westminster, MD: The Newman Bookshop, 1945), 203. See further discussion in
notes 9 and 10, below.

The Litany of the Saints is "one of the oldest liturgical offices in the West, . . . the model for all others. Only minor additions or changes have been made in it in the past thousand years or more, and these only by the Holy See," although there are official variants for the different circumstances of its use. The insertion of local saints is forbidden, to prevent deviation from this norm.[6] Present liturgical use minutely prescribes the formula for each of the canonical rites, in brief: 1) major occasions of blessing or exorcisms, 2) the vigils of Easter and Pentecost, and 3) the commendation of the dead.[7] The text of the litany from Bergamo is concordant with none of these, although it most resembles a truncation of the Easter Vigil litany. In the litany text below, points of divergence from this version are noted.[8] Additions, both textual and editorial, in Bergamo are in square brackets [ ]. Omissions are in angle brackets < >.

Litany of the Saints   BGbc 1209, 107v-111r

Kyrie eleyson. Christe eleyson. Kyrie eleyson.

Lord, have mercy. Christ, have mercy. Lord, have mercy.

Christe audi nos. Christe exaudi nos.

O Christ, hear us. O Christ, heed us.

Pater de celis Deus, miserere ei. Fili redemptor mundi Deus, miserere ei. Spiritus Sancte Deus, miserere ei. Sancta Trinitas unus Deus, miserere ei.

God, Father from heaven, have mercy on her. God the Son, redeemer of the world, have mercy on her. God the Holy Spirit, have mercy on her. Holy Trinity, one God, have mercy on her.

Sancta Maria, ora pro ea. Sancta Dei Genitrix, ora pro ea. Sancta Virgo virginum, ora pro ea.

Holy Mary, pray for her. Holy Mother of God, pray for her. Holy Virgin of virgins, pray for her.

Sancte Michael, ora pro ea. Sancte Gabriel, ora pro ea. Sancte Raphael, ora pro ea. Omnes sancti Angeli et Archangeli, orate pro ea. Omnes sancti beatorum spirituum ordines, orate pro ea.

Saint Michael, pray for her. Saint Gabriel, pray for her. Saint Raphael, pray for her. All ye holy Angels and Archangels, pray for her. All ye holy orders of blessed Spirits, pray for her.

Sancte Joannes Baptista, ora pro ea. Sancte Joseph, ora pro ea. Omnes Sancti Patriarche et Prophete, orate pro ea.

Saint John the Baptist, pray for her. Saint Joseph, pray for her. All ye holy Patriarchs and Prophets, pray for her.

Sancte Petre, ora pro ea. Sancte Paule, ora pro ea. Sancte Joannes, ora pro ea. Sancte Andrea, ora pro ea. [Sancte Marce, ora pro ea.] Omnes sancti Apostoli et Evangeliste, orate pro ea.

Saint Peter, pray for her. Saint Paul, pray for her. Saint John, pray for her. Saint Andrew, pray for her. [John and Andrew reversed, ed.] [Saint Mark, pray for her.] All holy Apostles and Evangelists, pray for her.

---

[6] Quoted and summarized from Musser, *Kyrie eleison*, 146, unnumbered footnote.

[7] Summarized from Musser, *Kyrie eleison*, 140, introduction to the Litany and unnumbered footnote. The litany text in full follows (140-46).

[8] In addition to comparison with "Litanies [*sic*] of the Saints," in Musser, *Kyrie eleison*, 140-46, I have compared the Litany of the Saints from Bergamo with those found in *Liber usualis* (Tournai: Desclée & Co., 1938), 756-59; Dom Gaspar Lefebvre, *Saint Andrew Daily Missal* (Bruges: Biblica, 1960), 1180-86, and *Collectio rituum pro dioecesibus civitatum foederatarum Americae Septentrionalis* (New York: Benziger Brothers, 1964), 200-202. No standard version even approaches the number of variants in Albertis' polyphonic litany.

<Omnes sancti Discipuli Domini, orate pro ea. Omnes sancti Innocentes, orate pro ea.>

<All ye holy Disciples of the Lord, pray for her. All ye holy Innocents, pray for her.>

Sancte Stephane, ora pro ea. Sancte Laurentii, ora pro ea. Sancte Vincenti, ora pro ea. [Sancte Alexander, ora pro ea. Sancte Domno, ora pro ea. Sancte Domnio, ora pro ea.] Omnes sancti Martires, orate pro ea.

Saint Stephen, pray for her. Saint Laurence, pray for her. Saint Vincent, pray for her. [Saint Alexander, pray for her. Saint Domno, pray for her. Saint Domnio, pray for her.] All ye holy Martyrs, pray for her.

Sancte Silvester, ora pro ea. Sancte Gregori, ora pro ea. [Sancte Martine, ora pro ea.] Sancte Augustine, ora pro ea. [Sancte Hieronime, ora pro ea] Omnes sancti Pontifices et Confessores, orate pro ea.

Saint Sylvester, pray for her. Saint Gregory, pray for her. [Saint Martin, pray for her.] Saint Augustine, pray for her. [Saint Jerome, pray for her.] All ye holy Bishops and Confessors, pray for her.

<Omnes Sancti doctores, orate pro ea. Sancte Antoni, . . . Sancte Benedicte, . . . Sancte Dominice, . . . Sancte Francisce, . . . Omnes sancti Sacerdotes et Levite, . . . Omnes sancti Monachi et Eremite, orate pro ea.>

<All ye holy doctors, pray for her. Saint Anthony, . . . Saint Benedict, . . . Saint Dominic, . . . Saint Francis, . . . All ye holy Priests and Levites, . . . All ye holy Monks and Hermits, pray for her.>

Sancta Maria Magdalena, ora pro ea. <Sancta Agnes, . . . Sancta Cecilia, . . . Sancta Agatha, . . . Sancta Anastasia, ora pro ea.> [Sancta Anna, ora pro ea. Sancta Grata, ora pro ea. Sancta Hesteria, ora pro ea. Sancta Eusebia, ora pro ea. Sancta Ursula, ora pro ea.] Omnes Sancte Virgines et Vidue, orate pro ea.

Saint Mary Magdalene, pray for her. <Saint Agnes, . . . Saint Cecilia, . . . Saint Agatha, . . . Saint Anastasia, pray for her.> [Saint Anne, pray for her. Saint Grata, pray for her. Saint Asteria, pray for her. Saint Eusebia, pray for her. Saint Ursula, pray for her.] All holy Virgins and Widows, pray for her.

Omnes Sancti et Sancte Dei, [orate] <intercedite> pro ea.

All holy men and women Saints of God, [pray] <intercede> for her.

[Here, the Bergamo litany eliminates many petitions for liberation from sin, for the church, and for the world, and three subsequent petitions beginning Agnus Dei. The Bergamo and standard litanies continue, as here—]

Christe audi nos. Christe exaudi nos.

O Christ, hear us. O Christ, heed us. [As in other occasions when the Kyrie does not follow separately, as part of the mass, the Bergamo litany appends here—]

Kyrie eleyson. Christe eleyson. Kyrie eleyson.

Lord, have mercy. Christ, have mercy. Lord, have mercy.[9]

[The Bergamo litany concludes:]

Oremus Pater noster.

Let us pray the Our Father.

[9] The translation of this litany is dervied and adapted from that in Musser, Kyrie eleison, 140-46 with emendations and additions by this author.

For a brief exegesis of the cycle's texts, let us return to the beginning and begin with *Oremus fratres carissimi*, the first motet. This text is an invocation, which exhorts those present to pray for the soul of the deceased woman. Beginning with the word *oremus*, the prayer is a suitable opening for a devotion. This text is nearly identical to one which follows the lowering of a body into the grave, given in ancient sources including a *Breviarium predicatorum* . . . (Venice: Giunta, 1515),[10] the supplicatory character of the text suits that action, with particular pleas for the exaltation of this most worthy woman.

The second motet, *Ne reminiscaris*, continues the crescendo of supplication with praise of the deceased and further prayer for her eternal rest. The eulogistic character of this text personalizes this prayer in a positive way that is not found elsewhere in the usual texts of the burial rites, which are otherwise heavily concerned with absolution from sin and escape from eternal damnation.[11] Crawford and Messing cite a variety of sources for phrases in this text, including antiphons for the seven penitential psalms and Saint Martin of Tours, and the introit of the Requiem Mass. They speculate that the remaining lines–the attributions of virtues–are commemorative of the deceased and, because they are the only lines that rhyme, they may derive in part from an anonymous litany for Albertus Magnus.[12] Like a litany, the lines have something of a formulaic character as well, which may indeed be a foreshadowing of the final work of the cycle.

The Litany of the Saints, which concludes the cycle, consummates the devotion by fulfilling the call to corporate prayer. In all of its variants, this litany begins with a prayer for mercy, followed by a supplication to Christ, and invocations to the Trinity and the Blessed Virgin. Following this standard beginning, saints are invoked individually within their classifications: angels and blessed spirits, patriarchs and prophets, apostles and evangelists, disciples and holy innocents, bishops and confessors, martyrs, doctors, priests and levites, monks and hermits, virgins and widows. On the vigils of Easter and Pentecost, the list of saints invoked in each class is substantially truncated, as indicated in Musser, cited above (n. 5). The Bergamo Litany seems to derive from this shortened pattern, but with significant additional deletions, (often of whole classes of saints, i.e., disciples, holy innocents, doctors, priests, levites, monks, and hermits). The Bergamo Litany also makes some significant deletions and additions of individual saints, discussed below.

[10] Crawford and Messing, *Albertis' Choirbooks*, 168-69; see n. 3.

[11] *Liber usualis*; Lefebvre, *Saint Andrew Daily Missal*; Sylvester P. Juergens, *The New Marian Missal* (New York: Regina Press, 1958); *Graduale Cisterciense* (Westmalle: Typis Cisterciensibus, 1960); and *Collectio rituum concur*. Although these sources are post-Tridentine, they do precede the major ritual reforms of the Second Vatican Council.

[12] Crawford and Messing, *Albertis' Choirbooks*, 169, citing Musser, *Kyrie eleison*, 203. The litany for Saint Albert includes many more such petitions. Only one of them is identical to that in the motet, "Vessel of all virtues." Metaphors for other virtues seem to have been scrambled between the litany and the motet, as if variants on a formulaic type. Examples for comparison from the litany for Albertus Magnus include: " Sure norm of prudence . . , Bright mirror of temperance . . , Living model of humility . . , Pure lily of chastity . . , True model of obedience . . , Bright gem of Bishops," etc. Musser's book sheds light on the great variability and creativity among litanies in general, as well as the many formulaic variants among petitions found in them.

Following the standard litany's catalog of the saints are petitions for intercession and mercy, and a lengthy series of petitions for liberation from sin, for the church, and for the world, which, with three subsequent petitions beginning *Agnus Dei*, are omitted in the Bergamo version. Both this version and the standard litany continue as they began: *Christe audi nos. Christe exaudi nos.* In concordance with the standard litany forms when not preceding mass, the Bergamo Litany adds: *Kyrie eleyson. Christe eleyson. Kyrie eleyson,* and concludes *Oremus Pater noster.* The *Pater noster*, prayed silently, also follows in the standard litanies, but, unlike the Bergamo Litany, they continue with Psalm 69, twelve versicles and responds, ten collects, and a closing set of three versicles and responds, none of which appear in the Bergamo version.

At the most macroscopic level, the Bergamo Litany differs strongly from the usual forms. This alone would weigh against its use for canonical rites, even without the substantial deletions of standard saints and substitutions of local ones listed in the Table below.

Table 1

Class of Saints	**Alterations**
Apostles, Evangelists	Andrew, John reversed, Mark added
Disciples, Holy Innocents	Collective petition omitted
Martyrs	Bergamasque saints Alexander, Domno, Domnio added
Bishops, Confessors, Doctors	Doctors' collective omitted
	Martin and Jerome added
Priests, Levites, Monks, Hermits omitted,	with Anthony, Benedict, Dominic, Francis
Virgins, Widows	Agnes, Cecilia, Agatha, Anastasia omitted
	Anne, Ursula, and (Bergamasque) Grata,
	Hesteria (Asteria), Eusebia added

In addition, as Crawford and Messing note, *Miserere ei* (Have mercy on <u>her</u>) is substituted for *Miserere nobis* (Have mercy on us), and *Ora pro ea* (Pray for <u>her</u>) for *Ora pro nobis* (Pray for us), in accordance with the form of this litany as used for commendation of the dead. It is these changes that led them to propose the litany's relationship with the two funeral motets that precede it in the manuscript.[13] This association is strengthened by the logical progression of the works' texts, which function as a single devotional unit. The substantial changes in the catalog of saints in violation of canonical restrictions point toward a personalization of the litany for a private rite. The particular changes also offer clues about identifying characteristics of the deceased, as well as confirmation of locale.

Not every change submits to easy explanation; many omissions may have functioned merely to shorten an already lengthy series of works. But several alterations are significant: Bergamo's Venetian sovereignty explains Saint Mark's appearance, which may also have emphasized a family's political allegiance within

---

[13] Crawford and Messing, *Albertis' Choirbooks,* 80, 168-70.

the convolutions of Bergamasque politics.[14] Bergamo and its environs are indicated
by the addition of numerous local saints. Saint Alexander, the patron of Bergamo,
escaped in the late third century from the martyrdom of the Theban Legion in
Switzerland, only to achieve it in Bergamo. Saint Domno was most likely the uncle
of Saints Domnio (Domneone) and Eusebia (see below), all three third-century
Bergamasque martyrs whose relics, entombed in the church of Sant' Andrea outside
the walls, were discovered in 1401.[15] The inclusion of Saints Martin, presumably of
Tours, and Jerome would indicate reverence for learning. Saint Anne, patroness of
motherhood, would suit a matron, and Saint Ursula, patroness of plague victims,
might signify the victim of a communicable disease. Grata, Hesteria, and Eusebia
round out the collection of Bergamasque saints with the city's most ancient and
revered holy women. Reportedly, Santa Grata carried Alexander's head from the
place of his execution to the tomb. Saint Hesteria (Asteria) was Grata's sister.
Both Grata and Asteria appear to have been holy women—matrons—rather than
virgins. As noted above, Saint Eusebia was another third-century Bergamasque
martyr, virgin, and niece of Saint Domno. Taking all the alterations together, the
textual emendations suggest as a dedicatee a matron of Bergamasque origin and
strong patriotic associations, who died of a communicable disease before her time,
who had family connections with learning and the military, and whose remains
may have been transported some distance.

Such personalization of the litany reinforces other unique adaptations
and composition of liturgical texts for a specific person and a unique purpose.
Although there is a near concordance of *Oremus fratres carissimi* with an old prayer
for interment, and the Litany of the Saints has substantial unaltered portions

---

[14] Bortolo Belotti, *Storia di Bergamo e dei Bergamaschi* (Milan: Casa Editrice Ceschina, 1940; republished
Bergamo: Banca Popolare di Bergamo, 1989), 3: 133-36, 221-22 ff., describes the long-lasting
strife and animosities following Venice's acquisition of Bergamo from Milan in 1427-28 and the
distubances that followed it for decades. Both Belotti and Luca Mazzoleni, "La faida degli Albani
e dei Brembati," *Le pagine del tempo: Fatti, uomini e luoghi del cammino humano*, back issue no. 1, ISSN
1720-3732, sec. 5, note that the continuing turbulence maintained Bergamo's ancient Ghibelline
and Guelf factions as partisans, respectively, of Milan, and Venice, into the sixteenth century.
Mazzoleni was found at http://www.fortepiano.it/PagineDelTempo/download/faida01.doc. This
article is cited by section because the page numbers vary according to one's printer. I note on 29
August 2010 that this web-published article is not now available at the website above.

[15] Discussion of Saints Domno, Domneone, and Eusebia is from Luigi Chiodi, " Dall' introduzione
del cristianesimo al dominio franco," in A. Caprioli, A. Rimoldi, and L. Vaccaro, eds. *Diocesi di
Bergamo* (Brescia: Editrice 'La Scuola,' 1988), 17, 19. There are a number of possible saints with
names similar to Domno and Domnio. Another source of Vitae is "Orthodox Europe: Latin
Saints of the Orthodox Patriarchate of Rome," with saints ordered calendrically by feast day: at
http://www.orthodoxengland.org.uk/stdjan.htm, and ff. (The three-letter abbreviation for month
precedes .htm, i.e. stdjan.htm, stdfeb.htm, stdmar, etc. in the web page address.) The presence of
these saints in the Orthodox calendar despite their absence from the conventional Catholic source
of Butler's *Lives* indicates their antiquity. Their presence in the Bergamo litany is also significant,
given the present canonical prohibition on inclusion of local saints. Unfortunately, although the
Orthodox calendar includes Saint Eusebia and Domnio, it lists Domnio as Eusebia's uncle instead
of Domno, whom it omits completely. Clearly, local tradition should prevail here. Other less likely
candidates from the Orthodox calendar include the Armenian martyr Saint Domno, whose ashes
were venerated in Brescia, and the saints Domninus, martyrs from Parma and Rome, respectively.

that follow its model as well as significant variations, the cycle's central motet, *Ne reminiscaris*, has no single model and appears to be a patchwork of phrases from various sources.[16]   None of these texts follows the precise wording of any of the regular services for burial, interment, or commemoration, or the Office of the Dead.[17] While they could be appended to any one of these rites, they also comprise in themselves (with the *Pater noster*) a textually functional whole. The works could have been used as a coda for any of the usual rites for the dead, or as a free-standing paraliturgical, or even extraliturgical private devotion. The origins, nature and adaptations, and composition of the texts suggest that the occasion for which these three works were written was the interment, translation, or later commemoration of a deceased woman of high standing. They appear to have been designed as a unit. From a textual standpoint, the foreshadowing of litany-like formulas in *Ne reminiscaris*, as well as the Bergamo Litany's textual echoing of opening and closing refrains, suggest the conceptual reshaping of the texts into a unity. Confirmation of this also appears in the musical design.

      The musical extent of these three works is considerable, occupying a total of six choirbook openings: *Oremus fratres*–83.5 breves; *Ne reminiscaris*–107 breves; and the litany–276 breves. The total length of 466.5 breves would have taken around fifteen minutes or more to perform without pause, not an insignificant amount of time, even for a fairly long-winded composer, and the concluding *Pater noster*, if chanted, would have added another two minutes. The clefs of the works are as follows: *Oremus fratres*–C3, C4, C4, F4; *Ne reminiscaris*–C3, C3, C3, F4; Litany of the Saints–G2, C2, C3, F3. The first two works have limited ranges overall, from F in the Bass to a' in the three upper voices, clearly set for *voci pari* or *voci mutate*, four-part men's voices–ATTB or TTTB.[18]   The litany at first appears higher, except that its clefs are what came to be known as *chiavette*, which indicated transposition down a fourth or fifth from the written pitch.[19]   Lowered a perfect fourth, the compass of actual pitches is from F in the Bass (which appears only once), to d'' in the Cantus, which also appears only once, in the final Kyrie; the Cantus range otherwise rises

---

[16] See Crawford and Messing, *Albertis' Choirbooks*, 80, 168-70.

[17] Modern sources consulted for the full rites include *Antiphonale monasticum pro diurnis horis* (Tournai: Desclée & Co., 1934); *The Hours of the Divine Office in English and Latin* (Collegeville, MN: The Liturgical Press, 1963); *Graduale Cisterciense* (Westmalle: Typis Cisterciensibus, 1960); *Breviarium Romanum* (Rome: Printers of the Holy See and the Congregation of Sacred Rites, 1960); *Liber usualis*; Lefebvre, *Saint Andrew Daily Missal*; Juergens, *The New Marian Missal*; and *Collectio rituum*.

[18] Frank Carey, "Composition for Equal Voices in the Sixteenth Century," *Journal of Musicology* 9 (1991): 300-42, discusses such works exhaustively; idem, "Voci pari, voci mutate," in *The New Grove Dictionary of Music and Musicians*, 2nd ed. (London: Macmillan, 2001), 26: 855-56, gives an abbreviated discussion.

[19] Patrizio Barbieri, "Chiavette," in *The New Grove Dictionary of Music and Musicians*, 2nd ed. (London: Macmillan, 2001), 5: 597-600, discusses the various authorities for this practice. He notes that the transposition could be either a fourth or a fifth down, under different circumstances. The earliest authority, Ganassi, mandates a fifth down. Banchieri advocates a fourth if there is a flat in the key signature and a fifth is there is not. For this work, Banchieri's transposition of a fourth best suits the low range of the bass voice as well as the key signature.

no higher than a'. This work, too, would suit four-part men's voices–ATTB or ATBB, which makes all three works suitable for the same ensemble.

The restricted ranges of these and other works for *voci pari* both complicates and simplifies the modal analysis. On the one hand, use of clef patterns to compare them with other works of more conventional scoring is not very helpful; on the other hand, the similar ranges of the three upper voices simplifies modal analysis somewhat, since their melodic patterns are consequently often similar. *Oremus*, ending on an F triad, with one flat, has *ambiti* that mostly fit mode 5, a major mode, described (after Glarean) by Cristle Collins Judd, as an *Ut*-mode.[20] Likewise, the litany, ending on a G triad (as transposed), with no flat, has *ambiti* that fit mode 8, also *Ut*. The case of *Ne reminiscaris* is a bit more complex, since its ending on an A triad (no flat) and the *ambiti* might suggest mode 2 (in relation to its transposition, a minor or *Re*-mode), but thematically and contrapuntally, there is very frequent reiteration of the half steps E-F and B-C. This gives this work a strong aura of the Phrygian, or *Mi*, tonality. As Judd observes, such mode 3 and 4 works may cadence on A even without a flat in the key signature. Based on the prevailing thematic *ambiti*, I would assign mode 3 to this motet, whose dark tonality provides a vivid contrast with the bright major modes of the works surrounding it.

Proceeding further into motivic analysis of the three works, we find that their textual coherence is reinforced by subtle motivic relationships. A three-note motive–a second enveloped by a third–appears in various forms in all three works. The forms of the motive are as follows: Original–rising second, falling third; Inversion–falling second, rising third; Retrograde–rising third, falling second; Retrograde Inversion–falling third, rising second. The alterations in the motive are diatonic–the intervals' qualities may vary.[21] Nonetheless, the motive's brevity and simplicity make it easily recognizable wherever and in whatever form it occurs. Its repetition lends it a familiarity that conveys a subtle unity among the three works. The motive first appears in the opening point of imitation of the first motet, *Oremus*, although it probably comes from the litany Cantus, where it begins nearly every internal petition: G-A-F in transposition, C-D-B-flat as written.[22] Table 2 lists appearances of the motive throughout these three works. Those that appear in subsequent musical examples are so noted.

---

[20] Cristle Collins Judd, "Modal Types and 'Ut, Re, Mi' Tonalities: Tonal Coherence in Sacred Vocal Polyphony from about 1500," *Journal of the American Musicoogical Society* 45 (1992): 428-67, discusses the complications entailed in application of monophonic modal criteria to polyphonic works, as well as Glarean's very useful and appropriate simplified classification of *Ut*, *Re*, and *Mi* tonalities.

[21] The use of the terms original, inversion, and retrograde is a convenience adapted from a more recent musical system; we need not feel hidebound by that system's anachronistic strictures any more than by the resemblance of the motive itself to one in a well-known science fiction movie– the important consideration is the audible pervasiveness of the basic motive, a third enfolding a second, throughout all three works, which would have been apparent to a Renaissance musician.

[22] In this original form of the motive, all three notes are structural, as they are in its thirty-eight iterations in the Litany (e.g., mm. 41-250, ex. 9 and 10). A similar three-note pattern that is the retrograde inversion appears in the Litany's first and last five petitions (ex. 8 below, mm. 1-18, 251-65, and ex. 11, mm. 261-265.) In this version, stated only nine times, the third note is set as an unaccented passing tone, which makes it slightly less obvious.

Table 2

Musical Work	Voice	Pitches	Form	Examples
Oremus fratres (mm. 6-10)	Cantus	F-G-E	O	1
(*fratres carissimi*)	Altus	C-D-B♭	O	
	Tenor	C-A-B♭	R I	
	Bassus	F-D-E	R I	
Oremus fratres (mm. 21-26)	Cantus	E-F-D	O	not included
(*de laqueo*)	Altus, Tenor	A-B♭-G	O	
	Bassus	D-E-C	O	
Oremus fratres (mm. 44-50)	Cantus	F-D-E, E-C-D	R I	not included
(*in sinu Habrae Isaac et Jacob*)	Altus	A-F-G	R I	
	Bassus	F-D-E	R I	
	Altus	E-F-D	O	
	Tenor	C-D-B♭	O	
	Bassus	A-B♭-G	O	
Ne reminiscaris (mm. 1-3)	Altus	E-D-F	I	3
(*Ne reminiscaris*)	(top voice)			
Ne reminiscaris (mm. 58-59)	Cantus	G-E-F	R I	5
(*caritatis speculum*)	Altus	E-C-D	R I	
Ne reminiscaris (mm. 87-93)	Altus	E-D-F	I	not included
(*Requiem eternam*)	Bassus	D-C-E	I	
	Cantus	C-B-D	I	
	Tenor	G-F-A	I	
(*dona ei domine*)	Altus	F-G-E	O	
	Bassus	D-E-C	O	
Ne reminiscaris (mm. 102-106)	Cantus	G-E-F	R I	7
(*luceat ei*)	Tenor	A-C-B	R	
	Tenor	G-A-F	O	
	Bassus	E-C-D	R I	
Litany (mm. 1-18, 251-65)	Cantus	G-E-F (transp.)	R I	8 & 11
(*Kyrie/Christe . . . audi nos*)		C-A-B♭ (writ.)	R I	
Litany (mm. 41-250)	Cantus	G-A-F (transp.)	O	9 & 10
(all internal petitions)		C-D-B♭ (writ.)	O	
Final triad roots, in order, Litany transposed		F-A-G	R	included

Abbreviations: O=Original form, I=Inverted form, R=Retrograde form (all diatonic)
not included = not included in this article's musical examples

The motive first appears at the initial point of imitation in *Oremus fratres:* in the Cantus, F-G-E; Altus, C-D-B♭; and loose retrograde inversion in the Tenor, C-A-B♭, and the Bassus, F-D-E (Ex. 1, mm. 7-10). It also appears on the text *de laqueo* in original form: Cantus, E-F-D; Altus and Tenor, A-B♭-G; Bassus, D-E-C; and in retrograde inversion on *in sinu Habrae Isaac et Jacob*: Cantus, F-D-E, E-C-D; Altus A-F-G, Bassus, F-D-E; as well as in original form: Altus, E-F-D; Tenor, C-D-B♭; Bassus, A-B♭-G. Other single-voice occurrences in the middle of melodies are also common.

The motive also appears several times in *Ne reminiscaris*: in inversion at the Altus (highest voice) opening, E-D-F (Ex. 3 below, mm. 1-3); also in retrograde inversion in Cantus and Altus on *caritatis speculum*, G-E-F and E-C-D, respectively Ex. 5, mm. 58-59); inverted in all voices on *Requiem eternam*: Altus, E-D-F (similar to the Cantus opening), Bassus, D-C-E, Cantus, C-B-D, Tenor, G-F-A; and on *luceat ei*: Cantus, G-E-F (retrograde inversion): Tenor, A-C-B (retrograde) and G-A-F (original); Bassus, E-C-D (retrograde inversion) (Ex. 7, mm. 102-6). The retrograde form also appears in the relationship of the final triads of all three pieces – F-A-G (with the litany transposed, as noted above).[23] Far from vitiating the motivic identity, the variety of forms, and the interchange of major and minor seconds and thirds permits a more widespread use of the motive throughout all three works, despite differences in mode and scale degree. The motive's brevity ensures its audible or subliminal recognition in whatever form, original, inversion, or retrograde, it is presented.[24] The motivic unity, however unconventional, of these three works compliments the textual affinities among them, and both textual and musical devices enhance and amplify the works' pious devotion.

The relationship between the cycle's texts and music further enhances the works' expressiveness. *Oremus fratres carissimi* begins with a four-voice statement of the word *Oremus*, which uses near homophony to convey unanimity of purpose (Ex. 1, mm. 1-6). Imitative entries in all voices follow on the words *fratres carissimi*, as if to denote the multiple brothers addressed. Albertis' practice in imitation in all his works I have investigated is unusually free. In addition to the diatonic motivic manipulations already discussed, he may enlarge or reduce an interval by a step, vary the text underlay, invert the motive, or even make significant melodic alterations, preserving only the motive's rhythmic identity. The opening measures (Ex. 1) show the motive treated in a loose retrograde between the entries of the lower and upper voices, which, if anything, enhances its depiction of the text.

[23] Given the muddy waters surrounding the assignment of monophonic chant modes to polyphonic works, as attested to in Judd, "Modal Types, and 'Ut, Re, Mi,'" it is presumptuous of me to assume that my modal assignments at the beginning of this analysis are those of the composer. But if they are, the mode numbers of the motets add up to that of the litany, 5 + 3 = 8, another possible indicator of the unified conception of the works.

[24] Although the exact technique described here is unusual, motivic repetition, thematic inversion, and retrograde have well-known precedents in Renaissance sacred music. While Albertis was clearly familiar with much of this repertoire, his lifelong residence in Bergamo, a bit off the beaten track, may have allowed him some individualism in compositional invention, apparent in the freedom with which he treats motives in much of his work, as well as in his way of exploiting here this motive's easy recognition.

Example 1: *Oremus fratres carissimi*, mm. 1-10. (I-BGbc MS 1209, ff. 105v-106r)

From this point, free counterpoint with some imitation prevails until paired imitation on the words *de laqueo huius seculi*, with a musical motive that echoes the opening point of imitation (Ex. 1, mm. 7-10). This alternation of techniques continues, with elegant and ever-changing textures and beautiful declamation. Certain phrases are appropriately highlighted: *cuius depositionis* with syncopated through-imitation, *diem commemoramus* with homophonic paired imitation. *Cum juditii dies advenerit inter sanctos et electos suos in parte dextera* depicts the teeming multitudes of the blessed with rich swirls of free polyphony, leading gradually to near-homophonic unanimity for the plea, *collocandam resuscitari atque sedere fatiat* (Ex. 2). The work closes with the invocation *Per Christum Dominum nostrum* stated twice homophonically in triple proportion. Here again, homophony conveys the unanimity of the plea.

Example 2: *Oremus fratres carissimi*, mm. 67-77. (I-BGbc MS 1209, ff. 105v-106r)

Ne reminiscaris shows similar creative richness, beginning with successive points of imitation–up to *pro anima matris nostre*. The opening motive is an inversion of the first point of imitation of *Oremus fratres*, which supports the musical relationship between the works (Ex. 3). The setting of this section of the text ends with all four voices repeating the words *matris nostre* in homophony (Ex. 4, mm. 19-22), which again expresses the mourners' unanimity.

Example 3: *Ne reminiscaris*, mm. 1-8 (Cantus and Altus parts inverted for clarity); order of voices from top to bottom, A-C-T-B.

Example 4: *Ne reminiscaris*, mm. 15-22. (Cantus and Tenor parts inverted for clarity); order of voices from top to bottom, T-C-A-B.

The next section of text utilizes two-, three- and four-voice homophony, occasionally enlivened by a single offset voice and by paired imitation on the words *optime sorores*. The list of virtues beginning with *gemma ecclesie* is set in similar homophony. Beginning at *norma doctrine*, two-voice homophonic echoes illustrate the mirror of charity (*caritatis speculum*) (Ex. 5). The two-voice pairings in this setting foreshadow the use of two-voice petitions in the subsequent Litany of the Saints, which reinforces Crawford and Messing's association of this portion of the text with litany formulas.[25]

Example 5: *Ne reminiscaris*, mm. 55-62. (I-BGbc MS 1209, ff. 106v-107r)

A later tutti section portrays the crowd of angels—*virtutes celorum*; then ascents in the lower voices depict their stealing away of the departed soul (*rapuerunt eam*) (Ex. 6, mm. 68-71).[26]

---

[25] Crawford and Messing, *Albertis' Choirbooks*, 169, citing Musser, *Kyrie eleison*, 203; noted above.

[26] "The following passages from St. Gregory the Great (Hom. 34, In Evang.) will give us a clear idea of the view of the Church's doctors on the point: 'We know on the authority of Scripture that there

Example 6: *Ne reminiscaris*, mm. 68-79, Cantus and Tenor parts inverted for clarity; order of voices, top to bottom, T-C-A-B. (I-BGbc MS 1209, ff.106v-107r)

In Example 6, measures 68-71, the four-voice imitation on the texts *O mater nostra* and *o quam desolatos*, the subsequent free polyphony, and the work's highest tessitura combine to express the mourners' distracted grief. This lamentation resolves in the prayer of all, *Requiem eternam dona ei Domine*, set in paired imitation to the same motive as the first point of imitation, creating a musical link between the texts (*Ne reminiscaris Domine . . .requiem eternam dona ei . . .*), as well as a recapitulation within this motet and a link to the rest of the cycle. The setting calms further to conclude with increasingly clear paired iteration of the closing supplication *et lux perpetua luceat ei* (Ex. 7).

Example 7: *Ne reminiscaris*, mm. 98-107. (I-BGbc MS 1209, ff. 106v-107r)

As seen in these examples, *Oremus fratres* and *Ne reminiscaris* show an almost madrigalistic concern for text painting, in a variegated tapestry of melodic, rhythmic, and textural devices, in addition to a humanistic clarity of declamation.

Such concern for declamation assumes an overriding importance in the cycle's third work, which has a very different character. Rather than a motet-like prayer setting, the third work is a homophonic litany, with only a hint of counterpoint in the opening and closing sections. Throughout the work, the syllables of the chant text, which would be freely intoned in monophony, are assigned definite

---

are nine orders of angels, viz., Angels, Archangels, <u>Virtues</u>, Powers, Principalities, Dominations, Throne[s], Cherubim and Seraphim.'" Hugh T. Pope, "Angels," in *The Catholic Encyclopedia*, vol. 1 (1904), as "New Advent," at http://www.newadvent.org/cathen/01476d.htm (italics mine).

rhythmic values, in the fashion of *cantus fractus*.[27]   Crawford and Messing note that "[Albertis'] music is based on the litany formula but does not agree exactly with any of the chant sources."[28]   Notwithstanding, from *Christe, audi/exaudi nos* (Ex. 8, mm. 13-28), the Cantus melody for all the petitions is nearly identical with the standard melody for this litany, with the one exception: that $B_\flat$ (B *fa*) replaces $B_\natural$ (B *mi*). Only the *Kyrie-Christe-Kyrie eleison* sections (Ex. 8, mm. 1-12; Ex. 11, mm. 262-65) diverge from their chant melody by using the Cantus melody from the *Christe, audi/exaudi nos* section (Ex. 1, mm. 13-18), no doubt for greater musical unity.   In the manuscript, the chant melody in the Cantus, with the other voices, is written a fourth higher than in my musical examples, which are transposed down by that interval, as indicated by their *chiavette*, in order to demonstrate the tonal relationships between the works in the cycle.   The first *Kyrie* begins with a slight offset of the Altus and Bassus before leading into settings of the *Christe* and second *Kyrie* in polyphonically-activated homophony, followed by similar but simpler settings of *Christe, audi nos* and *Christe, exaudi nos* (Ex. 8).   The subsequent petitions to the Trinity continue

Example 8: *Litany of the Saints*, mm. 1-23, transposed a perfect fourth down from the manuscript pitch. (I-BGbc MS 1209, ff. 107v-108r)

[27] "Il canto fratto è un tipo di canto cristiano liturgico eseguito con valori proporzionali: al contrario del cosiddetto gregoriano il cantus fractus possiede spesso una notazione con elementi mensurali, che indica con precisione il valore delle note." Marco Gozzi, ed. "Cantus Fractus – Canto Fratto," in *RAPHAEL (R̲hythmic A̲nd P̲roportional H̲idden or A̲ctual EL̲ements in Plainchant): elementi ritmico-proporzionali nel canto cristiano liturgico*, website and database of Progetto RAPHAEL, at http://www.cantusfractus.org/index.html, accessed April 13, 2008. Gozzi has also published extensively on this subject elsewhere.

[28] Crawford and Messing, *Albertis' Choirbooks*, 170

in the same style, following the model's change in tone, with slightly ornamented cadences on the second and fourth petitions. This second tone, from the chant litany, is that used for all subsequent petitions to the saints, and it echoes the first imitated motive of both motets (original form in *Oremus*, inversion in *Ne reminiscaris*). From this point, petitions to the Blessed Virgin follow swiftly in nearly identical four-voice settings. Subsequent petitions to the apostles, evangelists, most martyrs (with the exceptions of Saint Stephen and Saint Alexander, Bergamo's patron) and bishops and confessors are sung in duets with four-voice refrains on *ora pro ea*. Saints Stephen and Alexander receive four-voice settings (Ex. 9), as does the final collective petition in each group.

Example 9: *Litany of the Saints*, mm. 148-57, transposed a perfect fourth down from the manuscript pitch. (I-BGbc MS 1209, ff. 109v-110r)

Holy women are similarly addressed in duet (such as Eusebia), except for petitions to Saints Mary Magdalene, Anne, Ursula, and the collective petition, which are all treated in four voices (Ex. 10).

Example 10: *Litany of the Saints*, mm. 228-244, transposed a perfect fourth down from the manuscript pitch. (I-BGbc MS 1209, ff. 110v-111r)

Following the collective petition to all the saints, the sections on *Christe, audi/exaudi nos*, and *Kyrie/Christe eleison* return, their order reversed in a neat arch form and their music nearly identical with the work's opening. The final *Kyrie* is enhanced with imitative polyphony and a Cantus tessitura that rises a fifth above the rest of the work in a soaring melodic arc unrelated to previous themes, which provides an impressive finale (Ex. 11, mm. 266-271).

Example 11: *Litany of the Saints*, mm. 262-75, transposed a perfect fourth down from the manuscript pitch. (I-BGbc MS 1209, ff. 110v-111r)

The work concludes calmly, with a rhythmically imitative invitation to pray the *Pater noster*, each voice iterating a single note leading to a plagal resolution. This provides a transition to the devotion's conclusion, the *Pater noster*, presumably to be sung in monophony or said collectively, which brings to a chaste ending this exquisite devotional trilogy, with its elegant madrigalistic expression of lamentation and eulogy.

This noble musical tribute leaves us with the tantalizing question of who merited such an elaborate and unconventional obsequy. Crawford and Messing have proposed that the works commemorate an as yet unknown Mother Superior.[29] In my own researches, I have hitherto found no evidence of association of such a person with Gaspar de Albertis or Santa Maria Maggiore, nor have I found any appropriate woman in the time period proposed by Crawford and Messing–the mid to late 1520s.[30] But the works' texts do not exclude a secular woman. Some passages even suggest it. In *Oremus fratres carissimi*, both dearest brothers and sweetest sisters are called to pray for the deceased, who is called "our mother" no fewer than four times in the motets. And the only attribute that might suggest virginity, *castitatis exemplum*, is, in fact, applicable to a married woman, who can be a model of chastity—"purity from unlawful intercourse."[31] Allowing that the object of

[29] Crawford and Messing, *Albertis' Choirbooks*, 80

[30] Ibid., 69-72. Further discussion of this issue follows below.

[31] *The Compact Edition of the Oxford English Dictionary* (New York: Oxford University Press, 1971), 1: 385-86 microprint, 2: 300-301 original; the etymological discussion quotes Bauldwin's *Moral Philosophy* (1547-64), "The first degree of chastity is pure virginity and the second is faithfull matrimony." Further definitions, beyond the obvious one of abstinence from all sexual intercourse, include "Ceremonial Purity; Exclusion of meretricious ornament: purity of style, modesty, chasteness; and Exclusion of excess or extravagance: moderation, restraint." All of these might additionally be applicable to a woman meritorious of a tribute like this.

these devotions could be a married woman, it remains to find a woman sufficiently esteemed or of high enough station to merit such a tribute, a woman with both sons and daughters, whose circumstances explain this unusual paraliturgical or extraliturgical devotion, and who suffered a sufficient delay between death and interment to allow such extensive musical composition.

So far, I have found only one woman who fits the circumstances: Laura Longhi Albani, who died on March 23, 1540, at the age of 28.[32]   Laura Longhi was the niece and heir of Abbondio Longhi, the secretary to the famous *condottiere*, Bartolomeo Colleoni.[33] In 1531, she brought a dowry of 8,000 ducats and the castle of Urgnano to her marriage to Gian Gerolamo Albani, a rising star among the patriciate of Bergamo. The couple had seven children—three girls, and four boys—of whom the last died in infancy shortly after his mother's demise. Suffering from phthisis during her last pregnancy, she had gone late in 1539 to take the sea air at her kinsmen's house in Venice and died there the following spring. Her body was translated to Bergamo, at first resting in the church of Sant' Antonio fuori le Mura, then finally interred in the Carmelite monastery (the Carmine),with which the family maintained a longstanding association.[34]   Her death, after only eight years of marriage, was an occasion of great sorrow among Bergamo's grand families.

She left behind one of the most extraordinary figures of sixteenth-century Bergamo. Born January 3, 1504, Gian Gerolamo Albani received the Doctor of Laws from the University of Padua in 1529.[35] His father had died at the end of 1526, so Gian Gerolamo had assumed many responsibilities in the Venetian Republic, such that Doge Andrea Gritti named him *cavaliere aurato* (golden knight, equivalent in the sixteenth century to count palatine) in July 1529, the first of many honors.[36]

---

[32] Elisa Plebani Faga, "Lucia Albani: poetessa Bergamasca del Cinquecento," *Atti dell' Ateneo di Scienze, Lettere, ed Arti di Bergamo* 56 (1993-94), 105.

[33] Luca Mazzoleni, "La faida, sec. 6. "Giovanni Gerolamo Albani," in *Wikipedia*, at http://it.wikipedia.org/wiki/Giovanni_Gerolamo_Albani, accessed 29 August 2010, is also a well-researched article.

[34] Plebani Faga, "Lucia Albani," 105, presents the biographical details. The Wikipedia article lists the dowry. The family's association with the Carmine is documented in a tattered, partially destroyed, undated document in the Archivio di Stato di Milano, Archivio generale del Fondo di Religione 2911, which lists annual mass commemorations at the church of Santa Maria del Carmine as follows: "At the high altar, 24 per year for Cavalier Giacomo Albano, 40 for Count Francesco Albano; at the altar of Sant' Alberto, [one mass] sung for Lucia Albana; on 2 November [All Soul's Day], two torches of one pound on the monument of the most illustrious lord Cavalier Albani."

[35] Salvador Miranda, "Albani, Gian Gerolamo (1504-1591)," in "The Cardinals of the Holy Roman Church, Biographical Dictionary: Pope Pius V (1566-1572), Consistory of May 17, 1570 (III),"1998-2008, at http://www.fiu.edu/~mirandas/bios1570.htm. Another page of the website, http://www.fiu.edu/~mirandas/conclave-xvi.htm, records Albani's presence at conclaves of 1572, 1585, and 1590, with his death noted prior to the conclave of 1591.

[36] Mazzoleni, "La faida," sec. 6. From the *Comitato della valorizzazione della professionalità*, Network of Culture and Values, we learn that "La nomina Cavaliere Aurato era un'investitura nobilitante, essendo un riconoscimento di dignità. Intorno al secolo XVI, da quanto risulta dai documenti e dagli storici, i termini di Cavaliere Aurato e di Conte Palatino erano sinonimi." See http://www.covalori.net/-_Cavalieri_della_AURATA_MILIZIA.htm.

In 1543, he received an imperial diploma from Charles V, raising him (or confirming, or re-elevating him, it is unclear which) to the station of count.[37] In February 1555, he was appointed Collateral General of the Venetian Republic, which honor was celebrated by three days of continuous bell ringing and bonfires throughout Bergamo, followed on Sunday with the singing of the Te Deum in multiple processions. During this period, he also published four treatises of canon law, and in 1558, assumed the patronage of Bergamo's greatest poet, Torquato Tasso, who remained allied with the family, dedicating his verse to Lucia, daughter of Gian Gerolamo and Laura and a poet in her own right.[38] She (probably) and her father were both painted by Giovanni Battista Moroni, the great Bergamasque portraitist.[39]

In contrast to the esteemed respectability of Lucia and her sisters, their three brothers leavened their considerable talent with great notoriety in plotting the shooting of Achille Brembati, head of a rival family, during the elevation at mass in Santa Maria Maggiore on April 1, 1563. Judged by the Council of Ten in Venice to have inspired or at least failed to prevent the murder, despite his protestations of innocence, Gian Gerolamo was exiled to the island of Lesina for five years and thereafter perpetually from Venetian territory. His sons were also exiled. Two years later, in 1565, a request to free the Albani by the Sultan of Constantinople's ambassador to Venice was refused. And in 1566, Philip II of Spain, Holy Roman Emperor, ordered the immediate arrest and trial of the Albani if found in Imperial lands.[40] But meanwhile, back in Bergamo, essays at pacification between the two families began.

When in 1566 Michele Ghislieri became Pope Pius V, he began to press the Council of Ten for revocation of the exile of Gian Gerolamo Albani, who had saved Ghislieri's life from an angry mob when the future Pope was inquisitor in Bergamo some years before.[41] At the end of Albani's insular exile, in 1568, he was appointed

[37] Mazzoleni, "La faida," sec. 3 & 5, suggests that the controversy surrounding the legitimization of two children of Gian Gerolamo's great-uncle, Giacomo Albani, and the consequent disinheritance of his heirs presumptive, including Gian Gerolamo's father, Francesco, may have led to the suspension of the rank of count, if, indeed Giacomo had held it.

[38] Faga, "Lucia Albani, 105, and Mazzoleni, "La faida," sec. 6.

[39] Laura Lanzeni, "16th Century, Moroni, Portrait of Gian Gerolamo Albani, c. 1570" at http://www.nga.gov.au/TheItalians/Detail.cfm?IRN=161253&ViewID=2, discusses the portrait of Gian Gerolamo, now in a private collection. Carlo Andreoli, "Gentildonne italiane del '500, 3; at http://www.storiadellarte.com/articoli/gentildonne%20italiane%20del%20500.doc states that Moroni's portrait of the "Lady in Red," now in the National Gallery, London, almost certainly depicts Lucia. The articles reproduce both portraits; that of Gian Gerolamo also appears in Belotti, *Storia di Bergamo*, 4:173, as well as in the Wikipedia article cited above. A second portrait of Gian Gerolamo hangs in the Biblioteca Civica de Bergamo.

[40] The families had been at feud for several years, and its origins are obscure. In any case, disagreements in the early 1550s between Giovanni Battista Brembati, and Gian Gerolamo and son Giovanni Francesco Albani festered. In 1560, two Albani sons tried to ambush Brembati, who then plotted to assassinate Giovanni Francesco Albani in prison in Venice. Brembati was exiled upon discovery. These events preceded and provoked the infamous assassination of Achille Brembati in church. Mazzoleni, "La faida," sec. 3, 7.

[41] Ghislieri's unpopularity was due to his militant pursuit of Lutheran heretics, up to and including Bishop Vittore Soranzo, who was denounced twice. See Christopher Carlsmith, *A Renaissance*

Papal Governor of the March of Ancona; he took minor orders in 1569, and was appointed Cardinal May 17, 1570. Shortly thereafter, having applied to the Ancona governor for grain to relieve a famine in Istria and Dalmatia, the Council of Ten, embarrassed to discover Albani's elevation to the purple, revoked his exile. Albani responded graciously in letters accompanying the grain. In autumn of that year, the Albani were named to the Roman nobility and the Senatorial Order.[42]

Thereafter, the Albani sons' bans were also lifted. Giovanni Francesco, who had become a celebrated man-at-arms at the court of Constantinople, was ill with dropsy and took refuge in Rome with his father. Giovanni Battista took Holy Orders and later became Patriarch of Alexandria, and Giovanni Domenico took up arms for the King of France. Philip II also revoked his ban on the family. The city of Bergamo was content with a return to quiet stability and later reported peace between the Albani and Brembati families. Cardinal Gian Gerolamo lived his remaining years in peace and in 1590 was even considered for the Papacy. He died in 1591 and was interred in Rome. The two surviving portraits of Albani portray him in both his secular and ecclesiatical roles. Moroni, discussed in n. 38, shows him in secular panoply, while an anonymous portrait in Bergamo depicts him vested in a Cardinal's scarlet, wearing a biretta. Both probably postdate 1570.[43]

This brief excursion into a story worthy of, but too complicated for, an opera plot might seem irrelevant to the music under discussion, except that it confirms the remarkable talent and fame of Laura Longhi's family, which she died too early to see. Why then, should we suppose that the funeral works were written for her?

At some time between 1540 and 1544, Gaspar de Albertis was appointed titular rector of the parish church of Saint Agatha, the closest parish to the Carmelite convent, where Laura Longhi was ultimately buried. Indeed, the church is still known as Sant' Agatha del (or al) Carmine.[44] As the nearest secular priest to this monastery, he might well have played some role at Laura Longhi's translation and interment. Moreover, if Pietro Aron was correct, Albertis had been *maestro di cappella* at the Basilica of Santa Maria Maggiore since at least 1536.[45] Thus, in

Education: Schooling in Bergamo and the Venetian Republic, 1500-1650 (Toronto: University of Toronto Press), 235. Albani's orthodoxy displayed in this incident, which undoubtedly contributed to his later elevation to ecclesiastical honors, was also declared in his published works, in particular *De donatione Costantini Magni* (Cologne, 1535); *De cardinalatu ad Paulum III* (Rome, 1541); *Disputationes de immunitate ecclesiarum* (Rome, 1553); and *De potestate Papae et concilii* (Rome, 1554). See Mazzoleni, "La faida," sec. 6.

[42] Mazzoleni, "La faida," sec. 8

[43] Ibid. Other biographies of Gian Gerolamo Albani include F. Colleoni, "Il cardinale conte Gian Gerolamo Albani," *Rivista di Bergamo* (1931): 509-12; Bortolo Belotti, "Gian Gerolamo Albani, cardinale," in *Gli eccellenti bergamaschi* (Bergamo: La stamperia di Gorle, 1982), 3:17-26. Belotti's monumental *Storia di Bergamo*, mainly vol. 4, has much to say on Gian Gerolamo and the family, including a reproduction (112), of the anonymous second portrait of him as cardinal that now hangs in the Biblioteca Civica di Bergamo.

[44] Albertis' position at Sant' Agatha is discussed in my dissertation, "Gaspar de Albertis and Music at Santa Maria Maggiore," 1: 83-84.

[45] This letter, perhaps the most cited of the Aron-Spataro correspondence, appears in Vatican City Biblioteca Apostolica Vaticana, MS lat. 5318, fols. 183r-83v. It is the first document to award Al-

addition to being the parish priest, he had access to, and a working relationship with, Bergamo's finest singers, not to mention being, himself, the city's most prolific composer. These circumstances increase the feasibility of Albertis' writing and performing such elaborate funeral works for Laura Longhi Albani. And later, Albertis would certainly have renewed his contact with Albani in 1545, when the latter was elected Minister, the highest ranking lay post of the Consorzio della Misericordia Maggiore, the basilica's governing confraternity.[46]

In 1549, "Giovan Hieronimo Albano, Dottor et Cavagliero" was the dedicatee of *Il primo libro delle messe di pre Gasparo Alberti*, the first published collection of masses by an Italian composer.[47] A sixth voice in the final *Agnus Dei* of the second mass, *Missa Italia mia*, sings Albano's (*sic*) eternal praises.[48] This is the first and only concrete documentation of an association between Gian Gerolamo Albani and Gaspar de Albertis, but it must represent the culmination of a relationship begun years earlier. The dedication implies that Albani was the book's sponsor or underwriter, a significant investment, and certainly not one undertaken without knowledge of the composer.[49] Albertis' dedication also alludes to the count's recreations of poetry and music, which suggests some level of acquaintance between the two men, even in the absence of other known connections between them.[50] Albani had received one similar dedication five years before, for Scotto's publication of a book of madrigals by Gabriele Martinengo, who may have received Albani's patronage as a scion or associate of the Colleoni-Martinengo family, the employer of Laura Longhi's father.[51] Albani's sponsorship of both volumes would have recognized the

---

bertis the title of *maestro di cappella*, which appears only later in basilican and episcopal documents. See my dissertation cited above, 1: 77-78. 85-86. The correspondence is edited in full in Bonnie Blackburn, Edward Lowinsky and Clement Miller, eds., *A Correspondence of Renaissance Musicians* (New York: Oxford University Press, 1991).

[46] Albani's tenure in this post for the years 1545 and 1546 is documented in Bergamo, Biblioteca Civica, Archivio della Misericordia Maggiore, MS 1263, Terminazioni, vol. 20; he also served as Minister again in 1552 and 1553; see Terminazioni, vol. 21.

[47] Gasparo Alberti, *Il primo libro delle messe di pre Gasparo Alberti* (Venice: Scotto, 1549). The three masses of this print have been fully transcribed in Jeppesen, *Italia sacra musica: Musiche corali italiane sconosciute della prima metà del Cinquecento*. 3 vols. (Copenhagen: Wilhelm Hansen Musik Vorlag, 1962); and more recently in Gary Towne, *Opera Omnia Gasparis de Albertis*, Vol. 1: *Masses*. Corpus Mensurabilis Musicae 105 (Neuhausen-Stuttgart, American Institute of Musicology, 1999), which also includes their polyphonic models. The title and dedication pages are transcribed both in Jane Bernstein, *Music Printing in Renaissance Venice: The Scotto Press (1539-1572)* (New York: Oxford University Press, 1998), 373-74, and in Victor Ravizza, "Gasparo Alberti: Ein wenig bekannter Komponist und dessen Portrait," in *Festschrift Arnold Geering zum 70. Geburtstag*, 63-80 (Bern: Verlag Paul Haupt, 1972), 77-78.

[48] The dedicatory voice of the *Missa Italia mia* reads, "Nulla Albane tuum delebunt secula nomen, sed tibi magnanimo fama perhennis erit." The mass's model, Verdelot's setting of Petrarch's moving lament on the despoliation of Italy, has a political context worthy of Albani's career. Indeed, the mass itself may commemorate Albani's elevation to the station of count.

[49] The financing of music prints in sixteenth-century Venice, and what is known or implied about the role of patronage therein, is discussed in Jane Bernstein, *Music Printing in Renaissance Venice*, 109-20.

[50] As noted above, the dedicatory page is transcribed in Bernstein, *Music Printing in Renaissance Venice*, 374; and Ravizza, "Gasparo Alberti, "Ein wenig bekannter Komponist," 77-78.

[51] A full description of the print appears in Bernstein, *Music Printing in Renaissance Venice*, 373-75. It is also discussed in Knud Jeppesen, "A Forgotten Master of the Early 16th Century: Gaspar

talent of composers with whom he had close association, one of whom, Albertis, had paid eloquent tribute to Albani's beloved wife.[52]

Why then did the tribute not take the form of a more conventional liturgical setting? Madonna Laura died in Venice, and initial ceremonies would have been held there. The ceremonies in Bergamo would have been for the translation of her remains and interment, or perhaps a later commemoration.[53] The delay between her death and her translation to Bergamo would have allowed time for the composition of these three unique works, whose striking design may also incorporate a clever circumvention of recent restrictions on ritual display. In 1539, the city of Bergamo had enacted sweeping sumptuary laws, the *Pompe*, which regulated, among many other things, public rituals.[54] Funerals were limited to the participation of only one monastery, with only immediate family and household as mourners; further restrictions limited the number of candles and torches (and by extension, mourners) in the procession. The translation of Laura Longhi Albani, which followed the enactment of the *Pompe* by only a few months, might seem to have faced such constraints on its tributary magnificence, but Albertis' polyphony would have solved these dilemmas neatly. The cycle is not a conventional funeral

de Albertis," *The Musical Quarterly* 44 (1958): 311-28; and Ravizza, "Gasparo Alberti, "Ein wenig bekannter Komponist." Bernstein also discusses Martinengo's publication, 309-11, and an anthology to which he contributed, 828-30. She notes that Gabriele de Martinengo is unknown before his application to the Accademia Filarmonica of Verona in 1547, and she asserts he was therefore Veronese. However, I have noted in my dissertation, cited above, note 1, p. 17 and elsewhere, the presence at Santa Maria Maggiore of one Gabriele de Colionibus, roughly contemporary with Albertis, and a Franciscus de Martinengo, in the next generation. These associations bear further investigation, given that the two families were united in marriage and that Martinengo is a village, as well as a family name of Bergamasque nobility. The remaining music prints of this period by a Bergamasque composer, Francesco Bifetto's *Madrigali a quatro voci, Libro primo.* (Venice: Gardano, 1547) and *Libro secondo* (Gardano, 1548), are discussed in Mary Lewis, *Antonio Gardano: Venetian Music Printer, 1538-1569* (New York: Garland, 2005), 1: 555-57, 592-94. These are both dedicated to Rogerio, Conte di Calepio, whose estates lay northeast of Colleoni-Martinengo lands at Malpaga, Cavernago, and Martinengo and the nearby estate of Albani at Urgnano. The fashion of patronage of music prints by Bergamasque nobility seems to have been restricted to this small group of geographically proximate families.

[52] Bernstein, *Music Printing in Renaissance Venice*, 145-49, discusses the dedication of music prints as evidence of signorial patronage. Albani's patronage of Albertis' print seems largely to fit her third classification, in which "the musician composed something 'ready-made' and then sought out an individual patron." (The dedicatory voice to Albani in the third *Agnus Dei* of the *Missa Italia mia* could have been added, or that single mass could have been specially composed as an incentive to patronage.)

[53] Plebani Faga, "Lucia Albani," 105, describes the translation as without ceremony, in accordance with the sumptuary laws established November 4, 1539.

[54] The sumptuary laws, or *Pompe*, promulgated in six consecutive sessions of the City Council: Bergamo, Biblioteca Civica, *Azioni [del Concilio della Città di Bergamo] 1538-41*, ff. 166v-184r (Nov. 21, 25, 28, Dec. 3, 4, 10), were proposed earlier that year (April 24, May 12), and published in April 1540, as *Capitoli prohibenti le pompe della città di Bergamo* (Brescia: Damiano di Turlini, 1540). They were a substantial expansion of earlier statutes. See Angelo Pinetti, "La limitazione del lusso e dei consumi nelle leggi suntuarie bergamasche," *Atti dell' Ateneo di Scienze, Lettere, ed Arti di Bergamo* 24 (1915-17), 28. The laws concerning funerals, discussed in Pinetti, "La limitazione," 47-51, restricted the size and number of participants in the ceremonies but said nothing about the music. The funeral portions of the original statutes are in Azioni, ff. 178v-180v, Dec. 3, 4; transcribed in Pinetti, 74-75.

mass or office; it would not be sung in procession (assuming its present choirbook format—awkward for a performance in motion); it would only require four to eight singers, concordant with the usual performance practice at Santa Maria Maggiore; and any monastic involvement would likely have been the single Carmelite monastery. Thus although the cycle satisfies all of the restrictions of the *Pompe*, the polyphonic settings of this devotion exhibit an unparalleled and, for Bergamo, unprecedented musical sumptuousness, entirely fitting to the rank and regard for the beloved Laura—a striking and unusual tribute to a great and good lady.

There does remain the problematic issue of date. The Bergamo choirbooks have only three dates in them, which hover near the endpoints of their copying. The earliest date is December 8, 1524; the later two are August 8, 1541 and August 14, 1542.[55] Similar dates appear in documented copying noted in the church records: December 1, 1524, December 29, 1527, and February 23, 1541.[56] The great majority of the locally produced repertory, including the surviving portion in these manuscripts, was copied between these dates. But the current state of the three surviving choirbooks presents a very complex picture. They are the surviving remnants of an original set of nine or ten books; the degree to which fragments of other volumes in the collection have been added to the surviving ones cannot be determined with certainty, although Crawford and Messing have identified surviving portions of at least nine volumes.[57] Only two volumes were definitely commissioned in 1524. The others seem to have been products of Albertis' independent initiative. Although he was later paid for uncommissioned volumes, the creation of much of the collection seems to have been informal, and Albertis retained a strong proprietary interest in the books, to the extent that he took personal possession of them when he was forced into retirement in 1552.[58] The copying reflects the somewhat casual process, with a wide variety of styles on several papers.[59] As a result, the manuscripts' structure is very complex; Crawford and Messing discern no fewer than sixteen copying stages identified as Albertis and two as Associate, on nineteen different papers.[60] I have only praise for the meticulous care with which they describe and analyze papers, format, measurements, note and clef forms, and all other relevant details of these books.

The funeral works occur in a large section of MS 1209 that Crawford and Messing identify as Albertis 2. Although there is no documented date for this hand, they postulate a date not much after the documented date of Albertis 1 in 1524. I cannot contest their reasoning, but the complexity of the manuscripts leaves room for some flexibility in interpretation. A very distinctive characteristic of most of the Albertis hands is the use of tilted, rhomboid-shaped semibreves

[55] Towne, "Gaspar de Albertis," 1: 156-57; Crawford and Messing, *Albertis' Choirbooks*, 119-22, 136.

[56] Towne, "Gaspar de Albertis," 1: 73-75, 80, 154-55; Crawford and Messing, *Albertis' Choirbooks*, 61.

[57] Crawford and Messing, *Albertis' Choirbooks*, 78-81. See also, Towne, "Gaspar de Albertis," 159-67.

[58] Towne, "Gaspar de Albertis," 73-93; Crawford and Messing, 61-62.

[59] Crawford and Messing, 63-81

[60] Ibid., 22-25, 69-81

and smaller notes, in place of the upright lozenges favored by most contemporary scribes, who influence the earliest copying style of Albertis (Albertis I).[61]   To me, an increase in the tilting of the notehead develops with Albertis' increasing fluency and development of a personal and more unfettered copying style. The difference between these two styles is visible in Crawford and Messing's Plates I (MS 1207, 81v-82, and II (MS 1209, 29v-30r, both Albertis 1), and Plates III (MS 1209, 73v-74r) and V (MS 1208, 103', Albertis II).[62] It even seems to me that there is some further evolution of the hand between these latter two plates, with Plate V showing rhomboid noteheads with a more pronounced tilt and bold strokes, as well as a tendency to arch the horizontal strokes of breves. The funeral cycle copying style most resembles that of Plate V. Although it is impossible to assign a timeframe to subtle developments of personal style, such complex concerns surrounding the dating of these manuscripts may excuse some flexilibity in interpretation of the evidence.

This is good. Crawford and Messing's hypothetical date of the mid to late 1520s would place the composition of these works about fifteen years before the death of Laura Longhi Albani—an impossible historical paradox. And I must acknowledge that my inability so far to discover an appropriate dedicatee at the earlier date is no evidence that such a woman did not exist. On the other hand, the absence of an absolute date for this portion of these very complex manuscripts allows at least the possibility of these works' later origin. Given these ambiguities, Laura Longhi Albani is the best candidate so far for the great lady who inspired such a magnificent tribute: a woman of high station and a devoted wife and mother of celebrated men and women, whose tragic early death brought great sorrow to Bergamo and her family. Certainly she was a worthy receipient of such a tribute, even if we may never know with complete certainty that she was the mysterious matron memorialized.

[61] Ibid., 66-72.
[62] Ibid., 100-104.

Chère amie: The Mystery of the Unstamped Postcard

H. Colin Slim

Over the course of many years, I have observed that (beyond the odd glass of fine spirits) my great and good friend Bill Prizer has three abiding passions. They are: music; spy mysteries; and beautiful women—one need only glance at his wife, at whose marriage to the honoree I had the pleasure of attending more than twenty-five years ago in Santa Barbara. Distinctly a "minor" mystery, the ensuing tale addresses all three Prizer passions, namely: the last century's major composer, touring the US in 1937; a reluctant Russian spy already by that year, but turned by the FBI a decade later; and a former silent film star and vamp, who by 1937 was hardly the beauty of her heyday in the movies, but was in hot pursuit of the above-mentioned composer.

The mystery abides in a postcard I bought from J. and J. Lubrano at the 2004 AMS Annual Meeting at Seattle. It all happened quickly during a moment of weakness, thereby fracturing a successful two-year vow to make no further purchases of Stravinsky memorabilia.[1] The Lubranos's carefully typed transcription of the postcard for prospective customers lacked just one six-letter word. Recognizing it in Seattle quickly clinched the deal for me. Unfortunately, the only solid recollection by either Lubrano was that they had purchased it at Alexander Autographs, some time prior to March 2003. Its provenance can now, however, be established with reasonable certainty.

Once enclosed in a now lost stamped envelope perhaps discarded by its addressee, the postcard itself deprives us of the name of the writer's female friend—the "Chère amie" in the salutation—and of her location. Its front side displays a colored photograph entitled "Albuquerque New Mexico, From The Air." Identified as a "Photostint" for "Fred Harvey," it was "Made only by Detroit Publishing Co." (See Plate 1 on p. 328.) The card's obverse bears a message written in unmistakable and slightly impure French in black ink by an equally unmistakable hand. Headed "San Francisco 25 III 37," it reads:

[1] J & J Lubrano Music Antiquarians, *Antiquarian Music Materials Offered for Sale at the Annual Meeting of the American Musicological Society 2004* (Lloyd Harbor NY, 2004), 11, lot 157; after I informed the Lubranos that their lot 158 was not an autograph, they promptly withdrew it. For my former collection, see the *Annotated Catalogue of the H. Colin Slim Stravinsky Collection Donated by him to The University of British Columbia Library* (Vancouver: University of British Columbia Library, 2002).

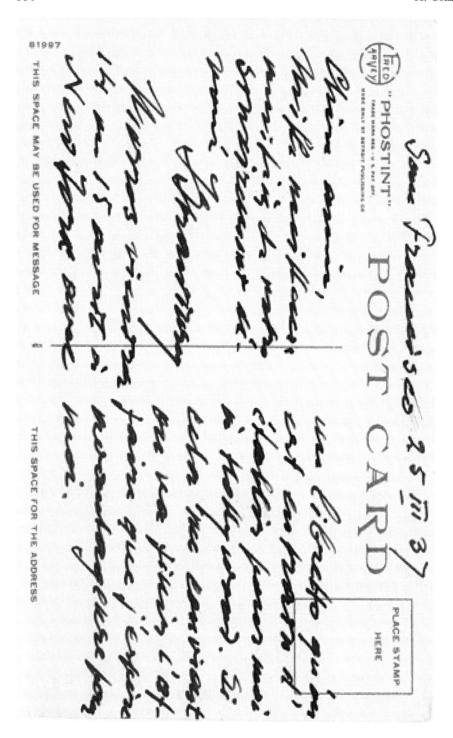

Plate 1: Postcard from Igor Stravinsky to Dagmar Godowsky, 25 March 1937

> Chère amie, / Mille meilleurs / amitiés de vostre / sincèrement dé- / voué / IStrawinsky / Morros viendra / 14 ou 15 avril à / New York avec / un libretto qu'on / est en train d'/ établir pour moi à Hollywood. Si / cela me convient / on va finir l'af- / faire que j'espère / avantageuse pour / moi.

This slightly enigmatic message may be translated thus:

> Dear lady-friend, A thousand best regards from your sincerely devoted I Stravinsky. Morros will come to New York on 14 or 15 April with a libretto that is in the process of being prepared for me in Hollywood. If it suits me, we will conclude this matter which I hope will be profitable for me.

The postcard raises the following questions, some more readily answered than others. First, where did Igor Stravinsky (1882-1971) obtain it, and who (or what) is Fred Harvey? Second, does Stravinsky's mention of a "libretto" being prepared for him in the world's movie capital signify some now unknown project for an opera? Third, who is Morros, why is he coming to New York, and what business, hopefully profitable for Stravinsky, is to be concluded there? Fourth, who is Stravinsky's unnamed woman friend, why is he imparting this information to her in French, and why did he send the postcard in an envelope instead of just stamping the postcard? A little sleuthing provides solid enough answers to most of these queries.

Stravinsky was still in San Francisco when he dated his card. Having entrained on 15 March from Los Angeles with his longtime friend Dr. Alexis Feodorovitch Kall (1878-1948), his violinist-colleague Samuel Dushkin (1891-1976), and Dushkin's wife Louise (they had married the previous year), the foursome had reached Santa Barbara later that day. There, at the town's Lobero Theater, he and Dushkin gave a concert on 16 March. In that beautiful seacoast locale, concert audiences have matured considerably. Writing two weeks later from Seattle's Olympic Hotel on 1 April, Stravinsky was to remind Dr. Kall (by then back in Los Angeles) about:

> the kind of thing that you heard in Santa Barbara, you remember, when somebody said to you that he didn't understand a thing in the whole concert— *Pulcinella*, *The Fairy's Kiss*, "Scherzo" from *Firebird*, and "Russian Dance" from *Petroushka* (mind-bending music)—but he understood only that Stravinsky— the violinist—was a remarkable accompanist.[2]

Arriving in San Francisco to conduct a single concert scheduled for 23 March, Stravinsky was interviewed there on Sunday the 21st by two music critics writing for leading newspapers of the city. The next morning, he rehearsed the San Francisco Symphony Orchestra, his self-annotated photograph showing him being introduced for the first time to its musicians by their conductor Pierre Monteux (1875-1964). That same afternoon sponsored by the city's Art Commission and the Russian

---

[2] See I. F. Stravinsky: *Perepiska s russkimi korrespondentami. Materiali k biographi*, 3 vols., ed. Viktor Varunts (Moscow: Kompozitor, 1998-2003) 3: 623-24, no. 1868, trans. Stanislav Shvabrin; for a different trans., see Stephen Walsh, *Stravinsky. The Second Exile: France and America, 1934-1971* (New York: Knopf, 2006), 63-64.

Music Society, Dr. Kall (who knew Stravinsky from about 1900 in St. Petersburg) delivered an appropriately-titled lecture at the Century Club: "Stravinsky as I Know Him," (one he soon repeated, on 13 September, after returning to Los Angeles). On 23 March Stravinsky conducted his *Symphony of Psalms* in the Civic Auditorium and it has been stated that he departed San Francisco the next day.[3] Our postcard does not necessarily belie this because its now lost envelope could have been mailed elsewhere.

Presumably, however, he left a day or two later, because, while entraining northwards with Dushkin and wife Louise, they had just two more West Coast engagements: a concert on the 30th in Tacoma, and one on the 31st in Seattle (the train trip from the Bay Area, then as now, consuming just one full day).[4] From Seattle, as noted above, he wrote Kall on 1 April. In that same letter he also reported that, on his way back to New York, the Dushkins would detrain at Louise's hometown of Cleveland, leaving him for almost a month to his own devices in New York. These consisted of rehearsals with and performance by members of the New York Philharmonic in the world premiere of *Jeu de cartes* with Balanchine and the American Ballet on the Metropolitan Opera's stage, part of a Stravinsky Festival on 27 and 28 April, which included *Le baiser de la fée* and *Apollo*.[5] He also had an assignation in the Big Apple, the continuation of an affair begun the previous year. From New York on 2 May, he wrote Kall that he would sail on the 5th "for Paris on the [S.S.] Paris."[6] Indeed, he did, and was photographed dining on board that ship together with the Dushkins, conductors Koussevitzky and Rodzinski, their wives, and several other passengers.[7]

He might just have bought his postcard in Detroit, its place of manufacture, where he had conducted the General Motors Symphony on 14 February 1937.[8] Early the following March, however, having played Winnetka, Illinois on the fourth, he and Dushkin (and the latter's wife) had boarded the train in Chicago for Los Angeles, where they arrived on the 8th. Thus I think it much more feasible that he got the postcard during the long refueling stop regularly scheduled (and to this day)

---

[3] See Vera Stravinsky and Robert Craft, *Stravinsky in Pictures and Documents* (New York: Simon and Schuster, 1978), 336-38.

[4] See Stravinsky. *Selected Correspondence*, 3 vols., ed. Robert Craft (New York: Knopf, 1982, 1985-86), 2: 303.

[5] Leonard Liebling, "Stravinsky Ballet in New York Premiere," *Musical Courrier* 115 (8 May 1937), 15, affirmed by Walsh, *Stravinsky. Second Exile*, 65. Martin Duberman, in *The Worlds of Lincoln Kirstein* (New York: Knopf, 2007), 330, states it was the Philadelphia Orchestra rather than the New York Philharmonic.

[6] Stravinsky: *Perepiska*, 3: 627-28, no. 1875.

[7] Complete photograph with all identifications and the ship as "S.S. Paris," in *Musical America* 57 (August, 1937): 4; both ship and its sailing date are incorrect in a severely cropped photograph in *Dearest Bubushkin. The Correspondence of Vera and Igor Stravinsky, 1921-1954, with excerpts from Vera Stravinsky's diaries, 1922-1971*, trans. Lucia Davidova; ed. Robert Craft (New York: Thames & Hudson, 1985), pl. 83, also incorrect in *Stravinsky. Selected Correspondence* 2: 303; both details correct in Walsh, *Stravinsky. Second Exile*, 66.

[8] *Stravinsky. Selected Correspondence*, 2: 302; Walsh, *Stravinsky. Second Exile*, 587, n. 6

at Albuquerque for the Atchinson, Topeka and Santa Fe Railway's "Super-Chief," then taking thirty-nine-and-a-half hours from Chicago to Los Angeles. Perhaps in Albuquerque he strolled to the Alvarado Hotel (built c.1926), belonging to a chain of restaurants founded by Fred Harvey (1835-1901). His company, by then an immensely successful enterprise and still bearing his name, sold postcards made by the Detroit Publishing Company, though Stravinsky could have found his postcard at almost any railroad stop with a Harvey restaurant on the way west.[9]

Upon the trio's arrival on 8 March at Los Angeles's Union Station, they were met by the conductor of the Philharmonic, Otto Klemperer (1885-1973), and by four Russian exiles, all but three of whom, like Stravinsky, hailed from St. Petersburg.[10] The exception, Modeste Altschuler (1873-1963) from Moscow, had founded the Russian Symphony in New York in 1903 (defunct by 1937), had given the first Stravinsky performances in the US, and was to lead his early song cycle, *The Faun and the Shepherdess*, Op. 2, on 10 March with the Los Angeles WPA Federal Symphony Orchestra in Trinity Auditorium.[11] Among the three Petersburgers greeting him was a former dancer for Diaghilev and a then-frequent choreographer for the Hollywood Bowl, Theodore Kosloff (1882-1956).[12] Stravinsky was slated to conduct the Los Angeles Philharmonic on the 12th and 13th, collaborating with Kosloff in what proved to be an enormously successful staged *Petrouchka* in the Shrine Auditorium.[13] Waiting at the train station was also his old buddy Kall who had been negotiating with both Kosloff and Klemperer on his behalf; and, most important for the unfolding of our little tale, Boris Mihailovitch Morros (1891-1963), the very person whose name the Lubranos had been unable to decipher on the postcard.

At this point a little background allows the missing pieces to fall readily into place. Stravinsky's American friend and supporter, author and bookman Merle Armitage (1893-1975), was managing his West Coast appearances with Dushkin. On the previous 4 November (1936), he had urged Stravinsky to consider writing

---

[9] See *The Great Southwest of the Fred Harvey Company and the Santa Fe Railway*, ed. Marta Weigle and Barbara A. Babcock (Phoenix: Heard Museum, 1996), xiii-xiv, 7, and 72; and Peter B. Hales and William Henry Jackson, *William Henry Jackson and the Transformation of the American Landscape* (Philadelphia: Temple University Press, 1988), 281. The Detroit Photographic Company (founded 1897) became the Detroit Publishing Company in 1904, the chief source of colored postcards (sometimes retouched to look more "modern"); among its biggest clients was the Santa Fe / Harvey restaurant and hotel enterprise.

[10] See "Composer Here for Premiere," *Los Angeles Times*, 9 March 1937, 17.

[11] See the announcement in the *Los Angeles Times*, 7 March 1937, pt. III, 5.

[12] On Kosloff's early career in Los Angeles, see Michael Morris, *Madam Valentino: The Many Lives of Natacha Rambova* (New York, London, Paris: Abbeville,1991), 36-63 and *passim*.

[13] A photograph (severely cropping ballerinas and sets) of Stravinsky rehearsing it in the Shrine Auditorium, in *Pictures and Documents*, 336, is from the now defunct *Los Angeles Evening Herald Express*, 12 March 1937, 1. According to Isabel Morse Jones, "Composer to Conduct 'Petrouchka' Ballet," *Los Angeles Times*, 7 March 1937, pt. III, 5, Stravinsky would also lead 'The Firebug' [*sic*]. He perhaps expresses his opinion of Kosloff in a mid-April letter to Kall from New York whence Kosloff had traveled: "I would rather see you than Kosloff," though he also recommends Kall ask Kosloff upon the latter's return about the success of *Jeu de cartes* (27-28 April) in New York; see Stravinsky, *Perepiska*, 3: 626, no. 1873 and 628, no. 1875, respectively.

music for a film with Morros, then the General Music Director for Paramount Pictures (1935-40): "[He proposes you] supervise or even write a film score while in the U.S.A. ...Morros [is a] graduate of the St. Petersburg Conservatory and says he knew you in his youth. He has ambitions for film music and is very charming. Perhaps you could be with the studio after your tour on the [West] coast is completed."[14] From New York on 10 March 1937, Morros was cabled by Dagmar Godowsky (1897-1975)—Stravinsky's East Coast assistant and daughter of the celebrated pianist, Leopold Godowsky (1870-1938)—that he should immediately sign up the composer. Three days later Morros duly invited Stravinsky to dinner in Beverly Hills. They "drew up a contract [never signed] under which Paramount would supply Stravinsky with scenarios, from which he would choose one to compose" for a fee of $25,000—a huge sum indeed in 1937 when one remembers that he was paid $5000 for *Jeu de cartes*.[15] On our postcard Stravinsky improperly wrote "libretto" for "scenario," the latter being the correct word in French as well as in English.

Even before Stravinsky had arrived in Los Angeles, Isabel Morse Jones had spilled the beans, on 7 March in that city's *Times*:

> It is strongly rumored about Hollywood that he is to stop a while and engage himself in creative work for the films. It will be of great interest if he finds another Diaghileff in a film director who will inspire him to write film music as gorgeous in color as his ballets.[16]

Concerning the scenario, when interviewed three weeks later in San Francisco, Stravinsky informed Alfred Frankenstein, music critic for the city's *Chronicle*, that:

> he plans to compose for Hollywood in the immediate future. . . . He has been in the film capital for the past two weeks making plans and laying the groundwork for a unique kind of picture. . . . [Stravinsky noted] "I shall not compose music in accompaniment to a photoplay...the story and the setting and all the rest will be written around the music, and the music will be composed in terms of the sound film. Thus the whole production will be conceived as a unit. I am not able at the present time to reveal the theme of the picture but it will not be

[14] Walsh, *Stravinsky. Second Exile*, 61, and 588, n. 25, Professor Walsh kindly supplying me from his notes this slightly expanded summary from Armitage's letter; on Armitage, see Slim, *Annotated Catalogue*, 261-63, item 86. Dorothy Lamb Crawford, *A Windfall of Musicians, Hitler's Émigrés and Exiles in Southern California* (New Haven and London: Yale University Press, 2009), 223, claims that the deal was initiated by Dagmar Godowsky through correspondence with Morros, although the date, 10 March 1937, of a wire from Godowsky to Morros is not supplied.

[15] First reported in Lawrence Morton, "Stravinsky in Los Angeles," *Festival of Music in Los Angeles* [program booklet] (Los Angeles: Los Angeles Philharmonic, 1981), 80; see Walsh, *Stravinsky. Second Exile*, 61 and 588, n. 26; and Crawford, *A Windfall*, 223-24, who gives the date of the contract as 11 March 1937. About *Jeu de cartes*, and Duberman, *Kirstein*, 329, respectively.

[16] Isabel Morse Jones, "Composer to Conduct," *Los Angeles Times*, 7 March 1937, pt. III, 5. She may have had this information from Kall, whom she admired and who, she noted, had aided Kosloff in the preparations for *Petrouchka*. See also Hal D. Crain, "Hollywood 20 March 1937," *Musical America* 57 (25 March 1937), 8: "Stravinsky . . . recently signed by Boris Morros to compose and arrange the music in a forthcoming film . . . ."

a Russian folk story." This work will not be undertaken on a regular Hollywood contract. Stravinsky will write and Hollywood will take it or leave it.[17]

On the same day Alexander Fried wrote in the *San Francisco Examiner* that

> he will NOT write a "mere accompaniment score for someone else's story.". . . and has signed no contract. "I have left them my subject. . . . They have given it to a noted writer. If I like what he does with it, I will then develop the story and music into an artistic unity." What is the nature of his possible film story? . . . All he would admit is that folklore . . . "interests him no more."[18]

The reader will hardly fail to hear the resemblance in the postcard of "If it suits me . . ." to his remark in French (his principal interview language) to Fried: "If I like what he does with it. . . ." Upon returning to Paris early in May, after having been essentially stymied in this enterprise in New York (as we shall see), he told an interviewer for *L'Intransigeant* on 19 May 1937 that "music must stop being the accompaniment to film. . . . I've suggested to our Hollywood friends that I provide them with the score for a film in the same way that one gives a ballet score to the scenarist."[19] And even as late as December 1939, when queried in San Francisco about the 1937 negotiations, he stated, not without some sour grapes: "Hollywood offered me lots of money. But it would not guarantee that I could do what I like. I like a lot of money. But I must also do what I like."[20]

As to the subject matter of this scenario, we have precious little information. Robert Craft suggests that it was called *The Knights of St. David* as cited in a letter from Kall to Stravinsky of 13 April 1937 (after Stravinsky had returned to New York).[21] Not surprisingly perhaps, no such screenplay is to be found listed in cinematic sources for the period. The eventual unraveling of this doomed enterprise was to require, however, several more months.

Not long after Stravinsky's return to New York from Seattle about 6 April, doctors there had diagnosed a recurrence of his tuberculosis. This did not prevent him from attending the New York premiere of Gian Carlo Menotti's *Amelia Goes to the Ball* on the 11th with Miss Godowsky, and a Paul Hindemith concert on the 15th, as well as from rehearsing for the coming Stravinsky-Balanchine Festival. In the same letter sent about the 19th that announced the return of his illness, he wrote Kall from the Sulgrave Hotel (where he had first stayed on 3 January), using stationery purloined from the Hermoyne in Hollywood:

---

[17] Alfred Frankenstein, "Just Where Is Stravinsky?" *San Francisco Chronicle*, 22 March 1937, 11.

[18] Alexander Fried, "Stravinsky Likes Idea of Writing for Movies," *The San Francisco Examiner*, 22 March 1937, 8.

[19] Walsh, *Stravinsky. Second Exile*, 61.

[20] Fried, "Stravinsky Fears Blow To Music During War," *The San Francisco Examiner*, 12 December 1939, 36.

[21] See *Stravinsky. Selected Correspondence* 2: 307, n. 52 and Walsh, *Stravinsky. Second Exile*, 588, n. 28; at my enquiry Professor Walsh kindly recalled that he too had seen this letter, perhaps now misfiled at the Paul Sacher Stiftung, Basle.

Morros and I agreed to abandon everything in Hollywood, and to go to New York on the 14th or 15th of April. And when these dates began to approach, Morros began to distance himself and did so to such an extent that I heard nothing more from him. The silly thing is that I took all this seriously and wasted time with people of so little interest to me.[22]

"Silly," or not, the matter of the scenario continued to bedevil him and he certainly ran into Morros again in Hollywood at a party given to honor John Barbirolli (1899-1970), who had conducted at the Bowl early in July 1940.[23] Fortunately so for the present narrative, because Stravinsky's annoyance with Morros reveals definitively, I believe, the identity of the "Chère amie" of the 25 March postcard. Yet, naming her may perhaps be better delayed until the reader knows something about the extraordinary career of Boris Morros.

Born eight to ten years after Stravinsky in St. Petersburg, Morros likewise studied at its University and, although not like him privately, with Rimsky-Korsakov (1844-1908) at the city's Imperial Conservatory of Music, having been a minor child prodigy on the piano and cello. Although his above statement indicates he knew Stravinsky in St. Petersburg, no further information is yet available about the extent of Stravinsky's friendship with a man a decade or so younger. Morros would have still been quite young when Stravinsky left Russia in mid-July 1914. Following the Russian Revolution, Morros was a conductor in Paris from December 1920 with the emigré cabaret troupe, Chauve Souris, formerly of Moscow, and he also directed opera elsewhere in France, Italy, and Egypt. Traveling with his troupe to New York early in April 1922, he emigrated permanently that year to the U.S.A. In 1923 he began working for Paramount in New York and then for five years was musical director for that company's films in Hollywood, ultimately forming Boris Morros Productions, Inc. in 1940; by 1944 he had his own music publishing company as well. Music scores for movies made while he was in charge of Paramount's Music Department in 1936-37 and a score by him in 1938 received nominations for Academy Awards. His most famous and successful film was probably *Wells Fargo* in 1937, for which he wrote the score, and though not a money maker, his most prestigious was *Carnegie Hall* (20th-Century Fox) of a decade later.[24] Either as cellist or patron, his name was attached to a string quartet performing in Los

---

[22] *Stravinsky: Perepiska* 3: 626, no. 1873, dated by Varunts about 16 April, and kindly translated by Michael Green; Walsh, *Stravinsky. Second Exile*, 64 and 589, n. 42, dates it firmly as 19 April.

[23] See *Rob Wagner's Script* 24 (20 July 1940): 27; this party may have followed Barbirolli's concert on 12 July which both Stravinskys attended; see *Bubushkin*, 12 July 1940.

[24] On Morros, see *The 1937-38 International Motion Picture Almanac*, ed. Terry Ramsaye (New York: Quigley, 1937[sic]), 648-49; *Music and Dance in California*, ed. José Rodriguez (Hollywood: Bureau of Musical Research, 1940), 407; *Index of the New York Times* for: 10 April 1922, 27 April and 24 September 1939, 7 April 1941, and 29 March 1944; Ken Bloom, *Hollywood Song. The Complete Film and Musical Companion*, 3 vols. (New York: Facts on File, 1995) 2: nos. 5246, 6018, 6708; and Richard Shale, *The Academy Awards Index* (Westport and London: Greenwood, 1993), 177, 378, and 383.

Angeles early in 1939.[25] In the summers of 1940 and 1941 we glimpse him at Hollywood parties. In the former, which included the Stravinskys, Mischa Elman, and Adolf Bolm, he "was aglow with good humor."[26] In the latter, given by the exiled composer Italo Montemezzi (1875-1952), among such guests as Artur and Mrs. Rubinstein, composers, singers and orchestra leaders, Jeanette MacDonald, Jan Kiepura, and Erich Korngold, was "Boris Morros wearing a modest shirt and his gorgeous smile."[27]

In the 1930s Morros was approached by a Soviet Russian agent. As he testified early in 1957 to the House Committee on Un-American Activities, it "all began" when solicited by this agent in 1933, while he was still living in New York. After his move to California in 1936, it continued with food packages sent to Morros' parents in Russia and again in 1942 (when Morros was making *Tales of Manhattan*), the agent also facilitating the emigration to the U.S. that year via Vladivostok of his ninety-six-year-old father. At some point in the early 1940s, frightened and feeling compromised, intimidated, and even menaced, Morros finally contacted the FBI. He and his wife lived in Beverly Hills and by March 1947 they also owned a suite in New York's Hampshire House. For a decade thereafter, until 19 January 1957, the Bureau used him as a counterspy. He stated that he had made sixty-eight trans-ocean voyages over a ten-year period, specifying that he was away every other month (i.e., slightly more than six trips per year). In January 1950, for example, he went to Moscow via Prague and Warsaw, ostensibly on business for his movie company and even carrying a print of his *Carnegie Hall* (1947). After his testimony, five articles by Francis E. Walter, Chairman of the Committee on Un-American Activities, appeared between 29 September and 3 October 1957 in the *Philadelphia Enquirer.* They revealed that Morros had been a counterspy for the U.S. from 1947 through early January 1957. On 20 January the FBI had had to cable him in Munich: "*Cinerama,*" a secret code "warning him of impending danger." He fled Europe immediately for the US. The *Enquirer* articles revealed that Morros had most recently testified on 16 August 1957 before the House Committee about his clandestine activities over the previous decade.[28] Two years later Morros published his own account, calling it *My Ten Years as a Counter Spy*.[29]

---

[25] See *Musical America* 59 (10 March 1939), 41.

[26] *Rob Wagner's Script* 24 (20 July 1940): 27.

[27] "Horrible Hollywood," *Rob Wagner's Script* 26 (19 July 1941): 24.

[28] The above paragraph is based upon *International Communism (Espionage). Excerpts of Consultation with Counterspy Boris Morros (August 16, 1957). Committee on Un-American Activities. House of Representatives, Eighty-Fifth Congress, First Session* (Washington: US Government, 1958), 7-20, and articles in *The New York Times*, 18 March 1947, and the obituaries "Boris Morros, a Film Producer, F.B.I. Counterspy, Dies at 73," 10 January 1963, 15, and "Morros, Who Duped Kremlin as Spy, Dies," *Los Angeles Times*, 10 January 1963, 3, the last giving his age as 68. Further, see Crawford, *A Windfall*, 168.

[29] (New York: Viking, 1959). Most books written about the Cold War do not even mention Morros, either from ignorance, or because of his relatively minor role as a spy. For a more significant musical spy, see Douglas Martin, "Henry Pleasants, 89, the Spy who Knew His Music," *New York Times*, 14 January 2000, B 11, discussing Pleasants in the US Foreign Service in Munich, Berne, and Bonn, and as a CIA station chief in Berlin during the 1950s.

During the earlier period of Morros' reluctant co-operation with the Soviet spy network, Stravinsky, who had sailed from New York on 5 May 1937, received a telegram in Paris from New York on 28 July. It read: "Morros of Paramount Pictures sailing Ile de France Thursday. [Richard] Copley [Stravinsky's US concert manager] saw him [in] Los Angeles. Nothing definite yet. Regards, Dagmar." By now, the reader will have guessed the identity of the female addressee of the postcard. Not only her above-mentioned wire from New York on 10 March urging Morros to sign up Stravinsky in Hollywood, but also this July telegram shows that it was Stravinsky's New York help- (and, apparently, bed-) mate, Miss Dagmar Godowsky, [30] to whom he sent his Albequerque postcard from San Francisco. Enclosing it in an envelope was for the sake of discretion, befitting a married man with four children, not to mention a mistress.

Godowsky emigrated with her family to New York near the close of 1914. During a seven-year stint in silent movies – she made at least twenty-four pictures between 1919 and 1926[31]—she was often in New York. She returned there permanently in June 1930 because her father had suffered a stroke that ended his concert career. She was remembered in New York by a Hollywood columnist as a young woman, who had been practically "an adopted child . . . in the Leopold Godowsky household." Dagmar had "the most classically beautiful head imaginable, the wit, innuendo and charm of her father, the generosity of spirit of her mother [died 1933], and the most erotic chuckle inherited from her own Rabelaisian concept of this silly world."[32]

In 1924 Dagmar wrote an article for *Photoplay* entitled: "She Wants to Be the Wickedest Woman on the Screen." She stated later that in films, "I was always type-cast as a vamp," and even her obituary read "'Vamp' of the Silent Screen."[33]

[30] Correspondence of Dagmar Godowsky and Stravinsky: 28 July 1937, film 95, Stravinsky archive, Paul Sacher Stiftung, Basel; on Copley (1875-1939), who also managed Josef Hofmann, see the obituary in *The New York Times*, 1 March 1939.

[31] For example: *Bonds of Honor* with Sessue Hayakawa in 1919; *The Altar Stairs* and *Souls for Sale* both with Frank Mayo in 1922 and 1923, respectively; *A Sainted Devil* with Rudolf Valentino, *Meddling Women* with Lionel Barrymore, and *Celebritypes* with Jascha Heifetz, all three in 1924. Her last film was *Borrowed Plumes* in 1926. See Evelyn Mack Truit, *Who was Who on Screen*, 3rd ed. (New York and London: Bowker, 1983), 278; Bernard Rosenberg and Harry Silverstein, *The Real Tinsel* (London: Macmillan, 1970), 254-64; Daniel Blum, *A Pictorial History of the Silent Screen* (New York: Putnam's Sons, 1953), 212, 215; John Kobal, *People Will Talk* (New York: Knopf, 1985), 56-70; Eugene Michael Vazzana, *Silent Film Necrology*, 2nd ed. (Jefferson, NC and London: McFarland, 2001), 201; and Anthony Slide, *Silent Players. A Biographical and Autobiographical Study of 100 Silent Film Actors and Actresses* (Lexington: University of Kentucky Press, 2002), 140-43, with pl.

[32] "Horrible Hollywood," *Rob Wagner's Script* 26 (27 September 1941): 18. The author is probably Bernadine Szold Fritz (1895-1982), whose first marriage (of four) was in 1922 to O.K. Liveright in New York. She moved to Los Angeles in 1939, and was a frequent contributor to *Script*; see the *Los Angeles Times*, 12 June 1977, pt. IX, 1, 8, and 22 February 1982, pt. II, 4 (obituary). Godowsky herself mentions Szold Fritz as the "first gossip columnist for the [*New York Daily] News*;" see Dagmar Godowsky, *First Person Plural. The Lives of Dagmar Godowsky* (New York: Viking, 1958), 128 and *Bubushkin*, 115, n. 9. In late November 1941, Szold Fritz gave a birthday dinner for Dagmar attended by both Stravinskys; see *Bubushkin*, 24 November 1941.

[33] See *Photoplay Magazine* 25 (May 1924): 86; Rosenberg and Silverstein, *Real Tinsel*, 262; and Louis Calta, *The New York Times*, 14 February 1975, 35, with a photograph taken in 1924.

She did not deny that among her initial conquests had been such luminaries as Charlie Chaplin, Sessue Hayakawa, Jascha Heifetz, Artur Rubinstein, to whom must be added Sergei Prokofiev (in 1919-21).[34] She possessed a wit matching her reputation. Twice married, first in Hollywood to movie actor Frank Mayo (1921; annulled 1926) and then back in New York for one day (but not that night, and quickly annulled) to a James D. Sloane shortly after her debut on Broadway in *The Rat* by David L'Estrange (pseudonym for Igor Novello and Constance Collier),[35] she was once asked by a matron at a party: "And how many husbands have you had, Miss Godowsky?" She replied: "Two of my own, darling, and most of my friends."[36]

Unfortunately, the closing three chapters of her 1958 autobiography, *First Person Plural*, were chronologically snarled and much pruned by her editors concerning the 1930s and later, and particularly about Stravinsky. As she said in 1964, "so many things were taken out."[37] Even so, it furnishes many details of her relationship with him, though not always in a satisfactory chronological order. First meeting him in New York early in January 1935 during his second U.S. tour, Dagmar promptly invited him and several other famous musicians to tea at the apartment on Riverside Drive that she shared with her recently widowed father. During this tour she also followed him, late in March, to Washington DC. In June of 1936, traveling with Josef Hofmann and wife (family acquaintances through her father), she pursued him to Rio de Janeiro where she also met his "charming" pianist son, Soulima (1910-94): "we got on right away."[38] But it was not the son she was after. Returning to New York, she initiated a correspondence on 10 September.[39] During Stravinsky's third trip to the U.S. in 1937, she served as his East Coast assistant, his first letter that year to her, on 3 March from Winnetka, was concerning his *Jeu de cartes*. Upon returning to Paris in mid-May, he continued the correspondence, his final letter of that year, 29 December, among many to her lamenting his wife's rapidly declining health.[40]

Like our postcard, one of his letters to her, "Paris, den 17 mai 1937," otherwise in German (often their language of correspondence), also begins: "Chère amie."[41]

---

[34] See Walsh, *Stravinsky: Second Exile*, 8; and Sergey Prokofiev, *Diaries 1915-1923: Behind the Mask*, trans. Anthony Phillips (Ithaca: Cornell University Press, 2008), 389-99, 402, 481, 559, 561, 565-67, 572, 574-75, 578, and pl. 20 (Dagmar).

[35] See Godowsky, *First Person Plural*, 145-50; on the annulment with Mayo granted in 1926 and financed by her father in 1925, see *The New York Times*, 16 and 20 February 1932, 28 and 34 respectively.

[36] Godowsky, *First Person Plural*, 11; differently quoted in Kobal, *People Will Talk*, 58.

[37] See Kobal, *People Will Talk*, 59 and 61. Stravinsky underlined many passages in his copy of *First Person Plural*; see *Pictures and Documents*, 639, n. 170, and 663-64, n. 10.

[38] *First Person Plural*, 217.

[39] *Bubushkin*, 92, n. 8.

[40] See *Illuminated Manuscripts, Illustrated Books, Autograph Letters and Music* (London: Christie's, 29 June 1994), 148-49, lot 124, and *Stravinsky, Selected Correspondence*, 2: 303.

[41] See the website: www.leopoldgodowsky.com/stravinsky.dagmar1.shtml (accessed 5 May 2007); and

His note from "Paris, 6.5.1938," although containing a few words in French and English, is mostly in German. Curiously, it addresses her (ungrammatically) as "Mein lieber Freund." It also nixes "Royal," perhaps the "Royal Gaillac" where he was wont to rendez-vous with his mistress, Vera Soudeikina (1888-1983).[42] Probably this salutation was as much for the sake of discretion with Vera (even though his note to Dagmar closes with "Herzliebste Küsse und Grüsse"),[43] as with his first wife, Catherine (1882-1939), still living though gravely ill. Another note he sent Dagmar from the TB sanatorium at Sancellemoz on 20 July 1939 employed the salutation: "Très chère amie."[44]

They corresponded during 1938, she writing him a mash note from New York on 22 February in German: "My only love. I love you so madly. . . . My blood pressure . . . would certainly go up if I were to see you."[45] Later that spring it probably did. Seeing off her friends, Josef Hofmann and wife in New York, she had somehow missed the announcement of the departure of the *S.S. Brittanic*, and thus had to disembark at Southampton on 23 April with only her purse, not even her passport. She arrived unexpectedly in Paris and went to Stravinsky's house in the rue Faubourg, invited by him (according to her) to meet both wife Catherine and mistress Vera. To judge by the sorrowful letter Godowsky wrote in English from the Hotel Edouard VII in Paris on 16 May to Stravinsky in Brussels,[47] a letter that he preserved in his 1938 scrapbook, he must have told her off shortly before he left that very morning with Soulima for a concert in Brussels.[47] A particularly poignant line in her letter paints the classic rejected lover who accepts all blame for a relationship's disintegration: "I am not reproaching you – but only myself, that *I* wasn't capable of making you care." At least as astonishing as his preservation of this utterly compromising letter were his instructions to Vera, his long-time mistress in Paris (since 1921): on the 21st to take buttermilk to Dagmar; and two days later, for Vera to visit Dagmar "regarding money matters."[48] In a word, just as he had long before arranged for Catherine to meet Vera, so was he now arranging for one mistress to meet the other.

Even so, neither his momentary rejection of Dagmar – in a letter of the late 1930s to Alexis Kall he calls her "the dangerous person" and his literary Argentine friend Victoria Ocampo recalled him saying in 1936 that "she has a bad

---

Walsh, *Stravinsky. Second Exile*, 66 and 589, n. 55. She was fluent in both French and German; see Godowsky, *First Person Plural*, 118-19.

[42] Stravinsky photographed Vera in 1923 at the "Royal;" see *Stravinsky, Selected Correspondence* 1: pl. between 202-3.

[43] See the website: www.leopoldgodowsky.com/stravinsky.dagmar2.shtml (accessed 5 May 2007). This letter of 6 May 1938 is briefly cited in Christie's *Illuminated Manuscripts*, 149 (paragraph 4).

[44] Correspondence of Dagmar Godowsky and Stravinsky: 20 July 1939, film 95, Stravinsky archive, Paul Sacher Stiftung, Basel.

[45] Walsh, *Stravinsky. Second Exile*, 80 and 592, n. 30.

[46] Godowsky, *First Person Plural*, 229-232.

[47] For her letter of 16 May, see *Babushkin*, 92, n. 8, and Walsh, *Stravinsky. Second Exile*, 80; for the Brussels program of 19 May, autographed by father and son, see Slim, *Annotated Catalogue*, no. 61.

[48] *Bubushkin*, 92: 21 and 23 May, respectively.

character"[49]—nor his long-standing relationship with Vera and their forthcoming marriage cooled his ardor and certainly not Dagmar's. He continued to use her as his US contact, telephoning on 25 May 1939 from Sancellemoz a four-page letter in German to her in New York about fixing the dates with Professor Edward Forbes for his 1939-40 Harvard lectures.[50] Arriving in New York on 30 September 1939, he was met on the dock by both Kall and Dagmar. Although he stayed nine days with Kall in the Sulgrave Hotel on East 67th Street, he certainly visited Dagmar in her hotel, the Navarro, prior to leaving New York with Kall on the 10th to take up his Harvard appointment. He also told her of his plans for marrying Vera who would be arriving in three months.[51] Thus on 27 October 1939, Dagmar wrote Kall in Cambridge: "I lose <u>every</u> thing [meaning Stravinsky] but weight and my cold (Ha-Ha) [—] good theme for a popular song."[52] Ostensibly to bring him some fine wine, she drove from New York to Boston early in November and according to Alexei Haieff (1914-94), Stravinsky attempted to have her visit him in his hotel room.[53] In any event, on 4 November she dined in Boston with him, Kall, and Kall's former piano student Adele Marcus (1906-95), by then at Juilliard and Stravinsky's future duo-pianist and soloist in 1940-41.[54]

In pursuing Stravinsky, Dagmar solicited Kall's sympathy and probably his connivance. Stravinsky's imminent second marriage did not hinder their relationship. After the death of Dagmar's boss, Richard Copley (February 1939), she worked for Stravinsky and, during 1940 she continued as his booking agent in New York.[55] On 11 December 1939 she wrote in German from New York, thanking her "Geliebter Freund" (by this time in San Francisco) for his postcard that had made her "<u>very</u> happy." She asked him to telephone, or wire, or write by air-mail after his second San Francisco concert on the 16th, closing her letter: "I embrace you, always yours, Dagmar."[56] She also arranged for an exhibition there of paintings by

---

[49] *Stravinsky, Selected Correspondence*, 2: 508, n. 12, and Walsh, *Stravinsky. Second Exile*, 49, respectively.

[50] Ibid., 508.

[51] See Godowsky, *First Person Plural*, 241-42; Department of Special Collections, Charles E. Young University Research Library, University of California at Los Angeles: Alexis Kall papers, 601, box 1, file Dagmar Godowsky; and Robert Craft, *An Improbable Life. Memoirs* (Nashville: Vanderbilt University Press, 2002), 198.

[52] Kall papers, 601, box 1, file Dagmar Godowsky, partially quoted in Walsh, *Stravinsky. Second Exile*, 107 and 597, n. 10.

[53] Craft, *Improbable Life*, 198, and also -- but this time -- told to him by St. John Perse, in Stravinsky and Craft, *Dialogues and a Diary* (Garden City: Doubleday, 1963), 197. Godowsky, *First Person Plural*, 241, writes of staying with a Dr. and Mrs. Whittemore on Beacon Hill. Perhaps Stravinsky did rent a hotel in Boston, but at this period he and Kall were rooming on the upper floor of Professor Edward Forbe's house at Gerry's Landing in Cambridge.

[54] Slim, "Unknown Words and Music, 1939-44, by Stravinsky for his longtime friend, Dr. Alexis Kall," in *Words on Music. Essays in Honor of Andrew Porter on the Occasion of his 75th Birthday*, ed. David Rosen and Claire Brook (Hillsdale, NY: Pendragon, 2003), 308.

[55] See Copley's obituary in *The New York Times* and Godowsky, *First Person Plural*, 238, respectively.

[56] Kall papers 601, box 1, file Dagmar Godowsky, 11 December 1939, signed: "Ich umarme Sie Stets Ihre/ Dagmar." In the same file, her undated letter [March 1940] to Stravinsky, "Dearest One …Do you miss me just a little bit? Please do!..." she signs: "Much love / always / Your Dagmar."

his elder son, Theodore (1907-69), in mid January 1940, about which forthcoming arrangements Stravinsky, in New York on 6 December, covered his tracks perhaps a little too casually—forewarning Vera (then still in Paris): "Of course, Dagmar is involved."[57] When his New York concert manager, Paul H. Stoes at 119 West 57th Street (successor to Copley), needed to reach him on 2 February 1940, he wrote c/o Dagmar Godowsky, though by this time Stravinsky and Vera had returned from Pittsburgh and were at the Great Northern Hotel in New York.[58] Dagmar frequently wrote Kall, a fellow heavy drinker: "Woof [Kall's nickname] dear. . . . Write to me as promised right away and I shall destroy [your letter] at once as promised—Am so anxious to learn how 'he' [Stravinsky] is. . . . How about the good-looking daughter [one of the Forbes's children?] 'he' told us about? I haven't had one drop of alcohol since you left. I will become again beautiful. . . . It seems only what one loves leaves one though."[59] Her reference to becoming "beautiful again" chiefly concerned a rapidly developing problem, her weight. Twenty years later in her autobiography she spoke of this herself: "I knew that I should lose at least fifty pounds . . . a generous waistline . . . a joyous Buddha," verbal descriptions not contradicted by a photograph made just at the time of her book's publication in 1958.[60]

Finally, late in the summer of 1941 she even moved from New York to North Bedford Drive in Beverly Hills, not all that far from the Stravinskys's newly-purchased house at 1260 North Wetherly Drive.[61] She first visited the Stravinskys on 3 September, Vera discreetly absenting herself for a while in order "that they might have had time for their explanations."[62] On 9 September the Stravinskys attended a drunken party at Dagmar's with author-playwright Mercedes de Acosta ("a very lady-like Lesbian").[63] Two days later the Stravinskys again encountered Dagmar at a dinner party given by her old family friend, Bernardine Szold Fritz.[64] On 13 September the wonderful gossip column, "Horrible Hollywood," often signed by the same Bernardine Szold Fritz in the lively and irreverent *Rob Wagner's*

---

[57] See *Bubushkin*, 14 January 1940 and *Perepiska* 3: 1939, no. 1974, differently translated in *Bubushkin*, 107. Through correspondence in the fall of 1939 with Soulima Stravinsky, Dagmar had also offered advice to Vera about entering the US; see *Bubushkin*, 100, letter 11: 4 November 1939.

[58] See Stravinsky, *Selected Correspondence*, 1: 439-440: 2 February 1940 and *Bubushkin*, 111: 1 February 1940.

[59] Kall papers 601, box 1, file Dagmar Godowsky, partially quoted in Walsh, *Stravinsky. Second Exile*, 114, who places her undated letter as c. January 1940, though perhaps it refers to the period after the Stravinskys and Kall had left the East Coast for Los Angeles the following May. One of the Forbes's daughters is seated next to Vera below her standing father, Edward, in the cropped departure photograph, 5 May 1940, in Robert Craft, *A Stravinsky Scrapbook 1940-1971* (New York: Thames and Hudson, 1983), 9, pl. 7.

[60] See Godowsky, *First Person Plural*, 4-5, and pl. entitled: "alone," facing 219.

[61] Godowsky, *First Person Plural*, 243-48, misspelling it "Weatherly;" Craft, *Improbable Life*, 197-98, and Walsh, *Stravinsky. Second Exile*, 129.

[62] *Bubushkin*, 3 September 1941; see also Godowsky, *First Person Plural*, 243.

[63] Ibid., 9 Sept and 26 May 1941, respectively.

[64] Ibid., 11 September, 1941.

Script (a Los Angeles journal with *New Yorker* aspirations), mentions Godowsky at a different evening party.[65] However, the next "Horrible Hollywood" documents a party Dagmar herself had given in September, almost certainly the above-cited bibulous one of 9 September. At this party, mobs of invitees came to her garden: "it lasted so late that Dagmar finally got very sleepy and went to bed, and is still in misery because she is afraid that she missed something." Among the guests were Mr. and Mrs. Artur Rubinstein, Mr. and Mrs. Igor Stravinsky, Mercedes de Acosta, Mr. and Mrs. Josef Hofmann, Erich Remarque, Mr. and Mrs. Richard Hageman, "and scores more."[66] Dagmar remained in Los Angeles throughout the war years, often visiting the Stravinskys and entertaining them at her place.

A group photograph of September-November 1941 was not taken at 1260 North Wetherly, but perhaps chez Godowsky at North Bedford Drive, to judge by its mountainous background (the Hollywood hills). It shows from left to right: Stravinsky; a standing George Martin (1902-c.1985, life companion of Stravinsky's long-time composer friend, Richard Hammond, 1896-1980); and a quite corpulent Dagmar, recognizable from her relatively late glamour photograph in her 1958 autobiography (facing p. 219). The 1941 photograph shows her chatting across an empty chair to Mercedes de Acosta. Perhaps either Vera or Hammond, both absent from the photograph, took it.[67] Throughout the war years, Dagmar, the inveterate name-dropper, still actively pursued Stravinsky (no longer as client or lover) and other "personalities" as part of her stable of famous folks.[68] By early 1948 she had returned to New York, living at Delmonico's Hotel on Park Avenue from where she visited the Stravinsky's on 16 April 1948 at the Ambassador while they were in New York for the premiere of *Orpheus*. With them, she attended it on the 28th, preserving its program.[69] Still later she lived in a rather shabby apartment though "in the fashionable block on West 57th Street,"[70] and, according to a *New York Times* obituary, her last residence was at 333 East 79th.

There is no question that at one time or another Stravinsky reciprocated

---

[65] *Rob Wagner's Script* 26 (13 September 1941): 26.

[66] Ibid., 26 (27 September 1941): 18.

[67] The photograph is reproduced in Walsh, *Stravinsky. Second Exile*, pl. 4 (bottom), between 204-05. Craft, *Improbable Life*, 118, states the wealthy Hammonds moved to the Hollywood hills late in 1941; see, for example, *Bubushkin*, 6 November. However, *Rob Wagner's Script* 26 (14 and 21 June 1941): 22 and 26, respectively, record Hammond and a George Marton [sic] at Hollywood parties before mid-June, Hammond already having bought property with intent to build. He was to take pictures of the Stravinskys at Torcello in September 1959 and of them and Martin at Venice in October 1958; see *Igor and Vera Stravinsky. A Photograph Album 1921 to 1971*, ed. Vera Stravinsky, Rita McCaffrey, and Robert Craft (New York: Thames and Hudson, 1982), no. 222, and Lisa Cox, *Music Catalogue 48* (Exeter, England: Lisa Cox Music Ltd, c. 2003), lot 129 (ill.), respectively. At Venice, 15 August 1958, Stravinsky inscribed words and tune of "Happy Birthday to You" on a sheet to George Martin; see Gary E. Combs, *Autographs* (New York: Gary E. Combs Autographs, Inc., February 2009), p. [11].

[68] See, for example, *First Person Plural*, 246, and *Bubushkin*, 11 August and 12 September, 1942; she was still in Los Angeles on 24 June 1947.

[69] See *Bubushkin*, 144 and *Illuminated Manuscripts*, 149, lot 124.

[70] Kobal, *People Will Talk*, 59; perhaps this is the "Buckingham on 57th" that Godowsky mentions in *First Person Plural*, 148.

her attentions, even if she had to admit that initially in 1936 "all the sparks were emanating from me."[71] To judge by the series of love letters she sent him, preserved in the Paul Sacher Foundation in Basle, her letters to him and in references to him in her letters to Kall in 1939-40 (with the latter's papers at UCLA), and in a series of items (alas now dispersed) auctioned at London by Christie's on 29 June 1994, their affair quickly turned torrid. (Among these dispersed items was a telegram from Boris Morros to Dagmar the contents of which would be interesting to know.) Not least, of course, are the references, even if slightly veiled, to him in her *First Person Plural.*

Interviewed in 1964 (but not published until after her death and the demise of both Stravinskys) as to whether she knew him well, Dagmar replied, obviously referring to the late 1930s: "I did *more* than know him! I looked after him all the time he was sick [1937, with tuberculosis in New York]. He was my great love. He was going to marry me. Then he got well [late summer, 1939] and he married that other woman [Vera, in March 1940]."[72] If Craft's observation about Stravinsky's obsession with "uberous bosoms" is accurate,[73] by the late 1930s Miss Godowsky amply filled the bill, like the similarly buxom Vera Soudeikina,[74] that "other woman," conveniently far away in Paris in 1937.

While Vera Stravinsky was alive—a nominal co-author with Craft for the 1978 *Stravinsky. Pictures and Documents*—Craft reported only that Stravinsky was horrified by Dagmar's autobiography.[75] When publishing Vera's diaries two years after her death, however, Craft went further and reported that Stravinsky "never denied the truth of her [Dagmar's] anecdotes about himself."[76] In his memoirs of 2002, Craft stated flat out that Dagmar was Stravinsky's lover during his visits to New York in 1935, 1937, and 1939, and to Rio de Janeiro with Soulima in 1936. He also insinuates that Vera retaliated in August 1936 with one of her former suitors, Baron Fred Osten-Sacken (1888-1974).[77] Faced with the same "evidence," but as unaware, as was Craft, of the franker admission by Dagmar in 1964 cited above, Walsh is far more cautious: "Did Stravinsky go to bed with Dagmar in Rio?" he asks.[78] The answer would seem to be yes, not only then but several times thereafter, and, as Walsh concedes, it seems highly likely that Craft, always close to Vera, obtained his information from her after Stravinsky's and Dagmar's deaths (1971 and 1975, respectively).

Even in our age of prurience, prying, and mass surveillance, we may never know for sure, and that is alright, too. Long before reading Charles Joseph's remarkable book, I for one, and surely many others felt and wondered even at a first hearing

---

[71] Godowsky, *First Person Plural,* 214.

[72] Kobal, *People Will Talk,* 61.

[73] *Pictures and Documents,* 387.

[74] See, for example, the 1932 photograph of Vera in *Igor and Vera Stravinsky,* 85, pl. 133, far left.

[75] *Pictures and Documents,* 663, n.10.

[76] *Bubushkin,* 92.

[77] Craft, *Improbable Life,* 115 and 197-98. In August 1936 Vera was at Wiessee in Bavaria (apparently with the Baron); see *Bubushkin,* 81, n. 2.

about the intense keening in Stravinsky's "Aria II," the third movement of his 1931 *Violin Concerto*. Joseph writes that "Aria II" had a special significance for the composer. Hearing it performed by Samuel Dushkin, his wife Louise reported that Stravinsky wept more than once, afterwards confiding to her that he had written "Aria II" for his wife Catherine by way of apology for his by then ten-year infidelity with Vera. Louise Dushkin could not have observed such tears when Stravinsky was conducting an orchestra with Dushkin as soloist. She probably noticed them when Stravinsky was at the piano accompanying Dushkin in this concerto, if we remember that Mrs. Dushkin (who married Samuel in 1936) traveled with them in 1937 and was presumably recruited to turn pages for Stravinsky. And perhaps he even wept over his present infidelity with Dagmar to his dying wife and to Vera.[79]

His Dagmar dalliance seems to have been the little man's last amatory adventure, for, so far as is known, once married to Vera, he remained faithful to her. This did not prevent him from flirting with attractive women, even married ones. Shortly before her death, my musical friend, the still attractive and vivacious Dorothy Ellis McQuoid Hopper (1911-1998), recalled for me a day in the spring of 1940 when she drove the Stravinskys house-hunting. The occasion may well have been 31 May (three weeks before they bought an automobile) for Vera wrote in her diary: "Drive around all day looking for a house" (they found one four days later, at 124 South Swall Drive).[80] In any event, Mrs. McQuoid recalled climbing an external staircase, Stravinsky directly behind her. He whispered: "Dorothy—vous avez un bel Popo [derrière]," at which, when this was repeated to Vera, both women laughed heartily.

What toll his liaison with Dagmar exacted on Vera remains unknown, even though clearly she knew about it. And in fact, their thirty-one year marriage has been celebrated as one of the happiest in the 20th century. We can only marvel that during this time of Stravinsky's additional infidelity—the "Dagmar years," roughly 1936 until his marriage to Vera in 1940 and perhaps the most difficult period of his adult life—he completed such masterworks as *Jeu de cartes*, *Dumbarton Oaks Concerto*, the *Symphony in C*, and some parts of *Danses concertantes*.

Acquired some three decades after Dagmar's demise, my postcard almost certainly figured in 1994 among several others in Christie's lot 124 comprising her treasured objects. As part of a great composer's legacy (not excluding his indiscretions), she rightfully conserved her memorabilia. They also contained a now-rapidly fading record of a successful, though by Cold War standards a relatively minor spy whose clandestine activities were, of course, unknown either to Stravinsky or to Miss Godowsky until the passing of another two decades.

---

[78] Walsh, *Stravinsky. Second Exile*, 50.

[79] Charles M. Joseph, *Stravinsky Inside Out* (New Haven and London: Yale University Press, 2001), 192.

[80] 31 May, 3, and 21 June 1940; for a photograph of Vera and the McQuoids taken in June 1940 by Stravinsky.

Musical Innovators and Innovations

Heinrich Isaac and Innovations
in Musical Style ca.1490

Keith Polk

When Isaac arrived in Florence in 1485 he was quickly immersed in a rapid flow of overlapping developments in musical style. We can trace the course of events clearest in secular composition because in the critical time span of concern here the manuscript sources for secular pieces have survived in greater quantity than those for sacred music. Moreover their chronology is much firmer, which allows us to follow the sequence of events with reasonable confidence. These collections verify the arrival of a new kind of three-part piece, based on imitation—a kind of piece which Helen Hewitt aptly described as "tricinia." Isaac seized on the potential of the innovations, used them in his own way, and established higher, indeed definitive, standards in the process. Ironies abound. The new manner evolved out of the French chanson, but was centered exclusively in Italian cities and courts. Many of the leading composers, Isaac for example, were neither French nor Italian. Moreover, Isaac worked intensely with the three-part texture between about 1485 and 1490, then he seems to have abandoned it almost completely, moving on to yet further innovations centered on textures involving four parts. The object here will be to emphasize how swiftly developments took place, and how central Isaac apparently was in the fundamental alteration of the musical vocabulary that resulted.

The Manuscript Sources

The argument put forward here rests on having some confidence of the dating of a select few core manuscripts. These are all Italian collections, many from Florence itself. Two groups are especially relevant, one including repertory from about 1480 or slightly earlier.[1] The other group, almost all assembled just after 1490, includes repertory that can be dated *ca.* 1490. A third and smaller set contains repertory written between *ca.* 1480-85. Fortunately for the present discussion this is the least important of the three, as scholarly opinion about the dating of what might be the key manuscript in this group, the Casanatense manuscript, has become divided. We shall come to this directly.

---

[1] The main interest in this study is usually in the most recently composed pieces contained in the manuscripts. It should be understood, of course, that all the collections considered here also contain items which were composed earlier—indeed, in some cases much earlier.

The first group includes most importantly three manuscripts: the Pixérécourt manuscript (Paris, Bibliothèque Nationale de France, f.fr. 15123, henceforth Pix, see the following note); Florence, Biblioteca Nazionale Centrale, MS Magl. XIX. 176 [F176]; and the "second" Riccardiana chansonnier (Florence, Biblioteca Riccardiana, MS 2356 [FR2356]).[2] These are all basically collections of songs, and are dominated by the French chanson. These sets are cited here primarily for a negative reason—they contain no pieces of what shall be identified as "tricinia." Their importance is that they show the state of the repertory up to about 1480, and to that date there is little sign of this later approach.

The second group, as indicated above, is that which consists of the manuscripts dating from just after 1490. The most central items are Florence, Biblioteca Nazionale Centrale, MS Banco Rari 229 (F229); Florence, Biblioteca Nazionale Centrale, MS Magl. XIX. 178 (F178); and Rome, Vatican City, Biblioteca Apostolica Vaticana, Cappella Giulia, XIII.27 (RCG). Slightly later, but containing similar repertory is Bologna, Civico Museo Bibliografico Musicale MS Q17 (BQ17).[3] As with the first group, these are song collections, and the French chanson, though usually untexted, still dominates. With this group, however, we find a full range of pieces that will also be included within the category of "tricinia." In any case, the emphasis here will be on those items in these collections which would seem to represent what musicians of the time would have considered the leading-edge styles.

With these two groups there is reasonable agreement among scholars concerning their dating. While some view, for example, that Pix might be slightly later than 1480, a consensus view is that the first group contains no repertory which can be dated after *ca.* 1480, while the second contains important contributions of pieces written between about 1485 and 1490. A third group is more difficult to place; this includes most importantly Bologna, Civico Museo Bibliografico Musicale MS Q16 (BQ16) and Florence, Biblioteca Riccardiana, MS 2794 (FR2794).[4] Actually these two can be reasonably securely dated between *ca.* 1485 and 1490—i.e., distinctly, though only slightly, before the second group. A more difficult problem is presented by the Casanatense manuscript (Rome, Biblioteca Casanatense, MS 3856, (RCas); this was dated by Lewis Lockwood as *ca.* 1481, but this dating has been challenged recently by Joshua Rifkin.[5] The issue is not yet resolved—but for the present discussion the precise dating of this manuscript is not critical. For our

---

[2] Henceforth these will be termed Pix, F176, and FR2356, borrowing the sigla of the ever useful David Fallows, *A Catalogue of Polyphonic Songs 1415-1480* (Oxford: Oxford University Press, 1999). For further details on the manuscripts, including the most important studies and editions, see his introductory section, "Source Abbreviations," 5-52. Another collection which might be mentioned consists of the Glogauer part books, Kraków, Bibliotheka Jagiellońska, MS Mus. 40098, hereafter Glog, which has been dated *ca.* 1480, and which contains segments for which the transmission origin was probably ultimately Italian.

[3] Again, following Fallows, these will be referred to as F229, F178, RCG, and BQ17.

[4] Henceforth BQ16 and FR2794.

[5] Joshua Rifkin, "Munich, Milan, and a Marian Motet. Dating Josquin's *Ave Maria . . . virgo serena*," *Journal of the American Musicological Society* 56 (2003): 239-50.

purposes it is sufficient to say that it dates from after 1480, but before 1492. It will then be included, but only provisionally, in this third group. Any pieces from RCas in the following discussion will be specifically noted.

These three groups of manuscripts provide a chronological outline. We can now turn to the development of the tricinia approach to see how it fits within this frame.

Pre-1480—Before Tricinia

While a more precise definition of tricinia will emerge in the course of the discussion, it can be said that these pieces were three-part, and rooted in the French chanson. An important characteristic for Hewitt in her original definition of this kind of piece was that they seemed to be tied to instrumental performance.[6] The issue of "instrumental" will not be dealt with in this study, however, as the concern here is the development of a musical style. At least for the short term the matter of performance medium is not relevant.

In the final decades of the fifteenth century the French chanson remained central to secular repertory in Italy. Interest in the northern repertory was lively, and new pieces and approaches evidently were rapidly imported to satisfy southern appetites. In about 1480 several layers may be distinguished. A somewhat older group, centered on Du Fay and Ockeghem, continued to be popular. A younger one includes Busnoys, Hayne, and Caron, all at the height of favor. In addition a still younger group of composers, including most importantly Compère, Martini, and Agricola, was just appearing on the scene. Note that no secular pieces by Isaac, Josquin, or Obrecht are found in any of the Italian manuscripts that can be dated before 1480 (or in any secular manuscripts anywhere for that matter).

While any overall summary will be coarse, certain features were generally present throughout all the groupings. As pointed out above, three parts was the norm. The pieces were based on text models, and almost always on fixed forms—with the rondeau being markedly the favored form. The texture was usually distinctly layered, with a basic discant/tenor duet, to which was added a contratenor. By about 1480 the discant and tenor often consisted of an imitative duet, but the contratenor tended to remain a freely-constructed part. Imitation in three parts was sometimes incorporated, but usually, if present, most often occurred at the beginning of a piece, or of a second major section. Melodic phrases tended to be long and subtly constructed. The use of short motives in through-imitation was not a part of chanson vocabulary as known up to about 1480. This summary can be qualified in that composers in the third group, each in his own way, were beginning to organize their musical thoughts in different ways.

Compère presents a most puzzling and remarkable profile. In general the transmission of his pieces follows exactly what we would expect of a man born about 1445 (i.e., a few years before Isaac and Josquin) and who is firmly recorded

---

[6] Helen Hewitt, ed. *Harmonices musices Odhecaton A* (Cambridge, MA: The Mediaeval Academy of America, 1942), 74-78.

in Milan by 1474. One piece of his (*Mes pensées*) was included in Pix; several in each of the manuscripts described above assembled in the 1480s, and even more in those assembled after 1490. He continues to be well represented in manuscripts and prints at the beginning of the following century. He produced both three- and four-part chansons. The three-part pieces reveal Compère being drawn in two directions. In one he follows the model of the older generation. In a piece such as *A qui dirai*, for example, the basic duet between discant and tenor is retained.[7] The melodic lines are rather long, and imitation appears, but is not used consistently. In the other, he tends toward more equal-voiced counterpoint, with the contratenor occasionally sharing in imitations. Moreover, particularly in ending sections, Compère at times uses such devices as sequence in an entirely modern manner. These were features which Isaac would incorporate to great effect in his tricinia— though Compère's approach only exceptionally shows the structural tightness that is so characteristic of Isaac.[8] Compère's four-part pieces are the most startling of all in that they represent a wholesale adoption of yet another, even more modern, style. This will be discussed further below.

One could be tempted to suggest a chronology for Compère based on style, but in fact in this regard he serves as a warning of the vagaries presented in manuscript transmission. The "late" four-part pieces may be put to the side, as their dating would indeed appear to be sound. The late style appears only in manuscripts or prints from after *ca.* 1495, and none of these pieces are found in earlier collections which include four-part repertory (F229, for example). For those in three parts, however, the chronology is odd—even bizarre. One of his most "modern" pieces, *Puis que si bien*, is included in the first layer of the Laborde chansonnier, which has been dated as early as 1465.[9] Then comes an apparent gap of at least ten years between this earliest piece and what follows. The one piece in Pix (*Mes pensées*)can

---

[7] For the sources and for editions of this piece see Fallows, *A Catalogue*, 88.

[8] An example of this second direction is *Ne vous hastez pas*. For the sources and editions see Fallows, *A Catalogue*, 294.

[9] Washington, DC, Library of Congress, MS M2.1 L25 Case. For a useful, concise description with bibliography, see Fallows, *A Catalogue*, 22. The piece occurs in three other sources, with the only attribution to Compère coming in the not always reliable Segovia manuscript (for the listings, see Fallows, *A Catalogue*, 334). Still, some features of the piece occur in other pieces by Compère—and, for that matter, even if *Puis que si bien* should not be by this composer, the style is very advanced for a dating of 1465. For an edited version of the piece see Ludwig Finscher, ed. *Loyset Compere. Opera omnia*, Corpus Mensurabilis Musicae 15 (Rome: American Institute of Musicology, 1972), 5: 45-46. It is important to note that the Laborde manuscript has recently been argued, quite persuasively, to be somewhat later, perhaps *ca.* 1470 by Jane Alden. See her "Makers of a Songbook: the Scribes of the Laborde Chansonnier" (Ph.D. diss.,, University of North Carolina, Chapel Hill, 1999). This was supplemented by her unpublished paper, "Open Borders: France, Burgundy, and Repertorial Exchange in the Fifteenth Century," presented at the national meeting of the American Musicological Society, Quebec City, November 2007. Both of these are updated in her monograph *Songs, Scribes, and Society: The History and Reception of the Loire Valley Chansonniers* (New York: Oxford University Press, 2010). Also useful is Clemens Goldberg, *Das Chansonnier Laborde, Studien zur Intertextualität einer Liederhandschrift des 15. Jahrhunderts* (Frankfurt am Main: Peter Lang, 1997), but this is superceded by Alden's discussions concerning dating and context.

be dated *ca.* 1480, and the next three or so are included in sources that would appear to date these pieces in the early 1480s (this number is more than doubled if RCas should be dated *ca.* 1481).   It should be noted that none of Compère's chansons are included in the several northern manuscripts that were evidently assembled in the 1470s, such as the Mellon and Cordiforme chansonniers, or the main layers of the Dijon manuscript.[10]   What is striking is that *Puis que si bien* is quite unlike the standard vocabulary of the 1460s and even the 1470s. At times the piece involves all three parts in imitative counterpoint; moreover, both the first major section and the ending include distinctive passages in sequence.

Without *Puis que si bien*, the manuscript repertory and known facts concerning Compère fit squarely with what one would expect of a musician born *ca.* 1445, with his pieces beginning to appear in manuscripts dated about 1480, and with maximum transmission between 1490 and 1510. In fact, in the landmark *Odhecaton* collection, it is Compère—not Isaac, Josquin, or Obrecht—who is the favored composer. *Puis que si bien*, if dated 1465, or even 1470, then posits a baffling gap in transmission, and seems completely at odds with the other available evidence for Compère's career trajectory.

Johannes Martini, who will figure prominently in the following section of the article, must be mentioned briefly here as well, for one piece of his, *La martinella*, was clearly beginning to circulate before 1480, and was probably written by 1475. Indeed, this piece has been much discussed, and it would appear to be similar to the tricinia repertory in a number of ways.[11]   The title, for example, seems to be in the same vein as such pieces as Isaac's *La morra* and Josquin's *La bernardina*. The piece was widely distributed, and is without text in all sources. Moreover, its structure would make it unlikely that it was based on any of the usual fixed forms. Yet in important ways it remains closer to the traditional chanson approach than the pieces which will be taken up shortly. The texture is still essentially based on a dialogue between discant and tenor, with the contratenor seldom sharing in the primary motivic material. The melodic lines tend to be relatively long, and the harmonic structure, as a consequence does not have the tight-knit quality which will characterize the later pieces.

One piece by Agricola (*Ay je rien fet*) was included in Pix, and was thus apparently composed slightly before 1480.[12]   *Ay je rien fet* remains firmly in what was then the traditional chanson style. Imitation occurs, but is not prominent, and is limited to the basic discant/soprano duet. The piece shows no features of what will emerge as the tricinia style. Nor is it, for that matter, anything like Agricola's

---

[10] The Mellon chansonnier is New Haven, Yale University, Beineke Library for Rare Books and Manuscripts, MS 91; the Cordiforme is Paris, Bibliothèque Nationale de France, Rothschild 1973 (i.5.13); the Dijon is Dijon, Bibliothèque Municipale, MS 517.

[11] For the most cogent discussion, see Lewis Lockwood, *Music in Renaissance Ferrara 1400-1505: The Creation of a Musical Center in the Fifteenth Century* (Cambridge, MA: Harvard University Press: 1984), 273-77.

[12] For sources and editions see Fallows, *A Catalogue*, 95-96.

later, and quite eccentric, compositions. Agricola is difficult to place in terms of his relationship to the developments which will be tracked below. Several of his pieces are included in the manuscripts containing repertory that probably dates from the early- to mid-1480s. For the most part these pieces from earlier in the composer's career remain more conservative. Yet one composition, *Si dedero*, breaks out of that mold, and is indeed one of the most widely distributed items of the era.[13] It is included in both BQ16 and in FR2794, as well as in RCas, and appears in all the manuscripts I have mentioned as belonging to the group dating from *ca.* 1490. The piece was undoubtedly widely known to musicians active in Italy by the mid-1480s. Its popularity may have some bearing on our topic, as it employs devices which might have been influential. All voices share in the contrapuntal interplay, i.e., they are not built on the frame of a discant/tenor duet. Motives figure prominently, and there is some use of extended sequence. Still, the piece creates a rather loose and rambling impression, quite different in total effect than the tight-knit quality which is so characteristic of Isaac. Moreover, after this early essay in this direction, Agricola seems to have explored a very different kind of musical approach.

Johannes Martini—*ca.* 1480-1485—Early Tricinia

Underlying an assessment of the events of the early 1480s is the assumption that the number of manuscripts available does allow a reasonably dependable view of the repertory as it was known in northern Italy up to the late 1470s. It would then follow that if pieces which might be termed early tricinia are not included in these collections, such pieces had probably not yet appeared on the scene. Another assumption relates to the dating of pieces by Johannes Martini. The first sure reference to this composer places him at the court of Ferrara in 1473, which would then make him probably at least ten years Isaac's senior. The appearance of his pieces in manuscripts suggests the same age difference. A further assumption is that the Martini pieces in the Casanatense manuscript represent a style that developed probably in the late 1470s to no later than about 1485 (and of course perhaps no later than 1481, if Lockwood's dating should prove to be correct). And the manuscript includes several pieces that I would suggest do represent a new approach to composition. The three-part *Tout joyeux* may serve as an example. It begins with a short motive, stated in the bass, which then runs through both of the other voices. This motive clearly outlines a triad from F rising to C, and cadences clearly after the third voice enters (with a small cadential extension). Then follows a series of imitative sections, most marked off with clear cadences. The final segment of the piece features a sequence in the discant voice, followed by a short melodic fragment, which is immediately repeated an octave higher, leading to the strong final cadence on F, the main tonal area of the piece. The model presented

---

[13] For a convenient edition of the piece, see Hewitt, *Odhecaton*, 339-40. It is with Agricola that some of the most difficult issues concerning the dating of RCas arise. The manuscript contains nineteen of his pieces, and while it is true that Agricola's music was circulating in Italy in the 1480s, this number of pieces would appear to be out of line with the general pattern of transmission of his music there—which saw a distinctive surge about 1490.

in this piece is similar to that of several others; an opening section in clear imitation in three parts, marked off by a strong cadence.[14] What follows in all these pieces is a string of imitative segments, each usually rather short. Individual lines will occasionally be active, and sometimes outline octave scale patterns (they are less energetic than those of Isaac's tricinia style, however). The pieces have a strong sense of tonal unity, with most cadences on the primary degree of the piece, though some may be on the fifth degree (F or C in the case of *Tout joyeux*). There is often a relatively strong marking-off point toward the middle of the piece. The final portion has the effect of a coda. This section usually includes some extended use of sequence or repetition (or both). The device of one of the voices receding into the background is not often found, but does occur in the example selected here. In some, the coda consists of, or includes, a segment in contrasting triple meter.

As with the mature tricinia, to be discussed in the next section, these pieces are exclusively transmitted in Italian manuscripts in the period *ca.* 1480-1500, and are given with titles or incipits, never with texts. The main composer of these pieces is Martini, but several are anonymous, with a small number by other composers.[15] The style of these pieces would appear be distinctive and new on the scene. This is a style which, for convenience, and perhaps for want of anything better, we might term fifteenth-century tricinia—but with the warning note that the term tricinia was not used in contemporary sources.

Isaac—*ca.* 1485-1490—Mature Tricinia

The general style of what I have termed the "mature tricinia" is essentially that enshrined in the *Odhecaton* and deftly described by Helen Hewitt.[16] As she observed, these three-part pieces begin with a clearly articulated initial phrase, usually, but not always, with a striking head motive. This head motive runs through all voices in imitation. The parts are subsequently active, usually involving motivic patterns that are especially effective in instrumental performance, often covering rather extended ranges. Patterns which emphasize the outline of an octave are frequently encountered. A characteristic device is a texture in which one voice recedes into the background in longer values, while the other two parts engage in sequential or repeated patterns. This often occurs toward the end of a piece, leading to a final cadential section. The overall formal schemes of the pieces are such that it seems most unlikely that they were based originally on any of the fixed forms.

Isaac's *Helas* and *La morra* provide examples which serve to define the style. Both of these pieces occur in the manuscripts dated *ca.* 1490, and were almost

[14] For an edition of *Tout joyeux*, see Edward G. Evans, *Johannes Martini, Secular Pieces*, Recent Researches in the Music of the Middle Ages and Early Renaissance I (Madison: A-R Editions, 1975), 71-73; for other similar pieces see *Fuga la morie*, 26-82; *Je remerchi dieu*, 40-42; *La pouverté*, 51-53; *Per fair tousjours*, 61-63; *Sans siens du mal*, 64-66.

[15] Anonymous pieces in F229 include nos. 30, 91, and 243. Also in F229 as no. 107 is a textless piece by the mysterious composer F. Rubinet. Josquin's *Il fantazies de Joskin*, in RCas without concordances, might also be placed in this category. Imitation in this piece is largely restricted to the discant and tenor, but the long concluding sequence seems related to the tricinia approach.

[16] Hewitt, *Odhecaton*, 74-78.

certainly written with Florentine audiences in mind, between about 1485 and 1490.[17] To the features described by Hewitt may be added further observations. The phrases, as in *Helas*, are usually quite short—except when extended by sequences and repetitive patterns. Cadences are frequent, well defined, and provide an underpinning to the overall tonal design. In *Helas*, for example, all cadences are on F or on C. All voices participate in the contrapuntal interplay. While each voice assumes its own role in cadences (i.e., the bass functions as a harmonic bass), all parts share equally in the melodic material—this last feature more than any other serves to distinguish the style from the chanson approach as known up to 1480.[18]

Helas introduces another element that seems to run through other pieces in the tricinia repertory, in that Isaac's setting represents a reworking of an earlier piece, Caron's *Helas que pourra devenir*. Howard Brown observed that Isaac's setting of *La martinella* in F229 also represents a fantasia on Martini's original.[19] As we shall see, this notion of reworking continued to fascinate Isaac as he turned increasingly to composition in four parts.

Isaac produced by far the most authoritative examples of tricinia up to about 1490. After about 1490 other composers appear to have worked with the tricinia approach. The most successful was Josquin des Prez, with the masterful *La bernardina*, but this piece made its first appears in contemporary sources in Petrucci's *Canti C* of 1504. At least two other Josquin pieces might be added: *Cela non plus* and the three-part version of *Si j'ay perdu*.[20] Neither of these is in sources from before

---

[17] For the sources of *Helas*, see Howard M. Brown, *A Florentine Chansonnier from the Time of Lorenzo the Magnificent. Florence, Biblioteca Nazionale Centrale MS Banco Rari 229* (Chicago: University of Chicago Press, 1983), 1: 209; for an edition, 2: 111-13; for the sources for *La morra*, 1: 211-13, for an edition, 2: 23-25.

[18] For additional examples by Isaac which would appear to be tricinia, see Brown's version of *La Martinella* (no. 192 in F229) and the textless pieces, nos. 230 and 253, also in F229. *Adieu fillette* is another, though known only from later sources (see Martin Picker, *Henricus Isaac: A Guide to Research* (New York and London: Garland, 1991), p. 100 for sources and editions), Note that the widely circulated *Benedictus* (probably first written as the *Benedictus* for the *Missa Quant j'ay au cor*), while it has some of the features of Isaac's tricinia, does not quite fit the tricinia pattern as seen in *Helas* and *La morra*. There is no firm division, for example, at roughly the midpoint. Similarly the textless piece included as no. 16 in F229, which is the *Christe* from the *Missa Chargé de deul*, also differs—it is, for example, a distinctly shorter piece. Similarly, another piece probably also from an unknown Mass is the item numbered 140 in F229. It should also be noted that some of Isaac's three-part pieces are more in the traditional mold. In the setting of *My My* in F229, for example, imitations are often restricted to the discant and tenor. The textless items numbered 249 and 251 as well as the *Serviteur suis*, all in F229, are written in the same vein. As this effort was in final proofs an article appeared by Warwick Edwards, "Isaac's Pre-Italian Songs: An Over-Optimisitic Hand-List," in *Essays on Renaissance Music in Honour of David Fallows; Bon jour, bon mois et bonne estrenne*, ed. Fabrice Fitch and Jacobijn Kiel (Woodbridge, Suffolk: The Boydell Press, 2011), 198-206. The subject of Edwards's article concerns the potential repertory that Isaac brought with him as he arrived in Florence in 1484/5, including the three pieces mentioned immediately above.

[19] Brown, *A Florentine Chansonnier*, 92-93; Brown also points out that a second setting of *La martinella* by Martini himself is itself a fantasia on his own original, 93-94.

[20] For editions of the pieces and a review of the sources, see David Fallows, ed., *Secular Works for Three Voices*, The New Josquin Edition 27 (Utrecht: Vereniging voor Nederlandse Muziekgeschiedenis, 1987). For reference to another three-part piece, *Il fantazies de Joskin*, see note 15 above.

1500; in fact, all of Josquin's mature tricinia seem to have been composed distinctly after 1490—i.e., Josquin may well have been following the model laid out by Isaac. Similarly, pieces by other composers, such as Ghiselin's *La alphonsina* and *La stanghetta* (perhaps by Weerbeke), also seem to have been composed after 1490.[21] Obrecht did not explore this approach in any substantive way. In fact, of thirty-four works included in the *New Obrecht Edition* of secular works, only nine are for three parts.[22] He certainly drew on features similar to those employed by Isaac—sequence for example, and phrases based on short fragmentary melodic ideas in imitation. Still, he did not produce any pieces that fit into the tricinia mold. His closest piece was perhaps his setting of *Tandernaken*, which is laced with sequences, short motives that are passed back and forth, and has a rhythmic liveliness much like that found in many tricinia. *Tandernaken*, however, is clearly a cantus firmus piece, and is tied to a very different strain of composition. Moreover its earliest main source is the *Odhecaton*, meaning that it while it might have been written earlier, it cannot be securely placed before the late 1490s.[23] Agricola, in such pieces as *Jay beau huer* and *A la mignonne*, would exceptionally approach the tricinia style—and was doing so by the mid-1480s.[24] As discussed above, however, the taut structure of such pieces as Isaac's *Helas* or Josquin's *La bernardina* was evidently not congenial to Agricola's interest. Most of his pieces produce a very different effect. One reservation in this potentially clear picture—some pieces which can well be included as tricinia, and are contained in the complex of manuscripts of *ca.* 1490 are anonymous. *La taurina* (in BQ16) is a particularly good example.[25]

In about 1490, in a startling move, Isaac seems to have abandoned the tricinia style almost completely, a course of events that can be followed clearly in contemporary sources. After relocating in 1496 to serve with Maximilian I at the Habsburg court, Isaac turned to four-part writing. Of some thirty-six pieces by Isaac in sources before 1496, only eight are in four parts. Of his German pieces, i.e., those based on German-texted songs and written after 1496, the figures are in essence reversed. Of the three-part German pieces, only *Der hund* is related to the tricinia style.[26] The others are mostly based on sacred tunes and represent a quite

---

[21] In Hewitt, *Odhecaton*, 325-27 and 387-88.

[22] Leon Kessels and Eric Jas, eds., *New Obrecht Edition*, vol. 17, Secular Works and Textless Compositions (Utrecht: Koninklijke Vereniging voor Nederlandse Muziekgeschiedenis, 1997).

[23] For a brief listing of the *Tandernaken* sources and settings, see Fallows, *A Catalogue*, 485-86. Note that the version which appears in Maastricht, Rijksarchief van Limburg, unnumbered musical fragments, fols. 26v-27, is actually drawn from the *Odhecaton*. In fact one other piece by Obrecht does incorporate tricinica-like elements: *Si sumpsero*, for which the earliest source is Petrucci's *Canti B* (see Helen Hewitt, ed. *Ottaviano Petrucci, Canti B, Numero Cinquanta, Venice, 1502* (Chicago and London: University of Chicago Press, 1967), 73, for a list of concordant sources). This piece was evidently designed as a motet, and in any case occurs in no sources before 1500.

[24] Both were included in F229; see Brown, *A Florentine Chansonnier*, nos. 127 and 174.

[25] The piece is in BQ16; see Fallows, *A Catalogue*, 532.

[26] For information on this piece, see Martin Picker, *Henricus Isaac*, 111-12.

different repertory than that of the tricinia. In Italian sources after *ca.* 1490, only *Adieu fillette*, in Petrucci's *Canti B*, continues in the three-part tradition.[27]

By 1500 most composers placed their primary focus in secular music on textures calling for four and more parts. Composers continued to write from time to time for three parts, but when they did so they were usually writing pieces which were clearly designed to be sung, often by non-professionals. The period of intense interest in what we have termed the fifteenth-century tricinia was a scant fifteen years. Then the style vanished, disappearing almost completely from the repertory soon after the turn of the century.

Isaac after 1490—The New Four-Part Vocabulary

While composers focused their main efforts in secular music on three-part textures until well into the 1480s, at about the same time that Isaac was cultivating the tricinia approach, he, and other composers as well, also turned increasingly to writing in four parts. This move is more complicated than that involved with the development of the tricinia style in that more composers are involved in more complex ways. Still, the picture for Isaac is relatively clear. F229 provides a reliable snapshot of how he focused his energies in his first years in Florence. The numbers tell the story. The manuscript opens with a kind of dialogue between Isaac and Martini, with nine pieces by Isaac, of which only three are in four parts. This reflects roughly the balance of his pieces in this collection as a whole, with eight pieces for four parts from a total of about twenty-five (the total is only approximate because of conflicting attributions).

Isaac from the very beginning seems to have arrived at an approach which he would continue subsequently. With *Mon pere m'a doné mari* (the fourth piece in F229), for example, Isaac has set a popular chanson. With this piece, and others like it, he has moved firmly beyond the fixed forms. The shape of this piece is cast as an A-B-A' with the opening section repeating (with slight variation) at the end. Phrases are concise, and cadences are frequent. The texture is imitative throughout—though imitations are often limited to discant and tenor. The closing A section presents an altered, but clearly recognizable version of the opening material, and moves to a short coda-like section which brings the piece to a firm close. Most of Isaac's early four-part settings appear to be based on popular French chansons.[28] Another well-known and masterful example is *E qui la dira*, which Petrucci included in the *Odhecaton*. This piece, as *Mon pere*, is based on a popular chanson, and it, too is in an A-B-A' form. It opens with the lower voices paired in imitation, answered by the upper two. This highly articulated structure is made even more emphatic as

---

[27] Hewitt, *Ottaviano Petrucci, Canti B*, no. 44, 79-80; 218-220.

[28] An exception is the curious but highly effective *Donna di dentro/Dammene un pocho/Fortuna d'un gran tempo*, also in F229. The first section of the piece is built around three different melodic ideas, though those of *Dammene un pocho* and *Fortuna* are the most prominent. The final segment of the piece (mm. 54-74 in Brown, *A Florentine Chansonnier*, II: 319-20) is a demonstration of Isaac's complete mastery of equal-voiced imitative counterpoint, based on the *Dammene* motive.

the opening section is repeated at the end (again with slight variation). The middle segment is, as was the case in the previous example, very short, here consisting of only two phrases (both in paired imitation, though here too slightly varied).

The shift in Isaac's interest to fuller textures is emphatically revealed in his settings of German songs—which we can assume were written after 1496. Of some thirty-eight pieces based on German texts, thirty-two are for four parts. These vary considerably in style; some are more homophonic settings of German melodies, usually in bar form, as in the setting of *Kein frewd*. Among the homophonic settings, although unusual both in its form and in placing the melody in the discant voice, is of course, the wonderfully expressive *Innsbruck, ich muss dich lassen*. More often the structures were more elaborate, involving chains of imitative phrases, sometimes with fascinating structures of altered repetitions, as in *Geiner, zancker, schnöpffitzer*. Isaac continued his interest in "fantasy" as seen in the settings of *In meinen sinn* (*In meinen sinn* I, appears to be a reworking of *In meinen sinn* II).[29] Probably the most intriguing aspect of Isaac's four-part writing, and perhaps ultimately the most important, is that he would from time to time introduce a melodic idea at the beginning of a piece, and this idea, or a motive drawn from it, would be reworked throughout the piece. Hints of this occur perhaps earlier, with Compère in his *Mes pensées*, for example, but Isaac would appear to be the first composer who placed this usage front and center. The approach fits with what Joshua Rifkin has described as "motivicity," that is, the "permeation of a polyphonic complex by a single linear denominator or set of denominators."[30] Both *La, la, hö, hö* and *Donna di dentro* show such organization, as does his masterful fantasy *La mi la so*. This would apparently reveal a maturing of Isaac's compositional process, as motivicity of this manner does not occur in his three-part, and presumably earlier, pieces. In any event, the sources reveal clearly that Isaac had made his first steps toward a modern approach to four-part composition probably in the late 1480s—and no later than 1490. In the 1490s he turned almost exclusively to writing in four and more parts.[31]

In assessing the significance of Isaac's shift to writing for four parts, we do need to bear in mind two points that were raised by Joshua Rifkin in his reading of a draft of this article. The first is that, in Rifkin's view, the essential shift was from the exploration of a vocabulary associated with one kind of piece ("instrumental chansons" in three parts) to quite a different vocabulary—an entirely separate compositional approach tied to a different genre (the "popular chanson" in four parts). The change was more complicated than simply an abstract interest in

[29] For sources and editions of Isaac's German pieces, see Picker, *Henricus Isaac*, 110-18.

[30] Joshua Rifkin, "Miracles, Motivicity, and Mannerism: Adrian Willaert's *Videns Dominus flentes sorores Lazari* and Some Aspects of Motet Composition in the 1520's," in *Hearing the Motet: Essays on the Motet of the Middle Ages and Renaissance*, ed. Dolores Pesce (Oxford and New York: Oxford University Press, 1997), 244.

[31] For sources and editions of *La mi la so*, see Picker, *Henricus Isaac*, 122; for a commentary on *La, la, hö, hö*, see Martin Staehelin and Eckhard Neubauer, "Türkiscke Derwischmusik bei Heinrich Isaac," *Von Isaac bis Bach: Studien zur älteren deutschen Musikgeschichte; Festschrift Martin Just zum 60. Geburtstag*, ed. Frank Heidlberger, Wolfgang Osthoff, and Reinhard Wiesend (Kassel: Bärenreiter, 1991), 27-39.

working with the potential of four parts. The point is a telling one, for certainly the newer style finds it most striking examples in settings of popular chansons, not in those of fixed form pieces. But as is so often the case, the situation is not completely a matter of black and white contrast. Such four-part pieces as *Je ne [me] puis vivre* (rondeau cinquain) and *Maudit soit* (bergerette) were settings tied to fixed forms. Moreover, *Donna di dentro*, cited above as an example of "motivicity" was obviously based on an Italian text. All three of these pieces are in F229, and represent relatively early examples of Isaac's writing for four parts. As Rifkin observed, however, these are all clearly exceptional pieces. Even with the settings of German texts the situation is blurred. Glog provides a large sampling of repertory, but dates from *ca.* 1480 (and contains no pieces by Isaac). Thereafter the sources are too scanty to provide a clear view. Certainly after about 1495 Isaac's overwhelming interest was in four-parts with German settings—but we have no sure examples of earlier German pieces (if he wrote any). In sum, yes, obviously Isaac's main interest in secular settings after *ca.* 1490 was in working with the potential of four-part composition, but, as Rifkin observed, this shift is a more subtle one than simply an interest in fuller texture. Rifkin's second point concerns to what extent Isaac's move to four parts in secular music is related to his writing of sacred settings, and the sacred settings are, of course, dominated by writing in four parts. This is a more refractory question. The sources for sacred music raise much more difficulty in terms of secure chronology. It is nonetheless true that during the 1480s and early 1490s Isaac certainly composed a vast quantity of motets and Mass settings calling for four parts. Any ultimate evaluation of Isaac's move to fuller textures in secular music will have to take into account how this move relates to his style in sacred compositions.

Before 1490 some composers had already made some moves toward what we might term more modern writing. Busnoys wrote several chansons in four parts—all apparently well before 1490. His *Acordes moy* begins, in fact, in much the same fashion as Isaac's *E qui la dira*—with a pairing of low versus high voices in imitation. While this opening segment creates much the same affect as later pieces—by both Josquin and Isaac—the continuation is, however, more subtly constructed; some imitation does occur, but the emphasis, as is usual for this composer, seems to turn to the spinning out of elegant lines. In short, while Busnoys hinted at the newer approach of through-imitation, he did not carry through in this manner. His interests lay elsewhere. Another striking example is the setting of *Je n'ay dueil* of Agricola. This piece begins with a beautifully constructed opening with imitation in all four parts. The next phrase continues with imitation between tenor and discant—then the texture dissolves into much more dense counterpoint. This presents a kind of curious inverse parallel; Busnoy's *Accordes moy* is a four-part piece which plays with imitation, but probably dates from late in his career, and is an exception among many pieces without any systematic use of this texture. Agricola's *Je n'ay dueil* is a similar piece which plays with imitation, but oddly dates from very early in his career. After this his interest was drawn in other directions.[32] Neither figure prominently in the exploitation of the potential of melodically interrelated contrapuntal voices which characterizes the period from 1485 to the end of the century and beyond.

Three other composers remain to be taken into account. Compère presents an odd case in that some of his earlier pieces were circulating in Italy by 1480, and generally his style at that point is more related to that of Busnoys and Hayne than to that which came into vogue in the following decade. Then Compère seems to have begun a move toward a radical style change. Beginning slightly before 1490, he, as was the case with Isaac, began to explore writing secular pieces in four parts. Probably the earliest example was *Ung franc archier*, which was included in F229, as well as in the *Odhecaton*. Imitation figures prominently in the piece, but melodic interplay occurs most often between discant and altus. The tenor and bass share a bit in the imitations, but the bass, especially, largely goes its own way. Still, phrases are short, and the motivic play is transparent.[33] Perhaps slightly later is *Je suis amie du fourrier*, which occurs first in RCG, then in several other sources. The opening begins with systematic imitation through all four parts. In the second half of the piece we see a feature that becomes ever more prominent in Compère's late chansons; the phrases become very short, with a patter effect from quickly repeated pitches. This approach becomes almost a trademark in the later four-part chansons by this composer. An example is *Nous sommes de l'ordre de Saint Babouin* included in the *Odhecaton*. This is an extraordinarily tightly organized piece. All parts share in the imitative interplay. The melodic phrases are distinctly clipped; they barely start when they bump up into a cadence—and many of the endings circle around the same pitch—namely C. In the final phrase all four voices work over a descending four note pattern, G-F-E-D, which is heard some twelve times in the space of four measures (in terms of modern notation).[34] The piece is a charmer: lively, clearly structured, and effective in performance. It is also utterly at odds with pieces written in the 1480s, or even up to the early 1490s. The parallels with Isaac are intriguing. None of their four-part pieces are included in the sources from the mid-1480s (provisionally including RCas, which does include a short section of four-part pieces at the end of the manuscript). In Compère's earlier pieces the four parts were perhaps not quite as smoothly coordinated as was the case with Isaac, but there is no question that by the early 1490s Compère had complete command of imitative technique involving all voices. For all his popularity in Italian sources, there is no evidence to show that Compère was in Italy in the crucial span between about 1485 and 1494. Isaac probably knew the music of Compère as his music was easily available in Florence. Whether Compère was up to date concerning Isaac

---

[32] For sources and editions of these two pieces, see Fallows, *A Catalogue*, 69 and 205. In another parallel, the two pieces are in both F229 and the *Odhecaton*.

[33] Similar in approach is *De les mon getes* (=*Volés oir un chanson*), which is in the apparently slightly later RCG. Note that the observations by Joshua Rifkin noted above in relation to the shift to four parts by Isaac also bears on Compère's similar shift—these new style pieces are an entirely different repertory, based on chansons in a popular style.

[34] Other pieces which draw upon the same devices include *Alons fere nos barbes*, *Gentil patron*, and especially, *Et don revenes vous*, all from sources dating from after 1500.

is an unknown—certainly Isaac's music had limited circulation in the northern manuscripts that have survived. In any case, the evidence would suggest that Compère at this time was likely developing his ideas independent of any direct "Italian" influence.

The stature and influence of Josquin concerning the issue at hand is difficult to assess. If pure numbers are any indication, Josquin was considered a formidable, but not yet a dominant composer in this era. F229 for example includes four of his pieces, compared to twenty-two for Isaac and about twenty for Martini. Similarly RCG includes fifteen pieces by Agricola, twelve pieces by Isaac, and only five by Josquin. F178 is more balanced between Isaac and Josquin with eight pieces each—but with some sixteen by Agricola. Even as late as the *Odhecaton* in 1501, while Isaac and Josquin are roughly evenly distributed with five or six pieces each, Compere and Agricola have more than double those numbers. Moreover, if we consider Josquin's four-part pieces circulating before about 1500, we find a distinctly small number, some six pieces, and most of these tend to recur throughout the sources. *Adieu mes amours* and *Un mousque de Biscay,* for example, are in RCas, and in all three of the sources I have identified as representing repertory *ca.* 1490. Josquin without question had complete control over four-part writing, but, as in *Adieu mes amours* he preferred to anchor his textures around canonic structures. That is, his textures tended to include more free material in the non-canonic voices, and be less transparently imitative than was the case with Isaac as in *E qui la dira* and *Donna di dentro.*

Similarly Obrecht also worked with four parts in secular pieces, but with him, too, pieces associated with the newer style are conveyed for the most part in sources that date after 1500.[35] Perhaps his most effective four-part song is *Tsat een mesken,* for which the earliest source is the *Odhecaton.* It can serve as a catalogue of devices in the new style. It opens with clear four-part imitative counterpoint, with a clearly profiled motive outlining the main triad which forms the tonal center of the piece. It cadences clearly and fairly often, with the slightly unusual feature of a first section being made up of a kind of internal A-B-A form. The final section begins with a contrasting homophonic section in triple meter, then moves to a conclusion with rapidly overlapping contrasts of high and low imitative duets. The piece is based on a borrowed tune placed in the tenor, but the counterpoint is so successfully interwoven that one is scarcely aware that this is a cantus firmus piece. *La tortorella,* which appears in both F229 and RCG, and which may date

[35] For no composer is the source situation more unsatisfactory than for Obrecht. Seventeen of his pieces are in Segovia, Archivo Capitular de la Catedral, Ms. s. s., which dates from the first decade of the sixteenth century. Many of these are not found in any other sources—but some may well have dated from much earlier. Two of his pieces are in RCas, which might tempt one to use the presence of these pieces to bolster an argument that the manuscript dates from after his first visit to Ferrara, in 1487-1488. Yet the absence of *La tortorella* in RCas, Obrecht's only Italian-texted piece, would seem to argue against this. That is, if Obrecht wrote this piece in conjunction with his first stay in Ferrara, as has been suggested, it would seem likely that it would have been included in this collection, which was clearly a representation of the repertory available in Ferrara. More on this point presently.

from Obrecht's visit to Ferrara in 1487-88, features imitation at its opening, but the piece is quite short, only one phrase which is repeated, plus a kind of coda. Probably from slightly later (it is included in RCG), *Wat willen wij* is some ways resembles *Tsat een meskin*, especially the concluding section which is in triple meter with prominent paired imitation between high and low parts. But in this piece the borrowed melody is less integrated than is the case with *Tsat een meskin*. *Lacien adieu* is conveyed in an even earlier source than any of the other four-part pieces (in Glog, which apparently dates from about 1480, though the version in this collection lacks the altus), but it has few of the more advanced features. Imitation is quite limited, and does not permeate all the voices. The most intriguing piece with regard to the present discussion is *Se bien fait*, included among the handful of four-part pieces in the concluding segment of RCas. It is broadly divided into two halves, with three sections in each half. Some level of imitation is incorporated into all segments except the final one (which hinges on the device of sequence). Only in the opening of the second half, however, do all parts share in the imitation. In the others at least one voice goes its own way in free counterpoint. Also, while the melodic phrases tend to be quite short, the piece often avoids strong cadences with the expected root of the chord in the bass (i.e., the endings are often what sound to modern ears either like first-inversion chords, or deceptive cadences on the sixth degree). While Obrecht certainly coordinated all four parts in imitative textures, he did not aim, at least in this early piece, for the taut and directed structures that we find in Isaac's four-part writing.[36]

As with the evolution of the tricinia, though more complex, the crucial years for the development of the concept of four-part, equal-voiced imitative counterpoint in secular pieces appear to be between about 1480 and 1490. Before 1480 composers were certainly aware of the device of imitation, but their textures in secular music were largely three-part and imitation was not incorporated in a consistent, continuous way. By 1490 each of the major composers—Compère, Josquin, Obrecht, and Isaac—were drawing upon imitation as a fundamental structural feature in songs in four (and sometimes more) parts, each in their own way. Compère was moving toward a highly concise formulation, with short motives in highly transparent textures. Josquin preferred the grounding of canonic writing. Isaac preferred an approach in which all parts were more free but interrelated by equally shared melodic material—and he appears to have developed this concept a few years before 1490.

Our evidence is of course incomplete. We have few manuscripts from the north for the critical years of concern here. Still, all the composers considered

---

[36] With *Se bien fait* the dating of the Casanatense manuscript could become crucial. It does seem unlikely that such fully realized four-part imitation could be dated as *ca.*1480 or a few years before— which would be the case if the collection did in fact date from *ca.*1481 as argued by Lewis Lockwood. On the other hand, the absence of *La tortorella*, as mentioned in the previous note might suggest a dating before *ca.*1487. Indeed, the styles and composers which are present, and those which are not (the absence of any pieces by Isaac is particularly striking), would suggest a date of *ca.*1485 or slightly earlier. "Style" and "repertory," however, seem to be potentially so elastic as to provide little secure footing.

in addition to Isaac—Busnoys, Agricola, Compère, Josquin, and Obrecht—are in fact amply represented in the complex of Italian manuscripts from *ca.* 1490. Their music was well known and prized—it is a reasonably safe assumption that pieces written in the north were quickly known in the south. That is, when Isaac began to work out his ideas of four-part writing, the works of Busnoys and Agricola formed a background, but their style was not the one toward which he was moving. He knew music of Compère, Josquin, and Obrecht, but pieces of theirs that he had available, too, were also not yet in the advanced style toward which he was working.

Some conclusions offered here are apparently well founded, while others are more speculative. Concerning the development of the tricinia approach, it would appear that the evidence is reasonably firm. The vocabulary did not exist previous to about 1480—or was at best only hinted at. Johannes Martini established most of the outlines of a new approach evidently about 1480. Isaac, soon after his arrival in Florence, expanded on the potential that he heard, and produced the first true masterworks in tricinia style. He worked extensively with three-part composition between about 1485-90, writing a series of pieces that achieved very wide circulation. In so doing he raised awareness of other composers active in Italy, notably Josquin and Ghiselin, of the potential of the new style, and they in turn also produced tricinia pieces. After 1490 Isaac, if the manuscript evidence is accurate, focused his energies on what he apparently felt was the richer potential available in four-part textures. Busnoys and Agricola perhaps laid the groundwork to a certain extent before Isaac began to emphasize four-part writing. The concept of structures integrated by imitative counterpoint was quickly realized by most of the important composers coming to maturity in the 1480s, but Isaac developed a distinctive, inventive and highly successful approach. This deserves to be emphasized as modern critical commentary often fails to recognize Isaac's versatility and originality. But whether he was "first" may be beside the point. Isaac produced a string of compositions: *Helas, La morra, Et qui la dira, La mi la so,* and, let us not forget, *Innsbruck ich muss dich lassen,* which all have to be counted as masterpieces. If we judge by their success with performers and audiences (and how else should we judge them?), Isaac simply must be included in anyone's list of the greatest composers of the Renaissance.

The Gaglianos:
*Two Centuries of Violin Making in Naples**

Guido Olivieri

For about two hundred years, from the end of the seventeenth century to the mid-nineteenth century, the Gagliano was the most important family of luthiers in Naples. Their art, transmitted from father to son for four generations, practically coincided with the history of violin making in Naples. The exceptional production of these makers, which covers the entire qualitative spectrum from outstanding to rather coarse instruments, was able to compete with the most famous North-Italian schools of violin makers and is still today in high demand.[1]

Violins and cellos made by members of the Gagliano family appear frequently in the lists of important international auctions, side by side with the celebrated instruments of the North-Italian families—Amati, Stradivari, or Guarneri—often attaining rather high prices. A 1709 violin by Alessandro Gagliano at Skinner auction in Boston fetched $205,000 in 2000, while another violin dated 1702 was valued at $204,000 at Christie's last year; a cello by Gennaro Gagliano, dated 1741, even reached the sum of £246,500 at Bonhams.[2] In 2007 a violin by Gennaro Gagliano was sold in London at a new record for that maker of $210,000.[3]

Abbreviations: ASBN: Napoli, Archivio Storico del Banco di Napoli.
ASC: Napoli, Archivio Storico del Conservatorio S. Pietro a Majella.

* This essay gathers the first results of a larger study I am conducting on the life and activity of the Gagliano violin makers. It is my homage to William Prizer's superb scholarship and a small token of appreciation for having been such a rigorous and patient mentor for me. I would also like to thank Timothy McGee and Neal Zaslaw for their invaluable suggestions. At the moment of the revision of this article, I have received news of a paper presented by David Bonsey at the 40th Annual Conference of the American Musical Instrument Society on the Gagliano family. Unfortunately I could not read this paper and I am not aware of the exact content of it.

[1] A recent article underlined the fame and popularity of these instruments stating that "The world is awash in Gaglianos" in Erin Shrader, "Gaglianos Galore," *Strings* 146 (Feb. 2007), 98-101 at 98.

[2] For the Boston's auction see Joanna Pieters, "News & Events," *The Strad* 111, no. 1317, (Jan. 2000), 8. The report on Christie's auction is by Caroline Gill, "Auction Report: New Internationalism," *The Strad* 118, no. 1406 (June 2007), 27. "The main attraction at Bonhams was a magnificent cello, which sold to a well-known musician. This Gennaro Gagliano, Naples 1741, came with an optimistic estimate of £220,000-280,000, and just managed the lower bracket of £220,000 (£246,500 with premium)." Anne Inglis, "Selling Fireworks," *The Strad* 111, no. 1318 (2000), 120.

[3] Caroline Gill, "The Best of Times," *The Strad* 118, no. 1402 (Feb. 2007), 24.

Instruments created by the Gagliano family form part of important collections worldwide. Three violins by Nicola and Giuseppe Gagliano have been acquired by the Royal Academy of Music in London, while other instruments of these makers are preserved in the collections of the Library of Congress, the National Music Museum of the University of South Dakota, and the Smithsonian Institution's Museum of American History, among other institutions.[4]

The irregular proportions adopted in the early instruments by the founding father of the dynasty, Alessandro Gagliano—especially their longer body, a characteristic shared with other South-Italian luthiers—makes some of these instruments more difficult to adapt to modern standards. But their rich tone and powerful voice are much in demand among many performers, particularly those committed to historically-informed performance practice. John Holloway and Fabio Biondi both play violins made by Ferdinando Gagliano in the 1760s; Catherine Mackintosh owns an 1803 Giovanni Gagliano as her modern violin; and Andrew Manze performs in concerts around the world with his 1783 violin by Giuseppe Gagliano, an instrument admired for its clear and sweet tone that he nonetheless describes thus: "of the ones coming out of the Gagliano workshop, this was probably third-rate, a budget violin."[5]

Yet despite all this interest, very little is known of this family of luthiers that dominated the production of violins and cellos in Naples. The activity of many of the Gaglianos – especially that of the earliest representatives – is still shrouded in mystery, while myths and legends characterize the reconstruction of their lives. The information on the careers of some are based solely on the dates recorded on the labels of the instruments they produced. Indeed, even a recent study examining some of the Gaglianos' finest instruments admits that the extraordinary story of this family is still "locked in the Archives of Naples; and likely to remain so, as the city records are notoriously incomplete, thanks to various acts of nature and mankind."[6]

It is perhaps time to shed light on and unveil some of the secrets of these prominent Neapolitan makers. This study presents the first documentary evidence on the activity of the Gagliano family and its relationship with the Neapolitan conservatories in the context of the history of violin-making in Naples in the seventeenth and eighteenth centuries.

---

[4] For the Royal Academy collection see David Rattray and Clarissa Bruce, *Masterpieces of Italian Violin Making 1620-1850: Twenty-Six Important Stringed Instruments from the Collection at the Royal Academy of Music* (London: Royal Academy of Music, 1991). Information on the Smithsonian Museum collection is in Pierre Ruhe, "Preservation or Incarceration?" *The Strad* 108, no. 1291 (Nov. 1997), 1230. For the National Music Museum collection, I have consulted the website at http://www.usd.edu/smm/. Several other instruments by Gagliano are preserved in the collection of instruments of the Conservatorio di S. Pietro a Majella in Naples as well as in numerous private collections.

[5] Catherine Mackintosh states: "My modern violin is an 1803 Giovanni Gagliano and that is fine for Brahms onwards—I just don't use a chin-rest for early 19th-century music and I have gut strings on it." See Jessica Duchen, "Practicing Performance," *The Strad* 106, no. 1261 (May 95): 484. Manze's comment is in Timothy Pfaff, "Masters of Early Music," *Strings* 13, no. 7, issue 77 (April 1999).

[6] John Dilworth, "Like Father, Like Son?" *The Strad* 115, no. 1365 (Jan. 2004), 36-43 at 36.

From its inception the history of violin-making in Naples was influenced by the intersection of two main traits: the presence in the city of workshops established by German makers and the impact of the North-Italian schools of luthiers.

It is well known that in some small German towns of the Bavarian region, especially in and around Füssen, a long tradition of instrument making had flourished since the Middle Ages. In Füssen the first guild of lute makers was already established in 1562, and a vigorous industry of violin making was well developed in the sixteenth and seventeenth centuries. The series of religious wars that ravaged Germany and central Europe in the early seventeenth century led to a rapid decline in the once lively commerce of instruments and to the consequent diaspora of entire families of makers. Although the German makers scattered throughout Europe—among the most famous was the Tieffenbrucker family in Lyon and Paris—many saw Catholic Italy as the safest place for the exercise of their art and a thriving country in which to practice their industry. These makers had a fundamental role in the formation and development of the luthier tradition in Italy. Some of the most important luthiers of the seventeenth and eighteenth centuries in Italy bear German names: a branch of the Tieffenbruckers in Venice and Padua; the Straubs in Milan, Venice, and Modena; Hans Kolb and David Tecchler in Venice and Rome; and Michael Platner in Rome. As in the rest of Italy, the earliest luthiers to establish their workshops in Naples during the first half of the seventeenth century were of German origin. The long list includes at least Matheus Daiser, Jörg Hellmeier, Georg Kaiser, Magnus Lang I, Christoph Railich, Michael Rauscher, Hans Schavitle, Georg Schiessler, Jacob and Michael Stadler, Lukas and Peter Steger, and Jacob Tiefenbrunner in the seventeenth century; and Georg Bairhoff, Thomas Eberle, Josef Joachim Edlinger, Magnus Lang III, Antonio Magnus, and Hans Man in the eighteenth century.[7]

Jörg Hellmeier was among the earliest makers to settle in Naples, dying there in 1626. He was probably a member of the large family of Hollmayr (or Hollmayer), German makers active in various Italian and European centers.

Georg Kaiser, who was originally from Rieden, near Füssen, moved first to Venice and Padua, where he probably worked with Wendelin Tieffenbrucker, and around 1605 arrived in Naples, perhaps together with Magnus Lang I. He was almost certainly a relative of Martin Kaiser, an influential figure in seventeenth-century violin making in Venice from whom Matteo Gofriller learnt his craft.[8] A document of 1615 indicates Georg Kaiser as the maker of an archlute for the use of the Viceroy Don Pedro Fernandez de Castro, Count of Lemos, a member

---

[7] This list, as well as some of the following information is extracted from the fundamental work by Richard Bletschacher, *Die Lauten- und Geigenmacher des Füssener Landes* (Hofheim am Taunus: F. Hofmeister, 1978).

[8] Stefano Toffolo, *Antichi strumenti veneziani 1500–1800: Quattro secoli di liuteria e cembalaria* (Venice: Arsenale editrice, 1987); and John Dilworth, "Fit for a King," *The Strad* 108, no. 1289 (Sep. 1997), 968.

of the Accademia degli Oziosi and one of the most cultured personalities in Naples.[9]

Before the plague that devastated the city in 1656, Jörg Hellmeier, Jacob and Michael Stadler, Georg Kaiser, Matheus Daiser, Magnus Lang, Michael Rauscher, Georg Schiessler, and Lukas and Peter Steger were all working in Naples. They were members of a confraternity established to bring together citizens and craftsmen of German origin that was located in the church of S. Maria dell'Anima dei Tedeschi, donated to the city's German citizens in 1586. According to the statutes of the Confraternita dell'Anima two of the four governors had to be chosen from among the craftsmen members.[10] Jakob Stadler certainly occupied a prominent place in the confraternity, since he was elected six times as governor between 1611 and 1644. Michael Rauscher was governor in 1620 and 1622, while Christoph Railich, member of a family of luthiers well established in Padua, was resident in Naples at least from 1668, where he married one Barbara de Mauro and became governor of the confraternity in 1670 and again in 1671.

It was also common for these craftsmen to establish family ties among themselves. In 1616 Kaiser's daughter Apollonia married Hans Schavitle,[11] another German luthier who on January 13, 1609 had been elected governor of the Confraternita dell'Anima. The luthier Magnus Lang I, born in Schwangau, had worked in Padua between 1597 and 1599, moving then to Naples probably together with Georg Kaiser. Here he was elected three times as governor of the confraternity in 1606, 1618, and 1624. His daughters Angela and Maddalena married, respectively, the makers Georg Schiessler (in 1628) and Matheus Daiser (in 1630).

The presence in Naples of Jacob Tiefenbrunner as a member of the Confraternita dell'Anima in 1667-68 is significant for the liaisons between the Neapolitan and later Mittenwald schools. Indeed, Jacob was probably a relative of Martin Tiefenbrunner, born in 1687 and in turn the godfather of Matthias Klotz, founder of the Mittenwald school.[12]

---

[9] The document is quoted in Gaetano Filangieri *Indice degli artefici delle arti maggiori e minori*, 1: 450, and reprinted in Francesco Nocerino, "Liutai del sedicesimo e diciassettesimo secolo a Napoli: contributi documentari," *Recercare* 13 (2001), 235-47, at 240. For the Count of Lemos see Otis H. Green "The Literary Court of the Conde de Lemos at Naples, 1610-1616," *Hispanic Review* 1, no. 4 (Oct. 1933), 290-308.

[10] A doctoral dissertation is presently in progress at the University of Rome Tor Vergata by Luigi Sisto on the Neapolitan luthiers during the Spanish domination (1503-1707), with the title "Napoli e le origini della tradizione liutaria italiana." Sisto also presented a paper at the annual conference of the Società Italiana di Musicologia in 2007 on "Aspetti sociali e sistema produttivo liutario a Napoli tra Cinque e Seicento. La Confraternita di S. Maria dell'Anima dei Tedeschi: storia, vita sociale, attività corporativa (1586-1717)," which discussed his systematic research of the archival funds of this congregation. The text of this paper was not available to me.

[11] In some documents he is indicated as "Sciaffitel."

[12] We note here that Vannes reports a violin of the Mittenwald school signed "Tentzel Benedikt, Napoli 1717." The Tentzel was in fact a family of luthiers active in Mittenwald in the 18th century. See René Vannes, *Dictionnaire universel des luthiers* (Brussels: Les Amis de la Musique, 1993), 1: 356.

Despite this significant presence of German makers in Naples, which certainly contributed to the birth of a local tradition of violin making, some documents seem to indicate that the production of violins in the early seventeenth century was still very limited and was soon overtaken by the North Italian schools. It seems likely that the best instruments were imported directly from what had already become the most famous school of luthiers in Italy, that of Cremona. Contacts between Naples and Cremona are confirmed as early as the first decades of the century. One of the earliest documents attesting the circulation of violins of Cremonese production dates back to 1620:

> To the Governors of the [Congregation of] Visita Poveri 10 ducats and on their behalf to Filippo Latino, these have been paid for the porterage of eight violins and one bass that he brought from the city of Cremona here to Naples to be used for the music of their conservatory and of this payment he remains satisfied.[13]

An inventory of the instruments owned in 1707 by the first violinist of the Neapolitan Royal Chapel, Pietro Marchitelli, shows that the violins of the Cremonese school were already preferred by the most eminent performers of the time. Marchitelli's collection includes several precious violins from the Amati workshop—here interestingly characterized as "old violins"—together with some other string instruments produced locally by the still today little-known luthiers Mancino and della Rocca:

> Seven old Violins from Cremona by Nicolò, Antonio and Geronimo Amati, three *violette* [violas], another violin by Mancini, one violin by Mr. Franceschino della Rocca, one guitar.[14]

The production of Alessandro Gagliano, the founder of the family dynasty, clearly demonstrates the influence of the two main traditions that coexisted in Naples.

---

[13] "Alli Governatori de Visita Poveri ducati 10 e per loro a Filippo Latino, dite se li pagano per la portatura di otto violini e uno basso che ha condutto dalla città di Cremona qua in Napoli per servizio della Musica del loro Conservatorio e resta sodisfatto." (ASBN, Banco dello Spirito Santo, giornale copiapolizze mat. 148, on January 3, 1620). Quoted in Francesco Nocerino, "Strumenti musicali a Napoli al tempo di Piccinni," in Clara Gelao, Michele Sajous, and Dinko Fabris, eds. *Il tempo di Niccolò Piccinni: Percorsi di un musicista del Settecento* (Bari: M. Adda, 2000), 62.

[14] "Violini di Cremona vecchi di Nicolò, Antonio e Geronimo Amati n. 7, Violette n. 3, altro Violino del Mancini, un Violino del Sig.r Franceschino della Rocca, una Chitarra." Document quoted in Ulisse Prota-Giurleo, "Breve storia del teatro di corte e della musica a Napoli nei sec. XVII-XVIII," in Felice de Filippis and Ulisse Prota Giurleo, *Il teatro di corte del Palazzo Reale di Napoli* (Naples: L'arte tipografica, 1952), 69. Mancino could be possibly identified with or at least related to the luthier Costantino Mancino. The activity of this luthier in the second half of the seventeenth century emerges in a single document of payment for a commission of numerous harmonic tables for the construction of calascioni and guitars: "A Giuseppe Antonio Galdieri ducati 18, tarì 1, grana 10, e per esso a Costantino Mancino a complimento de ducati 51.4.10 atteso l'altri ducati 33.3 l'ha ricevuti contanti, quali ducati 51.4.10 se li pagano per l'intiero prezzo, vendita e consegna fattali di numero 350 tompagni di calascione, e numero 452 detto de chitarra, quale con ditto pagamento resta intieramente soddisfatto e per esso a Pietro de Carluccio per altritanti" (ASBN, *Banco di San Giacomo*, mat. 461, 19 Agosto 1688, c.95); quoted in Nocerino, "Liutai," 242-43.

The earliest violins and cellos made by this luthier show a distinctive style whose model is closer to the German tradition than to the North-Italian one. Indeed this is not surprising considering the history of the Neapolitan tradition of violin making described above. One needs also to take into account that some German luthiers were still active in Naples when Alessandro started his workshop, and that others, such as Georg Bairhoff and Thomas Eberle, probably worked for some time in Gagliano's workshop—to the point that some of their instruments are often mistaken for Gagliano's.

A well-established tradition, however, still considers Alessandro to be a follower of the Cremonese school and more precisely a disciple of Antonio Stradivari. This association has been based essentially on the often unreliable surviving labels placed inside the instruments Alessandro made around 1700, in which he calls himself an "Alumnus Stradivari." To corroborate the belief in Alessandro's apprenticeship with Stradivari is also the story of his flight from Naples to escape punishment for a crime. One of the earliest and most imaginative accounts of this episode describes how the young Alessandro, son of a marquis of the same name, killed a man and was forced to "hide in a dense forest around Mariglianetto Borgo, and there as a pastime he started carving some instruments similar to the shape of violins in the tree trunks he found at hand."[15]

A more credible version was included in 1885 in De Piccolellis's book devoted to the Italian luthiers:

> Alessandro Gagliano was born in Naples around 1640 and since his youth had a passion for the study of music and as a pastime made a few mandolins and lutes, showing a certain predisposition and talent. In the Reign of Naples there existed at that time the deplorable custom of dueling. . . . Alessandro, following the common practice, became a very skilled swordfighter and, as he also had a bold temperament, it was easy for him to get into trouble. Indeed, one evening he was arguing with a young Neapolitan noble of the Mayo family, a very powerful family on account of its friendship with the Viceroy, the Count of Penneranda, when actions proved quicker than words and, swords having crossed, Alessandro's challenger fell dead on the spot. The duel occurred in the small square of Santa Maria La Nuova near the church of the Franciscans that a Bull of Pope Gregorio XIV had made inviolable, like all the other churches in the city. Thus Gagliano, fearing the consequences of his homicide, sought refuge among the friars and asked for their protection. Pennaranda was a strenuous opponent of dueling and was accustomed in such cases to treat it with extreme severity. . . . This was the situation, when it appeared prudent to the Cardinal of Naples, Ascanio Filomarino, who had taken the friars' side, to

---

[15] "… il s'enfonça dans une èpaisse forêt près de Mariglianetto Borgo, et là pour se distraire, il se mit à tailler dans les troncs d'arbre qu'il avait sous la main, des instruments dont la forme ressemblait à celle du violon…" Nikolai Borisovich Youssoupoff, *Luthomonographie historique et raisonnée: Essai sur l'histoire du violon et sur les ouvrages des anciens luthiers célèbres du temps de la renaissance par un amateur* (Frankfurt am Main: Ch. Jügel, 1856), 52.

save Alessandro by arranging his escape. He took all the necessary steps to have him secretly leave the convent, and at night, securely escorted by armed men, he took him to his villa in Mignaniello, from where Alessandro left for Rome. Alessandro moved on and, going from city to city, finally arrived to Cremona. There he had the opportunity to meet Stradivari and, observing the works of this luthier, Alessandro once again became inflamed with a passion for making instruments and entered the workshop of that great master as a pupil. He worked for about thirty years under the guidance of the illustrious luthier and acquired true mastery. Then, after such a long exile, having obtained an official pardon, he left Cremona and in the last days of the year 1695 saw his hometown again.[16]

Although there is no documentary evidence to confirm this legend, its profusion of details suggests that it was copied from a chronicle of the time. A few elements, however, make even this version suspicious. If Alessandro was indeed born in 1640 and the duel took place around 1664—this being the last year of Marquis of Peñaranda's reign—he would have returned to Naples to start up his independent workshop at the age of fifty-five and continued to make violins well into his eighties. Besides considering it unlikely that an artisan could start his activity in his late maturity—what is more, after spending about thirty years in a different city—one must also consider that in the 1660s Stradivari was still at the beginning of his career and therefore far from being the celebrated violin maker that he became later. It is also important to bear in mind that in most of the surviving labels Alessandro

---

[16] "Alessandro Gagliano nacque in Napoli verso il 1640 e fino dai suoi più giovani anni studiò con amore la musica e per diletto si diede a costruire qualche mandolino e qualche liuto, mostrando una certa naturale disposizione ed ingegno. Nel vicereame di Napoli esisteva a quei tempi la funesta piaga dei duellanti [...]. Alessandro, seguendo l'esempio comune, divenne un abilissimo spadaccino ed ebbe inoltre un'indole molto temeraria e tal da doverlo trascinare facilmente a qualche mal passo. Ed in fatti, avendo egli una sera attaccato briga con un nobile napoletano della famiglia Mayo, potente assai per l'amicizia che lo legava al viceré conte Penneranda, furono i fatti più pronti delle parole: ed incrociate appena le spade, il suo avversario cadde ucciso sul colpo. Avvenne il duello nel piccolo largo di Santa Maria la Nuova vicino alla Chiesa dei Francescani, resa inviolabile, come tutte le altre della città, dalla bolla di papa Gregorio XIV, onde il Gagliano, spaventato per le conseguenze che poteva avere tale omicidio, cercò ricovero dai frati, mettendosi sotto la loro protezione, in grazia del diritto d'asilo che essi godevano. Era il Penneranda strenuo persecutore dei duellanti, e soleva in simili casi trattarli con asprissimo rigore. [...] Stavano così le cose, quando parve savio partito al cardinale di Napoli Ascanio Filomarino, che si era mischiato nella faccenda per sostenere i frati, di ridurre in salvo Alessandro colla fuga. Procurò tutti i mezzi acciò segretamente si allontanasse, e nottetempo, con sicura scorta d'armati, lo diresse a Mignaniello in una sua villa, di dove lo fece partire per Roma. Alessandro spinse più innanzi i suoi passi, e di città in città giunse fino a Cremona. Quivi ebbe occasione di conoscere lo Stradivari, ed osservando le opere sue gli si riaccese la passione di costruire strumenti, ed entrò come scolare nella officina di quel grande maestro. Lavorò circa trent'anni sotto la guida dell'illustre liutaio, ed acquistò una vera abilità. Poi, dopo un così lungo esilio, avendo avuta notizia del suo perdono, lasciò Cremona e negli ultimi giorni dell'anno 1695 rivide la sua città nativa." Giovanni de Piccolellis, *Liutai antichi e moderni* (1885) (repr., Bologna: Arnaldo Forni, 1985), 31-32.

Gagliano stated only that he was a follower of Stradivari, without providing any further details. While we may safely assume that these labels referred to the by then famous Antonio Stradivari and were most likely used as an advertising stunt, the discovery of the last will of the celebrated luthier has revealed that his youngest son, Omobono, traveled to Naples probably around 1698 and spent two and a half years there.[17] It is certainly possible that Omobono Stradivari met Alessandro Gagliano and worked with him for a few months, and that this was enough to cause the Neapolitan maker to proclaim himself a disciple of Stradivari.

The lack of documentary evidence makes it extremely difficult to discern any grain of truth behind the legends surrounding the activities of the Gagliano family. However, new documents have emerged during this early stage of my research that provide precise information and firm data about the Gaglianos and their association with the Neapolitan conservatories. The four conservatories in Naples had evolved during the course of the seventeenth century from orphanages into full-fledged music schools. A complex administrative apparatus regulated the organizations of education and saw to the other needs of the *figlioli*, the young boys in training to become professional musicians. From the start these institutions had obviously to resort to luthiers in order to acquire and repair the instruments used by the *figlioli*. Some conservatories employed local makers on an occasional basis, while others, such as the Conservatorio of S. Maria di Loreto, hired them permanently among the official personnel, beginning with makers of harpsichords and organs, and later including makers of the string and wind instruments. Starting in the mid-seventeenth century the names, years of activity, and stipends of these "accomodatori d'istrumenti" were listed in the account books of the conservatories.

The first mention of Alessandro Gagliano appears in the list of the luthiers appointed at the beginning of the eighteenth century. In the *Libro Maggiore* covering the years from 1699 to 1703, the following makers are listed: Felice Cimmino, organ maker, and Matteo Cappello, who "from the first day of April 1699 has again started to serve the Conservatory for all repairs to violas and violins." Cappello worked for the conservatory until September 1701 and was temporarily replaced by Vito Antonio Albanese from March 9, 1702.[18] In June of the same year, Albanese ceded the post to Alessandro Gagliano, who was hired with a salary of 7.2.10 ducats per annum: "Alessandro Gagliano—1703 on 20 May, Ducats 3.3.15 to be paid through the Bank of S. Eligio for six months of salary up to December 11, 1702."[19] (see Fig.1.)

[17] On Stradivari's testament and Omobono's travel to Naples, see Carlo Chiesa and Duane Rosengard, *The Stradivari Legacy* (London: Peter Biddulph, 1998).

[18] It is possible that this maker belonged to a family of luthier of old tradition. An Orazio Albanese was active in Naples as a maker of viols in the second half of the sixteenth century. See Nocerino, "Liutai," 238.

[19] "Alessandro Gagliano -- 1703 @ 20 Maggio Ducati 3.3.15 pagabili per il Banco di S. Eligio per sua provvisione di mesi sei per tutto li 11 di Xmbre 1702 ut supra in esso banco." ASC, Conservatorio di S. Maria di Loreto, *Libro Maggiore* (1699-1703) (III.1.2.20), c. 289.

Figure 1: ASC, Conservatorio di S. Maria di Loreto, *Libro Maggiore* (1699-1703) (III.1.2.20), c. 289. (By kind permission of the Archivio Storico del Conservatorio di S. Pietro a Majella, Naples)

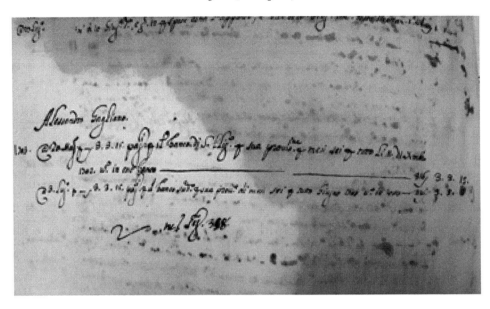

Figure 2: ASC, Conservatorio di S. Maria di Loreto, *Libro Maggiore* (1699-1703) (III.1.2.20), c. 289v. (By kind permission of the Archivio Storico del Conservatorio di S. Pietro a Majella, Naples)

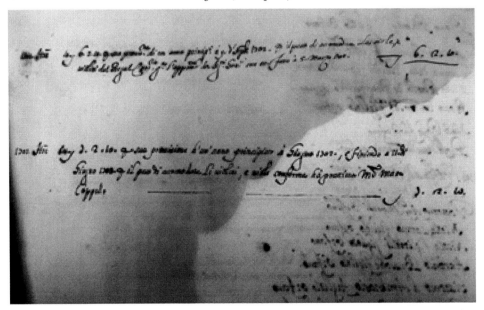

Figure 3: ASC, Conservatorio di S. Maria di Loreto, *Libro Maggiore* (1704-14) (I.22.7), c.358. (By kind permission of the Archivio Storico del Conservatorio di S. Pietro a Majella, Naples)

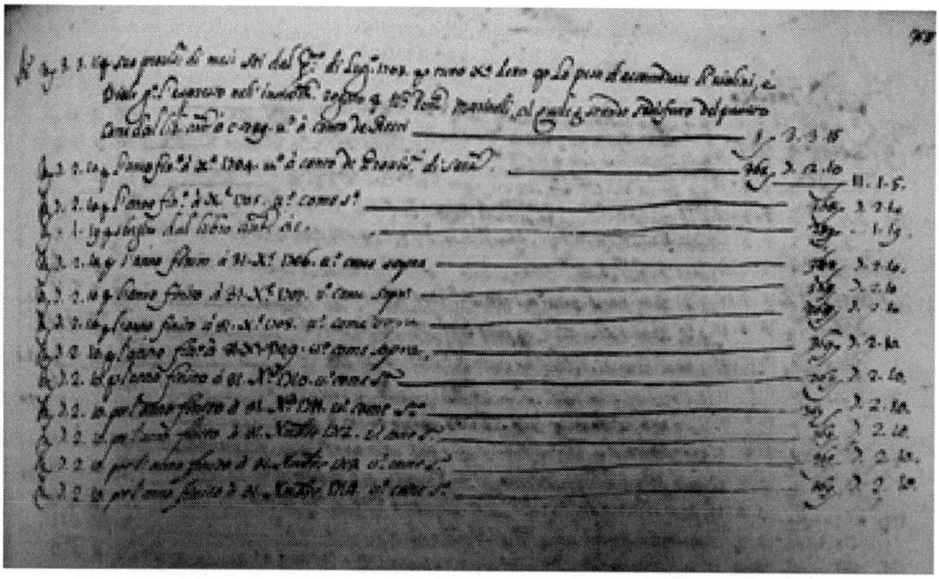

A note on the previous page reiterates that the salary of 7.2.10 ducats is awarded to Gagliano for one year of service "starting in June 1702 and ending on June 11, 1703 with the obligation of repairing violins and violas in the same way as carried out by Master Matteo Cappello."[20] (see Figure 2.)

Gagliano maintains his positions also in the years 1704-14 with the same obligations and an unaltered annual salary. But the *Libro Maggiore* further reveals the existence of a contractual agreement: (see Figure 3 above):

> Ducats 3.3.15 for his six months's salary from July 1 1703 until December of the same year with the obligation to repair the violins and violas according to the contract stipulated by the Notary Domenico Marinelli, to which we make reference, and he remain satisfied of the past, [he accepts] the balance as it appears in the preceding [account] book on c.289.[21]

The activity of Alessandro Gagliano at the Conservatory of S. Maria di Loreto ended in 1722, with the last payment being recorded in December of that year. All biographies place Alessandro's death sometimes between 1725 and 1735.[22]

---

[20] Ibid., c. 289v.

[21] "Ducati 3.3.15 per sua provvisione di mesi sei dal primo di Luglio 1703 per tutto Xmbre detto per lo peso d'accomodare li violini e viole giusta l'espresso nell'istromento rogato per Notar Domenico Marinelli, al quale ut supra stando sodisfatto del passato come dal libro antecedente a c. 289 ut supra a conto de Resti." Ivi, Conservatorio di S. Maria di Loreto, *Libro Maggiore* (1704-14) (I.22.7), c. 358.

[22] Luigi Francesco Valdrighi, *Nomocheliurgografia antica e moderna: ossia Elenco di fabbricatori di strumenti armonici* (1884) (repr., Bologna: Forni, 1967); Giovanni de Piccolellis, Liutai; Willibald Leo

I believe it is unlikely that Gagliano, having worked for about twenty years in the same conservatory, decided to retire from this secure position and either move to another institution or devote himself exclusively to the production of violins in his workshop. If not precisely in 1723, I would estimate the time of Alessandro's death as probably no more than a few years later.

Alessandro's successors at the conservatory of Loreto were three little-known luthiers: Emilio Sfrondato, from May 1723 to April 1726; Michele Sala, from September 1726 to August 1731; and Nicola Vinaccia, from October 1731 to March 1734. The last is the earliest-known member of an important family of instrument makers active in Naples in the second half of the eighteenth century. His name does not appear in any biographical repertory, but an archival document indicates that in the same year (1734), he was employed as a luthier at the Conservatory of Sant'Onofrio a Capuana.[23]

Between May and June 1734 the Gaglianos re-established their supremacy. Alessandro's eldest son, Nicola, probably the most talented member of the family, was hired as luthier at the Conservatory of Loreto. His activity there continued uninterruptedly for the entire period of fourteen years covered by the account book. (See Fig. 4 on p. 374.) It is certain that Nicola Gagliano kept his position at the Conservatory of S. Maria di Loreto for at least another ten years, as it is confirmed by a document dated November 14, 1758:

> Expenditures - To Magnifico Nicola Gagliano for three ducats, grana 3.15 via the Bank of S. Eligio for his salary of 6 months ended this month of November 1758, corresponding to his annual stipend of ducats 7.2.10 for the duty of repairing violins, cellos, and double basses in our Conservatory and Sacred House of Loreto, according to what has been agreed, and he remains satisfied ...[24]

Lütgendorff, *Die Geigen und Lautenmacher vom Mittelalter bis zur Gegenwart* (Frankfurt a.M.: Verlag von Heinrich Keller, 1913); and Henri Poidras, *Critical & Documentary Dictionary of Violin Makers, Old and Modern* (Rouen: Imprimerie de la Vicomté, 1928) all give 1725 as the year of death for Alessandro Gagliano. Vannes, *Dictionnaire*, puts the end of Alessandro's activity around 1728, while Cecie Stainer, *A Dictionary of Violin Makers* (London: Novello,1956) states that Alessandro died in Naples "around 1730." In his recent article "Like Father, like Son?" John Dilworth extends the activity of Alessandro to 1735.

[23] "Ducati 2.2.10 a Mastro Nicola Vinaccia, disse esserno per il semestre maturato alla fine di giugno 1734 per l'accomodi che fa alli Violini, viole, controbasso, ed altro delli figlioli del loro Conservatorio." ASBN, *Banco dei Poveri*, Account 1164, on July 7, 1734; quoted in Paologiovanni Maione, "Le carte degli antichi banchi e il panorama musicale e teatrale della Napoli di primo Settecento," *Studi Pergolesiani* 4 (2000), 1-129, at 76.

[24] "Esito – Magnifico Nicola gagliano per Ducati Tre, grana 3.15 per il Banco di Sant'Eligio per sua provvisione di Mesi 6 finidi nel corrente Mese di 9mbre 1758, alla ragione di ducati 7.2.10 l'anno per lo peso d'accomodare li Violini, Violoncelli e Contrabassi del nostro Real Conservatorio e Casa Santa di Loreto, giusta il convenuto, e resta sodisfatto [...]. ASC, Conservatorio di Santa Maria di Loreto, *Giornale dell'Introito et Esito* (1758-1762), c.37r. The document is published in Tommasina Boccia, "Documenti e regesti", in *Il museo della musica. Guida alla mostra*, ed. Luigi Sisto, Emanuele Cardi, and Sergio Tassi (Naples: Accademia organistica campana, 2002), 27. I am grateful to Luigi Sisto for making available this material.

Figure 4: ASC, Conservatorio di Santa Maria di Loreto, *Libro Maggiore* (1715-48), [I.23.3], ff. 183 r-v. (By kind permission of the Archivio Storico del Conservatorio di S. Pietro a Majella, Naples).[25]

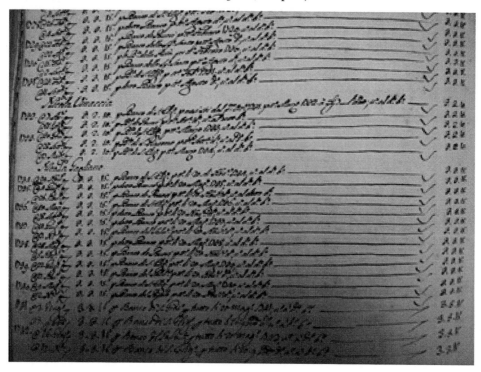

Nicola was also active as a luthier at the Conservatorio dei Poveri di Gesù Cristo around the same time. The documents related to the expenses for this conservatory in 1742 include the indication of a regular salary paid to "Nicola Cagliano" [*sic*] as *maestro* in repairing all the string instruments of the conservatory and other related duties for 8 ducats a year.[26] Another document in the same book records a payment for 1 ducat to "Mastro Nicola Cigliano" [*sic*] to repair a cello completely broken ("*rotta é tutta scassata*") of one of the *figlioli*.

The association of the Gagliano family with the Neapolitan conservatories extended over the entire eighteenth century and beyond. Some documents of the early-nineteenth century confirm that, even after the suppression of the four old conservatories and the creation of the Real Collegio di Musica a San Sebastiano, the Gaglianos remained the luthiers of choice. A list of all the repairs to the violins

---

[25] ASC, Conservatorio di Santa Maria di Loreto, *Libro Maggiore* (1715-48), [I.23.3], cc. 183r-v.

[26] "A di. d.o [Dec. 31, 1742] al Sig. Nicola Cagliano Maestro di Accomodare tutti li Istrum[en] ti di corde della Casa e Altro D. 8 per l'annata finita ut supra -----8." Naples, Archivio Storico Diocesano, Conservatorio dei Poveri di Gesù Cristo, *Libro d'Esito* (1742) [D51], f. 49v.

and bows of the students of the conservatory made between January and March 1816 bears the signature of Giuseppe Gagliano,(see Figs. 5 & 6 on p. 376), the second son of Nicola. This is clear evidence that Giuseppe was still active at the beginning of the nineteenth century, although apparently not as a violin maker.[27]

A later resolution of July 12, 1831 by the administration of the (now) Real Collegio di Musica rewarded a different member of the Gagliano family for his work in the manufacture and repair of instruments: "We pay to Antonio Gagliano 30 ducats and 14 grana for the cost of a violin and other new pieces made for the violin, cello, and double bass of this Collegio, in accordance with the estimate for this amount provided by Maestro Cerretelli."[28] The luthier named here is either Nicola's third son — who often collaborated with his brother Giuseppe on the manufacture of violins — or, more likely, Nicola's grandson, who belonged to the last generation of violin makers bearing this surname. Both Raffaele and Antonio, sons of Giovanni Gagliano, the last child of Nicola, started their activity as makers of violins in the family workshop, but their instruments are often of inferior quality, and they soon confined themselves to the production of strings for instruments.

By the mid-nineteenth century, the long tradition of the Gagliano family that started with Alessandro had been irreparably lost, but this family of violin makers had left its mark in the development of a Neapolitan school of luthiers: a school that created some of the finest instruments of the eighteenth century, still regarded as models by subsequent generations of luthiers inside and outside Naples.

---

[27] The two leaves are in ASC, Real Conservatorio di S. Sebastiano, Vol. Florimo, *Rari* 19.9, doc. 133. Many thanks to Dr. Tommasina Boccia, head archivist of the Conservatory, for pointing out this document to me.

[28] "Pagansi ad Antonio Gagliano ducati trenta et grana 14 per importo di un violino ed altri pezzi nuovi datti ai violini, violoncello, e contrabasso di questo Collegio, giusta la nota valutata per detta somma dal Maestro Cerretelli." ASC, Serie Amministrazione, Sottoserie Deliberazioni, *Registro delle Deliberazioni della Commissione Amministrativa del Real Collegio di Musica (8 gennaio 1831 – 27 Dicembre 1836)*, f. 13v. The document is reproduced in Boccia, "Documenti," 29.

Figs. 5-6: ASC, Real Conservatorio di S. Sebastiano, Vol. Florimo,
Rari 19.9, doc. 133. (By kind permission of the Archivio Storico del
Conservatorio di S. Pietro a Majella, Naples)

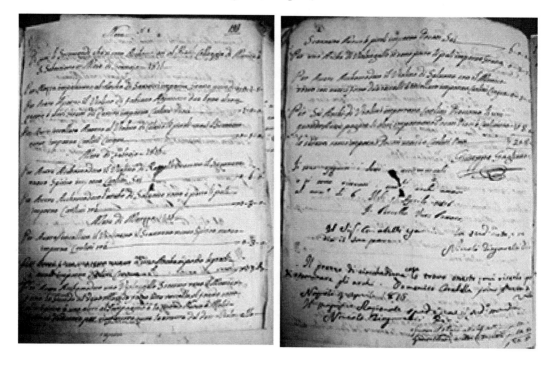

Jesuits and Music – Between the Periphery and the Center:
The City and the Jungle
T. Frank Kennedy, S.J.

Bernardus valles, montes Benedictus amabat;
Oppida Franciscus, sed magna Ignatius urbes.[1]

Bernardo loved the valleys, Benedict the mountains,
Francis the towns, but Ignatius the great cities.

—A Proverb

In the past thirty years scholars of the early modern period have turned to study an organization founded at the beginning of the period, one that almost from its inception established itself as a global organization: the Society of Jesus. Part of the success of the Jesuit enterprise stemmed from the ability of the Jesuits to present themselves through an international propaganda that allowed them flexibility and success in whatever culture they entered into. The Jesuits were above all others the ones who sold the image of themselves as those who lived and worked in the large cities, as the opening proverb expresses. But the fact is the order, though certainly well established in central institutions, never limited itself to those large cities. The Jesuits loved that image, but the reality was more complicated by its larger sense of mission, sometimes referred to as "Our Way of Proceeding."[2] If the principal insight of post-modernism is that there is essentially neither time nor place, nor narrative, nor historical events that are meaningful, what is left is the fact that all human beings of all time and all places are made up of the same stuff: intelligence, feelings, and a sameness that links all people of all time to one another.

I would like to propose and develop the hypothesis that the Jesuits, in their incredibly varied attempts to work for the care of souls, were captivated by the principal insight gleaned from the Spiritual Exercises of St. Ignatius that the

---

[1] This ancient proverb recurs throughout the existence of the Jesuit order. See John Padberg, "How We Live Where We Live," *Studies in the Spirituality of Jesuits* 20, no. 2 (1988), 29.

[2] "Nuestro modo de proceder" is the usual Spanish rendition of this phrase. See Marc Fumaroli, "The Fertility and the Shortcomings of Renaissance Rhetoric: The Jesuit Case," in *The Jesuits, Cultures, Sciences, and the Arts: 1540-1773*, John W. O'Malley, S.J., Gauvin Alexander Bailey, Steven J. Harris, and T. Frank Kennedy, S.J., eds. (Toronto: University of Toronto Press, 1999), 90-106.

love of God is present and manifested in all things. In a sense I am reducing a very complex unfolding of the history of the order to a single perspective, but nevertheless a perspective that sheds light on a search, a journey, a way of being perhaps, that for Jesuits implied a continual testing of their decisions. There seems to be an end product in this constant effort at discernment that resulted rather consistently in what we might now call the creation of culture. Whether or not the Jesuits were aware of it, they became creators of local culture that for them revealed an understanding of the human person that was as true in the Jesuit enterprise in Rome, Spain, Germany, and the rest of Europe, as it was in Brazil, China, Manila, New France, or Paraguay. Scholars know now that music was part of this enterprise in an ever-increasing manner, and indeed it may represent for us a model of the Jesuit enterprise in the early modern period.

This musical tradition not only amply characterized Jesuit chapels and colleges in Europe, but also throughout the far-flung mission lands of the "Old Society."[3] So not only in the great cities, but also the towns, villages, and remote missions – what the Jesuits accomplished in the large cities served as a complex paradigm to all the places the Jesuits were sent. What one discovers in the extant musical repertory is a continuous process of reconciliation, that is, a continuous representation through the music of the eternal questions of human identity. To use music as a paradigm for understanding what the Jesuits were doing, one needs first of all to focus on what the word "mission" meant to Jesuits of the "Old Society."[4] Today everyone has a mission statement, but the term mission was not generally used in the contemporary sense until the sixteenth century. In the early modern period the word recovered its more ancient apostolic/scriptural meaning. Before the sixteenth century the contemporary meaning of mission was conveyed by other terms and phrases like 'propagation of the Faith' or 'journeying to the Infidel.' The Latin Vulgate Bible uses the word *missio* in connection with the apostles and disciples of Jesus, but by the Middle Ages 'missions' almost exclusively referred to relations that were internal to the Holy Trinity – missions by then were part of a technical theological vocabulary. The Jesuits were among the first to inaugurate the new, or rather, revived apostolic usage, and were responsible for its widespread propagation.

In the "Formula of the Institute,"[5] the Jesuit's earliest document of approval of 1540, the first Jesuits spoke of this aspect of their goals as 'propagation of the faith' but later in the same document used 'missions' in the same regard.

---

[3] See for bibliography on Jesuits and music, T. Frank Kennedy, "Jesuits (Society of Jesus),"in *The New Grove Dictionary of Music and Musicians*, 2nd ed, Stanley Sadie, ed. (London: Macmillan, 2001), 13: 19-21. Most recently see O'Malley, *et al, The Jesuits, Cultures, Sciences, and The Arts, 1540-1773.* In volume I, see articles by Paulo Castagna, T. Frank Kennedy, Margaret Murata, and William J. Summers; in volume II, see articles by David Crook, T. Frank Kennedy, Franz Körndle, and Víctor Rondón.

[4] The "Old Society" refers to the order's existence previous to its suppression in 1773 and its consequent restoration in 1814.

[5] See "Formulas of the Institute of the Society of Jesus, Approved and Confirmed by Popes Paul III and Julius III," in *The Constitutions of the Society of Jesus and Their Complementary Norms* (Saint Louis: The Institute of Jesuit Sources, 1996), 3-14.

In subsequent years in their correspondence among themselves, they employed 'mission,' 'journey,' and 'pilgrimage' almost as synonyms to designate travel for the sake of ministry. Ten years after the first approbation of Paul III, Ignatius had substantially completed the 'Constitutions' of the order in which he wrote about "the distribution of the members in the vineyard of the Lord" where the word 'missioned' (being sent) emerged with prominence. Mission was now well on its way within the Society of Jesus to acquiring its contemporary meaning.

In the autumn of 1995, during a conversation with Madame Catherine Massip, the librarian of the Music section of the Bibliothèque Nationale in Paris, we both wondered why all the music manuscripts and prints associated with the pre-Suppression Society of Jesus had disappeared. Musicologists had recovered lots of documentary evidence about the rich musical tradition of the old Jesuit Colleges and chapels by then, but little of the music itself. At the time, we were in fact discussing the autograph manuscript of the Johannes Kapsberger opera of 1622, the *Apotheosis of Saints Ignatius and Francis Xavier*, which somehow found its way into the holdings of the Bibliothèque Nationale, and to my knowledge is the first complete score of any Jesuit opera to be rediscovered.[6] Soon thereafter, in 1996, the first recording of a small chamber opera, *San Ignacio*, from the Jesuit Missions of Paraguay appeared. It was reconstructed and teased out of a collection of manuscripts discovered in the remote Bolivian town of Concepción.[7] Now, twelve years later, a number of musicologists are gradually and painstakingly recovering the musical notation of the Jesuit enterprise.[8]

Embedded within the Jesuit references to music, art, poetry, and rhetoric one can see evidence of this vision. Overarching, macrocosmic themes in the construction of the ecclesial community are evident in the microcosm of the everyday culture of, for example, the indigenous townships of Latin American, but not only there. Theses themes are also evident in the order's center in Rome, in court culture of seventeenth- and eighteenth-century China as well as in the outreach to the Abenaki Indians in New France, to name but a few homes of the Jesuits. There is not essentially a difference between a Jesuit mission in Rome or

---

[6] *Apotheosis sive consecratio SS. Ignatii et Francisci Xaverii*, Bibliothèque Nationale, Département de Musique, Res. F. 1075. See also Franz Körndle, "Between Stage and Divine Service: Jesuits and Theatrical Music," in O'Malley *et al.*, *The Jesuits, Cultures, Sciences and the Arts, 1540-1773*, II: 479-97, in which Körndle discusses some polyphonic choruses by Lassus used in one of the Munich Jesuit dramas of 1577.

[7] The score for the San Ignacio was prepared by Bernardo Illari of the College of Music, University of North Texas at Denton. It remains unpublished. Both the *Apotheosis* and the *San Ignacio* have been released on Dorian Recordings #DOR-93243. The Dorian Recordings catalogue can be seen at www.dorian.com or info@dorian.com. The third opera discussed here, the *Patientis Christi memoria*, is also recorded on DVD and is included in the publication of *The Jesuits, Cultures, Sciences and the Arts, 1540-1773*, II, appendix 1.

[8] Paulo Castagna of the University of Sao Paulo, Brazil; Bernardo Illari from the University of North Texas; Victor Rondón from the University of Santiago, Chile; Franz Körndle of the Hochschule für Musik Franz Liszt in Weimar; and David Crook from the University of Wisconsin.

the rest of Europe, in New France, in China, or in Paraguay. For the Society of
Jesus there cannot really be a distinction between Jesuit art, Jesuit music, Jesuit
culture. There is only art for mission, music for mission, poetry for mission. It also
makes little difference where this all takes place—the great cities for sure, but just
as important were the mission townships and the mission journeys, whether in
Europe or elsewhere. From whatever perspective one enters into a consideration
of the Jesuit enterprise, the essential is present, but the degree of adoption and
accommodation for the particular situation is what may be different, normally only
slightly so.

Music was part of the Society's earliest works: certainly music in Jesuit
churches, but even more especially so in the colleges and missions, and it is most
especially connected with both the dramas and the public defenses of theses in
philosophy and theology.[9] I would like to consider three different operas from quite
different times and places that were all part of the Jesuit enterprise and which
exemplify the way Jesuits used music in their mission. We can also learn from these
three pieces a bit about music history and repertory. The first is one of the earliest
operas in the repertory, first performed in 1622 at Rome. The second is a chamber
piece intended for Holy Saturday, 1685, from the Royal College of Vienna. The
third is a small chamber opera from the Famous Jesuit Reductions of Paraguay,
around 1740 or so.[10]

In March 1622, as part of a week-long celebration of the canonization of
Ignatius and Francis Xavier, three dramas were performed at the Roman College,
one of them completely set to music, thus forming part of the development of
opera, that most baroque of musical forms. The title—*Apotheosis or Consecration of
SS. Ignatius and Francis Xavier*—refers to the ancient Roman practice of deifying
its heroes. The city of Rome suggests in the opera that the youths of the Roman
College perform the same rite for these two new saints. The music is in very early
Italian Baroque style and makes use of recitative, arioso or *mezz'aria*,[11] or simple
homophonic, madrigal-like dance choruses. The score has survived in one principal

---

[9] See especially T. Frank Kennedy, "Some Unusual Genres of Sacred Music in the Early Modern
Perio: The Catechism as a Musical Event in the Late Renaissance," in *Early Modern Catholicism: Essays
in Honor of John W. O'Malley, S.J.*, Kathleen M. Comerford and Hilmar M. Pabel, eds. (Toronto:
University of Toronto Press, 2001), 266-79, Paulo Castagna, "The Use of Music by the Jesuits in the
Conversion of the Indigenous Peoples of Brazil," in O'Malley *et al.*, *The Jesuits, Cultures, Sciences and
the Arts,*, 641-58; and Antony John, Louise Rice, and Clare Woods, eds. Domenico Allegri, *Music for
an Academic Defense* (Rome, 1617), Recent Researches in the Music of the Baroque Era 134 (Madison,
Wisconsin: A-R Editions, Inc., 2004).

[10] In addition to the previously mentioned two works in notes 6 and 7, the third work is the *Patientis
Christi memoria*, by Johann Bernard Staudt. The manuscript has two numbers MS 3887 and Mus.Hs.
18874, and is held in the Handschriften section of the Nationalbibliothek, Vienna rather than the
Musiksammlung.

[11] Domenico Mazzochi, in his description of the *mezz'arie* included at the end of the printed score of
his 1624 opera *La catena d'Adone*, states that an aria ought to be characterized by either by its strophic
nature, or by it lyricism. If it should lack one or the other of these characteristics, then Mazzocchi
would call it a *mezz'aria*.

source, an autograph manuscript in Paris.[12] Dramatic interest is held and reinforced by means of the strong visual character of the work and the structure of the music rather than by strong dramatic action. The musical structure is intensely regular, making use of a declamatory style in solos and choruses that seems to lack color on paper, but springs to life through timbral contrasts effected by the various continuo instruments: strings, organ, regal, harpsichord, virginal, lute, theorbo, harp, and Baroque guitar, as well as through appropriate ornamentation of the vocal line which often exhibits aria-like tunefulness. The rhythms of the choral writing, as well as the instrumental numbers, clearly define the many dance movements of the opera that are so essential to the spectacle. Dramatically and musically speaking, this work is a hybrid; it was obviously composed for a particular occasion, but represents a unique contribution to the development of opera as a form, precisely because of its combination of genres. The music and the drama combine to exude a didacticism so typical of the spirit of the Counter Reformation, yet it reaches beyond mere catechetical concerns in order to effect a new blending or reconciliation of Christian and Classical cultures.

This reconciliation of Christian and Classical cultures may offer some clues as to the meaning of this work, or at least may be the key to understanding why the Jesuit rhetoricians wrote pieces like the *Apotheosis*. In the first place, it is clear that the authors of the *Apotheosis*, as well as the other Jesuit dramas of the late sixteenth and early seventeenth century, were humanists, imbued with that Renaissance tradition which highly valued the classical tradition of drama and poetry, of philosophy, and moral values. What is also evident, though, is a special Jesuit spin on the humanist tradition, one that calls for a slightly different view. Though this work clearly partakes of the mission of the Jesuits, in a large city—Rome, perhaps the most important one for the Jesuits—it is more than a kind of blessing of pagan culture by means of the symbolizing inherent in the artistic enterprise. Actually it is a much more profound affirmation, one that clearly celebrates the human experience that is music, dance, poetry, and theater.

The *Apotheosis* represents a philosophy, no doubt stemming from Aristotle, that seeks to reconcile various philosophies of the person rather than replace, or worse, destroy them. Why would the Jesuits seek to celebrate the triumphal canonization of two major Counter Reformation figures with a ceremony that employs a ritual of ancient Roman religion? In short, there may be another level of meaning here, one that represents a different insight. What those authors were trying to reveal was a truth, not an exclusively confessional truth having to do with Christian Doctrine, but a truth about the unity of human beings. That what is true and good about humans is not something new with Christianity or restricted only to Christendom, but something that has always existed and is common for all people of all time. The piece breaks barriers and reconciles at the same time. This is the basic insight of the Spiritual Exercise of Ignatius Loyola that God was present in all things. There was nothing foreign to God's presence in the world.

[12] See note 6 above.

The second example is a small work from the seventeenth century at the Royal College of Vienna by the Baroque composer Johannes Bernhard Staudt (1654-1712), and exists within a collection of Jesuit dramas in the National Library of Austria. To give you an idea of how extensive this genre is, there are 236 drama manuscripts in the National Library of Vienna that pertain to the Jesuit drama in German speaking lands.[13] More than 117 of these manuscripts were for dramas that were produced in Vienna in the last quarter of the seventeenth century, especially under the patronage of Kaiser Leopold and his wife Eleonora. The other Jesuit school dramas in this collection pertain to Prague, Dillingen, Olmütz, Graz, Bohemia, Passau, Bruges, Innsbruck Klagenfurt, Linz, Augsburg, and the most significant number of dramas after the city of Vienna, Munich, with eighteen dramas from in the National Library there. This quite unexplored collection is a treasure trove of material for music historians and historians of the drama as well.

The Patientis Christi memoria (The Memory of the Suffering Christ) is one of the thirty-nine dramas that Johannes Bernhard Staudt (1654-1712) set to music while he was the chorus director at the Jesuit Professed House in Vienna, from 1684 until his death in 1712.[14] Staudt was born in Wiener Neustadt in 1654, and from 1666 to 1670 he was a boarding student at the Jesuit College in Vienna. In 1684 he became the music master for the students at his old college, and also was named a "freeman" of the city, indicating the kind of respect he commanded in Vienna.[15] Unfortunately, Staudt's reputation as a well-respected musician has not seemed to survive intact. What has come down to us in modern dictionaries of music history, and unfortunately repeated over and over, is a line, from an Austrian musicologist named Waltraute Kramer,[16] who in her 1961 dissertation entitled "The Music in Viennese Jesuit Drama from 1677-1711," glibly states that Staudt is "a technically well trained writer, prolific but deadened by routine." After re-quoting that line, most other scholars note that, after all, these dramas were didactic in purpose; hence there should be no surprise that they were routinely repetitive, and ultimately no offence should be taken. Listeners can agree or disagree, but in any case, one of the lessons the early music movement has taught us forty years after Dr. Kramer's comment is that we need to move beyond the concept of a closed musical canon, that only the great works of any age are passed on and worthy of our listening. What seems to be evident in this body of Jesuit music dramas or operas that we so far have been able to hear and study, is that if in the seventeenth century the genre seems to be a conservative one, and does not change as radically nor as quickly as opera in the public theater does, it's because the purpose is different. These works

---

[13] For all intents and purposes, this collection has remained hidden from musicologists because of its misplacement within the Handschriften collection rather than the Musiksammlung of the Nationalbibliothek in Vienna.

[14] See note 10 above.

[15] Walter Pass, "Staudt, Johann Bernhard," in *The New Grove Dictionary of Music and Musicians*, 2nd ed., Stanley Sadie, ed. (London: Macmillan, 2001), 24: 301-2.

[16] Waltraute Kramer, "Die Musik im Wiener Jesuitendrama von 1677 – 1711" (Doctoral diss., University of Vienna, 1961), 21ff, 310, 322.

are not first and foremost for entertainment. They teach, and on many levels as well: on the level of the music, on the level of the style of the text and poetry, and on the level of life-lessons offered for the students. The *Patientis Christi Memoria* and works like it were also reinforcing reminders for the adults present at the performances. For late twentieth century/early twenty-first-century observers didactic is such a negative and narrow word, but the actual vision here is broad.

Something to notice all the time with the use Jesuits make of music is that the genre in the hands of Jesuits is slightly different from the normal usage. This opera belongs to a small genre of music popular in Vienna from the 1660s to at the latest 1705 called *sepolcro*. The *sepolcro* is a sacred dramatic piece related to the oratorio, performed on Holy Thursday or Good Friday at the Hapsburg court chapels. The libretto is invariably based on the Passion or an Old Testament story that prefigured the Passion. The *sepolcro* tends to be shorter than an oratorio and in one structural part, rather than the oratorio's two-part structure. This particular Jesuit piece is in three sections called *Inductiones*, plus an epilogue, but in essence one large structural part lasting about forty minutes. The piece, unlike the conventional *sepolcro*, was performed not in the Church, but in the Jesuit theater of the Royal College in Vienna, and not on Holy Thursday or Good Friday, but on Holy Saturday. The text is an amalgam of quotations from scripture (Old and New Testaments) with freely composed poetry, reflecting on the reactions of the various allegorical characters to the facts of God's love for humankind as exemplified in the Passion of Christ.

The author of the text of *Patientis Christi memoria* is unknown. While thirty-four of the thirty-nine music dramas that Johann Staudt composed were for text settings of works by Fr. Johann Baptist Adolph (1657-1708), Adolph entered the Society in 1677 and was not assigned to the college in Vienna until after the 1685 date of *Patientis Christi memoria*. Thus, it cannot be his. The other great Jesuit dramatic writer of the seventeenth-century Vienna was the Austrian Jesuit Nicholas Avancini (1611-1686), and though he evidently kept writing dramatic texts while he was Provincial Superior and even as General Assistant in Rome, in none of his collected works, some of which have been printed, does the *Patientis Christi memoria* appear.[17] Fr. Adolph's plays seem to address more broadly the issues of society and its culture; they are often referred to as the culmination of Jesuit dramatic art in the baroque display of pomp and power, while the text of the *Patientis Christi memoria*, on the other hand, more resembles the type of play that Fr. Avancini composed: allegorical in nature, often emphasizing a moral teaching. If Avancini did not compose this text, and by 1685 he is already a General Assistant in Rome, then his strong influence on the actual Jesuit composer can be felt in the style and presentation of *Patientis Christi memoria*.

---

[17] Ludwig Koch, S.J., *Jesuiten-Lexikon* (Paderborn: Bonifacius-Druckerei, 1934), 15 and 142-43, and Carlos Sommervogel, Augustin De Backer, and Aloys De Backer, *Bibliothèque de la Compagnie de Jésus* (Brussels: O. Schepens, 1890-1909), "Adolph, Johann B," vol. 1, cols. 53-54 and "Avancinus, Nikolaus," vol. 1, cols. 668-80.

The sources of the text are: sacred scripture, *De Sacra Virginitate* by St. Augustine, and freely-composed poetic verses using metric schemes associated with the meters of Horace's *Odes,* especially the greater Sapphic meter, most often a four-foot verse.[18] In addition, a small part of the text of Augustine's *De Sacra Virginitate* is used as a background for the actual dramatic text. The full quote is stated before the beginning of the drama, but even the full quotation is slightly adapted, changing Augustine's "you" plural verb forms (Latin, *vos, vester*) to the singular (*tu, tuus*). The quotations from sacred scripture are also adapted. In the Latin text the scripture references are only incompletely given; the chapter is referred to, but never the verse. There is a sense that the librettist is using his memory of scripture to fit the general outline of the story. *Compassio*'s first line from the second chapter of the Prophet Jeremiah, "You heavens wonder greatly about this!" is joined with a line from 1 Peter, 3: "The just one has died for the unjust." Sometimes it is just part of a line and other times several lines are quoted from one chapter, but often not in the order in which they appear in the scripture. For instance, in the Epilogue *Genius Christi* (Spirit of Christ) sings from the Prophet Isaiah, 49, but the verses are out of order, cut, and put together again. The order is verse. 16 first, followed by half of verse 22, followed by the last phrase (six words) of verse 19 and finally verse 23, but only the third, fifth and sixth phrases of the six-phrase verse. *Pietas Christiana* (Christian Duty) follows with a quote from the Prophet Habakuk, chapter 3, where there is a word play with the original Hebrew text *Y'shua*, the verb meaning to cause to save. Hence the word savior is used, but in the Latin vulgate text the Hebrew *Y'shua* becomes Jesus, and in the original program of 1685 the words Deo and Jesus appear in capitals (DEO and JESU). In this libretto there is also a wonderful juxtaposing of Old and New Testament texts. In the middle of the first section (*Inductio*), *Memoria Passionis* (Memory of the Passion) sings a line from the second chapter of St. John's Gospel: "*Ipse est propitiatio pro peccatis nostris* (He is the very atonement of our sins)" along with a line from 3 Kings (1 Chronicles), 22, "*Pone sermones ejus in corde* (Take his utterances to heart.)." In the passage from *Chronicles* King David is ordering the building of the temple, while St. John is referring to Jesus as the temple, in the sense of the 'mercy seat.' These juxtapositions point towards reconciliation and linking of texts, perhaps proofs of scriptural truths. Depending on one's perspective, the combination of scriptural phrases in this libretto could be seen as accommodation, or simply as clarification, or both. Often the combination or rearrangement of verses creates a new contextual meaning without negating the context or meaning of the original.

Basic procedures of the Baroque era, ritornello, and fugue are evident throughout the work. *Durities Cordis* (Hardness of Heart) also has a real aria with a

---

[18] Here the metrical scansion is similar to the poetry of the *Apotheosis,* a Roman work of more than sixty years earlier. See the opening words of the allegorical character, "Hardness of heart," "Quae scena tristis? Saxis in istis,/ Funesta dolore, acerba maerore, Plena panditur atroce." (What is this sad scene? In this rocky place, with deadly pain, with bitter mourning, with full gloom it is reviled.) Or, Memoria Passionis' lines "Esto memor Creatoris, Tanta vi, qui te amoris. (Be mindful of the Creator, how he loves you with such great force)."

string ritornello accompaniment. He sings, "I want favors, I don't want pain!" Staudt uses the strings within the musical structure sparingly, always indicating serious business. The Epilogue uses a large ritornello that punctuates what amounts to a love duet between *Pietas Christiana* (Christian Duty) and *Genius Christi* (The Spirit of Christ). However, this love duet only happens after the earlier love/reconciliation duet of *Memoria Passionis* and *Pietas Christiana* in Act 2. *Memoria Passionis* sings, "Do you love me?" and *Pietas Christiana* responds, "one thing I ask of you without which I can not breath - I want you in my heart, where I cherish only you."

Finally, musicological research within the burgeoning field of colonial Latin American musical studies in the last decade or so has led to the discovery and classification of a new musical genre – one that may now be referred to as 'Mission Music.'[19] For a long time now, musicologists have been exploring the great cathedral archives that exist in Latin America: Mexico City, Guatemala City, Santa Fé de Bogotá, and Sucre in Bolivia. In the last twenty years, corollary research focusing on the local traditions of the various missionary townships throughout Colonial Latin America has begun to parallel the work in the great cathedral archives. The Jesuit corporate enterprise in Latin America has provided fertile ground for the study of this genre.

One of the famous Jesuit musicians of the Jesuit missions of ancient Paraguay was the Italian Domenico Zipoli (1688-1726). In the extant music from these missions by Zipoli are pieces that are utterly contemporary in the style of the mature Italian Baroque, yet they are tailored to the needs and realities of the more than thirty mission towns of the Province. Zipoli was born in Prato near Florence; he was organist at the church of the Gesù in Rome, as well as other Roman Jesuit institutions, before entering the Society on July 1716 (age 28) in Seville. Zipoli left Cadiz for the Rió de la Plata basin April 1, 1717, not even a full year after entering the Society. Zipoli continued his course of studies in Córdoba, Argentina, completing them in 1725. He died of tuberculosis on January 2, 1726 while waiting the arrival of a bishop for ordination.

San Ignacio is a small, hybrid work from the Paraguay Missions by Zipoli, a younger, Swiss Jesuit contemporary Martin Schmid (1694-1772), and a third, anonymous composer. This small chamber opera, from those last years of the Paraguay Province and before the expulsion of the Jesuits from Spanish lands in 1767, became for those twenty years or so a piece that captured the hearts of the native indigenous peoples (the Chiquitos) in such a profound way that, long after the Jesuits were expelled from the Spanish dominions in 1767, this work continued to be performed by the native peoples in what is now northeastern Bolivia. The earliest manuscript tradition of this small opera dates from 1755 in the township of Santa Ana in Chiquitos. But that is an inherited tradition that certainly began much earlier in the Guaraní townships of Paraguay. The work was used over and over for various festivities, especially St. Ignatius Day and the Visitation Days of the

---

[19] See T. Frank Kennedy, "Latin American Colonial Music: The Case for Mission Music as a New Genre," in *Sonus, A Journal of Investigations into Global Musical Possibilities* 21, no. 2 (Spring 2001), 27-38.

Provincial Superiors. The opera consists of two short acts: The Messenger and The Farewell. Act I represents the conversion and call of Ignatius and his experience of learning how to discern the will of God. Act II represents Ignatius' response to God's call, his friendship with Francis Xavier, and his sending of Xavier on mission to the East to preach and baptize. Like most operas, it is about love.[20] God as love sets Ignatius in motion, and the love of Christ that Loyola and Xavier share impel Francis to new worlds to share that news. In act II the only duet in the work is a love duet, or at least would be in secular opera, but its context is changed with Ignatius and Xavier sharing the mission of love. Love is the force that is in all things. It represents the aims, the means, and the music of the Jesuits in South America. *San Ignacio* stands in the middle, of several different cultures, creating a space for the confluence of differences and the understanding of peoples. Remember the Indians heard the story of Ignatius sending Xavier to the missions from their own township perspectives. They too were called to mission.

Although Kapsberger's *Apotheosis* and Staudt's *Patientis Christi Memoria* are not works that were composed by committee as was the Zipoli/Schmid/anonymous *San Ignacio,* all three stand as an examples of the flexibility and breadth of the Jesuit enterprise. They directly attest to a living creativity that ensured on a cultural level that what happened in these places, whether cities or jungles, was not ultimately imposed, but that shared templates of the western European tradition were exactly that —they were templates. They could be reused, mixed, and matched in various contexts with ease and on many levels: musical style, structural shapes, poetical or scriptural references, even the mixing of music and text with commentary, as well as the art work that accompanied these works in terms of staging and decoration. *Nuestro modo de proceder,* one of the favorite and common phrases of the Society of Jesus, is not a rule that is followed in detail. It is a method for each person and community to discover the deep humanity and connectedness inherent in the Christian vision.

---

[20] See Bernardo Illari, liner notes (4-6) to *The Jesuit Operas, Operas by Kapsberger and Zipoli,* Ensemble Abendmusik, James David Christie, Director, Dorian Records, DOR-93243, 2003.

From Santa Barbara to Xanadu:
Mildred Couper as West Coast Ultramodernist

Kristine K. Forney

Late nineteenth-century European composers, believing that harmonic systems encompassing the twelve-note chromatic scale had been fully exploited, led the way in experiments with microtonality. By the early twentieth century, one preferred approach among microtonal pioneers was quarter-tone music, using a system with twenty-four equal pitches to the octave. The most noted of the innovators of this new sound world were Alois Hába (1893-1973),[1] Ivan Wyschnegradsky (also Vyschnegradsky, 1893-1979),[2] Julián Carillo (1875-1965),[3] and the American mavericks Charles Ives, Henry Cowell, and Harry Partch. Rarely, however, does the name Mildred Couper (1887-1974) surface in this fascinating history. Couper's involvement in this ultramodern movement, and her connections with its better known exponents, are revealed through the extensive archival materials now housed at the University of California, Santa Barbara.[4] This study explores how Mildred Couper was a major conduit in the dissemination of microtonal music on the West Coast and highly influential in its reception by audiences and composers alike.

Born in Buenos Aires on 10 December 1887, Mildred was the seventh of eight children of Harriet Hathaway, a former opera singer, and Reginald Cooper, an exporter for a British firm. A true cosmopolitan, Mildred studied piano first

---

[1] Inspired by recitals given by Willi von Möllendorff on a quarter-tone harmonium, Hába's first quarter-tone works were written in 1917. See J. Vyslouzil, "Hába, Alois," in *The New Grove Dictionary of Music and Musicians*, 2nd ed. (London: Macmillan, 2001): 10: 630-33; and idem, *Alois Hába: zivot a dilo* (Prague: Panton, 1974).

[2] See Gottfried Eberle, "Ivan Wyschnegradsky, ein russischer Pionier der Ultrachromatik," *Neue Zeitschrift für Musik* 135, no. 9 (September 1974): 549-55; and the composer's own discussion, "La musique à quarts de ton," *La revue musicale* (October 1924): 231-34.

[3] Carrillo's earliest experiments with microtonality began in 1895, when he explored various division of the octave on the violin. See Gerald R. Benjamin, "Carrillo(-Trujillo), Julián," in *The New Grove Dictionary of Music and Musicians*, 2nd ed., 5: 193-96.

[4] My husband Bill Prizer first made me aware of this rich archive at USCB, knowing well my interest in unrecognized women musicians; it is appropriate then that this essay should appear in his honor. I would like to thank David Seubert of the Special Collections Department of the University Library, University of California, Santa Barbara, for his generous assistance with access to these archival materials.

389

in Germany (1902-07), then in Paris (1907-10) with Moritz Moskowski, in Rome (1910-14) with Giovanni Sgambati, and in New York with Alfred Cortot (1921-23). She was also a composition student of Nadia Boulanger, and was well acquainted with Cowell, Cage, Partch, and Stravinsky.

Mildred, or Mimi, as she was better known, met her husband, the landscape artist Richard Hamilton Couper, at a Paris art studio where they both studied. They met at the sign-in book, where they laughed over the similarity of their last names. Later, she told him "I gave my 'o' for 'u.'"[5] Mimi Cooper and Richard Couper soon married and settled in Rome, where they raised their young family—son Clive and daughter Rosalind. Richard Couper enjoyed a short but successful career in Italy, while Mimi played piano for his art shows. Living on the third floor of the enormous Palazzo Sonnino—a draughty edifice with few utilities and no baths—the Coupers circulated among Rome's most elite literary and artistic circles.[6] Mimi described in her autobiography that she was sponsored in Rome by the Steinway firm, who facilitated her introduction to a number of distinguished people:

> I met the brother of Peter Ilich Tchaikowsky at a party given by the Crowninshields at the American Academy of Rome, and, at his request, played the Waltz from the *Nutcracker* Suite. I went to a party at Sgambati's (my teacher) and met the brilliant Venezuelan pianist, Teresa Carreño, heard her play beautifully, and then Sgambati turned to me and said: "Now its your turn." I'm afraid I refused.[7]

The Couper family fled Europe at the outbreak of World War I, moving to New York City, where, in 1918, Richard Couper was an early victim of the Spanish flu pandemic that took millions of lives. Mimi began teaching piano in 1919 at The Mannes School (then the David Mannes Music School) in New York to support her two young children.[8] While at Mannes, Mildred was briefly a colleague of composer Ernst Bloch, who also wrote in quarter tones, and of experimental composer Johanna Beyer, who taught there from 1924 to 1927.[9] During the 1920s, Mimi became well connected with the new music scene in New York City.

[5] Mildred Couper papers, PA Mss 45, Box 11, Autobiography typescript, 1970, Department of Special Collections, University Libraries, University of California, Santa Barbara; available at http://www.geocities.com/sanbarart/couper-m/Autobio.htm (accessed 18 October 2008). Richard Hamilton Couper was the son of the American expatriate sculptor William Couper; he grew up in Florence at the Villa Ball, home of his grandfather, sculptor Thomas Ball.

[6] The Palazzo Sonnino, owned by the Italian politician Baron Sidney Constantino Sonnino (1847-1922), prime minister of Italy just prior to World War I, boasted an excellent library, according to Verne Linderman, in "Cosmopolitan Mildred Couper Has Shared Her Mind, Breadth of Vision with Neighbors for 22 Years," *Santa Barbara New Press*, 30 September 1951, B6.

[7] Couper papers, Autobiography, 1970.

[8] These dates based on the Couper entry in *The International Who is Who in Music*, 5th ed., ed. J. T. H. Mize (Chicago: Who is Who in Music, 1951).

[9] On Beyer, see John Kennedy and Larry Polansky, "'Total Eclipse': The Music of Johanna Magdalena Beyer: An Introduction and Preliminary Annotated Checklist," *Musical Quarterly* 80, no. 4 (Winter 1996): 719-78.

In 1927, Mimi Couper moved to the beachside community of Santa Barbara, California, where she resided the rest of her long life, actively teaching and performing. A formidable fixture of the Santa Barbara arts community, Mimi was a longtime music critic for the *Santa Barbara News Press*; she was a founding member of the Music Academy of the West, where she taught alongside Soulima Stravinsky, Darius Milhaud, and Lotte Lehmann;[10] she was the first woman instructor at the prestigious Cate School, founded in Santa Barbara in 1910;[11] she served as president of the Santa Barbara Music Society; and she was a notable patroness of music, frequently hosting salon concerts at Monteverde, her Italian villa in the hills above Santa Barbara (see Plate 1).[12]

Mimi Couper composed in a variety of genres, including much piano and vocal music, some chamber and orchestral works, and children's pieces (see Appendix I). Most of her manuscripts are now in the Special Collections division of the University of California, Santa Barbara library, but only a very few of her compositions were published: two collections of teaching pieces and her *Dirge* for two

Plate 1: Mimi Couper performing with the Stradivarius Quartet

[10] In "Music Academy of West Planning Summer Course," *Los Angeles Times*, 20 February 1949, D7, it was announced that Darius Milhaud would be the honorary director of the Academy and also serve as head of the composition department; Soulima Stravinsky would give master classes and private piano lessons; and Mildred Couper would offer courses in music theory.

[11] Although the first fulltime woman teacher, Katherine Forbes, was hired in 1942, the Cate School employed Mildred Couper from 1924 until 1949; see Cate School website at http://www.cate.org/public/histphoto.php?pcat=6&pindex=C (accessed 10 October 2008). Roger A Clarke, class of 1936 and a member of the Cate School faculty from 1949-1952, gave the school in 1993 a $15,000 bequest for a classical music collection in the name of his beloved piano teacher, Mildred Couper. Clarke wrote a tribute to Mildred Couper on the occasion of her death in 1974 (see note 97).

[12] Couper papers, Box 11. This photo, taken at her home Monteverde, shows one of Mimi's collectibles: a lampshade made from Gregorian chant. See the essay on similar lampshades at Hearst Castle by Alicia Doyle, in this volume. Mimi performed the César Frank Piano Quintet with the Stadivarius Quartet, which she called "one of my happiest memories." Couper papers, Autobiography, 1970.

pianos tuned a quarter tone apart, the latter published in 1937 in Henry Cowell's New Music Editions.[13] *Dirge* was clearly the most performed of her compositions, both in the United States and in Europe.

Couper first experimented with quarter tones in her work *Xanadu*, written in 1930 as incidental music for Eugene O'Neill's play *Marco Millions*. Like many American playwrights, O'Neill was well read in Eastern philosophy, and was especially interested in Taoism—indeed, he named his California home "Tao House." *Marco Millions* was premiered in 1927 in New York. The West Coast run of the play included performances at the Pasadena Playhouse, with Robert Young in the lead role, and at UCLA's Royce Hall, presented by the University's Dramatic Society. On 24-26 April 1930, *Marco Millions* was presented at Santa Barbara's Lobero Theater, with Mimi Couper and Malcolm Thurburn, the artist who contributed the stage murals for the play, performing the incidental music.[14]

This dramatic interpretation of Marco Polo's journeys through the Middle and Far East inspired Couper to evoke an Eastern sound; she wrote that "having heard some quarter-tone music in a New York recital, I decided this system would be appropriate for the Oriental setting of the play."[15] She achieved her desired effect through the use of the ultrachromatic scale with two pianos, explaining that she had the tuner raise the pitch on the second piano by a quarter tone, so that a chromatic scale played alternately, note by note, from one piano to the other, would produce the ultra-chromatic scale. This practical approach using two pianos eliminated the need for a specially-constructed instrument with two keyboards or extra keys, which other composers had utilized. Mimi described her working method for her quarter-tone compositions, noting: "When I lived on Orena Street [in Santa Barbara], I had three pianos in my music studio. The third piano was a small upright which was placed at right angles to my Steinway and tuned a quarter-tone high, so I was able to experiment in this medium with a hand on each keyboard."[16] She contended that experiments with string instruments, such as those of Julián Carrillo, were less satisfactory, because vibrato results in a variable pitch on each note.[17]

In addition to the two pianos, the manuscript score for *Xanadu* (see Plate 2) calls for various percussion instruments, including side drum, cymbals, Chinese gong, and wood block. These added instruments were apparently used for processions

---

[13] This work might have been selected by Gerald Strang, who managed the *New Music Quarterly* during Cowell's four years at San Quentin prison (1936-40). See Leta Miller, "The Art of Noise: John Cage, Lou Harrison, and the West Coast Percussion Ensemble," in *Perspectives on American Music, 1900-1950* (New York: Garland, 2000), 226. William H. Bailey's *Idles*, for piano and violin, was published in the same volume of *New Music* (January 1937). A selective list of Couper's compositions is found in Appendix 1 of this study.

[14] Couper's letters reveal that Thurburn was an aspiring amateur composer, much influenced by Scriabin and by polytonality. Thurburn had been close friends with Mimi since she and her future husband met him in Paris at the art school they all attended.

[15] Couper papers, Autobiography, 1970.

[16] Ibid.

[17] From a paper given in 1932 by Mimi Couper at the Mannes School of Music in New York.

Plate 2: Manuscript (p. 1) of Couper's *Xanadu*

and for dockyard scenes in the play. Couper's *Xanadu* is titled on the manuscript a "ballet" in five movements: *Largo, Andante, Scherzando, Allegro*, and *Allegro agitato*.[18] The *Santa Barbara Morning Press* reviewer called the production a "wonderful, colorful premier [*sic*]," singling out the scenic designs by Thurburn and the dancers, who heightened the drama with "their weird but artistic number in the throne room of the Khan." This weirdness must have been in part caused by the accompanying music by Mimi, although the reviewer simply noted her "musical arrangements" with no descriptive adjectives.[19] Mimi herself wrote, however, that "*Marco Millions* went over with a bang, and I received expressions of appreciation from many sources for the music."[20]

Subsequent performances of *Xanadu* were well received as she and Malcolm Thurburn traveled north up the California coast in 1932 through Carmel and Monterey to perform the work on one of Henry Cowell's New Music Society concerts, given on 15 May at the new YWCA in San Francisco's Chinatown.[21] This performance of *Xanadu* at an appropriately Eastern-inspired site was eclipsed, however, by the demonstration on the same program of the rhythmicon, a machine capable of performing complex rhythms, built for Henry Cowell by Léon Theremin.[22] The *San Francisco Chronicle* reported that Couper's work was "excellently written and finely played," and that the repeat performance strengthened the impression made by the first.[23] It soon became a tradition to perform Mimi's quarter-tone works twice on a concert, to give the audience time to become accustomed to the unusual sounds. The reviewer for the local Carmel paper, *The Carmelite*, described how "cross-rhythms played a quarter of a tone apart, weaving and interweaving, displaying their clear individuality by their independence of each other, arrived at last into a new and beautiful unity."[24] The *Monterey Peninsula Herald* critic appreciated the "awakening" effect of the music, noting that "new sensations arose to meet these new sounds."[25]

The opaque dissonances and dense clusters that envelop the pentatonic lines of *Xanadu* might well have evoked programmatic images from Samuel Taylor

[18] Couper papers, box. 1. (As enticing as the Abyssinian maid and her dulcimer is, any attempt to link Samuel Coleridge Taylor's famous poem with the style or structure of Couper's *Xanadu* would be highly speculative.)

[19] G. A. Martin, "Marco Millions' Is Termed Wonderful, Colorful Premier," *Santa Barbara Morning Press*, 25 April 1930, clipping.

[20] Couper papers, Autobiography, 1970.

[21] The YWCA was designed by the prominent architect Julia Morgan, who also designed the famous William Randolph Hearst estate, discussed by Alicia Doyle in this volume: "Let there be Light: Liturgical Manuscripts at Hearst Castle."

[22] Homer Henley, writing in the *Argonaut*, 20 May 1932, stated that "Mr. Cowell used his rhythmicon to accompany a set of violin movements which he had written for the occasion. ... The accompaniment was a strange complexity of rhythmical interweavings and cross currents of a cunning and precision as never before fell on the ears of man and the sound pattern was as uncanny as the motion."

[23] Quoted in "Quarter-Tone Music Concert," *Santa Barbara News Press*, 14 June 1932.

[24] Ibid.

[25] Ibid.

Coleridge's famous poem of the same name. Couper's *Xanadu* is an eclectic work, with Impressionistic parallelisms and whole-tone movement; it also evokes at times the motoric style of George Antheil's *Ballet méchanique*, a work that Mimi may have heard at its 1927 New York premiere. Her harmonic idiom is often secondal, with chords spaced over several octaves, a construct that Cowell suggests was inevitable in the development of music.[26] This, along with even more dissonant quarter-tone octaves and fifths that surely sounded "out of tune" to the unseasoned listener, suggest a possible influence from Indonesian instruments, with which Mimi was familiar, and possibly by Cowell's cluster tones pieces, such as his very Impressionistic-sounding *Snows of Fijiyama* (1924).

After the success of *Xanadu*, Couper continued to experiment with this microtonal technique, writing *Rumba* in 1932, followed in quick succession by *Anacapa* and a Prelude, and finally her *Dirge*, which she later arranged for violin and piano.[27] *Xanadu* and *Rumba* received another highly visible performance in 1939, when John Cage invited Couper to perform her works at the Seattle Cornish School, where he was an instructor. Cage had already premiered new American compositions in Seattle, including works by Henry Cowell, Lou Harrison, and Johanna Beyer.[28] Couper's music was again overshadowed on the program, this time by the premiere of Cage's *First Construction (in Metal)* for percussion ensemble, one of the most important works of his early career.[29]

It is fascinating to speculate what influence Couper's nonwestern-sounding, quarter-tone piano works might have had on Cage, who in the next year, wrote his first prepared piano work, *Bacchanale*. Although he had wanted to write another percussion work for this ballet, Cage was deterred by logistical factors that led him to use the piano in a nontraditional way, evoking an African character through the placement of metal weather stripping, screws, and small bolts in twelve piano strings. While more rhythmic than Couper's music, the prepared notes often sound dissonant and, indeed, microtonal.[30]

Mildred Couper may have been introduced to microtonal music and experiments in instrument construction during her early years studying in Europe. In particular, she could have encountered the early work of Julián Carrillo: he studied in Ghent and Leipzig from 1899-1905 (she was a student in Germany from 1902-07) and he gave a lecture in 1911 at the International Congress on Music in Rome while she was living there. He then came to New York in 1914,

[26] Henry Cowell, *New Musical Resources* (Cambridge: Cambridge University Press, 1993), 114-15.

[27] Couper's *Xanadu* and *Dirge* are recorded on Zeitgeist, *If Tigers Were Clouds*, American Composers Forum, 2003, CD.

[28] Leta Miller, "The Art of Noise," 227-30.

[29] On Cage and the Cornish School, see Miller, "The Art of Noise," 229-39. The sonic world of *First Construction in Metal* is already far removed from the Western tempered scale.

[30] Cage was clearly influenced as well by Cowell and the microtonal possibilities of the Theremin, as he noted in his lecture "The Future of Music: Credo," delivered in Seattle in 1937 and published much later as program notes; cited in Josiah Fisk, ed. *Composers on Music: Eight Centuries of Writings*, 2nd ed. (Boston: Northeastern University Press, 1997), 380-81.

where he served as the director of the American Symphony Orchestra and where the League of Composers and Leopold Stokowski presented his works in public concerts.[31] Mimi's lecture notes on microtonal music include mention of a quarter-tone piano in Moscow in 1863 (probably an instrument built by Prince Vladamir Odoyevsky),[32] as well as the groundbreaking work of many early experimenters, among them Alois Hába, Richard Stein, Ernest Bloch, Julián Carrillo, and Harry Partch. In tune with artistic currents in Russia, Couper was a great admirer of the music of Alexander Scriabin and she knew the writings and compositions of Ivan Vishnegradsky as well. Her exposure to quarter-tone music in New York included works by Ernest Bloch, her colleague at the Mannes School; his Hebraic rhapsody *Schelomo* was premiered there in 1917 and the Piano Quintet No. 1 (with quarter tones in the third and fourth movements) was written just after he left New York for Cleveland.

But Mimi's claim of "having heard some quarter-tone music in New York" most likely refers to the premiere of Charles Ives's *Quarter-Tone Pieces for Two Pianos*, performed by Hans Barth and Sigmund Klein at New York's Aeolian Hall on 14 February 1925.[33] At this famous event, she probably also heard the pre-concert lecture given by E. Robert Schmitz, the founder of the Franco-American Music Society, who spoke about Hába and the forward-looking ideas of Feruccio Busoni.[34] Ives had wanted the public to perceive his quarter-tone pieces as studies rather than completed works of art; he admitted that the way Barth "used the piano has done more harm than good in interesting people in quarter tones."[35] As a devotee of new music, Couper may well have read Ives's article that followed shortly after the concert, published in *The Franco-American Music Society Bulletin*. In it, he credits his father with promoting his interest in quarter tones and claims he wanted only to "open up some ears."

> It will probably be centuries, at least generations, before man will discover all or even most of the value in a quarter-tone extension. . . . Even in the limited and awkward way of working with quartertones at present, transcendent things may be felt ahead—glimpses into further fields of thought and beauty. . . . My

[31] Elliott Carter, "Expressionism and American Music," *Perspectives of New Music* 4, no. 1 (1965): 2-3.

[32] This was a piano tuned in just intonation that Russian theorist Prince Vladimir Odoyevsky had constructed; the instrument is found today in the museum of the Moscow Conservatory. Hugh Davies, "Microtonal Instruments," in *The New Grove Dictionary of Music and Musicians,* 16: 617-24. Cowell discusses this as well in *New Musical Resources,* 18. The original edition of this work is dated 1930, however, Cowell wrote much of it in 1918-19. One lecture on microtonality by Mimi Couper was given at the Music Academy of the West on 17 June 1953; see note 93.

[33] Barth and Klein performed *Allegro* and *Chorale* from *Three Quarter-Tone Pieces for Two Pianos;* also performed was a movement of a sonata by Barth.

[34] The pianist/composer Ferrucio Busoni called for the development of new, freer forms of musical thinking, advocating the use of third and sixth tones, in an effort to expand our musical perception, in *Sketch of a New Esthetic in Music,* trans. Theodore Baker (New York: Schirmer, 1911; reprint 1978). According to Cowell, in *Charles Ives and His Music* (Oxford: Oxford University Press, 1969), 101: "The quarter-tone concert aroused a good deal of laughter both then and later."

[35] Charles Ives, *Charles E. Ives: Memos,* ed. John Kirkpatrick (New York: W. W. Norton, 1972), 110-11.

father had a weakness for quarter-tones. . . . He would pick out quarter-tone tunes and try to get the family to sing then, but I remember he gave that up as a means of punishment.[36]

The first movement of the Ives set, a *Largo*, is mostly diatonic, using quarter tones as passing notes or suspensions, with some quarter-tone chords to heighten the dissonance. In the *Allegro*, he writes for two pianos, one tuned a quarter-tone sharp, but this work is less exploitive of the full range of intervals than Couper's writing.[37] The *Chorale*, voiced more densely than the other movements, may have been the most influential movement for Couper in her works.[38]

After the Ives premiere, which was panned by critic Olin Downes for sounding "a good deal out of tune,"[39] there followed a deluge of scholarly articles in the late 1920s, evaluating the pros and cons of microtonality. Some echoed Ives in promoting quarter tones as merely a theoretical study—Albert Wellek and Theodore Baker proclaimed that this was the language of dilettantes—"of those who, lacking inward capacity for individual expression, seek forcibly to enlist an external agency. . . . All the quarter tones in the world will not raise a commonplace conception to significance."[40]

A known admirer of the work of Ivan Vishnegradsky, Mimi's first acquaintance with his experiments might have been through an article entitled "The Possibility of Quarter Tone and Other New Scales" by Leonid Sabanneev, which acknowledged the Russian composer's compositions, along with those of Alois Hába's, claiming they merit attention but that much of the music was "academic." A follower of Scriabin, Sabeyneev viewed ultrachromaticism as the "music of the future," suggesting composers take an exclusive focus on an ultrachromatic melodic style.[41]

Igor Stravinsky, who later made Mimi's acquaintance, weighed in with his unenthusiastic view of microtonality as early as 1925 in a *Musical America* interview,

---

[36] Charles Ives, "Some Quarter-Tone Impressions," *Franco-American Music Society Bulletin*, 25, no. 3 (1925); reprinted in *Essays Before a Sonata and Other Writings*, ed. H. Boatwright (New York: W. W. Norton, 1962), 109-10. See also Maynard Soloman, "Charles Ives: Some Questions of Veracity," *Journal of the American Musicological Society* 40, no. 3 (Fall 1987), 447.

[37] The second and third movements of this set rework a number of pieces, most by Ives; on these borrowings, see J. Peter Burkholder, *All Made of Tunes: Charles Ives and the Uses of Musical Borrowing* (New Haven: Yale University Press, 1995), 276.

[38] Charles Ives, *Three Quarter Tone Pieces* (New York: C. F. Peters, 1968), with an introduction by Charles Ives and a preface by George Pappastovrou.

[39] Olin Downes, "Franco-American Musical Society," *The New York Times*, 15 February 1925, p. 26; cited in Peter Burkholder, ed., *Charles Ives and His World*, Bard Music Festival Series (Princeton: Princeton University Press, 1996), 292-93.

[40] Albert Wellek and Theodore Baker, "Quarter Tones and Progress," *Musical Quarterly* 12, no. 2 (April 1926): 237.

[41] Leonid Sabaneev, "The Possibility of Quarter-Tone and Other New Scales," translated by S. W. Pring, *The Musical Times*, 70, no. 1036 (1 June 1929), 501-04. Many other articles appeared in European journals that could have reached Couper as well, including Richard Stein, "Vierteltonmusik," *Die Musik* (1922-23), 510; Ivan Wyshnegradsky, "The Liberation of Sound," *Nakanounie* (7 Jan 1923); and Alois Hába, "The Quartertone Problem," *De Muziek* (1927), 109.

398   KRISTINE K. FORNEY

saying that the work of Hába sounded to him "like ordinary music just a little off. *Es klingt falsch*. That's all. They try to write the music of the future, strange unheard of combinations, and all they succeed in writing is quarter-tone Brahms."[42] Several years later, after a dinner with Hába in Prague, Stravinsky told the Czech press that "quarter tones seem to me simply like glissandos between pairs of half tones."[43] Indeed, this glissando effect is one of the unique features Couper employed in her compositions. Stravinsky apparently warmed up to quarter tones by 1931: during a visit with Hindemith in Berlin, he examined a specially-constructed piano with two keyboards capable of playing quarter tones:

> After a few minutes I had no difficulty in thinking in quarter tones. . . . As soon as you had got accustomed to the quarter-tones and comprehended what they are capable of, you found it was a construction that had always existed in your head. . . . Through quarter tones we are richer in the number of notes. But being richer in notes, we are not richer in any other respect.[44]

In 1933, Henry Cowell published his own "short list" of promising musicians and compositional trends. In it, he discredits the writings of several microtonal experimenters.

> One may mention Hans Barth, Dutch-American, who composes for quarter-tones, and Julián Carrillo, Mexican, who composes for quarter-tones and other intervals finer than a half step. Neither of these men can be considered a composer. Their music is meant to illustrate a system and serves its purpose. Other than as illustration, it has no importance.[45]

That Cowell later sought out and published Mildred Couper's *Dirge* in 1937 suggests that he viewed her work as having artistic merit.[46]

Los Angeles audiences and critics were generally receptive to experimental music during this era. Henry Cowell had organized the New Music Society in Los Angeles in 1925, and between that year and 1936, twenty-nine concerts were presented. New York critic Pierre Key warmed up West Coast audiences for quarter-tone music, first with his *Los Angeles Times* report on the 1925 Ives premiere

---

[42] Igor Stravinsky, interview in *Musical America* (10 January 1925); quoted in Stephen Walsh, *Stravinsky, A Creative Spring: Russia and France, 1882-1934* (New York: Alfred A. Knopf, 1999), 495.

[43] *Prager Presse*, 23 February 1930; quoted in Walsh, 495.

[44] See Vera Stravinsky and Robert Craft, *Stravinsky in Pictures and Documents* (New York: Simon and Schuster, 1978), 198. Although note 38 records Stravinsky's comments from the *New York World-Telegram* of 23 November 1937, the meeting in Berlin was most likely in October 1931, when Stravinsky premiered his Violin Concerto there. Vera's diary notes on 25 October of that year: at Hindemiths. Vera Stravinsky, *Dearest Bubushkin: The Correspondence of Vera and Igor Stravinsky, 1921-1954, with excerpts from Vera Stravinsky's Diaries, 1922-1971*, ed. Robert Craft, trans. by Lucia Davidova (London: Thames and Hudson, 1955), 53. I would like to thank Prof. H. Colin Slim for calling these citations to my attention and for his thoughtful reading of this essay.

[45] Cowell, *American Composers on American Music*, 11.

[46] As explained in note 13, Gerald Strang might have made this choice. Still, Cowell claimed that the works published in this series were mostly personal friends—"not because I published works by my friends, but because I became a friend of composers whose work I admired." Cowell, "About New Music," cited in Rita Mead, "The Amazing Mr. Cowell," *American Music* 1, no. 4 (Winter 1983), 72.

in New York City, writing that it evoked a "a strange after-sensation in the ears. . . . Orientalism was the strongly marked characteristic in the music" which the average listener may not find easy to hear; he continued, claiming "we have not attuned our hearing to such finely differentiated tones" and cautioned "Let us have progress but let it come gradually." Still, he joked that "up-to-the-minute music folk may begin to order, before long, quarter-tone pianos. . . . The use of such an instrument . . . puts something of a burden upon even the most ambitious and fantastically-inclined auditor. It is an instrument for an acquired taste . . . not unlike the olive."[47] A 2 February 1930 announcement in the *Los Angeles Times* promoted Hans Barth's upcoming recital, quoting the inventor on his quarter-tone piano.

> It opens a new language to music lovers. A new fluency of musical expression is immediately evident. The public, of course, must get used to it. Hearing it for the first time, one cannot pass judgment at once. Hearing a foreign language for the first time is very much the same thing. Sounds, for instance, which we think are beautiful in German may sound discordant and guttural in another tongue. But in time, the beauty of German or any other language is apparent, when the ear becomes accustomed to the intonations.[48]

A feature by Rosalind Shepard, in her *Los Angeles Times* column Home, Club and Civic Interests of Women, reported with enthusiasm on Barth's address to the Friday Morning Club. She noted that his presentation on the "piano of tomorrow"—the quarter-tone piano—was the first in the West, declaring that "it is a tribute to his artistry that the new harmonies, while strange and weird, were never disagreeable to the unaccustomed ear."[49] Pierre Key wrote the next month that "Hans Barth is a venturesome person, a quarter-tone pioneer, and a good one (almost, to my knowledge, the only one . . . at least hereabouts)."[50] Clearly Key did not know of Couper's imminent work, which was premiered the next month in Santa Barbara.

Los Angelenos had some previous familiarity with microtonal music, having heard performances by various musical groups from the Far East; a *Los Angeles Times* announcement of a visiting Japanese troupe in 1929 warned readers that "we will once again have a chance to try to distinguish quarter tones."[51] Concert-goers also heard the Asian-inspired compositions of Henry Eichheim, a Santa Barbara composer and friend of Couper who was also a founding member of the New Music Society in Los Angeles. Eichheim's own pioneering compositions foreshadow those of Cowell and Lou Harrison in his borrowings from Asian music,[52] and

---

[47] Pierre V. R. Key, "Pierre Key's Music Article," *Los Angeles Times*, 2 March 1925, A9.

[48] Hans Barth, quoted in an unsigned article, "Piano History Will Be Given by Inventor," *Los Angeles Times*, 2 February 1930, B12.

[49] Rosalind Shepard, "'Quarter-Tone' Piano Exhibited," Home, Club and Civic Interests of Women, *Los Angeles Times*, 9 February 1930, B19.

[50] Pierre V. R. Key, "Musical New York," *Los Angeles Times*, 9 March 1930, B21.

[51] "Japanese Drama Coming," *Los Angeles Times*, 15 December 1929, B14.

[52] As early as 1922, American audiences heard Eichheim's Eastern-flavored works: the Philadelphia Orchestra, under the direction of Leopold Stokowski, performed movements from the suite

Couper's autobiography notes the fascinating instruments Eichheim brought back from Indonesia.[53]

The Santa Barbara of Mildred Couper's era was a liberal-thinking center of artistic activity. One resident, David Strauss, the scion of the Strauss waltz-king family and an admitted modernist, sent a diatribe on music to the *LA Times* in 1930, the year that Mimi wrote *Xanadu*:

> If music is ever going to progress, the pianos will have to be burned. There must be no limit to tonal expressions in music. Instruments must be provided which are capable of expressing every shade of tones. Scales must not be permanent. They must be flexible. The western world has tuned its ear so long to the rigid scales of the piano that it cannot distinguish the fine shadings of the quarter tones, eighths, sixteenths, and so on.[54]

Even Santa Barbara's society folks welcomed Couper's experiments. A 1932 lecture-recital by Mimi and Malcolm Thurburn was announced on 14 June 1932 in the *Santa Barbara News Press*, proposing they would "make clear the mysteries of this little known subject," that is, quarter-tone music. The reviewer describes that the audience, at the Ripley home in Mission Canyon, gave the presenters an ovation, writing:

> The music at first fell strangely on the ear and often seemed dissonant. It was remarkable to discover, however, a much greater appreciation of the harmonies in Mrs. Couper's *Xanadu* when it was played a second time. . . . The listeners were led to see the infinite possibilities for new musical expression that will come with freedom from the restrictions of the diatonic scale . . . . *Xanadu* is remarkable for its clear, bell-like tones produced by the meetings of quarter tones, from which overtones arise.[55]

Mimi gave a similar lecture-recital to socialites in Montclair, New Jersey, where she warned the listeners that they would need to hear the works more than once, and then played all of her quarter-tone compositions. The *Montclair Times* noted that she "emphasized the preference for glissando effects, suggesting . . . that runs and trills could be carried to new heights, limited [only] by the extent of coordination possible between the two pianists." These runs and glissandi are a

---

Oriental Impressions. In 1929, Eichheim conducted *Java* with the Philadelphia Orchestra, the Boston Symphony Orchestra, and the Symphonie Orchestre of Paris. This is the first movement of a trilogy that also includes *Bali* and *Angkor*, all with gamelan instruments. On his relationship with Stokowski, who traveled to Asia with Eichheim in 1928, see http://www.stokowski.org/1929%20 Electrical%20Recordings%20Stokowski.htm (accessed 20 May 2011). Los Angeles audiences also heard Eichheim's *Burma* in 1929 at the Hollywood Bowl.

[53] Couper papers, Autobiography, 1970: "In our Art Museum, there is a room devoted to Henry Eichheim, showing many of the instruments he brought back from Bali." Henry Eichheim made five trips to Asia between 1915 and the mid-1930s, where he met with musicians, notated music he heard, and collected musical instruments. The Eichheim Collection is now housed in the Department of Music at University of California, Santa Barbara. Eichheim was one of the founding board members of the New Music Society of California, and he conducted Varèse's *Octandre* on the Society's first concert (22 October 1925, Biltmore Hotel, Los Angeles). See Mead, 37, 74.

[54] David Strauss, quoted in unsigned article, "Musician Would Burn Pianos," *Los Angeles Times*, 19 September 1930, p. 10.

[55] "Ovation Given Experimenters in Quarter-Tone Music Study," *Santa Barbara New Press*, [1932] clipping.

distinctive feature of her *Dirge*. Hearing the extensive use of minor keys, a listener asked "is all quarter-tone music sad?"[56] Her lectures also included a demonstration of various scales (ultrachromatic, chromatic, ¾ tone, 1¼ tone, etc.); her lecture notes were jotted on the first page of the score to *Anacapa*.[57] She explained to one audience that, to recognize a great composer, one must know the musical idiom of the day, because "he is certainly not going to talk in the language of the past."[58]

Harry Partch clearly had this attribute for greatness. Mimi Couper met Partch in 1932 when he stopped by Santa Barbara to discuss ideas with her for building a microtonal keyboard instrument; their ensuing correspondence spanned the 1930s. Her concept of quarter tones was anathema to Partch; he saw them as simple divisions of equal-tempered semitones that upheld "the very intonational paradigm that his just intonation system was attempting to contravene."[59] But Mimi was open-minded and encouraged Partch—indeed helped him—to design a keyboard that could accommodate his just intonation scale. With his keyboard design completed in August 1932, Partch applied—unsuccessfully—for a Guggenheim grant, using as his references composers Roy Harris, Richard Buhlig, Charles Seeger, and Mildred Couper. He did, however, get a Carnegie grant which allowed him to have his instrument—the Ptolemy—built in London. According to Bob Gilmore, one Carnegie official thought that Partch's Ptolemy resembled an adding machine, but was more like "a combination of a typewriter, checkerboard, Mah Jong, and chocolate fudge."[60] This organ-like instrument had 43 tones to the octave over a 3-octave range and 268 rainbow-colored keys.[61] Partch had it shipped home via the Panama Canal in April 1935, but needed Mimi to pay its transportation from the Los Angeles docks to Santa Barbara and to store it. He thereby dubbed her the "godmother of the chromatic organ."[62] This episode began one of the most difficult times in Partch's life, when he, feeling misunderstood, embarked

---

[56] Couper papers, Box 11, Undated clipping from *Montclair Times*. Mimi's connection with this city stems from her husband's art exhibitions at the Montclair Art Museum.

[57] The Prelude to *Anacapa* has notes for the demonstration: 1) ultrachromatic scale; 2) chromatic scale; 3) ¾ tone scale (starting on C, then C♯; 4) whole tone scale; 5) 1¼ tone (start on C, perfect 4ths); 6) diminished 7th; 7) minor, major 3rd (start 2nd on C, perfect 5ths); 8) glissando minor 3rds.

[58] Couper, quoted in Verne Lindeman, "Music Trends Pointed Out," *Santa Barbara News Press*, undated newspaper clipping.

[59] Bob Gilmore, *Harry Partch: A Biography* (New Haven: Yale University Press, 1998), 88.

[60] Robert M. Lester, secretary of the Carnegie Corporation, in a letter to Edward Murrow of the Institute of International Education, 9 April 1935; cited in Gilmore, 114. Gilmore notes too (121) that Couper encouraged Partch in November 1935 to give up his alienated hobo existence.

[61] See Harry Partch, "A New Instrument," *Musical Opinion* (June 1935) reproduced in Philip Blackburn, *Enclosure 3: Harry Partch* (Saint Paul: American Composers Forum, 1997), 48-49. Partch demonstrated the instrument with the aid of two Southern Californian sopranos: Rudolphine Radil and Calista Rogers.

[62] Partch notes, in *Bitter Music: Collected Journals, Essays, Introduction, and Librettos*, ed. Thomas McGeary (Urbana and Chicago: University of Illinois Press, 1991), 35: "I spent a week persuading the customs officials to admit the chromatic organ without duty. And through friends, a way is ultimately found. Its godmother, in Santa Barbara, has offered to keep it and pay for its transportation there." Blackburn, 475, claims the instrument was last seen in her garage in 1941, but was gone when someone went to retrieve it for Partch.

on a transient existence that he documented in his now-published journal *Bitter Music*. Mimi Couper was one of the few who stood by Partch, offering support to his iconoclastic ideas and feeding and housing him as well. A series of entries in the journal, including conversations with Mimi that Partch set to music, reflect his depressed state of mind and her unflagging encouragement (see Appendix 2). On 12 November 1935, he notes "I have been in Santa Barbara for four days and chromatic organ's godmother's bountiful table has sated one hunger." He continues, bemoaning the fate of his invention:

> Wake over Chromatic Organ the First.
> It is attended by Godmother, a few others, and myself.
> The 168 keys of the organ rest. They will not speak because of
> mechanical derangement. Their rainbowed colors are half chipped.
> I listen to funeral music—Brahms Opus 118, No. 6, which Godmother is
> playing—and gaze upon them. I am glad that no one notices me.[63]

Partch leaves a few days later, thinking that Mimi too does not understand him: she told him he was antagonizing people, that his existence had done something frightful to him, and begged:

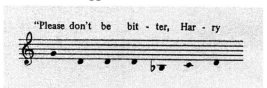

Mimi's quarter-tone music had attracted the attention of another prominent musician, Leopold Stokowski, conductor of the Philadelphia Orchestra, who wrote to her on 23 May 1935 (see Plate 3):

Dear Mrs. Couper,
I should like very much to meet you and hear your experiments in quarter tones. It is so kind of you to give me this opportunity. May I have your telephone number?

Sincerely
Leopold Stokowski[64]

Mimi later reviewed one of his concerts, noting he "has always been interested in exploring musical sound. He has shown a courage and singleness of purpose in this research that is probably unparalleled among musicians."[65]   As noted earlier,

---

[63] *Bitter Music*, 99-101. See Appendix 2 for the complete entries and music.

[64] Mimi saved the original letter, attaching a newspaper clipping about Stokowski's 90th birthday party in New York. Couper Papers, Box 11. Stokowski was then living in Santa Barbara at 224 Buena Vista Street. To the best of my knowledge, nothing came of this inquiry from Stokowski.

[65] Couper papers, Series IIIA, Writings, clipping. Stokowski gave the American premieres of *Rite of Spring, Pierrot lunaire,* and *Wozzeck,* among many other works. See José Bowen, "Stokowski, Leopold," in *The New Grove Dictionary of Music and Musicians,* 2nd ed. 24: 425-26.

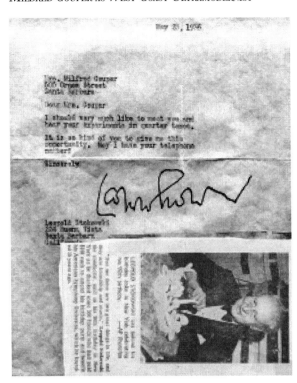

Plate 3: Letter from Stokowski to Mimi Couper

Stokowski championed the microtonal violin works of Mexican composer Julián Carrillo,[66] and he also recorded several compositions by Henry Eichheim.[67]

Mimi's work also came to the attention of the Polish-born French keyboardist Wanda Landowska, who like Mimi was a former student of Moritz Moskowski. Fascinated by Mimi's quarter-tone compositions, Landowska devoted most of a chapter in her 1937 yearbook *L'Année musicale* to Couper. The harpsichordist first rightfully recognized the long history of microtonality, beginning with the Greeks, but she claimed that Mimi's technique in *Dirge* was quite new. Landowska wrote of the "flowering of sonorities through which one walks, as though in a virgin forest," and noted the variety in its rhythmic patterns. She also remarked how she looked forward to the work's premiere in Paris, and the "ardent debates" that it would surely spawn.[68]

---

[66] In 1925, the League of Composers commissioned a work from Carrillo for its concerts; Stokowski heard this and commissioned a work for the Philadelphia Orchestra (*Concertino*, 1926). Stokowski wrote, "Luckily for America, we do not have to look to European musicians for this revolution, since everything is owed to an Indian who descends from the children of the Continent." Quoted in Gerald Benjamin, "Carrillo, Julián, in *The New Grove Dictionary of Music and Musicians*, 2nd ed. 5: 195.

[67] See note 52.

[68] Landowska discusses Couper's *Dirge* in some detail, noting that it was published but had not yet been performed publically. The original text of this essay is included in Appendix 3.

Couper's correspondence reveals that she took composition lessons with the French pedagogue Nadia Boulanger, who spent the years 1942-1944 in Santa Barbara as a guest of the Sachs family. In the summer of 1942, Mimi and Nadia worked together in Lake Tahoe, Nevada, at a ranch owned by the Sachs. Mimi documented her lessons with Boulanger in a series of letters.[69] The subject of microtonality came up in the first lesson: Mimi writes that

> she spoke of ¼ tones—and I don't believe she knew I was guilty of them—as a kind of cocktail for stimulating the senses but as something that is really bad for one. She wants to do away with unnecessary alterations—when one pupil came to her with very complicated altered harmonies, she said half laughing, 'if you could only do away with all the accidentals I believe it would be good.' . . . She said there is no future for atonality—it is dead.[70]

According to Mimi, Boulanger told her that "she did not think that women as a rule had creative talent," noting that she herself "felt she had the creative gift to lead others but not for self expression.[71]

Mimi's relationship with the Sachs family, whose daughter she instructed in piano, and with Boulanger, led to her first meeting with Stravinsky in Santa Barbara, captured in a famous photograph from late fall of 1944 at Featherhill Ranch in Montecito (see plate 4). Mimi treasured this photo, explaining in her unpublished autobiography how she came to have it.

> Mr. Sachs often had Stravinsky as a weekend guest. Igor Stravinsky is considered by many the greatest composer of our times. One day I arrived to give the two Marions their lesson [that is, Marion Sachs and neighbor Marion Baring-Gould],[72] and found the whole group posing for a photograph in the patio. Stravinsky saw me and asked me to join them, which I did.[73]

Also present in the photo are Vera Stravinsky, the hosts Arthur and Georgette Sachs, and three of Nadia Boulanger's students from her 1944 summer class at Edgewood College (Madison, WI): Sister Ignatia Céline (who had been hired as a tutor for the two young girls), the Canadian musician Jean Papineau-Couture (and his wife), and Abbé Elzear Fortier of Québec (who had come to Santa Barbara to study with Nadia). Couper later observed Boulanger and Stravinsky working together at the Sachs estate, and she noted with amazement that, when Stravinsky brought his latest score to show to Nadia, she "sat at the piano and played it at first sight."[74] Nadia informed Mildred that Stavinsky's genius will only be truly appreciated by future generations.

---

[69] Three letters written to Mrs. James Daley (Margaret Church), who was staying at Mildred Couper's house in the summer of 1942, dated 9, 12, and 29 August 1942, written from Glenbrook Inn and Ranch, Lake Tahoe, NV.

[70] Mildred Couper, Letter to Margaret Church, 9 August 1942, Couper Papers, Box 11. See Appendix 4 for the complete texts of her 3 letters about Boulanger.

[71] Mildred Couper, Letter to Margaret Church, 12 August 1942.

[72] Mildred wrote her composition *B.G.* for Marion Baring-Gould at Christmas, 1944.

[73] Couper papers, *Autobiography*, 1970. Photo in Couper papers, box. 11.

[74] Ibid. This anecdote is also recounted by society writer Litti Paulding, in "Nadia Boulanger Remembered Here," *Santa Barbara News Press*, 1 October 1957, on the occasion of Boulanger's 70th birthday.

Plate 4: Mimi Couper standing in back of the seated Nadia Boulanger. Stravinsky is standing to her right leaning forward. Montecito, 1944

In contrast to the conservative opinions toward microtonality of Nadia Boulanger and Stravinsky was the encouraging relationship she had with the eccentric theorist Ivor Darreg (aka Kenneth Gerard O'Hara),[75] whom she met through John Cage. Darreg is best known for coining the term "xenharmonic," referring to tuning systems not using equal temperament. Darreg was the author/ editor of the *Xenharmonic Bulletin* and the self-appointed president of the National Society for the Decriminalization of Microtones. In 1941, Mimi lent Darreg her copy of the Vishnegradsky treatise, *Manuel d'harmonie à quarts de ton*, which Darreg translated into English in a typescript now held in the Glendale (California) Public Library. In his introduction, he acknowledges Mildred Couper, "who lent me the French original . . . and who offered advice from her own experience with composition and performance in the quartertone system."[76] Darreg explains there was a lack of standardization in notation, keyboard layouts, and fingerings because "quarter-tonists were scattered about the world and usually were not aware of one another's

[75] Cage met Darreg (an anagram of Gerard, his given name) in Los Angeles in 1934. According to David Wolf, in the *Discussion Archive on History of Chords*, "Cage introduced Darreg to quarter-tone composer Mildred Couper and helped arrange an interview for Darreg with Schoenberg, who accepted him for study at USC. (Unfortunately, a few weeks before his first semester was to begin, Darreg had an operation that would leave him almost totally incapacitated for the next half century.)" Available at http:/boethius.ucsb.edu/www-talk/smt/2001jan.smt/0063.html. To mention only one example of Darreg's eccentricity, he lost all his teeth at a rather young age, a result of eating only canned soup (his mother did not cook). Not surprisingly, he suffered from high blood pressure his entire life. See Jonathan Glasier, "Ivor Darreg and Xenharmonics," *Perfect Sound Forever*, available at http://www.furious.com/perfect/xenharmonics.html (accessed 20 May 2011).

[76] Ivan Wyschnegradsky, *Manual of Quartertone Harmony*, translated from the French by Ivor Darreg, typescript dated November 1976, Glendale Public Library, 3. Darreg wrote many articles on microtonality; one of his earliest (1947) is "The Quartertone Question"; the complete musical writings of Darreg are available at hhttp://sonic-arts.org/darreg/contents.htm (accessed 20 May 2011).

existence."[77] He credits Couper with important modifications of Wyschnegradsky's notational system for flats, which he adopted in his own works (see Plate 5).[78]

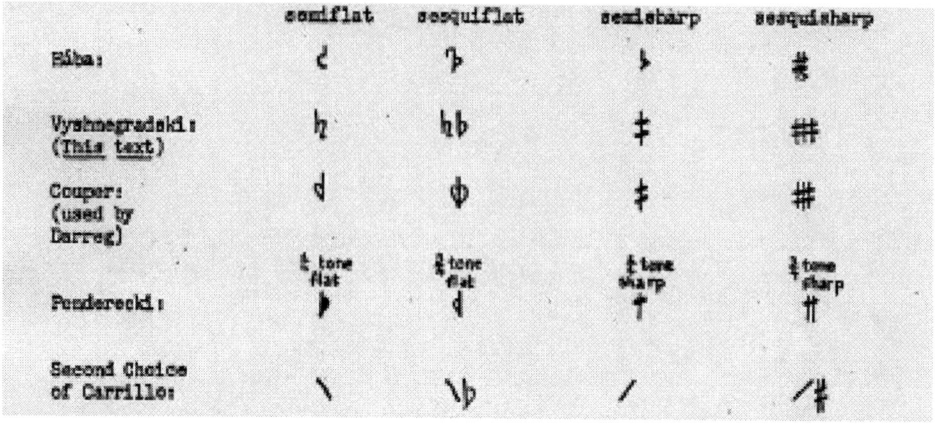

Plate 5: Darreg's table of notation systems. Introduction to Wyschnegradsky treatise.

As shown in Plate 6 below, Couper's system was an adapatation of the Italian Baroque violinist and composer Giuseppe Tartini's semi-sharp scheme to show semi-flat symbols, compared here with the modern Sagittal notation system, which provides a universal set of microtonal accidentals.[79]

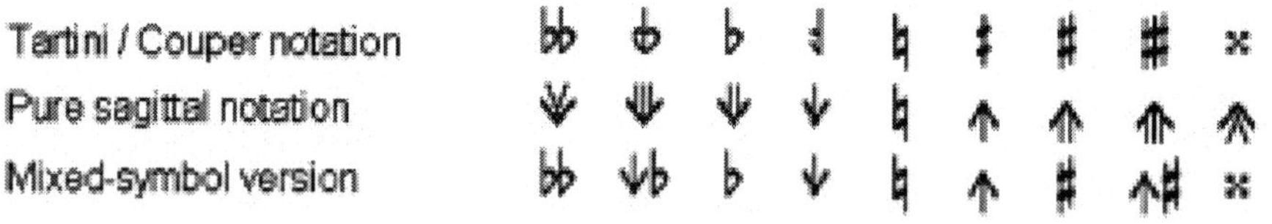

Plate 6: Comparison of modern microtonal notation systems.

Couper used this new notational system only once that I can determine in her works: in the arrangement of her *Dirge* for violin and piano. Of course, her two-piano works had no need of these special symbols. In the violin part, she first used Vishnegradsky's semiflat (or ¼ flat) symbol, but created her own for the sesqui- or ¾ flat; the symbols for sharps are from Tartini's notation (see Plate 7).[80]

---

[77] Ibid., 4.

[78] Ibid. Darreg writes "even though in my quartertone compositions I use the Couper modification of the Vyshnegradski system, which differs only in the flat-signs . . . I have left all of Vyshnegradski's semi- and sesquiflats intact in his text."

[79] George D. Secor and David Keenan, "Sagittal, A Microtonal Notation System," *Xenharmonicôn: An Informal Journal of Experimental Music* 18 (2006), available at http://www.sagittal.org/sagittal. pdf (accessed 20 May 2011). This is a comprehensive system for notating musical pitch in all possible scales and tunings—a universal set of microtonal accidentals, equally suited to extended just intonation, equal division of intervals, or anything in between. It is called Sagittal (arrowlike) because it uses various arrow-like symbols, pointing up or down to indicate raising or lowering of pitch.

[80] Couper papers, box. 1.

Plate 7: Manuscript of violin part to *Dirge*

Mimi's unflagging interest in modernism is revealed through her review of the New York scene in spring 1939, on the occasion of the first New York World's Fair; here, she informs her Santa Barbara readers that there is growing interest in contemporary art and music in New York, "although there are still many who persistently close their ears to these developments." She notes "a very significant event" in March being the *Versus* exhibit at the Architectural League, while asserting that music—"fluid architecture"—was still in an early phase of development. She singled Tom Adrian Cracraft, as "a forward-looking musicologist . . . [and] pioneer in the science of new musical color . . . who is arousing much interest in the New York World's Fair with his electrical band," providing the composer of the future with not only these new timbres, but also "new scales and harmonic combinations made possible by the use of the higher overtone series." She further considered the New York concert scene for a period of several weeks in April 1939, assessing that "the proportion of new to old is pretty evenly balanced." She went on to list all the living composers whose music was performed, claiming that "ten years ago, such an array of contemporary works could not have reached the New York concert stage."[81]

Later in her career, Mimi may have forseen that quarter-tone music was beginning to lose its luster. The brief biographical entry (that she most likely penned) in the 1948 edition of *Music and Dance in California and the West* states that Couper "formerly experimented and concertized in quarter-tone music."[82] Still, Mimi continued to promote her works: one notable performance was in 1951, when she and American composer Ingolf Dahl performed her *Dirge* and *Rumba* at one of the famous Los Angeles "Evenings on the Roof" concerts, held on 19 November 1951.[83] Although this was a California composer's concert, Charles Ives's quarter-tone piano works were also performed.[84] While the review headline read "Music by California Composers Pleases," Couper's works were not fully appreciated: "Listed as exemplifying the quarter-tone system," wrote the reviewer, "one can justifiably report this contribution as simply a musical stunt."[85] Nevertheless, Mimi continued

---

[81] Mildred Couper, "Interest Growing in Contemporary Music, Critic's Survey Reveals," *Santa Barbara News Press*, [April 1939], clipping. The composer mentioned are: Roy Harris, Roger Sessions, Theodore Chanler, Ernst Krenek, Leo Soerby [*sic*], Robert Russell Bennett, Charles Wakefield Cadman, Harold Morris, Robert Delaney, Robert Sanders, Igor Stravinsky, Serge Prokofieff, Benjamin Britten, Hunter Johnson, Aaron Copland, and Robert Palmer.

[82] *Music and Dance in California and the West*, 3d ed., ed. Richard Drake Saunders (Hollywood: Bureau for Musical Research, 1948), 188. She advertised herself in this same dictionary (p. 295) as pianist, teacher, composer, lecturer, and music critic for the *Santa Barbara News Press*.

[83] "Roof Artists Will Go North," *The Los Angeles Times*, 16 September 1951, E7, reported that 6 Evenings on the Roof concerts were given in Santa Barbara: 3 at the Lobero Theater and 3 at Monte Verde [*sic*]. The Couper archive at UCSB preserves a recording of *Dirge* made by Mildred Couper and Violet Koehler.

[84] Dorothy Lamb Crawford, *Evenings On and Off the Roof: Pioneering Concerts in Los Angeles, 1939-1971* (Berkeley: University of California Press, 1995), 97. Also performed on this concert were works by Paul Pisk, Andrew Imbrie, William O. Smith, and George Hyde.

[85] A.P.Q., "Music by California Composers Pleases," *Los Angeles Times*, 21 November 1951, A6. Albert Goldberg, in his *Los Angeles Times* column, "The Sounding Board. A Study in Contrasts"

her relentless promotion of new music in Santa Barbara; Dorothy Crawford records that several programs were sent there, "where Mildred Couper owned a beautiful home called Monteverde, which became one site—along with the Lobero Theater—of touring programs by Roof musicians."[86]

Mildred Couper's legacy is her pivotal role as a maverick female composer and supporter of quarter-tone music within the orbit of West Coast avant-garde musicians.[87] That Couper earned the respect of such avant-garde leaders as Cowell, Partch, and Cage, amid the misogynistic atmosphere of the era, is remarkable.[88] It is well known that within the modernist cultural milieu there lurked a deep-seated bias against women. Ives, for example, famously remarked that "a good dissonance is like a man,"[89] and in an article entitled "The Feminization of Music," published in the 1922 *Music Teachers Association Proceedings*, a faculty member from the Peabody Conservatory railed about the increasing sentimentality of music.[90] Furthermore, it was Cowell's custom to use women to do his bookkeeping and the day-to-day routine work for his ventures;[91] indeed, the experimental composer Johanna Beyer served as Cowell's personal secretary during the four years he was in prison.[92] It

---

(13 February 1949), relates that Alois Hába was castigated by delegates to the 1948 International Congress of Musicians in Prague for his quarter-tone music: "White as a sheet," Goldberg writes, "Hába stood up before his accusers and defended his right to his way of thinking." Goldberg entertains his readers in his Sounding Board column of 16 December 1951 (p. E6) with this quarter-tone anecdote from a 1951 interview he conducted with Samuel Barber: when asked by a commanding general of the Air Force "why don't you write for quarter-tones," Barber (then a private in the Air Force) explained that, since his symphony would be played by the BSO, it would not be feasible. The general quipped, "What's the matter, don't they have quarter tones? We will take care of that—the Air Force has all the latest equipment."

[86] Crawford, 97.

[87] The term "maverick," generally associated with males, is used here with trepidation after its adoption by Sarah Palin.

[88] See "Search for the Modern, Early 20th-century Mavericks," in *American Mavericks*, ed. Susan Key and Larry Rothe (Berkeley and Los Angeles: University of California Press, 2001), 32-35. This misogyny was rampant among composers (see notes 87 and 88 below) as well as educators and critics.

[89] This now infamous quote is the title of a documentary on the life of Ives, written and directed by Theodor William Timreck et al, originally released in 1976 as a motion picture by the New York Foundation for the Arts, then released in 1988 as a part of the Metropolitan Museum of Art home video collection. On Ives and misogyny, see especially Judith Tick, "Charles Ives and Gender Ideology," *Musicology and Difference: Gender and Sexuality in Music Scholarship*, ed. Ruth A Solie (Berkeley: University of California Press, 1993), 87-106; and Frank Rossiter, *Charles Ives and His America* (New York: Liveright, 1975), 28-37.

[90] Harold Randolph, "The Feminization of Music," Papers and Proceedings of the Music Teachers National Association, 1922 (Hartford, CT: Music Teachers National Association, 1923), 198. Mary Herron DuPree, "The Failure of American Music: The Critical View from the 1920s," *Journal of Musicology* 2, no. 3 (Summer 1983): 311, cites Deems Taylor's complaints about the domination of women as patrons and the public for music has led to a "sentimentality" and claimed that "this well-nigh complete feminization of music is bad for it." DuPree also emphasizes Ives's obsession for manliness, "which results from his distaste for the 'effeminate' quality which pervaded American musical culture" (see note 89 above).

[91] Rita Mead, *Henry Cowell's New Music, 1925-1936: The Society, the Music Editions, and the Recordings* (Ann Arbor, UMI Press, 1981), 38.

[92] Kennedy and Polansky, "Total Eclipse," 720.

was a difficult road for an individualist female composer, and few broke through this barrier. An exception was Ruth Crawford Seeger, who enjoyed success during her brief career as a composer and who is now viewed as one of the most original voices of her time. The evidence suggests that Mildred Couper crossed this frontier as well, to be recognized by the likes of Harry Partch, John Cage, Henry Cowell, Leopold Stokowski, and Igor Stravinsky. Her strong commitment to education linked her to two female "giants" of her time: Nadia Boulanger and Wanda Landowska. Perhaps most importantly, Couper sought to educate the public about this new world of sound. She continued her lectures on microtonality in Santa Barbara, including the gifted students at the Music Academy of the West in her audience. Ronald Scofield described a 1953 lecture in Santa Barbara in detail:

> Yesterday afternoon Mrs. Mildred Couper of Santa Barbara discussed and demonstrated "Microtones in Music," especially in reference to the use of quarter tones in which she has experimented for some years.
>
> Quarter tones are only a primary step in freeing music from the chromatic scale, she revealed, citing the work of Harry Partch of California, who has divided the octave in 43 microtones, according to the overtone series, and has invented many instruments to play these intervals. Carrillo of Mexico has written music for quarter tones, eighth tones and 16th tones, Mrs. Couper said, and listed some of the other composers who use quarter tones as: Alois Hába, for string quartet, small orchestra, harmonium, and piano as well as a complete opera in quarter tones; R. H. Stein of Germany for piano and clarinet; Grecchi of Italy, an opera; Ernest Bloch and Bartók have occasionally employed quarter tones in their music. Ivan Vischnegradsky of Paris has invented a quarter-tone piano, and written some of the most important music in this medium, she added. For herself, she said she has returned to the piano as the instrument best suited to reveal the values of quarter-tone music, without leaving the impression of out-of-tune playing.
>
> Mrs. Couper demonstrated with phonograph records the minute gradations of the microtones, and then showed the contrast in the quarter-tone scale by playing on two pianos. With the assistance of Dr. John Gillespie [Professer of Music at UC Santa Barbara], she played two of her compositions, *Dirge* and *Rumba*, which revealed a fascinating new tonal texture of overtones as well as new possibilities in melodic lines, arpeggios, and harmonic relations.
>
> The composer did not claim microtones represent the music of the future but she felt that there would always be a small group of musicians interested in exploring this field, which held great possibilities for enriching our musical experiences.[93]

A *Santa Barbara News Press* article confirms that she took her expertise to another cultural mecca: apparently her lectures on quarter-tone music were "anticipated with great interest in Santa Fe and many are joining the course to hear Mrs. Couper's exceptional talents in presenting such material," referring to

[93] Ronald Scofield, *Santa Barbara News Press*, 18 June 1953.

her 1953 "Listening to Music" lecture series, presented at Santa Fé's Eidolon Arts School. Couper was even responsible for another Santa Barbara musician taking up experimental compositional techniques: her friend Countess Madeleine de Bryas turned to music in the 1950s after a distinguished career as a French diplomat.[94] One of Santa Barbara's resident royalty, the Countess's music was performed on many occasions in the channel city.[95]

Mimi remained true to modernism to the end, showing her ability to recognize cutting-edge art in her introduction to an exhibition catalog of paintings by Kelly Frear, a leader in the Texas modernist school and a core member of the so-called "Fort Worth Circle." Here she revels in the fanciful traits of his canvases amid a discussion of the artist's pantheistic philosophy, closing with the comment that "one might almost say that he foretells the art of the future."[96]

By the time Mildred Couper died on 9 August 1974, she was best remembered for her ardent patronage of the arts, as well as her dedicated teaching at Santa Barbara's most esteemed institutions. Former student Roger A. Clarke, of the Lobero Theater, called her "a woman of great courage and high ideals," noting how Santa Barbara was enormously in her debt for her leadership in the city's cultural life, and the Canadian conductor/pianist Reginald Stewart, who headed the piano department at the prestigious Music Academy of the West, claimed that with her death, "one of the strong pillars of our musical structure was removed. It was as though a light that had shone upon us all had suddenly been extinguished."[97] With this renewed interest in her creative efforts, Mildred Couper can now be recognized as the true maverick she was; her musical contributions, appreciated by the most famous of colleagues—including John Cage, Harry Partch, and Henry Cowell—mark her as an important harbinger of West Coast modernism.

---

[94] Madeleine de Bryas is the author of *A Frenchwoman's Impressions of America* (New York: The Century Company, 1920). She first traveled to Santa Barbara in 1918 as a representative of the American Committee for the Relief of Devastated France.

[95] Mary Ann Callen, "Resident Royalty Find New Life Here," *Santa Barbara News Press*, 14 December 1958, D1.

[96] "An Exhibition of Paintings by Kelly Fearing, Saturday, August 25, 1962," with a catalog introduction by Mildred Couper, photocopy, UCSB archive.

[97] Letters to the Editor, *Santa Barbara News Press*, 11 August 1974.

Appendix 1

SELECTED LIST OF COMPOSITIONS BY MILDRED COUPER[98]

Published compositions

1925   *We Are Seven* (children's pieces, J. Fischer)
1937   *Dirge* (New Music Editions)
1938   *Seven More* (children's pieces, J. Fischer)

Quarter-tone compositions, all for 2 pianos tuned a quarter-tone apart

1930   *Xanadu*
                    Largo
                    Andante
                    Scherzando
                    Allegro
                    Allegro agitato
1932   *Rumba*
193?   *Prelude* and *Anacapa*
193?   *Dirge*
                    arr. violin and piano, using new notational symbols

Other notable works (with reviews or other commentary)

                Variations on "The Irish Washerwoman"
                    Solo piano (performed by Shura Cherkassky as an encore,
                        Bethlehem, PA, 1943)
                    2-piano arrangement
                    Orchestral arrangement, performed in Los Angeles, Dec. 1945
                        (Werner Janssen Orchestra) on concert with LA debut of
                        Leon Fleischer (age 17)
1941   Piano Quintet, *And on Peace Earth*, written for Homer Simmons
1949   *Gitanesca*, for 2 pianos; arranged for trio and first performed 1949
                The Days of Our Lives, for violin, oboe, piano
                Passacaglia for clarinet, 2 violins, viola, cello and piano, later rescored
                        for flutes, oboes, clarinets, bassoons, 3 horns, trumpets,
                        trombone, tuba, drums, piano, ;2 vlns, viola, cello, double bass
                The Nine Muses, piano, performed 1965

---

[98] This list includes only published works, her quarter-tone compositions, and other frequently
performed compositions. Complete list of Couper's works available at http://wingedsun.com/
couper-m/Music.htm

Children's pieces (unpublished)

1944   *B.G.,* for piano, dedicated to Marion Baring-Gould
        Barnyard Cogitations and *Fur and Feathers*, children's pieces set to
           verses by Ogden Nash

Appendix 2

HARRY PARTCH'S COMMENTS ABOUT MILDRED COUPER
FROM *BITTER MUSIC*, NOVEMBER 1935.

November 12—Santa Barbara

Something to eat, a dry place to sleep, and sometimes a smile—they seem like little things.

But they are not always easy. Five days ago I begged at fourteen houses in San Luis— at fourteen sets of steps I mortified myself—and when I was through I held a can of milk and a can of pea soup. Not even these would I have gotten had I not insisted on my need like a homeless please-eyes dog.

True, there was a Sally kitchen. I went there twice, the limit of meals allowed, and since they want you to move. It is always move, move, move—where? Nobody knows or cares.

They gave me beans and skimmed milk, and it tasted good. A can of milk and a can of pea soup—not enough to satisfy that night's hunger, let alone the accumulated hungers of the day, and the day before that, and that, and that.

And not even enough misery of mortification to end it. And all around me spirits.

That hover like humming birds over flowers. Is there honey for the suckling? Now I have been in Santa Barbara for four days and chromatic organ's godmother's bountiful table has sated one hunger.

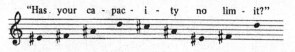

I look at her sadly.   asks Daughter.

Wake over Chromatic Organ the First.

It is attended by Godmother, a few others, and myself.

The 168 keys of the organ rest. They will not speak because of mechanical derangement. Their rainbowed colors are half chipped off.

I listen to the funeral music—Brahms Opus 118, No. 6, which Godmother is playing—and gaze upon them. I am glad that no one notices me.

Today I dress the body—cementing the colors back on before leaving.

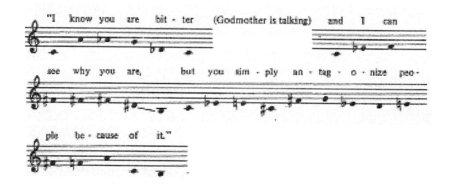

I continue her thought but do not say—"Work with them, as they work, and thereby deny your existence."

I wipe the dust from the body with my handkerchief. The mask fretwork smiles.

Tears weary, wither, and blow away.

November 14

I am walking about in the park and find forty-four cents in dimes, nickels, and pennies at a spot in the grass.

"How lucky," I say as I go away, but I turn to look back and see a fat man scratching in the grass on the spot.

Instinctively I start back, with the forty-four cents in my hand ready to present. Before I get to the fat man, I also see a stylish lady in a shiny car, its motor idling, waiting.

I turn and disappear quickly into the bushes.

November 15—Leaving Santa Barbara

(Godmother is talking as she drives me part of the way to Ventura),

Sans home or hope—the wanderer still lives, does things, says things, thinks things. I am thinking that if I have done nothing more than show these I perhaps have done a service.

"It is only through the ferment of experience and bitterness that evils are corrected (I am replying). If all feelings were suppressed, there would be no voice.

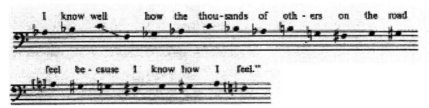

She, who had courageously supported herself and her children for many
years and is now debt-ridden, inssts I take a dollar.

We then agree that life is a siege of anguish, she smiles, and we part.

Appendix 3

LANDOWSKA'S WRITING ABOUT MILDRED COUPER

Wanda Landowska, *L'Année musicale* (1937), chapter XIII, 63-65:

L'Amérique nous adresse une oeuvre pour deux pianos écrite par Mme Mildred
Couper, sous le titre de: *Dirge, Chant funèbre*. L'auteur de cette composition étrange
qui mérite un examen approfondi est née à Buenos-Ayres où elle reçut sa première
éducation musicale complètée en Allemagne, à Paris et à Rome. Après avoir
donné des leçons de piano neuf années durant dans un Institut musical de New-
York city, Mildred Couper se rendit en Californie. Là elle organisa un studio à
Santa-Barbara pour effectuer des expériences de musique en quarts de tons. Son
premier ouvrage réalisé dans ce sens fut un ballet: *Xanadu* interprété au cours
de la pièce d'Eugène O Neills: *Marco Millions*, représentée au théâtre Lobero de
Santa-Barbara. En dehors des ouvrages en quarts de tons, Mme Mildred Couper
composa notamment un opéra dansé d'après des paroles de Malcolm Chuburn
[*sic*]. *Le Chant funèbre* que nous recevons n'a pas encore été joué en public, l'édition
précède l'exécution. Le second piano doit être accordé un quart de ton plus
haut que le premier; aucune altération ne figure à la clé. Les dièzes comme
les bémols sont placés devant chaque note, ce qui supprime totalement l'usage
des bécarres. La technique présentée par Mme Mildred Couper et qui semble
nouvelle était familière aux Grecs de l'Antiquité. Des études faites dans le monde
entier tentent à la remettre en honneur. Un movement très net se dessine en ce
sens et peut-être dans quelques generations, la musique en quarts de tons, après
une éclipse de plusieurs siècles retrouvera-t-elle la vogue qu'elle connut durant
une longue période de l'histoire. Il faudra longtemps pour s'habituer à la subtilité
des harmonies nouvelles ainsi créées; au début, elles paraîtront étonnamment
fausses; la tessiture de la voix et celle des instruments devront être modifiés; après
de sérieuses études, les chanteurs parviendront à interpréter les oeuvres difficiles
qui leur sont offertes et les instruments, accordés de manière différente subiront,
eux aussi, d'importants changements. Le système actuellement en usage sera
remplacé par un autre infiniment plus compliqué, plus riche en sonorités. Dans
le *Chant funèbre* de Mme Mildred Couper, on peut compter jusqu'à vingt-trois
altérations dans une même mesure, l'impression causée au premier moment
par l'accord différent de deux pianos n'est pas agreeable, mais une certain
accoutumance se fait; lè tout est de partir d'un point de vue nouveau: les fausses

notes n'existent pas. L'abondante floraison de sonorités à travers laquelle nous nous promenons comme dans une forêt vierge surprend mais ne déçoit pas. Le rythme, dans l'oeuvre de Mildred Couper, subit, lui aussi d'importantes fluctuations: measures à 5, 7, 8/4, remplacées par des mesures à 2, 3, 6, ou 9/8. Nous attendons maintenant la présentation de cette oeuvre dans un concert où elle ne manquera pas de soulever d'ardentes polémiques que l'avenir se chargera de résoudre.

Appendix 4

COUPER'S LETTERS ON BOULANGER COMPOSITION LESSONS

Letter of 9 August 1942, from Mildred Couper to Margaret Church (Mrs. James Daley)
From Glenbrook Inn and Ranch, Lake Tahoe, Nevada

Dear Margaret,

Well, I read in the [San Francisco] Chronicle that you came off with flying colors in your concert; congratulations! I would have given anything to hear it. Wasn't it a very stimulating experience! I don't know if you will be surprised or not at a decision I have taken. Nadia Boulanger is here for the rest of the month & I started lessons with her yesterday. There is no doubt about it, she has a master mind. I will try to give you an idea of these lessons, using you for a diary (I hope you don't mind). I shall ask you to keep the letters & let me have them eventually. I never seem to be able to write a diary but in writing to you I can get a better impetus by passing on what Boulanger gives me. I decided to take the Walt Whitman song to her, the one you took away. She went over (mentally) the first part very intently making one or two minor suggestions; when she came to the middle part, however, where "the bows turn, the freighted ship, tacking, speeds away," she shook her head & asked me if I really felt that was good. I confessed I had had difficulty with the rapid passage & she said it was too much according to a pianistic pattern & had very little to do with the rest of the song. She therefore recommended re-writing all the middle part—then she gave a long talk on the importance of discarding everything that is not really good in one's own opinion. I told her I was often in doubt, & she said if something is <u>really</u> good one <u>knows</u> it. The first part, she said, was in the mood of the words and rang true (also the end). She then discoursed at length about the necessity of getting back to the early masters, Bach, Mozart, Haydn (she loves him) & using their methods—she said we cannot get away for long from dominant harmonies. She spoke of ¼ tones, & I don't believe she knew I was guilty of them—as a kind of cocktail for stimulating the senses but as something that is really bad for one. She wants to do away with unnecessary alterations—when one pupil ~~who~~ came to her with very complicated altered harmonies she said half laughing "if you could only do away with all the accidentals I believe it would be good." They tried it that way and it is now a published work!!! She said there is no future for atonality--it is dead. This constant leaping in large intervals destroys any feelings of climax because the means for one are used up. She also thinks that large orchestral works are on the wane—throughout she would illustrate at the piano with quotations from a Haydn quartet or some other chamber work & with such miraculous precision & point! I have been given food for thought in one lesson which will last one a long time. I am trying to rewrite the middle section of the song & it is the hardest thing I ever did. Perhaps I am too old a dog?
Much love,
Mildred

Letter of 12 August 1942, from Mildred to Margaret
From Glenbrook Inn and Ranch, Lake Tahoe, Nevada

Dear Margaret,
A letter from Radiana [Pazmor] tells me you played beautifully last Thursday. I
knew you would! She seems to have been more impressed with Rebecca Clarke's
work than by the compositions of the mere male faction. This interests me because
Mme Boulanger told me that she did not think that women as a rule had creative
talent. She said of herself that she felt she had the creative gift to lead others but
not for self expression. I do not think she was being personal when she told me
this. Today I had a fascinating lesson. I took her the first three movements of the
Dance of Life—she was a good deal more enthusiastic about this than about the
Whitman song; a few helpful suggestions I shall carry out, but there is no need for
extensive rewriting—three cheers! The song is giving me the dickens of a time. By
the by did you give it to Goldschmitt? Because I think the changes I am making
are improving it very much—Mme B[oulanger] is hipped on the subject of strict
metronomic time, & on this I cannot completely agree altho[ugh] I know what she
means—she is fed up with the laxity of pulse that many professionals show. She is
intensely religious & secretly believes, I am convinced, that nobody who is not a
Catholic can be a good musician. She thinks the most important thing in life is self-
discipline. The one thing particularly I like about her as a teacher is the fact that
she never suggests a change of style; that is probably why her pupils are so varied.
Her principal advice is to be sincere & to discard more than one writes. We all had
lunch at the Sach's today, the three men who are studying with her and myself. It
was lots of fun.
More anon
Much love,
Mildred

Letter of 29 August 1942, from Mildred to Margaret
From Glenbrook Inn and Ranch, Lake Tahoe, Nevada

I had my last lesson with Boulanger today. I took her the song that I had rewritten
at her suggestion (Aboard, at a Ship's Helm) & she thinks it is immensely improved;
I also took her the worked over version of "The Dance of Life." She read it over
very carefully, made a few minor suggestions & appeared to like it very much.
I feel enormously encouraged. Of course, all this rewriting has retarded me in
accomplishing what I had set out to do this summer—but I can go on at home & I
feel so much clearer in my mind about what lies ahead. Mme Boulanger is always
very stimulating—she has the most active mind I have ever encountered—she will
pause over a phrase & then bring up several examples from the great composers to
back up her criticism, sometimes about only one badly placed note; what's more

she will jump into the middle of some phrase at the piano that perfectly illustrates her point. She seems to have the entire literature of music at her finger's end— not only piano music but orchestral, chamber & vocal. She tells me I must guard against a tendency to write chords to punctuate the first beat & suggests that I use a more contrapuntal style. She spoke a great deal about the teaching of children. She adores children but has never taught them as she is only interested in teaching professionals. She thinks I have accomplished a great deal with little Marion Sachs & is surprised because she knew how apparently tone deaf she was—she is against reading those biographies of the composers to children. She has a horror of the superficial tendency to know facts about great men & to overlook their works. I do not agree with her about this as I think the children are stimulated to read & play the music when they hear what the composers have accomplished. In the case of Marion Sachs it has had a definite result. Those three lessons with Boulanger have made the whole summer worthwhile.

Mildred

Mysteries and Secrets Revealed

❧❧

Let there be light:
Liturgical Manuscripts at Hearst Castle

Alicia M. Doyle

Lampshades with panels made out of folios from a chant manuscript would typically stand out in even the most opulent of homes, but at newspaper magnate William Randolph Hearst's estate La Cuesta Encantada (The Enchanted Hill) located near San Simeon, California, they fail to raise even an eyebrow amongst visitors who pay to take one of four guided tours. The only child of mining investor, publishing icon, and later U.S. senator George Hearst, William Randolph built what is popularly known as "Hearst Castle" between 1919 and 1947.[1] Since 1958, thousands of visitors each year have filed through the grounds, all within an arm's reach of priceless cultural artifacts gathered by Hearst through years of exhaustive purchasing. Designed by architect Julia Morgan, the estate's grounds are as theatrical as Hearst's famed "news" stories.[2] Some of the most popular tour destinations are the enormous pools—the outdoor Neptune Pool (featuring four seventeenth-century Italian *bas-reliefs*) and the indoor Roman Pool (decorated from ceiling to floor with one-inch square mosaic tiles that are blue, orange, and transparent; the transparent tiles have fused gold inside).

---

[1] Hearst's home was bequeathed to the state in 1957. The first tours were similar in scope to today's "Tour 1," see: http://www.hearstcastle.org/. My most sincere thanks to the curator of Hearst Castle, Jana Seely, who was extraordinarily accommodating during my examination of the lampshades and chant book. Additional thanks to Jeff Payne, who was a font of historical information based on decades of experience as a docent and Hearst Castle collections registrar, and to Hoyt Fields, Museum Director at Hearst Castle, who approved my initial research request.

[2] Julia Morgan's client-centered approach to design was a perfect match for Hearst's capricious architectural desires. Established as an architect in the San Francisco area, Morgan is recognized as a pioneer amongst women architects in the early twentieth century. A good introductory resource to the work of Morgan can be found in: Sara Holmes Boutelle, *Julia Morgan, Architect* (New York: Abbeville Press, 1995); Richard W. Longstreth, "Julia Morgan: Some Introductory Notes," *Perspecta* 15 (1975), 74-86; and details pertaining to her designs can be found within the materials housed in the Julia Morgan Collection, Special Collections, California Polytechnic State University, San Luis Obispo, California. This archival resource contains architectural drawings and plans, office records, photographs, correspondence, project files, student work, family correspondence, and personal papers from the estate of Julia Morgan.

Although it is remarkably devoid of objects created in the spirit of modernism or other contemporaneous trends, the tremendous collection at Hearst Castle contains extraordinary bits and pieces of world history assembled in a truly eclectic fashion. From a tour, one can see objects dating back to the Eighteenth Dynasty of Egypt (sixteenth-eleventh centuries BCE) capriciously positioned next to European treasures from the nineteenth century.

Coveted personal invitations to the castle were often awarded to famous visitors such as Franklin Roosevelt, Winston Churchill, Cary Grant, and Charles Lindberg. At his estate, Hearst famously insisted on a casual atmosphere made clear by his insistence on paper napkins and bottles of Heinz ketchup (which were situated alongside eighteenth-century Mexican silver candlesticks) on a massive antique dining table located in the Refectory. Hearst's informal intent is in dramatic contrast with the ostentatious *mise-en-scène* of the Refectory itself, where the wall behind the table is adorned with an early sixteenth-century Flemish tapestry depicting Daniel at the court of Nebuchadnezzar that in turn is flanked by fourteenth-century Spanish choir stalls.

Given his role in politics and media, Hearst's musical tastes understandably have not been the central focus of any biographical studies of note. He was, however, also the son of a music teacher, Phoebe Apperson Hearst, and music played more than a minor role in the "courtly pastimes" at Hearst Castle. When I was wandering the halls of the castle during my research visit, I was reminded of the years I spent as Bill Prizer's student at UC Santa Barbara. It is with great fondness that I remember his scholarship on the music of courtly love and the lively seminar discussions of north Italian court life in Florence, Modena, Ferrara, and Mantua. In particular I recall being impressed by the cultural literacy of the elite Sforza, Estensi, Medici, and Gonzaga families. In some way I believe Hearst felt he was continuing the cultural splendor of these Italian Renaissance families by decorating his home with European artifacts and entertaining contemporaneous political idols. While Hearst certainly was not a patron of the arts in the way that Isabella d'Este or Lorenzo de' Medici had been, he showed a keen interest in incorporating music and musicians at his coastal retreat.[3] In addition to political celebrities and Hollywood film stars, Hearst frequently invited musicians to his home as guests. Other evidence of his interest in music includes the presence of record players in several rooms at the castle, two Wurlitzer Apollo player pianos on site, and an impressive collection of piano rolls and records.[4]

---

[3] "Courtly Pastimes" is a reference to William Prizer's *Courtly Pastimes: The Frottole of Marchetto Cara* (Ann Arbor, Mich.: UMI Research Press, 1980).

[4] There are over a hundred piano rolls at Hearst Castle. The collection contains a wide variety of popular tunes along with classical works including Verdi's *Aïda*, Mozart's *Gloria*, Wagner's *Parsifal*, and many pieces by Chopin. The rolls are in a storage closet next to the musician's balcony that opens from the second floor into the Refectory.

Music was also a determining factor in the architectural design of the castle, as witnessed by the balcony in the Refectory where musical performances (both spontaneous and planned) took place. The selected décor in the Assembly Room includes a nod to music in the form of a nineteenth-century manuscript chant book, as does a set of lamps in the third-story Gothic Suite, the shades of which are fashioned out of folios from a separate chant manuscript.[5] This study is dedicated to these decorative musical items.

Discussions of Hearst's political and cultural ideology are a common theme in his biographical literature and his conspicuous consumption has been addressed by most.[6] This consumption is immediately apparent at his home near San Simeon. The message the castle sends is clear: if you have enough money, you can buy history and move it to the United States.[7] Political, cultural, and moral arguments aside, this home is a fascinating historic attraction, providing insight into an exuberant collector's mindset.[8] To a scholar of liturgical music manuscripts these items—the lampshades in particular—fall under the category of morbidly fascinating and deserving of examination beyond the velvet ropes of the tour routes.

Physical Description: The Lampshades

There are a total of fourteen lampshades comprised of folios from a chant manuscript at Hearst Castle.[9] Ten are currently on display in Hearst's private

[5] There is, to my knowledge, limited use of manuscript folios as lampshades. On lampshades from one or two fourteenth-century antiphoners, see Morné Bezuidenhout, "The Franciscan Lampshade Fragments in Port Elizabeth," *SAMUS: South African Journal of Musicology* 16 (1996), 1-9. An involved Google image search did turn up two other lampshades for sale by antiques dealers and an image of a lampshade appearing to be made out of chant manuscript leaves at the home of ultra-modernist Mildred Couper in Montecito, CA. http://wingedsun.com/couper-m/MusicPh.htm (accessed November 18, 2009). For more on Mildred Couper, see Kristine Forney's article on pp/387ff of this volume.

[6] David Nasaw's *The Chief: The Life of William Randolph Hearst* (New York: Houghton Mifflin Company, 2000) is an excellent biographical study of Hearst. Of particular interest are details culled from Hearst's private correspondence with Julia Morgan.

[7] Hearst even bought two monasteries (one from the twelfth and another from the thirteenth century), had them dismantled, stone by stone, and shipped to the U.S. Neither was rebuilt in his lifetime. Portions of the monasteries have since been partially rebuilt and can be seen today as the chapter house at the Abbey of New Clairvaux in Vina, in Northern California, and the Monastery of St. Bernard de Clairvaux in Miami, Florida.

[8] The collections of other late nineteenth- and early twentieth-century entrepreneurs who at one time called California home (Getty, Sutro, Huntington, Doheny, etc.) are equally as revealing of the collectors themselves as hyperextensions of contemporaneous cultural values.

[9] There are also six lampshades made out of indenture papers in the suite, all written in English. According to Seely, several of the indenture papers appear to have been written on pre-printed forms. She indicated that one of the shades in the Gothic Study (associated with lamp 529-9-2179) has a lion and unicorn heraldic etching with the following printed in a circle: "Sold by T. David's Stationer in Cliffords Inn Fleet Street." Dates visible on the lampshades include 1697, 1745, and 1848.

third-story Gothic Suite (Tour 2), and one is on display in the Visitor Center (free to view without purchasing a tour). The remaining three shades are currently held in the basement of the castle.

Hearst's private Gothic Suite in the main house was clearly designed to evoke a "gothic" atmosphere. The resulting space is neo-gothic in aesthetic, but the objects are not wholly medieval in origin. The suite was one of Hearst's frequent architectural afterthoughts, and after considerable reverse engineering and complicated construction, it was added on to the main building (Casa Grande) in the late 1920s and early 1930s. Since it is on the third story, a private elevator was also built in an existing stairwell to ease transport.[10]

Five of the ten music lampshades in this suite illuminate the Gothic Study, the main room within the Gothic Suite (located above the second floor Cloister Bedrooms, and Doge's Suite, also Tour 2). In this impressive room with double clerestory windows and an open-beamed roof seemingly supported by gothic arches, the chant lamps stand in front of wall-to-wall bookshelves.[11] Below the fifteenth-century Spanish ceiling (again, not quite "Gothic"), the lampshades definitely appear at home, complementing and enhancing the ancient and solemn characteristics of the design (See Figure 1).

Five other lampshades serve to light the Gothic Sitting Room, which is at the south end of the study. Flanked by a Gothic chest, a French Gothic mantel, and a late fifteenth-century French cupboard, the lampshades add further gravitas to the "ancient" theme of the suite.[12]

As noted above, there are three additional lampshades in storage in the basement at the castle. Although, according to paleographic evidence and liturgical content (to be discussed later), they appear to be part of the set, the vellum of all three is a distinctly darker color and one is in visible disrepair. Finding three shades in the basement was unexpected, as only two were catalogued prior to my research visit in 2008.[13]

The shade in the Visitor's Center and nine of the ten chant lampshades on display in the Gothic Suite are each comprised of five folios of vellum on rounded frames; the tenth is comprised of four flat panels. Two of the shades in the

---

[10] This small elevator accommodated three adults semi-comfortably. The most amusing aspect of this device was that at the ground-floor level the door was quite likely to open into a group of surprised and curious tourists.

[11] The volumes of these shelves, although numerous, pale in comparison to the collection of the second-floor Library which houses 4,000 volumes. The arches disguise steel girders.

[12] The chest and mantel are called "Gothic" in Thomas Aidala's Hearst Castle San Simeon (New York: Hudson Hill Press, 1981), 144. Whether or not they are truly of the Gothic era or Gothic in style is unclear.

[13] Jana Seely found the lampshade while bringing out the two damaged shades in preparation for my visit in January of 2008.

Figure 1: Hearst Castle Gothic Study. Wikicommons. The chant shades are on the perimeter in this room; the shades made of indenture paper are on the table in the center.

Figure 2: Hearst Castle six-panel lampshade with one panel upside down (in basement). Photo by author.

basement (including the more damaged shade) are also the four-sided flat-panel type. The newly discovered shade in the basement is unique in the collection, as it is comprised of six panels on a rounded frame. This six-panel lampshade also has one panel that was sewn in upside down (see Figure 2).

All fourteen of the chant lampshades at the castle appear to have been assembled from folios removed from one antiphoner.[14] The repertory the lampshades transmit is that of Holy Week: specifically, the office of Matins for Maundy Thursday, Good Friday, and Holy Saturday with two pieces for Lauds (one from Maundy Thursday, one from Holy Friday) and two belonging to Vespers from Maundy Thursday.[15]

Several of the lampshades display modestly decorated capitals. Generally, the decorated capitals fall into two stylistic categories: those that are mainly black, with a crosshatch design and accents in green and blue, as seen in Figure 4 on facing page; and those that are red and blue, on a field of red, as seen in Figure 2. There is a single ornate gilded capital on the flat-panel shade in the Gothic Study (see Figure 3 below).

Figure 3; Hearst Castle Trapezoidal shade with gilded capital "C." Text is from Vespers of Feria V in Cena Domini, "Calicem salutaris."

[14] To identify the repertory of the lampshades I used the text search engines of CANTUS: A Database for Latin Ecclesiastical Chant, and the La Trobe University Library Medieval Music Database as well as Dom René-Jean Hesbert, *Corpus Antiphonalium Officii*, 6 vols. (Rome: Herder, 1963-79).

[15] Three lampshades in the Gothic Suite are made entirely out of leaves transmitting portions of Psalms 21, 26, 37, and 39 and do not contain music. The stenciled text is written in the same style and color as the folios of the text on the music lampshades, and they were most likely were a part of the same manuscript.

The music on all of the shades was stenciled in black ink, on a red five-line staff that was drawn with a rastrum. The rubrics were clearly marked in red and the text was also stenciled. Several panels have been repaired with linen thread; most likely these repairs were done while each was still a part of a manuscript, as the repairs have nothing to do with the shade frames. Prior to having been made into lampshades, the original manuscript appears to have been in use, as there is significant evidence of wear in the lower corners of the panels, which would have been the lower corners of the actual folios. In addition, there is more recent damage to the shades that is clearly the result of years of candlelight, followed by years of electrical light, shining through the shades.[16]

Remarkably, the lampshade panels were sewn together in fairly contiguous liturgical order, with the repertory from the office of Matins during three days in Holy Week (Maundy Thursday, Holy or Good Friday, and Holy Saturday) mostly grouped together, although the entire liturgy is not represented. Many of the folios appear to have been chosen for the sake of their decorated capitals (including the panels containing only psalm texts), but several of the panels are devoid of capitals or any other items of significant visual interest. The majority of the panels are sewn so that the skin side of the parchment is on the exterior of the shade. The four-panel lampshades and the unique six-panel lampshade, however, are sewn together with the hair side of the vellum on the exterior, accounting for the darker color of these shades. Figure 4 shows the only example of adjacent hair/skin lampshade panels.

Figure 4: Adjacent hair-to-skin panels on lampshade at Hearst Castle.

[16] The material on the inside of each panel has been severely faded due to light and heat exposure, although it is still possible to identify the music and text. In this study, only the exterior material is under consideration.

[17] Nasaw describes in some detail the extent of Hearst's collecting operation, including a humorous anecdote describing how Hearst was often not able to find objects he had purchased amongst his many treasures in *The Chief,* 297-302.

Hearst, "the great accumulator," is reported to have spent at minimum one million dollars a year on his collections. So great was his consumption, he not only had to buy warehouses for storage, but he also had to hire a staff to keep track of his numerous purchases.[17] Given these circumstances, one wonders how important any individual item was to him, let alone a set of lampshades in one of his massive homes.

Yet a series of communications with Julia Morgan makes it quite apparent that these lampshades were of particular interest to Hearst. There are no fewer than four articles of correspondence between the media mogul and the architect that specifically mention the lampshades.[18] Below are excerpts from the correspondence:

From Julia Morgan to W. R. Hearst on 2/4/1935:

> On Saturday we shipped you by express two of the lamp shades made from the leaves from the choral book. We will be glad to have your comments on these before finishing the remaining four.

From W. R. Hearst to Julia Morgan on 6/29/1935:

> I particularly requested that there should not be any varnish or any stain of any kind put on these parchments shades. I am sending this one back as it has been ruined.

From Julia Morgan to W. R. Hearst on 7/5/1935:

> Your request "not to allow any stain or varnish on the parchment shades" was carefully followed. The shade complained of was the one sent from San Simeon to the shade maker to copy, and was returned to San Simeon, attention of Mr. Williams, to be put with he other three of the original attempt.

From W. R. Hearst to Julia Morgan on 7/9/1935:

> Many thanks for your letter of July 5th regarding the parchment shades. The four shades in my Gothic living room (West side) have shrunk from their frames. Could these possibly be repaired?

From the correspondence, it is clear that for Hearst the visual condition of the shades was of primary import. In the letter dated June 29, 1935, Hearst was very specific in his desires, in his statement that "there should not be any varnish

---

[18] William Randolph Hearst-Julia Morgan. Unpublished letters: February 4, June 29, July 5, July 9, 1935. Julia Morgan Collection, Special Collections, California Polytechnic State University, San Luis Obispo, California. I am grateful to Ken Kenyon, formerly in Special Collections at Cal Poly San Luis Obispo, for his guidance and for locating the correspondence that specifically mentions the Hearst Castle lampshades.

or any stain of any kind put on these parchments shades." Further evidence of his interest in the presentation of the shades is found in his declaration that one of the shades "has been ruined" by use of varnish or stain. Curiously in Julia Morgan's response, dated July 5, 1935 she indicates that the lampshade "being complained of" was actually a shade sent to the shade maker to copy and then returned to "the other three of the original attempt." It is not clear which, if any, of the shades currently on display are copies. None of the shades in the castle transmit duplicate music or text and, after examination of the vellum and ink, none appear to be reproductions. The question remains as to which lampshade had upset Hearst. Of the chant lampshades at the castle, four of them—the unique six-panel shade and the three shades comprised of four-panels—are sewn with the hair side of the vellum on the exterior, resulting in a darker patina that might be misinterpreted as having been varnished. While one of these darker-toned shades is on display in the Gothic Study, the other three are out of sight in the basement.

It is reasonable to assume that these shades in the basement are "the other three of the original attempt" Julia Morgan mentioned in the correspondence of July 5, 1935. The sole "ruined" shade that remained on display then was probably spared banishment due to the fact that it alone has the most beautiful decorated initial of the entire set. (See Figure 3.)[19] The discussion of the visual condition of the shades between Hearst and Morgan did not end there, however, as Hearst went on to note on July 9, 1935 that the four shades in his "Gothic living room (West side)" had shrunk and he requested that they be repaired.[20] It is not known whether his request was granted; however, most of the shades have now pulled away at least slightly from their frames, and none show that they were repaired to fit their frames.

Hearst's concern in the correspondence over aesthetic quality of these items and their placement in his private suite indicates that the shades were at minimum of some decorative importance to "the Chief," and it is likely that the panels were not chosen for their liturgical content, but rather because they imparted an ancient "gothic" quality.

Physical Description: The Chant Book

In the same way the chant lampshades add to the *gravitas* of the Gothic Suite, a large book of chant adds a sense of solemnity to the décor of the Assembly Room on the

[19] It is possible that a duplicated shade was made, but is no longer on site. Record keeping in the early days of the California Parks tenure at the castle was incomplete.

[20] The Julia Morgan Collection, July 9, 1935. I would like to express my sincere thanks to Craig Russell (California Polytechnic State University, San Luis Obispo) for reading an early version of this paper and providing support (with characteristic enthusiasm) for my idea that the shades **did** matter to Hearst.

[21] *Astiterunt reges* is the first antiphon for Matins on Good Friday.

Figure 5: Hearst Castle Antiphoner, fol. 40v-41r. Photo by author.

first floor. From the late 1950s until recently, the chant book was often positioned in the room to display various openings that feature an item of visual interest. For example, in several historic photos, the manuscript opening 40v-41r was on display in December (see Figure 8 on p. 00). Easily seen on Guided Tour #1 (the "Experience Tour"), this particular opening was probably chosen because of the decorated "A" in red and gold at the beginning of the antiphon *Astiterunt reges*. Despite being liturgically inappropriate, this particular decoration provided an added bonus in that it matched the Christmas décor nicely.[21] (See Figure 5, above)

More recently, in May of 2006, a Conservator examined the chant book. At that time it was noted that the book is in "good condition," and it was suggested that the book be displayed in a closed position for preservation. Since this suggestion was made, the chant book has been kept in a closed position on a foam support covered in cardinal-colored velvet.[22]

Bound in heavy medium-brown calf leather over wooden boards and secured with brass and iron fittings, the closed book originally had four rollers, one of which is now missing. Measuring 34.75" x 25.25" x 5", the book is comprised of leaves of guarded conjugate vellum arranged in twenty fascicles of six leaves, and

---

[22] The conservator, Kathleen Orlenko (Santa Clara, CA), referred to the antiphoner as a "Missal (Chant Book)" in her report. It is her expert measurements that I rely upon in this examination.

one single leaf at the end. The leaves are arranged hair-to-hair, skin-to-skin. Like the lampshades, each folio has a maximum of five staves (five-lines each) drawn with a rastrum in red ink. The music and chant text are stenciled in black, and the rubrics are in red. The modestly decorated capitals are variously in blue, green, red, yellow, and gold, or a combination of several of these colors. Periodically the capitals are further enhanced with decorative flourishes in identical or contrasting colors.[23] Although the book is not luxurious, the size of the festal description (as seen in Figure 5) certainly takes up an extravagant amount of space, indicating that this manuscript emerged from a professional scriptorium that produced books for wealthy institutions.[24]

All of the leaves are intact, with minor repairs and damage to a few. Contradictory information is listed in the Hearst Castle Accession/Inspection Record, where the condition of the book is described as having an extremely gouged and scuffed binding and that the

> paper [is] extremely soiled & extremely cuckled [sic]. Previous tears of endpapers have been sewed. Several fore-edges have been mended. Vellum is extremely brittle & discolored.[25]

This description is misleading as the manuscript is actually in remarkable condition, showing little if any wear from either use or display. The assessment of discoloration was probably due to the appearance of natural color differentiation between the hair and skin sides of the vellum, which most likely was an unfamiliar sight to the examiner.[26]

Inventory and Repertory

Like the folios that make up the panels of the lampshades, this chant book is also an antiphoner, containing Matins, Lauds, and Vespers antiphons and responses as well as portions of two masses, all for Holy Week.[27] The first leaf contains (upside down) part of the Matins Responsory text for Good Friday "vi: ¿Quómodo convérsa."[28]

---

[23] The catalog records consistently remark that the manuscript contains "approximately 117 pages." There are, in fact, 121 vellum leaves. The "approximately" comes no doubt from the inaccurate numbering of the leaves; leaf 99 is not numbered, and two leaves are numbered 114.

[24] Many thanks to William Summers who observed that the "wasted" space on folios such as that shown in Figure 5 are indicative of production for a wealthier client.

[25] Department of Parks & Recreation Hearst Castle Area Accession/Inspection Record, 11/12/1985, p. 2. The author suspects that the pages were viewed as wrinkled, or "cockled."

[26] According to Seely, the examiner who described the nature of the manuscript as poor was a not an expert art historian, or appraiser, but rather a seasonal State Park employee who did office work transcribing information from historic inventories and other available materials.

[27] There are only two antiphons for Vespers in the chant book; they are from the Holy Friday series and are included on the last folio (117).

[28] The entire responsory is: *Vinea mea electa, ego te plantavi: Quomodo conversa es in amaritudinem, ut me crucifigeres, et Barabbam dimitteres.* In this opening flyleaf, there is no music. The style of the script and the punctuation are the same as the full responsory (with music) found on folios 48r-51v.

Figure 6: Hearst Castle
Chantbook Title Page,
f. 1r. Photo by author.

This inclusion of the distinctly Spanish use of the inverted question mark is reflective of an Iberian or colonial origin. The inclusion of the text here appears incidental, although it is related to the repertory that follows. Figure 6, above, is the title page, including some relationship with Guadeloupe.

The inventory of the manuscript is quite standard and transmits nine antiphons and nine responsories for each of the three nocturs of Matins. (See Table 1 on facing page.)

Although the precise origin is unknown (discussed below), Hearst and the art collectors who sold him the manuscript thought that it had come from Spain. As part of the décor in the grand Assembly Room, it reflects Hearst's fondness for ancient Spanish art and architecture. The manuscript certainly is in harmony with the surrounding artifacts; however, despite its rather large size, it is almost unnoticeable in the imposing space.

History and Provenance of the Chant Book and Lampshades

When Hearst purchased the chant book in 1929 it was listed in the American Art Association sales catalog as item #406, an "Illuminated Missal on Vellum: Chorale." Apparently based solely on information from this catalog, all subsequent descriptions of the manuscript as part of the Hearst collection mistakenly describe the antiphoner in the same way. Item #406 (for which Hearst paid $90.00) was only one of several items purchased that day. Amongst the objects that he bought was another considerably older chant book, item #405 from the same auction (see transcription of Auction Catalog on facing page.[29] Item #405 may well have been the source of the lampshade folios, as discussed below.

Table 1. Inventory of Hearst Chant Manuscripts

Folio	Text	Feast
f.1v-31r	Responses for Matins	Feria Quinta in Coena Domini
f. 31v-35r	Responses for Lauds	Feria Quinta in Coena Domini
f. 35r-40v	Proper chants for Mass	Maundy Thursday
f. 41r-73r	Antiphons, psalm cues, responses for Matins	Feria Sexta in Parasceve
f. 73r-77v	Antiphons, psalm cues, responses for Lauds	Feria Sexta in Parasceve
f. 78r-82v	Tracts	Pre-sanctified
f. 83r-111v	Responses for Matins and Lauds (no rubric)	Holy Saturday
f. 112r-117r	Tracts and alleluia (with verse)	Holy Saturday
117v	Alleluia, psalm cue for the first antiphon for Vespers (inc.)	Holy Friday

American Art Auction Catalog Description of Item 405.

Illuminated Missal on Vellum: Chorale. Spanish, XVII Century.
Approximately one hundred and eighteen pages of Gothic lettering and
musical scores, the first page beautifully illumnated. Leather covers
bound in brass and enriched with perforated brass bosses. Length, 28
inches; width, 19 inches.

American Art Auction Catalog Description of Item 406.

Illuminated Missal on Vellum: Chorale. Spanish, dated 1826.
Approximately one hundred and seventeen pages of Roman lettering

[29] The manuscripts were purchased from the Don Luis Ruiz Collection (Madrid, Spain), through a

and musical scores, with illuminated capitals and rubrics, the title page
dated MDCCCXXVI. Covered in brown leather enriched with brass
mounts. Length, 34 inches; width, 25 inches.

After being purchased from the Luis Ruiz sale, item #406 was received in
New York in April of 1929 and sent to "the Hill" on May 29, 1929, where it was
newly cataloged as item #4071 in Box 3, "Books." ("The Hill" was an affectionate
term Hearst had for his home near San Simeon.) Once the book was shipped to
California it was stored in the San Simeon warehouse until the 1950s. In 1951
Fidelity Appraisal appraised it at $50.00 and in 1957 the chant book was moved
into the Assembly Room at Hearst Castle. Although it is possible that the book was
on display in different positions, a historic photo from the Sarah Holmes Boutelle
collection taken by Cecilia Bancroft Graham shows the book displayed in a closed
position on a long low wooden table.[30]

Pinpointing a specific provenance within Spain for either the chant book or
lampshade panels is difficult, as the styles of text, music, and decoration found
in each of them are not unique to any particular region; similar examples are
found across Iberia.[31] Whether Spanish or Portuguese, an Iberian origin for the
lampshade manuscript fits what we know about Hearst's collecting strategies, as
he did buy many items he assumed were from Spain. This makes all the more
tempting a hypothesis that the lampshade panels were fashioned from leaves of
the other chant book Hearst purchased at the American Art Association auction
in 1929, item #405 (see catalog transcription above). The description of this
manuscript's size and other characteristics in the sales catalog certainly support this.
Further evidence that item #405 was likely the source of the lampshade panels is

---

sale at the American Art Association held on January 24-26. Spanish Collection of Don Luiz Ruiz
(New York: American Art Association, Inc., 1929), 79-80. The auction catalog is available today at
the Getty Museum in Los Angeles, the Arts Library at the University of California, Santa Barbara,
and The Art Institute of Chicago. The copy at the Arts Library at University of California, Santa
Barbara (on microfilm), is missing pages 79-132. The copy at the Art Institute includes handwritten
annotated amounts for the sale of each item. The catalog from the Luis Ruiz sale is listed as #5472
in Harold Lancour, *American Art Auction Catalogues, 1785-1942; A Union List* (New York: New York
Public Library, 1944), 241.

[30] The curator of the collection, Jana Seely, provided a variety of historical documents describing
the chronicle of this antiphoner to me during my research. Much of this documentary information
comes from the Provenance file. The description as a "choral missal" is consistent, with one slightly
more inaccurate entry in 1957 describing it as "Illuminated Missal on Vellum. Chorals, Spanish…"

[31] A *flickr®* search using "libro coro" turned up several images of a similar-looking manuscripts,
including one currently on display at the Cathedral of Burgos (Spain), and one at the Igreja de São
Francisco in Évora, Portugal, each bearing a strong resemblance to the lampshade panels. Another
flickr® search turned up images of a manuscript dated 1834 currently on display at the Museo de
Música de la Catedral de Pamplona (displaying the introit "Suscitabo mihi" from the *Missa pro
Eligendo Summo Pontifice*). This Pamplona source is visually quite similar to the Hearst chant book
in the decorated capitals and simple style of the stenciled text, as well as containing five staves per
page.

the remarkable gilded capital on the sole four-panel shade in the Gothic Study. This unique occurrence is directly in line with the description of item #405 in the AAA catalog as containing a single "beautifully illuminated" page. (See Figure 3.)

Unfortunately, the Hearst Corporation sold item #405 in 1957, and the Hearst Castle staff is under strictest orders to keep all buyers information confidential. So, although there is no "smoking gun," the circumstantial evidence is compelling and adds to the means, motive, and opportunity that Hearst had to create gothic lampshades out of his purchase.

For both the chant book and the lampshade panels, supporting evidence for a Spanish or colonial provenance is based upon the purchase from a Spanish dealer who claims to have been selling Spanish objects, and the fact that the rubrics in both consistently employ the Spanish "Aña" for Antiphon (Antífona). Additional information from the title page of the chant book led to a comparison of it with items in the collection at the Real Monasterio de Nuestra Señora de Guadalupe (Royal Monastery of Santa María de Guadalupe) in Extremadura, Spain. The monastery, a Hieronymite house until secularization in 1835, boasts a sizeable collection of large *libros corales* (choir books) similar in size to the panels of the Hearst lampshades and the folios of the chant book. Unlike many of the Guadalupe manuscripts, the Hearst chant book and lampshades are devoid of border decoration. There are strong paleographic resemblances in the text, music, and decorated capitals between several of the Guadalupe sources and the Hearst lampshades, but not the chant book. [32]

While several characteristics of the manuscripts from the monastery in Spain bear a resemblance to the Hearst lampshades, a book exhibiting even more similarity is on display at the Igreja de São Francisco in Évora, Portugal. Note in particular the decorated capitals, which are in blue and red. (See Figure 7 on p. 436.) Additionally, like the panels of the Hearst lampshades, the Évora manuscript does not display elaborate illuminations or border decoration.

Addressing the origin of the Hearst chant book, there are even fewer leads. The repertory and decorations in the chant book are unremarkable, making a comparison to other sources difficult. However, one source now in Pamplona shows promise for future comparison. The manuscript, inscribed with the date 1834, is on display at Catedral de Santa María la Real in Pamplona. This Spanish

---

[32] Many of the Guadalupe sources are similar in size to what the lampshade manuscript probably measured: 28" by 35". It is not evident from the lampshades whether the source manuscript originally had border art, but it seems unlikely because there is a great deal of empty space on the bottom edge of most of the lampshade panels. A few of the Guadalupe manuscripts are represented in Fr. I. Acemel y Fr. G. Rubio, *Guía Ilustrada del Monasterio de Ntra. Sra. De Guadalupe*, 2nd ed. (Barcelona: Industrias Gráficas, 1927), 72, and Fr. Arturo Alvarez *Guadalupe: Arte Historia y Devocion Mariana* (Madrid: Ediciones Studium, 1964), 329. Further comparison can be made using Elías Tormo y Monzó, *The Monastery of Guadalupe Art in Spain, [published] under the Patronage of the Hispanic Society of America* (Barcelona: Hijos de J. Thomas, 19--), 32-33. Most of these Guadalupe sources that bear a resemblance to the lampshade panels are from the early sixteenth century.

Figure 7: Choirbook on display at the Igreja de São Francisco in Évora, Portugal. Wikicommons.

Figure 8: Choirbook on display at the Catedral de Santa María la Real in Pamplona, Spain. Wikicommons.

manuscript is equally as unremarkable, and at the same time visually quite similar to the Hearst chant book.[33] (See Figure 8.)

The information on the title page of the Hearst chant book, although enticing, has not served to pinpoint Guadalupe as a locus. The current archivist at the Biblioteca del Real Monasterio de Guadalupe examined the title page and informed me that none of the books in the archive bear the same dedication. However, this does not entirely discount the possibility of the book having been originally from Guadalupe as manuscript production during the first half of the nineteenth century was high at the monastery.[34]

In a search for a point of origin having to do with Guadalupe, another entirely plausible possibility emerged in that the manuscript might be of Spanish colonial origins, where the Virgin of Guadalupe has a large cult following. Of particular interest is the collection of *libros coros* at the Franciscan convent and colegio of Guadalupe in Zacatecas, Mexico.[35] If the Hearst manuscript was in fact from Mexico, this would complicate things since Don Luis Ruiz sold it as a Spanish item. The simpler explanation is that the chant book is from Spain and at this point, the Pamplona manuscript remains the closest match.

Conclusion

Despite the fact that no specific provenance can be firmly assigned, clues surrounding the history and origins of the lampshades and chant book remain quite intriguing yet elusive. Both objects contain characteristics that resemble other unexamined manuscript sources (those mentioned above in Spain, specifically Guadalupe, Pamplona, Burgos; and the source located in Évora, Portugal) and these manuscripts certainly warrant further examination. A comprehensive comparative study of items of liturgical import from this region is made quite difficult by several contributing factors, including the secularization in 1835, and the subsequent relinquishment of the choir books to antiquarians and others who had little understanding of their true value or function.

Like the hunt for the meaning of Rosebud in the filmic version of Hearst in Orson Welles's *Citizen Kane*, the Holy Week repertory of both the lampshades and chant book cries out for a psychological investigation or a spiritual explanation. Alas, it appears that the liturgical items were only valued for their perceived

---

[33] This source was found near the time of submitting this article and will be the subject of further comparative study.

[34] Many thanks are due to Antonio Ramiro Chico, archivist at the BRMG, for taking the time to check the collection for any similar indication on the title page.

[35] For a comparison to Mexican sources see Federico Sescosse, *El Colegio de Guadalupe de Zacatecas.* (Mexico: Fondo Cultural Bancen, 1993), 92-93. I wish to thank John Koegel (California State University, Fullerton) for his insight into a possible Mexican provenance.

"gothic" appearance and their function was to adorn the physical space in the Assembly Room and the lamps in the Gothic suite, lamps that in Hearst Castle served to provide light, rather than enlightenment.

Solving the Mystery of Francesco Corteccia's Book of Counterpoints

Frank A. D'Accone

Among the many sacred works Francesco Corteccia composed during his thirty-year tenure as master of the Florentine chapel is a set of propers for the principal feasts of the church year, or counterpoints on the plain chants of solemn Masses, as he called them.[1] They appear without ascription in a unique manuscript from the historic music collection of the Florence Cathedral, now in the library of that city's Opera di Santa Maria del Fiore. The volume is mentioned in the first surviving inventory of Cathedral holdings from 1651. There it is described as "a book also in manuscript of old Introits of 137 folios by various authors which are [still] used, [and it] begins Et filius datus est nobis."[2] It is one of several Cathedral volumes that preserve works by Corteccia, some also without ascription but known to be his from contemporaneous manuscripts and prints. These and Corteccia's own words from various times in his life offer ample evidence of his long-range plan

---

[1] Corteccia (27 July 1502-7 June 1571) was the leading Florentine composer of his generation. Trained at the Cathedral's School of Chant and Grammar, he was a clerk at the Baptistry of San Giovanni for over a decade and was ordained a priest in 1531. He was chaplain and organist there before assuming the leadership of the chapel, reorganized in 1540 under the aegis of Duke Cosimo de' Medici. Corteccia was also chaplain and then canon of the Medici church of San Lorenzo. Although he would later style himself as the Duke's "maestro di cappella," he held no formal position at court. The fundamental study of his life and career is Mario Fabbri's "La vita e l'ignota opera-prima di Francesco Corteccia musicista italiano del Rinascimento," *Chigiana* 22, N. S. 2 (1965), 185-217. A modern edition of the book of counterpoints, edited by David J. Burn and me, has recently been published by the American Institute of Musicology as volume 13 of Music of the Florentine Renaissance (MFR), Corpus Mensurabilis Musicae 32 (Middleton, WI: 2009). Page and measure numbers in references to examples here are to that volume.

[2] The inventory, with extensive commentary, has been published by Gabrielle Giacomelli in "Due granduchi in cent'anni (1621-1723): continuità e tradizione nel repertorio della cappella musicale di Santa Maria del Fiore," *"Cantate Domino": musica nei secoli per il Duomo di Firenze: Atti del convegno internazionale di studi, Firenze, 23-25 maggio 1997*, ed. Piero Gargiulo, Gabriele Giacomelli, and Carolyn Gianturco, Atti del VII centenario del Duomo di Firenze 3 (Florence: Edifir, 2001), 195-218. The book of counterpoints (I Fd, II-46) is listed as No. 11 in the inventory: "Un libro simile manuscr[itt]o d'Introiti vecchi di c. 137 di varij autori e si adoperano comincia Et filius datus est nobis." (Ibid., 215) Corteccia himself referred to the propers in this volume as "contrappunti nuovaments fatte sopra il canto fermo delle messe solenne." See note 7 below.

to furnish the chapel singers with up-to-date settings of the texts and prayers they performed in polyphony at various services throughout the church year. The book of counterpoints was one of several large-scale works he put his hand to, though unlike others initiated early in his career, he never finished it.

Corteccia's works, of course, were not the only ones in the chapel's repertory. The contents of several Cathedral volumes made under his supervision include music by composers of a previous generation as well as his own. Masses, motets, Magnificats, and psalms by Carpentras, Verdelot, Morales, Willaert, Layolle, and Jacquet, to name a few, provided a truly international repertory alongside those by Corteccia, whose works, in the main, are preserved in discrete collections devoted to his music alone.[3] Several of these volumes, Corteccia's and the others, were copied between 1545 and 1565 by his friend and colleague Gian Piero Masacone, the doyen of sixteenth-century Florentine copyists.[4] The volumes are mentioned in the 1651 inventory, though, unlike Corteccia's book of counterpoints, they are described as "no longer in use."[5] The book of counterpoints, apart from some

---

[3] These are I Fd, Mss. II-4, II-11, II-27, II-28, copied by Gian Piero Masacone, and II-6bis, II-13, II-45, II-46, II-49. The volumes are described in *Census-Catalogue of Manuscript Sources of Polyphonic Music 1400-1550*, vol. 1, ed. Charles Hamm and Herbert Kellman (Neuhausen-Stuttgart: American Institute of Musicology, Hänssler-Verlag, 1979), 237-41.

[4] See note 3. Gian Piero di Niccolò Masacone was Corteccia's colleague at San Lorenzo for many years and it was there that he pursued his vocation throughout his long career. The best known of Masacone's works is a set of partbooks, now in the Newbury Library that have been edited by H. Colin Slim, *A Gift of Madrigals and Motets*, 2 vols. (Chicago: Chicago University Press, 1972). An up-to-date account of Masacone's activities and of newly recovered manuscripts he copied is given by Philippe Canguilhem, "Lorenzo Corsini's 'Libri di canzone' and the Madrigal in Mid-Sixteenth-Century Florence," *Early Music History* 25 (2006), 1-57. Payments to Masacone from the Cathedral for copying music manuscripts are given in my "Sacred Music in Florence during Savonarola's Time," *Una città e il suo profeta. Firenze di fronte al Savonarola, Atti del convegno internazionale (Firenze, 10-13 dicembre 1998)*, ed. Gian Carlo Garfagnini (Florence: Sismel, 2001), 353-54; reprinted as Chapter VI in my *Music in Renaissance Florence: Studies and Documents* (Aldershot: Ashgate, 2007). In his time Masacone (1497-1573) was a living link to Florence's musical past. As a young clerk at the Baptistry, he was evidently a pupil of Heinrich Isaac after the composer's return to Florence in 1512. Proof of their relationship appears in a document which shows him receiving on Isaac's behalf the salary due the older composer from his pension as honorary leader of the Florentine chapel. The document, I Fd, VIII. 1. 134, *Quaderno di Cassa* (1515-1516), fols. 47v-48r, reads:

[fol. 47v] MDXV

Arrigho di Ugho d'Isac cantore de' dare adì 28 di febraio [1516] Fl Quattro larghi d'oro in oro portò Giovanpiero di Nicolò chericho di San Giovanni contanti per conto di suo salario—Fl... L. 28

E adì 10 di maggio Fl 4 larghi d'oro in oro portò ser Francesco di Benedetto cartolaio contanti—Fl...L. 28

E adì 5 di luglio L. 20 pli portò ser Francesco di Benedetto—Fl...L 28..

E adì 17 di detto L. otto pli portò Giovampiero di Nicolò contanti—Fl.... L. 8

[written below] 28

[5] "Non si adopera più" is said of three of Masacone's volumes, I Fd II-4, II-27, II-28, while the fourth, I Fd, II-11, is qualified with the words "se ne adopera poco." (Giacomelli, "Due granduchi," 215.) A facsimile of this last, with an introduction by me, is in *Florence, Archivio dell'Opera di Santa Maria del Fiore*, MS 11, Renaissance Music in Facsimile 3 (New York and London: Garland, 1987).

subsequent additions, is in the hand of Michele Federighi, Corteccia's one-time pupil and principal copyist of his works in later years.[6] Precisely when Federighi began copying it is not known, but several of the propers were already in the chapel's repertory before the end of Corteccia's life.

This much is made clear by Corteccia's own words regarding them. Unlike his hymns, responsories, and motets, which he mentioned on several occasions throughout his career, Corteccia spoke about his propers only once. It was in the dedication to Cosimo de' Medici of a presentation volume containing the final, revised version of his Hymnary that Federighi copied towards the end of the 1560s. The dating is approximate, but earlier revisions of some of the hymns are documented to within a few years of that time and in the dedication Corteccia addressed Cosimo as Second Duke of Florence, a title he hardly would have used in 1570 when Cosimo was created Grand Duke of Tuscany. Here is what Corteccia said:

> And these [hymns] then such as they may be, I dedicate and present to Your Excellency's most illustrious name, humbly beseeching that you deign to accept them with your usual magnanimity, so that encouraged by such approval, I shall eagerly be able not only to fulfill the promises already made of motets, Lamentations and, furthermore, counterpoints newly composed on the plain chants of solemn Masses but also to be ever mindful of other things in which I can likewise give pleasure and be useful.[7]

Corteccia had mentioned his motets and Lamentations, along with his responsories and hymns, as early as 1544 in a dedication to Cosimo of one of his madrigal books.[8] At the time he said he was readying those works for the printer and would soon be making Cosimo a gift of them. But he was unable to follow through on his promise—perhaps because court subsidies were denied him—and it was only toward the end of his life that he began publishing his sacred music, at his own expense. Two volumes of responsories and other music

---

[6] During the course of his long career Federighi († 31 May 1602) was a chaplain, canon, and ultimately abbot of San Lorenzo. In addition to the just-mentioned Hymnary, he made other copies of Corteccia's hymns, responsories, and music for Holy Week. These are preserved in a section of I Fd, Ms II-45; in I Fl, Ms C ; and in the first section of I Fl, Ms N. In this last Federighi entered his name and the year, 1561, on fol. 8v, shortly after beginning his work, and on fol. 52r, the date he completed it, 3 March 1561/62. See my "Updating the Style: Francesco Corteccia's Revisions in His Responsories for Holy Week," *Music and Context: Essays for John M. Ward*, ed. Anne Dhu Shapiro (Cambridge, MA: Harvard University Press, 1985), 38; reprinted as Chapter II in my *Music and Musicians in 16th-Century Florence*.

[7] The dedication in facsimile and in English translation are in Francesco Corteccia, *Hymnary according to the Use of the Roman Church and of the Florentine*, MFR 12 (1996), lxv-lxvii. An English translation first appeared in Glen Haydon's "The Dedication of Francesco Corteccia's *Hinnario*," *Journal of the American Musicological Society* 13 (1960), 112-16.

[8] The dedication in facsimile and in English translation are in Francesco Corteccia, *The First Book of Madrigals for Four Voices*, MFR 8 (1981), xxvii, xxx.

for Holy Week appeared in 1570, and two books of motets were issued by June of the following year, within weeks of his death.[9] In his last will and testimony Corteccia bequeathed his musical estate to Michele Federighi and directed him to see the rest of his works through the press using profits from the sale of those already published to do so.[10] Federighi was unable to comply, and in the end much of Corteccia's output remained in manuscript. The elegant copy of the Hymnary, with Corteccia's name emblazoned across its title page, early on found its way into the ducal collection, while the book of counterpoints, without attribution and in only the one performing copy, stayed in the Cathedral's music library, where, as the 1651 inventory reveals, they formed part of the repertory for many years after the composer's death.[11]

Federighi planned the book of counterpoints in two distinct sections: a main one devoted exclusively to Corteccia's propers for feasts from the Temporale and the Sanctorale entered in the chronological order of the church year, and a subsidiary one containing music for Vespers and other services appropriate for days covered by the propers. Later, a number of additions were made to the manuscript. Several consisted of textual emendations or replacement settings reflecting Tridentine liturgical changes. These point to Corteccia having composed the propers in the main section before the new Roman Missal was published in 1570 and corroborate his statement in the dedication of the Hymnary from a year or so earlier. Whether the set was as complete as he envisioned it at that time, however, is uncertain, for he referred to the counterpoints as "newly composed," a hint, perhaps, that he was still putting the finishing touches on them. In any case Corteccia's own testimony is that he composed a set of propers long after most of his other sacred works. This, Federighi's role in their transmission, the post-Tridentine emendations and additions to his manuscript after 1570, and knowledge that it was in the Florentine Cathedral's music collection for decades before the 1651 inventory was made, all leave no doubt that the anonymous propers are indeed Corteccia's.

If it were certain that Corteccia composed no more of them after he mentioned them, and if the manuscript were still as Fedrighi originally left it, that would be more than enough evidence to turn the page on the book of counterpoints. And as for the later additions, if they were confined to post-Tridentine emendations and replacement settings, their presence would be self-explanatory--an *aggiornamento*

---

[9] For the responsories, with the dedication in facsimile and in English translation, see Francesco Corteccia, *Music for the Triduum Sacrum*, MFR 11 (1985). The motets, with the original dedication and an English translation, are discussed extensively by Ann Watson McKinley in "Francesco Corteccia's Music to Latin Texts," 2 vols. (Ph.D. dissertation, University of Michigan, 1963), 1: 118-34, 321-99.

[10] Corteccia called him "mio creato" in the will, portions of which were published by Mario Fabbri, "La vita e l'ignota opera prima," 202-3.

[11] David Sutherland was the first to suggest that Cathedral manuscript I Fd, II-46 contained Corteccia's counterpoints. See his "A Second Corteccia Manuscript in the Archives of Santa Maria del Fiore," *Journal of the American Musicological Society* 25 (1972), 79-85.

of Corteccia's propers that kept them in line with new liturgical requirements. Scattered among the later additions, however, are ten settings of propers whose texts remained the same after Trent. These are intended for seven feasts not included in the main corpus and, to add to the mix, half of the new settings are in Federighi's hand. Inevitably, the question of Corteccia's authorship arises. Are these pieces his? Was he still working on them when Federighi made his first redaction of the manuscript? Is this why Federighi later returned to it? If they are Corteccia's, how can we know this? And how can we know whether he composed the other newly added propers that are not in Federighi's hand? The origins of these additions, it stands to reason, lie behind the mystery of the book of counterpoints—a mystery not of the classic kind that Bill Prizer is so fond of reading, but a mystery nonetheless that required some musicological detective work to solve. In the following pages I offer a solution to this "whodunit" that I dedicate to him in celebration of our many years of friendship.

Solving the mystery, as I saw it, required an approach on two fronts: the first, through a study of the manuscript itself that would establish Federighi's original plan and explain how later insertions related to it; and second, through musical analysis that would establish stylistic norms in the propers by Corteccia on the basis of evidence just cited and discover whether or not those norms are present in the later additions. I should note immediately that Corteccia's propers are in a style that is unlike anything else in his known *oeuvre*. This is not so remarkable, however, because a different aesthetic underlies their composition, one that seeks to recreate the sound of extempore performance as he knew it.

First, we turn to the manuscript. The book of counterpoints survives in its original form. Bound in parchment over stiffened cardboard, perhaps in the late seventeenth century, its front cover is marked "Introiti 46" in pen above an older design that encircles the earlier inventory number "11." In 1651 it was described as containing introits—read propers—and consisting of 137 folios. It still has same number of folios and there is no evidence that there were ever any more or any less. These measure 465 x 315 mm. and are all lined with twelve staves. There are seventeen gatherings in the manuscript, grouped into two distinct sections: the first, of twelve gatherings (folios 1-97); the second, of five (folios 98-137). All of the gatherings are quaternions except for the third, where a single sheet (fol. 25) was tipped in at the end in order to complete one of the cycles. An old sheet bearing the table of contents on its recto precedes the coeval guard sheet and pastedown on the back cover of the volume.

Federighi employed standard copying procedures and entered the parts of the pieces—most of them are for four voices—on the facing sides of each opening, cantus and tenor on the verso, altus and bassus on the opposite recto. For the occasional five-voice piece, he entered the extra part on one or another of the sides. Normally, he copied two cycles within a gathering. When he needed to extend a cycle beyond the gathering, he copied the parts across the last verso of its last folio onto the first recto of the next gathering. In the first section such conjugates occur between gatherings 1-2, 2-3, 8-9, 10-11, and 11-12. He left ten openings blank within these gatherings, notably folios 11v-12r, 32v-33r, 69v-73r, 93v-97r. Otherwise, he might leave the first recto of a gathering blank, as he did with that of the first gathering—which remains blank to this day—and begin copying on the gathering's first opening (the verso of the first folio and the recto of the second). He then copied through the gathering and concluded the last piece of a cycle on the verso of its penultimate folio and recto of its last one, leaving the last verso blank. In the main corpus he did this between gatherings 3-4, 4-5, 5-6, 6-7, 7-8, 9-10, thus leaving another large number of openings blank. In the second section he also left the opening between gatherings 14-15 blank, although his copying there was almost continuous, leaving only the last five sides of the last gathering unfilled. He did this as well on a few occasions in the first section, at the end of gatherings 4, 9, and 12, an indication, I believe, that he anticipated the addition of more material—either by himself or by others—which is, in fact, what eventually happened in those places and on every other side he left blank, except for the very first folio.

Federighi initially copied fifty-one of the manuscript's sixty-eight pieces. Forty-one of them form the main corpus of the first section. With two exceptions, this contains settings of an introit, Alleluia, and communion, in that order, for fourteen major feasts.[12] For Octave of Christmas he gives only an Alleluia and his rubrics indicate that the introit and communion are the same as at Christmas. Easter includes a setting of the gradual verse, an exception that necessitated adding an extra sheet, as noted, so that the cycle would fit within the third gathering.[13] Federighi originally copied ten items into the second section of the manuscript, six hymns (all with several stanzas) by Corteccia, and a few other multi-stanza works by Verdelot and Richafort. Interspersed within the two sections are seventeen new pieces, two minor additions, and textual emendations to three existing propers. These were entered later by by Federighi and fourteen new hands.[14] A few more statistics about the additions, for which I ask the reader's

---

[12] They are: Christmas, 25 December (folios 1v-5r); Octave of Christmas=Circumcision, 1 January (5v-7r); Epiphany, 6 January (7v-11r); Purification of the Virgin Mary, 2 February (12v-18r); Easter (18v-25r); Ascension (26v-32r); Pentecost (34v-41r); Corpus Christi (42v-49r); Nativity of St. John the Baptist, 24 June (50v-57r); St. Lawrence, 10 August (58v-63r); Assumption of the Virgin Mary, 15 August (63v-69r); Birth of the Virgin Mary, 8 September (74v-79r); Sts. Cosmas and Damian, 27 September (as patron saints of the Medici their feast was celebrated as a major one in Florence, 79v-85r); All Saints, 1 November (85v-92r).

[13] A later hand copied the final words, "Congregavit eos" of the gradual verse, *Confitemini*, now sung on Easter Tuesday, above the plain chant which has those of the Easter verse, *Misericordia*. Below the cantus part with the *Misericordia* text, the same hand recopied the music and underlaid it with the Tuesday text.

[14] Besides the ten new propers, there are the following: three new replacement settings of Tridentine assigned psalm verses, one for the Pentecost introit (folios 41v-42r) and two for the Ascension introit (11v-12r, 49v-50r); an antiphon and canticle for the Blessing of the Candles on 2 February (25v-26r); two settings of the *Deo gratias* versicle (73v-74r, 113v-114r); and at the end, a psalm verse in falsobordone (136v-137r). Minor supplements include a recopied portion of the chant for the All

indulgence, will serve to place them within the manuscript's context and provide some insight into what must have been Corteccia's principal aim in undertaking the project. All of these late arrivals supplement Federighi's original ground plan in one way or another, though they disrupt the chronological order he so meticulously observed in the main corpus. Nevertheless, the outlines of the volume's design show that folios he left blank became logical places for new additions. In my discussion of these I shall limit my remarks to the ten settings of propers for seven other feasts that were not initially included.[15] None of these feasts has all three items—introit, Alleluia, and communion—as do those of the main corpus.

Five propers for three of the new feasts were added by Federighi himself. Like the propers for the fourteen feasts of the main corpus, these exhibit certain stylistic features that both unify and distinguish them as the work of a single composer. Two of the subsequently added propers for two new feasts, written in hands similar to Federighi's, show many of these same features, as do two more for another new feast copied by an unrelated hand. This leaves only one piece, in a hand quite different from all of the others, that seems foreign to the group as a whole. I find no features in it that mark Corteccia's propers as the work of an authentic musical personality. The compositional procedure Corteccia adopted in the propers is quite different from his usual one, as I said. But it is purposely so, because by opting for an approach in which formal, harmonic, and imitative developments were secondary considerations, he was able to capture the boldness and immediacy of improvised church polyphony and to contrast finer points of its idiosyncrasies with more formal artifices of written part music.[16] All of his propers

---

Saints' Alleluia (90r) and a supplementary "Sicut erat" for a psalm setting copied earlier by Federighi (122v-123r). Emphasizing the desire to keep Corteccia's music relevant are three of the original propers with later textual emendations reflecting Tridentine substitutions of psalm verses, namely, the already mentioned Easter gradual and the introits for Pentecost and Nativity of the Virgin (21v-22r, 27v-28r, 75v-76r).

[15] They are: Holy Spirit in Lent, introit (between Ascension and Pentecost, folios 32v-34r); St. Andrew, 30 November, Alleluia (inserted between Nativity of St. John the Baptist and St. Lawrence, 57v-58r); Dedication of a Church, introit (inserted between Assumption of the Virgin Mary and Birth of the Virgin Mary, 69v-71r); Common of a Virgin not at Martyr and Annunciation of the Virgin, introit (also inserted between Assumption and Birth of the Virgin, 71v-73r); St. Zenobius, Florentine bishop, 25 May, introit and Alleluia (inserted near the end of the main corpus, 92v-95r); Common of Apostles and Evangelists, introit and Alleluia (inserted between the end of the main corpus and the first hymn of the subsidiary section, 95v-98r); and Common of a Confessor not a Bishop, introit and Alleluia (inserted at the end of the subsidiary section, 133v-136r). I am grateful to Michael K. Phelps for his assistance in determining the volume's original design and in identifying the various hands that made these later additions.

[16] There was a widespread tradition of improvised polyphony long before Corteccia's time. The fundamental study is Ernest Ferand's "Improvised Vocal Counterpoint in the Late Renaissance and Early Baroque," *Annales musicologiques* 4 (1954), 129-74; a relevant bibliography is given in the entry on Improvisation, II: Western Art Music by Imogene Horsley, Michael Collins, Stewart Carter *et al* in *Grove Music Online* (accessed 19 January 2008). More or less contemporaneous with Corteccia's propers is Ippolito Camaterò's volume *Li introiti fondati sopra il canto fermo del basso....*, published in 1574. Camaterò claims in its preface that the music represented written examples of what his choir

are four-voice elaborations of chant melodies, except for an apparently unfinished three-voice Alleluia for St. Andrew's Day, one of the later additions. The chant is sung without interruption from beginning to end by the bassus and is notated in neumes that have the value of a semibreve of the mensural notation of the upper parts. All of the pieces except for the Christmas Alleluia are in imperfect time with imperfect prolation.

Throughout the various cycles the cantus, altus, and tenor unfold above the bassus in lively, independently conceived melodies that make little or no reference to the chant. The upper voices rarely pause for rests, seemingly oblivious of one another as they weave a dense, non-imitative texture that is as richly triadic as it is meandering in modal ambiguity. Occasional dissonant clashes between two or more of them add spice to the mixture, though the individual parts are always consonant with the chant. Parallel fifths are sometimes allowed. Forward-moving melodies, fleeting harmonies, and overlapping phrases find occasional resolution in briefly touched upon cadences. These often seem abrupt, arrived at in passing and then only because of a desire to mark the end of a word or to signal the end of a melodic phrase. Such places often lie far afield of the closing cadence that defines the final of the mode. Brief forays into triple division of the semibreve in one part against the normal duple division of the others produce a sense of increased rhythmic activity, while sudden octave leaps in one or another of the upper parts will thrust it into momentary prominence. All of this, of course, is intended to evoke the spirit and sound of improvised music, the kind of performances that many of the gifted singers in Corteccia's chapel were doubtless capable of giving and probably had given over the course of many years.

Several features—mannerisms, we might call them—appear frequently throughout Corteccia's propers. Some, such as those just mentioned, fit well within the context of a style that purports to recreate the sound of improvised polyphony. Others hint at means of organizing materials the composer himself might have invented. Foremost among the latter is a two-part "characteristic" phrase of one-and-a-half to three breves (or more) in length between the bassus and cantus in contrary motion. It may stand alone or it may appear at the beginning, within, or at the close of a larger passage that sets a word or two of the text. The mode of the chant does not determine its use. Usually, the bassus begins on E (or F) and ascends a fourth (or a third) by step to the A above, while against it the cantus, two octaves higher, descends a third by step, from E to C, forming a 4-3 suspension with the bassus before dropping to B and then resolving on C. The inner voices change from piece to piece. The resulting sound is a deceptive cadence within a C mode, which more often than not is remote from the central mode of the chant.

---

at Udine Cathedral was accustomed to improvise. For this and an example of the music, see Max Schneider, *Die Anfänge des Basso Continuo und seiner Bezifferung* (Leipzig: Breitkopf & Härtel, 1918/ R 1971), 64, note 1; 163-65. Another example is furnished by Ferand in his *Improvisation in Nine Centuries of Western Music* (Cologne: Arno Volk Verlag, 1961), 85-87.

Ex. 1: p. 9, mm. 1-5[3]

The characteristic phrase is present throughout the set, in introits, Alleluias, and communions, and its appearance is predictable only in so far as the chant melody, irrespective of mode, ascends from E or F to A. Whether it takes the form just described or is slightly varied, its sound is unmistakable. This is true of the beginning of the Christmas communion, where, after the intonation "Viderunt omnes," all voices enter with the words "fines terrae" and a repeated note in the chant occasions an ornamented resolution of the suspended C in the cantus.[17] (Ex. 1 above.) Another slightly varied Ex. is found at the opening of the Alleluia for Assumption Day, in the fifth mode.[18]   Here, in the length of two-and-a-half breves, as the upper voices sing "Alleluia," the chant ascends by step from its initial C to A.   Two octaves above it the cantus also begins on C and reaches E via a downward third and two consecutive rising fourths before descending one step and then another to C, which is suspended before it is resolved into the deceptive cadence. This same material, except for the first two beats, recurs during the course of the Alleluia. (Ex. 2)

Ex. 2: p. 95, mm. 1-4[1]

[17] Except for Alleluias, the incipits of the propers are sung in plain chant.
[18] The same Alleluia but not its verse was reused for Common of Apostles, discussed below.

Ex. 3: p. 46, mm. 1-3

Another of Corteccia's mannerisms is his use at the onset of a piece of a brief phrase, two to three breves long, which makes a fleeting cadence as the first word or words of the text are sung by the upper parts. In the Pentecost communion, after the intonation on "Factus est," all voices enter with the word "repente" and quickly form an authentic cadence on D, the dominant note of the mode, before moving on. (Ex. 3 above.) An altogether illuminating Ex. of Corteccia's practice comes from the opening of the Alleluia for Birth of the Virgin Mary. Here, for the first statement of "Alleluia" the chant in the bassus ascends a third by step from F to A, while above it, the cantus embellishes its initial C. The upper voices unite briefly in a deceptive cadence for the last syllable, "ia," before continuing on with it through another, slightly longer passage. This latter is none other than the characteristic phrase. (Ex. 4)

Ex. 4: p. 102, mm. 1-4[1]

At the polyphonic opening of the Corpus Christi communion "Quotienscumque," the upper voices sing "manducabitis" in a brief phrase, and again the cadence is on the D dominant of the mode. In this instance because the chant rises to the F above middle C, Corteccia composes a tenor that moves below the bass to furnish

Ex. 5: p. 56, mm. 1-4[1]

the root of the triad. Generally, he treats the tenor in this manner whenever the bass is in a high register and he prefers the sound of a root-position chord to that of its first inversion. (Ex. 5 above.)

Repetitions of short passages from one section of a piece to another occur a number of times. These seem antithetical to the improvisatory spirit of the setting and to the supposedly spontaneous nature of the added voices yet they are justified by analogous passages in the chant. For the most part such passages are literal repetitions, as in the Ascension introit, where the material of the psalm verse ending perfectly matches that at the close of the doxology. The same pattern of repetition is found in the verse opening of the Pentecost introit and that of the doxology following. In the cycle for All Saints, such repetitions occur in both the introit and in the Alleluia. In this last, a few notes at the end of the Alleluia are varied to better accommodate the last words, "reficiam vos," at the end of its verse. (Ex. 6). Whether in improvised performances those who sang the upper parts could repeat note for note materials they had previously sung to a different text is open to question.

Ex. 6: p. 120, mm. 27-31; p. 121, mm. 42-46

Ex. 7: p. 9, mm. 18-22

There are a number of instances in the propers where Corteccia altered the received melody for his own purposes. Usually, the change involves the penultimate note of the chant melody.   In these cases the second note of the modal scale is replaced with the dominant note, a simple substitution that provides an authentic cadence for the close. Examples are plentiful, and here suffice it to cite the end of the Christmas communion, where the penultimate E is substituted by an A and an authentic cadence on the D final of mode 1. Clearly, Corteccia was willing to bend rules if he determined that his setting required a more definitive close than could be had by strict adherence to the chant melody. (Ex. 7 above.) In some propers where the penultimate note is supplanted by the dominant Corteccia used yet another approach to the cadence. In these pieces he brought the parts to a close on the penultimate note and capped them with a fermata. Then, above the sustained final in the bassus he added a codetta in which the upper parts sing the notes of its triad. The closes of the St. Lawrence Alleluia and its verse provide a typical Ex. of this approach. (Ex. 8)

Ex. 8: pp. 86-87, mm. 21-27; p. 88, mm. 43³-49

Corteccia's practice in his written polyphony is to order his structures so that, in addition to a well-defined final cadence on the tonic, cadences at the ends of larger phrases or entire sections emphasize the tonic or closely related points such as the subdominant and dominant. Such tonal bias is not always apparent in these improvisatory-style pieces, but a desire to affirm the modal final in one way or another is often in evidence. In the Alleluia for Purification of the Virgin Mary, as in a few other propers with a D final, Corteccia retained the chant's penultimate E but made sure to compose a C in one of the upper voices against it. In performance the C would be raised in accordance with the conventions of musica ficta, thus yielding a convincing cadence.[19] (Ex. 9).

Ex. 9: p. 66, mm. 29-32

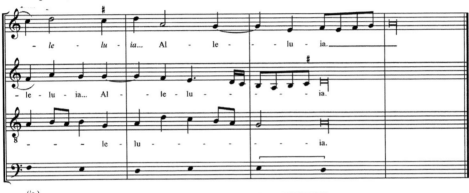

Now we turn to the propers that constitute the later additions to the book of counterpoints. Each of the five added by Federighi exhibits one or several of the features just illustrated. A brief phrase sets the first word of the introit for Confessor not a Bishop, and at the end of the antiphon the penultimate note is replaced by the dominant C before the F final of mode 6.[20] (Ex. 10 on p. 454.)

There is some repetition of material among the various sections of the piece, particularly at the closes of the psalms and doxology, which also substitute the dominant C for the penultimate note of the melody. Similar treatment is found at the end of both the Alleluia and verse for this same feast of Confessors. The introit and Alleluia for Common of Apostles and Evangelists, though copied later, bear Federighi's signature, "Michael scribebat," an indication that Corteccia was still working on his counterpoints for some time after Federighi finished the manuscript's first redaction. The Alleluia for Apostles and Evangelists, with only a slight change, has the same music as the just-cited Assumption Alleluia of the main corpus.

---

[19] Corteccia's version of the chant differs from the one in the *Liber usualis* (p. 1363), whose penultimate note is F.

[20] Corteccia's chant is no longer used for this feast. With a few variants his version of text and music is found in modern edition in *Graduale Sacrosancte Romanae Ecclesiae. . . Editio parisiensis Juxta Vaticanum* (Paris: Société d'Éditions du Chant Grégorien, 1909), [38].

Ex. 10: p. 132, mm. 31-35

Its verse, however, is different, and though it lacks any typical features—a not uncommon occurrence in many of the pieces Federighi copied—there is nothing about it that precludes Corteccia's authorship. The question arises as to whether it was Corteccia himself who reused an earlier Alleluia, to which he appended a newly composed verse as he attempted to bring his work to a timely close, or whether it was Federighi who did so as he sought to create a more complete cycle by using whatever was in Corteccia's *Nachlass*, in this case the verse without its Alleluia.

A similar situation arises with the introit, "Mihi autem," for the same feast. This bears Corteccia's signature right at the start with the next two words, "honorati sunt," set to a short phrase that comes quickly to a cadence on the dominant A of mode 2.[21] (Ex. 11, below) At the end the chant's penultimate E is retained, and the C in the cantus, which will be raised in performance, assures a satisfying cadence on the D final.

Ex. 11: p. 125, mm. 1-4[1]

[21] Corteccia often treats authentic and plagal forms of a mode as having the same dominant as well as the same final.

As in other instances, the closes of both of the following sections, the psalm verse and doxology, are treated in the same way. Although neither of these displays any of the typical features, their sound, especially the opening of the doxology, differs little from pieces in the main corpus. What is noteworthy about this introit for Common of Apostles and Evangelists is that it shares its psalm verse and doxology with the introit for Dedication of a Church, Federighi's other late addition. The antiphon in this piece, "Terribilis est," also announces Corteccia's authorship with the opening phrase for the words that follow, "locus iste." (Ex. 12)

Ex. 12: p. 145, mm.. 1-4[1]

Its ending too retains the penultimate E of the chant, above which the predictable raising of the C in the tenor will again provide an appropriate close on the D final of mode 2. As before the question of Corteccia's role in assembling the piece arises: did he himself transfer materials from one introit to the other, or did Federighi, having only the antiphons at hand, simply lift the psalm verse and doxology from the one in order to complete the other? Both scenarios are plausible because at this late stage the primary aim of composer or copyist would have been to make the book of counterpoints as complete as possible.

Of the five remaining propers that were copied later, three can be attributed to Corteccia with a reasonable amount of assurance, the fourth has a few of the stylistic elements just described, and the fifth has none of them. In the St. Andrew Alleluia, written in a hand close to Federighi's, a brief opening phrase is soon followed by the characteristic phrase. It recurs soon after, this time, slightly varied. (Ex. 13 on p. 456.) At the close, as he did in the main corpus, Coreteccia retains the penultimate F of the melody, which is in mode 1. It produces an indecisive cadence. But he compensates for the lack of a strong dominant-tonic close with an extended codetta on the D final.[22]

---

[22] I believe that the St. Andrew Alleluia comes down to us as a three-voice piece because it was unfinished at the time of Corteccia's death.

Ex. 13: p. 59, mm. 1- 8[1]

Another hand copied the introit, "Statuit ei Dominus," and the Alleluia for St. Zenobius. The introit begins with a typically short opening phrase. A variation of the characteristic phrase appears later in the introit at the words "in aeternum" and then again in the doxology (Ex. 14). At the end a cadence on the D final is treated in the usual manner, as the C in the cantus rises above the penultimate E of the bassus.

Ex. 14: p. 70, mm. 24-27

A short phrase also introduces the Alleluia for St. Zenobius. (Ex. 15) The chant's penultimate and final notes, F and D, are retained in both the Alleluia and its verse, which share almost similar endings. All in all the music for this feast,

[24] The syncopated passage is presented one other time in the psalm verse, but with a different melody in the bass, which now begins A, G, F before continuing with G, A.

[25] The three are Holy Thursday, Good Friday, and Whit Monday. The later added introit for Dedication of a Church is suitable for both the Cathedral and the Baptistry. In Florence the Consecration of the Cathedral occurred on the feast of the Annunciation. Given the significance of the feast, it is highly unlikely that Corteccia would have neglected to set the appropriate texts

Ex. 15: p. 72, mm. 1-3

though not in Federighi's hand, is so similar in sound to the pieces in the main corpus that Corteccia's authorship can hardly be doubted.

This is not so of the introit for Common of a Virgin not a Martyr, which, as I said, is in a hand very different from all of the others. It mimics some features of Corteccia's improvising style but makes its point primarily through frequent use of running passages in smaller note values and occasional couplings of thirds and sixths in the upper parts. Like many of the propers in mode 2, however, two of its sections close with a cadence on D that is approached by a C in the cantus above the penultimate E of the chant melody. Lack of any correspondences with other works and, more important, the sound of the piece make it highly unlikely that it is Corteccia's. Its insertion on folios left vacant by Federighi, an opening between propers for two feasts of the Virgin Mary, offer evidence of continuing efforts—here unsuccessful, in my opinion--to ensure the usefulness of the book of counterpoints.

I have kept discussion of the introit, "Dum sanctificatus," for the Mass of the Holy Spirit in Lent for last because it raises interesting questions of authenticity, even though a strong case can be made for attributing it to Corteccia. Copied by a hand close to Federighi's, the similarities it shares with works in the main corpus are easily identified. Among them are allusions to the characteristic phrase in the introit antiphon, a clash between two of the upper parts on a strong beat, and manipulation of harmony by setting the tenor below the bassus when the chant moves into a high register. A passage containing three successive semibreves in the cantus syncopated against the even semibreves of the chant is even more conspicuous.[23] The cantus here is reminiscent of the characteristic phrase but differs in that the two notes, E, D, following the initial C are twice their usual value. They proceed to the suspended C, which drops to B before settling on A. The same

---

[23] It is not unique because three syncopated semibreves in succession occur also in the latadded verse of the Alleluia for Confessors. They do not outline the characteristic phrase, as here. Corteccia's usual practice is to have no more than two successive semibreves in syncopation.

passage, set to the words "et dabo vobis spiritum," appears near the close of the introit antiphon, shortly after the beginning of the psalm verse and then again near the close of the doxology. (Ex. 16)

Ex. 16: pp. 142-43, mm. 53-56[3]

Its last appearance comes about because of the repetition of the entire psalm verse, which is tacked onto new material that begins the doxology. Wholesale repetition of this sort appears only in the later added propers, and it seems to me that it represents another instance of the composer—or the copyist—seeking a quick way to bring the piece to an end.[24]

   The appearance of cambiata figures in semiminims in the cantus perhaps offers the most significant reason for questioning Corteccia's authorship of the piece. In the last instance, to the words "inquinamentis vestris," the cambiata figure is stated sequentially three times—the fourth is cut off at mid-point—as the chant melody descends from G to D. (Ex. 17)

Ex. 17: p. 142, mm. 45-48

[24] The syncopated passage is presented one other time in the psalm verse, but with a differemt melody in the bass, which now begins A, G, F before continuing with G, A.

to polyphony. Perhaps he did, earlier in his career, and these were in a volume with other settings of a Cathedral liturgy for 25 March that is no longer extant. For the 1651 list of feasts see my "The Musical Chapels at the Florentine Cathedral and Baptistry during the First Half of the 16th

Century," *Journal of the American Musicological Society* 24 (1971), 1-50, particularly 33-36; reprinted as Chapter I in my *Music and Musicians in 16th-Century Florence*. Many of the feasts are listed in earlier reports concerning the singers' duties. (Ibid., 4-5, 10, 26-7)

It is unlike anything in the entire book of counterpoints, surprising in its recourse to such facile embellishment. If it is Corteccia's, it may have been a lapse on his part, perhaps composed at a time when he was struggling to finish the piece. On the other hand, if it is the work of one his pupils, it represents another valuable addition that was accepted as such by the singers of the Florentine chapel, who were still performing from Corteccia's book of counterpoints long after most of his other works had disappeared from the repertory.

These nine newly added propers raise the number of cycles, or partial cycles, in the collection to twenty, which assuredly enhanced the volume's usefulness and contributed to its longevity. In this, its final form, it contains music suitable for all but three feasts celebrated with Masses at the Cathedral as late as 1651.[25] The feasts are mentioned in a list from that year of the chapel's duties, which normally included Vespers on Sundays and feast days at the Cathedral and Masses on Sundays and other feast days at the Baptistry. Masses at the Cathedral, it bears emphasizing, were reserved for principal feasts. Propers for the few days when the chapel performed Masses at the churches of San Lorenzo and Santa Maria Novella and at the Palazzo Vecchio also find a place in the book of counterpoints. But prominently lacking are propers for eight other feasts that were customarily sung in polyphony at the Baptistry. It is difficult to believe, if not downright inconceivable, that Corteccia would not have considered composing music for those occasions as well.[26] Their absence could mean that he began his project with settings for Cathedral feasts and that he did not live long enough to begin the others.

If Corteccia's plan was to write cycles of propers for all of these other feasts, his book of counterpoints would have been as ambitious in scope as his Hymnary. That the music of the propers that comes down to us represents what he actually managed to finish seems more than likely in view of the incomplete state of the later added cycles: two copied by Federighi and the one for St. Zenobius all lack a communion; St. Andrew is represented by an Alleluia alone;[27] and Dedication of a Church has an introit only. Together with the absence of cycles appropriate for the Baptistry,

---

[25] The three are Holy Thursday, Good Friday, and Whit Monday. The later added introit for Dedication of a Church is suitable for both the Cathedral and the Baptistry. In Florence the Consecration of the Cathedral occurred on the feast of the Annunciation. Given the significance of the feast, it is highly unlikely that Corteccia would have neglected to set the appropriate texts to polyphony. Perhaps he did, earlier in his career, and these were in a volume with other settings of a Cathedral liturgy for 25 March that is no longer extant. For the 1651 list of feasts see my "The Musical Chapels at the Florentine Cathedral and Baptistry during the First Half of the 16th Century," *Journal of the American Musicological Society* 24 (1971), 1-50, particularly 33-36; reprinted as Chapter I in my *Music and Musicians in 16th-Century Florence.* Many of the feasts are listed in earlier reports concerning the singers' duties. (Ibid., 4-5, 10, 26-27)

[26] This would be particularly true for at least four of them: Indulgence of St. John the Baptist, Beheading of St. John the Baptist, Finding of the Holy Cross, and Exaltation of the Holy Cross because they were already among the Baptistry's principal feasts when Corteccia became master of the chapel in 1540. ("The Musical Chapels," 26-27.)

[27] The introit for Common of Apostles, however, could also be used for this feast.

these remnants of a near successful attempt to include a complete set of cycles for Cathedral Masses in the book of counterpoints lead to a final observation about Federighi's manuscript, and that is, that from the very beginning it was intended for use at the Cathedral. Whether Corteccia envisioned a similar volume for the Baptistry alone will remain a matter of speculation. But what does seem clear is that his plan to compose cycles for all Cathedral feasts was well along when death overtook him and provided the final clue to solving the mystery of the book of counterpoints.

"Other" Musics in Sixteenth-Century Venice

Iain Fenlon

> "There you may see many Polonians, Slavonians, Persians, Grecians,Turks,
> Iewes, Christians of the famousest regions of Christendome, and each
> nation distinguished from another by their proper and peculiar habits."
>
> —Thomas Coryate (1611)

On 1 May 1491, Isabella d'Este wrote to her agent Giorgio Brognolo with the request that he procure for her a young black girl, with the intention that she be trained as a servant. This is just one of a number of attempts by the Marchioness to buy black slaves in Venice. Their presence in the city is not unusual; Marin Sanudo mentions black African gondoliers, and several of them are shown in Carpaccio's paintings.[1] The episode itself is not only a reminder of Isabella's legendary enthusiasm for the curious and exotic, an apparently "insatiable appetite"[2] which extended to paintings, antique marbles, and musical instruments,[3] but is also a reminder of the status of Venice as a great entrepôt, the "Hinge of Europe" as it has been called by one historian.[4] From as early as the thirteenth century, Venetian traders had been bringing back slaves from the Aegean and Black seas, and the trade grew appreciably in the decades after the Black Death as the need for cheap labour increased.[5] By the sixteenth century black faces were an not uncommon sight in the elite environments of Renaissance Italy, and their presence was much prized.

---

[1] Paul H. D. Kaplan, "Isabella d'Este and Black African Women," in Thomas F. Earle and Kate J. P. Lowe, eds., *Black Africans in Renaissance Europe* (Cambridge: Cambridge University Press, 2005), 125-54.

[2] Clifford M. Brown, "*Lo insaciabile desiderio nostro de cose antique:* New Documents on Isabella'd'Este's Collection of Antiquities," in Cecil Clough, ed., *Cultural Aspects of the Italian Renaissance: Essays in Honour of Paul Oskar Kristeller* (Manchester: Manchester University Press, 1976), 324-53.

[3] William F. Prizer, "Isabella d'Este and Lorenzo da Pavia, 'Master Instrument-Maker,'" *Early Music History* 2 (1982): 87-127. My friendship with Bill Prizer goes back to the early 1970s when, sitting at adjacent desks on an almost daily basis, we both worked in the Archivio di Stato in Mantua. I am extremely grateful to Kris Forney for the opportunity to write in honour of Bill on this occasion. For further on Isabella and Lorenzo da Pavia, another of her agents in Venice, see Clifford M. Brown and Anna Maria Lorenzoni, *Isabella d'Este and Lorenzo da Pavia. Documents for the History of Art and Culture in Renaissance Mantua* (Geneva: Librairie Droz, 1982).

[4] William H. McNeill, *Venice: The Hinge of Europe, 1081-1797* (Chicago: University of Chicago Press, 1974).

[5] Charles Verlinden, "Le recrutement des esclaves à Venise aux XIVe et XVe siècles," *Bulletin de l'Institut Historique Belge de Rome* 39 (1968): 83-202.

Such arrivals, if dramatically different and recognizably "other," were just one element in the rich racial mix of early modern Venice. The sixteenth-century city was not only one of the largest in Europe but also one of the most cosmopolitan. The characterization of the Piazza San Marco which stands at the head of this essay, published in Coryate's book of travel reminiscences of 1611,[6] also underlines the fact that the city's large foreign population included substantial colonies of Germans, Arabs, Flemings, Greeks, and all manner of Slavs, not to mention those perennial outsiders: the Turks and the Jews.[7]

Some of these foreign enclaves were concentrated in the area around the Rialto, where they maintained vital business interests,[8] but sizeable numbers were also congregated in other parts of the city; there they maintained cultural practices from their places of origin including musical traditions both learned and popular, composed, written down, oral, and improvised. The little that can be recovered helps modify the picture of the musical life of a center dominated by the Basilica di San Marco and the more important institutions of the city, by the compositions of Andrea and Giovanni Gabrieli and their contemporaries, and by the practice of written polyphony, both there and in parish churches and confraternities.[9]

The health of Venetian commerce was but one motive for the considerable influx of outsiders in the sixteenth century; a reputation for security from outside aggression, and for a degree of religious toleration, both of which were significant considerations in this most turbulent of centuries, were also important. According to one interpretation of the Venetian census of 1509, somewhere between 2.6% and 3.0% of the population of the city was then made up of foreigners.[10] Since it has been estimated that in the decades immediately before the vicious plague of 1575-77, which carried off approximately one third of its inhabitants, the population of Venice stood at about 150,000,[11] perhaps as many as six to eight thousand people were then classed as outsiders. In addition to questions of numbers and percentages, sixteenth-century Venice was also the most ethnically diverse of all European

[6] Thomas Coryate, *Coryat's Crudities: Hastily gobled up in five moneths travells in France, Savoy ...* (London, 1611).

[7] For a rapid overview see Alvise Zorzi, *La vita quotidiana a Venezia nel secolo di Tiziano* (Milan: Rizzoli, 1990), ch. 4.

[8] For the character of the area, see Donatella Calabi and Paolo Morachiello, *Rialto: le fabbriche e il ponte, 1514-1591* (Turin: Einaudi,1987), 16-40, which deals with the period before the fire of 1514.

[9] The literature on music in sixteenth-century Venice is large. Some sense of the present state of scholarship can be gained from three recent contributions: Elena Quaranta, *Oltre San Marco: organizzazione e prassi della musica nelle chiese a Venezia nel Rinascimento* (Florence: Olschki, 1998); Jonathan Glixon, *Honoring God and the City: Music at the Venetian Confraternities, 1260-1807* (New York: Oxford University Press, 2003); Iain Fenlon, *The Ceremonial City: History, Memory and Myth in Renaissance Venice* (New Haven and London: Yale University Press, 2007).

[10] Brunehilde Imhaus, *Le minoranze orientali a Venezia, 1300-1510* (Rome: Il Veltro, 1997), 48.

[11] This is one figure, but modern calculations of the population of the city vary; see for some of them Daniele Beltrami, *Storia della popolazione di Venezia dalla fine del secolo XVI alla caduta della Repubblica* (Padua: CEDAM, 1954); Mirto Etonti and Fiorenzo Rossi, *La popolazione del Dogado Veneto nei secoli XVII e XVIII* (Padua: Cleup, 1994); Eugene Rice, "Recent Studies on the Population of Europe, 1348-1620," *Renaissance News* 18 (1965):180-87.

cities on account of its extensive trading links with the East, a vast network which had been gradually built up by Venetian merchants since the early middle ages. Black gondoliers aside, the most visible of all these foreign communities was that of the Turks. Incorporated into narrative paintings by Carpaccio and endlessly discussed and illustrated in Venetian printed books, they were a source of both fascination and fear for early modern Venetians.[12] The flood of celebratory books and pamphlets that appeared in Venice after the victory over the Ottoman fleet at Lepanto in 1571 revealed not only this, but also the wealth of dialects spoken in the city, a clear indication of the diversity of the resident population.[13]

Foreign communities not only brought much-needed skills to their adopted city; their presence also encouraged a certain degree of social mobility and, at least in times of peace, a measure of toleration.[14] At the same time, they also fostered the formation of a cultural dialogue between centre and periphery, with stylistic influences and material objects travelling in both directions. In a historical sense this is most obviously true of Venetian contacts with Byzantium and the East,[15] but similar processes of assimilation, adaption, and appropriation also involved territories such as the trading posts along the eastern shores of the Adriatic, and the islands in the Aegean and eastern Mediterranean that were under Venetian control. Deposits of all kinds, from fortifications to fountains, and paintings to printed books, survive in these places as memorials to their cultural encounters with Venice, and sometimes as reminders of the artistic consequences of political domination. Buried among these often damaged and sometimes ghostly archaeological presences are the occasional residues of musical exchange.

The most documented of all the foreign "nations" in Venice is that of the Germans, who lived and traded from the Fondaco dei Tedeschi next to the Rialto bridge. The building itself, which still survives (though in much altered condition), was maintained by the Venetian government, who leased it in turn to the community. Religious devotion took place in the nearby church of San Bartolomeo, which contained an organ whose shutters were painted by Sebastiano del Piombo, and an altarpiece commissioned by Albrecht Dürer.[16] Of all the foreign communities the Germans were perhaps the best assimilated, a feature that was noted at the time; it was not confined to the merchant class, but also included the porters and boatmen necessary to its successful operation. In addition, outside the Fondaco proper many

---

[12] Paolo Preto, *Venezia e i Turchi* (Florence: G. C. Sansoni, 1975); Steve Ortega, "Ottoman Muslims in the Venetian Republic from 1573 to 1645: Contacts, Connections and Restrictions" (PhD diss., University of Manchester, 2001); Bronwen Wilson, *The World in Venice: Print, the City, and Early Modern Identity* (Toronto, Buffalo, and London: Toronto University Press, 2005), 221-48.

[13] Manlio Cortelazzo, "Plurilinguismo celebrativo," in Gino Benzoni, ed., *Il mediterraneo nella seconda metà del '500 alla luce di Lepanto* (Florence: Olschki, 1974), 121-26.

[14] Stephen Ell, "Citizenship and Immigration in Venice, 1305 to 1500" (PhD diss., University of Chicago, 1976).

[15] See, for a recent synthesis, Deborah Howard, *Venice and the East: The Impact of the Islamic World on Venetian Architecture, 1100-1500* (New Haven and London: Yale University Press, 2000).

[16] Peter Humfrey, "Dürer's Feast of the Rosegarlands: A Venetian Altarpiece," *Bulletin of the Society for Renaissance Studies* 4 (1986): 29-39; idem, "La festa del Rosario di Albrecht Dürer," *Eidos* 2 (1988): 4-15.

Germans lived and worked in different parts of the city as bakers, shoemakers, weavers, physicians, and printers, while others were engaged in a the textile trade and the jewelry business.[17] Taken as a whole the community represented both a broad social range and a decent spread of commercial and professional activities which brought considerable benefits in terms of social and cultural integration. This can be observed in the days following the victory of the Holy League over the Turks at Lepanto in 1571, when the Germans were quick to organize public celebrations. They decorated their Fondaco with tapestries and torches, and for three successive nights the Venetian crowds were treated to displays of fireworks accompanied by music.[18]

Similar patterns of assimilation can be observed in relation to other North European enclaves such as the Flemings, many of whom were wealthy merchants. Here, too, there are occasional glimpses of musical activity. According to the inventory of the possessions of Francisco Vrins, drawn up in 1604, he owned not only "un clavizimbano con suoi piedi," but also "una spinetta" kept in one of the upper rooms.[19] Similarly, Carlo Helman, evidently a man of substance, included among his possessions not only silver, brocades, and paintings—including works allegedly by Veronese and Titian ("una Santa Maria Maddalena")—but also "un manicordo vecchio" and "un clavicembano" ("in portico").[20] Both Vrins and Helman lived in the parish of Santa Maria Formosa. Flemings seem to have congregated in this area, and Dutch merchants continued to gravitate there throughout the seventeenth century. One, Giacomo Stricher, had trading links with Smyrna, Constantinople, Genoa, Livorno, the Netherlands, England, and France. With a large house in the Campo, and a documented capital of 200,000 ducats in cash, he was one of the wealthiest immigrant merchants in the entire city.[21] At a different professional level, the careers of Jacques Buus and Adrian Willaert underline the importance of Flemish immigrants for the artistic and musical life of Venice. About Willaert's economic and personal circumstances nothing much is known, but Buus was evidently a figure of some social standing, at least to judge from the existence of his profile medal and his ability to bear the costs of publishing his own works.[22]

[17] Paolo Braunstein, "Appunti per la storia di una minoranza: la popolazione tedesca di Venezia nel Medioevo," *Strutture familiari, epidemie, migrazioni nell'Italia medievale*, Rinaldo Comba, Gabriella Piccinni, Guiliano Pinto, eds. (Naples: Edizioni scientifiche italiane, 1984), 511-517; Carolin Wirtz, "Mercator in fontico nostro," in Susanne Winter, ed., *Presenze tedesche a Venezia* (Rome and Venice: Storia e Letteratura, 2005), 1-26 at p. 3.

[18] Ernst H. Gombrich, "Celebrations in Venice of the Holy League and of the Victory of Lepanto," in *Studies in Renaissance and Baroque Art Presented to Anthony Blunt on his Sixtieth Birthday* (London and New York: Phaidon, 1967), 62-68.

[19] Wilfred Brulez, *Marchands flamands à Venise*, I (1568-1605) (Brussels and Rome: Institut Historique Belge de Rome, 1965), 630-43.

[20] Greta Devos and Wilfred Brulez, *Marchands flamands à Venise*, II (1606-1621) (Brussels and Rome: Institut Historique Belge de Rome, 1986), 799-811.

[21] For Stricher, see Alexander Cowan, "Foreigners and the City: The Case of the Immigrant Merchant," in Alexander Cowan, ed., *Mediterranean Urban Culture, 1400-1700* (Exeter: University of Exeter Press, 2000), 45-55.

[22] Fenlon, *The Ceremonial City*, 70.

Equally distinct, if inevitably less integrated into general cultural praxis, were the Jews.[23] The foundation of the Ghetto was not an intentional government policy, but rather an accidental consequence of the war of the League of Cambrai. In 1509, Jewish moneylenders, fearful of the anti-Venetian armies of the alliance which were advancing with speed, fled across the lagoon; once they had established themselves in the city, the authorities, realizing their social utility, allowed them to stay.[24] A few years later, in response to pressure from the clergy which had consistently advocated their expulsion, the Jews were allocated a small and self-contained island in the north of the city which subsequently became known as the Ghetto Nuovo.[25] Heavy wooden gates, installed on the two bridges which led to it, were locked at sunset and opened at dawn.[26] This was in 1516. Twenty-five years later the Ghetto was enlarged by the addition of the adjacent Ghetto Vecchio, to which it was connected by a bridge.[27] This not only located the community within the topography of Venice, but also established it functionally within the operations of Christian society, as Francesco Sansovino recognized.[28]

Nonetheless, throughout the century, relations between the authorities and the Jews were often turbulent, particularly during the years between the siege of Malta and the battle of Lepanto.[29] As with the Turks, the Venetians had always regarded the Jews with a mixture of wariness and toleration born of expediency; conscious of their importance for Venetian trade, the authorities had usually left both in peace. But with the growing Ottoman threat to Venetian possessions in the Mediterranean during the War of Cyprus, official attitudes began to harden. In 1568, thousands of copies of Hebrew books were destroyed and others censored on the grounds that they had been published unexpurgated, and although

[23] For overviews of the cultural life of the Ghetto, see the old but still valuable picture presented in Cecil Roth, *The History of the Jews of Venice* (Philadelphia: Jewish Publication Society of America, 1930), and the lively account in Brian Pullan, *The Jews of Europe and the Inquisition of Venice, 1550-1670* (Oxford: Blackwell, 1983), 145-98.

[24] Robert Finlay, "The Foundation of the Ghetto: Venice, the Jews and the War of the League of Cambrai," *Proceedings of the American Philosophical Society* 126 (1982): 140-54; Ennio Concina: "Owners, Houses, Functions: New Research on the Origins of the Venetian Ghetto," *Mediterranean Historical Review* 6 (1991-92): 180-89.

[25] For the area before the establishment of the Ghetto, see Ennio Concina, "Parva Jerusalem," in Ennio Concina, Ugo Camerino, and Donatella Calabi, eds., *La città degli ebrei. Il ghetto di Venezia; architettura e urbanistica* (Venice: Albrizzi, 1991), 112-24.

[26] Benjamin Ravid, "Curfew Time in the Ghetto of Venice," in Ellen E. Kittell and Thomas F. Madden, eds., *Medieval and Renaissance Venice* (Urbana and Chicago: University of Illinois Press, 1999), 237-75.

[27] Benjamin Ravid, "The Religious, Economic and Social Background and Context of the Establishment of the Ghetti of Venice," in Gaetano Cozzi, ed., *Gli ebrei a Venezia: secoli XIV-XVII* (Milan: Edizioni di Comunità, 1987), 211-59, and the same author's essay "The Venetian Ghetto in Historical Perspective," in Mark R. Cohen, trans. and ed., *The Autobiography of a Seventeenth-Century Venetian Rabbi: Leon Modena's "Life of Judah"* (Princeton: Princeton University Press, 1988), 279-83.

[28] Francesco Sansovino, *Venetia citta nobilissima et singolare, descritta in XIIII libri* (Venice, 1581), f. 136v.

[29] See Benjamin Ravid, "The Venetian Government and the Jews," in Robert C. Davis and Benjamin Ravid, eds., *The Jews of Early Modern Venice* (Baltimore and London: Johns Hopkins University Press, 2001), 3-30.

Hebrew books were printed and published again in some number after 1568, and Venice gradually regained its position in the trade, this revival took place in an increasingly threatening atmosphere. In 1570, Marc' Antonio Giustiniani, accused of clandestinely importing Hebrew texts printed on the island of Cephalonia, was brought before the Inquisition and subjected to a gruelling trial.[30] The peak of anti-Jewish feeling was reached a few months later, just after the loss of Cyprus, when the Senate voted to expel the Jews from the Ghetto; it was not until after 1573 that relations returned to some sort of normality.[31] In the chequered history of Venetian relations with its Jewish subjects, these years mark a low point as the ruling elite, for political reasons, abandoned tolerance in favour of repression.[32] This policy, which involved the wholesale destruction of Hebrew books, was clearly aimed at the suppression of religious ritual.

This uneven history may help to explain the almost total lack of documentation of music in the Ghetto during the late sixteenth century. In terms of musical practice, activities there are largely shrouded in silence, and no sixteenth-century sources of polyphony (assuming that they ever existed) have survived. (The note of qualification is necessary because of the untypical status of Salamone Rossi's settings of the Song of Solomon, which cannot reflect common practice in contemporary north Italian synagogues).[33] Occasional archival references reveal that the community included musicians, dancers, and music teachers, some of whom were active as professionals, but beyond that little is known before the arrival of Leon Modena.[34] According to a brief aside in his autobiography, Modena assumed the leadership of a Jewish music academy, the Accademia degl' Impediti, during the summer of 1628. He was also responsible for one of the first choral performances of the Jewish liturgy at the Sephardic synagogue on the feast of Simhat Torah, a celebration marking the annual cycle of public readings from the Torah, which attracted the attention of large numbers of curious Christian observers.[35] The life of the Venetian Ghetto, the first of its kind in Italy (though soon to be much imitated elsewhere in the peninsula), fascinated both citizens and visitors; as such it soon became a regular feature of the early tourist experience.[36]

[30] Paul P. Grendler, "The Destruction of Hebrew Books in Venice, 1568," *Proceedings of the American Academy for Jewish Research* 45 (1978): 120-29.

[31] See Benjamin Ravid, "The Socioeconomic Background of the Expulsion and Readmission of the Venetian Jews 1571-73," in Phyllis Cohen Albert and Frances Malino, eds., *Essays in Modern Jewish History: A Tribute to Ben Halpern* (Rutherford, NJ: Fairleigh Dickinson University Press, 1982), 27-55.

[32] Michele Jacoviello, "Proteste di editori e librai veneziani contro l'introduzione della censura sulla stampa a Venezia, 1543-1555," *Archivio storico italiano* 151 (1993): 40-44.

[33] Don Harrán, *Salamone Rossi: Jewish Musician in Late Renaissance Mantua* (Oxford: Oxford University Press, 1999).

[34] For what little is known, see Israel Adler, *La pratique musicale savante dans quelques communautés juives en Europe au XVIIe et XVIIIe siècles*, 2 vols. (Paris: La Haye, 1966), 1: 43-154 [? 54?], and Don Harrán, "Jewish Musical Culture: Leon Modena," in Davis and Ravid, eds., *The Jews of Early Modern Venice*, 211-30.

[35] Howard E. Adelman, "Leon Modena: The Autobiography and the Man," in Cohen, trans. and ed., *The Autobiography*, 19-49, at p. 31.

[36] Benjamin Ravid, "Christian Travelers in the Ghetto of Venice: Some Preliminary Observations,"

Figure 1:
Playing the shofar on the feast of Rosh
Hashanah in the Campo del Ghetto,
2008.

Witnessed by many, Jewish religious practices, both then and now, were the principal
contribution of the community to the soundscape of the city.

As for the rest, the Albanians, Dalmatians, and Greeks all maintained their
own churches and charitable institutions. Long established though they were, these
communities of immigrants from the eastern shores of the Adriatic were not so
easily absorbed into Venetian society. For about a century, beginning in about 1540,
the Usoks, in practice an organization of no more than a thousand men, regularly
robbed and plundered the Dalmatian islands and the smaller craft that sailed the
waters of the northern Adriatic.[37] If for the Venetians the problem was insoluble, for
the islanders the question of allegiance was not always straightforward. Dalmation
informers, discontented with the rigours of Venetian rule, were at work even in
Venice itself; in 1586, it came to the notice of the Council of Ten that an official
from Lesina, Francesco da Bruzza, routinely reported the departure of every
vessel to the Usoks.[38] Suspicion of the Albanians was equally strong, since some
of the greatest threats to Venetian shipping came from pirates based in Valona
and Durazzo, and in the early seventeenth century their galleys even occasionally
appeared in the upper Adriatic.[39] In Venice itself, the Albanians mostly settled in

---

in Stanley Nash, ed., *Between History and Literature: Studies in Honor of Isaac Barzilay* (B'nei B'rak:
Hakibbutz Hame'uchad, 1997), 110-50.

[37] Alberto Tenenti, *Piracy and the Decline of Venice, 1580-1615* (Berkeley: University of California Press,
1967), 3-15.

[38] Ibid., 5.

[39] Ibid., 18-20.

Figure 2:
The Scuola degli Albanesi

the parishes of San Moise and San Maurizio,[40] where the Scuola degli Albanesi, built in 1531 as the focal point for the community which had been established in this area of Venice since the thirteenth century, engaged Carpaccio[41] to decorate its *albergo*. So too did the Schiavoni whose *scuola*, which lies in the middle of the area between the church of the Pietà and the Campo San Lorenzo, preserves its cycle of paintings also by Carpaccio. Yet while independent traditions and religious rituals were preserved, some measure of engagement with Venetian mainstream culture also took place, particularly in the case of the Orthodox Greeks.

Of all these communities, this was the largest. The fall of Constantinople in 1453 had caused a wave of immigrants from Constantinople including, famously, Cardinal Bessarion, whose large donation of Greek and Latin manuscripts became the foundation collection of what is now the Biblioteca Nazionale Marciana.[42]

---

[40] See Freddy Thieret, "Les communautés grecques et albanaises à Venise," in Hans-Georg Beck, Manoussos Manoussacas, and Agostino Pertusi, eds., *Venezia, centro di mediazione tra Oriente e Occidente (secoli XV-XVI): aspetti e problemi*, 2 vols. (Florence: Olschki, 1977), 1: 217-31; Alain Ducellier, et al., eds., *Les chemins de l'exil: Bouleversements de l'Est européen et migrations vers l'Ouest à la fin du Moyen Age* (Paris: Armand Colin, 1992).

[41] Patricia F. Brown, *Venetian Narrative Painting in the Age of Carpaccio* (New Haven and London: Yale University Press, 1988), 7.

[42] For an overview, see Deno Geanakoplos, *Byzantium and the Renaissance: Greek Scholars in Venice* (Cambridge, MA: Harvard University Press, 1962), and the more recent synopsis in Nigel G. Wilson,

Scholars from outside Greece itself were also attracted to Venice, which by 1500 had become the most important centre for Greek learning anywhere in Europe. Manuscripts as well as men had made the journey from Constantinople, and it was in Venice that many texts were copied by a whole colony of Greek scribes (the best known of whom is George of Trebizond) for clients both inside and outside the Italian peninsula. It has been estimated that, by the end of the sixteenth century, there were between four and five thousand Greeks in Venice. Certainly there were enough to sustain a printing and publishing trade; while some of the books were clearly destined for export, others must have been bought locally.[43] Before Aldus Manutius opened his press in 1494-95, only a few Greek titles had been printed in Venice, but these included a Missal in Croatian with Glagolithic script, a market for which could otherwise only be satisfied by the printers of Cetinje in Dalmatia.[44] By the time of his death in 1515, Aldus had published most of the most important Greek classical texts then known.[45] A small number of native Greek printers living in Venice, among them Zacharias Callierges (who in collaboration with his fellow Cretan Nicola Vlastò founded the first exclusively Greek press in the city), also contributed to its development as the major centre for the production of Greek texts of all kinds, including liturgical books.[46] It is from these that we gain the clearest picture of the music regularly sung and heard by the Greek community in Venice as we do for that of the Ghetto. But somewhat unexpectedly, a small amount of liturgical polyphony has also survived. During the late fifteenth century, Ioannes Plousiadenos, the spiritual director of a small Greek colony in Venice, composed one (or possibly two) communion verses in primitive two-voice polyphony,[47] possibly

From Byzantium to Italy: Greek Studies in the Italian Renaissance (London: Duckworth, 1992), 124-56. On Bessarion's books see Lotte Labowsky, *Bessarion's Library and the Biblioteca Marciana: Six Early Inventories* (Rome: Edizioni di storia e letteratura, 1979).

[43] Giorgio Fedalto, "Le minoranze straniere a Venezia tra politica e legislazione," in Beck, Manoussacas, and Pertusi, eds. *Venezia centro di mediazione*, 1: 143-62, at p.149; Linos Politis, "Venezia come centro della stampa e della diffusione della prima letteratura neoellenica," in Beck, Manoussacas, and Pertusi, eds., *Venezia centro di mediazione*, 1: 443-82; Enrica Follieri, "Il libro Greco per I greci nelle imprese editoriali romane e veneziane della prima metà del Cinquecento," in Beck, Manoussacas, and Pertusi, eds., *Venezia centro di mediazione*, 1: 483-508.

[44] James G. Ball, "The Greek Community in Venice, 1470-1620" (PhD diss., University of London, 1984), 160.

[45] On Aldus and his enterprise in general, see Martin Lowry, *The World of Aldus Manutius: Business and Scholarship in Renaissance Venice* (Oxford: Blackwell, 1979), especially 111-16; 141-42; 149-52 and, at a more technical level, Nicolas Barker, *Aldus Manutius and the Development of Greek Script and Type in the Fifteenth Century* (New York: Fordham University Press, 1992). His contribution to the dissemination of classical scholarship is treated in Ralph Hexter, "Aldus, Greek, and the Shape of the 'Classical Corpus,'" in David S. Zeidberg and Fiorella Gioffredi Superbi, eds., *Aldus Manutius and Renaissance Culture: Essays in Memory of Franklin D. Murphy* (Florence: Olschki, 1998), 143-60.

[46] There is a considerable literature on this subject; see, *inter alia*, Manusos Manoussakas and Konstantinos Staikos, eds., *L'attività editoriale dei Greci durante il Rinascimento italiano (1469-1523)* (Athens: Ministero greco della cultura, 1986), 127-42, and Georghios Ploumidis, "Le tipografie greche di Venezia," in Maria Francesca Tiepolo and Eurigio Tonetti, eds., *I greci a Venezia: atti dei convegno internazionale di studio, Venezia, 5-7 novembre 1998* (Venice: Istituto veneto di scienze, lettere ed arti, 2002), 365-79.

[47] Dimitri Conomos, "Experimental Polyphony, 'According to the ... Latins,'" in Late Byzantine Psalmody," *Early Music History* 2 (1982): 1-16.

in imitation of the simple improvised style (also occasionally written down),
described by the Paduan theorist Prosdocimus as *cantus planus binatim*.[48] It is highly
likely that polyphony of this kind, which was the *lingua franca* of confraternities and
parish churches throughout Italy, would have been performed in Venetian churches
(including San Marco) in the fourteenth and fifteenth centuries and even later.

It is probable that a similar manner of singing was adopted by the Venetian
Greeks for use in a liturgical context. The evidence comes from a doxology and
two settings of the Creed (sung in the Western church but not the Eastern),
composed in the early fifteenth century for the ruler of the island of Lefkas (which
lies between Corfu and Cefalonia in the Ionian archipelago), by Manuel Gazes,
whose compositions circulated elsewhere in the Eastern Mediterranean, reaching
Lesbos and even Crete.[49] Another composer and copyist, the Cypriot Hieronymus
Tragodistes (Geronimo Cantore), who studied for three years with Gioseffo Zarlino,
wrote a four-voice setting of the final troparion of the Easter canon; this survives
in a manuscript that probably belonged to Cardinal Alvise Cornaro, a Venetian
patrician family with strong connections to the island.[50] Such merging of cultures,
on the borders of written and oral practices, which must have been far more
common than indicated by notated records, would have been further facilitated by
the experiences of Roman clergy returning from service in the Venetian colonies.

In addition to the Greeks and the Jews, the musical and liturgical needs of
other foreign communities were also served by Venetian publishers. The Armenian
enclave, which mostly consisted of merchants whose presence is attested to by
documents as well as by a number of spectacular tombs in Venetian churches, was
another. The first book in the Armenian language to be published in Venice appeared
in 1511, and a psalter was issued in 1566.[51] Small in size in comparison to other
immigrant groups, the Armenians were clustered around the church of Santa Croce
and the adjoining hospital in the Sottoportego degli Armeni at San Zulian.[52]

Sixteenth-century Venetian conceptions of the "other" would also have
embraced immigrants from the *terraferma*. The influx of newcomers from these
regions inevitably quickened in the course of the fifteenth century as the boundaries
of the Venetian state were relentlessly pushed westwards, and further impetus to
the process occurred after 1494, as the effects of the French invasions began to
be felt more strongly elsewhere in Italy. The image of Venice as a safe haven in
the midst of general Italian turmoil at the end of the 1520s, as the last Republic

[48] F. Alberto Gallo, "The Practice of *Cantus Planus Binatim* in Italy from the Beginning of the 14th to the Beginning of the 16th Century," in Cesare Corsi and Pierluigi Petrobelli, eds., *Le polifonie primitive in Friuli e in Europa* (Rome: Torre d'Orfeo, 1989), 14-23.

[49] Michael Adamis, "An Example of Polyphony in Byzantine Music of the Late Middle Ages," in *Report of the Eleventh International Musicological Society Congress, Copenhagen 1971*, 2 vols. (Copenhagen: Hanson, 1972), 2: 737-47.

[50] Oliver Strunk, *Essays on Music in the Western World* (New York: W. W. Norton, 1974), 79-93.

[51] Giorgio N. Gianighian, "Segni di una presenza," in B. Levon Zekiyan and Aldo Ferrari, eds., *Gli Armeni e Venezia: Dagli Sceriman a Mechitar: il molmento culminante di una consuetudine millenaria* (Venice: Istituto veneto di scienze, lettere ed arti, 2004), 59-73 at p. 59.

[52] Ibid., 70.

collapsed in Florence and a half-savage Lutheran soldiery brutally sacked Rome, has been exaggerated, for these were also troubled times for Venice itself. After the Treaty of Bologna of 1529, a new vision of Venice's international role was shaped; in what has been described as "a remarkable paradigm shift on the part of the Venetian ruling elite," the Venetians rapidly replaced the previous image of a militant, self-confident Republic with that of Venice as the haven of peace and the home of the *Pax Veneziana*.[53] In these circumstances, many aspects of Venetian economic life benefited from the skills and enterprise of a new wave of immigrants; many came from elsewhere in Italy,[54] but others continued to arrive, as they had done for decades, from Venetian possessions on the *terraferma*.

The example of Bergamo is instructive. In a *relazione* written at the beginning of the seventeenth century, the Spanish diplomat Antonio de la Cueva, Marchese of Bedmar, touched on three themes commonly found in contemporary descriptions of Bergamo and its inhabitants: the poverty of the city and its *contado,* the need to emigrate in order to escape from the risk of starvation, and the aptitude of the Bergamaschi for commercial enterprise as a result of which many "hanno palagi, possessioni, e richezze grandissime."[55] These three characteristics echo down the centuries, from Bandello's *novelle* and the reports of the Venetian *rettori* of the city onwards, and together they constitute the main explanation for the significant presence of Bergamaschi in Venice in the early modern period.[56] Certainly many of them worked in lowly circumstances; Bedmar identifies the job of portering, carrying goods from one part of the city to the other, as something of a Bergamasque speciality, to which should be added that of courier.[57] In terms of the accuracy of the picture that Bedmar paints, there can be little doubt of the poor

[53] Elizabeth G. Gleason, "Confronting New Realities: Venice and the Peace of Bologna, 1530," in John Martin and Dennis Romano, eds., *Venice Reconsidered: The History and Civilization of an Italian City-State, 1297-1797* (Baltimore and London: The Johns Hopkins University Press, 2000), 168-78.

[54] For one example considered in detail, see Luca Molà, *La communità dei Lucchesi a Venezia: Immigrazione e industria della seta ner tardo medioevo* (Venice: Istituto veneto di scienze, lettere ed arti, 1994).

[55] Italo Raulich, "Una relazione del marchese di Bedmar sui veneziani," *Archivio veneto*, n.s. 16 (1898): 16. On Antonio de la Cueva, see Franco Gaeta, "Venezia da 'stato misto' ad aristocrazia 'esemplare,'" in Gianfranco Folena, ed., *Storia della cultura veneta*, vol. 4, bk. 2, Girolamo Arnaldi and Manlio Pastore Stocchi, eds., *Dalla controriforma alla fine della Republica* (Vicenza: Neri Pozza, 1984), 469-70.

[56] See, for example, M. De Grazia, "Note sull'emigrazione bergamasca dei secoli passati, sulle postee sui Tasso," in *Le poste dei Tasso, un' impresa in Europa* (Bergamo: Commune di Bergamo, 1984), 171-76. For the relazioni of the rettori, see Amelio Tagliaferri, ed., *Relazioni dei rettori veneti in Terraferma*, vol. XII: Podesteria e capitanato di Bergamo (Milan: Giuffrè, 1978), with useful comments on the subject in the introduction (by Bruno Polese) on pp. xv-xvi. A general overview of the Bergamasque presence in Venice is given in Andrea Zannini, "L'altra Bergamo in laguna: La communità bergamasca a Venezia," in Aldo De Maddalena, Marco Cattini and Marzio A. Romani, eds., *Storia economica e sociale di Bergamo*, vol. 2, *Il tempo della serenisssima* (Bergamo: Fondazione per la storia economica e sociale di Bergamo, 1995), 2: 175-93.

[57] See Alessandra Sambo, "Il lavoro portuale," in *Storia di Venezia*, vol. 12, *Il Mare*, Alberto Tenenti and Ugo Tucci, eds. (Rome, Istituto della enciclopedia italiana, 1991), 850-51; Bonaventura Foppolo, "La compagnia dei Corrieri Veneti," in *Le poste dei Tasso*, 51-85.

conditions in sixteenth-century Bergamo which forced so many of its inhabitants to seek their fortunes elsewhere.[58] Whether or not it was quite so easy for the sons of Bergamasque porters to become wealthy in Venice must remain something of an open question, but together with the Friuliani, they have undoubtedly left distinct traces of their own musical culture.[59] Distant echoes of their presence surface, among other places, in Orazio Vecchi's *L'Amfiparnasso,* which includes a dialogue between Capitan Cardon and Zanni who sing in Spanish and Bergamasque dialect respectively, and a scene in which a chorus of Jews is heard offstage.[60] The Jews also appear in Banchieri's *Barca di Venetia,* an evocation of a journey along the Brenta canal between Venice and Padua, where they are joined by a Brescian merchant in the parodistic madrigal "La trai nai nai nai nai," while other passengers include a music teacher from Lucca, a Florentine bookseller, five professional singers including a German, and a group from various places in the lagoon including Mazzorbo, Murano, and Chioggia.[61] An ensemble of "vecchietti chiozzotti" also show up in Banchieri's *Festino,* a musical depiction of the Venetian celebration of Giovedi Grasso, which occurred during the carnival season.[62] If these examples represent more general north Italian perceptions, Giovanni Croce's *Mascarate* speak with a more local voice. This sequence, which is divided into six sections, each devoted a single group defined by trade, class, or place of origin (fishermen, "magnifici," women from Burano), concludes with a piece in Friuliano.[63] Here the tradition goes back at least to Antonio Molino, one of the leading figures of the *commedia dell'arte,* who was one of the first actor-poets to recite in a number of different dialects.[64] Included in his repertory were texts in Venetian, Bergamasque, and the invented "stil strathiotesco," a mixture of Greek and Italian meant to approximate the language of Greek mercenaries who wandered along the Riva degli Schiavoni. Andrea Gabrieli, Willaert, and Rore all set his poetry to music, as did a number of non-Venetian composers including Giaches de Wert.[65] In his *Greghesche et giustiniane,* Andrea Gabrieli included no fewer than fifteen settings of texts by Molino.[66]

---

[58] Brian Pullan, "Town Poor, Country Poor: The Province of Bergamo from the Sixteenth to the Eighteenth Century" in Ellen E. Kittell and Thomas F. Madden, eds., *Medieval and Renaissance Venice,* 213-36.

[59] For consideration of which, see Nicholas Davidson, "'As Much for its Culture as for its Arms': The Cultural Relations of Venice and its Dependent Cities, 1440-1700," in Cowan, ed., *Mediterranean Urban Culture,* 197-214.

[60] Orazio Vecchi, *L'Amfiparnaso* (Venice, 1597).

[61] Adriano Banchieri, *Barca di Venetia per Padova. Dilettevoli madrigali a cinque voci* (Venice, 1605).

[62] Adriano Banchieri, *Festino nella sera del Giovedi grassi avanti cena* (Venice, 1608). For the feast of Giovedi Grasso, see Edward Muir, *Civic Ritual in Renaissance Venice* (Princeton: Princeton University Press, 1981), 160-64.

[63] Giovanni Croce, *Mascarate pacevoli et ridocolese per il carnevale a 4.5.6. & otto voci* (Venice, 1604).

[64] For an overview, see Paolo Fabbri, "Fatti e prodezze di Manoli Blessi," *Rivista italiana di musicologia* 11 (1976): 182-96; Manlio Cortelazzo, "I fatti e le prodezze di Manilio Blessi strathioto: titolo e nome imitati o parodiati?" *Quaderni veneti* 29 (1999) 177-80.

[65] As in *Di Manoli Blessi il primo libro delle greghesche* (Venice, 1564).

[66] See Andrea Gabrieli, *Greghesche et iustiniane* (Venice, 1571); Alfred Einstein, "The Greghesca and the Giustiniana of the Sixteenth Century," *Journal of Renaissance Music* 1 (1946-47): 19-32.

Such examples are a gentle reminder that the Venetian sixteenth-century concept of the "other" embraced not only the obvious categories of Jews, Turks, Slavs, North Europeans, and non-Christians from the East, but also natives from the towns and cities of the *terraferma*. The Venetian liturgical soundscape, which embraced not only the sounds emanating from parish churches, convents, and monasteries, but also the cantillations from the synagogue in the Ghetto, orthodox chants from the Scuola dei Greci, and the music from the meeting-halls of the other foreign "nations," was in consequence both complex and cosmopolitan. Heard in *campo* and *calle*, as well as in private and public enclosed spaces, these "other" musics added a further dimension to the already rich texture of Venetian devotional practice. To these sounds, elusive as they are, should be added the noise of everyday existence in the Piazza, which in the sixteenth-century was close in atmosphere to an Arab souk.[67] Our conceptions of the urban sound of early modern Venice, undoubtedly over-refined and restricted as it is to elite musical experience, need to take them into account, not merely to fill out and diversify the sonic panorama. Such sounds also played a crucial role in the way that topographical and social spaces were mapped out and recognized. In the same way that some parts of the city were identifiable through the noises of industrial or artisanal activity (Dante refers to the sounds of the Arsenal in the *Inferno)*, so too the songs, street cries,

Figure 3:
The Scuola dei Greci

[67] See Iain Fenlon, "Noise in the Square: St. Mark's in the Sixteenth Century," in Franco Bernabei and Antonio Lovato, eds., *Sine musica nulla disciplina: Studi in onore di Giulio Cattin* (Padua: Il Poligrafo, 2006), 221-34.

church bells and devotional music of the foreign communities carried cultural and symbolic meanings that delineated boundaries and could both repel and encourage social interaction.[68] Recognition of this fact encourages a more complex view of Venetian society than that of the traditional tripartite division into a ruling caste of patricians, a semi-privileged group of citizens, and an underclass without civic rights. At the same time it undermines the conventional view of Venetian parishes as microcosms of the wider city, each with its own individual character but essentially made up of the same basic elements.[69] At a more immediate level, it also recuperates sounds of the Venetian early modern urban landscape that have been largely undetected by the conventional period ear.

[68] For which, see Jacques Attali, *Noise: The Political Economy of Music*, trans. Brian Massumi (Minneapolis: University of Minnesota Press, 1985); David Garrioch, "Sounds of the City: The Soundscape of Early Modern European Towns," *Urban History* 30 (2003): 5-25, at p. 6.

[69] For a contrary view, see Ennio Concina, *Venezia nell'età moderna: Strutture e funzioni* (Venice: Marsilio, 1989), 165-76, esp.170-71 and, along the same lines, the treatment of the .

You Gotta Play Hurt and Other Reflections
on Composers and Their Lot*

Michael Beckerman

Introduction

When Dan Jenkins wrote his rascally novel *You Gotta Play Hurt* he was hardly thinking about musicians or musicologists. It's a raucous look at the world of sports magazine journalism, with sleazy agents, pampered athletes, mean-spirited corporate hacks and the usual bunch of wealthy hangers-on. However, the protagonist, Jim Tom Pinch, is, like us, a writer, who bullied and bloodied by generations of self-serving, talentless and power-hungry editors, comes to the realization identical to the title words of the novel and of this paper. These are the words of Jim Tom:

> Here's the deal: by the time the games come around at the Final Four, you're lethally bored from three days of going to dreary press conferences to find out if any player has failed a drug test, from loitering and gossiping in the hotel lobby with the nation's coaches in the hope of getting a scoop, an item, a quote. You're suicidally hung over from going to three nights of ice-sculpture parties and winding up each evening in the hospitality room, drinking eccentric brands of whiskey in the company of wobbling, nostalgia-stricken SIDs and lost-in-the-past sportswriters like yourself. This is where you remind the younger writers that you gotta play hurt. It's where you allow them to prod you into telling the same old tales of yesteryear. So you talk far too long about the day when all of the athletes and coaches in all of the sports were infinitely more heroic and infinitely more accessible, days when all the writers chain-smoked and no writers jogged or drank nonbeer, days when you could hear the words being made on the paper by the deadline muse that lived in your typewriter, days when this guy and that one wrote literature that still gets quoted today by young sportswriters with taste and a sense of history, whose ranks were growing a damn sight thinner every year, it seemed.

---

* This essay is an edited version of a talk I gave on the occasion of Bill Prizer's retirement. Since almost all the information contained within can be found in a few minutes of (easy) internet searching;, and because the hero of the piece, Jim Tom Pinch (the alter ego of Dan Jenkins, and I'm sure some part of my dear colleague Bill Prizer), would think documentation a merely fusty tradition; and because I am not trying to argue a thesis; and mostly because my strong feelings about Bill's retirement are woven through this essay, whether of not a word of it is true— for all those reasons you will search in vain for footnotes. Gosh, except for this one.

I intend to take Dan Jenkins far more seriously that I'm sure he was ever intended to be taken and ask what kinds of things happen when composers "play hurt," and just what, if anything, we can learn from it.

It's pretty obvious that the main musical prototypes for "playing hurt" in the popular imagination come from the Mozart of the *Requiem* composition (perhaps even the sweaty, yellow Mozart from *Amadeus*), late Schubert and especially Schumann, half the career of Tchaikovsky, and almost all of Beethoven's. And of course, we cannot forget blind Bach dictating the *Art of the Fugue*. All these would be fruitful subjects to explore. Today, though I'm going to put on some "sub-specialty" spectacles, and look at a few examples of "zatni zuby a hraj!" or playing hurt in Czech (it actually means something like "grit your teeth and play!").

In my efforts, I have tried to match the two primary spins of a proper retirement paper—the celebratory and the elegiac—by juxtaposing several classic examples of the burgeoning field of Downer Studies with inspirational moments framed, of course, by Dan Jenkins's cheerful romp.

O Viola!

The first example is tragic and wrenching. And the general circumstances have been treated by Derek Katz in his study of Bedřich Smetana's final quartet in *The Musical Quarterly*.

On March 12 1883 Smetana completed his Second String quartet. The differences between this work and his First String Quartet, "From My Life," explored in Katz's article, illustrate the difference between "playing" hurt and being hurt. When Smetana began to suffer the effects of tertiary syphilis, the effect was somewhat paradoxical: not only was there no lessening of creative power, on the contrary, one could argue that his compositions became even more powerful. They include such works as the cycle *Má vlast*, the operas *The Kiss*, *The Secret*, and *The Devil's Wall*, and the two string quartets. The former "From My Life," written when the composer was at the height of his powers, is a reflection on his life and the onset of disease, about being hurt, at least in the final movement. When the latter was written, the composer had to struggle merely to compose.

In fact, the music Smetana wrote at this time goes to the heart of what one aspect of "playing hurt" might mean at its worst, because he had been advised by his doctors that composing was apt to make his mental condition worse.

> My whole family fears that I could possibly lose my ability to read and write, and that I could become an idiot. I work secretly in short periods, and not as before.

Like the player who suits up with a concussion or partially torn tendon, Smetana's choice had to have been a brave one.

Around seven months after he completed the Second Quartet, Václav Vladivoj Zelený reports that Smetana made the following remark: "I'm writing one more thing, but only to show what happens in the mind of a musician when he's in the kind of state I'm in." Suffering at this time from hallucinations, and unable to recognize friends and family, the composer wrote the final sketches for his incomplete opera *Viola* based on Shakespeare's *Twelfth Night*. It is difficult to know just what was written when, because many of the sketches and letters from around this time are undated. But the material contains exquisite passages, as well as seemingly incoherent ones.

While his music from these desperate days may have been occasionally xtraordinary, his prose at the time was of a different stripe, and of a different world:

> Oh, Viola, tell the gentlemen in Prague how my soul is moved to tears-tears-tears. From Act I I send you divine melodies so you can enjoy these parts in full delight...Some transform me into an angel—nothing else from the beginning—the numbers do not exist. It will not set the world on fire, but it will awaken admiration. Glory to *Viola*.

And in a final page he writes "Glory to Her" and then "Poslední arch," or "Final Sheet."

There is a difference between playing hurt and being hurt (so that one cannot continue to play). When one plays hurt, one of two things happen; one might be playing in something like "constant pain," but one also might find that in the playing the pain disappears. While this may have happened at the beginning of process of composing *Viola*, we cannot begin to imagine what happened at the end.

On Dvořák Having Played Hurt

Let us now look to another kind of work related to mental disorder, but in this case, pathological joy.

Dvořák in the New World. Dvořák, in the words of critic James Creelman "sitting in the dark with his teeth clenched," Dvořák "afraid of everything, afraid of the tram wires" in the reminiscences of his son Otakar. Dvořák writing most of his American works in the shadow of anxiety and panic. Dvořák, self-medicating, swilling beer by the gallon—a ten-dollar weekly budget for the sudsy stuff at a time when it was a nickel a pail. The following infamous "reflection" from the pianist, critic and public intellectual James Huneker:

> But Borax! I left him swallowing his nineteenth cocktail. "Master," I said, rather thickly, "don't you think it's time we ate something?" He gazed at me through those awful whiskers which met his tumbled hair half-way: "Eat. No. I no eat. We go to a Houston Street restaurant. You go, hein? We drink the Slivavitch. It warms you after so much beer."

But also this: Dvořák leaving New York in May 1893 having completed a full draft of the *New World* Symphony and traveling across the "endless" dry expanse of Pennsylvania, all the way to Iowa. Dvořák coming to Spillville, Iowa, that "mother colony" of Czech immigrants where one might still hear the tingle of 1840s Czech, grandmother's Czech. Dvořák telling a woman his first day in Spillville, "imagine, when I walked in the woods along the creek, I heard the birds singing for the first time in six months!" and in a matter of two days exhaling the flip side of hurtness, an ecstatic work, the sketch for the *American* Quartet. The whole thing was finished in a matter of two weeks. (Dvořák wrote "I am satisfied. It was done quickly.") Alleging pathology, of joy or despair, is one thing, demonstrating it another. We are early on taught to say, and to point out to our students, that the statement "Mozart being sad wrote sad music," is trite and unsatisfying.

But the exuberance of this work is astonishing and even unprecedented, from its twin octave ambits, to its almost incoherent pentatonic fanfares. By the time the *American* Quartet was written, there was already something of an autobiographical tradition in the *Czech* String Quartet, one that will be augmented by Janáček at the end of his life. Since Dvořák was a violist—and I believe Derek Katz has made this point—it is as if he is celebrating his own return to health, and superhuman vigor. About recovery, more at the end of this paper.

Janáček: Tying the Black Ribbon 'Round Jenůfa

In Smetana's case, it was personal illness that plunged the composer into a frightful world of haunting shadows. But sometimes one's worst nightmares are the illnesses of others. The story of how Janáček came to finish the opera *Jenůfa* while his beloved daughter Olga was dying of typhus is perhaps as awful as it is inspiring. But it is a remarkable example of a certain combination of total self-absorption and selfless devotion.

This is from the memoirs of Janáček's maid:

> The sicker Olga became, the more obsessed she became with her father's new opera. And sensitive as he was, he put his pain about Olga into his work, the suffering of his daughter into Jenůfa's suffering. And that tough love of Kostelnicka—that's him, there is much of his own character in this part.

She also claims that the exquisite "Zdravas král'ovno" or *Salve Regina* from *Jenufa* was composed with Olga in mind, that Janáček wrote it about her.

We may also recall the heartrending moment, recorded by both the maid and Janáček's wife Zdenka when Olga said something like "Daddy, play me Jenůfa, I will never hear your opera in the theater." "Leoš sat down at the piano and played," recollected Zdenka, "I couldn't bear it and ran off again to the kitchen." Olga died several days later, and Janáček placed a page of the manuscript in her coffin. At the end of his copy of the play he wrote "18 March 1903, the third week after the terrible mortal struggle of my poor Olga. Completed." The work was dedicated to her and in his autobiography of 1924 Janáček wrote "I would bind *Jenůfa* simply with the black ribbon of the long illness, suffering and laments of my daughter Olga and my little boy Vladimir."

Klein's Last Concert

In the case of Janáček and Jenůfa, there are two corroborative witness accounts, in addition to Janáček's own comments. But my penultimate example is merely a whiff of an historical event, although, I think this is true for much of what we call history. It takes place in a concentration camp, and I am not even sure which one. Although I am sure which one is it not, for after almost three years in Ghetto Theresienstadt (Terezin), where he became a formidable force in the camp's musical life, Gideon Klein was loaded on a freight car in October of 1944 and transported, along with Pavel Haas, Viktor Ullmann, Hans Krása , and more than a thousand others, to Auschwitz. Within a day or so, most of the trainload was gassed, but Klein survived until January 1945, as a prisoner at the Fürstengrube mining camp. The incident I'm about to describe took place in either Auschwitz or Fürstengrube—and this is impossible to fully determine, since the only witness to it has died.

In addition to his work as a composer, Klein had distinguished himself as one of the fine pianists in the Czech Republic before the war. Only twenty-one at the time of his incarceration, he continued to compose and performed many concerts in Terezin.

The story, as it has come down to us, is as follows: a group of prisoners are standing naked in a room, waiting for a medical examination. There is an SS guard present, and a piano. Bored, the guard asks if any of the prisoners can play. Klein says yes, and sits down at the keyboard. We do not know what he plays, but according to the witness, Hans Schimmerling, he surprised some of his listeners. Instead of playing something light to please the guard, and perhaps win himself some favors, he offers something serious. Schimmerling is not a musician, and does not know what the piece is, but he says, "Bach or Beethoven or some such thing."

What did Klein play? We know the pieces he played in Terezin, we know his specialties: the Bach *Toccata, Adagio and Fugue in C Major,* Beethoven's Op.110, the Janáček *Sonata*, Suk's *Of Life and Dreams*, Mozart's late *Adagio in B Minor* and Schumann's *Fantasy in C Major.* A few weeks before this event, he had completed his last work, a String Trio. Did he play the variations movement from this at this, his last concert appearance?

The curtain opens, and curtain closes. History. We don't know what he played, or how he thought about it. Everything is a guess. We try to peek inside to see what happens, but it all happens so quickly, and then it is impossible to reclaim.

Klein plays, and plays hurt. But that's all we know. The concert is probably in early November, 1944. He dies or is killed in late January 1945, just as the camp is liberated.

Martinů's Seventh Quartet, BAB, and a Return to Health

There are other ways to "play hurt" or to come to terms with being hurt. In the summer of 1946 Bohuslav Martinů was at the top of his game. After a harrowing escape from Europe in 1941, he had become a kind of star in American public musical life. His symphonies were performed by the best orchestras, and he was making a living by commissions and teaching. Recommended by Koussevitzky as an instructor at Tanglewood's summer music program, he was ready to guide a new generation of students. On the evening of July 17th, after everyone had gone to bed, Martinů stepped out onto the terrace outside his room, and for some reason, still not fully understood, fell ten feet off the balcony onto the concrete surface below, and almost died. His recovery from a fractured skull was slow and uncertain, and he heard buzzing sounds for the rest of his life.

By October of 1946, he was composing again, He completed a work for small orchestra, the *Toccata a due canzoni* and then wrote nothing but chamber music for the next fourteen months: the Sixth String Quartet, the Madrigals for Violin and Viola, and the Oboe Quartet. Included with these was the Seventh String Quartet, a work described by biographer and cataloguer Harry Halbreich as "unproblematic." I'd like to look briefly at one problem in his Seventh Quartet and ask whether or not it might be a response to "playing hurt."

The slow movement of the quartet opens fervently with entrances meant to suggest imitative counterpoint and the sensibility of a chorale. Descending scale passages with staggered entrances suggest Martinů's madrigal style. After a fantasy-like middle section the opening repeats.

But almost precisely four-fifths of the way through (m. 69 of 86) Martinů introduces—for the first and last time—a brand new theme marked *dolce expressivo*.

Tom Hanks' character in the movie *A League of Their Own* famously remarked that "There's no crying in baseball." And we might echo this with: "There's no introducing main themes right near the end!" Okay, there are some exceptions: rondos, after all, introduce new episodes, right up to the end, sometimes there is a bit of fresh material in a coda. What does *new* mean anyway? Etc. etc. But you have to look a long way to find examples of such things in opening or middle movements. One of my favorite exceptions is the opening movement from Mozart's K.375 *Wind Serenade* where an entirely new idea, the best idea of the piece, is introduced after the development. Mozart not only makes it work, but it seems so comfortable that one forgets how utterly rare the practice is. The reasons for not employing such a formal strategy are obvious in a rhetorical sense; it threatens the form and threatens closure. Doesn't it?

By means of attempted explanation I am going to introduce a main new idea myself very near the end of my paper. I'll call the idea BAB, and it is a simple alphabet soup reminder that rather than ABA, which implies that the main ideas of any statement are at the beginning and the end, the reversal suggests that quite often the best stuff is in the middle, or even, the real stuff is in the middle, that middles are primary: "A" not "B." So what's going on in the middle movement of the Martinů Seventh String Quartet?

I would like to suggest a connection between the opening of Martinů's slow movement and the opening of a far more famous work: the slow movement from

Beethoven's Op. 132 String Quartet. And by doing this I would like to suggest that— keeping Martinů's circumstances in mind—this quartet movement is his own *Heilige Dankgesang*, and that it is based on the Beethoven quartet. With its contrapuntal textures, its measured tone, and prayer-like gestures, it apes the "Veni creator spiritus" sections of Beethoven's work, especially the middle section of the movement.

And if this is the case, then the explanation for the new theme might be clear as well. Though the five-part form of Beethoven's movement involves elaborations of the opening section in sections three and five, the composer labels the second section: "Feeling new strength." It is certainly possible to hear Martinů's improbable late theme, *dolce espressivo*, with its parallel filigree work and decorative trills as his own "new strength," announcing, softly but firmly, both a return of his health, and a return of his inner core.

From this vantage point, Martinů had played hurt, and he'd gotten better; he had fallen and gotten up. (His wife said something like, "He's got the hard head of a Czech peasant.") He had survived something arguably even worse than running away from the Nazis and improbably returned to something like full strength. A happy conclusion to an unfortunate event!

Conclusion

Dan Jenkins' *You Gotta Play Hurt* also ends joyously, as joyously as the wedding in Janáček's *Cunning Little Vixen*: Jenkins writes: "So it was happy endings all around, the only known happy endings in the modern history of magazine journalism!" Everything gets sorted out in this novel: the right people get sacked, the right people get promoted, and some very bad folks get some very special punishments.

And such a joyous conclusion is clearly the way to close, because Bill Prizer's extraordinary time at Santa Barbara is also ending joyously. Over the course of many seasons he has stuck with the home team and made it a winner. Year after year, he has played healthy, he has played hurt, and he has always, always, played magnificently.

Preface to the Writings of
William F. Prizer

Nel "bel paese là dove 'l sì suona":

Bill Prizer in Mantua[1]

Gilberto Scuderi

In July 2007, upon returning to Mantua from a holiday in the Dolomites, I found an email from Kristine Forney, the wife of William Prizer, waiting for me in my inbox. She had invited me to write an essay for *Sleuthing the Muse*. Without any sense of my chosen subject, I answered her at once, expressing that I was delighted to have this opportunity and I would accept with joy her invitation to write for the Festschrift honoring Bill. My spontaneous wish was to write my essay with a more talkative, less academic style, the kind one would use between friends, without forgetting, however, the formal style (*tono alto*) that one should maintain for these important occasions. To write honoring a friend is to assume a great responsibility. It is not like writing a review of that person's work, no matter how important or prestigious that review might be. It is more, because the value of such an essay amounts to something much more important: the affection of friendship. I needed to write this with feeling, and to offer—with sensibility and with the labor of a developed study—a work made with purpose (the kind one might use in their approach to treating a work of art, at least as much as one *can* do in a short essay). Thus, I began remembering when I first came to know Bill at the Biblioteca Comunale Teresiana, where I worked: it was 1981 and in the reading room there was this young Californian (in reality, a Virginian, belonging to a family which had resided in America since the seventeenth century, and with two notable ancestors: one, Thomas Bragg, was the Governor of North Carolina from 1855-59; the other, Braxton Bragg, a General in the Confederate States Army during the Civil War). He was a young professor with a small blond beard and a tuft of hair that fell across his forehead (Bill still has this same tuft of hair and beard). He was busy with a document in "an Italian" of the fifteenth or sixteenth century (a kind of Lombardian-Venetian dialect), a written language not easy even for a modern, educated Italian to understand. In particular, Bill was lingering on a difficult word, of which neither of us could understand the meaning. Finally, after very close analysis and with the help of a dictionary of Mantuan dialect, we gave sense to that word.

---

[1] Gilberto Scuderi is the librarian of the Sala Manoscritti and Libro Antico at the Biblioteca Comunale Teresiana, Mantua, Italy. He is an historian, journalist, and contributor to *Gazzetta di Mantova* (the oldest Italian newapaper, founded in 1664), and a poet of Mantuan dialect. I would like to thank Stefanie Tcharos for the English translation of this text.

As we took a break, Bill told me he came to Mantua the first time during spring and summer of 1972 with a travel grant from the University of North Carolina, and then he came again during the summers of 1974 and 1975 with grants from the University of Kentucky to continue his research. Thus, from 1972 on, every year or two, Bill returned to Mantua to carry on his research at the Archivio di Stato and Biblioteca Teresiana. This to and fro from the United States to "the fair land there where the *sì* doth sound"[2] was done in a way that, besides knowing the ins and outs of the town's history, which the large majority of Mantuans ignore, Bill would note the particulars of everyday life. Bill would tell me: "This ancient palace was recently restored—two years ago it was crumbling..." (a fact that I had completely forgotten!) and "this stone tablet from the fifteenth century says this..." In this way, we wandered around Mantua: it was I who accompanied Bill to see the tablet which was on the corner near Palazzo Arrivabene, or was it Bill who accompanied me? Or was it that we arrived there together? In any case it is the tablet that bears the snake of Aesculapius;[3] but, also, the palace is situated in the ancient *contrada* which also bears the coat of arms of the Snake (in Mantua during the fifteenth century, there were twenty districts: Eagle, Griffon, Ox, Leopard, Camel, Horse, Unicorn, Ship, Vermilion Lion, etc.) These are only a few details of our simple urban passages together: simple, but rich in history, of those powerful and those humble, of princes and of the people, the kind that give a sense of which those who come from afar can appreciate, of which those on the "inside" are not capable of understanding, due to carelessness or habit, or just mental laziness. But perhaps it is normal that it is this way. In fact—at least we say in Italy—that it was a Frenchman, Alexis de Tocqueville, in his *De la démocratie en Amérique*, who understood more profoundly than Americans themselves, the social and political reality of the United States during the 1830s and '40s.

So I realized my new friend was (and is) an authority on the history and the music of the town where I was born. I landed the job of librarian in 1979, seven years after Bill had first come to the Teresiana. In October 1974 there was a scholarly conference, organized by the Accademia Nazionale dei Lincei and by the Accademia Virgiliana di Mantova with the support of the President of the Italian Republic,[4] at which Bill presented some early fruits of his Mantuan research.

---

[2] "il bel paese là dove 'l sì suona." Dante, *Inferno* XXXIII, 80. I have used Henry Wadsworth Longfellow's translation of the *Inferno*.

[3] See Giancarlo Malacarne, "I serpenti di Esculapio stanno in via Arrivabene," *Gazzetta di Mantova*, 3 August 1994, 23. Recently, eight ancient inscriptions, transcribed and translated by Professor Rodolfo Signorini, have been printed on plaques made of Plexiglas, and have been posted on the wall beside each tablet. The project continued throughout 2008 with five other tablets. In all, there are fifty tablets catalogued. See Valeria Dalcore, "Un tour fra le 'pietre,'" *Gazzetta di Mantova*, 12 September 2007, 23, and Paola Cortese, "Tutta Mantova di lapide in lapide," *Gazzetta di Mantova*, 14 September 2007, 32.

[4] William F. Prizer, "La cappella di Francesco II Gonzaga e la musica sacra a Mantova nel primo ventennio del Cinquecento," in *Mantova e i Gonzaga nella civiltà del Rinascimento: Atti del Convegno, Mantova 6–8 ottobre 1974* (Verona: Mondadori, 1977), 267–76.

I soon began to acquire a background in a new discipline (of which I remain a disciple today): the music of the Renaissance, a subject I knew hardly anything about. At that time I was, in fact, a working student. After having studied in the Faculty of Letters, I enrolled in that of Political Science at the University of Bologna: hence, in 1981, I received my degree in American History. It was thus natural that I would hold in great esteem my precious friendship with an American. Bill's interests in the history of his country were principally focused on seventeenth and eighteenth centuries; I, instead, concentrated on the nineteenth century. My university thesis was titled *Cattaneo e l'America: la pubblicistica milanese della Restaurazione e del Risorgimento*, in which I reflected—in addition to how America had been represented in Italian newspapers and reviews—on the Italian federacy movement (defeated after 1861, with the affirmation of a unified and centralized state). The victor had been Cavour, of which Carlo Cattaneo (Milan, 1801–Castagnola, Lugano, 1869) was the most authoritative representative, and a great admirer of the American political system, especially the concept of liberty (of speech, of press, and commerce), so much so as to consider the idea of a United States of Europe, based on the American model.

In general, I was interested in the American native populations, and in Italian travelers who went to the United States (for many, a moral gymnastic in the land of liberty, while Europe lay flat in large part due to the oppression of the autocratic governments). I was also interested in the Mantuans involved in subversive plots, who after the revolts in 1820–21 and 1830–31 and due to the revolution of 1848, found political asylum and refuge beyond the Atlantic Ocean; among these was Tullio Suzzara Verdi, who became a medical consultant to President Lincoln. I was interested in the revolvers and rifles that Colonel Samuel Colt presented in December 1859 to the Italian cause—"to our Italian friends," i.e., Garibaldi, who was preparing to invade Sicily and southern Italy. Last, I followed the notices in local newspapers and in the Archivio Storico Comunale of Buffalo Bill's Wild West Show that arrived in Mantua with fifty-nine wagons and a train of coaches on 17 April 1906—800 people, replete with cowboys, Sioux, Cheyenne, Crow, and Pawnee Indians, as well as 500 horses—planting their tents in the park of the Villa Te,[5] beside the magnificent Palace that Giulio Romano constructed

---

[5] I list my essays and articles on the United States: on the Nullification Ordinance with which South Carolina forbade federal officers to collect duty fees within its borders, from 1 February 1833, "Gli Stati Uniti in un articolo milanese del 1833," *La Tribuna di Mantova* 22, no. 9 (1979), 25–26; "Carlo Cattaneo e gli Stati Uniti d'America," *Atti e memorie del Museo del Risorgimento di Mantova* 17 (1980–81), 5–34; "Immagini di vita americana nella corrispondenza e nell'attività pubblicistica di Carlo Cattaneo (1844–1862)," *Archivio trimestrale* 7 (1981), 183–97; "Tullio e Ciro Suzzara Verdi: due mantovani in America," *Quadrante Padano* 3, no. 4 (1982), 38–39; on Cattaneo's essay, printed at Milan in 1862 on *Il Politecnico*, against the racial and racist theories of the authors of *Types of Mankind* (the American anthropologist Josiah C. Nott and the Swiss archaeologist George R. Gliddon—with a posthumous contribution of the American physician and naturalist Samuel G. Morton), printed in Philadelphia in 1857, "Obiettività scientifica," *Sapere* 85, no. 849 (1982), 4–5; "Gli Stati Uniti d'America nelle riviste milanesi della Restaurazione e del Risorgimento," *Atti e memorie del Museo del Risorgimento di Mantova* 18 (1982–83), 43–79; "Indiani d'America nelle riviste milanesi della Restaurazione e del Risorgimento," *Archivio trimestrale* 9 (1983), 159–74; "Le armi di Colt per Garibaldi," *Quadrante Padano* 4, no. 1 (1983), 39; on the exhibition *Views of a Vanishing Frontier* (Omaha, Fort Worth, San Francisco and Washington), "Immagini di una frontiera

between 1524 and 1535 outside the walls of the town to create a residence of pleasure and amusement for Federico II Gonzaga, so that Federico had a place to keep his prized horses and also his lover Isabella Boschetti.

It was due principally to Federico's mother, Isabella d'Este[6] (in 1490, bride to Marchese Francesco II Gonzaga, Federico's father), who was present at Mantua from 1490 until her death in 1539, that the town became an important center of production of secular music, a courtly music that by the beginning of the sixteenth century had become a genuinely Italianate genre of music. Isabella was personally engaged in the search for new music and in the acquisition of instruments for the court,[7] including *viole da mano, viole da gamba, lire da braccio, liuti grandi alla spagnola,*

scomparsa," *Quadrante Padano* 5, no. 4 (1984), 55; "Il viaggio di Tocqueville sul lago Oneida," *Quadrante Padano* , no. 3 (1985), 58–59; on Giacomo Costantino Beltrami, who searched for the source of the Mississippi in 1823, "Un bergamasco tra gli indiani d'America," *Gazzetta di Mantova*, 26 June 1987, 20–21; on Giovanni Capellini, geopaleontologist of the University of Bologna, who visited the United States in 1863, "Un naturalista nel paese dei pellirosse," *Gazzetta di Mantova*, 24 September 1987, 18–19; on Samuele Mazzucchelli, who lived in the United States from 1828 until 1843, "Un frate milanese tra gli indiani," *La Martinella di Milano* 42, no. 2 (1989), 46–47; on a refugee in the United States from 1824 to 1831, "Giacomo Sega. Vita di un intellettuale mantovano (1794–1859)," *Civiltà Mantovana*, N.S. 23–24 (1989), 103–25; "Buffalo Bill a Mantova," *Quadrante Padano* 10, no. 3 (1989), 67–68; on the Italian view of the United States in the first half of the nineteenth century as a model of liberty and progress, "E l'Italietta guardava alla cuccagna americana. Le simpatie di Cavour, Garibaldi, Gioberti e Cattaneo," *Gazzetta di Mantova* 26 February 1993, 28.

Unpublished is my article, written in 1984, on Francesco Arese (Milan, 1805; Florence, 1881), who, implicated in the insurrection movements of 1831, in 1837 during his exile, traveled to New York (where he found his friend Charles Louis Napoleon Bonaparte, the future Emperor of France, Napoleon III), then to Chicago, St. Louis, and Fort Leavenworth, and going up the Missouri, always further to the West, where a Sioux chief invited him to dinner, the main course of which was dog roasted over the coals, and where in the solitude of the prairie, he improvised mimed dialogues between two Indian warriors named Eagle and Running Cloud. See Francesco Arese, *A Trip to the Prairies and in the Interior of North America, 1837-1838: Travel Notes* (New York: Harbor Press, 1934) and idem, *Da New York al selvaggio West nel 1837. Le note di viaggio del conte Arese*, ed. Luisa Cetti (Palermo: Sellerio, 2001), translated from idem, "Notes d'un voyage dans les prairies et dans l'intérieur de l'Amérique septentrionale," in Romualdo Bonfadini, *Vita di Francesco Arese* (Turin–Rome: L. Roux e C., 1894), 445–544. Francesco Arese's mother was Antonietta Fagnani, celebrated by Ugo Foscolo in the ode *All'amica risanata*. Antonietta Fagnani (married to Count Marco Arese and already the mother of two girls, with whom Foscolo carried on a love affair in Milan, between 1800 and 1802) was ill during the winter of 1801–02 and recovered in the following spring.. The ode, a salute to the recovery, was written in April 1802, when passion was dwindling, and published in *Poesie di Ugo Foscolo,* (Milan: Destefanis, 1803); now in Foscolo, *Le poesie*, ed. Marcello Turchi, 3th edition (Milan: Garzanti, 1979), 13–18. On the affair, see Enzo Mandruzzato, *Foscolo* (Milan: Bur, 1991), 102–14.

[6] See Prizer, "Una 'virtù molto conveniente a madonne': Isabella D'Este as a Musician," *Journal of Musicology* 17 (1999), 3-56.

[7] See Prizer, "Marchetto Cara and the North Italian Frottola" (Ph.D. diss., University of North Carolina, Chapel Hill, 1974) 1: 8–13 and 22–25; idem, "Lutenists at the Court of Mantua in the Late Fifteenth and Early Sixteenth Centuries," *Journal of the Lute Society of America* 13 (1980), 5–34; see also, idem, "Music in Ferrara and Mantua at the Time of Dosso Dossi: Interrelations and Influences," in *Dosso's Fate: Painting and Court Culture in Renaissance Italy*, eds. Luisa Ciammitti, Steven F. Ostrow, and Salvatore Settis (Los Angeles: The J. Paul Getty Research Institute for the History of Art and the Humanities, 1998), 290–308. On the Mantuan repertory, see also Prizer, "Local Repertories and the Printed Book: Antico's Third Book of Frottole (1513)," in *Music in Renaissance Cities and Courts: Studies in Honor of Lewis Lockwood*, eds. Jessie Ann Owens and Anthony M. Cummings (Warren, MI: Harmonie Park Press, 1997), 358–59; and idem, "A Mantuan Collection

clavichords, and organs[8] to play "divinissima musica di diversi stromenti."[9] "Through her determined sponsoring of musicians and secular Italian vocal music, Isabella had significantly shaped the cultural policy of the court of Mantua and had aided in the creation and development of the new genre of the frottola."[10] However, already by 1490, during the year of her transfer from Ferrara to Mantua, she demonstrated an early desire to study the art of singing, and therefore requested that her father, Ercole, lend her the composer Johannes Martini as teacher.[11] Her wish was granted.[12]

Mantua was therefore "the cradle of Italian Renaissance music. Isabella d'Este and her musicians were the first to transform the oral tradition[13] into a new tradition of written music."[14] In an interview granted in 1994 to the *Gazzetta di Mantova*, Bill said: "There was music of the church: it was in these years that the chapel choir of the Cathedral of Mantua was founded. Then there was secular music of the court, written by two important Veronese composers who were resident in Mantua: Bartolomeo Tromboncino[15] and Marchetto Cara.[16] Then there was popular music performed in the streets." And obviously, people danced. "There were dances held at the princely courts and outdoor dances held in the country, as in one case from 1511, at a *festa* in Pietole,[17] where Francesco II Gonzaga was

---

of Music for Holy Week, 1537," in *Renaissance Studies in Honor of Craig Hugh Smyth* (Florence: Giunti Barbèra, 1985) 1: 613–25. On the frottola, see also idem, "Wives and Courtesans: The Frottola in Florence," in *Music Observed: Studies in Memory of William C. Holmes*, eds. Colleen Reardon and Susan Parisi (Warren, MI: Harmonie Park Press, 2004), 401–15.

[8] See Prizer, "Isabella d'Este and Lorenzo da Pavia, 'Master Instrument-Maker,'" *Early Music History* 2 (1982), 87–127.

[9] Prizer, "Bernardino Piffaro e i pifferi e tromboni di Mantova: Strumenti a fiato in una corte italiana," *Rivista italiana di musicologia* 16 (1981), 172.

[10] Prizer, "Una 'virtù molto conveniente a madonne,'" 10.

[11] Ibid., 12.

[12] Ibid., 47.

[13] See Prizer, "The Frottola and the Unwritten Tradition," *Studi musicali* 15 (1986), 3–37.

[14] Translated from Scuderi, "La musica pop al tempo dei Gonzaga. Cosa si suonava a Mantova 500 anni fa? Risponde il musicologo William Prizer," *Gazzetta di Mantova*, 9 July 1994, 35.

[15] See Prizer, "Isabella d'Este and Lucrezia Borgia as Patrons of Music: The Frottola at Mantua and Ferrara," *Journal of the American Musicological Society* 38 (1985), 6–11 and 15–17, as well as idem, "Renaissance Women as Patrons of Music: The North-Italian Courts," in *Rediscovering the Muses: Women's Musical Traditions*, ed. Kimberly Marshall (Boston: Northeastern University Press, 1993), 193–96 and 199–201. See also Prizer, "North Italian Courts, 1460–1540," in *The Renaissance: From the 1470s to the End of the 16th Century*, ed. Iain Fenlon, Man and Music 2 (London: The Macmillan Press Limited, 1989, and Englewood Cliffs, NJ: Prentice Hall, 1989), 133–55.

[16] See Prizer, *Courtly Pastimes: The Frottole of Marchetto Cara* (Ann Arbor, MI: UMI Research Press, 1980), and idem, "Marchetto Cara at Mantua. New Documents on the Life and Duties of a Renaissance Court Musician," *Musica disciplina* 32 (1978), 87–110. Cara was *maestro di cappella* at Mantua from around 1511 until his death in late 1525. See documents (the originals in the Archivio di Stato di Mantova), in *Courtly Pastimes*, 207 (letter of Francesco Gonzaga, 20 March 1511, concerning his new chapel) and 208 (letter of Francesco Gonzaga to Massimiliano Sforza, 9 December 1512, in which the Marchese names Cara "maestro de la mia capella").

[17] Pietole (the ancient Andes), the village where Vergil was born in 70 B.C.

supposed to have danced with an old peasant."[18] This episode from June 1511 was recounted by Bill in his 1991 article from the *Journal of Musicology*: "Francesco no longer wanted to dance due to heat and tiredness, but the old woman did not want to stop, so that his Excellency had to finish the *ballo* with her."[19]

Another genre of dance was made popular by the nineteen-year-old new Duke of Milan, Massimiliano Sforza (son of Ludovico il Moro and Beatrice d'Este, sister of Isabella), who arrived in Mantua in November 1512 for a masked ball given in his honor: in the *sala grande* of the Palazzo San Sebastiano, he danced *in maschera* with his aunt Isabella, with Laura da Luzzara, and other grand dames.[20] As a duke, Massimiliano did not demonstrate a great preparation to govern, but showed great expertise in his ability to party,[21] and, as he already experimented with in Mantua, "a dansare et stare in piacere,"[22] to dance and to find pleasure. Another nice scene that reveals the human side of the Gonzaga court, as evidenced in documentary sources, was in 1537, when Federico II commanded Roberto d'Avanzini and Paolo Poccino "to come immediately to Mantua as quickly as possible" to play and sing— —I think a lullaby ("Because it is necessary for the Marchese, our son, to sleep"); Francesco III was at that time four years old.[23]

I was deeply interested in this aspect of my town's past life, so much so that I began to search out any CD recordings I could find, all very rare, of *danze e canti carnascialeschi* of the Italian Renaissance: I experienced much joy when I read on the CD's plastic cover the names of Cara or Tromboncino, so that I could hear their compositions (however, I understood the music very little, and even today I have not made great progress in this regard). At this very moment, as I write at my computer to honor Professor William F. Prizer, I am listening to Marchetto Cara's barzelletta, *Mentre io vo per questi boschi*,[24] and in a few minutes I will hear Cara's frottola, *Non è tempo d'aspectare*,[25] and Tromboncino's canzone, *Che debb'io far*.[26] Of

---

[18] Translated from Scuderi, "La musica pop al tempo dei Gonzaga," 35.

[19] Prizer, "Games of Venus: Secular Vocal Music in the Late Quattrocento and Early Cinquecento," *Journal of Musicology* 9 (1991), 35 and 56.

[20] See Prizer, *"Facciamo pure noi carnevale*: Non-Florentine Carnival Songs of the late Fifteenth and Early Sixteenth Centuries," in *Musica Franca: Essays in Honor of Frank A. D'Accone*, eds. Irene Alm, Alyson McLamore, and Colleen Reardon (Stuyvesant, NY: Pendragon Press, 1996), 193; and idem, "Secular Music at Milan during the Early Cinquecento: Florence, Biblioteca del Conservatorio, MS Basevi 2441," *Musica disciplina* 52 (1998), 30, originally read at an international symposium on Francesco da Milano on the five hundredth anniversary of his birth. On the symposium, see Scuderi, "I Gonzaga 'festaioli,'" *Gazzetta di Mantova*, 9 November 1997, 43. On the carnival songs, see also Prizer, "Petrucci and the Carnival song: On the Origins and Dissemination of a Genre," *Venezia 1501: Petruci e la stampoa musicale, Atti del convegno internazionale di studi, Venezia, Palazzo Giustinian Lolin, 10–13 ottobre 2001* (Venice: Edizioni Fondazione Levi, 2005), 215–51.

[21] See Prizer, "Music at the Court of the Sforza: The Birth and Death of a Musical Center," *Musica disciplina* 43 (1989), 142–93. See also Scuderi, "I Gonzaga 'festaioli,'" 43.

[22] Prizer, "Bernardino Piffaro e i pifferi e tromboni di Mantova," 170.

[23] Prizer, "Lutenists at the Court of Mantua," 30.

[24] See the text and the music in Prizer, *Courtly Pastimes*, 519–23.

[25] Ibid., 95.

[26] Ibid., 89.

course, I was devastated to find out that on 21 July 1499 Tromboncino—in the words of Isabella d'Este, writing to her husband Francesco—"killed his wife with great cruelty," seemingly without an ounce of remorse; rather he believed it his "right to punish his wife" if he "found her in error."[27] So Trombonicino incurred the wrath of Marchese Francesco; he was later rehabilitated, but by 1505 he left Mantua.[28]

The time that I have spent together with Bill in Mantua and also at times in Florence (which amounts to about one week every two years) is always spent happily, easily, and in a state of grace. Usually, we begin with the "exchange of books ceremony"—Bill gives me his essays and I give Bill the books and essays (which I receive free when I review them) printed in Mantua since the last time we saw each other. Then, when Bill has ended his day of work at the archive or in the library, and I finish mine, we stroll around the town or the countryside until we find a good restaurant or inn. So a good part of our time we spend sitting at a table (ah, the delicious Italian cooking! The exquisite Mantuan cuisine that finds roots in the gastronomic art of the Gonzaga's chefs), to chat about a number of topics that range historically and personally—such as Lorenzo de' Medici, or the sonnets of Burchiello,[29] or the *Facezie* di Poggio Bracciolini (the protagonists of the tale are a Mantuan miller and his wife),[30] or the *Novellino* (in this short story, Castellano da Cafferi of Mantua, who was the podestà of Florence around 1240, had to settle a quarrel between two gentlemen),[31] or the *Novelle* di Matteo Bandello (a gentleman of Mantua runs to the Palazzo San Sebastiano to speak with Marchese Francesco Gonzaga),[32] or the short story of Franco Sacchetti (in which, for a word said in jest about one of his retainers, Lodovico I Gonzaga confiscated his entire fortune of two thousand *bolognini*),[33] or the extraordinary letters Floriano Dolfo sent in 1494 to the Marchese Francesco from the thermal

[27] Ibid., 57. "The same day the Registro necrologii had the entry, 'Antonia, wife of Bartolomeo Tromboncino, died in the Contrada Bovis from wounds and remained ill for the space of one hour.'" Ibid. Tromboncino "Aveva sposato un'Antonia mantovana, la quale trovata infedele, uccise a pugnalate..." Antonino Bertolotti, *Musici alla corte dei Gonzaga in Mantova. dal secolo XV al XVIII. Notizie e documenti raccolti negli Archivi Mantovani* (Milan: G. Ricordi & C., 1890), 12.

[28] Prizer, *Courtly Pastimes*, 58.

[29] *I sonetti del Burchiello*, ed. Michelangelo Zaccarello (Turin: Einaudi, 2004).

[30] See Poggio Bracciolini, *Facezie*, ed. Marcello Ciccuto (Milan: Bur, 1983), 402–4.

[31] See *Il novellino*, ed. Guido Favati (Genoa: Bozzi, 1970), 330. *Il novellino* is an anonymous work written by a Florentine author between 1281 and 1300.

[32] See Matteo Bandello, *Tutte le opere*, ed. Francesco Flora, 4th edition (Milan: Mondadori, 1966) 1: 137.

[33] See Franco Sacchetti, *Il Trecentonovelle*, ed. Emilio Faccioli (Turin: Einaudi, 1970), 165–66. Faccioli (Goito, 1912–Florence, 1991) was director of the Biblioteca Teresiana di Mantova from 1947 to 1952, and from 1969 he taught at the Università di Firenze, first as a free docente, then as Professor of Lingua e Letteratura italiane. See *Per Emilio Faccioli. Studi e testimonianze*, ed. Maurizio Bertolotti (Mantua: Biblioteca comunale and Istituto mantovano di storia contemporanea, 1993). The volume contains a bibliography of Faccioli's writings (1935–91), edited by Cesare Guerra, 133–55.

baths of Porretta,[34] or even about our cats (Kristine and Bill have two, Chiara and Pierrot; I only one, Cleopatra,[35] and it's fair and sacrosanct that they also should get to participate in the celebrations honoring Bill).

We laugh and crack jokes too, pleasantries of course, but most times what we say in jest is not just a trifle but things connected to literary, artistic, or musical subjects—an oasis of peace in a world too often cruel. These are the things that are meaningful—music, art, literature, "gli studi leggiadri"[36] (in reality "le sudate carte"),[37]

[34] See Floriano Dolfo, *Lettere ai Gonzaga*, ed. Marzia Minutelli (Rome: Edizioni di Storia e Letteratura, 2002), pp. 18–23. See Pasquale Stoppelli, "Facezie oscene inedite di Floriano Dolfo a Francesco I Gonzaga," *Belfagor* 32 (1977), 685–96. The letters are found in the Archivio di Stato di Mantova, Archivio Gonzaga, 1143–46. In the essay's title, "Francesco I" is actually Francesco II. In the letter to Francesco II of 28 November 1494, Dolfo mentions "la morte del Conte Zoanne de la Mirandula," which took took place "dopo la inofficiossima morte del Polliciano."Both died in Florence: Angelo Poliziano in September and Pico della Mirandola in November. Dolfo, *Lettere ai Gonzaga*, 26. On Poliziano, see Davide Mattellini, "Quando 'Orfeo' cantò a Mantova," *La voce di Mantova*, 28 September 1994, pp. 24–25. See also below note 49.

[35] Cleopatra was born in Mirandola (like Pico), in October 2004. I dedicated to her several lines of my poem in Mantuan dialect, *Inferan* XXXI, 167–84 and XXXII, 1–8: "... E m'arcord Cleopatra in sal cossin, / picinina, ch'l'ha pers al prim dentin. / Mezza persiana e mezza norvegesa, / tutta bianca col pél longh e molzin, / la stava a panza insù longa distesa / par buscar le carezze, on angilin: / s'a t'an gh'i a favi, la fava l'offesa / e la t'dava on colpin con al sanfin / e po, par dimostrart i sentiment, / Cleo la tirava fòra i onge e i dent! / E mi, gran pàndol fòra dl'ordinari, / ... mós, paté! / Mi, bìgol doppi grand com on armari, / dal bechèr, dal droghér avanti e indré, / e on gioran sì e un no dal vetrinari,... / ... Av giuri che / compagn cme mi gh'n'è tanti: l'è mia on scherz / quand as dis che l'amor l'è propia sguerz. // Par fars i dent Cleopatra la sgagnava, / oltr a on sorghin da pezza e a 'na balina, / tutt quell ch'a gh'era in cà ch'agh capitava. / Ronfand e sgnavoland, a la gattina / gh'piaseva i libar: cme la gogolava / intant ch'la sbrisolava la *Divina*, / mandand in strazz i vers originai / par la cartera... dal Mai!..." ("... And I remember Cleopatra on the cushion, when she was little, having lost her first tooth. Half Persian and half Norwegian, all white with a long and soft coat, she was lying on her back stretched out to accept carresses, a little angel: if you didn't stroke her, she was offended and dealt you a light blow with her little paw and then, to show you her feelings, Cleo extended her claws and bared her teeth! And I, big simpleton that I am... mousse, pâté! I, a great simpleton, square as an armoire, went back and forth to the butcher and grocer, and sometimes to the veterinarian... I swear there aren't many like me: it's not a joke when people say that love is blind. To sharpen her fangs Cleopatra bit a small stuffed mouse and a little ball, all that I could find at home. Snarling and meowing, the kitten liked books: how she mrrred while shredding the *Divine [Comedy]*, reducing to strips the original verses to the paper mill... of Maglio!..."). Scuderi, *Inferan*, with a note by Mario Artioli, 2nd ed. (Mantua: Il Cartiglio Mantovano, 2005), 251 and 253–54. This is why there has not survived even an autograph comma of Dante: perhaps he too had a cat.

[36] Giacomo Leopardi, *A Silvia*, 16. Now in Leopardi, *Canti*, ed. Niccolò Gallo and Cesare Garboli, 3rd ed. (Turin: Einaudi, 2007), 172.

[37] Leopardi, *A Silvia*, 15. It pleases me to remember that Gaetano Salvemini thought that the Italian people in the nineteenth century had boasted of only four men of genius. Of these, the first two were Giacomo Leopardi and Carlo Cattaneo ; the third was Cavour, whom Salvemini, however, because of his own political viewpoint, admired very little, and the fourth was the historian of literature Francesco De Sanctis. See Salvemini, introduction [written in its original form in Cambridge, MA, in September 1948: Salvemini held the chair of history of Italian civilization at Harvard University from 1934 to 1949] to *Scritti sul Risorgimento*, in idem, *Opere* II: 2, ed. Piero Pieri and Carlo Pischedda, 2nd ed. (Milan: Feltrinelli, 1963), 9. See also idem, *Dizionario delle idee*, ed. Sergio Bocchi (Rome: Editori Riuniti/L'Unità, 2007), 43. On Cattaneo's great influence on Salvemini, see Salvemini, "Carlo Cattaneo," introduction to *Le più belle pagine di Carlo Cattaneo scelte da Gaetano Salvemini* (Milan: Treves, 1922), i–xxxi, and Giuseppe Armani, introduction to Salvemini,

"et benedette sian tutte le carte"[38] and the good cooking, to save the Earth from violence? So, to gladden (ah, Lorenzo the Magnificent's *Canzona di Bacco*: "Chi vuol esser lieto, sia"),[39] I placed Bill in my poem in Mantuan dialect *Inferan*, in *ottava rima* very liberally inspired by the *Inferno* of Dante.[40] In canto XXXI, 100–110, I imagine one of the Giants, the Bomb Man, who gives the Earth a shake: "... l'è rivà on rintron / che pussè fort al pöl sol al Signor. / L'era l'Om Bomba che con on stosson / l'ha fatt on tarremot, cal brutt villan, / che in California agh völ quattar Big One. / ... To màdar, che spigott!, / ho ditt: 'Addio battell, son zà sepolt!,' / a Bill, da botta, a gh'è 'ndà zó 'l salott, / a Nibal gh'è restà gnanca l'arvolt; / Scipion, povrett, al viv in 'na roulotte...."[41] ("... there arrived a huge roar. . . It was the Bomb Man who with a jolt caused an earthquake, that boor, which in California equaled four Big Ones.... S.o.b., what a fright!, I have said: 'Farewell ship [i.e., All is lost], I'm already buried!,' Bill's living room is, at once, collapsed; not even Hannibal's wine cellar is left; Scipio, poor devil, lives in a trailer..."), It's to exorcise the evil, to dispel the melancholy that sometimes grips us all. It's to be happy.

To be cheerful but I hope more serious, in September 2007 one of the topics I proposed to Bill was the emblem or monogram of Isabella d'Este: YS, where Y and S, which are superimposed and thus entwined, form the f in Francesco, in this way creating "a love symbol (YSf) of their married life—the tie between wife and husband marquises of Mantua."[42] My suggestion, or fantasy, was pertinent to the Y of Isabella and to its possible connection with the Y of Pythagoras, which through its bifurcation is the symbol of a choice between two paths: one of vice, the other of virtue.[43] One could also apply the Pythagorean Y to two other possible directions that a governing person could choose: "one the broad way of 'tyrants,' the other the straight and narrow way of the 'adepts' or inspired mystics."[44]

I partiti politici milanesi nel secolo XIX (Milan: Linea d'Ombra, 1994), 7–15. Now in Armani, *Un'idea di progresso. Da Beccaria a Galante Garrone* (Reggio Emilia: Diabasis, 2005), 167–75. See also idem, "Interpreti di Cattaneo: da Ghisleri a Salvemini," in idem, *Cattaneo riformista. La linea del "Politecnico"* (Venice: Marsilio, 2004), 97–123.

[38] Now in Petrarch, *Canzoniere*, ed. Piero Cudini, 6th ed. (Milan: Garzanti, 1980), 86. It is verse 12 of the celebrated sonnet, the incipit of which is "Benedetto sia 'l giorno e 'l mese e l'anno," which was also set to music by Franz Liszt.

[39] Now in Lorenzo il Magnifico, *Poesie*, ed. Federico Sanguineti, 2nd ed. (Milan: Bur, 2001), 377 and 378.

[40] See the flattering reference to *Inferan*: "in the poem, real and imaginary vicissitudes take inspiration from Dante's *Inferno* and from the everyday news." Translated from Belf. [Carlo Ferdinando Russo, review], "Giuseppe Armani, Noticine, a cura di Gilberto Scuderi, edizione non venale per gli amici di Giugi, Mantova, 2006," *Belfagor* 61 (2006), 746.

[41] Scuderi, *Inferan*, 248–49.

[42] Translated from Malacarne, "Il segno di Isabella. Stemmi, motti, imprese,"in *Isabella d'Este. La primadonna del Rinascimento* (Quaderno di Civiltà Mantovana), ed. Daniele Bini (Modena and Mantua: Il Bulino and Artiglio, 2001), 192. See also, ibid., the monogram.

[43] Frances A. Yates, *The Rosicrucian Enlightenment* (London: Routledge & Kegan Paul, 1972), 56.

[44] Ibid., 58. See also (ibid., ill. 16, between 56 and 57) the German satirical print of 1621, held by the British Library, with the caricature of Frederick V, king of Bohemia, on the Pythagorean Y, who had taken the wrong road.. In 1620 Frederick was defeated in the battle of White Hill, near Prague, and his short reign—he was called the Winter King—ended.

Moreover, for women, the Pythagorean Y could signify the bifurcation between marriage and the religious life, *aut maritus, aut murus*:[45] marriage or the cloister, the husband for Isabella, the religious life for the blessed Osanna Andreasi (d. 1505); her veneration, widespread in Mantua, was officially recognized in 1515 by Pope Leo X.[46] In 1515, Isabella, who was devoted to the blessed Osanna, ordered from her tutor (and secretary to her husband Francesco) and man of letters Mario Equicola,[47] the prayer *In conservatione divae Osannae Andreasiae mantuanae oratio ad d. Isabellam estensem Mantuae principem*, which was made to follow an oration published in 1505 in the appendix alla *Beatae Osannae mantuanae vita* by the monk Francesco da Ferrara, and the biography of the blessed Osanna, included in *Via & porta paradisi, ac omnium virtutum*, by the Monteolivetan monk Girolamo, printed in Mantua in 1507.[48]

Of course, I am not the only friend Bill has had in Mantua. First among them is Maestro Claudio Gallico, musician and musicologist of wide fame, who died on 24 February 2006 at the site of the Accademia Nazionale Virgiliana (where he was president) during a break from rehearsal in the Teatro Accademico for *Orfeo*, which he had been conducting.[49] I'm certain that Professor Gallico himself would have written an essay honoring Bill for *Sleuthing the Muse*. Upon being introduced by Claudio Gallico, on 19 September 2002, Bill delivered a lecture at the Archivio di Stato di Mantova: "Una nuova fonte per la vita musicale e spirituale a Mantova intorno al 1500." In his lecture he discussed the manuscript 676 of Bibliothèque Nationale de Paris: a "libro di coro" that contains 114 instrumental works, laudi,

---

[45] See Filippo Lovison, "Donne e riforma della Chiesa in epoca moderna," Abstract of Papers Read at the XIV convegno di studio dell'Associazione italiana dei professori di Storia della Chiesa: Le donne nella Chiesa in Italia, Rome, Centro Studi Storici dei PP. Barnabiti 12–15 September 2006, 9.

[46] See ibid., 8.

[47] Nel *Libro de natura de amore di Mario Equicola secretario del illustrissimo s. Federico II Gonzaga marchese di Mantua* (Venice: Lorenzo Lorio da Portes, 1525), l'autore ricorda, col titolo di "Perigynecon," il *Marii Equicoli Oliuetani De mulieribus ad d. Margaritam Cantelmam* (1501). See Paolo Cherchi, "Equicola, Mario," in *Dizionario biografico degli italiani* (Rome: Istituto della Enciclopedia Italiana, 1993), 43: 34. This work by Equicola, of 1501, was perhaps printed at Ferrara by Lorenzo Rossi: see Stephen Kolsky, *Mario Equicola the Real Courtier* (Geneve: Librairie Droz, 1991), 319, or perhaps in Mantua: see Cherchi, "Equicola, Mario," 34.

De mulieribus was dedicated to Margherita Cantelmo, that is, Margherita Maroscelli, widow of Sigismondo Cantelmo, who entered the convent named "della Cantelma," founded by Isabella d'Este in1534. See Vasco Restori, *Mantova e dintorni* (Mantua: L'Artistica, 1915), 163–64; see also *Stradario della città di Mantova*, ed. Enrico Grazioli and Gilberto Scuderi (Mantua: Comune di Mantova, 1984), 84.

[48] See Monica Bianchi, *Artigiani e mercanti nella Mantova antica*, presentazione di Gilberto Scuderi (Mantua: Il Cartiglio Mantovano, 2007), 65.

[49] *L'Orfeo* was staged at the Teatro Accademico (Bibiena) the evening of 24 February 2007, on the four hundredth anniversary of the first performance and the first anniversary of the death of Claudio Gallico. We are referring to famous *Fabula di Orpheo* of Angelo Poliziano (*fabula* to be understood in the Latin sense of staged representation), rewritten by Alessandro Striggio for the music of Monteverdi and performed on 24 February 1607 in a hall of the Palazzo Ducale of Mantua. See Giorgio Bernardi Perini's introduction to *L'Orfeo: favola posta in musica da Claudio Monteverdi*, ed. Paola Besutti (Mantua: Tre Lune, 2007), vi–vii. Poliziano composed the *Fabula di Orpheo* at Mantua in 1480 "in tempo di dua giorni, intra continui tumulti [di festa]." See Poliziano, *Stanze. Orfeo. Rime*, ed. Davide Puccini (Milan: Garzanti, 1991), 145–46, and idem, *Poesie italiane*, ed. Saverio Orlando, 4th ed. (Milan: Bur, 1994), 109. See also note 34 above.

canzone, and frottole, which Bill demonstrated were of Mantuan provenance, as proven through a few particulars: beyond language, of course a *koinè* of northern Italy between the fifteenth and sixteenth centuries, the manuscript reveals two verses—"Apresso il sancto ucello n'è uno sì degno. / Griffom! Che bella insegna ha nostro nome!" ("Close to the holy bird [the eagle] there is one as worthy. / Griffon! What a wonderful coat of arms bears our name!")—which refer to two *contrade* of Mantua: Aquila and Grifone, with abutting borders. In a strambotto there is also reference to "il Turco" the (nickname of Marchese Francesco II Gonzaga) and his wife Isabella.[50] In September 2007, Bill told me he knew the name of the copyist of the manuscript, who perhaps was a figure at the Gonzaga court.

In addition to Maestro Gallico, other Mantuan friends of Bill include Isa Melli, teacher of literature at the Conservatorio of Mantua, and Anna Maria Lorenzoni, who for many years worked in the Archivio di Stato and whose collaboration with Clifford M. Brown (University of Ottawa) produced ample research[51] on the relationship between Isabella d'Este and the "intarsiatore et maestro da istrumenti musici,"[52] the wood-worker and master instrument-maker, Lorenzo da Pavia, a relationship which also interested Bill;[53] there is also Roberto Navarrini, who was vice-director at the Archivio di Stato of Mantua, director of the same in Brescia, and now, since 1992, is professor of archival studies at the University of Udine. There are many others—the complete list would become too long. Bill is a Virginian, a Californian and, like Stendhal was a Milanese, Bill is a Mantuan. In an interview, Bill once said, "By now I feel at home. I have been very fortunate because I have found many friends: waiters, professors, musicians, and people of every class."[54] Here is a passage from a letter Bill sent me from Santa Barbara, California, 16 December 1992:

> It was truly a great pleasure to see you and other friends this past summer. I enjoyed so much spending time with you and others. It is very interesting to me to hear Mantuans speak at a certain level of erudition. It is not only pleasurable, as I've said, but I learn very much, at times I think I learn more this way than at the archive and the library.

Bill is a sensitive person (he is a man of the South)—in reality it is we who have learnt many things from him, many things that regard the culture of our city. In every way, with these gentle words, Bill has given me the awareness that even I could be erudite!

---

[50] On "Turcho, Turcho et Isabella" and "Apresso il santo ucellone" ("Close to the holy bird"), see also Prizer, *Courtly Pastimes*, 32–33. "Turcho" was also the name of one of Francesco's horses, and "isabella" also means a "bay-colored mare." See ibid., 179.

[51] Clifford M. Brown, with the collaboration of Anna Maria Lorenzoni, *Isabella d'Este and Lorenzo da Pavia: Documents for the History of Art and Culture in Renaissance Mantua* (Geneva: Librairie Droz, 1982).

[52] Brown and Lorenzoni, "Isabella d'Este e Giorgio Brognolo nell'anno 1496," *Atti e Memorie dell'Accademia Virgiliana di Mantova*, N.S. 41 (1973), 101.

[53] See above note 8.

[54] Translated from Scuderi, "La musica pop al tempo dei Gonzaga," 35.

If I were permitted to give an aesthetic judgment of Bill's letters, I would describe them as incredibly clear and perfectly comprehensible like everything he writes (like his essays—possessing all five qualities, also a sixth, as indicated by Italo Calvino in the *American Lessons*, the five lectures he gave at Harvard in 1985: lightness, quickness, exactitude, visibility, multiplicity and also consistency). Of Bill's letters, I especially love his opening lines, which are exceptional: for example, before there was email, when Bill sometimes had not written me for long periods, every letter which I received started with that which I have called "Bill's autoflagellation," in which he charged himself with every sort of adjective— in the clearest Italian—that he could express his most profound regret—but I cannot write these adjectives here. They are just too harsh! I would like to read Bill's letters to his other friends to compile an anthology of his autoflagellations. But now, with the advent of email, the "autoflagellations" have diminished due to the increased frequency of our correspondence. I, however, miss the pre-emails of golden times: the autoflagellations were wonderful. Not even the flagellant confraternities of Mantua were so fabulous in their atonement for their own sins!

On 5 September 2006 Bill was in Mantua, on the very day of the opening of the ex-church of Madonna della Vittoria (now to be used as a museum and space for exhibition and concerts),[55] the church originally built by Marchese Francesco II as an ex-voto to celebrate the fortunes of his armies in the battle of Fornovo, which he fought as commander of the league of the Italian states on 6 July 1495 against King Charles VIII of France.[56] Niccolò Machiavelli exhorted that trumpets, drums, and *pifferi* were used during military operations to cheer on the troops. And, in fact, on the day of the Assumption (15 August 1495), in a pavilion of the encampment of Federico II, a High Mass was sung "cum cantori et musici electi,"[57] precious singers and musicians who played *pifferi* and trombones— —wrote Federico's secretary Jacopo d'Atri in his chronicle of the campaign—an assertion authoritatively confirmed from the Marchese Federico in a letter to his wife Isabella: a "solemne messa," "cum cantori, piphari et tromboni."[58]

---

[55] See Prizer, "Paris, Bibliothèque Nationale, Rés. Vm.⁷ 676 and Music at Mantua," in *Trasmissione e recezione delle forme di cultura musicale: Atti del XIV congresso della Società Internazionale di Musicologia, Bologna, 27 August–1 September 1987, Ferrara–Parma 30 August 1987*, eds. Angelo Pompilio, Donatella Restani, Lorenzo Bianconi, and F. Alberto Gallo (Turin: EDT, 1990) 2: 235–39. On Prizer's lecture, see Paolo Bertelli, "Mantova musicale: ritrovato un codice," *La voce di Mantova*, 20 September 2002, 18.

[56] The reopening of the desanctified church (that for a long time had housed an automobile repair shop) took place after many years of being completely closed, and after five years of restoration, the second floor's problems were still not resolved. Among the many people who came to the reopening, there was near Bill and me, Dario Fo, who in 1997 won the Nobel Prize for Literature. In recent years, Bill has come to Mantua in the first week of September, exactly at the time of the annual Festivaletteratura. In 2007, the Nobel Prize winners Nobel Wole Soyinka and Orhan Pamuk were in the city at the same time Bill was there.

[57] Prizer, "Bernardino Piffaro e i pifferi e tromboni di Mantova," 174–75.

[58] Ibid., 175.

On 6 July 1496, the first anniversary of Federico's 'victory'[59] of Fornovo, the painting of the Madonna by Mantegna[60] (the one we find today in the Louvre) was transported from the new church of Mantua to Palazzo San Sebastiano.[61]

> All the religious orders, together with the greater part of the populace, gathered at San Sebastiano where the image of the glorious Virgin that Andrea Mantegna had finished, decorated most solemnly, was raised onto a large platform, and above it was a youth dressed as God the Father and two prophets on each side [of him]; on one side [of the platform] were three little angels who sang certain laude, and on the other, the twelve apostles.[62]

During the procession, along the streets of Mantua, the lauda composed by Bartolomeo Tromboncino[63] resounded:

> Hail Mary, Queen of Heaven and Earth,
> Holy Virgin and Mother of the Highest God.
> True protector of this godly land
> That is without her full of every wicked evil.
> Rise, people, claps your extended hands,
> Beg her to intercede for you with her holy Son.
> Thou, Mother, hear this thy land,
> And watch over its Prince and his house. Amen.[64]

---

[59] The battle had an uncertain result. Francesco Gonzaga believed he had won. In reality, Charles VIII, in retreat, succeeded in opening a passage and in arriving safely in Asti, towards France, on the road home.

[60] This is how Andrea Mantegna, in a letter to the Marchese Francesco II, depicted the King of France: "King Charles had a great deformity, both of the eyes, large and protruding, and also of the nose, large, aquiline, and deformed, balding and with thinning hair, and he was an "homo piccolo et gobo" ("little and humpbacked man"). What a difference between Charles VIII and Francesco Gonzaga, whom the Pistoian chronicler Francesco Ricciardi, detto Ceccodea, called "Ector troiano (the Trojan Hector)." Antonio Tosti, *Storie all'ombra del malfrancese* (Palermo: Sellerio, 1992), 28.

[61] Before the conclusion of the restorations, the palace was opened on 6 July 2006, only for the day celebrating the anniversary of the hanging of Mantegna's canvas, which took place 510 years earlier, in 1496. For the occasion, a copy of the painting was shown in the ex-church.

[62] "Tuti li religiosi si adunoreno a San Sebastiano cum la mazore parte del populo, dove era exaltata la imagine de la gloriosa Verzene che ha fornita messer Andrea Mantinea suso uno tribunale grande adornato molto solemnemente, et sopra ad essa imagine gli era uno zovene vestito da Dio Patre et dui propheti da ogni canto, da li ladi tri anzoletti che cantavano certe laude et per contra vi erano XII apostoli." Letter of Sigismondo Gonzaga to Francesco Gonzaga, in Archivio di Stato di Mantova, published also in Prizer, "*Laude di Popolo, Laude di Corte:* Some thoughts on the Style and Function of the Renaissance Lauda," in *La musica a Firenze al tempo di Lorenzo il Magnifico: Congresso internazionale di studi, Florence 15–17 June 1992,* ed. Piero Gargiulo (Florence: Olschki, 1992), 190. See also Prizer, "Court Piety, Popular Piety: The *Lauda* in Renaissance Mantua," Abstract of Paper Read at the Fifty-seventh Annual Meeting of the American Musicological Society, Chicago 6–10 November 1991 (Madison, WI: A-R Editions, 1991).

[63] See Prizer, "Laude di Popolo, Laude di Corte," 180–81.

[64] "Ave Maria, regina in cielo e in terra, / vergene sacra e madre del summo Idio. / Vera fautrice de questa alma terra / ch'è senza de lei sempre ogni mal rio. / Hor su, popul, le man d'estende e serra, / pregela te concedi al figliol pio. / Tu, madre, exaudi questa terra tua, / avendo in cura el principe e casa sua. Amen. Ibid, 191 and the music, 192-93.

If one day, on the streets of Mantua, such an ancient procession unraveled as an historical recreation of that long ago festive event, we would know—to the credit of Professor William F. Prizer—what music to play and which words to sing.

Biography and Writings of
William F. Prizer

BIOGRAPHY

William Flaville Prizer II was born on 27 October 1943 in Petersburg, Virginia. He completed his B.A. in Music History and Trumpet at Duke University (1967) and his M.Mus. in Trumpet at Yale University (1969), writing a thesis entitled "Some Bolognese *Sonate con Tromba*: Edition and Commentary." During his years at Yale, he performed professionally in various orchestras in New York and New England. He then went on to study musicology at the University of North Carolina, Chapel Hill, where he earned his Ph.D. (1974), with a dissertation on "Marchetto Cara and the North Italian Frottola," under the direction of Howard Smither and James Pruett. While in Chapel Hill, he taught trumpet and French horn at North Carolina Central University and was instructor of trumpet at University of North Carolina, Greensboro and Chapel Hill. Bill was appointed Assistant Professor (and Associate Professor) of Music at the University of Kentucky (1973-79); he then moved to the University of California, Santa Barbara, where he taught for twenty-nine years (appointed Professor of Music, 1987) and served as Department Chair (1995-1999). He also taught as Visiting Professor of Musicology at the University of Michigan for three summer terms (1982, 1984-85).

Among many honors, Bill served as Editor-in-Chief of the *Journal of the American Musicological Society* (1989-1992) and was twice the Leopold Schepp Fellow at Villa I Tatti, the Harvard Center for Italian Renaissance Studies in Florence. He has been the recipient of grants from the National Endowment for the Humanities, the National Humanities Center, the American Philosophical Society, and the University of California. He lives during the year in Westlake Village (Thousand Oaks), California, with his wife, Kristine K. Forney, and their two cats; they summer at their cottage in the Thousand Islands, in upstate New York.

The following is a list of his published and forthcoming works.

BOOKS AND EDITIONS

Giuseppe Torelli, *Sonata a cinque con tromba, G. 6.* New York: Mentor Music, 1972.

Josquin Desprez, *Qui belles amours a.* Oxford University Press Early Music Series, 1975.

Libro Primo de la Croce (Rome: Pasoti and Dorico, 1526). Canzoni, Frottole, and Capitoli. Yale University Collegium Musicum, Second Series, vol. 8. Madison, Wisconsin: A-R Editions, 1978.

Courtly Pastimes: The Frottole of Marchetto Cara. Studies in Musicology, No. 33. George Buelow, general ed. Ann Arbor: UMI Research Press, 1980.

IN PROGRESS

Music at the Court of Mantua, 1475-1540. Variorum Collected Studies Series. Aldershot: Ashgate, 2009.

Courts, Carnivals, and Courtesans: *Italian Song ca. 1500.* Forthcoming.

ARTICLES

"Performance Practices in the Frottola." *Early Music* 3 (1975): 227-35.

"La Cappella di Francesco II Gonzaga e la musica sacra a Mantova nel primo ventennio del Cinquecento." *Mantova e i Gonzaga nella civiltà del Rinascimento, Atti del Convegno organizzato dall'Accademia nazionale dei Lincei e dall'Accademia virgiliana, con la collaborazione della città di Mantova, sotto l'alto patronato del Presidente della Repubblica italiana Giovanni Leone : Mantova, 6-8 ottobre 1974,* 267-76. Verona: Mondadori, 1977.

"Marchetto Cara at Mantua: New Documents on the Life and Duties of a Renaissance Court Musician." *Musica Disciplina* 32 (1978): 87-110.

"Lutenists at the Court of Mantua in the Late Fifteenth and Early Sixteenth Centuries." *Journal of the Lute Society of America* 13 (1980): 5-34.

"Bernardino Piffaro e i pifferi e tromboni di Mantova: Strumenti a fiato in una corte italiana." *Rivista Italiana di Musicologia* 16 (1981): 151-84.

"Isabella d'Este and Lorenzo da Pavia, 'Master Instrument Maker.'" *Early Music History* 2 (1982): 87-127.

"A Mantuan Collection of Music for Holy Week, 1537." *Renaissance Studies in Honor of Craig Hugh Smyth*, edited by Andrew Morrogh, 1: 613-25. Florence: Giunta Barbéra, 1985.

"Isabella d'Este and Lucrezia Borgia as Patrons of Music: The Frottola at Mantua and Ferrara." *The Journal of the American Musicological Society* 38 (1985): 1-33.

"Music and Ceremonial in the Low Countries: Philip the Fair and the Order of the Golden Fleece." *Early Music History* 5 (1985): 113-53.

"The Frottola and the Unwritten Tradition." *Studi Musicali* 15 (1986): 3-37.

"Music at the Court of the Sforza: The Birth and Death of a Musical Center." *Musica Disciplina* 43 (1989): 141-93. Originally commissioned by the Archer M. Huntington Gallery at the University of Texas at Austin in conjunction with the exhibition, *The Sforza Court: Milan in the Renaissance.*

"North Italian Courts, 1460-1540." *The Renaissance Era.* Volume 2 of *Music and Society*, edited by Stanley Sadie, 133-55. London: Macmillan, and Englewood Cliffs, NJ: Prentice-Hall, 1989.

"Paris, Bibliothèque Nationale, Manuscript Rés. Vm.^{7} 676 and Music at Mantua." In *Atti del XIV Congresso della Società Internazionale di Musicologia: Trasmissione e recezione delle forme di cultura musicale*, edited by Angelo Pompilio *et al.*, 2: 235-38. Turin: EDT, 1990.

"Games of Venus: Secular Vocal Music in the Late Quattrocento and Early Cinquecento." *Journal of Musicology* 9 (1991): 3-56.

"Renaissance Women as Patrons of Music: The North-Italian Courts." In *Rediscovering the Muses: Women's Musical Traditions*, edited by Kimberly Marshall, 186-205. Boston: Northeastern University Press, 1993.

"*Laude di popolo, laude di corte*: Some Thoughts on the Style and Function of the Renaissance Lauda." In *La musica a Firenze al tempo di Lorenzo il Magnifico.* Congresso internazionale di studi, ed. Piero Gargiulo, 167-94. Florence: Olschki, 1993.

"The Study of Patronage at Italian Courts." *Actas del XV Congreso de la Sociedad Internacional de Musicologia*, vol. 2 [= *Revista de Musicología* 16 (1993)]: 622-24.

"Instrumental Music / Instrumentally Performed Music ca. 1500: The Genres of Paris, Bibliothèque Nationale, MS Rés. Vm.^{7} 676." *Le Concert des Voix et des Instruments à la Renaissance. Actes du XXXIV Colloque International d'Études Supérieures de la Renaissance*, edited by Jean-Michel Vaccaro, 179-98. Paris: Éditions du Centre National de la Recherche Scientifique, 1995.

"Local Repertories and the Printed Book: Antico's Third Book of Frottole (1513)." In *Music in Renaissance Cities and Courts: Studies in Honor of Lewis Lockwood*, edited by Jessie Ann Owens and Anthony Cummings, 347-71. Warren, MI: Harmonie Park Press, 1997.

"*Facciamo pure noi carnevale*: Non-Florentine Carnival Songs of the Late Fifteenth and Early Sixteenth Centuries." *Musica Franca: Essays in Honor of Frank A. D'Accone*, ed. Irene Alm, Alyson McLamore, and Colleen Reardon, 173-211. Stuyvesant, NY: Pendragon Press, 1997.

"Secular Music at Milan during the Early Cinquecento: Florence, Biblioteca del Conservatorio, MS Basevi 2441." In *Essays in Honor of Nino Pirrotta* [= *Musica Disciplina* 52 (1998)]: 9-57.

"Music in Ferrara and Mantua at the Time of Dosso Dossi: Interrelations and Influences." In *Dosso's Fate: Painting and Court Culture in Renaissance Italy*: *Acts of the International Conferences on Dosso Dossi and his Works*, edited by Luisa Ciammitti, Steven F. Ostrow, and Salvatore Settis, 290-308. Los Angeles: The J. Paul Getty Research Institute for the History and Art and the Humanities, 1998. Shorter version of "Music in Ferrara and Mantua," below.

"Una 'virtù molto conveniente a madonne': Isabella d'Este as a Musician." In *Essays in Honor of H. Colin Slim* [= *Journal of Musicology* 17 (1999)]: 3-56.

"Music in Ferrara and Mantua in the Late Fifteenth and Early Sixteenth Centuries: Interrelations and Influences." In *Res Musicae: Essays in Honor of James W. Pruett*, edited by Paul R. Laird and Craig H. Russell, 75-95. Warren, MI: Harmonie Park Press, 2001.

"Charles V, Phillip II, and the Order of the Golden Fleece." In *Essays on Music and Culture in Honor of Herbert Kellman*, edited by Barbara Haggh, 161-88. Paris: Centre d'Études Supérieures de la Renaissance/Klincksieck, 2001.

"The Music Savonarola Burned: The Florentine Carnival Song in the Late 15th Century." *Musica e Storia* 9 (2001): 5-33.

"Brussels and the Ceremonies of the Order of the Golden Fleece." *Revue Belge de Musicologie* 55 (2001): 69-90.

"Wives and Courtesans: The Frottola in Florence." In *Music Observed*: *Studies in Memory of William C. Holmes*, edited by Colleen Reardon and Susan Parisi, 401-16. Warren, MI: Harmonie Park Press, 2004.

"Reading Carnival: The Creation of a Florentine Carnival Song." *Early Music History* 23 (2004): 185-252.

"Petrucci and the Carnival Song: On the Origins and Dissemination of a Genre." In *Venezia 1501: Petrucci e la stampa musicale*, edited by Giulio Cattin and Patricia dalla Vecchia, 215-51. Venice: Fondazione Levi, 2005.

"Cardinals and Courtesans: Secular Music in Rome, 1500-1520." In *Italy and the European Powers: The Impact of War, 1503-1530,* edited by Christine Shaw, 253-77. History of Warfare 38. Leiden: Brill, 2006.

"Siena and Northern Italy: The Secular Music of the Republic in the Early Sixteenth Century." *L'ultimo secolo della Repubblica di Siena: Arti, cultura e società. Atti del Convegno Internazionale,* ed. by Mario Ascheri, Gianni Mazzoni, and Fabrizio Nevola, 501-15. Siena: Accademia Senese degli Intronati, 2008.

"Secular Music in Siena in the Early Sixteenth Century: Pietro Sambonetto's *Canzone, Sonetti, Strambotti, et Frottole, Libro primo* (1515)." In *La la la . . . Maistre Henri: Mélanges de musicologie offerts à Henri Vanhulst,* ed. Christine Ballman and Valérie Dufour, 71-87. Centres d'Études Supérieures de la Renaissance. Turnhout, Belgium: Brepols, 2009 (enlarged version of "Siena and Northern Italy," above)

"The 'Virtue' of Lorenzo Lotto: A Musical Intarsia in the Basilica of Santa Maria Maggiore in Bergamo." In *Uno gentile et subtile ingenio: Studies in Renaissance Music in Honour of Bonnie J. Blackburn,* ed. M. Jennifer Bloxam, Gioia Filocamo, and Leofranc Holford-Strevens, 617-26. Centres d'Études Supérieures de la Renaissance, Collection Épitome musical. Turnhout, Belgium: Brepols, 2009.

DICTIONARY ARTICLES

New Grove Dictionary of Music and Musicians, 6th ed., ed. Stanley Sadie. London: Macmillan, 1980.

> *Ana, Francesco d'; Ansanus, S.; Antenoreo, Onofrio; Cara, Marco; Lauda, 2. Polyphonic; Ludovico Milanese; Lulinus Venetus, Johannes; Lurano, Filippo da, Pesenti, Michele; Tromboncino, Bartolomeo.*

The New Grove Dictionary of Music and Musicians, 2d ed., ed. Stanley Sadie and John Tyrell. London: Macmillan, 2001.

> *Alessandro Mantovano; Ana, Francesco d'; Ansanus, S.; Antenoreo, Onofrio; Cara, Marco; Dupré, Elias; Lauro, Hieronymo del; Lodi, Pietro da; Ludovico Milanese; Lulinus Venetus, Johannes; Lurano, Filippo da' Niccolo Patavino; Niccolò Piffaro; Pesenti, Michele; Piccolomini, Niccol;, Rossino Mantovano; Stringari, Antonio; Tromboncino, Bartolomeo.*

Die Musik in Geschichte und Gegenwart, 2d ed., ed. Ludwig Finscher. Personenteil 13: 951. Kassel: Bärenreiter, 1994-. S.v. "William F. Prizer."

Contributors to the Volume

Contributors to this Volume

Michael Beckerman is the Carroll and Milton Petrie Professor of Music and Department Chair at New York University. A specialist in Czech and Eastern European music, as well as music in concentration camps and music in film, he holds the Janáček Medal from the Czech Republic, is a Laureate of the Czech Music Council, and is a recipient of the ASCAP Deems Taylor Award for his work on Dvořák. He was Bill's colleague at UC Santa Barbara for nearly ten years, before leaving for NYU.

Bonnie J. Blackburn is a member of the Faculty of Music at Oxford University and a freelance editor. She specializes in music and music theory of the fifteenth and sixteenth centuries. Among her many publications is *Music for Treviso Cathedral in Late Sixteenth Century: A Reconstruction of the Lost Manuscripts 29 and 30* (RMA, 1987), and she edited *A Correspondence of Renaissance Musicians* (Oxford, 1991), *Music in the Culture of the Renaissance and Other Essays by Edward E. Lowinsky* (Chicago, 1989), as well as the *Opera omnia* of Johannes Lupi. She is a Corresponding Member of the AMS and a Fellow of the British Academy.

Frank D'Accone is Professor Emeritus at the University of California, Los Angeles. His work focuses on Italian music of the Middle Ages, Renaissance, and Baroque eras, notably in Florence and Siena. His monograph *The Civic Muse: Music and Musicians in Siena during the Middle Ages and the Renaissance* (University of Chicago, 1997) won the Roland Bainton Prize from the Sixteenth-Century Society. He has also written on Alessandro Scarlatti operas (Pendragon, 1985), and edited the music of Francesco de Loyolle as well as numerous volumes in the Renaissance Music in Facsimile series. He has served as General Editor of the series Corpus Mensurabilis Musicae and as co- editor of *Musica Disciplina*. He received the University of Pisa's Galilei Prize for his contributions to Italian culture, and he is also a Fellow of the American Academy of Rome, and an Honorary Member of the AMS.

Alicia M. Doyle is Associate Professor of Music and Associate Department Chair at California State University, Long Beach. Her research areas include medieval liturgical music and Latin American music. She has authored many ancillary resources that accompany the music appreciation text *The Enjoyment of Music*. She completed her MA degree at UCSB under Bill's tutelage, writing on Florentine carnival-song manuscript, and subsequently turned her interest toward chant, writing her dissertation on a tenth-century Aquitanian troper.

Iain Fenlon is a Fellow and Professor of Music at King's College of the University of Cambridge. A specialist in Italian music of the Renaissance and early Baroque eras, he is author of, among other books, *Music and Patronage in Sixteenth-Century Mantua* (Cambridge, 1980), *Music and Culture in Late Renaissance Italy* (Oxford, 2009), *The Ceremonial City: History Memory and Myth in Renaissance Venice* (Yale, 2007), and *Piazza San Marco* (Harvard, 2009). He and Bill first met as fellows at Villa I Tatti, the Harvard Center for Italian Renaissance Studies.

Kristine K. Forney is Professor of Music and Area Director of Musicology at California State University, Long Beach. Her work focuses on sixteenth-century music in the Low Countries, including the printing/publishing trade in Antwerp, and she has edited several volumes of music in the Garland Sixteenth-Century Chanson series. She is also co-author of the pre-eminent music appreciation text *The Enjoyment of Music* and editor of *The Norton Scores*. She was a PhD student at University of Kentucky when Bill took his teaching post there, and after both moved to California, they married in 1984.

Beth Glixon is Instructor of Musicology at the University of Kentucky. She specializes in the history of opera in seventeenth-century Venice as well as social history of musicians there. She is a founding member of the Society of Seventeenth-Century Music and is the author of numerous articles as well as the monograph *Inventing the Business of Opera: The Impresario and His World in Seventeenth-Century Venice* (Oxford University Press, 2007), which she co-wrote with her husband, Jonathan Glixon.

Jonathan Glixon is Professor of Music and the Provost's Distinguished Service Professor at the University of Kentucky. His research interests include music in Venice from the Middle Ages through the eighteenthth century, as well as archival studies and early music performance practices. In addition to many articles and papers, he is the author of *Honoring God and the City: Music at the Venetian Confraternities (1260-1807)* (Oxford University Press, 2003) and co-author, with Beth Glixon, of *Inventing the Business of Opera: The Impresario and His World in Seventeenth-Century Venice* (Oxford University Press, 2007), published in the AMS Studies in Music series.

James Haar is Distinguished Professor Emeritus at the University of North Carolina, Chapel Hill and a past President of the American Musicological Society. A specialist in fifteenth and sixteenth-century Italian music, notably the madrigal, he has written many articles and books, including *Essays on Italian Poetry and Music in the Renaissance, 1350-1600* (Ernest Bloch Lectures, University of California, 1987); *The Italian Madrigal in Early Sixteenth Century: Sources and Interpretation* (Cambridge, 1989), with Iain Fenlon; and is the editor of *European Music, 1520-1640* (Boydell, 2006). He has also edited many scholarly editions of Italian music and serves as the General Editor of the Recent Researches in the Music of the Renaissance series (A-R Editions).

Daniel Heartz is Professor Emeritus at the University of California, Berkeley, and an Honorary Member and past Vice-President of the American Musicological Society. His research has focused on sixteenth-century music printing, dance music, and humanism, as well as eighteenth-century opera and the classical style. Among many honors, he has been awarded the Kinkeldey Award twice: first for his study of the Parisian printer Pierre Attaingnant; and, more recently, for *Music in European Capitals: The Galant Style, 1720-1780* (Norton, 2003). Two further studies on eighteenth-century music have followed, comprising an impressive trilogy.

Leofranc Holford-Strevens is Consultant Scholar-Editor at Oxford University Press. He is a classicist and remarkable linguist who in recent years has turned his abilities to musicology. Among other studies, he is author of *The History of Time: A Very Short Introduction* (Oxford, 2005) and several books on the Latin scholar Aulus Gellius. He co-edited, with his wife Bonnie J. Blackburn, *Florentius de Faxolis* (Harvard, 2010) as well as Uno gentile et subtile ingenio: *Studies in Honour of Bonnie J. Blackburn* (Brepols, 2009).

Thomas Forrest Kelly is the Morton B. Knafel Professor of Music at Harvard University. His main fields of interest are chant and performance practices. He was the recipient of the Kinkeldey Award for *The Beneventan Chant* (Cambridge. 1989), and is the author of the *First Nights: Five Musical Premieres* (Yale, 2000) and *First Nights at the Opera* (Yale, 2004), among many other publications. He is a member of the American Academy of Arts and Sciences, an honorary citizen of the city of Benevento, and a Chevalier de l'Ordre des Arts et Lettres of the French Republic.

T. Frank Kennedy, S.J. is the Canisius Professor of Music at Boston College, and is also the Director of the Jesuit Institute and the Rector of the Jesuit Community. He is a specialist in early Baroque music, especially that of Jesuits, and has edited several early Jesuit operas, two of which are now recorded. He was Bill's first doctoral student at UCSB; his 1982 dissertation was on "Jesuits and Music: The European Tradition, 1547-1622."

Anne MacNeil is Professor of Music at University of North Carolina, Chapel Hill. Her research areas include music of the sixteenth and seventeenth centuries, music and spectacle, the commedia dell'arte, and music and ceremony in the lives of noblewomen. She is a Fellow of the American Academy in Rome, and is the author of *Music and Women of the Commedia dell'Arte in the Late Sixteenth Century* (Oxford, 2003) and the editor of *Selected Poems of Isabella Andreini* (Scarecrow, 2005). She has also served as editor of the journal *17th-Century Music*.

Alison Sanders McFarland is Associate Professor of Music at Louisiana State University. Her research interests focus on Renaissance sacred music and papal patronage and music in Rome, particularly the music of Cristóbal de Morales, and twentieth-century English music, notably of Ralph Vaughn Williams. Bill directed her 1999 dissertation, "Cristóbal de Morales and the Imitation of the Past: Music for the Mass in Sixteenth-Century Rome."

Margaret Murata is Professor of Music at the University of California, Irvine. A specialist in Italian Baroque opera and cantata as well as the revival of *arie antiche*, she is the author of many studies, including *Operas for the Papal Court* (UMI, 1981), and she is the editor of the Baroque volume in the revised *Strunk's Source Readings in Music History* (Norton, 1998). Most recently, she collaborated with Dinko Fabris in *Passaggio in Italia: Music on the Grand Tour in the Seventeenth Century* (Brepols, 2012). She is a former President of the Society for Seventeenth-Century Music and Vice-President of the AMS.

Guido Olivieri is a Lecturer in Music at the University of Texas, Austin. His research interests focus on eighteenth-century music, including social, cultural, and political influences on the circulation of music and musicians. He has held research fellowships at the University of Liverpool and Columbia University, and was awarded a Mellon Postdoctoral at the University of Michigan. Bill directed his 2005 dissertation on "The 'Fiery Genius': The Contribution of Neapolitan Virtuosi to the Spread of the String Sonata (1684-1736)."

Alejandro Enrique Planchart is Professor Emeritus at University of California, Santa Barbara, and taught previously at Yale University, where he founded the early music ensemble Cappella Cordina He is a leading scholar on the music of the Middle Ages and early Renaissance era, notably of Guillaume Du Fay. His many publications include *The Repertory of Tropes at Winchester* (Princeton, 1977) and editions of *Beneventan troporum corpus*, with John Boe (A-R Editions, 1989) and of *Missae Caput* (Yale, 1964). He has also conducted many recorded performance of early music for Lyrichord and Musical Heritage Society. He hired Bill for the position at UC Santa Barbara in 1979, and they were colleagues there for nearly thirty years.

Keith Polk is Professor Emeritus at the University of New Hampshire. A specialist in instrumental music of the Renaissance, and especially the wind band, his publications include the monograph *German Instrumental Music in the Late Middle Ages* (Cambridge, 1992) and he edited *Tielman Susato and the Music of His Time: Print Culture, Compositional Technique and Instrumental Music in the Renaissance* (Pendragon, 2005). He is also an accomplished performer on modern and natural horn player.

Katherine Powers is Associate Professor and Director of the Graduate Studies Office at California State University, Fullerton. Her research areas include the spiritual madrigal, musical iconography, and women musicians in Sweden. Bill directed her 1997 dissertation on "The Spiritual Madrigal in Counter-Reformation Italy: Definition, Use, and Style."

Colleen Reardon is Professor of Music at University of California, Irvine. Her research focuses on music in Siena in the sixteenth and seventeenth centuries, and she is the author of *Agostino Agazzari and Music at Siena Cathedral, 1596-1641* (Oxford, 1993) and *Holy Concord within Sacred Walls: Nuns and Music in Siena, 1575-1700* (Oxford, 2002). She also co-edited Festschriften in honor of William C. Holmes and Frank D'Accone.

Gilberto Scuderi is the librarian of the Sala Manoscritti and Libro Antico at the Biblioteca Communale Teresiana, Mantua. He is a specialist in the Mantuan dialect and, remarkably, in American history. Gilberto has been an immense help to Bill in his work in Mantua and in translating dialect to Italian.

Richard Sherr is the Caroline L. Wall '27 Professor and Department Chair at Smith College. His work centers on music of the fifteenth and sixteenth centuries, including the singers of the Papal Chapel, and also on Gilbert and Sullivan operetta. His publications include the monograph *Papal Music Manuscripts in the Late Fifteenth and Early Sixteenth Centuries* (Hanssler, 1996), *Papal Music and Musicians in Late Medieval and Renaissance Rome* (Oxford, 1998) and *The Josquin Companion* (Oxford, 2000), the latter two which he edited. He is also General Editor of the Sixteenth-Century Motet series of Garland publications, for which he edited numerous volumes.

H. Colin Slim is Professor Emeritus at University of California, Irvine. He is a specialist in sixteenth-century Italian music, musical iconography, and, more recently, Stravinsky. He is a past President of the American Musicological Society, an Honorary Member of that society, and winner of the Kindeldey Award for his study *A Gift of Madrigals and Motets* (Chicago, 1972). Among his many publications are editions of *Music Nova* and *Keyboard Music at Castell'Arquato*, and he is also author of the *Annotated Catalogue of the H. Colin Slim Stravinsky Collection*, which he donated to the University of British Columbia.

Jeremy L. Smith is Associate Professor of Music at University of Colorado, Boulder and co-editor of this volume. He works on music of the English Renaissance, music and politics, and progressive rock. He is author of numerous studies, including a monograph on Thomas East and an edition of William Byrd's *Psalmes, Sonets and Songs* in the Byrd Edition. Bill directed his dissertation on "The Career of Thomas East, Elizabethan Music Printer and Publisher (1997)."

Gary Towne is Professor of Music at the University of North Dakota. His research focuses on sixteenth-century Italian music, notably in Bergamo. His publications include an edition of the masses of Gaspar de Albertis, in the composer's collected works. He was Bill's second PhD student at UCSB, with a 1985 dissertation on "Gaspar de Albertis and Music at Santa Maria Maggiore in Bergamo in the Sixteenth Century."

Susan Forscher Weiss holds a joint appointment in the Peabody Conservatory and the Department of German and Romance Languages of Johns Hopkins University. She specializes in Italian music and sources of the fifteenth and sixteenth centuries as well as music pedagogy in the Middle Ages and Renaissance. Among her publications are a facsimile edition of Bologna MS Q18 and *Music Education in the Middle Ages and the Renaissance* (Indiana, 2010), which she co-edited. Bill served as an outside member of her doctoral committee, advising her work on Bologna, MS Q18.

Blake Wilson is Professor of Music at Dickinson College. His research areas include music of Renaissance Italy, performance practice, and the interaction of oral and written music traditions in the culture of Renaissance Florence. In addition to many articles, he is the author of *Music and Merchants: The Laudesi Companies of Republican Florence* (Oxford, 1992) and *Singing Poetry in Renaissance Florence: The Cantasi Come Tradition* (1375-1550) (Olschki, 2009).